Zambia

Africa: Policies For Prosperity Series

Series Editors

Christopher S. Adam and Paul Collier

For the first time in more than a generation, sustained economic growth has been achieved across Africa – despite the downturn in global economic fortunes since 2008 – and in many countries these gains have been realized through policy reforms driven by the decisive leadership of a new generation of economic policymakers. The process of reform is continuous, however, and the challenge currently facing this new generation is how to harness these favourable gains in macroeconomic stability and turn them into a coherent strategy for sustainable growth and poverty reduction over the coming decades. These challenges are substantial and encompass the broad remit of economic policy. Each volume in this series brings leading scholars into the policy arena to examine, in a rigorous but accessible manner, the key economic challenges and policy options facing policy makers on the continent.

BOOKS PUBLISHED IN THIS SERIES

Kenya: Policies for Prosperity
Edited by Christopher S. Adam, Paul Collier, and Njuguna Ndung'u

Zambia: Building Prosperity from Resource Wealth
Edited by Christopher S. Adam, Paul Collier, and Michael Gondwe

Zambia

Building Prosperity from Resource Wealth

Edited by Christopher S. Adam, Paul Collier,
and Michael Gondwe

OXFORD
UNIVERSITY PRESS

OXFORD

UNIVERSITY PRESS

Great Clarendon Street, Oxford OX2 6DP
United Kingdom

Oxford University Press is a department of the University of Oxford.
It furthers the University's objective of excellence in research, scholarship,
and education by publishing worldwide. Oxford is a registered trade mark of
Oxford University Press in the UK and in certain other countries

First Edition published in 2014
Impression: 1

Published in the United States of America by Oxford University Press
198 Madison Avenue, New York, NY 10016, United States of America

British Library Cataloguing in Publication Data
Data available

Library of Congress Control Number: 2014944699

ISBN 978-0-19-966060-5

As printed and bound by
CPI Group (UK) Ltd, Croydon, CR0 4YY

Series Preface

Policies for Prosperity

Since the mid-1990s the economic prospects for Africa have been transformed. The change has been uneven: some countries remain mired in conflict and economic stagnation. But for many macro-economic stability has been achieved – even through the global economic crisis – and far-reaching policy reforms have been put in place. For these countries, growth prospects in the early 21st century are much brighter than at any time during the final quarter of the last century. But converting favourable prospects into sustained growth and decisive poverty reduction requires a degree of good luck, good policy formulation, resources, and a lot of good economic management. For policy improvements to be sustained they must be underpinned by more fundamental shifts in political power; sectional interests ruling through patronage must be defeated by the public interest. For the shift in power to be decisive, the achievements of individual reformers must be locked in through the development of institutions. The challenges are formidable: they range beyond the conventional agenda of macro-economic management, infrastructure provision, and the improvement of the investment climate. For example, land policy, which has usually been left dormant, will need to be rethought in the face of high population growth rates and growing urbanization. Trade and industrial policies will need to be rethought so as to engage more effectively with changing global opportunities. The continent will need to develop adaptive policies in the face of rapid climate change.

Many of the successes of recent decades have been wrought by the progressive leadership of a new generation of policymakers. To build on these successes, this same generation needs both the support of, and restraint by, an informed and engaged society. This is the fundamental philosophy of this series: informed societies are strong societies. If citizens are to hold governments to account they require information, debate and dispassionate analysis on the challenges and choices confronting countries and their people. This is especially relevant in the realm of economic policy where path-dependency is powerful and the consequences of choices are far-reaching and long-lasting.

In many industrialized economies there is a long tradition of informed debate and analysis sustained in large measure by high-quality financial journalism. In Africa, by contrast, while a dynamic and often fearless free press is now quite widely established, it still lacks a tradition of solid, durable, and independent writing on economic policy. As a result local debate is too often ill-informed or is perceived to be driven by the agendas, and cheque-books, of sectional interests and international organizations.

There is now considerable academic research on the issues that matter for Africa and it could potentially inform Africa's debates. But to date it has been disconnected from them. Increasingly, academics write only for other academics rather than to inform the public. With this series of books we seek to build bridges between the evidence from solid research and contemporary policy debates. Each book aims to bring together the best international and domestic scholars with policymakers working on economic policy issues across the continent. Throughout, our contributors are required to write with clarity, avoiding academic jargon, but equally avoiding advocacy. Focusing on the key issues that matter for a society, each chapter aims to leave readers better able to draw their own conclusions about important choices.

Christopher S. Adam
Paul Collier
Series Editors
Oxford, July 2014

Foreword

The road to development is one of the most treacherous to tread and yet when successful it brightens the countenance of all citizens of a country. When it doesn't seem to produce the desired results, a sense of gloom and hopelessness engulfs the nation. Finger pointing becomes the order of the day, laying the blame on one or other section of society. It is unbelievably rare for the real source of the failure to be blamed – or the real source of good to be included in the praise for economic success. Yet it should be obvious to all stakeholders that the most important underlying factor of every economic success or failure is the nature of the policies that are adopted and their implementation.

I am delighted that this book, *Zambia: Building Prosperity from Resource Wealth,* has outlined the key policies that have been adopted and implemented in Zambia in the recent past. It is also interesting to note that the book has been written at a time when it is crucial to move the country out of the vicious cycle of poverty after a decade of appreciable growth. Furthermore, the publication of the book coincides with the 50th Anniversary of Zambia's Independence.

Developing countries such as Zambia have learned important lessons from the recent global financial crisis of 2008–09 and the on-going sovereign debt problems of the euro area. Important among these is that the policies that have led to economic growth and development in developed economies in the last five decades may not be the ones to propel developing countries to higher income levels. It will take new ideas and a different mix of policies to develop our economies and lift our people out of poverty.

Drawing on the work of authors who come from a variety of disciplinary backgrounds, the book sets out a rich discussion of what policies Zambia needs to adopt going forward in order to ignite development that can put paid to the suffering of a larger portion of the population under the pangs of poverty. These policies are expected to deliver sustainable development that ensures that the benefits of economic growth accrue to a larger portion of the population. Various policies are proposed for Zambia in this book, in areas including: growth strategies in Part I; macro-economic policy choices in Part II; the supply side: production, trade and infrastructure in Part III;

while public service delivery and the political economy of reforms are discussed in Part IV.

The book is unique not only because it is forward-looking but also because it has a rare blend of Zambian and international authors who are prominent in their areas of expertise, therefore making the recommended policy options richer. This also ensures that the book has benefited from the local and international experience, which most books on Zambia lack.

It is clear that this book will be of interest to practising policymakers in government, quasi-government institutions, academics, students and co-operating partners. It will also form a firm foundation and reliable reference for policymaking and discussion on Zambia for many years to come.

Alexander B. Chikwanda
Minister of Finance,
Republic of Zambia

Acknowledgements

This book is the product of the collaboration between numerous institutions and individuals, foremost of which is the Bank of Zambia under the leadership of its current and former governors, Michael Gondwe and Caleb Fundanga: their vision and commitment to the project has been invaluable. The Bank of Zambia gratefully acknowledges financial support provided by the UK Department for International Development (DFID) through its continued support to the Bank's training and capacity development efforts. The many Bank of Zambia staff who appear as contributing authors to this volume bear witness to the value of this support. As editors, we would particularly like to acknowledge the support of the Economics Department of the Bank of Zambia; the University of Zambia; the National Council for Construction; the Zambia Revenue Authority; and the World Bank office in Zambia. We also thank Alan Whitworth, who served as DFID-Zambia's liaison for the project, helping us to keep the project moving. Finally, we thank our friend and colleague from Oxford, Rose Page, for her superb management of the project from Oxford and especially for transforming a disparate set of chapters into a coherent and elegant manuscript.

Christopher S. Adam
Paul Collier
Michael Gondwe
July 2014

Contents

Contents

List of Illustrations

List of Tables

List of Contributors

Editors

Christopher S. Adam is Professor of Development Economics at the University of Oxford and a Research Associate at the Centre for the Study of African Economies

Paul Collier is Professor of Public Policy at the Blavatnik School of Government and Director of the Centre for the Study of African Economies, University of Oxford

Michael Gondwe is the Governor of the Bank of Zambia

Contributors

Michael Bratton is University Distinguished Professor of Political Science and African Studies at Michigan State University, US

Samuel Bwalya is an Economist at UNECA, Addis Abba, Ethiopia

Massimiliano Calì is a Trade Economist with the International Trade Department at the World Bank

Adriana Cardozo is a Consultant on Latin America and the Caribbean at the World Bank

Collins Chansa is a Health Economist attached to the World Bank Zambia Office as Health Systems Specialist

Nic Cheeseman is the Hugh Price Fellow in African Politics and the Director of African Studies at the University of Oxford, UK

Francis Chipimo is the Director, Economics Department, Bank of Zambia

Robert Conrad is an Associate Professor of Public Policy and Economics in the Sanford School of Public Policy at Duke University, US

Shanta Devarajan is the Chief Economist of the Middle East and North Africa Region of the World Bank

Robert Ford is a Senior Lecturer in Politics at the University of Manchester, UK

Chungu Kapembwa is a Senior Researcher in the Economics Department, Bank of Zambia

Alexander Lippert is an Analyst at Goldman Sachs

Peter Lolojih is a Lecturer at the University of Zambia

Sylvester Mashamba is the former Executive Director at the National Council for Construction (NCC), Zambia

Gibson Masumbu is an Economist based in Lusaka, Zambia

Isaac Muhanga is Assistant Director of Market Analysis, Financial Markets Department, Bank of Zambia

Mulenga Musepa is the Assistant Director in the Governor's Office and Executive Assistant to the Governor, Bank of Zambia

Chiwama Musonda is an Economist with Acumen Consulting Limited, Zambia

Austin Mwape is a Senior Financial Sector Consultant with AFTFE, World Bank and formerly Deputy Governor of Operations, Bank of Zambia

Vinayak Nagaraj is the Chief Economic and PFM Advisor to the New Zealand Aid Programme

Francis Ndilila is the Principal Architect at Ndilila Architects & Associates, Zambia

Emmanuel Mulenga Pamu is Director of the Financial Markets Department, Bank of Zambia

Jonathan Pycroft is an Economist at the Institute for Prospective Technological Studies (IPTS), European Commission, Spain

Gaël Raballand is a World Bank Senior Public Sector and Governance Specialist, formerly based in Zambia

Sherman Robinson is a Research Fellow at the Institute of Development Studies, UK

Anthony Simpasa is the Principal Research Economist in the Research, Networking and Partnerships Division of the African Development Bank

Neo Simutanyi is the Executive Director at the Centre for Policy Dialogue, Zambia

Mirja Sjoblom is an Economist with the Health Nutrition and Population Group at the World Bank

Monique Vledder is a Senior Health Specialist at the World Bank

Alan Whitworth is a Senior Economist with DFID Pakistan

Ivan Zyuulu is the Assistant Director, Balance of Payments and Debt, Economics Department, Bank of Zambia

I

Growth Strategies for Zambia

1

Growth Strategies for Zambia: Harnessing Natural Resource Wealth for Sustainable Growth

Michael Gondwe and Emmanuel Mulenga Pamu

1.1 Introduction

Zambia is endowed with abundant natural resources, not only the copper for which it is well known, but also many other minerals, as well as resources such as water, forests and substantial farm land. The key challenge for the economy is to translate these resources into sustainable development.

Shortly after independence, Zambia experienced a period of rapid economic growth supported by prevailing high copper prices. However, the fall in the international price of copper from 1974 put an end to this rapid economic growth. Perceiving the fall in the international price of copper as a temporary phenomenon, the Zambian Government resorted to borrowing both domestically and externally to maintain consumption and investment at previous levels. External borrowing resulted in Zambia accumulating a huge external debt that halted the country's economic development. During the boom, however, the high copper prices generated a significant Dutch Disease effect, with adverse consequences on non-booming sectors such as manufacturing and agriculture that might have otherwise sustained growth.

Commentators have argued that it would have been better if the government had assumed the boom was temporary and had encouraged the country to save a much higher proportion of its copper revenue than it did. This would have generated a more modest growth in consumption and, at the same time, would have defused the incipient Dutch Disease, as most of the foreign exchange inflows would have been reflected in current account surpluses and a build-up of savings abroad.

The persistently low prices of copper in the 1980s and 1990s made the mines economically unviable, so that after the change of government in 1991, privatization of the mines became inevitable as the new government rolled out its policy of economic liberalization.

The 2000s saw a completely different trend in the international price of copper, as it rose to unprecedented levels. At the same time, Zambia benefited from debt relief initiatives under the Heavily Indebted Poor Countries (HIPC) initiative and the Multilateral Debt Relief Initiative (MDRI) in 2005. Zambia's external debt fell from around 190 per cent of GDP in 2000 to 10 per cent of GDP in 2011. Thus Zambia had a new equilibrium with improvements in both its current and capital accounts. The country saw a reversal in growth trends from the economic stagnation that was experienced during the 1990s.

Per capita income grew at 2.5 per cent during the period 2002–05. A rapid expansion of mining and construction was the key driver of growth during this period. The mining sector was supported by the recapitalization of the mines and buoyant commodity prices, while increased private construction activities saw the construction sector grow.

This chapter examines how the legacy of the development agreements negotiated with the private mine owners at the time of privatization still hamper the realization of Zambia's growth and development potential and how this has created inconsistencies in Zambia's macro-economic figures. The chapter also looks at how growth in other sectors can be accelerated when infrastructural constraint is eliminated through mobilization of sufficient resources from the mining sector. Section 1.2 examines some generic aspects of growth strategies; Section 1.3 describes the inconsistencies in Zambia's macro-economic performance; and Section 1.4 prescribes strategies for mobilizing resources. The chapter concludes with an analysis of how resource mobilization can ease infrastructural constraints in various economic sectors.

1.2. Generic aspects of growth strategies

1.2.1 *Leadership and governance*

Zambia has made significant strides in entrenching democratic tenets as evidenced by the successful elections of September 2011, and the peaceful handover of power from the Movement for Multi-party Democracy (MMD) to the Patriotic Front (PF).

It is gratifying to note the PF Government has adopted a policy of zero tolerance against corruption. The issue of corruption and nepotism is central to the attainment of sustainable economic growth in Zambia. In the past, public resources have been misapplied through corruption and revenues have also been lost through corrupt practices. It is therefore important that the anti-corruption commission is strengthened and given operational autonomy. It is important to acknowledge that recently the office of the Auditor General has independently revealed several abuses of public resources in government ministries. Zambia's tax revenue to GDP ratio can be improved and therefore increase resources for development if the opportunities for corruption are reduced. In Kenya, for example, tax revenues increased as a result of increased compliance following administrative reforms that reduced opportunities for corruption.

It is also important that the regulations and procedures, as stipulated in the Zambia Public Procurement Authority (ZPPA) Act, are followed in the public sector to ensure transparency, integrity, and efficiency.

Market allocation and openness: Zambia's trade policy has remained substantially unchanged since the liberalization process started in 1992. That reform process removed exchange and other controls; privatized state-owned enterprises; eliminated almost all import and export licences, and abolished all export bans. The country's aim was to pursue an outward oriented, export-led strategy based on open markets and international competition. After periods of stagnation in the 1990s and contraction of industrial output, the economy registered higher growth rates the following decade averaging 5 per cent per year.

Macro stability and sustainable public finances: Zambia has implemented prudent macro-economic policies since 2003. As a result, Zambia reached the completion point under the Highly Indebted Poor Countries (HIPC) initiative, which earned the country a debt write off under both the HIPC initiative and the Multilateral Debt Relief Initiative (MDRI). Inflation declined to single digit of 8.6 per cent in 2006, for the first time in 30 years and remained in single digit of 8.9 per cent in 2007. This trend was blown off track by the global financial crisis that saw inflation rise to 16.6 per cent in 2008. However, as the global economy recovered, inflation declined to 9.9 per cent in 2009. Since then inflation has been maintained at single digit levels, with the latest figure standing at 7.2 per cent at the end of 2013.

Future orientation: The government has demonstrated commitment to the long-term development of the country by easing infrastructural constraints through investing more in the transport sector by way of the Link Zambia 8000 project and by restructuring the Railway System of Zambia. Furthermore, there are plans to re-establish a national airline. In the energy sector, the government has allocated some of the resources from the proceeds of the $US750 million Euro Bond issued in 2012 to the energy sector.

1.2.2 Reducing youth unemployment

Zambia's economic performance has been strong with broad-based growth since 2001. However, poverty levels and unemployment have remained high. A major concern has been that formal sector employment has remained almost stagnant since 1998, and that most employment growth has been recorded in the informal sector of the economy. Of the 4.6 million Zambians reported to be employed, over 80 per cent are in the informal sector. In order to address the problem of unemployment, especially among the young, the government has developed a strategy for creating 1,000,000 new formal jobs over the next five years. In order to create these jobs, economic growth above 8 per cent is necessary. For this to occur, economic growth must be driven by those sectors in which Zambia has a comparative advantage and in which labour intensive activities can be most effectively used to expand output and employment. Four growth sectors have been identified as having the greatest potential to achieve employment, growth, and value addition and expand Zambia's economic base. These are the agricultural, tourism, construction, and manufacturing sectors.

The implementation of the strategy will require an estimated total of K25 billion over a period of five years. Thus domestic resource mobilization is critical to the success of the strategy.

At the core of all the generic strategies described above is the mobilization of adequate resources to finance growth and development. While Zambia has an opportunity to do so using its natural resources, some inconsistencies in the macro figures indicate that urgent remedies are required to arrest the situation.

1.3 Inconsistencies in Zambia's macro-economic performance

Despite the positive developments of the 2000s, Zambia has remained weak as it cannot generate enough resources from the booming mining sector to support its development efforts. Despite the high copper prices in the 2000s, Zambia's macro-economic experience has been contrary to what conventional wisdom would assume. Firstly, there has been no evidence of Dutch Disease effects as was the case in 1970s and, secondly, government fiscal performance has not been consistent with improved current account balances. Both themes are discussed in detail in later chapters in this volume.

1.3.1 Dutch Disease effects

The Dutch Disease effects arising from an increase in copper prices are expected to work through the resource movement effects and the spending effect. The resource movement effect implies a movement of labour from the non-tradables sector and the non-booming tradables sector, such as agriculture and other non-traditional exports in the case of Zambia, into the booming tradables sector, which is the copper mining sector. These movements constrain supply in the non-tradables sector, leading to an increase in the price of non-tradables relative to tradables. This channel appears not to be powerful in Zambia principally because of the prevailing high levels of unemployment. According to the government's 2008 Labour Force Survey, urban unemployment stood at 33 per cent, while formal sector employment stood at 511,338 out of a population of 13.8 million. Moreover, any adverse effect that might have been expected in the agricultural sector has been neutralized as the country has recorded bumper harvests since 2009.

The spending effect arises from increased spending by the booming sector as wages in this sector increase in line with increased incomes. The real exchange rate appreciates as the price of non-tradables increases relative to tradables, the prices of which are fixed internationally. The non-booming tradables sector thus suffers a further resource movement effect as resources move into the non-tradables sector, further constraining supply in this sector.

One way of analysing the macro-economic impact of high copper prices in Zambia is to look at the response of the real exchange rate to changes in the international price of copper. Copper prices had been on an upward trend since March 2003. They declined sharply in June 2008 at the height of the global financial and economic crisis but recovered after December 2008 (see Figure 1.1).

As shown in Figures 1.1 and 1.2, the real exchange rate has remained fairly constant despite the rising international price of copper. The real exchange rate appreciated up to the fourth quarter of 2008, and then depreciated to a new level and remained there for most of 2009 and 2011. With

Figure 1.1 Copper prices US cents/lb

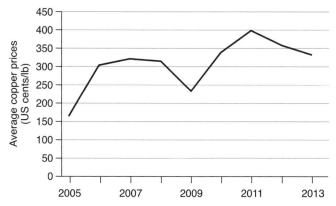

Figure 1.2 Real exchange rate

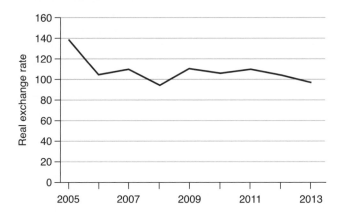

the sharp increase in the international price of copper, conventional wisdom would suggest a corresponding appreciation in the real exchange rate.

The argument behind this phenomenon is that with insufficient absorption of the mineral rents into the domestic economy, either by way of higher wages in the booming sector, higher payment obligations for domestic goods and services, or higher taxes that would finance higher expenditures, there would be no Dutch Disease effects. Thus the Dutch Disease effects would be absent when the rents are absorbed by external debt service or by the accumulation of assets abroad. In Table 1.1, we see that Zambia recorded current account surpluses from 2009 to 2011. In the same period, the financial account balance recorded negative balances reflecting either loan repayments, remittance of profits and dividends, or accumulation of foreign assets abroad.

The central lesson from these stylized facts is that when natural resource rents are foreign-owned, standard Dutch Disease effects may not be observed unless some measures to increase the share of the rents are implemented by the government through tax and other reforms. The opportunities for spending and indeed absorption are both limited by the inadequacy of resources that are made available to the government, and the private sector, from natural resource rents. This is a new phenomenon that is applying to the Zambian situation.

Table 1.1 Selected balance of payments accounts in $US millions

Year	2008	2009	2010	2011	2012
Current Account Balance	(1039)	538	1,143	236	(53)
Financial Balance	816	(172)	(1076)	(429)	(520)

Source: Bank of Zambia 2011 Annual Report

This is why the trends in the exchange rate are not consistent with the trends in the international price of copper. In the initial stages, when copper prices began to rise, we saw the Zambian Kwacha appreciate after a long period of persistent depreciations. In fact, during the previous period, the Zambian Kwacha was more biased towards depreciations. Thus the high copper prices seen during the 2000s saw the Zambian exchange rate exhibit a different pattern of movement, from being biased towards depreciations.

1.3.2 Fiscal performance

Unfortunately, when the mines were privatized in the 1990s, investors in the sector were offered very attractive tax incentives that shielded them from paying higher taxes as the copper prices rose. As a consequence, despite copper making up more than 70 per cent of total exports, the contribution to tax revenues is relatively small compared with other countries. In 1992, when the mines were owned by the state and copper prices averaged $US2,280 per ton and production was 400,000 tons, the government was able to collect $US200 million in revenues and other remittances. In 2004, when the mines had been recapitalized and the copper prices had risen to $US2,868 and copper production was 400,000, the government only received about $US7 million in revenues.

Thus, the increase in earnings from exports did not translate into improved fiscal performance, especially in the aftermath of the financial crisis. The fiscal balance as a proportion of GDP improved from 2000 began to fall after 2007 and has continued to decline as shown in Figure 1.3.

Figure 1.3 Fiscal balance as per cent of GDP

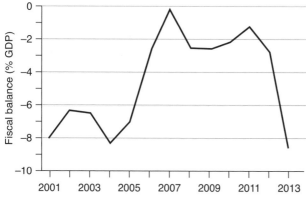

1.4 Strategies for mobilizing domestic resources

Zambia has huge infrastructural needs that have to be financed. In addition, the economic sectors, which are engines of economic growth, require resources for them to overcome the constraints that they confront. At a time when donor countries are facing their own fiscal challenges, domestic resource mobilization has become more important. One way of enhancing domestic resource mobilization is to look again at the mining tax regime to ensure that adequate taxes are collected from the mines. Measures also need to be implemented to improve tax administration and ensure adequate funding to the Zambia Revenue Authority.

Another strategy for enhancing domestic resource mobilization is the development of the financial sector. According to the 2009 survey on financial inclusiveness (2009 Finscope survey), only 37 per cent of the Zambian population has access to financial services. As a result, the Zambian economy has a high currency to deposits ratio and these resources can be mobilized so that they contribute to economic growth and development.

Following the adverse effects of the financial crisis on the mining companies, the windfall tax was withdrawn and, as a consequence, Zambia has experienced some inconsistency between positive performance in the external sector and fiscal performance (see Table 1.2). In 2010, Zambia recorded the highest current account surplus in many years and yet the fiscal deficit increased to 3.1 per cent of GDP from 2.4 per cent recorded in 2009.

Therefore, the Zambian Government has an opportunity to improve its fiscal performance on the revenue side and thus provide the needed resources for accelerating growth in various economic sectors and financing poverty-reducing schemes.

1.5 Easing infrastructure constraints

1.5.1 *Transport communications and infrastructure*

In Zambia, the transport system encompasses road, rail, air, water, and pipeline. The dominant mode of transport is road, followed by rail. However,

Table 1.2 Fiscal deficits and current account deficits, 2009–11

	2009	2010	2011
Fiscal Balance (% of GDP)	(2.4)	(3.3)	(3.0)
Current Account Balance (% of GDP)	4.2	7.1	1.2
Financial Account Balance (millions of US dollars)	(173)	(1076)	(429)

very little investment has been made in the air-transport sector. The information and communication technology (ICT) subsector is gaining prominence with the rapid technological advancement that has been experienced worldwide in the past decade. Zambia needs resources to further develop its road, rail, water, and air-transport infrastructure so as to unlock the potential that Zambia has in various economic sectors such as agriculture, tourism, and mining. In particular, the rail system has not performed well for many years and has contributed to increased congestion on Zambian roads as more Zambians acquire motor vehicles.

1.5.2 *Energy*

With the exception of petroleum, Zambia is richly endowed with a range of energy sources, particularly woodlands and forests for wood fuel, hydropower, coal, and new and renewable sources of energy. Woodlands cover 66 per cent of the country's total land area and provide about 70 per cent of its energy requirements. With some of the best river resources and hydro-electric potential in Africa, Zambia ought to be a major exporter of power to the region. The country's hydropower resource potential stands at an estimated 6,000 MW, while the installed capacity is a mere 1,715.5 MW. Major sources include Kafue Gorge, Kariba North Bank, and Victoria Falls. Apart from the Kariba-North Bank extension, there has been no significant investment in generation capacity since 1977. The mines consume about 68 per cent of Zambia's electricity, while households use only 19 per cent. As investments in the mining sector increase, Zambia needs the resources to invest in electricity generation.

Paradoxically, Zambian electricity tariffs are among the lowest in Africa, well below the level necessary to attract investment. Meanwhile, the government has insufficient resources to spend on basic health and education services, let alone to invest in power. Clearly, Zambia needs to mobilize adequate resources for investment in power generation. The tariffs to the privatized mines are at subsidized rates. To ensure the Zambia Electricity Supply's (ZESCO) long-term financial health and sustainability and to enable investment to proceed, mining tariffs need to be renegotiated at a level that covers both capital and operational costs. This is an alternative avenue to taxation for raising resources from the mining sector.

ZESCO supplies power at a wholesale level to the Copperbelt Energy Corporation (CEC), which acquired ZCCM's transmission and distribution network and which retails power to the individual privatized mines. The publicly owned mines benefited from low tariffs for most of the 1980s and 1990s while ZESCO had excess capacity. These tariffs were then entrenched during the privatization negotiations. In 2006/2007, ZESCO was selling to CEC at a loss of one half of a US cent/KWH. In 2006, the negotiated tariff rates for the new mines, Kansanshi and Lumwana, were below the rate at which ZESCO sold to CEC (IPA Energy Consulting 2007:9).

Furthermore, to the extent that the Zambian Government subsidizes oil imports, the government is also subsidizing the mining sector. In effect there may be a net transfer of resources from government to the mining sector.

1.5.3 *Agriculture*

Zambia is well endowed with resources for agricultural development, possessing a conducive climate, abundant arable land, and labour and water resources, yet the economy has not unlocked most of this potential. Zambian agriculture is dominated by smallholder farmers, of which there are 800,000.

Agriculture employs 67 per cent of the labour force, even though it contributes only 21 per cent to GDP (World Bank, 2007). The sector also supplies the agro-manufacturing industries, which account for 12 per cent of export earnings. Of the country's 752,000 square kilometre landmass, 58 per cent is suitable for arable use – however only about 14 per cent is currently under cultivation. Furthermore, although the country accounts for 40 per cent of the water resources in Southern Africa, only 6 per cent of the irrigation potential is utilized, making agriculture predominantly rain-fed and highly prone to weather, and thereby creating wide variations in output.

Lack of technological development has contributed to modest productivity in the sector. The technology used in Zambia is, in most cases, very basic. Despite the wealth of technological developments that are known to enhance agricultural productivity, few are available to the majority of poor farmers. Many farmers use only simple farming implements such as the hand hoe. Technologies such as fertilizer, improved seed and water management techniques are also underutilized.

Zambia's current land tenure system comprises customary land constituting 94 per cent of the total land area in Zambia, while state land constitutes 6 per cent (Ministry of Lands, 2006). Land tenure reform must be undertaken to ensure that farmers can have security of tenure and thus increase investment in farmland.

Agricultural policies in Zambia need to be reoriented from the current price-support system, which gobbles up an enormous amount of resources, to the provision of the basic infrastructure from the resources saved. Government has been spending huge sums of money every year to purchase maize at prices in excess of the market price, and then selling that same maize at prices lower than it paid for it. The resources released by this reorientation can then be used to invest in in infrastructure such as irrigation.

1.5.4 *Tourism*

Zambia's tourism sector has great potential as the country is endowed with vast wildlife resources, has a diverse culture and natural heritage and enjoys good weather. Zambia has 19 national parks and 22 game-management areas, covering 22.4 million hectares. Government strategy in this sector should be to create an enabling environment through private sector participation. This should be done through the provision of adequate infrastructure and legislation and encouraging balanced community involvement aimed at poverty reduction in rural areas.

1.5.5 *Mining*

The Zambian economy has been dominated by the mining sector for more than 70 years. In the period 1965–75, copper accounted for 95 per cent of export earnings and 45 per cent of government revenues. Although copper exports constitute about 30 per cent of GDP in Zambia, mining revenues have remained relatively low. This has been driven by a combination of generous development agreements, signed with the international mining companies in the 1990s at the time of privatization, and the fact that most of these mines had to undertake large capital expenditures to revive production and therefore had losses that had to be carried forward to reduce their taxable income. As a result, Zambia's mining revenues have been low compared with other mineral producers, despite a relatively high share of mining exports in GDP. Mineral exports, as a percentage of GDP, are in excess of 30 per cent while mineral revenues, as a percentage of GDP, are less than 4 per cent. This underscores the urgent need for measures to enhance the contribution of the mining sector to revenues commensurate with the sector's contribution to exports.

1.5.6 *Manufacturing*

The manufacturing sector has great potential for job creation due to its forward and backward linkages with other sectors in the economy. The manufacturing sector grew rapidly after independence, during the period 1964–73, mainly due to high copper prices that facilitated the establishment of local import substituting industries, largely servicing the mining sector. The sector's performance was adversely affected when copper prices fell and oil prices increased in the 1970s. The sector's performance is constrained by the lack of infusion of new technology, the high cost of borrowing, and foreign competition. The leading subsector in manufacturing has been food, beverage, and tobacco, accounting for more than two thirds of total value added, followed by textiles and leather, and leather products. The performance of textiles and leather, and leather products, has been adversely affected by increased imports, especially from China.

Government interventions should focus on addressing constraints that seem to negatively impact the manufacturing sector. Specific interventions include assisting enterprises particularly the Medium, Small, and Micro Enterprises (MSMES) to access affordable finance, removal of administrative barriers to the establishment of enterprises, improvement of regulatory frameworks, and establishment of multi-facility economic zones in order to increase export oriented industries.

1.5.7 *Science and technology*

Zambia has about 1,000 scientists and engineers per million population who are engaged in research and development, which is insufficient given the fact that more than two million Zambians have post-secondary school education. Most of the funding for research and development has been donor-funded. This has been exacerbated by the fact that the private sector has been inclined towards trading. Science and Technology needs to be embedded as a culture in the key economic sectors in order to attain competitiveness in the production of a wide range of goods and services.

1.6 Conclusion

Zambia is a country endowed with abundant natural resources that can be harnessed to put the country on a sustainable development path. Foreign ownership of mining companies and attractive tax incentives has limited the amount of resources that the economy can absorb from increased mining revenues. This is exacerbated by implicit subsidies to the mines through lower tariff rates charged to the mines by some public utility companies and VAT refunds that are so huge that the mines have no incentive to convert their foreign exchange earnings into Kwacha to settle domestic obligations. As a result, Zambia has recorded an inconsistency in its macro numbers, with a depreciating exchange rate when the current account of the balance of payments is in surplus as copper prices rise. Furthermore, high copper prices have not been translated into improved fiscal performance. It is, therefore, recommended that urgent measures be undertaken to ensure that an increasing amount of foreign exchange earned from natural resources is absorbed into the economy either through taxes or payments for domestic goods and services.

2

Zambia: A Time of Big Opportunities and Tough Decisions

Paul Collier

2.1 Introduction

Zambia is archetypal in both its political system and its economy. Politically, Zambia has a strong claim to being among the most democratic countries in Africa. Its economy has long been defined by the extraction of copper. Development based on resource extraction raises distinctive political issues of sustainability: a non-renewable natural asset is being depleted, and its price on world markets is subject to large fluctuations. Hence, Zambia's overall economic progress depends critically upon how democracy interacts with the management of natural resources: is resource depletion used to fund the accumulation of other assets, in particular addressing the accumulated deficit of infrastructure, or is it used to finance an unsustainably high level of recurrent expenditure? Are periods of high prices used as opportunities for high savings, or are recurrent expenditures ratcheted up?

In Section 2.2, I discuss how democratic pressures affect overall economic policies, setting the Zambian experience in the broader context of African and other developing countries that, like Zambia, have genuine electoral democracies and I compare them to the many countries that are less democratic. In Section 2.3, I focus more specifically on the political economy of balancing the needs of the present with responsibility towards the future. Again I set the Zambian experience in the broader context of the global experience of developing countries. Finally, in Section 2.4, I examine the implications for current government policy priorities.

2.2 The economic implications of genuine democratic accountability

Zambia is an exemplary democracy. Indeed, it stands out in Africa as a country in which governments and presidents have been sufficiently circumscribed by checks and balances that they have not been in a position to abuse the power of incumbency to the extent of denying their opponents the opportunity to gain power. Not only has Zambia regularly held multi-party elections, but also Zambian elections have repeatedly resulted in a change of government. Since 1991, there have been constitutional changes of power as a result of elections – between parties and between presidents. This is the most convincing testimony to the fundamental decency of the Zambian electoral process.

In any genuine democracy, pressures from the electorate loom large in economic policy. To understand these pressures it is helpful to set the Zambian experience in the wider context of the global experience. Sir Winston Churchill famously described democracy as the worst system of government except for all the others. This continues to be an apt description. It is clear that the pressures on economic policy coming from democratic accountability to citizens are not always benign, both globally and in Zambia. However, accountability does provide a check on the abuse of power that becomes evident when democracies are compared to autocracies, of which Africa has had much unfortunate experience.

Recent research into the effects of democratic accountability on economic performance substantiates Churchill's proposition. Judged on the criterion of economic growth, democracies have less variance than autocracies. They are not able to achieve the fabulous growth rates of Chinese autocracy because implementation of policies cannot be as swift and ruthless. However, they avoid the catastrophic collapses all too familiar during African autocracies. Therefore, democracy produces a less risky overall environment.

But recent research on Africa enables us to be much more precise about the effects of elections on economic policies. I have recently explored this issue. My research, conducted in collaboration with Lisa Chauvet, analyses not only Zambia, but all African countries and indeed all other developing countries for which data are available, from 1970 to 2005. We measure economic policies annually using World Bank ratings, the Country Policy and Institutional Assessment, and also include an international measure of economic governance (Chauvet and Collier, 2009). Our question is, how are policies and economic governance affected, year-by-year, by an election?

We arrive at three key findings. The first is that elections only have a significant effect on policy if they are properly conducted. This is an important comment because many elections in Africa, and elsewhere, are sham events with the government using the power of incumbency to skew the results. I have studied such fraudulent elections extensively (Collier and Vicente, 2011; Collier and Hoeffler, 2014). Sham elections produce economic policies that look like those of an autocracy rather than those of a genuine democracy. An implication of this is that the pressures from electoral competition on economic policy in Zambia are likely to be much more intense than in much of the rest of Africa, where standards of electoral conduct are significantly lower – as revealed by the greater power of incumbents to remain in office.

Our second finding is that, viewed over the long term, those developing countries with decent elections such as Zambia tend to have better economic policies and economic governance than countries that are autocratic in form if not in name. In other words, Churchill was right.

However, economies are not viewed in the long term, but in the here-and-now of how policies are currently changing, and Zambia is no exception. Our final finding bears this out. Those developing countries with decent elections tend to have an economic policy cycle that coincides with their electoral cycle. This is indeed a familiar phenomenon from elections in the developed economies and is known as the political business cycle. The cycle is characterized by three phases: in describing them I will begin with the phase when politics is most prominent, namely the run-up to an election. During this phase the incumbent government is tempted to look good to voters by implementing policies that have a quick beneficial impact, even if they have an adverse subsequent legacy. Economists label these policies as populist. The pressure for populist policies reveals itself in the global data. Economic policy typically deteriorates significantly in the year before an election. For example, governments tend to reduce spending on public investments that will not pay off until after the election, while increasing spending on consumer subsidies. In the worst cases, governments try to win elections by printing money, realizing that the inflationary consequences will not be felt until after the election. Recognition of this problem has been the major impetus behind the greater independence given to central banks around the world in recent decades.

The second phase in the electoral cycle is the period immediately following an election. We again find that this is typically a period of poor economic policies. There are likely to be two distinct reasons for this. One is that the pressures faced during the run-up to the election leave an unfortunate legacy. Chickens hatched during that phase come home to roost after the election.

The populist measures adopted in the year prior to the election will give rise to economic difficulties in the following year. In the past, Zambia has suffered from just such a legacy problem. For example, in the final months before the 1991 election President Kaunda sharply increased public spending, financed by an enormous expansion of the money supply. This was a strategy of desperation, and it proved unsuccessful as Kaunda was decisively swept out of power. However, unsurprisingly, following the election the successor government inherited a severe bout of inflation. Economic policies also tend to deteriorate in the aftermath of an election because during the election the contestants tend to compete on promises which sound attractive to voters but which are costly to implement. After the election, the winner is faced with the painful choice of implementing promises that may prove to be excessively expensive or explaining to voters why implementation will have to be deferred. For example, in Zambia during the election campaign of 2011, the winning party promised to create many more local governments, which proved to be a popular commitment. Since the election this, combined with fuel subsidies and wage increases, has severely burdened the budget. As a result, the fiscal deficit has risen sharply to around 8 per cent, which is clearly unsustainable.

If these two phases were the only consequences of genuine electoral competition, then it would be hard to reconcile these results with the statement that democracy is good for economic performance. However, there is a crucial third phase, which is the mid-term period. In this phase the government has dug itself out from the consequences of its election commitments and is not yet faced by the need to garner votes through electorally appealing, short-term measures. A key finding of Chauvet and Collier is that the mid-term is the key phase in which democratically accountable governments adopt good policies. Accountability ensures that political leaders are well-intentioned, and the mid-term gives them the power to think about and implement good policies even if they may take some years to pay off: after all, successful leaders have second terms.

In 2014, the Zambian Government reached the middle of its first term. The implication is that it has arrived at the critical period during which good democratic governments make the hard choices that yield long-term economic success. The consequences of these choices are magnified because of copper. Zambia's copper reserves considerably enlarge the range of policy choices, which creates both opportunities and dangers.

2.3 Back to the future: Zambia's second chance at managing copper

Zambia's copper is a depleting natural asset. Unusually, Zambian society has faced the same opportunity twice, namely that of depleting its natural asset and using the revenues to accumulate other, more productive assets.

The first opportunity was during the long period from independence to about 2002. In retrospect, this can be seen as an entire cycle of copper extraction, taxation, and spending of the resulting revenues, ending in the complete depletion of known copper reserves. At independence, Zambia was endowed with a huge reserve of copper, but by 2002 nearly all of the known copper reserves that were commercially viable at the prices then prevailing had been exhausted. Indeed, the sector appeared to be a liability rather than an asset. An indication of this was that the private operator, Anglo-American, pulled out. It is therefore important to assess how well the Zambian governments, which managed the economy during these four decades, succeeded in capturing revenues from this resource depletion and converting them into productive assets.

Unfortunately, the first complete cycle of copper extraction was a failure. Revenues automatically accrued to the state because copper extraction was nationalized. However, successive governments did not use the revenues from copper to accumulate productive assets. Instead, they were used to finance consumption subsidies for the population and production inefficiencies in the state-owned copper company. In reality, the policy was even worse: not only were revenues from copper used for these recurrent purposes rather than for investment, they were also used as the implicit collateral for international sovereign borrowing. In turn, the borrowed money was again used for consumption subsidies and production inefficiencies. Hence, far from accumulating assets, the country accumulated debts. As a result, by the end of the copper extraction period in 2002, Zambians were no better off than they had been at independence. I recall an elderly Zambian at the time aptly summing up the past mistakes in economic policy with the comment, 'What will our children say of us?'

Natural resource extraction is usually unforgiving of errors; once the resource has been exhausted the opportunity is over. As of 2002, it looked as though Zambia had missed its opportunity. However, fortuitously, two important external changes since 2002 have given Zambia a second chance. Firstly, the world price of copper has risen very strongly, transforming mines that were unviable into profitable operations. The high price also triggered investment in new mines, opening up substantial new reserves that are commercially viable within the foreseeable price range. Initially, mistakes were made in the design of taxation so that the foreign companies that replaced Anglo-American provided little revenue to the government, but taxation was gradually increased. Secondly, the millennium triggered a global movement for debt forgiveness, *Jubilee 2000*, which, in due course, largely cancelled much of Africa's debt, including that of Zambia.

As a result of these two fortuitous developments, the government elected in 2011 faced approximately the same opportunities as those faced by the first government after independence half-a-century earlier. As then, the prospective revenues from copper are substantial and the country is not burdened by debt, but the copper will gradually be depleted to exhaustion, so the revenues are intrinsically unsustainable. This second chance has given

Zambia a huge opportunity to finance development from its own resources. It can potentially address the accumulated deficit in infrastructure by radically increasing the rate of productive investment, financed by the new revenues from copper. It can even accelerate this process by using future resource revenues as collateral for borrowing.

However, it is essential to recognize that previous Zambian governments that faced the same opportunity completely failed to harness it. History does not just happen; powerful forces usually drive policy mistakes, so that the default option in any society is for the same mistakes to be repeated. Hence, a crucial question for Zambian society is whether enough has changed since that first 30 years of independence to prevent a repeat of the missed opportunity constituted by the first period of copper depletion? Clearly, the new circumstances are different in one important respect. Fifty years ago, Zambia's copper mines were owned by the state, now they are owned privately. One implication is that an effective fiscal regime is now more important than it was then. The papers by Adam et al., and by Conrad in this volume discuss the implications.

2.3.1 Learning from the past

Once this question is posed, it is at once apparent that there are two important differences between then and now. The first difference is that Zambians now have the benefit of hindsight. The society has lived through a huge missed opportunity, and so there is good reason to expect politicians, officials, and ordinary citizens to have learned from that searing experience. Societies are not condemned to repeat history; indeed they often learn from it. For example, Germany is currently the most successful economy in Europe, with an enviable record of good macro-economic management. However, the fundamental reason for this success is that Germans learned from their previous history of catastrophically bad macro-economic management, during which the society collapsed into hyperinflation. That experience of hyperinflation became, in effect, an investment in the education of the German people in the importance of prudent policies. Has an analogous learning process occurred in Zambia? Evidently, the critical policy is somewhat different – not hyperinflation but the accumulation of productive assets as copper is depleted.

2.3.2 Pressures due to democracy

The second difference is that Zambia is now a genuine democracy. During the first period of copper extraction, over the years when copper prices were high so that revenues should have been devoted to investment, Zambia was a one-party state. So, it is pertinent to ask how much difference might democracy make to the prudent management of copper revenues?

Since Zambia is at the beginning of this new period of copper depletion, the best guide is again to turn to international evidence from developing countries in Africa and elsewhere that have substantial natural resources and are also democratic. In research with Anke Hoeffler, I studied all those countries for which there is data, and examined whether they were able to harness natural resources for sustained growth to their political systems (Collier and Hoeffler, 2009).

We found that a clear pattern only emerged once we distinguished between two distinct aspects of democracy – electoral competition and checks and balances. As discussed earlier, some societies that appear superficially to be democracies do not have genuine electoral competition – they are shams. However, there can be no doubt that Zambia has active electoral competition. The other aspect of democratic systems, checks and balances, also varies greatly between states. In some states the government of the moment faces few restraints on its decisions, whereas in others there are a great many restraints, such as an independent judiciary and a range of other potential veto points. Political scientists, country-by-country, have counted the number of such veto points and we used this to measure the degree to which checks and balances restrained governments. Elections are an easy aspect of democracy to establish; they are periodic events that can be organized even in severely troubled conditions. In contrast, checks and balances are not events but processes. They take time to establish, and therefore are usually quite weak in societies that have only recently become democratic.

We found that resource-rich economies were distinctive in how the political system, as measured by the degree of electoral competition and the number of checks and balances, affected growth. In countries without significant natural resource wealth, electoral competition raised the growth rate and checks and balances were not important. In effect, for resource-scarce countries, elections themselves appeared to be a sufficient check on government behaviour and further restraints were redundant. However, resource-scarce economies differ from resource-rich ones in two critical respects. Firstly, their governments need to tax citizens in order to generate revenues. In contrast, resource-rich economies have much less need to tax citizens – revenues come from resource taxation. A consequence is that there tends to be less pressure from citizens to use revenues well. Secondly, resource-scarce economies have less need to invest government revenues because the revenues are not unsustainable – they are not going to expire due to resource depletion. Hence, not only are citizens more inclined to scrutinize how government spends money, they have less need to worry that government is not investing enough.

In contrast to the effects of electoral competition and checks and balances in resource-scarce economies, we found that in resource-rich ones electoral competition was damaging for growth whereas checks and balances were beneficial. In effect, if a government faced intense electoral competition, but was then unrestrained by checks and balances on its decisions, it was tempted into populist policies. The chapter by Cheeseman in this volume addresses the pressures for populism in Zambia. We found that resource-rich democracies could outperform less democratic societies, but only if they had strong checks and balances.

These results are a clear warning to Zambia. In Zambia electoral competition is indeed very fierce, but, being a relatively young democracy, strong checks and balances have yet to be built. An implication is that if Zambia follows the global pattern, its political system will tend to push government decisions towards populism rather than entrenching the good stewardship of resource revenues.

2.4 Priorities for policy: copper extraction, investment, and sovereign borrowing

Having reached the mid-term phase, when democratic governments adopt the policies that pay off in the long term, the Zambian Government has an opportunity to put three distinct sets of policies into place. Firstly, these are policies that directly shift resource allocation from current consumption to investment. Here the government has already made preliminary moves to curtail subsidies and increase investment projects. Secondly, they must build the capacity to design, select, and implement investment projects well. It is not enough to increase investment spending; projects must be productive. Thirdly, they must put in place the checks and balances that ensure that these policy changes persist, so that they are not abandoned during the pressures of the other two phases of the political business cycle. I take these three priorities in turn.

2.4.1 *Reining in current expenditure*

A fundamental principle of sound management of revenues from the depletion of natural assets is that a substantial proportion of the revenues should be devoted to the future. Quite what proportion is sensible is a matter of judgment, but a prudent minimum is somewhere in the range of 30–50 per cent. For example, the Ghanaian parliament recently passed a law requiring that at least 30 per cent of the new oil revenues should be used for savings and investment. The savings decision is complicated by the fact that, in addition to the gradual depletion of the physical resource, its price is subject to large fluctuations on world markets. Hence, the savings rate needs to reflect a judgement on whether the copper price is above or below its long-term level. To date, the proportion of copper revenues devoted to the future in Zambia has been far too low. Indeed, the present rate of savings out of copper revenues, properly accounted, appear to be negative. Figure 2.1, which shows an estimate of the national savings rate adjusted for copper depletion, suggests that the savings rate has been declining since around 2003 and had become negative by 2010. This is because future copper revenues are being pre-empted to fund an unsustainably large budget deficit caused predominantly by increases in recurrent expenditure such as public sector wage hikes.

Therefore, an urgent priority is to reduce recurrent spending. In a democratic society such decisions are always politically painful because vested interests use their political freedom to protest against cuts that disadvantage them. Yet globally, many low-income democracies have achieved fiscal stability over the past two decades, so substantial reductions in recurrent spending have proved to be entirely possible. In the current Zambian context, there will be insufficient space to raise the rate of investment out of resource revenues to sustainable levels without significant reductions in recurrent spending.

An important aspect of the successful management of the shift in spending from consumption to investment is for politicians to explain to citizens why such a strategy is wise. Almost all households have children and so can appreciate the potential importance of postponing gratification for the sake of future opportunities. Managing natural resource extraction adds extra punch to this argument because the current generation of adults are the stewards responsible for managing the depletion of the country's natural

Figure 2.1 Gross, net, and adjusted savings, 1980–2010

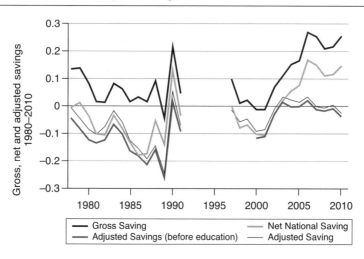

Source: World Bank

asset. Good stewardship requires that revenues from depletion be used to benefit the next generation, not just the present one. Here, Zambia's history of failed stewardship is potentially a major asset. Ordinary citizens can readily appreciate that Zambia is poor today only because previous generations failed in their responsibility towards their children. It is but a small step from this recognition to finding the resolve not to repeat that mistake.

2.4.2 *Investing in investing*

In tandem with reining in recurrent spending, Zambia needs to build the capacity to invest well in productive assets. Investment is always specific and so the design, selection, and implementation of projects are critical. Given the accumulated shortages of public capital in Zambia, it should be possible to undertake projects that yield high social returns. However, it is also entirely possible for public investment to be dissipated in worthless projects induced by vanity or corruption; such projects are littered across Africa.

Building the capacity to create good projects is in itself an investment: hence, a good way of conceptualizing the process is 'investing in investing' (Collier, 2010). A useful initial step in improving the capacity to invest is to benchmark Zambia's current capacity. Here a new index developed by the IMF – the Public Investment Management Index – provides a guide. The Fund has rated over 70 developing countries on four different aspects of the project cycle: design, selection, implementation, and evaluation. Each component is scored over a 0–4 range, high scores indicating better management. Zambia's overall rating, at 1.87, is the same as Ghana, but well behind Botswana at 2.35 and South Africa at 3.53. However, more can be learnt from the component scores that from the overall average. In Table 2.1, I compare Zambia on these ratings with some other pertinent countries. Such a comparison is potentially useful in indicating the priorities for improvement.

The table suggests that the priorities for building Zambian investment capacity are at the project design and project implementation stages. These are the two areas where Zambia is markedly weaker than comparable African countries. Project design can, initially, be contracted out to foreign companies

Table 2.1 Public investment management

	Design	Selection	Implementation	Evaluation
Zambia	1.50	2.80	1.87	1.33
Botswana	3.00	2.40	2.00	2.00
Rwanda	2.50	2.00	3.20	1.33
South Africa	4.00	4.00	2.80	3.33
Ghana	1.33	2.40	2.40	1.33
Tanzania	0.33	1.60	2.27	1.33

and foreign expertise can be brought in. This has been the major strength of Botswana, as its high score indicates. Hence, by simply adopting Botswana's practices at the design stage, Zambia could double this component of its rating. Similarly, at the implementation stage the country to emulate is Rwanda. Rwanda has achieved remarkable improvements in implementation by the simple expedient of insisting on personal responsibility for clearly specified and monitored objectives, backed up by penalties for failure. Since Zambia's project selection process is better than that in either Botswana or Rwanda, this act of learning could be a reciprocal process: Zambia has as much to teach as to learn from others. Finally, Zambia could improve its evaluation capacity by learning from South Africa. Were Zambia to improve these three components of its public investment management to equal these models its overall management would rise to being one of the very best among all the countries rated by the IMF. In the process, it would get a much higher return from any given investment effort.

Zambia's project selection is relatively good. However, in some other countries a rapid scale-up in the quantity of public investment led to deterioration in the process of selection, notably Nigeria during its first oil boom and Kenya during its coffee boom. Therefore, it would be prudent to strengthen the process of project selection further. Good project selection is partly technical and partly political. The technical aspect is to be able to assess the costs of a project relative to the benefits – the technique known as cost-benefit analysis. This requires a substantial team of professional economists, typically placed within the Ministry of Finance. The political aspect of good project selection is that the technical assessment coming from cost-benefit analysis has to be defended against lobbying from special interests, which are not concerned about the benefits and costs to society but only about the benefits and costs to themselves.

2.4.3 *Building checks and balances*

Recall that democratic societies rich in natural resources require particularly strong checks and balances in order to harness the opportunity for development. Young democracies such as Zambia do not start with strong checks and balances; they have to be built. Checks and balances are veto points that can block government decisions and so governments are often wary of helping to build them – all governments prefer untrammelled power. However, the statistical evidence suggests that for resource-rich countries, untrammelled government power inhibits economic development. Therefore, governments need to look beyond their own short-term interest in forcing decisions through, to the longer-term interest of the society in having clear rules and institutions empowered to enforce them.

The successful management of resource depletion is a process that lasts for a generation, not just for the lifetime of a single government. Rules and institutions provide consistency in the design and implementation of policy over this long horizon. Rules guide future decisions. Institutions are teams of public officials with the mandates and skills that enable them to implement the rules.

The key challenges to good management are that revenues fluctuate from year-to-year due to volatility in world copper prices, and that extraction gradually depletes copper reserves so that the revenues will not be sustained. Each of these challenges requires a rule supported by an institution.

One pair of rules and institutions concerns volatility. Chile is the global leader in building the rules and institutions for managing public finances in the face of fluctuations in the world price of copper. The Government of Chile has established an independent team of technical experts that produces an annual assessment of how the current world price of copper stands relative to the likely price in the long term. Since the Zambian Government needs the same information, the most straightforward solution may well be for it to incorporate this independent assessment into its own decision procedures. Zambia would need to build a stabilization fund similar to that of Chile; such a fund, which would hold only foreign financial assets, could be managed under the auspices of the Bank of Zambia.

Over-and-above managing volatility, the gradual depletion of the endowment of copper ore needs to be offset by investment in infrastructure. This involves three key rules. One concerns the proportion of revenues that are saved; the second concerns the process by which savings are invested in assets; and the third concerns recourse to borrowing.

The savings rule, which indicates how much of the resource revenues should be devoted to assets in order to offset depletion, firstly needs to make allowance for volatility. For example, if a Chilean-type stabilization rule is established, each year there will be flows into or out of a stabilization fund. The post-stabilization revenue would then become the relevant revenue figure out of which savings should be made to offset depletion. A helpful principle in determining the appropriate savings rate needed to offset depletion is that it should gradually rise over time. For example, it might start at 30 per cent of copper revenues, analogous to Ghana's initial savings rate out of oil revenues, and then gradually rise, year-by-year, so as to be close to 100 per cent by the time copper is close to final exhaustion. Exhaustion may not be for several decades, so that the savings rule might increase the required savings rate very gradually at only around 1 per cent each year, but this would make a substantial difference over the long term.

The second rule concerns the choice of assets from these savings. I have already discussed the procedures appropriate for domestic investment. It is helpful to legislate rules that require due procedures to be followed in the design, selection, implementation, and evaluation of public investment projects – the Ministry of Finance being the appropriate institution for assessing projects. There is also, sometimes, a case for parking savings in foreign financial assets. Zambia is short of infrastructure so, over the longer term, all the copper revenues that it saves should be invested domestically. However, if the funds available for investment build up rapidly the available finance may exceed the capacity to invest it well domestically for a time. This is particularly likely as a result of sovereign-bond issues.

The third rule concerns foreign borrowing to finance infrastructure. The government has already embarked upon sovereign borrowing. In 2012 it was able to raise $750 million at an interest rate of only 5.625 per cent. This was a major vote of confidence in the government by the international financial community. In 2014, the Zambian Government plans to raise an even larger sum from a bond issue. However, even at this modest rate of interest, the money is only repayable if a high proportion of it is soundly invested. In 2012, however, part of it had to be used to finance an overrun in agricultural subsidies and so was used for recurrent spending, resulting in ratings downgrades. If, for example, only half of the borrowed money were used for the future, with the other half used for recurrent spending, the break-even rate of return on investment would need to be over 11 per cent in dollar terms. Hence, a sensible precautionary rule for sovereign borrowing is that all the money raised should be used for investment.

Since there are high fixed costs for issuing bonds, it is sensible to borrow in large amounts, such as $1bn. However, the capacity to invest well cannot be increased in such massive steps, so that some of the money borrowed will need to be parked abroad for a while, being drawn down gradually as investment projects are prepared. There is a wide spread between the interest rate that Zambia is paying on its borrowed money and what it can get on world markets, so this raises the true cost of borrowing.

Some infrastructure projects generate revenues that make them self-financing. It may be better to finance such investments through project finance rather than sovereign borrowing, since this leaves the government unencumbered. Project finance also provides a legal structure whereby revenues generated by the project are pre-committed to service the debt borrowed for the project. This structure provides an in-built discipline that guards against bad projects, since it will only be possible to borrow the money if there is convincing evidence that the project will yield a return that is higher than the cost of its finance.

The case for financing infrastructure from sovereign borrowing is strongest where, although the rate of return to society on the project is high, only a small proportion of these returns can be recovered through the tax system. For example, social infrastructure, such as schools and hospitals, does not directly recover its return through charges to users; and only around one fifth of the social return to the economy is captured through taxation. Hence, even if such projects yield a high social return, they will never generate enough revenue for the government to meet the obligations of debt service and repayment. Instead, repayment will depend upon tax revenues from copper. Such investments are worth doing, but they effectively mortgage future copper tax revenues.

A potentially serious problem with sovereign borrowing to finance infrastructure that does not generate enough revenues to pay for itself is that it can open the door to projects that have low social rates of return. Interest groups and politicians have many pet projects. Sometimes this is because the project would advantage them; sometimes it is because the project is glamorous, or fits some idea of progress for which there is little underlying justification. It is vital that there be an effective defence against such projects since they pre-empt future revenues from copper. Hence, an important rule is that all projects funded by sovereign borrowing should be subject to independent cost-benefit analysis.

The rules suggested above can provide guidance both for those officials in government who are tasked with implementing them and for those whose job is to scrutinize public decisions. While the primary *loci* for the institutions of implementation are the Ministry of Finance and the Bank of Zambia, the main *locus* for the institutions of scrutiny is parliament. Specialist parliamentary committees need to develop both a thorough understanding of why the rules matter, and a flow of usable information on the behaviour of the institutions tasked with implementation so that they can properly monitor how well Zambia's copper is being harnessed for the development of the nation.

2.5 Conclusion

When Zambia was a one-party state its governments so mismanaged the opportunity presented by a valuable endowment of copper that the entire resource was exhausted without sustainable benefit. Zambia is now one of the most democratic countries in Africa. Fortuitously, the country has a second chance to harness a copper endowment for development, and so a pertinent question is whether the switch to democracy will lead to a happier outcome. A defining feature of democracies is that they are accountable to citizens, and in the long run this will deliver better and less risky economic management than is typical of undemocratic societies. However, democracies find the conversion of natural resource wealth into sustained prosperity particularly difficult to manage. Populist pressures can easily drive governments into using resource revenues for recurrent spending rather than devoting them to productive investment. To resist such pressures, the international evidence suggests that in resource-rich democracies strong checks and balances through policy rules, institutions with clear mandates for implementation, and powerful institutions for scrutiny of decisions, are needed.

Zambia has a high level of recurrent expenditure relative to investment. Governments have found spending pressures difficult to resist because, as a young democracy, it does not yet have strong checks and balances. The time when democratic governments are best able to implement policy improvements is during the middle of their term of office. The Zambian Government has arrived at this moment. It faces the daunting challenges of rebalancing public spending towards investment, while at the same time building the rules and institutions that lock the society into good stewardship of resource revenues. If it is able to achieve this agenda, future generations of Zambians will no longer have just cause to complain about their elders.

References

Chauvet, L. and P. Collier (2009). Elections and economic policy in developing countries. *Economic Policy*. 24(59): 509–550

Collier, P. (2010). *The Plundered Planet*. Oxford: Oxford University Press.

Collier, P. and A. Hoeffler (2009). Testing the neo-con agenda. *European Economic Review*. 53(3): 293–308

Collier, P. and A. Hoeffler (2014). Do elections matter for economic performance? *Oxford Bulletin of Economics and Statistics*. DOI: 10.1111/obes.12054

Collier, P. and P. Vicente (2011). Violence, bribery and fraud: The political economy of elections in sub-Saharan Africa. *Public Choice*. 153(1–2): 117–147

3

Growth, Employment, Diversification, and the Political Economy of Private Sector Development in Zambia

Adriana Cardozo, Gibson Masumbu, Chiwama Musonda, and Gaël Raballand[1]

3.1 Introduction

For several decades, Zambia has been struggling to diversify its economy beyond the mining sector. Examples of economic diversification among mining companies are not numerous. This chapter investigates why economic diversification may have failed up to now and what could be done in the future to improve and add value to diversification.

Zambia has strengthened its macro-economic fundamentals (see Chapter 2). Economic growth in Zambia rebounded in the last decade, showing remarkably stable average gross domestic product (GDP) growth of 5 per cent, which is an improvement on the poor growth observed during the 1980s and 1990s, which resulted in a large reversal in social development.[2]

A year after independence from Great Britain, Zambia was the second richest country in Africa in 1965 but by 1997 it was the only country, out of those with data available, where human development – measured by the Human Development Index (HDI) – was lower than that observed in 1975 (Mphuka, 2002). If one considers a more recent period, Zambia's HDI fell by 0.17 per cent annually between 1990 and 2007; the HDI decreased from 0.495 in 1990 to 0.481 in 2008 (United Nations Development Programme, 2009).

Poverty has significantly worsened since the mid-1970s, with the decline in per capita income resulting from slow economic growth. Stagnation and crisis were associated with the contraction of mining and the failure to diversify (Duncan et al., 2003). Despite robust growth in more recent years, aggregate poverty rates in Zambia have declined only slightly and remain high. The majority of Zambia's poor (80 per cent) lives in rural areas and is at least nominally engaged in small-scale agriculture (Ianchovichina and Lundstrom, 2009). Nine in every ten households in Zambia perceive themselves to be poor. Among the households that perceived themselves to be poor, 50 per cent considered themselves to be moderately poor while 40 per cent considered themselves to be extremely poor (CSO, 2010).[3]

Large income inequality and informality could be explained by the employment and production structure of the country. Each of the recent highest-growth sectors in Zambia (mining, construction, financial services, and tourism) only employ formally approximately 1–2 per cent of the population. The vast majority of the workforce is self-employed (55 per cent) or employed as an unpaid family worker (26 per cent). Formal private sector employees only account for 7 per cent of the working population of around 4 million people, while Government employees represent 5 per cent of the working population (World Bank, 2010).

Using an institutional approach, this chapter demonstrates that in a country where rents are important (owing to the importance of the mining industry aggravated by the fact that the country is landlocked), a lack of economic/trade diversification enables capture and rent-seeking behaviour to prosper, which then perpetuates the status quo, in turn limiting economic diversification. A vicious circle could then be in place. If it is assumed that many sectors are captured by monopolists or cartels, despite discourse on economic/trade diversification, the reality could be different and, in this context, it could be extremely difficult to see new sectors and business actors emerging.[4]

Some possible options would be to open up some sectors to internal and external competition with the aim of improving productivity of small and medium companies by, for instance, starting initiatives in order to increase access to finance and knowledge, or to ensure better infrastructure.

3.2 Growth has not translated into formal employment and trade diversification

3.2.1 *A lack of trade diversification*

There have been difficulties in translating the marked improvement of economic growth and the positive evolution of macro-economic variables in recent years into formal employment and trade diversification.

31

In 2009, export concentration was close to the value achieved in the early 1990s, after having reached levels that reflected a much lower concentration at the end of that decade.[5] In Zambia, the Hirschman-Herfindahl Index (HHI)[6] has increased from 0.5 in 2006 to 0.68 in 2009. This relatively large change is associated mainly with increased exports in copper, which represent a large share of total exports in the country. HHI values for Zambia corresponding to previous years suggest that the index declined from 0.70 in 1990–92 to 0.26 in 1999–01 (Yagci and Aldaz-Carroll, 2004).[7]

Zambian exports of intermediate goods, comprising mainly copper products, accounted for 75 per cent of total exports in March 2010, while raw materials accounted for 18 per cent. The share of consumer goods exports was as low as 6.6 per cent. Non-traditional exports – which include sugar, maize, cotton, tobacco, flowers, and vegetables – modestly increased from 2000 to 2003 and have gained some dynamism since then. Nevertheless, the largest increase in exports results from copper and its derivatives and is associated with higher prices, partly driven up by demand from China.[8] Exports grew rapidly in the last decade (Figure 3.1).

China is now the world's largest consumer of copper and has secured access to this resource through purchases of mines and the construction of a copper smelter in Zambia. As a result, from 2002 to 2006 Zambia's exports to China rose seventeen-fold, as a percentage share, to account for 3.5 per cent of the total copper exports. Likewise, Switzerland's share of Zambian exports grew from 3 per cent in 2002 to 20.3 per cent in 2006 after the acquisition of two major copper mines by the Swiss and because of the fact that several major commodities traders are based in Switzerland (Carmody, 2009; Carmody and Hampwaye, 2009).[9]

Figure 3.1 Total imports and exports

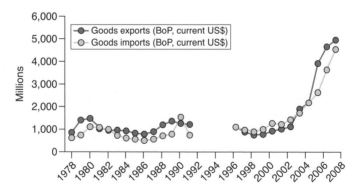

Source: World Development Indicators, 2009

Imports contracted as a result of the sharp exchange rate depreciation at the beginning of 2009 and there was a surge in imported investment goods as a result of increased private investment in mining. In 2007, investment goods (machinery and mechanical equipment) accounted for 24 per cent of imports, followed by mineral fuels (12 per cent), and vehicles (10 per cent). Other imports consist of electrical machinery, iron and steel, plastic products, fertilizers, and inputs for the mining industry (OECD, 2008: 621). The Southern African Development Community (SADC) is Zambia's main trading regional partner for both exports and imports, followed by Asia and Europe (including Switzerland).

3.2.2 The employment question

In the last few decades, the country has been experiencing difficulties in generating formal employment. According to the Central Statistical Office (CSO), the formal sector accounts for about 10 per cent of national employment levels (350,000 in the private sector and fewer than 140,000 in the public sector). Each of the highest-growth sectors in Zambia (mining, construction, financial services, and tourism) only employs approximately 1–2 per cent of the population. While larger firms drive the economy, they only employ 7 per cent of the workforce (Figure 3.2). The vast majority of the workforce is self-employed (55 per cent), employed as an unpaid family worker (26 per cent) (OECD, 2008), or estimated to be unemployed.

With the exception of the trade sector, formal employment has not grown substantially in the last few years (Table 3.1).[10] The trade sector contributed significantly to job creation between 2000 and 2008, growing by 60 per cent. In 2000, the sector employed 52,336 people; in 2008 this number had grown to 87,296. The employment levels in mining grew by nearly 40 per cent in the same period. Employment creation was very low in agriculture and

Figure 3.2 Employment breakdown in Zambia

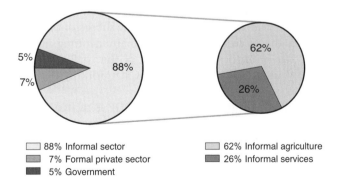

88% Informal sector	62% Informal agriculture
7% Formal private sector	26% Informal services
5% Government	

33

Table 3.1 Employment levels, 2000–08

Year	Agriculture	Mining	Manufacturing	Construction	Trade
2000	59,377	35,042	47,782	13,828	52,336
2001	59,248	34,966	47,679	13,798	52,223
2002	43,819	37,245	67,752	2,406	50,812
2003	42,543	53,888	54,008	3,576	37,918
2004	65,136	46,078	45,340	5,787	44,460
2005	65,496	32,103	40,151	7,953	67,521
2006	66,597	32,611	53,021	11,589	57,451
2007	59,030	48,318	53,152	14,731	63,901
2008	60,265	47,910	45,287	14,075	87,296

Source: CSO labour force survey 2005 and CSO quarterly employment enquiry 2008

construction, only growing by around 2 per cent between 2000 and 2009. Manufacturing, however, recorded a decline in employment levels; in 2000 the sector employed 47,782 people but in 2008 this had fallen to 45,287 people.

3.3 Growth decomposition trends

According to official statistics, agriculture, forestry, and fishing account for 73 per cent of employment in Zambia and 19 per cent of total GDP. Large commercial farmers produce most agricultural exports, 80 per cent of the country's milk, 75 per cent of wheat, and 70 per cent of soybeans and poultry. However, a large part of productive agricultural areas (about one third) has low productivity and is used by small peasants for subsistence agriculture. A small number of large businesses drive exports and productivity, whereas a massive number of informal businesses record low productivity and only provide incomes for one or two persons.

Manufacturing accounted for 9.3 per cent of GDP in 2009, a slight decrease compared with the year 2000 (9.8 per cent). The subsector of food, beverages, and tobacco has the largest share in total manufacturing, followed by the textile and leather industries, whose share of the GDP decreased from 1.7 per cent in 2000 to 0.9 per cent in 2009 (CSO Monthly Bulletin, February 2010).

Lower participation of manufacturing in GDP is related to higher textile imports in the latter years as a result of strong appreciation of the Kwacha and higher competition from Chinese producers.[11] Higher shares and dynamism of construction and housing compensated for the disappointing

Table 3.2 Growth rates in selected economic sectors

	2001	2002	2003	2004	2005	2006	2007	2008	2009*
Agriculture, Forestry and Fishing	-2.6	-1.7	5.0	4.3	-0.6	2.2	0.4	2.6	7.1
Mining and Quarrying	14.0	16.4	3.4	13.9	7.9	7.3	3.6	2.5	15.8
Manufacturing	4.2	5.7	7.6	4.7	2.9	5.7	3.0	1.8	2.5

*Preliminary.
Source: Central Statistical Office Zambia (2010)

performance of manufacturing, reflecting the effect of larger copper revenues and the appreciation of the Kwacha.

Growth within services was mainly driven by growth in community and social services, real estate, and business services, and wholesale and retail services (Millennium Challenge Account, 2009). On the contrary, tourism experienced a sharp decline and other tertiary sectors decelerated (IMF, 2010). Although the share of mining in total GDP is only 8 per cent, its influence on the economy is large, mainly via reserves and effects on the exchange rate. For instance, between 1974 and 1988, when external receipts from copper dropped 23 per cent, access to foreign exchange, as well as the government's budget, was severely affected (Saasa and Carlsson, 2002; Fraser, 2007).

Of the major economic sectors, the wholesale, retail, and trade sectors had the largest average share of the GDP over the period 2000 to 2009, contributing 18 per cent on average to overall GDP.

The growth in the sectoral share of GDP varied considerably between 2000 and 2008, as shown in Figure 3.3; construction had the largest growth over

Figure 3.3 Comparative share of GDP, 2000 and 2008

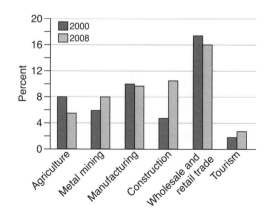

35

the same period. The mining sector also grew remarkably during the same period, recording an overall growth. The contribution of tourism (restaurants, bars, hotels) to GDP grew, whereas wholesale and retail trade, and agriculture declined.

Growth of the construction sector can possibly be explained by several factors, such as mining development; large publicly-funded programmes, such as a large stadium and road rehabilitation projects;[12] and also several privately-funded projects.[13] Growth of the construction sector could also be explained by the fact that, as a result of a Dutch Disease effect, aid inflows (in infrastructure) and mining foreign direct investment have been crowding out some investment in the tradable sectors. Moreover, this sector depends relatively heavily on public procurement, i.e. it is capital intensive, which means that it may have led to the strengthening of a few large companies.

Even though it is rather difficult to explain the construction boom without doubt, what is important is the fact that this boom has not had a large impact on formal employment.

Manufacturing recorded a modest growth rate of 3 per cent during the period 2000–09; however, the eight subsectors of manufacturing experienced various extents of growth rates (Figure 3.4). Growth in manufacturing was mainly prompted by chemicals, rubber and plastic products (9 per cent), paper and paper products (7 per cent), wood and wood products (6 per cent), non-metallic mineral products (6 per cent), and food and beverages (5 per cent).

Figure 3.4 Average growth rates for manufacturing subsectors (2000–09)

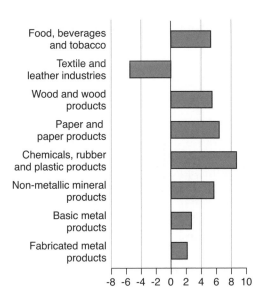

The basic metal product and fabricated metal product subsectors also recorded positive average growth of 3 per cent and 2.5 per cent respectively (Figure 3.4).

3.4 The dualistic structure of the private sector

The private sector in Africa is dominated by a dual structure. The formal private sector usually belongs to a small number of large enterprises, often foreign-owned, that generate a large share of the national output. The remaining private sector is composed of a large bulk of micro-, small-, and medium-sized enterprises (MSME) that are predominantly owned by local, indigenous entrepreneurs[14]. MSMEs are, on average, less productive than foreign-owned enterprises, a fact that also holds elsewhere but with a wider gap in Africa than in other regions. Differences in productivity are explained mainly by the education levels of managers and employees; access to technology and capital; firm size; and market access. However, recent studies point to firm size as a key factor that allows firms to increase their productivity as they grow (World Bank, 2010).

Productivity increases as firms grow in size, gain experience (firm age), and are able to access new markets. In Africa, the stark size difference explains a large part of the performance gap between domestically owned and foreign-owned enterprises. For instance, small-sized enterprises have a low chance of learning by doing or learning by exporting as a result of their isolation from foreign markets and even to markets beyond the boundary of their location. Moreover, limited agglomeration processes impede development of backward and forward linkages between firms. Although firm size makes a difference, recent studies show that the two significant constraints to fostering the existence of indigenous owned firms in Africa is access to finance and the manager's educational background (World Bank, 2010).

3.4.1 *The productivity differential*

In Zambia the productivity differences between large firms and MSMEs is extreme. Workers in the average micro-enterprise in the agricultural and service sectors make up only about a sixth of the number of workers in average large firms in the same sectors. The difference for workers in manufacturing and retail firms is a ninth (Conway and Kedia, 2010).

The Zambia Business Survey, which is the first comprehensive, nationally representative survey of MSMEs across all nine provinces in Zambia depicts these differences. Its analysis shows that agricultural firms dominate the MSME sector, while large firms are dominant in more diverse sectors. Out of the total number of MSMEs, 70 per cent are in agriculture; 21 per cent are in the retail sector; and 2 per cent are located in the service industry, for example hotels, restaurants, and transport. Manufacturing comprises only 3 per cent of the sample, mainly small agro-processing activities.

Typically, agricultural firms have very low start-up capital and have informal working arrangements, such as unpaid family members or cash payment of salaries. Output tends to be larger than sales, given that part of the output is used for the farm's own consumption, or is bartered or given away. For agricultural firms, land size and location are key factors. An increase in land size by 10 per cent is associated with a 1.6 per cent increase in productivity and an increase of 10 per cent of capital endowment is associated with a 1.8 per cent increase in productivity. The location in rural areas is undoubtedly associated with higher productivity, particularly to those firms close to railway lines. Farmers situated along railway lines have 62 per cent higher productivity compared with those located elsewhere.

Estimates of total factor productivity indicate that a 10 per cent increase in capital endowment leads to a 2.6 per cent increase in productivity in non-agricultural firms and to a 1.8 per cent increase in productivity in agricultural businesses.

For non-agricultural firms, location plays an important role; productivity is 37 per cent higher for those located in non-rural areas and 30 per cent higher for those located along railway lines. Access to financial services also plays a significant role for non-agricultural firms. Those without access to banks are estimated to be 44 per cent less productive. An increase of 10 per cent in capital endowment leads to a 2.6 per cent increase in productivity in non-agricultural firms.

3.4.2 *Wage and profitability differentials, and the issue of trading against manufacturing*

A survey of small and medium-sized companies gave an indication of profitability levels among the small enterprises. However, field interviews with informal business operators indicated that profit margins were higher during

Table 3.3 Average monthly wages between large and small economies

Sector	SEs	LEs	Difference %
Agriculture	249,537	560,000	44.6
Construction	335,833	2,012,719	16.7
Manufacturing	252,128	1,496,345	16.8
Services	337,019	1,888,145	17.8
Tourism	334,567	1,661,275	20.1
Trading	312,727	1,661,275	18.8
Transport	337,759	2,687,259	12.6

Source: Zambia Business Survey and *CSP 2008 Employment Enquiry

the period 2000–06. Those in trading attribute this to the fact that the exchange rate was relatively stable during that time. Since 2006, margins have gone down, especially for those involved in cross-border trading.

Table 3.3 shows the difference in the wage levels between the large and small enterprises[15]. Wages in small enterprises are much lower than in large ones, especially in trading and construction.

What is also striking is the fact that between small entrepreneurs, wages are much higher in the trading sector than in the manufacturing sector (almost 25 per cent more)[16]. This fact probably explains why the informal retail-trading sector has mushroomed in the last decade[17]. Obviously, it is difficult to estimate the number of Zambians involved in the informal trading sector; however, some conservative estimates suggest several hundreds of thousands of individuals involved in this activity, which probably explains why MSMEs are much more involved in trade than in large companies (Figure 3.5).

Figure 3.5 Sectoral distribution of MSMEs and large firms

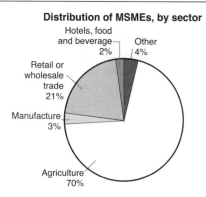

Distribution of MSMEs, by sector

Hotels, food and beverage 2%
Other 4%
Retail or wholesale trade 21%
Manufacture 3%
Agriculture 70%

Distribution of large enterprises, by sector

Hotels, food and beverage 9%
Retail or wholesale trade 9%
Other 44%
Manufacture 24%
Agriculture 14%

Source: Zambia Business Survey

39

Unlike other sectors such as tourism, manufacturing, and mining, companies in the wholesale and retail trade sectors seem to experience fewer barriers at entry. Additionally, capital requirements are not as binding as in other sectors. All that is needed is reasonable start-up capital – borrowing is usually not needed (compared with manufacturing). Education is also a constraint that is not as binding as in other sectors, and profit margins are much higher than in manufacturing, with profit margins commonly above 15 per cent. Therefore, trading (especially informal) is not as risky as manufacturing – it is easier to enter into the market and is more profitable, which can also explain why few individuals take the route into manufacturing compared with trading.

3.5 How to strengthen/formalize the second sector to enable it to diversify?

In terms of employment, poverty alleviation, and number of enterprises, the second sector is of crucial importance. This section is dedicated to understanding what the specific constraints to MSMEs are in Zambia and what could possibly be done to increase their productivity and to minimize the dualistic nature of the Zambian economy.

3.5.1 *What are the constraints borne by small enterprises?*[18]

Firstly, location proves to contribute significantly to observed productivity. For non-agricultural firms, a rural location is associated with a 37 per cent decrease in productivity. Firms along railway lines have a 30 per cent higher productivity relative to firms in other areas.

Secondly, as discussed previously, the retail trade sector is 37 per cent more productive than the services sector (the excluded sector).

The third explanation of productivity is based on the human capital of the firm's owner. In Zambia, the educational attainment of the owner contributes positively to productivity in both agricultural and non-agricultural firms, but the effect is only statistically significant in non-agricultural firms. Completing secondary school raises productivity in non-agricultural firms by 26 per cent relative to those led by owners with less education, but the increase in productivity as a result of vocational or university education is less (and statistically insignificant). While the average productivity of firms with more educated managers is shown to be greater, these regression results imply that much of the observed productivity difference is a result of complementary factors such as access to infrastructure and business services, etc.

Fourthly, access to infrastructure and inputs proves to make a significant contribution to productivity in both non-agricultural and agricultural firms. Four measures of access are tested: access to the electric grid, access to piped water, access to banking services (checking and saving accounts), and access to lending services.[19] In non-agricultural firms, access to electricity is associated with 24 per cent higher productivity; access to banking services is associated with 44 per cent higher productivity. These are significantly different from zero. In agricultural firms, electricity and access to water raise productivity by 52 per cent and 23 per cent respectively; access to lending leads to a 44 per cent increase in productivity. Thus, there is a sizeable positive effect from extending the physical availability of each of these inputs or services; the magnitude of the effect differs depending upon whether the firm is agricultural or non-agricultural.[20]

It is also worth noting that while these four hypotheses have significant power in explaining productivity, there is much cross-firm variation left unexplained. These explanations cover 26 and 25 per cent of the variation in non-agricultural and agricultural firms respectively. The remaining variation can be interpreted as the component of productivity observed by the owner but unobserved by the econometrician.

3.5.2 *How can these firms transition to higher productivity outcomes?*[21]

Some policy initiatives to increase productivity (and competitiveness) for small Zambian businesses need to be initiated, such as physical access to basic business inputs and services, with the hope of increasing productivity in consequence.

Extend access to finance

Survey results show that firms in districts with access to banking and lending services are more productive than others. In addition, there is a positive correlation between the firms' use of banking and lending services and productivity. Figure 3.6 illustrates the results of an analysis of firms in the Zambia Business Survey. Large businesses have near-universal access to banking services for transactions and insurance. Nearly 85 per cent use banking services for saving and over 45 per cent receive credits from the banking sector. By contrast, the MSMEs that dominate the survey have much lower access. Only 11 per cent use banks for transactional purposes and only 0.9 per cent have insurance services. Fewer than 8 per cent use saving instruments, while only 2.3 per cent receive financial credits.

As is evident, small enterprises are much less likely to use banking services. There could be three reasons for this. Firstly, small enterprises may not have physical access to banking services – the financial institutions may not exist in their district in Zambia. Secondly, small enterprises may be unable to

Figure 3.6 Access to financial products in MSMEs versus large firms

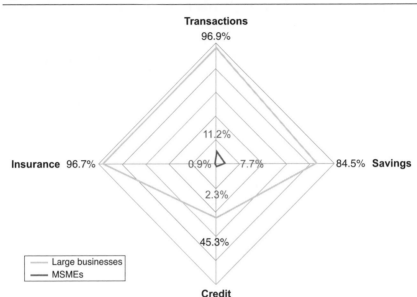

afford the financial products offered by the financial institutions. Thirdly, small enterprises may have no need for financing or, more generally, choose not to use the available financing.

A similar decomposition based upon the use of financial credit instruments indicates an even more striking conclusion: only 2 per cent of small businesses have access to credit. The reasons are the same: either the businesses have no physical access to banking or the financial products are too expensive. There is an additional, complementary, reason: these small businesses do not, for the most part, keep the financial records necessary to document a credit application. By contrast, remembering that 45 per cent of large businesses use financial credit, the lack of access to credit disadvantages small businesses relative to large ones.

Increase access to infrastructure

Productivity analysis shows that both agricultural and non-agricultural firms are far more productive when they have access to infrastructure – electricity, cell phones, and water. Among MSMEs, coverage for these services is currently very low. Even in provinces along line of rail, only about 6 per cent of rural MSMEs and 25 per cent of urban MSMEs are connected to the power grid.

Transportation infrastructure is also perceived as a serious constraint, particularly in rural areas.

Improve access to basic education

MSMEs with better-educated owners are more productive than other MSMEs in both the agricultural and non-agricultural sectors. However, many of the MSME owners only have basic levels of education, particularly in rural areas. About half of MSME owners in rural areas have no education or only a primary education, and about 45 per cent have only a secondary education. In rural areas, very few people have any vocational training and virtually none have a university education in either urban or rural areas. In addition to the direct effect of improving education, there are also strong connections between education and other forms of investment. The return to improving physical infrastructure – whether for irrigation or access to telephone banking – will be lower unless concomitant investments in education are made.

However, simply improving physical access to infrastructure or to financial services will not eliminate the constraints that MSMEs in Zambia face. The performance of MSMEs also has to be improved. MSMEs will always suffer from a lack of economies of scale and, as mentioned earlier, the competency and capacity of the company's owner is probably just as important as these other factors. That being said, it may also explain why some donor-funded projects aimed at supporting private sector development may not have been as successful as anticipated,[22] as access to finance is difficult to achieve (especially for MSMEs), vocational training is a long-term strategy, the majority of this type of project does not really tackle infrastructure issues, and, above all, as long as trading remains as profitable as it is compared with manufacturing, few projects of this type can really succeed.

Moreover, in an economy where rents could be potentially important, what is important for leaders in a market is to prevent competition (internal and external), even though it would consist of neglecting competitiveness abroad. There is lack of a level playing field in some sectors in Zambia – which goes against strengthening the competitiveness of the second sector – which would mean strengthening competition and, therefore, possibly reducing rents.

3.6 A political economy approach of economic diversification

In this section, we investigate the impact of the political economy of the private sector on economic diversification.

Two major characteristics impact Zambia's economy: being landlocked and being an economy based mainly on mining. It is widely known that both aspects contribute to increasing rents.[23] The rent-seeking risk of the mining industry has been studied relatively extensively in the literature. Auty (2001) describes the impact of abundance of natural resources on economic development, such as mining production.

The proliferation of rents in landlocked countries has been studied less and derives from the fact that landlocked countries trade/produce small volumes in isolation, which is conducive to rent capture by a few monopolists (with the assistance of some public officials).[24]

An important question to ask is if those characteristics interact and affect economic diversification. Aside from a macro-perspective through the Dutch Disease model, until recently the link between the political economy of the private sector/the extent of rents and economic/trade diversification had not been studied rigorously. Recently, Starosta de Waldemar (2010) demonstrated, using a large sample of more than 130 countries between 1995 and 2007 and a highly disaggregated export database comprising more than 5,000 products, that a high level of rent-seeking activity has a large impact on the diversification of exports. In countries where rent-seeking is a widespread practice, the number of products being exported will be smaller and its value more concentrated in certain goods.

3.6.1 *The vicious circle of rents and economic diversification*

In a country where rents are important (owing to the importance of the mining industry and aggravated by the fact that the country is landlocked), a lack of economic/trade diversification enables capture and rent-seeking behaviour to prosper, perpetuating the status quo, which then prevents economic diversification, potentially leading to a vicious circle. If it is assumed that many sectors are captured by monopolists or cartels, despite discourse on economic/trade diversification, the reality could be different and, in this context, it could be extremely difficult to see new sectors and business actors emerging. Indeed, low trade volumes and low diversification make it easier for 'monopolists' to capture a rent or a sector. Thanks to collusion with the public sector, some barriers to entry are put in place in order to prevent external and internal competition. A lack of competition enables the monopolist to inflate selling prices thanks to a dominant position and perpetuating rents. The dominant position of a monopolist in a sector favours a status quo, which then weakens the coalition of interest in favour of major reforms (and the ones in favour of reforms are too weak to achieve any major impact). This then translates into inflated prices in most sectors, therefore undermining the competitiveness of all the non-mining sectors; hence, diversification remains a challenge and low volumes enable the monopolists to prosper (Figure 3.7). The only remaining option for the majority of the population (if they cannot afford rent) is to live from the informal economy to start informal competition in some niches with possible high returns (that is also why, in this context, trading appears more suitable because there is a demand for cheaper products as locally-manufactured products' prices are inflated).[25]

Figure 3.7 A political economy lens of economic diversification

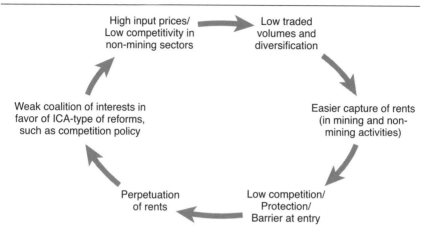

Source: Author's representation

Could this analytical framework be relevant for Zambia? How does the Zambian economy function from an institutional perspective?

As described earlier, the Zambian economy has a dualistic nature for which the political economic context has a role to play. In most of the major manufacturing and services sectors in Zambia (sugar, cement, beef, beer, telecoms, retail, etc.) there is usually one large company with more than 50 per cent of the total market share; the remaining 50 per cent is fulfilled by some medium, small or nano-sized companies (usually fulfilling a slightly different demand/taste).

The strategy of monopolists is usually threefold: firstly, limiting competition from outside the country; secondly, limiting input exports (if produced in Zambia); thirdly, limiting internal competition as much as possible. That is where public sector regulations can help some of these large companies to perpetuate their current market share. Indeed, limiting competition from outside the country is ensured by peak tariffs but even more importantly by non-tariff barriers, such as standards (the government requirement that all sugar being sold in Zambia for domestic consumption must be fortified with Vitamin A, which is specific to Zambia).[26] Limiting input exports can be realized through the ban of cattle exports.[27] Finally, limiting competition is ensured through interference in the work of the Competition and Consumer Protection Commission (CCPC) and other business practices.

As explained above, small or nano-sized companies thrive,[28] despite the fact that their productivity is low. In contrast to large companies, these small or nano-sized companies do not have enough social capital, which means that they do not have enough knowledge/connection to improve the quality of their products, finance business expansion,[29] or influence regulation/ competition in their favour.[30]

The impact of the predominance of monopolists in many sectors of the Zambian economy is both direct and indirect. A direct impact is that selling prices are inflated. It is the basic of economics (and the reason why antitrust legislation was established in the USA in 1890 with the Sherman Anti-trust Act). The CCPC documented such behaviours in several sectors in Zambia[31]. It was especially obvious when prices started to fall substantially in one sector when a major competitor began operations. Indirectly, if input prices are inflated in several sectors, downstream sectors are so affected that they become uncompetitive outside the country and the finished product prices are also inflated cumulatively. If, for instance, it is assumed that cement price is inflated, construction prices will also be inflated.

The lack of competition in Zambia today is mainly a result of two main factors:[32] (i) CCPC capacity constraint and (ii) the influence on the CCPC to make decisions that limit competition. The Competition and Fair Trading (CFT) Act (1994) introduced a code of conduct for all businesses that prohibited anticompetitive trade practices such as the formation of cartels and collusive tendering. The Act stipulated which business practices were considered anticompetitive or unfair. This Act followed the process of liberalization of the Zambian economy and its transition from a command to a market economy.

The CFT Act (1994) was repealed and replaced by the Competition and Consumer Protection (CCP) Act (2010)[33] in 2010, primarily to improve competition law enforcement and consumer protection. This will be enabled by the fact that the new law provides definitions of various competition and consumer protection terms, which were not defined in the preceding legislation. Like the CFT Act (1994), the new Act has provisions that deal with anticompetitive practices and has defined what may amount to anticompetitive practices. In order to capture as many anticompetitive practices as possible, including those that may not meet the requirements of anticompetitive conduct, Section 8 of the CCP Act (2010) states that 'any category of agreement, decision or concerted practice which has at its object or effect, restriction or distortion of competition to an appreciable extent in Zambia is anticompetitive and prohibited.'

Despite these improvements in the legal and policy frameworks, the new law does not provide for autonomy of the CCPC, hence the likelihood that political interference may influence its investigations and decisions.

3.6.2 CCPC capacity constraint

The CCP Act (2010) Number 24 of 2010 of the Laws of Zambia empowers the CCPC to safeguard and promote competition; to protect consumers against unfair trade practices; and also to provide for the establishment of the Competition and Consumer Protection Tribunal (to deal expeditiously with cases of appeal rather than the High Court, as in the case of the previous legislation). The Act also provides for the continued existence of the Zambia Competition Commission (ZCC),[34] which has been in operation since 1997, and renaming it as the CCPC in 2010. The Act is made up of 10 parts and these are Preliminary; Establishment of the CCPC; Restrictive Business and Anticompetitive Trade Practices; Mergers; Market Enquiries; Sector Regulated Activities; Consumer Protection; Investigations and Determinations by CCPC; Setting up the Competition and Consumer Protection Tribunal; and General Provisions.

The weakness of the ZCC first derived from the fact that relevant legislation for the ZCC did not provide a clear test that would provide a basis for judging anticompetitive conduct. It appeared that a test of competition co-existed with a test of general public interest; however, the competition test was not clearly defined. International practice mostly uses a consumer welfare test, while a minority of jurisdictions use a total welfare test that embraces consumer and (business) producer welfare. A competition test can co-exist with a public interest test, but the boundaries need to be clearly drawn.

Moreover, the CCPC has been faced with a lack of data from companies and business associations. It is especially problematic because of a limited staff and budget. The main source of funding is through monthly grants provided by the government's Ministry of Commerce, Trade and Industry (MCTI). The annual allocation was reduced by 35 per cent from ZMK3.1 billion in 2009 to ZMK2.0 billion in 2010. According to the CCPC, budget allocations and/or disbursements normally cover only a third of its planned activities/programmes for any given year.[35] Therefore, the budget is not predictable and not dependent on annual work plans submitted by the CCPC to the MCTI, which means that the CCPC's budget mainly covers the wage bill; therefore, operations, such as law enforcement, investigations, surveillance, and processing court cases, suffer. Under the new Act, however, the CCPC has been empowered to fine a maximum of 10 per cent of the annual turnover of businesses that violate the competition and/or consumer provisions rules of the Act. The Act does not only provide administrative powers to the CCPC, but also a broader scope of enforcement provisions.

3.6.3 *Influence on the CCPC to take decisions to limit competition*

A review of CCPC decisions over the last few years reveals that the CCPC was influenced to take decisions that do not necessarily contribute to increased competition. As a result, out of 252 cases handled by the CCPC since 2000, only one case[36] was rejected by the CCPC (a rejection rate of 0.4 per cent),

Table 3.4 Tabulation of CCPC approvals and rejections for mergers, acquisitions, and takeovers

CCPC mergers, acquisitions, and takeovers

	2000	2001	2002	2003	2004	2005	2006	2007	2008	2009
Approvals	31	16	22	34	23	26	25	27	30	18
Rejections	–	–	–	–	–	1	–	–	–	–

which does not compare with the benchmarks of other such institutions (Table 3.4).

3.7 The policy implications of low pressure for economic diversification

Informal enterprise operators see different roles for both the government and cooperating partners in developing the sector. Increasing access to finance appears to be an important role for both the government and donors. Donors are also seen as critical in increasing skills and training, whereas the government should provide infrastructure, business services information, and better health services (Figure 3.8).

Currently, the high cost and limited range of financial services limits the number of MSMEs that can afford these services. Enhancing access will require

Figure 3.8 Main priorities according to small business owners for GRZ and donors

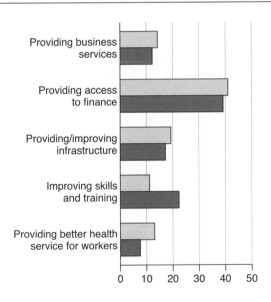

changes in service delivery, such as a significant enhancement of banking infrastructure and/or the adoption of alternative distribution strategies, and also a substantial reduction in fees. The introduction of general packet radio service (GPRS) based correspondent banking models, where local retailers are used as bank agents to facilitate cash deposits and withdrawals, is of interest. Models like this, which have been introduced successfully in Kenya (M-Pesa) and the Philippines (G-Cash), could significantly improve access to banking services in Zambia. One solution of particular significance is the Quick Pay Zoona service, which is used by the cotton industry in Choma and Katete.

However, what is probably even more important is to break the vicious circle of rents and the lack of competition. The objective would be to spark off competition between the first and second private sector in Zambia in order to increase the coalition of interests in favour of change.

Is it realistic to set this as an objective in the current context? One alternative could be to launch some experiments with small and medium-sized companies to assess what could be implemented successfully instead of trying to develop a sector *ex nihilo*. Some options could be to finance some experiments on how to better cluster/agglomerate resources between small companies in order to provide increased financing for a cluster of firms with the hope that it would lead to the establishment of large companies (based on the models of spontaneous clusters studies by the World Bank (2010)). Some alternative options would be to find out whether collective infrastructure would have a major impact on the productivity of small firms. Another option would be to see if the collective action of firms and public disapproval of the abuse of the market share by a monopolist would have any impact on the commercial/business practices of the dominant actor. These are only initial thoughts on where to start in order to contribute to economic diversification with new tools – in the current context political statements may not necessarily translate into economic diversification, and then income generation and poverty reduction.

Appendix

Table 3.A1 Percentage changes in GDP by kind of economic activity

	Base value	Commodity tax cut	
		Value	%age change
Traded agriculture	2,260.4	2,324.2	2.82%
Non-traded agriculture	5,2131.1	5,148.8	-1.23%
All agriculture	7,4373.5	7,473.0	-0.01%
Traded manufacturing	4,410.5	4,398.8	-0.27%
Non-traded manufacturing	26,102.6	26,110.2	0.03%
All manufacturing	7,952.7	7,947.2	-0.07%
Traded services	2,878.5	2,937.7	2.06%
Non-traded services	19,682.0	19,624.0	-0.29%
All services	22,560.4	22,561.7	0.01%
All non-agriculture	30,513.2	30,509.0	-0.01%
Total production	37,986.7	37,982.0	-0.01%

Source: Central Statistical Office Zambia, 2010

Table 3.A2 Share of the main ten products in total exports

Industry	2008 Exports as a share of total exports (%)	2004 Exports as a share of total exports (%)	Change
00 All industries	100	100	0
74 Copper and articles thereof	64.31	43.35	20.86
26 Ores, slag and ash	15.11	1.99	13.12
81 Other base metals, cements, articles thereof	5.85	16.41	-10.56
24 Tobacco and manufactured tobacco substitutes	1.41	3.87	-2.46
17 Sugars and sugar confectionery	1.26	2.36	-1.1
85 Electrical, electronic equipment	1.24	0.82	0.42
84 Boilers, machinery; nuclear reactors, etc	1.1	0.24	0.86
10 Cereals	1.01	2.76	-1.75
52 Cotton	0.77	9.32	-8.55
27 Mineral fuels, oils, distillation products, etc	0.71	1.76	-1.05
25 Salt, sulphur, earth, stone, plaster, lime and cement	0.66	1.17	-0.51
11 Milling products, malt, starches, inulin, wheat gluten	0.65	0.47	0.18
71 Pearls, precious stones, metals, coins, etc	0.63	1.98	-1.35
99 Commodities not elsewhere specified	0.55	0.01	0.54

Source: International Trade Center, Trade Performance HS: Exports and imports of Zambia

Notes

1. Adriana Cardozo, consultant, Latin America and the Caribbean, World Bank; Gibson Masumbu, consultant, Economic Policy and Private Sector Development, Zambia; Chiwama Musonda, economist, Zambia; Gaël Raballand, senior public sector and governance specialist, World Bank. The authors would like to thank Boris Branisa for inputs and Kapil Kapoor, Anna Morris, Julio Revilla, and Marie Sheppard for comments.
2. The macro-economic environment in Zambia is detailed in Chapter 1.
3. Income inequality is high in Zambia and has not changed much between 1991 and 2004. The estimated Gini coefficient was close to 50 per cent in 2004. For that year the income share held by the richest quintile was 57 per cent, while the poorest quintile had an income share of only 3 per cent.
4. This finding also emerges from the last Investment Climate Assessment (ICA) carried out in Zambia (World Bank, 2009).
5. International comparisons show that the HHI remained almost unchanged for the average Least Developed Countries, with a value of 0.49 in 2006 and 0.48 in 2009.
6. It is a measure of the degree of export concentration approaching one when there is a high degree of export concentration.
7. Meliak (2008) reports an HHI value of 0.30 for Zambia in 2004.
8. Currently, Zambia applies very few non-tariff trade barriers. On the whole, imports are restricted solely for health reasons and exports of maize must be authorized owing to concerns over food security. An export tax also exists on scrap metal, which is considered an important input for manufacturing.
9. However, Switzerland is not the final destination of the production; more probably it is emerging Asian markets.
10. Moreover, growth has also not translated into poverty reduction in rural areas.
11. The largest textile factory in Zambia closed in 2007.
12. Road Sector Investment Programme Phase Two (ROADSIP II) is an investment worth $US1.6 billion over a ten-year period which is co-financed by governments and cooperating partners.
13. According to the Central Statistical Office (CSO), at independence Zambia's construction industry employed more than 74,000 people out of a population of four million people; 45 years later, out of a population of 13 million people, the industry only employs 13,500 in the formal sector.
14. Most of the small enterprises are more likely to employ people on a part-time basis or employ relatives that are usually 'unpaid'.
15. In nominal terms, there has also been some considerable growth (in wage levels between 2006 and 2009) and variation between sectors. The average earnings have been highest in the mining sector (K1,700,000 in 2006 increasing to K4,600,000 in 2009). Earnings in construction also increased from K700,000 to K2,100,000 in 2008. Manufacturing earnings increased from K750,000 to K1,500,000; in trade, however, the increase has been from K700,000 to K1,600,000. Agriculture has had rather static wage levels at K560,000.
16. Based on interviews: before the depreciation of the Kwacha, margins were commonly above 50 per cent.

17. Incentives for formalization are low as tax evasion is, for instance, a major source of extra profit in this sector and sanctions are scarce.
18. This section builds mainly on Conway et al. (2010) and presents a quantitative analysis of small and medium-sized firm surveys in Zambia in 2008–9.
19. These are measures of physical access – are these inputs or services available? The explanatory variables are 0 if no access and 1 if access, whether or not the firm chooses to use those inputs or services.
20. It is important to note that these physical-access variables are defined geographically – if the region has no banks, for example, there is no physical access to banking services. There could also be other differences across regions that contribute to the effect attributed to physical access to electricity, water, banking services, or lending.
21. For further details, see Conway et al. (2010).
22. This is the underlying message of the evaluation of donor-funded projects in the private sector.
23. Economic rent is defined as an excess distribution to any factor in a production process above the amount required to draw the factor into the process or to sustain the current use of the factor. Economic rent can be collected as royalties or extraction fees in the case of minerals, oil, and gas. Economic rent is closely related to producer surplus. Related to the concept of rent in economics, rent-seeking occurs when an individual, organization, or firm seeks to earn income by capturing economic rent through manipulation or exploitation of the economic or political environment rather than by earning profits through economic transactions and the production of added wealth. Rent-seeking generally implies the extraction of uncompensated value from others without making any contribution to productivity, such as by gaining control of land and other pre-existing natural resources or by imposing burdensome regulations or other government decisions that may affect consumers or businesses. While there may be few people in modern industrialized countries who do not gain something, directly or indirectly, through some form or another of rent-seeking, rent-seeking in the aggregate sense can impose substantial losses on society. The modern use of the word 'rent' is not directly equivalent to its usual meaning of a payment on a lease, but rather stems from Adam Smith's division of income into profit, wage, and rent. Rent-seeking behaviour is distinguished in theory from *profit-seeking* behaviour, in which entities seek to extract value by engaging in mutually beneficial transactions.
24. See Arvis et al. (2010) for an explanation of the impact of low volumes in landlocked countries on logistical costs.
25. This is consistent with Guttiérrez-Romero (2010) who found out that 'the higher the initial wealth inequality the larger the size of the informal economy and the higher wealth inequality will be in the long-run'. This also explains why there is a missing middle in this type of economies as the only companies unable to avoid taxes and regulation are the middle ones (Klapper and Richmond, 2011). Moreover, in this environment small, informal firms can increase their productivity as much as formal firms as the enforcement of regulations are low in both cases (Gelb et al., 2009).
26. See Ellis et al. (2010) for more details on the impact of the government policy in the sugar sector. No other country in the region has a similar requirement.

27. The official justification is because of diseases, which is understandable. However, it greatly benefits the leader of this industry.

28. See Fox and Steel (2010) for this trend in East and Southern Africa. This is mainly a result of demographic and economic factors: formal job employment does not generate enough jobs per year to absorb the increase in the active population.

29. Even the political economy is at play for trading activities. All marketers belonged to Zambia National Marketeers Association (ZANAMA); however, after political differences surfaced the ZANAMA executive and a few members became aligned with the ruling Movement for Multi-Party Democracy (MMD) government. They have benefited from preferential treatment, including the loan scheme that has been introduced for ZANAMA members. However, to access it they had to be true 'blue' members. The scheme is intended to help members who have faced challenges with collateral and security requirements demanded by financial institutions. The intention is to empower members by graduating from small-scale to bigger businesses and migrate into the formal sector. The soft loan is provided at a 10 per cent interest rate and is payable after one month. The repayment period has resulted in slow repayment. The other challenge is that this fund is being managed or administered by the executive, instead of an independent fund manager. The ZANAMA headquarters are in Kitwe and the main operational markets are run by local authorities. It is also worth noting that other markets in provinces, including those in Lusaka, have been dominated by members of the opposition parties probably because of the cash generating function of trading in Zambia.

30. That is also probably why holdings prosper in Zambia. One such holding in the agro-processing industry is Zambeef, which diversified its product line (business activities) into other related activities, such as milk processing, and chicken, egg, palm oil, and flour/bread production, etc.

31. Investment climate assessment for Zambia presents the same finding on the prevalence of monopolists in the country.

32. Economic history and the nature of Zambia's industrial base may also explain why the competition environment was not favourable at the time the ZCC was created.

33. Restrictive business and anticompetitive trade practices are specified in Sections 8–23 of the Act. The types of business behaviour that have been scrutinized by the Act are:

    - Prohibition of Anticompetitive Practice, Agreement, or Decision (Section 8);
    - Horizontal Agreements (Section 9);
    - Vertical Agreements (Section 10); Severability (Section 11);
    - Other Horizontal and Vertical Agreements (Section 12);
    - Inter-connected Bodies Corporate (Section 13);
    - Share or Supply Threshold for Authorization of Restrictive Agreements (Section 14);
    - Share of Supply Threshold for Establishing Existence of Dominant Position (Section 15);
    - Prohibition of Abuse of Dominant Position (Section 16);
    - Determination of Relevant Product Market (Section 17);

- Application for Exemption (Section 18); Determination of Application for Exemption (Section 19);
- Amendment of Exemption (Section 20); Revocation of Exemption (Section 21); Exemption in Respect of Professional Rules (Section 22); and Publication of Grant or Revocation of Exemption (Section 23).

34. Currently, the CCPC has a total staff establishment of 22 professionals but some of the positions are not filled and staff turnover has always affected operations and continuity/institutional memory. The CCPC has one main office in Lusaka, which has the mandate to execute all competition and consumer-related cases countrywide, but in the course of 2011 established an office in Kitwe to cover cases in Northern Region.

35. Government contention had been that the ZCC (now the CCPC) could raise its own resources through notification fees and other types of fees collected, just like the Zambia Weight and Measures Agency (ZWMA), Patents and Companies Registration Agency (PACRA), Zambia Bureau of Standards (ZABS), and many more. However, the biggest challenge has been how many mergers, acquisitions, or takeovers of considerable magnitude take place in a given month or year to supplement government grants.

36. This case is under litigation and involves the application for the takeover of the jet fuel facility at Lusaka International Airport.

References

Arvis, J-F., Marteau, J-F., and Raballand, G. (2010). *The Cost of Being Landlocked*. Washington, DC: World Bank.

Auty, R. (2001). *Resource Abundance and Economic Development*. Oxford: Oxford University Press.

Carmody, P. (2009). An Asian-driven economic recovery in Africa? The Zambian case. *World Development* 37: 1197–1207.

Carmody, P. and Hampwaye, G. (2009). Inclusive or exclusive globalization? Zambia's economy and Asian investment. *Institute for International Integration Studies IIIS Discussion Paper No. 297.*

Central Statistical Office Zambia (CSO) (2010). *The Monthly*, 83: February 2010. Available at: <http://www.zamstats.gov.zm> (last accessed 10 March 2012).

Conway, P., Kedia, M. S. (2010). *Who's Productive in Zambia's Private Sector? Evidence from the Zambia Business Survey*. Washington, DC: World Bank, Available at: <http://siteresources.worldbank.org/INTAFRICA/Resources/zambia_biz-survey.pdf> (last accessed 10 March 2012).

Duncan, A., Macmillan, H., and Simutanyi, N. (2003). Zambia. Drivers of pro-poor change: an overview. *Oxford Policy Management*: 1–72.

Ellis, K., Singh, R., and Musonda, C. (2010). Assessing the economic impact of competition: findings from Zambia. *ODI Working Paper*. Available at: <http://www.odi.org.uk/resources/details.asp?id=4959&title=competition-economic-impact-zambia> (last accessed 10 March 2012).

Fox, L. and Steel, W. (2011). What is driving the growth of informal firms in Africa? Unpublished mimeograph.

Fraser, A. (2007). Zambia: Back to the future? *University of Oxford Working Paper* 2007/30.

Gelb, A., Mengistae, T., Ramachandran, V., and Shah, M.K. (2009). To formalize or not to formalize? Comparisons of microenterprise data from Southern and East Africa. *CGD Working Paper* 175.

Guttiérrez-Romero, R. (2010). The dynamics of the informal economy. *CSAE WPS/2010-07*.

Ianchovichina, E. and Lundstrom, S. (2009). Inclusive growth analytics, framework and application. *World Bank Policy Research Working Paper* No. 4851.

International Monetary Fund (2010). *IMF Country Report* No. 10/17.

Klapper, L. and Richmond, C. (2010). Patterns of business creation, survival, and growth: evidence from a developing country. *Labour Economics* 18: S32-S44.

Meilak, C. (2008). Measuring export concentration: the implication for small states. *Bank of Valletta Review* 37: 35–48.

Millennium Challenge Account (2009). Constraint analysis to inclusive growth in Zambia. Unpublished mimeograph.

Mphuka, C. (2002). *HIPC Study: The Case of Zambia*. Lusaka: Jubilee-Zambia.

Organisation for Economic Co-operation and Development and African Development Bank (2008). *African Economic Outlook 2007/2008*. Paris: OECD and ADC, 615–630.

Sassa, O. and Carlsson, J. (2002). *Aid and Poverty Reduction in Zambia: Mission Unaccomplished*. Uppsala: The Nordic Africa Institute.

Starosta de Waldemar, F. (2010). How costly is rent-seeking to diversification: An empirical approach. *Proceedings of the German Development Economics Conference, Hannover 2010*. Verein für Sozialpolitik, Research Committee Development Economics.

United Nations Development Programme (2009). *Human Development Report Zambia*. Lusaka: UNDP.

World Bank (2009). *Second Investment Climate Assessment. Business Environment Issues in Diversifying Growth*. Washington, DC: World Bank.

World Bank (2010). *Zambia Business Survey. The Profile and Productivity of Zambian Business*. Washington, DC: World Bank.

Yagci, F. and Aldaz-Carroll, E. (2004). Salient features of trade performance in eastern and southern Africa. *Africa Region Working Paper Series* 76. Washington, DC: World Bank. Available at: <http://www.worldbank.org/afr/wps/wp76.pdf> (last accessed 10 March 2012).

II

Macro-economic Policy Choices

4

Increasing Public Revenue and Expenditure Efficiency in Zambia

Samuel Bwalya, Shantayanan Devarajan, Vinayak Nagaraj, and Gaël Raballand

4.1 Introduction

For most of its independent history, fiscal policy in Zambia has been characterized by high levels of expenditure (30 per cent of gross domestic product (GDP)) and relatively lower tax revenues, leading to large levels of borrowing and dependence on grants. As a result of poor economic policies, revenues from the country's main export – copper – diminished gradually between 1970 (11 per cent of total revenues) and 1999 (negligible per cent of total revenues), leaving the revenue base dependent on trade and income taxes, which were vulnerable to global commodity prices and domestic economic conditions. At the same time, public expenditures were inefficiently allocated and utilized, leading to unsustainable spending patterns that required the contraction of substantial amounts of debt in addition to an excessive dependence on grant assistance. As a result, debt levels exceeded 200 per cent of GDP, leading Zambia to apply for, and eventually receive in 2005, assistance under the 'Highly Indebted Poor Countries' initiative.

Despite a rebound in Zambia's macro-economic performance over the last decade, and some recent improvements in public expenditures, a number of problems with fiscal policy remain unresolved. One of the main reasons for their persistence, despite substantial overall progress in constraining aggregate fiscal expenditure, is the lack of transparency and accountability of public expenditures. In turn, this lack of accountability has affected the quality of expenditures, as well as revenue collection. Consistently poor quality spending over the last few years has undermined taxpayers' willingness to pay their taxes voluntarily, the benefits from which they see as insignificant. In the absence of a strong fiscal social contract between the government and citizens, the outcome of public spending will most likely continue to remain weak despite increased external pressure for transparency and financial accountability. As a result of this vicious circle, the government is likely to continue to remain revenue-constrained.

This chapter attempts to trace the root problems inhibiting further transparency and accountability, and then presents an original scheme to increase fiscal space, public expenditure efficiency, and accountability in order to improve prospects for higher growth and poverty reduction using fiscal policy instruments. Unless concerted efforts are made to bolster domestic revenue mobilization and increase public expenditure efficiency and service delivery, the effect of fiscal policy on growth and poverty reduction in the future will not be very different from what Zambia has experienced in the past.

4.2 Recent developments in fiscal policy in Zambia

4.2.1 *Fiscal trends and fiscal efficiency*

Government efforts and achievements in enhancing fiscal space in Zambia can, as a first attempt, be discerned by studying trends in three major sources of public finances, namely tax and non-tax revenues, grants, and government borrowing (domestic and foreign).[1] Table 4.1 shows trends in public resource mobilization between 2002 and 2010.

In order to create macro-economic stability and stimulate private sector-led economic growth, the government restructured its fiscal programmes and brought fiscal balances to sustainable levels. This was achieved in 2004 when the overall fiscal deficit was lowered to 2.9 per cent from 6 per cent in 2003. The decrease was accomplished by reductions in public expenditures from 31.2 per cent of GDP in 2002 to 26.6 per cent in 2004. The fiscal space created enabled the government to reduce its borrowing to 0.8 per cent of GDP in 2004 from 6.5 per cent of GDP in 2003, thereby increasing the opportunities available for private sector financing and containing an important source of inflationary pressures. This re-alignment of fiscal resources meant that about three-quarters of total government expenditure was financed through tax revenues and government borrowing (see Table 4.1 for more details).

Zambia's fiscal position was further strengthened when it received debt reductions under the Heavily Indebted Poor Countries (HIPC) and Multilateral Debt Relief Initiative (MDRI) initiatives, reducing the external debt stock

Table 4.1 Trends in public financial resource mobilization by revenue source

	2002	2003	2004	2005	2006	2007	2008	2009	2010 (Prelim)
Total Revenue and Grants (excl. HIPC)	26.20	24.90	23.00	23.00	21.50	23.30	22.90	20.00	20.60
Revenue	17.90	18.00	18.20	17.40	16.90	18.70	19.00	16.00	17.80
Tax revenue (excl. mining)	17.50	17.30	17.40	16.60	15.50	16.50	16.50	14.00	14.60
Mining taxes	0.00	0.10	0.10	0.40	0.60	1.40	1.40	1.00	2.20
Non-tax revenue	0.40	0.60	0.70	0.40	0.80	0.70	1.10	1.00	1.00
Grants	8.30	7.00	5.50	5.60	4.60	4.60	3.90	4.00	2.80
Budget Support	2.00	1.10	1.00	1.70	1.10	1.30	1.20	1.40	1.20
Project	6.30	5.80	4.50	3.90	3.50	3.30	2.70	2.70	1.50
Financing	5.51	6.51	0.77	2.64	18.59	0.24	2.30	2.70	3.30
External financing (net)[2]	4.26	1.50	0.88	0.74	0.43	0.32	0.48	0.60	0.70
Net domestic financing	1.25	5.01	-0.11	1.90	19.01	-0.08	1.82	2.10	2.60
Overall fiscal balance	-5.10	-6.00	-2.90	-2.70	-1.60	-1.30	-1.50	-2.70	3.30
GDP nominal	16,260	20,470	25,997	32,456	39,223	45,669	53,706	64,616	76,015

Source: Adapted from Whitworth, 2009 and updated based on information from MOFNP and ZRA

from 86 per cent of GDP in 2005 to 8.8 per cent of GDP in 2006 (Table 4.2). This helped to reduce the overall deficit further to 1.6 per cent of GDP in 2006. This level was maintained through to 2008, until the onset of the global financial crisis.

Having managed to bring the overall fiscal deficit within manageable limits, concern has now shifted to the sustainability of such limits in the future and the more efficient use of public resources for growth and poverty reduction. The question of fiscal sustainability can be examined by assessing the sustainability of public revenue streams. Further, fiscal prudence on the expenditure side is critically dependent on the strength of governance institutions and their ability to induce greater public expenditure efficiency, transparency, and accountability (see Sections 4.4 and 4.5).

Table 4.2 Zambian debt stock and servicing position per cent of GDP

	2002	2003	2004	2005	2006	2007	2008p	2009b
External debt								
Debt stock	178	156.2	126.6	87.1	9.0	9.8	10.6	2.1
Interest	1.3	1.1	0.6	0.4	0.2	0.1	0.1	[x]
Domestic debt								
Stock	11.3	16.6	13.5	12.9	12.5	10.6	9.5	2.8
Interest	2.8	2.9	2.3	1.8	1.6	1.6	2.9	[x]

Source: Adapted from Whitworth, 2009

The issue of revenue sustainability in Zambia is, ironically for a mineral resource-rich country, less of a concern. Following the initial decline of the mining industry in the 1980s and 1990s, the majority of revenues arose from sustainable sources (non-mining tax revenues), with more volatile natural resource-based revenues from the copper industry making an insignificant contribution to the treasury. Alongside expectations of robust economic growth, non-mining tax revenues are expected to remain the largest share of the fiscal resource base. In addition, the contribution of grants to the budget has been declining steadily since 2002, reaching 11.7 per cent in 2010 from a high of 25.8 per cent in 2002. This trend is expected to continue even under fairly moderate assumptions about economic growth and tax system buoyancy.

In recent years, the Zambian government has shifted its policy stance from contracting only highly concessional loans to actively seeking non-concessional loans for projects of 'high economic return' (MTEFs 2007–2009, 2008–2010, 2009–2011, 2010–2012/National Budgets 2009, 2010, 2011). The aim is to raise this borrowing to finance important public projects that are capable of stimulating private sector activity and income from which additional tax revenues can be mobilized to finance future debt servicing and repayment obligations (Mintz and Smart, 2008). In fact the government, under strict fiscal rules, may be justified in borrowing to finance public investments and repaying the debt with future tax revenues. In this way, the government would be able to smooth the tax burden across generations and generate dynamic efficiency gains in the economy.

However, public expenditure efficiency and accountability remain quite low, making it difficult to rationalize such a recommendation in the Zambian context. As an example, sector strategies, in general, reflect optimism bias and are typically prepared without coherent links to other government strategies. They are broadly defined and overly ambitious, and as the pre-screening process is a simple, formal exercise (Le et al., 2010), they often accommodate investment proposals without any prior feasibility or cost/benefit analyses. Moreover, the whole process of screening and appraising project proposals relies exclusively on the responsibilities of the Ministries, Provinces and Spending Agency (MPSA). There is no formal structure in place at the Ministry of Finance and National Planning to independently appraise these projects. In addition, large public projects are often budgeted as 'construction-only', with little or no attention paid to the longer-term recurrent expenditures involved in running and maintaining these assets. Two examples that acutely demonstrate this problem are the health and education sectors, where large infrastructure drives in recent years have been accompanied by inadequate fiscal space for staff recruitment and supplies (Tjoa et al., 2010). Large public projects, therefore, suffer from problems at the initial project selection stage all the way through to the spending, project execution, and management of

Figure 4.1 Trends in total public expenditures as per cent of GDP

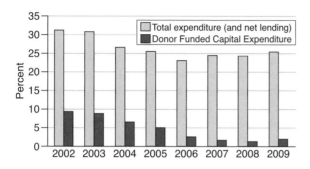

Source: MOFNP

assets once created. While Zambia's macro-economic fundamentals can justify some limited foreign, non-concessional financing at this stage, the government would probably do better to restrain both foreign and domestic non-concessional borrowing in the short-term until a sound public investment management system that can resolve some of these concerns is in place and working effectively.

In the medium-term, the growing level of domestic (non-concessional) borrowing poses a threat to future fiscal space. To alleviate this, one proposal that has been put forward in recent years is to substitute domestic borrowing with more concessional (and, in certain cases non-concessional) foreign borrowing. The aim would be to strengthen the country's fiscal position by trading off high-interest domestic debt for low-interest foreign debt, allowing for greater crowding-in of private investment in the domestic economy. What makes such an operation more feasible in Zambia is that its natural resource exports provide a steady source of foreign exchange, partially mitigating foreign exchange risks. Such an experiment was announced in 2009 as part of the International Monetary Fund's (IMF) Extended Credit Facility (ECF), with an initial $US200 million of international reserves and highly concessional IMF resources used to retire domestic debt (IMF Memorandum of Economic and Financial Policies 2009). While the exact impact of the operation is not measurable, rates on government securities fell sharply during the period after the announcement was made, although this could well have been a result of other factors (such as increased domestic banking competition).

4.2.2 The role of donors in fiscal efficiency

Aid flow to Zambia has decreased in recent years, in both absolute and relative terms, but remains well within its historical range (Figure 4.1). Among countries in the region, aid per capita to Zambia is near the median – lower than in Malawi, Mozambique, and Tanzania, but higher than in Botswana, Namibia, Angola, and South Africa. However, donors in Zambia face increasing pressure for development results. Budget support (through both general and sector-wide approaches) assumed a major role in 1990s and 2000s, although project-based aid continues to be the most important instrument in terms of the total level of financing provided to the Zambian Government.

Beuran et al. (2011) present impact evaluations for recent donor operations in Zambia across various programmatic sectors: education, health, public sector reform, private sector development, and general budget support. The analysis of the projects studied reveals two principal conclusions. Firstly, most aid-funded projects have been relatively, or very, successful in terms of their immediate outputs. Schools are built, roads rehabilitated, access to social services improved, and relevant administrative and legislation reforms adopted, and so on. Secondly, results have been much more limited with regard to the quality of service delivery and the achievement of broader development objectives such as improving educational attainment, decreasing transport costs, raising the competitiveness of Zambian companies, and reducing rural poverty.

They also found that donors have low leverage, especially with regard to governance issues, which may lead to decreased accountability and even promote complacency on the part of Zambian society, and may ultimately undermine public spending efficiency because it enables the government to continue with a certain lack of accountability.

4.3 Policies and strategies to improve public revenue mobilization

4.3.1 Overview of the tax system

The performance of Zambia's revenue system depends on a number of factors that determine the tax base and the cost of collection (tax effort). These factors not only include tax policy and administration but the whole range of economic, political, and institutional factors that affect the productivity of the country's revenue system.

Zambia's revenue system was more productive in the first few years following the establishment of the Zambia Revenue Authority (ZRA) in 1995, with revenue collection exceeding 18 per cent of GDP. In subsequent years, revenues fluctuated at around 17 per cent until 2004, when they started to fall, reaching 16.1 per cent in 2006. This decrease in performance was attributed to a number of factors, including decreases in the efficiency of tax administration and changes to the tax regime that focused on generous tax incentives and exemptions. One challenge has been the level of funding available to the ZRA to execute its mandate. Efforts have been made to increase operational funding to the ZRA over the last few years and funding subsequently increased to 2.4 per cent of total revenue collection in 2008 from 1.9 per cent in 2006. This contributed, in part, to the increase in revenue collections to 18.0 per cent of GDP in 2007 and 2008, demonstrating that adequately resourcing tax administration functions could improve public revenue mobilization, especially when accompanied by adequate tax policy reforms.

Establishing an optimal and stable taxation regime for Zambia's copper sector has been a major challenge for authorities over the last decade. Revenues from copper contribute only 7 per cent of total tax revenues. In an effort to reverse this trend, the government adjusted the mineral tax regime in 2008. One of the main amendments was the inclusion of a windfall tax aimed at increasing tax collections at well-defined international copper price triggers. In the midst of the global economic crisis, the tax was repealed in 2009 and replaced with a variable profit tax that would be more sensitive to the unique cost structures of mines in Zambia.[2]

4.3.2 The history of the Zambian tax system

The Zambian tax structure has changed considerably over the last two decades. Prior to 1995, trade taxes were the major source of tax revenue for the government, accounting for 50.6 per cent of total tax revenues. After the introduction of sweeping tax and administration reforms in 1995, which also included the introduction of a value added tax (VAT) to replace the archaic sales tax system, its contribution to total tax revenues increased from 12.8 per cent in 1995 to around 38.3 per cent between 1996 and 2000. Starting in 2000, however, the contribution of domestic VAT contribution started to decline steadily, reaching a low of 23.3 per cent in 2004. This decline resulted, in part, from a reduction in both domestic VAT rate and excise duty rate, which fell from 20 and 18 per cent respectively, in 1995 to 17.5 and 14 per cent. Most importantly, however, the reduction in VAT collections was also attributed to an increase in exemptions.

The contribution of trade taxes to tax revenue also fell from 52.3 per cent in 1995 to a low of 23 per cent in 1998. This is largely attributed to tariff reductions associated with the implementation of multilateral and regional trade liberalization initiatives. In recent years, trade taxes, which include collections of import VAT, have gradually increased, accounting for 41.7 per cent of total tax revenue in 2008 (see Table 4.3).[3]

Direct taxes have shown the greatest improvement in terms of revenue collections since 1995. The contribution of direct taxes has risen from 34.9 per cent of total tax revenue in 1995 to 48.5 per cent in 2008. This performance is consistent with the expectation that as trade tax collections decline, the tax base shifts inland and collection of domestic taxes should increase to compensate for the fall in revenues from trade taxes such as import duties.

Table 4.3 Revenue performance by tax type, 2005–09, per cent of GDP

	2005 %	2006 %	2007 %	2008 %	2009 %
Income Taxes	7.6	7.5	8.4	8.7	8.0
VAT	5.0	4.6	4.9	4.1	4.5
Excise Duties	2.4	2.1	2.6	2.5	2.9
Import Duties	2.0	1.8	2.0	2.2	2.3
Other duties	0.01	0.02	0.02	0.38	0.29
Total	17.0	16.19	17.9	18.0	18.1

Source: ZRA and MOFNP

However, despite these increases, the tax gap under domestic taxes remains high (as much as 50 per cent) and the stock of tax arrears was around 7.5 per cent of GDP in 2008.

Pay As You Earn (PAYE) accounts for over 65 per cent of total income tax revenue. The contribution of PAYE to total tax revenue recorded the highest growth rate since 1995; increasing from 16 per cent in 1996 to 32.6 per cent in 2004, before declining to 31.2 per cent in 2005. In comparison, company taxes only grew from 6.2 per cent in 1995 to 8.2 per cent in 2005, while mineral royalty declined steadily from 5.2 per cent in 1995 to 2.3 and 1 per cent in 1996 and 1999 respectively.

The performance and contribution of mineral tax revenue continues to be a major source of concern. A number of factors have contributed to the problem, with the most significant being political economy factors related to Zambia's history. For example, the reduction of the mineral royalty rate from 3 per cent pre-privatization to 0.6 per cent post-privatization has been a major contributor to the poor mineral revenue base. The decision to reduce this rate, as an incentive for private investment, was made during a very difficult time in Zambia's economic history, necessitating generous incentive provisions to restimulate the copper sector.

The mining tax regime has since been revised (with royalties restored to the 3 per cent level) and is expected to contribute over $US438 million in additional tax revenue annually. There is an opportunity to capture additional revenue from the mining sector by ensuring that all base metals jointly mined and produced with copper are accounted for tax purposes. This will require a further review of the mining licensing regime and tax legislations to ensure that residual minerals jointly mined with copper are also optimally taxed.

4.3.3 *Tax policy improvements*

The soundness of Zambia's tax system depends on an enabling tax policy that optimally balances the fundamental principles of effectiveness, efficiency, and equity. One trade-off that has posed a challenge to the health of Zambia's tax collections has been the provision of fiscal incentives. The effectiveness of these incentives in investment depends on how they are designed and implemented. If poorly designed, they can significantly erode the tax base and reduce public financial resources available to finance public goods and services.

Zambia has one of the most generous fiscal incentive regimes in the Southern Africa Development Community (SADC) region, with negative marginal effective tax rates (METR) for most of the sectors, including manufacturing (Bolnick, 2004). In addition, indirect tax regimes are greatly punctured with exemptions and frequent suspensions of indirect taxes on excisable products and services. For instance, while administration of VAT has posed challenges, the VAT regime has a long list of exempted and zero-rated products that, over time, have reduced the productivity and performance of the tax. Our estimates, based on data obtained from the ZRA, show that rationalizing VAT exemptions on food and agricultural products, books and newspapers, water and sewerage services, and domestic transportation would increase revenue collection by as much as 0.2 per cent of GDP, while removing zero-rating on packaged tours and removing import exemptions for VAT would increase VAT revenues by 0.14 per cent of GDP. Together, these would increase the contribution of VAT revenues to 7.2 per cent of GDP from 4.8 per cent of GDP in 2007, thereby re-aligning VAT performance to the regional average of about 5 per cent of GDP. However, these tax proposals are difficult to enact politically, as some of these proposals have been previously rejected as being regressive and anti-poor. Similarly, exemptions on excisable and dutiable goods and services can also be rationalized to increase tax revenue by an additional 0.2 per cent of GDP.

Further improvements in tax revenue mobilization can be achieved by reviewing the corporate taxation regime. Corporate rates across sectors are so highly differentiated that they distort efficient resource allocation. There is also significant scope to increase the share of corporate tax revenue in total revenue by restructuring and rationalizing the corporate tax rates and tax incentives and exemptions across sectors. In the long-term, tax policy should be geared towards greater harmonization of corporate tax rates and tax incentives across all sectors to enhance efficiency in resource allocation in the economy. However, harmonizing corporate tax rates and tax incentives across sectors is much more difficult to achieve in practice as there are legitimate structural differences and socio-political reasons that justify differentiated tax treatment across sectors.[4]

4.3.4 *Increasing non-tax revenue*

Non-tax revenues in Zambia can contribute more to public finances if properly designed and implemented. Between 1995 and 1997, charges, levies, and fees collected as non-tax revenue by different government departments averaged 5.5 per cent of total government revenue. Thereafter, non-tax revenue declined significantly, accounting for 2.2 per cent of total revenue between 1999 and 2007 and increased to 5 per cent in 2008, largely as a result of the increase in passport renewal fees. There is great potential to improve the performance and contribution of non-tax revenue to government revenue and, by implication, to domestic financial resources available to finance the provision of public goods and services in the country.

The greatest potential to increase non-tax revenues lies in streamlining local revenue systems and improving revenue collection on land rates and property taxation. Local authorities, especially those in major cities, have an adequate revenue base from which to collect local revenues to finance the provision of local public goods and services within their respective jurisdictions. However, inadequate devolution of responsibilities from the central government to local authorities and central government transfer to urban local authorities have created systemic dependence of local authorities on central government funding, thereby diluting their incentives to sharpen their revenue collection efforts to enable them to become more self-reliant.

The impending execution of the recently approved de-centralization policy should lead to a re-examination of fiscal transfer systems in a bid to provide incentives to local authorities to increase the collection of non-tax revenues. De-centralization will also help to make the local authority more accountable to the local population from whom they will collect revenues, both in terms of service delivery and accountability in the use of such resources, subsequently laying a strong foundation for enhancing local participation and improving local fiscal governance. Further, accounting systems for non-tax revenue by public departments needs to be improved both in terms of transparency and accountability, as well as how appropriated funds are spent by collecting public agencies.

4.3.5 *Improving tax administration*

Efforts to strengthen tax administration can be traced from 1994, when legislation was passed to establish a semi-autonomous revenue administration – the Zambia Revenue Authority (ZRA) – by merging the former Income Tax Department and Customs and Excise Department, and subsequently abolishing sales tax and introducing VAT.

In 2006, the ZRA began to implement further reforms aimed at modernizing tax administration to improve efficiency and service delivery. Critical components of the reform involved merging the VAT and Direct Taxes Division into a single Domestic Taxes Division, and implementation of a segmented, but functionally integrated, organization structure for domestic tax administration. This has involved the creation of a robust Headquarters Department, responsible for providing support services (planning, budgeting, monitoring), as well as a Large Taxpayer Office and Field Delivery Departments, which cater to medium and small taxpayers. Tax operations and systems are currently being re-engineered and tax legislations reviewed to support greater efficiency in tax administration. Additional reforms are also being implemented in customs administration and include installation of mobile scanners, the implementation of one-stop border post initiatives, and the client accreditation programme. These reforms are expected to lead to better service delivery, operational efficiency, and improved compliance management, and consequently to increased revenue collection. Although there are no precise estimates of the revenue impact of these reforms at this time, they are expected to have a significant positive impact on revenue collection.

There remains significant room to improve the tax collection effort. The level of compliance, especially among the small and medium taxpayers, is less than 50 per cent and many income earners are still unregistered for taxes. Tax collection efforts should be streamlined to increase taxpayer registration and the development of educational programmes to bring more taxpayers under the tax net. In parallel, the development of a modern information database and management system to support management decision-making is also expected to yield significant increases in tax revenue. Finally, strategies and efforts to collect back taxes (tax arrears), especially from parastatal companies, will also increase amount of tax revenues collected to finance development programmes and will help to improve the predictability of tax revenues and make fiscal policy instruments more effective.

There is also a need to improve external revenue oversight institutions, such the Auditor General's Office, in order to ensure proper accounting practices and service delivery standards. In addition, the administration needs to continuously review and strengthen efforts to prevent and investigate corruption, and keep both perceived and actual occurrences to a minimum in order to create and sustain public confidence in the country's revenues system. In particular, the tax administration should continue to implement the Integrity Committee initiatives and invest in developing the capacity and authority of the Internal Affairs Unit to investigate and prosecute corruption cases involving ZRA employees. Efforts to reduce occurrence and high perceptions of corruption, tax fraud, and tax evasion by enforcing tax laws fairly and equitably across all taxpayers is critical in demonstrating transparency and commitment to the principles of good governance. Good revenue governance practices create the public confidence in the revenue systems needed to promote and sustain quasi-voluntary tax compliance. It is important to emphasize that efforts to promote good revenue governance practices cannot be effective unless accompanied by similar efforts on the expenditure side. This later aspect of fiscal governance is discussed in Section 4.4.

4.4 Creating fiscal space by increasing the accountability, transparency, and efficiency of public expenditure

Strong public investment management (PIM) policies and procedures, anchored in the Ministry of Finance, are crucial; PIM is being developed in Zambia (see Box 4.1 for more details on the golden rules of PIM).

Box 4.1 The golden rules of public investment management (PIM)

These elements would minimize major risks and provide an effective process for managing public investments:

1. Investment Guidance and Preliminary Screening. A first level screening of all project proposals should be undertaken to ensure that they meet the minimum criteria of consistency with the strategic goals of government.

2. Formal Project Appraisal. Projects or programs that meet the first screening test should undergo more rigorous scrutiny of their cost-benefit or cost effectiveness. The project selection process needs to ensure that projects proposed for financing have been evaluated for their social and economic value. The quality of *ex-ante* project evaluation depends very much on the quality of the analysis, which, in turn, depends on the capacity of staff with project evaluation skills. Investment in training in project evaluation techniques is an important aspect of an effective public investment system.

3. Independent Review of Appraisal. Where departments and ministries (rather than a central unit) undertake the appraisal, an independent peer review might be necessary in order to check any subjective, self-serving bias in the evaluation.

4. Project Selection and Budgeting. It is important that the process of appraising and selecting public investment projects is linked in an appropriate way to the budget cycle even though the project evaluation cycle may run along a different timetable.

5. Project Implementation. Project design should include clear organizational arrangements and a realistic timetable to ensure the capacity to implement the project.

6. Project Adjustment. The funding review process should have some flexibility to allow changes in the disbursement profile to take account of changes in project circumstances. Each funding request should be accompanied by an updated cost-benefit analysis and a reminder to project sponsors of their accountability for the delivery of the benefits.

7. Facility Operation. Asset registers need to be maintained and asset values recorded. Ideally, countries should require their operating agencies to compile balance sheets, on which the value of assets created through new fixed capital expenditure would be maintained.

8. *Ex-post* Project Evaluation. *Ex-post* project evaluation of completed projects should focus on the comparison of the project's outputs and outcomes with the established objectives in the project design. Good practice suggests that the project design should build in the evaluation criteria and that learning from such *ex-post* evaluations is used to improve future project design and implementation.

Source: Rajaram et al. (2008), Ley (2009)

However, a diagnostic in this area concluded that:

... public investment management (PIM) remains largely inefficient and certain key functions of project evaluation are missing or in rudimentary forms. To succeed, all the pieces of reforms have to be woven into a coherent framework targeting the weakest links in the PIM system. Multiple factors, including the absence of necessary institutions, unclear institutional mandates, weak capacity, lack of vertical and horizontal coordination, and misaligned incentives drive the inefficiency of PIM. This also implies that pure technical solutions do not guarantee success. As a result [the paper] suggests that strengthening of the challenge function of the Ministry of Finance in Zambia is critical for better PIM but a gradual, incentive-compatible approach is probably necessary in the current context.

Le et al. (2010)

4.4.1 *Zambia's public financial management and budgeting framework*

The World Bank's 2003 Public Expenditure Management and Financial Accountability Review found that many of Zambia's public finance laws and regulations were not enforced, leading to a breakdown of administrative systems and procedures for the control of expenditure. This was further complicated by a lack of audit systems and enforcement of the Auditor General's recommendations (World Bank, 2003).

By 2005, when Zambia's first Public Expenditure and Financial Accountability (PEFA)[5] Assessment was carried out, a number of improvements had been recorded. A follow-up PEFA assessment in 2008[6] provided evidence of a number of improvements in the areas of budget credibility, comprehensiveness, and transparency; controls in budget execution, including an improved internal audit; transparent procurement procedures, coverage, and improved methodology for external audit; and permitting public access to Public Accounts Committee hearings.

Over the last decade, Zambia's planning and budgeting system has come under substantial scrutiny, first as a result of HIPC obligations, and then as a result of both government and cooperating partner-driven initiatives.[7] As a result, there has been a significant effort to improve linkages between strategic planning, budgeting, and budget execution, with the aim of improving results and service delivery. This includes the adoption of a medium-term expenditure framework (MTEF) in 2003 – a more focused five-year planning system with the Fifth National Development Plan. More recently, the adjustment to a new budget cycle in synch with the financial calendar (a concern which had been identified in the 2008 PEFA assessment as the single largest impediment to improved PFM in Zambia), the adoption of a Single Treasury Account, and the strengthening of audit functions have further cemented PFM reforms in Zambia.

However, while Zambia has managed to set in place many of the major top-level systems for effective planning, budgeting, and financial control over the last five years, there remains substantial work to be done in ensuring that these measures trickle down to spending agencies. In part, the inability of the government to track expenditures at lower levels of aggregation has led to large variations across expenditure types and categories. As a further complication, supplementary budgets are applied for and obtained with ease, further reducing national budget transparency and parliamentary oversight.

In 2010 the Open Budget Index (OBI), published by the International Budget Partnership, Zambia obtained a score of 36 per cent on the Index, compared to South Africa's 92 per cent (the highest scoring government; International Budget Partnership, 2010). In comparison to its regional peer group, Zambia ranks among the worst, with only fragile/post-conflict states ranked poorer. The principal factor dominating Zambia's poor performance on the Index relates to the poor design and availability of its main budget estimates document, known commonly as the 'Yellow Book'. In its current form, the Yellow Book contains detailed proposed financial estimates, along with previous year expenditure details. The document does not, however, contain any documentation providing reasonable justification for expenditure or any measures of performance against strategic objectives set for each expenditure item. As a result, parliament and the general public do not have adequate information to hold the government accountable for its expenditures or to better understand financial outlays for future years.

It could be argued, however, that the design of the OBI questionnaire and the ranking system unfairly portray the Zambian budgeting system as furtive. For instance, editors amended Zambia's self-reported classification as a result of guidelines prohibiting the inclusion of the MTEF as a 'supporting budget document'. In the Zambian context, however, one of the principal roles of the MTEF is to serve as a supporting budget document by providing the macro-economic and fiscal policy framework that underscores the production of the Yellow Book estimates. As a result, the classification policy penalized Zambia by moving it from the highest (or second highest) score to the worst in nearly 10 per cent of the questionnaire. Notwithstanding methodological issues, Zambia's ranking on the OBI highlights the need for transparency and ease of access to information by stakeholders.

4.4.2 *Low public expenditure efficiency*

Low public expenditure efficiency seems to be recurrent in Zambia. In 2010, in a public expenditure review, Revilla (2010) stated that 'the most important challenge in the coming years will be to improve the efficiency of public spending and its impact on the social and economic sectors'. Like most developing countries, the Zambian government has a constrained budget; furthermore, however, the efficiency of public spending is low, largely because of poor planning, a poor procurement process, poor supervision of public works and projects, and lack of detailed post-project evaluations. Spending on social services has remained constant relative to GDP and, while expenditure on road infrastructure and agriculture has grown relative to GDP, this has been the result of questionable investments in major roads and a poorly targeted 'Fertilizer Support Program', which have had a very limited impact on economic growth and poverty reduction (Revilla, 2010).

A recent, and compelling, example concerns the roads sector in the country. In this sector, an effective investment policy is based on four pillars: (i) a sound and sustainable strategy; (ii) sound planning and prioritization techniques; (iii) efficient and transparent procurement processes; and (iv) efficient and transparent implementation/supervision of projects. Raballand (2010) demonstrates that the current implicit strategy for roads investment should be amended. It is even more important that the value for money of road contracts (which is currently low as a result of inadequate procurement processes and contracts implementation) should be improved dramatically. Otherwise, some funding in this area should be questioned.

Apart from maintaining the road network in its current condition (fair and good), measures such as the simplification of clearance procedures or rationalizing the presence of controlling agencies at borders would have, by far, the highest impact on reducing transport prices for international trade.

As far as planning and oversight is concerned in this sector, the Ministry of Finance and National Planning has not appeared to play its role of oversight institution to make public investments more efficient. In 2009, the Office of the Auditor General conducted procurement, financial, and technical audits in the roads sector. Some findings were problematic for efficiency of public spending in this area. On the side of procurement, the Office of the Auditor General highlighted the following:

- the keeping of records, notices, and advertisements and documents was in such a manner that quick retrieval was impossible;
- there was over-commitment by the awarding of too many/too large contracts in 2008 (with an over-commitment of $US200 million compared with the budgeted $US180 million);
- the allowance of inadequate bidding periods (and without de facto differentiation depending on contract value);
- a lack of transparency in the selection of Road Development Agency (RDA) bid evaluation committees;
- a lack of consistency by the RDA bid evaluation committees with the tendency of the tender boards at the RDA to ignore the bid evaluation

committees' recommendations, which is contrary to procurement rules in Zambia;

- engineers' estimates were not used when carrying evaluations, which made it difficult to ascertain the reasonableness of bids.

On the financial and technical aspects, the audits highlighted that:

- several contracts were running without supervision;
- the RDA does not usually hold contract negotiation meetings despite inconsistencies in the evaluation and poor contract documents;
- many contracts were not signed or dated;
- some performance bonds were never submitted;
- payments to contractors and consultants are frequently delayed;
- irregular instructions were given to contractors, for example with regard to paying RDA staff and the servicing of motor vehicles;
- decisions on contract price variations were, in some cases, not justified by the contractor;
- in cases where supervision of the contracts was performed by the RDA, supervision funds were paid through the contractor, thereby raising issues of objectivity.

All of these factors led to poor quality works that are documented in the hundreds of pages of documents based on several dozens of contracts. It also concurs with a comparative study on road unit costs and 'red flags' in sub-Saharan Africa, which discovered that, despite a perceived relatively strong control of corruption, Zambia had one of the highest recurrent number of red flags[8] in the project documents reviewed (along with Mozambique, Kenya, and the Democratic Republic of Congo, and behind Nigeria and the Republic of Congo).

4.4.3 *How can it be explained – the lack of accountability and political economy factors*

Zambia has in place a system of oversight institutions in that it has both internal and external checks and balances. These checks and balances are instituted by different institutions whose combined role is to ensure that the country has accountable, transparent, and credible institutions so as to limit inefficiencies in public spending, thereby securing public resources.

However, these institutions have usually failed to fully implement their stated mandate. This is mainly because of the fact that some Controlling Officers are at the whim of the appointing authority. This trend has been improved since 2003 with the introduction of performance contracts in the

Zambian public service. Owing to politicization of the civil service, the sanctioning system is weak, and collusion between auditors and controlling officers occurs rather frequently (Mwangala, 2010). Governance challenges that have come to light over the years (the most recent being in the health sector) also explain the lack of progress in implementing changes or reforms that improve service delivery to the public, or the failure over the years of the executive to follow through on public policy implementation. Political interference during project selection and project management seems to be pervasive in certain sectors and could explain the relatively low value for money of some projects in Zambia. Therefore, in order to improve public investment management, some governance reforms will have to be undertaken in parallel with technical measures.

4.5 What can be done to increase public spending efficiency?

There remains a pressing need for the government to increase public output and service delivery to the population. This includes both the quantity and quality of services delivered per unit of public financial resources currently at its disposal to spend. Increasing public expenditure efficiency will require the government to reform and strengthen its budgeting processes (especially in areas of budgeting, budget execution, monitoring, and financial reporting) and public expenditure accountability. Simultaneously, there must be greater emphasis in expanding the absorptive capacities of government spending agencies, a number of which are too undercapitalized and understaffed to be able to deal with large capital projects. These improvements can be attained by improving budget institutions and public expenditure oversight institutions in order to increase public transparency and accountability, particularly in the area of public expenditure management. Some progress has been made with regard to budget execution, mainly by re-aligning national budgeting and approvals to be made early enough to allow expenditures to be undertaken for a full twelve-month fiscal year from January to December.

A single treasury account has been established and is being tested to improve the management of public resources and to support monetary policy implementation. These reforms should be implemented rapidly to improve budget execution and monitoring, increase the absorptive spending capacity of spending agencies, and assist fiscal and monetary policy coordination. Furthermore, the government needs to improve its budget and expenditure institutions to ensure broader consultation and participation of non-state actors in the fiscal governance of the country (Bwalya et al., 2011). This will help circumvent some policy and institutional failures that result from poor coordination as a result of information asymmetry.

There is much room for improvement in the area of financial accountability and transparency. The easiest and most direct reform would be to reformat the book of budgetary estimates (the 'Yellow Book'). In its current format, the book serves only as a collection of numerical estimates, without any explanation or narrative. The inclusion of summaries describing each programme and how it links to the government's longer-term strategies and the medium-term macro-economic and policy environment (along with risks and opportunities) would provide stakeholders – in particular members of parliament – with a more useful evaluating and referencing tool. In addition, producing a 'people's budget', which summarizes the budget in commonly accessible language, and publishing the Yellow Book and other budget documents online, would further strengthen the transparency of the budgeting process and allow for greater civic participation.

In the longer term, reforms need to focus on better systems that define and measure budgetary performance. Revilla (2010), for example, recommends a drastic overhaul of the classification of budgetary programmes and suggests a reclassification of programmes along strategic and thematic areas, along with the clear identification of responsible institutions/entities. Bird also calls for the development and inclusion of performance-based indicators focusing on quantity, access, quality, and efficiency of outputs for each programme in the budget, and for these indicators to be eventually integrated into the budgetary allocation process. Finally, a stronger internal and external auditing system, in particular placing greater emphasis on following through the recommendations of audits and parliamentary committees, is also an important area for longer-term reform.

4.6 Concluding remarks and a way forward?

Increasing demand from citizens for the accountability of officials is increasingly sought by donors and civil society organizations. The Public Expenditure Management and Financial Accountability Review concluded: 'Only through greater disclosure of information on resources and liabilities of the State will it be possible for Zambians to develop credible strategies for tackling the economic challenges ahead' (World Bank, 2003). If governments are not held accountable to citizens, the efficiency of public spending is likely to remain low.

It is also well known that taxation sets up the interaction between citizens and the State, with the former holding the latter accountable. Brautigam (2008) stresses that 'state-building is shaped by societies, and taxation is a strategic nexus between the state and society'. As citizens pay higher taxes, they demand better services, which require better public expenditures. What Karl (2007) calls the *participation deficit*, 'a lack of connection between subjects and the state, which breaks any sense of ownership of public resources or consequent citizen engagement', seems to be one of the most important challenges for oil or mineral economies. The linkage has even been highlighted as central to avoiding the natural resource curse in natural resource-rich countries (OECD, 2008). Governments in oil-rich or mineral-rich countries gather less revenue from domestic taxation (Henry and Springborg, 2001) and are therefore not held accountable (Moore, 2007; Bornhorst et al., 2008).

In most oil-mineral-developing economies, a small elite captures most rents whereas the poor benefit from some subsidies and do not expect much from the government/local authorities. The bulk of the population lives from employment in the informal sector and as they pay little or no taxes they do not expect large investments in public goods by the government.

As in most developing countries, civil society organizations in Zambia are involved at the planning stage (their impact is marginal) but not during the execution and supervision of projects (Economics Association of Zambia, 2009), which translates to limited accountability to citizens/taxpayers. In Zambia, the Economics Association of Zambia undertook an analysis of public expenditure reviews and their impact on public efficiency spending (Economics Association of Zambia, 2009). It was found that information on domestic and external debt stock of the public institutions is not adequate or comprehensive[9] because it excludes revenues and expenditures of the wider public sector, including local authorities and semi-autonomous bodies. Moreover, donor funding is not comprehensively captured.

In terms of accountability and controls, the parliament does not fulfil its role, mainly because of the executive branch's tendency to regularly submit supplementary expenditures after the adoption of the budget and its inability to have recommendations and sanctions enforced.

What is therefore critical is to improve public expenditure *accountability*, firstly by improving the design, budgeting, and execution of public projects in general, and more specifically by streamlining public procurement systems to ensure that public projects are awarded transparently and competitively, and that they are properly supervised and evaluated. Parliamentary oversight of the budget and, in particular, public expenditures and public projects must be strengthened as its members have a mandate to ensure that projects in their respective constituencies are properly executed. This role is often diluted by party patronage, poor budgetary documentation, and inadequate de-centralization of the public service delivery system to enable effective participation at a local level. Therefore, strengthening parliamentary oversight should invariably be complemented by reforms to enable greater public disclosure and scrutiny of public expenditures, and facilitation of the greater participation of civil society organizations, the media, and citizens in general, in monitoring budget execution, public expenditures, and projects.

Governments generally become more accountable in the manner they use public resources when citizens themselves are able to hold politicians accountable for their actions and demand public services for the taxes they pay. With the exception of those that are employed formally, the majority of the citizens pay taxes indirectly and therefore do not perceive themselves as contributing to public revenues. Consequently, they lack the necessary incentive and drive to demand better public services, accountability, and efficiency in the manner that politicians spend their tax money; hence, the ballot is not effectively used to remove underperforming political leaders from government. In this context, taxation needs to be more broad-based and effective in order to motivate citizens to demand better public services and greater accountability for public expenditures (even though, from an efficiency perspective, indirect taxation may be better).

Furthermore, when a significant portion of the national budget is financed through grants from cooperating partners, and non-state actors lack detailed information on how such monies are to be spent, one would not expect citizens to be that interested in scrutinizing and holding the government accountable to how such grants are spent. In fact, countries where aid resources finance a greater share also tend to have weak fiscal accountability and the efficiency of aid expenditure is low, especially when donor and civil society oversight is weak. Citizens will generally lack the incentive and voice to hold the government accountable to how they spend donor aid resources.

Usually, efficiency of the public sector is tackled primarily through technical measures either aimed at better collecting public revenues or at making public spending more efficient. In many countries, these technical measures are expected to reduce vested interests and corruption. The main issue is that without accountability vis-à-vis citizens, technical measures are less likely to reduce the impact and power of vested interests and then are bound to fail in many instances.[10]

In any case, without shaping a fiscal social contract through the taxation of citizens, the outcome of public spending will probably remain low despite increased external pressure for public transparency as a condition for access to increased aid resources. The line of argument is straightforward: citizens are more likely to hold their governments accountable when they have to pay more taxes; as a result, governments have incentives to design and implement policies that improve the welfare of the population – see, for example, Moore (2004). However, in a poverty-ridden country, where the proportion of the population paying taxes is small, the current tax system is likely to remain an impossible vehicle for creating sufficient incentives for citizens to demand increased fiscal transparency and accountability of public officials. That is why we would also propose that mineral revenues be increased to a level where it is feasible to redistribute it in the form of transfers to all citizens and then taxing them in order to create/recreate a fiscal contract between citizens and the government – this scheme is described in Devarajan et al. (2010).

Notes

1. Fiscal space can also be created by rationalizing public expenditures, a matter deferred to Section 4.4.
2. See Chapter 5, Conrad, R., Mineral taxation in Zambia.
3. Import VAT contributes over 60 per cent of total trade taxes, and import duty and trade excise account for the rest. From 2007, import VAT deferment was only applicable on imports of capital goods, meaning that collections under import VAT consequently increased trade tax revenues in 2007 and 2008, while net domestic VAT collections declined as VAT refunds substantially increased. The performance of VAT as a tax type is illustrated in Table 4.3, where domestic VAT and import VAT are added together. Import duty continued to decline as tariffs were reduced under the various regional trade agreements that Zambia has ratified.
4. For example, the tax regime for agriculture is quite generous, with the lowest corporate tax rate of 15 per cent on income from farming, 50 per cent depreciation allowance per five years of farming improvements, 20 per cent capital expenditure for one cost incurred for the production of coffee, tea, bananas, citrus fruits, and similar plants, and a further 100 per cent allowance on farm works on farm land (i.e. stumping, land clearance, etc.). This compares favourably with the tourism and manufacturing sectors, where the corporate rate is 35 per cent, and 10 per cent and 50 per cent for initial and depreciation allowances respectively. All these incentives are in addition to those given to priority sectors under the Zambia Development Agency Act, which are explained later.
5. The PEFA is the internationally agreed diagnostic tool for public financial management.
6. Zambia has agreed to undertake the review every three years. The next assessment is due in 2012.
7. This includes work done under the Public Expenditure Management and Financial Accountability programme, as well as individual support projects from the World Bank and the Department for International Development.
8. The main patterns are as follows: (i) the difference between contract price and read-out bid price is more than 10 per cent; (ii) the winning bid not the lowest bid accepted for detailed examination; (iii) more than seven months from bid opening to contract signing; (iv) half or more firms that buy bidding documents do not bid. See Alexeeva et al. (2008) for more details.
9. The Public Expenditure Management and Financial Accountability report pointed out that: 'First, expenditure reports are prone to errors and inconsistencies that are difficult to find and to reconcile. Second, reporting tends to be significantly delayed because of the various levels of compilation required. Third, the focus on bookkeeping tasks distracts accounting staff from more meaningful analysis of the data and trends. Fourth, the delays and inconsistencies greatly diminish the ability of MFNP to provide sufficient oversight and control over the nature of the expenditures. Because of these inadequacies, the MFNP has found it difficult to provide an accurate, complete and transparent account of its financial position to Parliament and other stakeholders, including the general public and donors.' (World Bank, 2003).

10. It is worth noting that accountability vis-à-vis citizens is easier to achieve in open and democratic societies relative to closed and authoritarian countries.

References

Alexeeva, V., Padam, G., and Queiroz, C. (2008). Monitoring Road Works Contracts and Unit Costs for Enhanced Governance in Sub-Saharan Africa. *Transport Paper* 21. Washington, DC: World Bank.

Beuran, M., Raballand, G., and Revilla, J. (2011). Improving aid effectiveness in aid-dependent countries based on lessons from Zambia. *Centre d'Economie de la Sorbonne Working Paper* 2011.40.

Bolnick, B. (2004). *Effectiveness and Economic Impact of Tax Incentives in the SADC Region.* Gaborone: USAID/SADC Tax Subcommittee.

Bornhorst, F., Gupta, S., and Thornton, J. (2008). Natural resource endowments, governance, and the domestic revenue effort: Evidence from a panel of countries. *IMF Working Paper* 08/170.

Brautigam, D. (2008). Introduction: Taxation and state building in developing countries. In: Brautigam, D., Fjeldstad, O., and Moore, M. (eds) *Taxation and State-Building in Developing Countries: Capacity and Consent.* Cambridge: Cambridge University Press.

Bwalya, S.M., Phiri, E., and Mpembamoto, K. (2011). How interest groups lobbying to influence budget outcomes in Zambia. *Journal of International Development*; 23: 420–442.

Devarajan, S., Le, T.M., and Raballand, G. (2010). Increasing public expenditure efficiency in oil-rich economies: A proposal. *World Bank Policy Research Working Paper* No. 5287.

Economics Association of Zambia (2009). *Public Expenditure Reviews in Zambia: A Review of Literature.* Lusaka: Economics Association of Zambia.

Henry, C. and Springborg, R. (2001). *Globalization and the Politics of Development in the Middle East.* Cambridge: Cambridge University Press.

International Budget Partnership (2010). *Open Budget Index 2010.* Available at: <http://www.internationalbudget.org/what-we-do/open-budget-survey> (last accessed 12 August 12 2011).

Karl, T.L. (2007). Ensuring fairness: The case for a transparent fiscal social contract. In: Humphreys, M., Sachs, J., and Stiglitz, J. (eds) *Escaping the Resource Curse.* New York: Columbia University Press.

Le, T.M., Raballand, G., and Palale, P. (2010). Public investment management in Zambia – diagnostic and recommendations. In: Revilla, J. (ed.) *Zambia – Public Expenditure Review.* Washington, DC: World Bank.

Ley, E. (2010). Exhaustible resources and fiscal policy: Copper mining in Zambia. In: Revilla, J. (ed.) *Public Expenditure Review.* Washington, DC: World Bank.

Mintz, J.M. and Smart, M. (2008). Incentives for public investment under fiscal rules. In: Perry, G.E., Serven, L., and Suescun, R. (eds) *Fiscal Policy, Stabilization and Growth.* Washington, DC: World Bank.

Ministry of Finance and National Planning (2006). *Economic Report for 2005.* Lusaka: Ministry of Finance and National Planning.

Moore, M. (2004). Revenues, state formation, and the quality of governance in developing countries. *International Political Science Review* 25: 297–319.

Moore, M. (2007). How does taxation affect the quality of governance? *IDS Working Paper* 280.

Mwangala, P. (2010). Review of oversight institutions in Zambia. *Mimeo* Ministry of Finance and National Planning.

Organisation for Economic Co-operation and Development (2008). *Governance, Taxation and Accountability*. Paris: Organisation for Economic Co-operation and Development. Available at: <http://www.oecd.org/dataoecd/52/35/40210055.pdf> (last accessed 9 September 2012).

Raballand, G. (2010). Welfare of roads investments impact – the case of Zambia. In: Revilla, J. (ed.) *Zambia – Public Expenditure Review*. Washington, DC: World Bank.

Rajaram, A., Le, T.M., Biletska, N., and Brumby, J. (2008). *A Diagnostic Framework for Assessing Public Investment Management*. PRMPS, PREM Network. Washington, DC: World Bank.

Revilla, J. (2010). *Zambia – Public Expenditure Review*. Washington, DC: World Bank.

Tjoa, A., Kapihya, M., Libetwa, M., Lee, J., Pattison, C., McCarthy E., and Schroder, K. (2010). Doubling the number of health graduates in Zambia. *Human Resources for Health* 8: 22.

World Bank (2003). Zambia – Public Expenditure Management and Financial Accountability Review. *Report 26162-ZA*. Washington, DC: World Bank.

5

Mineral Taxation in Zambia

Robert F. Conrad

5.1. Introduction

This chapter examines Zambia's fiscal regime for minerals. The discussion begins with a description of the regime in an international comparative context. Section 5.3 contains a framework to evaluate the country's minerals policy in the context of the broader fiscal regime and is followed by an evaluation of the regime and proposals for both short- and long-term reforms. Emphasis is placed on developing a foundation upon which the policy and administrative apparatus can evolve through time. A brief summary completes the analysis.

The government appears to be committed to increasing the public return from mining via increased enforcement, review of existing contracts, and changes in the fiscal regime, such as the recent increase in royalty rates and restrictions on the use of hedging.[1] In general, there appears to be room for government to achieve this objective. Increasing government's return is not costless, however, and it is important that government decision-makers think systematically about how greater returns are achieved. The chapter argues that an incremental approach where administrative enhancements are coupled with rationalization of the various revenue instruments is preferable to imposing additional charges without rationalization of existing instruments.

5.2. Comparative mining fiscal regimes

Table 5.1 briefly summarizes Zambia's fiscal regime.[2] Tables 5.2, 5.3, and 5.4 contain comparative information about the current structure of royalties, profits taxes, and excess profits taxes (and other matters) respectively, across

Table 5.1 Zambia's minerals regime

A. Profits tax

Item	Treatment
Tax rate	Mining companies – 30% General rates – 35% Lusaka Stock Exchange listed companies – 33% Banks – 35% Mobile telecommunications operators, income above K250 million – 45% Farming – 10% Companies under the Zambia Development Agency Act – 0% first 5 years, 50% reduced rate years 6–8, 25% reduced rate years 9 and 10[3]
Accounting standards	Accrual basis
Thin capitalization rules	Thin-capitalization rules apply to thinly capitalized companies and the ratio of debt-to-equity should not exceed 3:1[4]
Depreciation	Capital expenditure on the improvement or upgrading of infrastructure will qualify for an improvement allowance of 100% Equipment, plant, machinery and other capital expenditure will be claimed at a rate of 25% per annum[5]

B. Indirect tax

Item	Description
Value added tax (VAT)	Standard VAT rate of 16%[6] Cash accounting for VAT for companies carrying out mining operations[7]
Customs duties	Levy/tax charged on imported goods at the following rates: 0–5% capital equipment and raw materials 15% intermediate goods 25% finished goods Customs duty is charged on the customs value[8] A holder of a mining right is exempt from customs and VAT duties for all machinery and equipment required for exploration or mining actvities[9] A 15% export duty on concentrate was imposed in 2008 but subsequently repealed
Excise duty	Excise duties are levied on specific classes of goods manufactured in, or imported into, the country[10]

a set of comparator countries.[11] Zambia's regime is a variant of a traditional royalty tax regime in which the government charges a royalty and then imposes the generally applicable tax regime, with, perhaps, special provisions for mining.[12] There is a supplemental revenue charge (based on the ratio of taxable income to measured sales), as well as equity participation retained as part of the privatization process and held by Zambia Consolidated Copper Mines (ZCCM-IH).[13] This system has resulted, in part, from the privatization

process and was modified significantly in 2008 and again in 2010. The royalty
rate has been increased twice, first to 3 per cent and then to 6 per cent, and
a variable profits tax was introduced. A variant of the windfall profits tax
was enacted in 2008 but was repealed in 2009.

The centrepiece of the Zambian mining tax system is the royalty. Globally,
royalties are used widely and most are *ad valorem* (see Table 5.2). Australia
(Northwest Territories) and Canada (both British Columbia and Saskatchewan)

Table 5.2 International comparison of mineral royalties – copper and gold

Country	Rate – copper	Rate – gold	Definition of base
Australia (NSW)	4%	4%	Ex-mine value
Australia (NT)	18%	18%	Net value of mineral
Canada (BC)	15%	15%	2% net current proceeds + 13% net revenue
Canada (Sask.)	5/10%	5/10%	Net profits based on unit sales
Chile	0–5%*	Unclear	Total sales, varies by volume
China	2%+Rmb‡ 7/ton	4% per unit charge	*Ad valorem* royalty + per unit charge
DRC	2%	2.5%	Net sales value
Indonesia	4%	3.75%	Net sales
Kazakhstan	5.7%	5.0%	Mineral extraction tax based on revenue
Mexico	None	None	None
Mongolia	5% (base rate)	5%	Sales value
Peru	1–3%	1–3%	Gross sales
Russia	8%	8% (6% concentrate containing gold)	Value of mineral resources
South Africa	Unrefined: 0.5+ (EBIT/(gross sales*9*))*100, max. 7% Refined: 0.5+ (EBIT/(gross sales*12.5))* 100, max. 5%	Unrefined: 0.5+ (EBIT/(gross sales*9))*100, max. 7% Refined: 0.5+ (EBIT/(gross sales*12.5))* 100, max. 5%	EBIT = earnings before income Taxes and gross sales
USA (AZ)	At least 2%	At least 2%	Gross value
USA (NV)	Up to 5%	Up to 5%	Net proceeds
Zambia	3% (6% in 2012)	5%	Gross value

*Peru: 2010 proposal to double rates for most minerals to 2–6%, copper to 5%, gold to 10%,
unclear when effective. Chile: temporary increase on copper royalty rate up to 9% for 2011
and 2012
‡Rmb = China Yan Renminbi 1Rmb = 0.15 USD (as of January 2011)
Data correct as of 2011.
Additional comparative royalty rates are available on request
NSW: New South Wales; NT: Northern Territory; BC:British Columbia; Sask: Saskatchewan;
DRC: Democratic Republic of the Congo; AZ: Arizona; NV: Nevada

are exceptions, with rates in these mining areas higher as a result.[14] *Ad valorem* royalty rates for copper vary, generally ranging between 0 per cent and 8 per cent. Zambia's 3 per cent and new 6 per cent rate falls between these extremes. The rates, however, may be misleading because the base to which the royalty rate is applied also varies across countries. The bases, even for *ad valorem* charges, are generally some measure of output value: how the base is measured will determine the effective rate and the administrative aspects of application.[15]

Some countries, such as Peru and South Africa, use variable rate royalties which might be interpreted as a type of excess profits tax scheme or, alternatively, a type of price participation system common among private sector participations (see following discussion).[16] Special note should be made of recent proposed changes in Chile and Australia. Beginning in 2011, Chile has introduced a variable system on a voluntary basis for two years. The rates revert back to previous levels after the two-year period. The benefit for those choosing the higher rates will be that stabilization agreements will be extended for ten years after the rates revert. After a review of the entire tax system, Australian analysts proposed that the states repeal their *ad valorem* royalties and substitute a type of resource rent tax system for mining. The law enacted in November 2011 will impose a charge of 30 per cent on returns (measured in terms of a mine's net present value) in excess of a long-term bond rate plus 7 per cent.

Standing alongside the royalty in most jurisdictions is a profits tax (see Table 5.3), in some cases, such as Zambia and South Africa, imposed as a variable profits tax on mining in addition to the standard income tax. Profits tax rules are generally applied uniformly across industries, but there are industry-specific provisions for each sector, including mining. Two aspects of mining are addressed specifically in most tax laws: exploration and development. Zambia provides for immediate expensing of both exploration and development. This is the method employed in a number of other countries (Australia and Canada), though some countries (Mongolia) employ capitalization and amortization. Differences, perhaps significant, in effective tax rates will result from this variation across countries because of the relative size of exploration and development expenditures to total measures of profitability both in total and at the margin.

Many countries impose a value added tax (VAT) that, as a destination-based consumption tax, should, in principle, be imposed in the mining sector. However, given the zero-rating of exports combined with the large import content of mining operations, mining companies are frequently in a perpetual excess credit position. This means that refunds would have to be paid to the investors on a monthly basis, which can be challenging for liquidity-constrained governments. Sometimes governments resort to ad hoc methods (such as exempting production or exempting imports) in an effort to reduce

Table 5.3 International comparison of profits tax policy

Country	Profits tax rate	Treatment of exploration expenses	Treatment of development expenses
Australia	30%	Immediate expensing	Immediate expensing
Canada (federal) Canada (BC) Canada (Sask.)	16.5% (2011) 10% (2011) 10%	Immediate expensing	Immediate expensing
Chile	20% first category tax + global complementary + additional tax on non-residents	Immediate expensing	Immediate expensing
China	25%	Amortized	Amortized
DRC	40%; 30% for mining companies	Unknown	Immediate expensing
Indonesia	25%	Amortized	Amortized
Kazakhstan	20%; branch profits tax of 15%	Immediate expensing	Immediate expensing
Mexico	30%	Unknown	Unknown
Mongolia	10% up to MNT* 3 billion; 25% thereafter	Amortized pre-production 5 years SL‡	Amortized 5 years SL
Peru	30%	Unknown	Unknown
Russia	20%	Immediate expensing	Amortized over 5 years
South Africa	28%; branch profits tax of 33%	Immediate expensing	Immediate expensing
USA (federal) USA (AZ) USA (NV)	15-35% on residents/30% branch profits tax AZ – 6.97% NV – no tax	70% first year, then 5 years SL	70% first year, then 5 years SL
Zambia	35%; 30% for mining companies + 0–15% variable profits tax	Immediate expensing	Immediate expensing

*MNT = Mongolia Tugrik; 1 MNT = 0.0008 USD (as of 24 January 2011)
‡SL = straight line depreciation method
Data correct as of 2011.
Additional information on other aspects of the profits tax is available on request
BC: British Columbia; Sask.: Saskatchewan; DRC: Democratic Republic of Congo;
AZ: Arizona; NV: Nevada

Table 5.4 International comparison of excess profits taxes, VAT, and trade taxes

Country	Excess profits tax	VAT	Import duties	Export duties
Australia	RRT – 30% on a measure of the present value	Standard GST rate 10%	5% general rate	Exempt
Canada	No	Standard GST rate 5% (BC 12%, Sask. 5%)	Exempt: most minerals	Exempt
Chile	No	Standard VAT rate 19%	10% on mining equipment	Exempt
China	No	Standard VAT rate 17% (gold exempt)	Exempt	Exempt
DRC	No	13% sales tax (10 or 3% for mining companies)	Exempt: mining companies	Exempt: mining companies
Indonesia	No	Standard VAT rate 10%, pre-production purchases of machinery and equipment exempt	Taxed	Exempt
Kazakhstan	0–60% on portion of net income exceeds 25% of deductions	Standard VAT rate 12%	Taxed	Exempt
Mexico	No	Standard VAT rate 16%	Exempt if used in production of exports	Exempt
Mongolia	Rates vary from 5% to 15% when output is concentrated	Standard VAT rate 10%	5% on mining equipment	Exempt
Peru	No	Standard VAT rate 19%	0–17%	Exempt
Russia	No	Standard VAT rate 18%	0–25% of customs value (oil drilling platform 15%)	35–65% on minerals
South Africa	No	Standard VAT rate 14%	Taxed	Exempt
USA	No	States and localities may impose sales tax	Taxes; rates vary by country and commodity	Exempt
Zambia	0–15% variable profits on copper producer	Standard VAT rate 16%	Taxed	Unclear

Data correct as of 2011.
Addional comparative data available on request
DRC: Democratic Republic of Congo; RRT: resource rent tax; GST: General Sales Tax; British
 Columbia; Sask: Saskatchewan; VAT: value added tax

or to eliminate the need for the investors to pay VAT on inputs and collect refunds for exports.

Finally, tariffs can be used for revenue (such as the uniform tariff in Chile), for protection (on finished goods in particular), or both. Rates in Table 5.4 vary by country, which reflects protection motives at least in part. Given the export nature and lack of domestic input supply, mining investors may enjoy reduced rates or exemptions (Mexico). Russia is the only major mineral-producing country that imposes export charges; those charges are generally limited to oil and gas.[17]

5.3. Fiscal analysis framework

A government of a country endowed with mineral assets might perform five different economic functions, four of which have direct financial consequences:

- manage the resource on behalf of the population;
- impose and administer the general tax regime;

Table 5.5 Summary of potential government functions in the natural resource sector

Function	Financial payments to government	Financial and opportunity costs
Ownership function (stewardship of the reserve base)	Financial returns to ownership: bonus auction bids royalties (including variable royalties) excess profit schemes	Reduction in wealth via accumulated extraction Lost diversification
General tax function	Personal income tax Profits tax VAT Tariffs Property tax	Distortions in private sector decision-making Administrative and compliance costs
Passive investment function	Dividends Capital gains Interest (if passive investment is via loans) Price participation agreements	Less diversification (both domestic and international) given investment budgets Foregone current government expenditures (such as debt reduction or education)
Operating company	Returns to management (in addition to dividends and capital gains)	Further losses in diversification Lost efficiency in public sector enterprises

VAT: value added tax

- take equity positions in some, or all, mining operations;
- use state enterprises as operating companies;
- regulate the mining industry (health and safety, environmental, and other regulatory functions).

The total cash flow to government, and the risks borne by the economy, will be affected by how many functions are undertaken and the choice of instruments. Moreover, the payment streams are only a partial measure of the gross benefit to government. For instance, a government might forego tax revenue in order to require a mining company to purchase inputs from domestic sources.[18] Such a requirement might benefit domestic suppliers, on a net basis, if the value of supplying the goods and services is greater than their opportunity costs. Economic costs are also imposed and thus it is essential that the gross benefit be balanced against the real costs in order to ensure positive economic returns, including the growth of the economy.

Some benefits and costs of each of the four revenue-generating functions are summarized in Table 5.5 and a description is provided in the following section.

5.3.1. *Manage the resource on behalf of the population*

A country must determine how mineral ownership rights are allocated. State ownership of subsurface rights is common in most countries. Ownership may be at the national level (Zambia) or at the subnational level (Canada). Mineral ownership means that a government's assets (or balance sheet) will include the value of the subsurface rights in addition to other assets, such as assets of state enterprises, government buildings, and the power to tax (an intangible asset). If a deposit is developed, then the government may receive financial flows from a variety of sources, including land rents, bonus payments, royalties, and resource rent charges.[19]

The type of payment, the timing, and the amounts will depend on a country's legal framework, how extraction rights are awarded, the quantity and quality of the deposit, and other factors. It is important to note that the government is responsible for the speed with which resources are exhausted and thus can use these instruments, along with production quotas to the extent quotas are not redundant, to influence how much operators develop and determine extraction within and between time periods.

Resource extraction is not costless to any economy. At a basic level, the wealth of the economy is reduced with cumulative extraction. In addition, the government closes off options for different contractual forms or methods for awarding contracts to different investors by determining a particular contract form and choosing a particular operator (either public or private sector entity). The government, and society more generally, foregoes the use of surface rights and other rights resulting from the need for such assets in the production of subsurface minerals. Finally, the government must administer the fiscal regime, as well as monitor – and, hopefully, actively husband – the resource base.

At a more aggregate level, extraction may change the diversification of the economy's asset base. A resource discovery increases the variety of assets in the economy, which is reversed as the reserves are depleted. Significant resource discoveries can affect domestic relative prices, which can have adverse effects on non-resource sectors. For instance, the price of non-tradables may rise because, at least in the short run, the stock of non-tradable assets may have to be re-allocated between pre-existing economic activities and new mining activities resulting from an appreciation of the real exchange rate. Sector-specific losses may result – in traditional export sectors in particular – and such costs are part of the real cost of resource development (and to the extent they occur, should be part of any mineral evaluation).

5.3.2. *Impose and administer the general tax regime: return for rights to taxation*

The right to tax is vested in the state. This asset enables governments to accrue economic resources from the private sector without directly supplying goods and services in exchange. That is, unlike the private sector, the government does not have to sell a good or service to generate revenue. As a general rule, the mining sector should be treated like any other sector with respect to overall tax policy, particularly with respect to the use of direct taxes and VAT.

Three elements of the income tax are, however, particular to mining: the treatment of expenses for exploration, development, and reclamation. All three elements, however, have similar counterparts in non-mining industries: exploration is effectively searching and is similar to research and development; development is a type of self-constructed asset; and reclamation is similar to expenses related to plant closure (disposal of hazardous waste, restoration, and other issues). A significant issue in the VAT treatment of mining is related to the export nature of production and the use of imported inputs, particularly during the initial investment stage. One implication is that VAT refunds would be significant if standard VAT treatment is afforded to the mineral sector. These problems, however, are similar to any new investment where imported inputs are required and the output is designed for export. In emerging economies, this is the case with manufacturing in general.

The costs of developing a generally applicable tax system include administration and compliance costs. Such costs are complicated by the asymmetric nature of the information structure. Taxpayers have access to information about revenues and costs while tax administrations may have little or no means to independently verify that information. In addition, incentive compatibility is absent in a tax system because there is not a direct transfer of goods or services in exchange for tax payments. An additional cost of a generally applicable tax system is the adverse economic incentives created by lack of direct exchange. Incentives are created to change investment and labour supply decisions, which may reduce real net national income.

5.3.3. Take equity positions in some, or all, mining operations

Some countries, including Zambia, have chosen to take equity positions in particular mining enterprises. Potential financial gains include dividends from shares and capital gains. Such gains are not costless, even if shares are so-called free equity. The government, as a minority shareholder, may be adversely affected by decisions made by those with majority positions, particularly in countries where transparent corporate governance is lacking and shareholder protection is weak. The government and economy more generally may bear three additional costs.

Firstly, the government now owns rights to physical capital and intangible assets held by the mining company in addition to holding the reserves. Thus, the government is taking a longer position in mining and there will be a higher correlation between overall government revenues and mineral prices (or returns to mining more generally), unless the government pursues an active risk diversification strategy. Secondly, the economy will be less diversified, all else equal. Funds used to invest in mining enterprises could have been used to invest in other domestic and international assets (with perhaps higher marginal returns), in addition to reducing the society's exposure to mineral price risk. Finally, there is an additional cost that is common to both passive and active equity positions. The government may be placing itself in a direct conflict of interest. Taxes reduce profits and environmental standards may reduce profits. Thus, the government must actively trade off implementing effective tax and regulatory policies with reduced financial gains from asset ownership.[20]

5.3.4. Use state enterprises as operating companies

State enterprises may take a majority interest in mining enterprises and may themselves become operating companies. Potential dividends and capital gains increase with larger equity interests, and the government can directly affect the operating decision of the enterprise, which, in turn, may affect both the level of financial benefits and their distribution.

One cost of using state enterprises as operating companies includes greater financial costs (relative to passive equity ownership), making the economy even more dependent on mineral production for government revenues. That is, this strategy increases risk bearing in minerals, unless mitigated by other means, and decreases the diversification of the economy. Potential conflicts of interest are greater relative to passive equity participation. In addition, there is the risk that state-operated companies will be less efficient relative to private sector counterparts, unless those enterprises are placed in competitive situations in both the output and input markets.

5.3.5. *Summary*

In summary, governments may accrue financial benefits from mining in different ways. If form follows function, then the structure and levels of the financial flows will depend on the different types of functions undertaken by the government. This implies that concentrating on the 'total take' may be inappropriate because the economic objective is to maximize the net social benefit from mining (or any other activity) and the 'total take' is a measure of the gross financial benefit without regard for the structure of the costs required to accrue various components of the gross benefits.

In addition, cross-country comparisons of total take may be misleading unless adjustments are made for the number and structure of functions undertaken by the government. For instance, mineral rights on private lands are not held by the government in the USA. The US federal government does not collect mineral factor payments in this case. In addition, there are no state-owned mining enterprises in the USA. Chile, however, has both a state mining enterprise and state ownership of reserves. Thus, comparing the gross benefits (or total take) between the USA and Chile would be misleading, absent adjustments for the payment streams that flow to private parties in the USA (royalties and returns to ownership of mineral enterprises), but to the state in Chile. That is, the total take to the economy could be the same in the USA as it is in Chile, but the distribution of that revenue is different, resulting in a different measure of government revenues.

5.4. Evaluation and analysis

As noted previously, Zambia's mineral fiscal regime is built around a royalty combined with the generally applicable corporate tax (including some withholding taxes on remittances to non-residents), a variable profits tax, and an element of equity participation.

This structure is reasonable given the history of the sector's development and the current situation. Policymakers and the general public should, however, consider improving each element so that the system as a whole can function in a more coordinated fashion. This section contains an evaluation of the current regime, followed by a discussion of the themes that might serve as guidance for refining and implementing a reform.

5.4.1. Diagnosing current problems with the mining tax regime

Revenue mobilization

General and mining-specific revenue statistics are reported in Tables 5.6–5.9. It is clear that the revenues were not significant in the immediate post-privatization period and have improved since the changes in 2007 and 2008.[21] The revenue increase after 2005 may reflect the amortization of loss carry-forwards resulting from the reorganization of the mineral sector (corporate taxes began to increase), the use of deemed prices for the royalty and for the income tax for some producers, better mineral prices, and improved monitoring. The royalty, once modified, seems to be the most stable revenue source, with the profits tax taking a larger proportion of total revenues during periods of relatively high prices (Table 5.6). The shares of mineral revenue to total tax revenue (including royalty) have also been increasing recently and by the end of the period exceed minerals' share in gross domestic product (GDP) (Tables 5.7–5.9). Mineral revenues should be a greater share of total revenue relative to sector value added because the government is collecting royalties on a factor of production; a phenomenon unique to the mining industry.

On balance, it appears that the revenue situation is improving, but this does not imply that revenues are either adequate or reasonable. The number of mines actually paying tax is known to be relatively few. Perhaps more mines will begin to pay a reasonable amount once stabilization agreements expire and monitoring is improved. Expensing provisions – the ability to set 100 per cent of capital expenditure against the current-year tax liability – may hamper revenue collection, even with improved enforcement, because mines appear to be making frequent incremental investments. Thus, given the current regime, the government might expect only marginally higher revenue, except for the royalty, which may imply that the revenue system is neither adequate in a dynamic system nor stable over the longer term.

Structural issues

While the basic structure of the royalty tax regime, as modified and adjusted since 2008, is reasonable, the additional variable rate profits tax raises a number of concerns (see the following). Two general problems with the weak regulatory and administrative framework are apparent. Firstly, the tax system is replete with special incentives, both for mining and across sectors, which

Table 5.6 Mining sector revenue by type of charge and relevant ratios

Year	1995	1996	1997	1998	1999	2000	2001	2002	2003	2004	2005
Company tax*	8.00	–	–	–	–	2.00	2.00	1.00	–	–	1.00
Withholding tax/dividends	–	–	–	–	–	–	–	–	1.00	2.00	3.00
Mineral royalty	29.00	17.00	19.00	17.00	13.00	4.00	7.00	3.00	8.00	4.00	39.00
Export duty	–	–	–	–	–	–	–	–	–	–	–
Windfall tax	–	–	–	–	–	–	–	–	–	–	–
Mining revenue total	37.00	17.00	19.00	17.00	13.00	6.00	9.00	4.00	9.00	6.00	43.00

Year	2006	2007	2008	2009	2010	2011
Company tax*	160.00	603.00	464.00	401.00	1,244.48‡	2,477.03‡
Withholding tax/dividends	–	–	–	–		
Mineral royalty	59.00	68.00	238.00	235.00	412.00	857.15
Export duty	–	–	178.00	15.00		
Windfall tax	–	–	126.00	–		
Mining revenue total	219.00	671.00	1,006.00	651.00	1,656.48	3,334.17

*Nominal million kwacha.
†Variable profit tax included after 2008.
‡Includes lump sum settlements for disputed taxes arising from imposition of new royalty, windfall tax, and variable profit tax.
Source: Zambia Revenue Authority.

Table 5.7 Importance of mining in gross domestic product (GDP) and in total government revenue

Year	1995	1996	1997	1998	1999	2000	2001	2002	2003	2004	2005
Nominal GDP*	3,005.10	3,950.20	5,140.20	6,027.90	7,447.70	10,121.30	13,193.70	16,324.40	20,551.10	25,993.10	32,041.50
Mining GDP*	432.90	476.80	510.90	378.30	281.30	416.10	518.90	575.10	564.80	809.60	1,030.90
Ratio of mining value added to GDP	14.41%	12.07%	9.94%	6.28%	3.76%	4.11%	3.93%	3.52%	2.75%	3.11%	3.22%
Ratio of total revenue from mining to mining GDP	8.55%	3.57%	3.72%	4.49%	4.62%	1.44%	1.73%	0.70%	1.59%	0.74%	4.17%

Year	2006	2007	2008	2009	2010	2011
Nominal GDP*	38,560.80	46,194.80	54,839.44	64,615.58	77,666.59	93,963.82‡
Mining GDP*	1,612.50	2,037.20	1,998.94	1,682.14	2,837.77	3,825.36
Ratio of mining value added to GDP	4.18%	4.41%	3.65%	2.60%	3.65%	4.07%
Ratio of total revenue from mining to mining GDP	13.58%	32.94%	50.33%	38.70%	58.37%	87.16%

*Nominal million kwacha.
†Gross domestic product is believed to be underestimated in Zambia and in other mining countries because of valuation methodologies employed for mineral exports and production more generally.
‡Preliminary.
Source: Zambia Revenue Authority (see notes to Table 5.6).

Table 5.8 Shares by type of payment to total mineral revenue

Year	1995	1996	1997	1998	1999	2000	2001	2002	2003	2004	2005
Company tax	21.62%	0.00%	0.00%	0.00%	0.00%	33.33%	22.22%	25.00%	0.00%	0.00%	2.33%
Withholding tax/dividends	0.00%	0.00%	0.00%	0.00%	0.00%	0.00%	0.00%	0.00%	11.11%	33.33%	6.98%
Mineral royalty	78.38%	100.00%	100.00%	100.00%	100.00%	66.67%	77.78%	75.00%	88.89%	66.67%	90.70%
Export duty	0.00%	0.00%	0.00%	0.00%	0.00%	0.00%	0.00%	0.00%	0.00%	0.00%	0.00%
Windfall tax	0.00%	0.00%	0.00%	0.00%	0.00%	0.00%	0.00%	0.00%	0.00%	0.00%	0.00%
Total mining revenue	100.00%	100.00%	100.00%	100.00%	100.00%	100.00%	100.00%	100.00%	100.00%	100.00%	100.00%

Year	2006	2007	2008	2009	2010	2011
Company tax	73.06%	89.87%	46.12%	61.60%	75.13%	74.29%
Withholding tax/dividends	0.00%	0.00%	0.00%	0.00%	0.00%	0.00%
Mineral royalty	26.94%	10.13%	23.66%	36.10%	24.87%	25.71%
Export duty	0.00%	0.00%	17.69%	2.30%	0.00%	0.00%
Windfall tax	0.00%	0.00%	12.52%	0.00%	0.00%	0.00%
Total mining revenue	100.00%	100.00%	100.00%	100.00%	100.00	100.00%

Table 5.9 Mineral revenue share by type of charge

Percentage of mining tax to total collections by type of tax					
Year	2005	2006	2007	2008	2009
Company tax	0.22%	23.02%	49.30%	34.29%	29.14%
Withholding tax/dividends	1.25%	0.00%	0.00%	0.00%	0.00%
Mineral royalty	100.00%	100.00%	100.00%	100.00%	100.00%
Export duty	0.00%	0.00%	0.00%	93.68%	88.24%
Windfall tax	100.00%	100.00%	100.00%	100.00%	100.00%
Mining revenue total	0.78%	3.46%	8.20%	10.54%	6.74%

are tantamount to an individualized tax system. Such complexity makes administration impossible, particularly when tax administrators may not have access to specific provisions of the individualized development agreements or other contractual provisions.[22]

Secondly, definitions and rules are not clear, there appears to be significant discretion about how tax provisions are applied, and public information about how the rules should be applied is scarce. This situation raises the potential for honest taxpayers to exploit the legal ambiguity for their benefit, for dishonest taxpayers to evade taxation, for corruption within the tax administration, and for inevitable, but what might otherwise be unnecessary, disputes. For example, the quantities used as a basis for the royalty vary by producer. Some pay royalty on extraction, others on concentrate, and still others on production of smelter output. This means that effective rates are not uniform and that adverse marginal incentives (such as for inefficient downstream processing) may exist.

5.4.2. Corrective actions

This diagnosis leads to a number of corrective actions.

Correctly measure price and quantity

The first is the need to correctly measure prices and quantities for royalty calculation. Determining the output price (P) and quantity (Q) are the most important variables in any mining fiscal regime. Under current law, the government should accrue more than $0.49 from a $1 increase in total revenue (either by an increase in the price holding quantity fixed, or an increase in quantity holding the price fixed), holding all else constant. That is, a \$1 increase in revenue should increase the royalty by \$0.06 (0.06*\$1), the profits tax by \$0.29 (0.3*\$0.97), and the dividends to ZCCM-IH by \$0.14 (0.2*(1–0.3)*\$0.97), assuming that ZCCM-IH holds a 20 per cent equity interest. The value of \$0.49 is a lower bound for a profitable firm because the variable profit charge may increase government revenue by a greater amount. Price and quantity (particularly quality-adjusted quantity) are only estimates in the mining industry in the best possible situations and so the government has every reason to seek improvements in the measures of both.

In addition to potentially increasing government revenue, improving the measurement of price and quantity has several benefits. Firstly, audits could be more accurate because auditors would be able to measure input/output ratios and other audit indicators. Secondly, companies could increase efficiency by identifying excessive production losses at each step in the chain of domestic value added. Thirdly, determining export values and GDP would be easier and more accurate. Finally, revenue forecasting and receipts estimation could be improved, in addition to providing better information for overall macro-economic management.

It appears that Zambia is not capturing these benefits because of the ambiguity in the definitions used to measure prices and quantities. On prices, until the government's capacity to compute 'arms-length' prices is developed, it makes sense to use deemed prices such as the London Metal Exchange (LME) price for the computation of the royalty. The LME price is known, cannot be manipulated by any party, and is publicly available at little cost. The price should be computed by the government and supplied to both the producers and the general public so that everyone has knowledge of the price to be employed for the prior month.

Similar issues surround the measurement of quantity for royalty purposes. Currently, depending on the firm, the royalty in Zambia may be applied to concentrate, either at the time of export or sale to domestic smelters, smelter output (cathodes), or production. This means that the effective royalty rate, and, perhaps, the income tax rate, may vary across firms. To illustrate, assume that the LME price is based on 100 per cent pure copper (for simplification purposes) and that the LME price is \$8,000 per ton. A royalty of 3 per cent imposed on the transfer in London would accrue \$240 to the government. Pure copper is not exported from Zambia, however, and even if pure copper were exported, the true economic border price would be less than \$8,000 because of transportation costs.[23] For instance, if concentrate in Zambia is 50 per cent copper, then simply using the LME price would imply that the deemed value of copper concentrate would be \$4,000 per ton of concentrate when the LME price is \$8,000. Of course, this value is too high relative to any true economic value. Smelting, storage, transportation, insurance, and waiting are all costly activities. Thus, the effective royalty rate will be more than 3 per cent when the LME price is used as the benchmark price and no other adjustments are made. Suppose that smelting and transport costs are $5,750 per unit of concentrate and that two tons of concentrate are required to produce one ton of copper cathode. The value per ton of copper concentrate would be $2,250 in this case. The value of $2,250 may correspond to a deemed net smelter return[24] for concentrate for our purposes, and thus the effective royalty will be 5.33 per cent.[25]

Two points follow. Firstly, international comparisons of royalties are of little or no value without knowing the base to which the rates are applied.[26] For instance, the royalty might be applied to ore and not concentrate. Secondly, there may be variation in effective rates across mines in Zambia depending on the stage at which the royalty is imposed. To the extent possible, such incentives should not be present because inefficient domestic processing may result. To minimize administrative difficulties, and to avoid the problems of imposing a royalty on imported ore, the Zambian Government should impose the royalty as far upstream as possible and use the LME price (however defined) as the measure of value. The charge should be imposed on 'production' and not 'sales' for royalty purposes. At a minimum, the government should attempt to impose the royalty on concentrate. The combination of an exogenous price for the royalty (the LME price) and the quantity recommendation means that administration for the royalty becomes similar to administration for the excise tax. That is, a mine (and/or concentrator) effectively becomes a bonded warehouse (like a cigarette warehouse) where the most important administrative consideration is control of quantity. As a consequence, the government collects a royalty regardless of production losses at the concentrator or smelter, thereby avoiding the need to measure own concentrate for smelters that are part of integrated operations with the result that the first 'measurable' point is not the first 'marketable' point. The government is selling a scarce resource and thus should not be penalized by (or benefit from) inefficient (or particularly efficient) processing. In effect, 100 per cent of the copper is used to produce smelter output even though less than 100 per cent of the copper is sold to another party in the form of smelter output. This means that variations in effective rates will be less variable if the measure of output is more uniform across producers.

There are some drawbacks from such a system. Notably, producers may be concerned about the arbitrary nature of using the LME price for a commodity whose value is highly, but not perfectly, correlated with the LME price. In effect, using the LME price, all else equal, shifts more of the risk for changes in downstream production and distribution costs from the government to the producer.

If Zambia is competitive in its pricing at 6 per cent of the LME price, then the gains from simplification and transparency outweigh these costs. It is important that Zambian authorities increase their efforts to maintain comparative information on prices, transport costs, processing costs, and other international statistics so that Zambian experts can review Zambia's competitive position.

Diligently monitor production

These measurement issues are the most important concerns, but diligent monitoring of production should be part of the basic regime regardless of how royalties are computed. As noted, the government owns the reserves and is selling those reserves to a producer. Thus, the government (and the general population) has the right and the need to know, as well as the responsibility of measuring and monitoring, the quantities transferred to the producers. This responsibility includes reasonable access to data and the right to take samples. If government agencies do not have the equipment or expertise to perform their own testing, then the government should contract with independent agencies until such time as the infrastructure necessary to supply independent valuations exists.[27]

Clarify rules and definitions

Definitions and operational valuation rules affect the profits tax, as well as the dividends and other payments to minority shareholders. Clarification of the tax rules and regulations should be improved, and it might be possible to make such changes without amending the statute. Some specific issues and recommendations are discussed in the following. The first is the importance of monitoring both domestic intra- and inter-mine transactions, as well as international transactions to limit the prevalence of transfer pricing (deliberately mis-invoicing the true value of transactions so as to shift profits to corporate units paying the lowest tax rates or to those where accumulated losses can be used to extinguish tax liabilities). Some mines export concentrates, others sell concentrate to domestic smelters on an arm's-length basis, and others sell smelter output. In addition, some vertically-integrated operations process concentrate on a tolling basis, at least with respect to concentrate imported from the Democratic Republic of the Congo.[28] The industry structure indicates that transfer prices on domestic transactions for ring-fenced activities will have to be monitored, as well as transfer pricing for international transactions.

Fix (or eliminate) the variable profits tax

The final corrective action is to fix the variable profits scheme, which appears to be based on the South African variable royalty tax. Under this scheme, the ratio of taxable profit to sales (however defined) is computed. If this ratio is greater than some value (0.08), then an additional charge is applied to some measure of profits. This charge makes little economic sense even in a pure form, and is only marginally related to standard notions of excess profit, except, perhaps, as some adjusted measure of the return to invested capital net of tax depreciation. To understand the concern, note that the ratio can be expressed as unity less the ratio of average cost (AC) to price (P) for any given level of production and sales (Q), or:

$$\frac{P*Q - AC*Q}{P*Q} > 0.8 \text{ or } 1 - \frac{AC}{P} > 0.08$$

This ratio is an average of profit to sales. It is an indicator generally used in finance as a crude measure of some average margin. It is neither an indicator of profitability nor of comparative profitability across firms. Accordingly, it should be not be used as an investment criterion. As a practical matter, the trigger value of 0.08 (or any value) is some measure of the normalized profit margin (normalized using the price). That is, the variable profit charge will become effective if:

$$0.92P - AC > 0$$

Another way to say this is the trigger value will be equal to 0.08 if price is equal to 1.087 of the average cost. One might infer that the value of 0.08 is some proxy for presumed real (net of inflation) return to capital, but this is not the case because it is easy to show that if the necessary return to capital were included, then 0.08 would be equal to the ratio of the total return to capital divided by sales, or:

$$0.08 = \frac{P*Q - AC*Q}{P*Q} = \frac{r*K}{P*Q}$$

where r is defined as return to capital (after depreciation) and K is the value of the capital stock.

That is, the trigger rate of 0.08 is equal to the required return on capital, r, times the ratio of the value of the capital stock to sales. The latter ratio is unknown and is certainly not constant across investments, particularly on a measured annual basis. Thus, without knowing the value of the capital stock, any inference about the trigger value being some required return on an accrual basis is questionable at best.

The basic problem with the methodology is that it is an average, but excess profit, if it is to be defined at all, is a total value, not an average. Thus, it is possible for one mine to have a large net present value, a large capital cost, and a large margin on some measure of profits to sales, while another mine has a high ratio (greater than 0.08 in this case) with negative returns to true equity (or may even be technically bankrupt).

These issues can be illustrated via a numerical example. Suppose Firm A has a ratio of taxable profit to sales of 0.1, while Firm B's ratio is 0.06. Firm A will pay the variable charge, while Firm B will be exempt. Firm B's profits, however, could be 1,000, while Firm A's profits could be 100 – hardly an indicator that Firm A should be paying additional charges relative to Firm B.

A simpler way to achieve a proxy for the level of incremental profits is to make the additional charge a function of the price.[29] For instance, a variable royalty would have a similar result if the trigger price were equal to 1.087 of some publicly-available price. That is, if the LME price were less than 1.087 of a base price, then the variable charge would not be active. In effect, the presumed margin over average cost would be the same as the system described in the previous section. There is no strong case for using a .087 margin; rather, the trigger should be computed annually and it might be based on one standard deviation above the mean of the historical LME price adjusted for inflation. This means that the charge will become effective only about 16 per cent of the time when prices are unusually high.

A variable rate royalty of this kind has been introduced in the Canadian province of Alberta (a two-part charge on oil) and recently in Chile (as a temporary measure), among other places. This charge has a number of advantages. Firstly, in addition to being transparent, the industry is familiar with the charge. Such charges are known as 'price participation agreements' and are common in the industry. For instance, a smelter commonly receives a proportion of the price above some base price as part of contractual process regimes. ZCCM-IH has some price participation agreements with firms in which it holds equity. In effect, the variable charge is a type of risk-sharing system in which the beneficiary shares the upside gain, presumably in exchange for a lower base price. Given the common use of these agreements, industry representatives can hardly complain about a government selling reserves and receiving this type of compensation.

Moreover, the system might approximate a flat-rate income tax. Conrad (2008) has shown that a variable royalty might be used to approximate a flat-rate income charge and provides some examples. Thus, a variable rate charge, if the rates are relatively reasonable, is not a 'progressive charge' when measured relative to the appropriate base (economic income).[30]

There are costs, including the fact that the government needs to balance the benefits of a flat-rate royalty relative to those from a variable royalty. In particular, the base royalty rate might be set a bit lower if a variable component is added. For instance, the base rate might be 4 per cent if there is no variable component; with a variable scheme, the base rate might be 3 per cent if the price is less than some trigger price and 6 per cent on the 'increment' above the trigger price. Note the variable component is on the marginal increment and not on the entire value if the observed price is above the trigger. Thus, the government might have to trade off some increased variability in revenue for higher expected revenue if a variable royalty is considered.

Modify (or do not renew) stabilization clauses

Stabilization clauses are part of the existing mineral agreements in Zambia. It might be in Zambia's best interest to let the existing stabilization clauses expire or to modify stabilization regimes in the future, at least for new investments. Most companies have had at least ten years to recover their capital plus a reasonable rate of return from their investments. These privatized projects were operated inefficiently in the past, but the mineralization was known, there was access to markets, and there were some assets.[31] Thus, risks were reasonable and ten years is an adequate time to capture a basic return on capital given these circumstances and relatively high mineral prices. Existing investors should, accordingly, be subject to any modifications to the current fiscal rule on existing and incremental investments or at a minimum not benefit from more restrictive stabilization regimes.

Stabilization provisions for future investments may be another matter. Stabilization provisions have been used to protect mining investors from capture. That is, a mining company makes significant investments in exploration and development that *ex post* are not movable. Thus, a country might induce a company to invest with attractive terms, but then increase effective rates arbitrarily once the investment is made. The investor will not leave as long as short-run variable costs are covered, but any competitive return on the entire investment may be lost. This concern is valid and some stabilization might be employed as long as Zambia is in a transition.

That said, stabilization should be neither one-sided nor unbounded. With regard to the former, any stabilization provision should provide stabilization for both parties. One-sided stabilization is a situation in which the investor is protected from tax increases, however defined, but may opt to switch regimes if taxes are lowered. Such a practice should be abandoned. That is, investors should not be allowed to take advantage of tax decreases, however defined, at their discretion.[32]

With respect to the latter issue, there may be at least three methods to limit stabilization.[33] Firstly, the stabilization provision should be limited in time. The government might consider providing a stabilization period sufficient for the investor to reasonably expect to recover their capital investment plus some return before being exposed to unforeseen changes in the fiscal regime. Secondly, the government might provide stabilization from de facto discriminatory changes in the fiscal regime. Some claim that a stable fiscal regime is necessary in order to attract investment. The USA and most developed countries would not satisfy this criterion because, at least in the USA, significant changes in tax law are made during almost every legislative session.[34] What taxpayers need, and should expect, is to be treated in a non-discriminatory fashion. With regard to mining stabilization, stabilization might first be limited to the royalty and excess profits regime because these charges are not generally applicable. Stabilization of the overall profits tax, the VAT, or other taxes, such as excise taxes, might be resisted, however, unless it can be demonstrated that the changes as applied are discriminatory. Finally, stabilization should not be free. Zambia might adopt the Chilean model and offer stabilization in exchange for higher rates (for instance, increased royalty rates).

Address minority ownership

ZCCM-IH holds a minority interest in the privatized mines, has taken an equity interest in other mines, and has price participation agreements with some corporations in which it has equity participation. Results reported from ZCCM-IH are less than what one might anticipate given the significant time lag since privatization, the periods of high copper prices, and efforts to rationalize the mining industry's operations. In particular, the government, as 87.5 per cent owner of the holding company, has received few, if any, dividends from ZCCM-IH.

There are a number of reasons why this might have occurred. ZCCM-IH has been obligated to assume significant debts from the predecessor national company. These debts include accrued pension benefits and other severance costs for employees laid off as a result of the privatization. There also appear to be outstanding lawsuits against the predecessor company that have not been resolved and a significant environmental legacy project.

There might be other reasons for the weak financial performance, including the nature of the contractual relationships between the holding company and the majority investors. None of these contractual relationships are publicly available.

The government of Zambia holds 87.5 per cent of ZCCM-IH and should rapidly renew the process of holding the company accountable for its significant investments. In effect, expenditures by ZCCM-IH are a type of off-budget financing that would benefit from full disclosure and public discussion. In addition, ZCCM-IH is a state enterprise with the immediate implication that it is accountable not to the government but to the people of Zambia, who should have information sufficient to make informed decisions about the company's performance. Thus, the government should require ZCCM-IH to publish all contracts and agreements between ZCCM-IH and the companies in which it holds equity, including the exact nature of any price participation agreements, any carried interests, and other relevant information about the nature of the relationships. The government and the public more generally have a responsibility and the right to monitor how their assets are being used. In addition, there is little foundation for confidentiality of financial agreements between ZCCM-IH and the companies in which it invests because of the public nature of the ownership. Finally, the company should provide a public report of the status of legacy expenses, the rules under which they are being amortized, and any underlying liability to the government of Zambia more generally.

This will lead to a more active process of bringing ZCCM-IH, including the flows between the government and ZCCM-IH, into the normal budget process and reporting the net position of the company as part of the budgetary accounts. The flows to and from ZCCM-IH can then be evaluated within the overall budget guidelines established by budgetary legislation.

ZCCM-IH may also play an important role in protecting its interests and those of the government against the majority shareholders. The majority shareholders may exert significant influence over the financial practices of the operating company, but management of the operating companies should seek to maximize shareholder value, regardless of who owns the shares. Such an objective may be jeopardized when there is a majority shareholder that seeks to maximize its own returns and that can influence the operating and financial decisions of the operating company. Some of these decisions may adversely affect the returns to minority shareholders. The problem is similar in substance to manipulation of prices to reduce profits tax and similar rules should be applied in the financial accounts to protect the minority shareholder. For instance, the majority shareholder may influence the transfer price for copper between the operating company and a related company. A low price might effectively transfer profits at the expense of the minority shareholder. A second example is a situation in which the majority shareholder makes loans to the operating company, and then the operating company uses the interest on the loans to reduce its profits and dividends. Given the numerous transactions between the majority shareholder and the operating company, it is important for ZCCM-IH and the government of Zambia more generally to exercise due diligence with respect to all major transactions between the related parties. Thus, the government should use the protections provided by corporate law to minority shareholders, both locally and internationally, to ensure that the majority shareholder's return is proportional to its true equity interest. This due diligence can be achieved only by requiring the operating company to report all, or at least all significant, transactions between the majority shareholder and the operating company, complete with a description of the basis for the transactions, the methodologies employed, and the financial values involved.

In summary, it is important for ZCCM-IH and the government to ensure that their financial interests are protected by publishing information and acting in a consciously self-interested professional manner to monitor the transactions between the related parties.

5.5. Summary

Zambia's fiscal regime for mining has begun to improve and it is important to increase the momentum for reform. I believe the recommendations presented here are consistent with the new government's commitment to transparency and increased revenue yield. Such reforms should provide (i) a stable policy environment that allows the country to capture a competitive return for its natural assets, and (ii) a more neutral fiscal regime that is both transparent and consistent with sound economic principles.

Notes

1. The increase in the royalty rate and change in hedging were part of the 2012 budget. Statements by representatives of the new government about the desire to increase revenue from mining can be found in numerous press reports, including Els (2011), Topf (2011), Mfula (2011), and Schneider (2011).
2. No evolution of the fiscal regime is supplied. Excellent reviews are found in Adam (1995), and Adam and Simpasa (2009), among other sources.
3. Deloitte (2013) *Doing Business in Zambia: A Unique Flavour*, pp. 52-4. Available at: https://www.deloitte.com/assets/Dcom-India/Local%20Assets/Documents/Africa/Doing_Business_in_Zambia.pdf (last accessed 8 April 2014).
4. Deloitte (2012) *Zambia Highlights 2012*. Available at: http://www2.deloitte.com/content/dam/Deloitte/global/Documents/Tax/dttl-tax-zambiahighlights-2012.pdf (last accessed 8 April 2004).
5. Deloitte (2013) pp. 52-4.
6. Deloitte (2013) p. 56.
7. Deloitte (2013) p. 54.
8. Zambia Revenue Authority. Available at: https://www.zra.org.zm/commonHome Page.htm?viewName=CustomsTaxes (last accessed 8 April 2014).
9. Ministry of Mines and Minerals Development. Available at: http://zambiamining.com/tax-regime-incentives/ (last accessed 8 April 2014).
10. Deloitte (2013) p. 57.
11. The information supplied is only a summary. Detailed tables can be supplied by the author or can be found in Conrad (2010).
12. A royalty is a payment to the owner of the reserves (usually some level of government) that is proportional to the purchase price of ore at the time of extraction.

13. ZCCM-IH is the state-owned residual holding company resulting from the privatization of ZCCM at the end of the 1990s. ZCCM-IH maintains the state's equity participation in individual mines, and is obliged to extinguish a range of residual liabilities of the former ZCCM, principally pension and environmental obligations.

14. Mineral rights are vested in the Canadian provinces and are shared between the states and federal government in Australia.

15. For the present purposes, the effective rate is defined as the ratio of the charge to the economic definition of the base. For instance, the effective rate for an *ad valorem* royalty will be the amount paid per unit/economic value of unit used to compute the charge. The denominator's value may or may not be related to the value used in practice. The Zambian royalty is an example. The royalty is the LME price of copper multiplied by the metallic content of the commodity (ore, concentrate, ingot) at the point where the charge is imposed. By definition, the LME price will not be equal to the value of the quantitative measured employed unless by accident.

16. It is common for transactions between both related and unrelated parties in metal mining to have price participation clauses as part of their contracts. For instance, the contract between a mine concentrator and a smelter may contain provisions in which the smelter obtains a proportion of the excess above the base price.

17. The Russian export tax in its current form was imposed after the financial crisis in 2008 to sop up gains to domestic producers from the significant devaluation of the ruble.

18. In addition, fiscal revenue losses might be direct or indirect. A direct revenue loss would result if a government explicitly reduced a payment in return for domestic sourcing. The loss might be indirect if the government simply required domestic sourcing; as costs to the firm are higher than without the rule, profits taxes paid by the mine would be reduced by more than the increase in taxes paid by the supplier.

19. The value of the reserve base might change even if the deposit is not developed. For instance, governments should expect a competitive return from holding reserves because, at a minimum, reserves are assets from an economic perspective. Thus, a government holding assets in the ground is forgoing selling those assets, or converting them into cash or other tangible (intangible) assets that accrue cash income. Thus, a government needs to be aware of this opportunity cost of developing deposits and should hold reserves as long as the returns are at least as great as those forgone costs.

20. It is sometimes claimed that the ability to influence corporate decisions via board membership afforded by share ownership is a benefit for government. Influence is limited, however, when the government is a minority shareholder. It should also be noted that the government is a sovereign state and has the power to regulate and influence corporate decisions directly by government action. This power, if properly and appropriately applied, may be more important relative to the benefits of holding minority positions.

21. Revenue figures are on a receipts basis and thus represent neither charges actually payable nor the correct timing of accruals. For instance, payments in 2008 might represent charges (including interest and penalties) arising from any prior year. Thus, it is not possible to discuss the effect of particular policy changes given these differences.

22. The government claimed that the negotiated agreements of November 2010 would be uniformly applied, but it is not possible to evaluate this claim unless documents are made public and administrative procedures are made uniform.

23. A person wishing to purchase copper cathodes would have to pay the LME price plus transport from London to Zambia for copper cathodes from non-Zambian sources. Domestic sellers of copper cathodes would receive only the LME price less transport on exports, leaving the transport cost differential to be arbitraged between buyers and sellers. Competition among suppliers, to the extent that competition exists, would result in a domestic price (measured in foreign currency) equal to the LME price less transport. This basic dynamic will be used to determine the efficient price for current purposes.

24. Again, a competitive measure of the net smelter return will not, in general, be equal to the arm's-length price for two unrelated parties unless certain assumptions are made; assumptions that are not applicable in practice.

25. Two factors may be responsible for any difference in the competitive price of smelter output relative to concentrate. Firstly, competitive processing costs are strictly positive. Secondly, production losses occur. That is, more than two tons of 50 per cent concentrate are required to produce one ton of copper in smelter output because recovery is less than 100 per cent.

26. For instance, a royalty of 5 per cent is imposed on the net smelter return in Mongolia. Whether the 6 per cent royalty in Zambia is lower or higher relative to the Mongolian royalty depends on whether the net smelter returns in Mongolia are lower or higher (in an economic sense) relative to the effective base in Zambia, all else equal.

27. At a minimum, there needs to be better coordination between the Central Bank, tax departments, Ministry of Finance, and Ministry of Mines on obtaining samples and reconciling differences in measurement.

28. Hedging is common for large, integrated mining companies. Valuation issues are raised because of the vertical integration present in some firms, the fact that consolidated reporting for corporate profits tax purposes is not allowed in Zambia, and the presence of related party transactions.

29. There is a serious question about whether any type of excess profits scheme is needed if the recommendations made in this chapter are enacted in addition to other reforms. The combined fiscal return to the government, including increased profits from ZCCM-IH, should increase significantly if the proposals are enacted. Risk-sharing is significant given the structure of the profits tax and equity participation. Thus, Zambia's risk-adjusted return from owning reserves may be significant, at least in terms of a competitive return, and effective tax rates may be sufficient to reduce, or to eliminate, the need for any excess profits tax.

30. That is, a variable royalty might approximate a flat-rate income tax. Progressivity should be defined with respect to economic profit on a flow basis (or net present value on a stock basis) and, if progressive, the average effective rate should increase with the measured base.

31. In addition, it appears that the investors who participated in the privatization were not burdened with at least some of the liabilities, such as accrued pensions, from the predecessor ZCCM.

32. To the extent that one-sided stabilization is retained, the option should be irrevocable. A tax decrease is clear when rates fall holding the base constant, but what constitutes a tax decrease may not be clear in other situations. For instance, if the government changes the foreign exchange provisions, then whether a particular taxpayer will benefit with lower taxes depends on the facts and circumstances. Taxes could be lower in some years and higher in others. Taxpayers should not be allowed to switch from one regime to another. That is, if the taxpayer switches to the new regime, then that election should be irrevocable for the term of the stabilization agreement. See Daniel and Sunley (2010) for alternative methods to modify stabilization provisions.
33. Stabilization should be limited to the fiscal regime to the extent applied. That is, the investor should be subject to current labour laws, environmental laws, and other statutes as modified. In addition, stabilization should be limited to parties to the agreement and should not be extended to service providers or to any related party.
34. It may not be variability of the tax system that is important, but the environment in which changes take place. Taxpayers may adapt to frequent tax changes if the process is transparent, participatory, and non-discriminatory.

References

Adam, C. (1995). Fiscal adjustment, financial liberalization and the dynamics of inflation: Some evidence from Zambia. *World Development* 23: 735–700.

Adam, C., Simpasa, A.M. (2009). Harnessing resource revenues for prosperity in Zambia. *OxCarre Research Paper* 36

Conrad, R.F. (2008). Using a variable royalty to approximate a profits tax in mining (or any other sector). Unpublished mimeo.

Conrad, R.F. (2010). *Fiscal Regime for Mining in Zambia: A Survey and Analytical Framework.* Unpublished. London: International Growth Centre.

Daniel, P., Sunley, E. (2010). Contractual assurances of fiscal stability. In: Daniel, P., Keen, M., McPherson, C. (eds) *The Taxation of Petroleum and Minerals: Principles, Problems and Practice.* Washington, DC: International Monetary Fund. 405–424.

Els, F. (2011). Zambia minister says miners must 'brace for tough decisions'. Available at: <http://www.mining.com/2011/10/17/zambia-minister-says-miners-must-brace-for-tough-decisions> (last accessed 14 March 2012).

Mfula, C. (2011). Zambia's new govt wants more of foreign miners' revenue. Available at: <http://www.ibtimes.com/articles/222155/20110929/zambia-mine-mining-sata-copper.htm> (last accessed 14 March 2012).

Schneider, J. (2011). Experts weekly: what next for Zambia? Available at: <http://thinkafricapress.com/zambia/experts-weekly-what-next-sata> (last accessed 14 March 2012).

Topf, A. (2011). Zambia suspends issuing mining licences, calling system 'inefficient' Available at: <http://www.mining.com/2011/10/21/zambia-suspends-issuing-mining-licences-calling-system-inefficient> (last accessed 14 March 2012).

6

Monetary Policy and the Exchange Rate in Zambia

Isaac Muhanga, Ivan Zyuulu, and Christopher S. Adam

6.1 Introduction

Textbook economics teaches that in the long run money is neutral to growth: what matters, and what must be of central importance in thinking about long-run growth and development, is the evolution of relative prices and the fiscal and institutional structures that combine to promote efficient growth-promoting resource allocations. However, over the short- to medium-run – the horizon over which policy decisions are actually made – monetary policy matters enormously. It matters directly because money, or more precisely inflation and inflation volatility, has powerful effects on saving and investment behaviour, on the choice of economic activity and on labour allocation over the short to medium-term, which in turn influence growth. And it matters indirectly because inflation also has impacts on fiscal behaviour and on financial development and capital flows. Maintaining a coherent and credible monetary regime, which sustains low and predictable inflation – which in turn demands a broader degree of macro-economic coherence – is thus central to effective broader economic management.

For much of first three decades of independence, Zambia – influenced to some degree by the prevailing orthodoxy – adopted an economic policy regime that effectively asked monetary and exchange rate policy to do 'too much', at least viewed from a contemporary perspective. The idea of 'too much' here stems from the so-called 'impossible trinity' of monetary policy which states that in the medium term policymakers cannot use its monetary instruments to both target the exchange rate (to promote competition or, conversely, to keep imports cheap) and manipulate aggregate demand (through the interest rate and the money supply) unless tight controls on capital flows can be enforced. This is exactly what happened in Zambia from the mid-1970s and particularly during the 1980s, but only in a very extreme and unsustainable manner. The political economy of economic policy at the time reflected the alignment of the interests of a highly centralized state and a powerful, urbanized industrial labour force that had grown up around the mining sector, so that real wages were kept 'too high' and the cost of capital and imported consumer goods 'too low', relative to their long-run equilibrium. Monetary policy was central to sustaining this disequilibrium: the official exchange rate was hugely over-valued and (official) interest rates kept extremely low. The resulting anti-export bias, excess aggregate demand and extreme credit-rationing placed enormous pressure on the current account, only part of which was alleviated by donor inflows and foreign capital (see for example, Bates and Collier, 1993).

The only way the imbalance could be reconciled was through increasingly distorting controls on the balance of payments, initially through capital account controls but increasingly on current account flows as well. But as theory and evidence from elsewhere tells us, when the underlying macro-economic disequilibrium is severe, capital controls can only be effective for a short period. Thus, foreign exchange rationing fuelled widespread smuggling and mis-invoicing of trade, out of which emerged a deep and active parallel exchange rate market.

A central element in the dismantling of this regime was the rapid and profound liberalization of both money and exchange rate markets and an explicit commitment to a floating exchange rate regime combined with a money supply anchor for prices. This commitment to let the exchange rate float was further reinforced by the new MMD government's decision in January 1994 to fully liberalize capital account transactions, making it the first country in Africa to do so (albeit with consequences for the capital account that would come back to haunt the mining industry in the 2000s, as discussed in Chapter 9 by Adam et al.).

It has been argued that, along with wholesale privatization and the elimination of domestic price controls, this radical policy shift was an essential element in attempts by the Third Republic to signal a decisive break with previous approaches to macro-economic management.[1] It may have been a necessary move, given the political and economic legacy of the time, but what is of interest now is to ask whether this particular monetary policy regime remains best-suited for the Zambia of the 21st century, particularly given the structural characteristics and potential shocks that it is likely to face over the coming decades.

Such an assessment covers a wide range of issues – more than can be covered in a single chapter. Some are technical and reflect the structure of the economy and its exposure to external factors, while others are more closely concerned with capacity and the coordination of monetary and fiscal policies. The analytic section of this chapter, presented in Sections 6.4 to 6.6, is an assessment of how, over the period since liberalization in 1993, monetary policy has served to shape the evolution of output, prices and the exchange rate in the face of external shocks. Based on this, we offer some thoughts about the future direction of monetary policy in Zambia. Before launching into the quantitative analysis, however, we set the scene by discussing some guiding principles and the challenges shaping the design of monetary policy in Zambia.

6.2 Some guiding principles

A monetary regime defines the institutional framework to deliver monetary policy and the constraints under which monetary policymakers operate. Most contemporary governments would subscribe to the view that the role of monetary policy can be reduced to three core functions: firstly, to deliver low and stable inflation; secondly, conditional on this, to moderate fluctuations in the path of domestic output by judicious tightening or loosening of the stance of monetary policy as circumstances dictate; and thirdly, more indirectly, to support the smooth functioning of the payments system and the financial system more generally, so as to promote the efficient market-based allocation of credit and pricing of risk in support of efficient investment and growth.

How these objectives are best met, given country characteristics and the universal constraint of the impossible trinity, is a subject of extensive debate. Contemporary monetary theory sees the reconciliation of the first two objectives emerging from the 'constrained discretion' systems typified by the inflation targeting regimes commonly found in the OECD and among an increasing number of middle- and low-income countries. The essential feature of these regimes is a transparent, verifiable and credible commitment to a publicly-announced target for inflation, which, in turn, serves to anchor inflation expectations and to tie the authorities' hands in a way that minimizes their incentives to act in a time-inconsistent manner.[2] With expectations thereby anchored, space is created for the authorities to pursue output stabilization.[3]

This still leaves the question of how the central bank should deploy its policy instruments to hit its inflation target. Conventional theory presents the discussion in terms of the authorities setting a policy instrument – the cost of funds under a standing facility which is used to steer short-term market rates from which the spectrum of interest rates are established – raising it when expected future inflation appears to be exceeding the target and vice versa when expected inflation falls below target. In principle, the same function can be performed under a monetary targeting framework through the manipulation of balance sheet instruments to influence the path of the money supply consistent with the same path for the real interest rate. In either case, deployment of policy instruments needs to be accompanied by a communication strategy that makes public the evidence and analysis that informs rate-setting decisions and devote substantial resources to public information and direct engagement with key stakeholders. This comprehensive communication strategy applies both when inflation is on target and, a fortiori, when it is off target, in which case additional disclosure requirements may be placed on the central bank to explain deviations and specify remedial action to return inflation to target, for example through the 'Open Letter' mechanism used by the Bank of England.

The final function, that of financial sector development, is necessarily less direct – it depends on the idea that low and stable inflation combined with a credible monetary policy are essential ingredients in nurturing an environment in which savings are effectively mobilized and intermediated and where participants are increasingly able to trade risk. We say little about this function in this chapter; later chapters in the book focus specifically on issues of capital market development and regulation.

6.3 The challenges to conducting monetary policy

This description sets the bar high and, in practice, only a few emerging market and low-income countries can be counted as full-fledged IT regimes. In practice, the reality is more complex and many countries, including Zambia, operate what may be called a hybrid regime in which targets for inflation exist and where there is a public commitment to a flexible exchange rate, but where a wider set of shocks and constraints mean that the authorities' policy reaction function is less sharply drawn. Moreover, robust structures for communication and verification are only just being developed and core analytical capacity – in inflation forecasting and developing robust models of the transmission mechanism, for example – only just being built.

For Zambia, at least four general challenges contribute to this complexity. Firstly, the conduct of monetary policy in a small open commodity-dependent economy must grapple with the challenge of responding to supply shocks emanating from the volatility in copper prices, fuel and electricity prices and agriculture. The problem here is that when shock emerges from the demand-side – for example, unanticipated public expenditure – the impact of the shock on output (or more strictly on the deviation of output from its trend) on the one hand and inflation on the other is positively correlated since excess demand increases both the output gap and inflation. For supply shocks, however, the direction of correlation tends to be negative – an adverse shock to agricultural output reduces the output gap but increases inflation. As Adam et al. (2011) argue, in industrialized countries shocks tend to come predominantly from the demand-side, whereas in developing and emerging-market countries, supply-side shocks tend to play a much larger role.

This simple distinction poses a major challenge for the conduct of monetary policy. The essential problem is as follows: with demand shocks moving output and inflation in the same direction, an interest rate rise or a tightening on monetary growth, designed to bring inflation back on track, will simultaneously serve to eliminate the excess output gap. This 'divine coincidence' – the fact that demand shocks dominate and that a policy reaction targeting inflation also targets output – goes a long way to explaining the attraction of IT in industrialized countries. With supply-side shocks output and inflation will move in opposite directions. One instrument is now no longer sufficient: acting to stabilize the inflationary consequences of a supply shock risks exacerbating the adverse output effects and vice versa. This brings to the fore the essential problem of monetary policy that, with a single instrument, policymakers must confront the trade-off between competing objectives (in this case inflation and output stabilization). This is, of course, a generic 'instruments and objectives' problem, but, as Frankel et al. (2007) amongst others show, when supply shocks dominate, the case for the strict inflation targeting is undermined by the tendency for the strategy to exacerbate output volatility.

It is worth noting that the conventional response in these circumstances is to distinguish between core components of inflation – those where domestic policy has leverage – and these non-core components of inflation and to bring to bear the apparatus of IT only on the core component of inflation, reacting to movements in non-core prices only to the extent that they have second-round feedback effects on core inflation. This approach makes sense in developed countries where non-core components account for a relatively small share of the overall CPI, so that focusing monetary policy on the stabilization of core inflation goes a long way towards stabilizing overall inflation without drawing the authorities into destabilizing responses to supply-side shocks. In developing countries, where non-core items account for a large share of the CPI, targeting core inflation would mean that the authorities would end up targeting only a small share of the overall consumption basket. Even if an IT regime was extremely successful in stabilizing core inflation, this may still co-exist with high volatility in headline inflation if the evolution of prices of non-core items is volatile: trying to control overall inflation in these environments would require the authorities to lean much more heavily on their policy levers, with the attendant risk of greater volatility in output and interest rates.

The second challenge is reconciling exchange rate objectives with the primacy of the inflation objective. Even though a new understanding of the limits of monetary policy has emerged since the early 1990s, the multiple objectives have not entirely disappeared, with concerns about the path and volatility of the exchange rate still playing a dominant role in Zambia. While contemporary thinking about monetary policy makes a clear and unam-biguous case for prioritizing the inflation target over the exchange rate, this does not imply that the exchange rate should be ignored – not least because it plays a central role in forecasting inflation – but rather that it should be made clear that the authorities are not beholden to any specific value of the currency. Practice may be more complex, however. Buffie et al. (2008), for example, suggest that, when fiscal policy reacts to variations in aid or commodity price flows, some more active degree of exchange rate interven-tion may be desirable, especially if the private sector's demand for money reacts strongly to changes in the expected degree of fiscal dominance. These arguments are particularly powerful in environments where domestic prices are sticky or where other forms of market imperfection (e.g. credit rationing) mean that the effects of exchange rate volatility on real resource allocation are highly geared. But navigating these considerations requires coherence both at the level of policy and in terms of communication.

6.3.1 *The exchange rate appreciation of 2005*

The sharp, short appreciation of the nominal and real exchange rate in 2005 and 2006 illustrates very clearly the Buffie et al. (2008) point. Since the rise in copper price in 2003, the exchange rate tended to appreciate. While the appreciating currency has helped the Bank of Zambia hit its inflation target – especially given the rise in world prices of oil and imported food at the time – the Bank's tight adherence to its monetary target drew it into a first-order monetary policy error in 2005, which, temporarily, severely exacerbated the exchange rate appreciation and imposed extremely heavy costs on the export and import competing sectors of the economy. This error was not directly attributable to the management of the boom in copper prices but arose from problems with managing debt relief. Nonetheless, it highlights a well-known problem associated with strict adherence to reserve money programmes in the face of the positive shocks to domestic money demand that can occur during periods of surging export earnings or capital inflows. The HIPC/MDRI initiative in 2005 had two self-reinforcing effects. The first was a direct fiscal benefit: debt relief reduced pressure on domestic deficit financing requirements, *ceteris paribus*, and reduced the supply of domestic money. However, at the same time successful completion of the debt relief exercise had a powerful effect on the private sector demand for the Kwacha. With expectations of credibly lower inflation and higher growth prompting there was a sharp portfolio shift towards the Zambian Kwacha by the domestic private sector. Concerned to hit the monetary targets they had agreed with the IMF, the authorities did not accommodate this powerful demand shift but rather sought to stick to the now 'too tight' monetary targets. The result was a sharp overshooting of the exchange rate which severely eroded the competitiveness of non-copper export and import competing sectors of the economy. The authorities' attempts to stick to their money targets drew them into bond sterilization which exacerbated the problem as foreign investors. Taking full advantage of the liberalized capital account, these investors entered the government debt market to take advantage of high domestic interest rates, thereby further appreciating the exchange rate.

The policy error in this episode stemmed directly from the vulnerability of a strict money anchored programme in the face of portfolio shifts. In such circumstances, the appropriate monetary policy response would have been to accommodate the shift in money demand, most readily through unsterilized foreign exchange rate intervention. Unsterilized intervention increases the money supply but this is exactly what is required to meet the increased demand for the Kwacha at the prevailing exchange rate.

The response to events of 2005 and 2006 therefore represented a major monetary policy error. However, what is more important is that, in sharp contrast to earlier decades, the error was short-lived and the authorities moved very quickly to re-establish a coherent – and apparently credible – monetary framework. Thus from mid-2006, the stance of monetary policy was relaxed and the excess appreciation of the exchange rate was eliminated – the real exchange rate returned to its (appreciating) trend by early 2007. It was from this period that the authorities began intervening more heavily in the foreign exchange market, building an increased reserve buffer but, at the same time, moderating the tendency for the real exchange rate to appreciate.

The key lesson here is probably not that the authorities pursue a pure float but rather that they establish a credible commitment that the inflation target will take precedence when there is a conflict between objectives. However, as O'Connell (2010) notes, the literature offers very little guidance on how multiple instruments, e.g. a policy interest rate and foreign exchange intervention, ought to be deployed when imperfect capital mobility allows the monetary authority some scope to reconcile domestic with external objectives. Little is known, for example, regarding the appropriate scale of intervention or the degree to which intervention should be sterilized.

The third challenge consists of a weak transmission channel of monetary policy. The effectiveness of monetary policy and the credibility of any regime will depend on how reliably, and how quickly, observable policy actions influence inflation and other real variables; in other words, on the nature of the transmission mechanism. The textbook macro-economic model derives from the research and experience of the OECD, in which the interest rate channels of transmission, in which short-run interest rate decisions are transmitted directly to long-term interest rates, which, in turn, influence the interest-sensitive components of aggregate demand and hence moderate expected and actual inflation. In the open economy setting, this effect is augmented by the exchange rate channel: higher interest rates appreciate the exchange rate, which reduces net exports and thus the output gap. In addition, exchange rate appreciation directly reduces the domestic cost of imports.

For less mature emerging markets and for pre-emerging markets, where the financial sector is often much less developed, these traditional channels may be less powerful and much less stable (Mishra and Montiel, 2012) so that the short- to medium-run link between money grow, or nominal depreciation and domestic inflation and output, is harder to identify.

In settings such as Zambia, where monetary policy still tends to be exercised through operations on the central bank's own balance sheet – domestic credit policy, bond operations, and foreign exchange sales – and where the banking sector has been dominated by oligopolistic commercial banks, interest rates tend to play a less important role.

Finally, the question of fiscal dominance continues to cast a long shadow over monetary policy. One of the most dramatic achievements of the economic reforms of the early 1990s was the resolute determination of the government to stand firm against excessive fiscal expenditure; the cash budget of the period 1992–96 was only the most public demonstration of this commitment (Adam and Bevan, 1999). It was this as much as anything else that allowed a coherent monetary policy to emerge. However, the dragon of fiscal indiscipline is, of course, never completely slain, so an important consideration becomes the capacity of alternative monetary regimes to offer an effective bulwark against recurring fiscal indiscipline.

6.4 Sources of volatility and the conduct of monetary policy

In this and the following sections we draw these ideas together to examine how these different shocks interact with the conduct of monetary policy. As noted previously, the specific conduct of monetary policy depends on the authorities' chosen exchange rate regime. Since independence, Zambia experimented with the full gamut of exchange rate regimes (N'gambi, 2006, Table 6.1), with the half-century falling neatly into two halves, the first a period of relatively fixed exchange rates – accompanied by a large and highly distortionary parallel market – and the second quarter-century, a period of a relatively clean float – one of the longest uninterrupted periods of regime stability in post-independence sub-Saharan Africa.

After adopting the flexible exchange rate regime in 1991, the nominal exchange rate adjusted rapidly before establishing relative stability after 2003, save for strong appreciation after reaching the Heavily Indebted Poor Country

(HIPC) initiative Completion Point in April 2005 and obtaining debt relief under the Multilateral Debt Relief Initiative in 2006. On the other hand, the bilateral real effective exchange rate exhibited an appreciating trend since 2000 (Figure 6.1).

Table 6.1 A half-century of exchange rate regimes in Zambia

1964 – 1982   Fixed Exchange Rate Regime
1983 – 1985   Crawling Peg (with parallel market exchange rate)
1985 – 1987   Floating Exchange Rate Regime (parallel market premium declines)
1987 – 1991   Fixed Exchange Rate Regime (re-emergence of parallel premium)
1991 –   Floating Exchange Rate Regime (with full exchange rate unification)

Figure 6.1a Zambian exchange rate developments

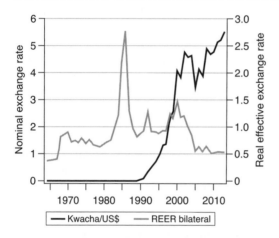

Figure 6.1b Domestic inflation

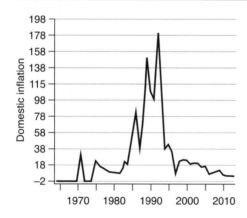

These can be clustered into three broad groups. The first are supply-side shocks emanating from the volatility in the international terms of trade. As Cashin et al. (2002) noted, Zambia can be characterized as a 'commodity currency', meaning that movements in the world price for copper overwhelmingly determine the terms of trade, at least in the medium term. However, at higher frequencies, volatility in aid and in input prices, such as oil, also move the terms of trade. The other principal source of supply-side volatility emanates from the effect of climatic variation on agricultural output (which is overwhelmingly rain-fed). On the demand side, the principal source of volatility emanates from the fiscal domain as spending shocks. Finally, with an open capital account, the economy is vulnerable to volatility from private capital flows, either reflecting changing global conditions (changes in risk perceptions, global interest rates, etc.) or as an endogenous response to domestic policy actions.

In the face of these challenges, the conduct of monetary policy can be described as eclectic, at least in the short-run, with the authorities responding differently to otherwise similar economic shocks at different times. This is understandable as monetary policymakers do not exist in a (political) vacuum; the weight placed on different objectives including objectives that are not even under the control of the monetary authorities. In the post-1990s, monetary policy particularly seems to have a fairly stronger linkage to exchange rate volatility concerns than conventionally expected, driven largely by the importance of such external shocks to the economics and politics of Zambia.

We wish to investigate how the policy environment has evolved and been shaped by the presence of unforeseen economic shocks. In this effort, we employ impulse response functions based on the structural vector autoregression (SVAR). Impulse response functions describe the dynamic response of current and future values of economic variables in a model to a hypothetical one-off economic shock to the model economy, holding other variable shocks unchanged. In this manner, the SVAR and impulse response functions help us diagnose and understand the short-run economic dynamics that monetary policy seeks to influence.

6.5 Methodology and model specification[4]

The dynamic evolution of the economy can be described by the following structure:

$$A_0 Y_t = B(L)Y_t + C\varepsilon_t \qquad (1)$$

where Y_t is an $n \times 1$ vector of endogenous variables, A_0 is $n \times n$ contemporaneous coefficient matrix, $B(L)$ is a p-th degree matrix polynomial in the lag operator L, C is $n \times n$ diagonal matrix and ε_t is an $n \times 1$ vector of white-noise orthonormal structural shocks. In other words, the shocks' properties are such that they exhibit a covariance-variance matrix of $E[\varepsilon_t \varepsilon_t'] = C\varepsilon\varepsilon'C' = \Omega$ with all off-diagonal elements equal to zero.

Equation (1) in its structural form cannot be estimated directly (due to the feedback inherent in the system[5]). We therefore re-parameterize it in its reduced form

$$Y_t = D(L)Y_t + u_t \tag{2}$$

where $D(L) = A_0^{-1}B(L)$, and $u_t = A_0^{-1}C\varepsilon_t$

The covariance matrix of the reduced form is given by

$$E(u_t u_t) = A_0^{-1}C\varepsilon\varepsilon'C'A_0^{-1} = \Sigma$$

The transformation of (1) into (2) shows that the error terms (u_t) are a linear combination of the orthogonal structural shocks (ε_t). Although the shocks are serially uncorrelated with zero mean and a constant variance, they are however correlated with each other such that, unlike the matrix Ω, the covariance-variance matrix Σ is non-diagonal.

Although (2) can be estimated, its structure presents a problem because it is not possible to recover the underlying structural shocks unless the equation is transformed back into a structural form that exhibits uncorrelated shocks. This transformation can be achieved by imposing some identification restrictions on the parameters. Specifically, noting that the reduced-form residuals are simply a linear combination of the structural form innovations, (i.e. $u_t = A_0^{-1}C\varepsilon_t$), we can preserve this structure by introducing some exclusion restrictions on the matrices A and C.

Taking note that $E(\varepsilon_t \varepsilon_t) = I$, this imposes $(n^2+n)/2$ restrictions on the $2n$ unknown parameters in A and C. We therefore need to introduce at least an additional $(3n^2-n)/2$ restrictions to identify the model.

There are a number of ways of identifying an SVAR. We use the Choleski form decomposition, which involves recursively ordering variables in such a way that structural shocks contemporaneously affect only succeeding variables. That is, variables pre-dating others are assumed to have contemporaneous effects on those coming after them, but not vice versa. As in Bernanke (1986), Blanchard and Watson (1986) and Sims (1992) among others, this will involve orthogonalizing the reduced form residuals by imposing restrictions on the contemporaneous matrix derived from economic theory rather than merely triangulating. Thereafter, we derive the impulse response functions to examine the dynamic responses of the variables to innovations within the SVAR.

6.6 Data issues and model identification

6.6.1 *Data issues*

Monthly data spanning from March 1993 to November 2013 is used in the estimation. The time-span is preferred as it largely represents the time when the economy has been under a liberalized regime with markets playing a more prominent role than before. All data was obtained from the Bank of Zambia and Central Statistics Office of Zambia. We express data in annual growth rates except for the US Fed rate (FFR), the Treasury bill rate (TBR) in levels. We test each one of the series for stationarity and having established non-stationarity in the series, we build the model on the basis of first differences rather than levels. The model is therefore a short-run model.

The variables chosen for the model are summarized in Table 6.2 below. The impact of external market conditions on Zambia is proxied by the international copper price (CP) and the US federal funds rate (FIR), while the rest of the variables represent the domestic economy. Inclusion of foreign variables for the Zambian economy is important for us to appropriately capture the underlying responses of domestic variables in the midst of these external market conditions. The most obvious intuition for utilizing CP and FIR as proxy for foreign market conditions is that the domestic economy as a whole and the monetary authorities must confront volatility from external shocks.

6.6.2 *Model identification*

To identify the SVAR, we use short-run restrictions of the model parameters. We build the external block on the following assumptions. The US Federal funds rate is not conditioned by any of the variables included in the model. In other words, the Zambian economic policy environment does not influence US monetary policy. Likewise, we further assume that copper prices do not depend on domestic economic developments. However, copper prices do

Table 6.2 Variables used in the SVAR system

Abbreviation	Definition of variable
FIR	US Federal funds rate
CP	Annual growth rate of copper price
Y	Annual growth rate of domestic mineral production
CPI	Annual growth rate of domestic consumer price index
M	Annual growth rate of domestic monetary aggregate (broad money)
TBR	Average Treasury Bill rate
EX	Log of ZMK/US$ exchange rate

121

respond to monetary policy changes in the world's major economies. Indeed, as a number of studies have found, commodity prices generally do respond strongly to changes in monetary policy actions of the major industrial economies (Cody and Mills, 1991; Awokuse and Yang, 2002; Lunieski, 2009). We therefore treat these variables as exogenous. Our analysis of the dynamics of domestic variables is conditioned on these exogenous external factors.

The five equations in the domestic block are built on the following assumptions. The first equation, the output equation, assumes no contemporaneous reaction of output to domestic variables in the model. Money, consumer prices and the exchange rate are assumed to affect output with some considerable lag. To that extent, we treat output, Y, as a non-policy variable.

The second equation describing the evolution of the money stock, assumes that the quantity of money supply held by agents reacts to fortunes implied by positive shocks to output. The effects of inflation, Treasury bill interest rate and exchange rate on money supply are assumed negligible. To the extent that agents can hold both foreign currency and domestic currency as bank deposits, we believe that inflation, interest rate, and exchange rate only have an effect on relative proportion of foreign currency in money holdings rather than the quantities. The equation can further be enriched by the experience that to some extent a domestic monetary policy reaction function in addition to economic agents' wealth portfolio re-alignment activities does matter. Authorities in Zambia follow an IMF-supported economic programme that emphasizes regulating monetary aggregates in order to control inflation.

The third equation depicts the inflation process which we assume is dependent on developments in output demand and supply conditions as well as in the exchange rate. This assumption is not unwise. For instance, Zambia's agriculture output is itself heavily dependent on rainfall and mining is vulnerable to international investor sentiments, both of which domestic policy can do little about. Yet, it is hard to discount the contemporaneous effects of these output shocks on inflation. Furthermore, the exchange rate is a vital variable in inflation expectations in the economy. With many consumer goods imported, exchange rate movements are more or less immediately reflected in domestic prices.

The fourth equation is built on the assumption that developments in the Treasury bill interest rates depict monetary sterilization activities. Under the auspices of the IMF, Zambia's monetary policy regime can be designated as monetary targeting. Under this arrangement, the core aspect of decision-making has been projections of 'desired' inflation, from which money supply targets are subsequently derived. In the transition to modernising monetary policy, authorities set up a liquidity sterilization account into which excess cash raised over and above the fiscal requirement was deposited.

Although this sterilization arrangement worked well in reigning in inflation, challenges regarding economic modelling and forecasting remained. As a direct consequence of this, a monetary policy reaction function tends to respond to inflation surprises in a somewhat backward looking, rather than forward looking, manner. In other words, once the inflation rate has been observed, decisions to adjust policy are taken. In practice, policy response implies increased or decreased liquidity sterilization operations which themselves have an impact on the Treasury bill interest rate. One therefore can rely on the Treasury bill rate to characterize a monetary policy shock. As in Bernanke and Mihov (1996)[6] policy shocks emerge from policymakers' relative preference for output or inflation and the policymakers' lack of adequate information on the current state of the economy. These two factors combined could be interpreted as monetary policy shocks and show up as part of the Treasury bill rate equation. We therefore model the equation as a quasi-monetary policy reaction function.

The fifth and final equation basically incorporates the exchange rate as a shock-absorbing variable in the sense that both foreign and domestic shocks 'hit' the exchange rate. This is reasonable given that Zambia is a small, yet open, economy with a fully liberalized balance of payments regime. Table 6.3 summarizes these assumptions.

6.6.3 Impulse response functions and analysis

Having estimated the model, we can summarize the results and insights by means of selected impulse response functions. These show the response of each of the variables to shocks to the other variables in the model by tracing the predicted response of each variable in response to a shock to one of the other variables. In order to focus on the interaction of monetary policy with the rest of the economy, we limit our attention to the response functions of output, inflation, monetary policy and exchange rate to each other. It is these interactions that shape the monetary policy debate in Zambia.

Figures 6.2a to 6.2d depict the responses of each of the endogenous variables to various other variable shocks included in the model. Figure 6.3 shows the responses of each variable to shocks to the world price of copper, arguably the principal external driver of the Zambian economy.[7] Notice that in this case the figures report the response of different variables to the same temporary shock.

Table 6.3 Short-run parameters (restrictions on contemporaneous matrix)

Variables	Y	M	CPI	TBR	EXR
Y	1	0	0	0	0
M	β_{43}	1	0	0	0
CPI	β_{53}	β_{54}	1	0	β_{57}
TBR	β_{63}	β_{64}	β_{65}	1	0
EXR	β_{73}	β_{74}	β_{75}	β_{76}	1

Figure 6.2a Response of output

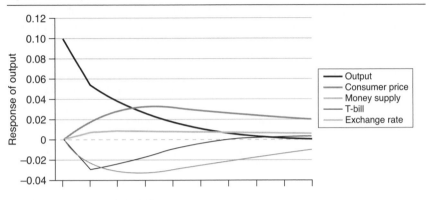

Figure 6.2b Response of inflation

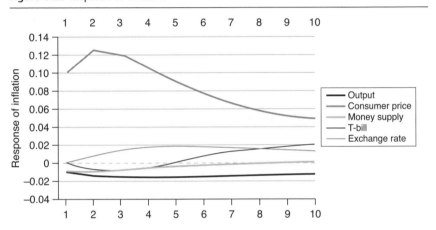

Figure 6.2c Response of Treasury bill rate

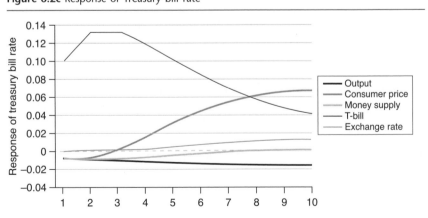

Figure 6.2d Response of exchange rate

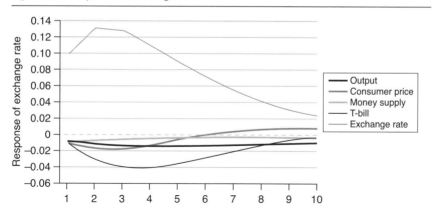

Figure 6.3 Response functions to world copper prices

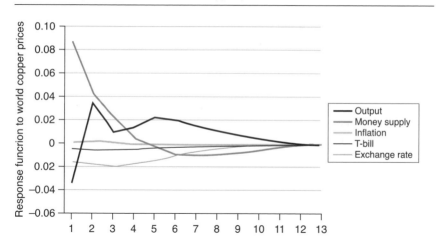

Taken together, these response functions paint a relatively conventional picture of the macro-dynamics of a small open commodity dependent economy. We start by considering how copper price movements impact the vector of endogenous variables (Figure 6.3). The responses are predictable. After the first period (month), aggregate output rises sharply and remains elevated for approximately 12 months after the shock. Over this period, the exchange rate appreciates which in turn tends to dampen any inflationary pressures emanating from the income effect of rising copper prices. The shape rise in the money supply over the shock is consistent with a policy of leaning against exchange rate appreciation in which the authorities accumulate reserves. However, since the money supply measure here

125

is inclusive of foreign current deposits the response is also consistent with public sector reserve accumulation being accompanied by similar private sector responses. The fact that domestic inflation hardly responds may help explain the passive monetary policy response, as proxied by movements in the Treasury bill rate.

Turning next to the economy's response to domestic sources of variation, we note that the short-run behaviour of output follows directly from theory: demand shocks, represented by excess money growth, and inflation shocks increases output in the short run, while interest rate and exchange rate shocks lead to a decrease in output. In the short run, these real macro-economic dynamics are entirely conventional; higher interest rates affect the ability of firms to cost-effectively expand their production, while for an economy that is highly dependent on imports, a depreciating exchange rate seems to immediately raise costs of importable inputs.

A similarly conventional pattern emerges when we look at inflation and exchange rate dynamics, with output shocks having a deflationary impact and exchange rate shocks a more persistent inflationary impact, with this latter response lending some support to authorities' concern about exchange rate developments. Interest rate impacts lead to lower inflation, the effect that peaks at about two periods.

Taken together, these impulse response functions give a valuable perspective on the authorities reaction function that describes a conventional countercyclical policy stance (Figure 6.2c) with interest rates tightening in the face of positive inflation and exchange rate shocks, although in both cases with a lag. By contrast, the response to output shocks appears to be mildly procyclical. What is most notable, though, is that policy appears to be more highly geared towards inflation control than the exchange rate.

6.7 Conclusions and future policy implications: Towards inflation targeting

In recent years, the Bank of Zambia has embarked on a process of re-orienting the conduct of monetary policy away from an emphasis on balance-sheet aggregates (money targets) and towards an explicit interest rate target. The Bank believes an interest rate target is far more transparent and easier to understand than a money growth rate target, allowing for a clearer and more readily verifiable approach to communicating the central bank's intentions. In April 2012, the central bank introduced a policy interest rate at an inaugural 9.25 per cent. To tighten the transmission of policy rate changes to bank credit demand, the central bank further required that commercial banks set their lending rates off this policy rate (effectively, the policy rate became the base lending rate). Implementing the interest rate policy involves conducting liquidity operations in order to steer the interbank overnight interest rate to fluctuate closely around the policy rate. In transition, however, reserve money levels still remain actively looked at, mainly within the context of IMF programmes.

In this chapter, we have demonstrated the interaction between monetary policy and the exchange rate in Zambia. Obviously, this relationship is quite complex even for a small economy with less sophisticated financial markets. Using the SVAR technique, the chapter sought to identify how structural shocks included in the SVAR system dynamically affect each other and what this has implied for the practical conduct of monetary policy. This exercise becomes important for policy design and timing. The general finding is that foreign factors, including movements in copper prices, are informative in designing domestic policy responses.

Drawn on the complexities of these empirical relationships, coupled with increasing conviction among monetary policy designers that the economy has changed in a fundamental way, an interest rate-targeting framework has consequently been developed and seen as a more pragmatic method of conducting policy. Going forward, developing financial market structures that ensure the efficacy of such interest rate targeting will remain a surmountable challenge.

Notes

1. The post-independence history of Zambia spans three Republics. The First Republic ran from independence in 1964 until 1973 when the Second Republic was born with the creation by President Kaunda of a one-party state. The introduction of multi-party electoral politics, and Kaunda's defeat at the hands of the Movement for Multi-party Democracy (MMD) in 1991 ushered in the current Third Republic.
2. The rationale is that expected inflation feeds into current price and wage-setting behaviour so that a credible inflation target thus leads to price and wage-setting behaviour today that is consistent with, and therefore validates, the forecast.
3. If the authorities' commitment is credible, then the private sector's price and wage setting will be conditional on this expectation and not on short-run inflation developments. In technical terms, this will flatten the Phillips curve, thereby giving monetary policy short-run traction on output.
4. This section is relatively technical. Readers can skip directly to Section 6.6.
5. The feedback is due to the fact that each endogenous variable in the structural VAR is correlated with the contemporaneous error terms of other endogenous variables. Standard estimation techniques require that regressors should not be correlated with error terms.
6. What does the Bundesbank target? WP 5764 NBER.
7. We do not report the response functions for world interest rate shocks although these are available on demand.

References

Adam, C.S. and Bevan, D.L. (1999). Fiscal restraint and the cash budget in Zambia. In: Collier, P. and Pattillo, C. (eds), *Risk and Investment in Africa*. London: Macmillan.

Adam, C.S., Maturu, B.O., Ndung'u, N.S. and O'Connell, S.A. (2011). Building a Kenyan monetary regime for the twenty-first century. In Adam, C.S., Collier, P. and Ndung'u, N.S. (eds) *Kenya: Policies for Prosperity*. Oxford: Oxford University Press.

Awokuse, T.O., Yang, J. (2003). The information role of commodity prices in formulating monetary policy: A re-examination. *Economics Letters* 79.

Bernanke, B.S. (1986). Alternative explanations of the money-income correlations. *Carnegie-Rochester Conference Series on Public Policy* 25.

Bernanke, B.S., and Blinder, A.S. (1992). The federal funds rate and the channels of monetary transmission. *The American Economic Review* 82.

Bernanke, B.S., and Mihov, I. (1995). Measuring monetary policy. NEBR Working Paper.

Blanchard, O.J., and Watson, M.W. (1986). Are business cycles all alike? In: Gordon, R. (ed), *The American Business Cycle: Continuity and Change*. Chicago: University of Chicago Press.

Buffie, E., Adam, C., O'Connell, S. and Pattillo, C. (2008). Riding the wave: Monetary responses to aid surges in low-income countries. *European Economic Review* 52: 8 1378–95.

Cashin, P., Cespedes, L., and Saha, R. (2002). Keynes, cocoa and copper: In search of commodity currencies, *IMF Working Paper* 02/223.

Lunieski C. (2009). Commodity price volatility and monetary policy uncertainty: A GARCH estimation issues. *Political Economy*, 19.

Mishra, P., and Montiel, P. (2012). How effective is monetary transmission in low-income countries? A survey of the empirical evidence. *IMF Working Paper* 12:143.

O'Connell, S.A. (2010). Inflation targeting in Africa. In: Aryeetey, E., Devarajan, S., Kanbur, R. and Kasekende, L. (eds) *The Oxford Companion to the Economics of Africa*. Oxford: Oxford University Press.

Sims, C A. (1992). Interpreting the macro-economic time series facts: The effects of monetary policy. *European Economic Review*, 36.

7

Financial Markets and Resource Mobilization in Zambia

Francis Chipimo[1]

7.1 Introduction

This chapter addresses the challenge of resource mobilization from both internal and external sources of finance, if Zambia is to sustain high levels of economic growth and achieve upper middle-income status by 2030. At the centre of this challenge is the role played by the financial sector in the savings and investment decisions of households and firms in Zambia. The chapter also provides an assessment of how the current policies being pursued in the financial sector help or hinder resource mobilization. Our focus is exclusively on private sector resource mobilization, with a focus on both debt and equity instruments.

This chapter is organized as follows. Section 7.2 provides a summary of the recent financial sector developments and the current structure of the financial sector in Zambia. Section 7.3 provides a framework for understanding the role of financial markets in resource mobilization in Zambia, drawing upon the extensive literature that exists on the role of information costs on the saving and investment decisions of households and firms. This literature also provides valuable insights on the nature of the financial institutions that we observe. Section 7.4 outlines some of the key challenges that need to be addressed to enhance resource mobilization and financial sector development in general. Section 7.5 concludes.

7.2 Financial sector developments in Zambia[2]

7.2.1 *Zambia's investment needs 2011–15 and towards achieving the vision 2030*

In the recent past, Zambia has been able to mobilize both domestic and external resources to drive economic growth, with real GDP growth averaging 6.2 per cent per annum between 2003 and 2012. This growth has been facilitated by the financial sector reforms that have taken place over the past 20 years. In early 2011, the government launched the Sixth National Development Plan (SNDP) 2011–15, focusing on infrastructure and human capital development. These were seen as the key binding constraints to expanding economic growth, diversifying the economy, and reducing poverty and inequality. Under the SNDP, infrastructure development involves collaboration between the public and private sector in delivering projects through public private partnerships (PPPs), particularly in the areas of energy and transport and communications.

The SNDP envisages infrastructure spending over the plan period amounting to K26.8 trillion or approximately 34.5 per cent of GDP in 2010, covering transport infrastructure, energy and housing. Investment in human development is estimated at K18.1 trillion or 23.3 per cent of GDP in 2010. This will be directed at health, education and skills development, and water and sanitation. In the energy sector, for example, additional generating capacity of approximately 1,867 MW is expected to be created by 2018, which is nearly double current production capacity. The cost of this investment is estimated at US $3.7 billion. This additional power supply should create self-sufficiency in Zambia's own energy consumption as well as expand export capacity and earnings – further diversifying Zambia's export base. (Ministry of Energy, 2010).

Clearly, Zambia's investment needs will require an unprecedented mobilization of resources from both domestic and external sources, with 25 per cent projected to come from external financing and the balance from both tax revenues as well as domestic borrowing. Beyond the SNDP, Zambia has also adopted a long-term vision that seeks to transform the country into a prosperous, middle-income nation by 2030. A diagnostic country study by Vivien Foster and Carolina Dominguez (2010) on Zambia's infrastructure needs suggests that for Zambia to raise its level of infrastructure development to that of developing countries outside of Africa, annual investment of approximately US $1.6 billion was required over a ten-year period. This indicative infrastructure spending included investment in power, transport, irrigation, information and technology, and water and sanitation infrastructure. It was also estimated that given the planned expenditure commitments, and taking into account the possibility of some efficiency gains in the utilization of resources, Zambia faced a potential annual funding gap of approximately US$500 million. It is with this background that we now turn to a description of the structure of Zambia's financial sector, as well as financial sector developments and economic growth in Zambia.

7.2.2 Structure of the financial sector in Zambia

The financial sector in Zambia is dominated by the banking sector, which accounted for 71 per cent of the assets of all financial intermediaries in 2012 (Table 7.1). Then comes the pensions and insurance industry, which accounts for 23.3 per cent of total sector assets and the microfinance institutions (MFIs), which account for only 2.8 per cent of total assets. With respect to nominal GDP, the banking sector accounted for 33.3 per cent, while the pensions and insurance industry and the microfinance sector accounted for 11 per cent and 1.3 per cent respectively in 2012.

The Lusaka Stock Exchange (LuSE) had a market capitalization representing 46.8 per cent of GDP at end 2012. LuSE is still shallow, with few stocks that are actively traded, and still lacks liquidity. The secondary market trading of government bonds in 2012, for example, was a monthly average of 15 trades worth approximately US $27 million. However, as with many other emerging markets, recent growth has been impressive and capital markets remain an

Table 7.1 Total assets of financial intermediaries in Zambia in 2012

In K billions Sector	Number of institutions	% of total assets of financial intermediaries	Percent of nominal GDP
Banking sector	19	70.9	33.3
Leasing sector	8	0.7	0.3
Building societies	4	0.9	0.4
Micro-finance institutions (MFIs)	35	2.8	1.3
National Savings and Credit Bank (NSCB)	1	0.6	0.3
Development Bank of Zambia (DBZ)	1	0.8	0.4
Pension funds (Voluntary schemes)*	46	7.4	3.5
National Pension Scheme Authority (NAPSA)	1	12.7	6.0
Insurance industry	23	3.2	1.5
Total assets of financial intermediaries		100.0	46.9
Lusaka Stock Exchange (LuSE) market capitalization	1	99.7	46.8

Source: Bank of Zambia (BoZ), Lusaka Stock Exchange (LuSE), Pensions and Insurance Authority (PIA)
*Does not include the Public Sector Pension Fund (PSPF) and the Local Authorities Superannuation Fund (LASF), both of which are in deficit

important part of the solution to the greater need for resource mobilization, both domestic and external, if Zambia's economy is to continue to grow at a rapid pace. Demirguc-Kunt and Levine (2001) show that as economies develop the role of non-bank financial intermediaries such as insurance companies and pension funds as well as the capital market play an increasingly significant role in the financial sector. However, whether a financial sector is predominantly banks based or market based is not seen as providing an advantage to economic growth.

7.2.3 *Financial sector developments 1992–2013*

Prior to 1992, Zambia's economy was dominated by the government, which had direct ownership of the key enterprises in most sectors of the economy and implemented pervasive controls on the returns to labour and capital through price and incomes policies. Zambia's financial sector was repressed, with direct controls on prices (interest rates and the exchange rate), external flows (current and capital account controls), and credit provision (quantitative credit ceilings). This ultimately led to disintermediation, as resources were misallocated and productive enterprises had no advantage over unproductive enterprises in their ability to access financial resources.

From 1992, a concerted and broad programme of economic reform was implemented incorporating structural reforms as well as trade and financial sector liberalization. In the financial sector, administrative controls were removed such as directed credit, controls on interest rates and the operation of a fixed exchange rate. The financial sector reforms also included the establishment of new regulatory bodies such as the Securities and Exchange Commission (SEC), the Zambia Competition Commission (ZCC), and the Pension and Insurance Authority (PIA). They also included revisions to the legislation governing the supervision of the financial sector, with the amendment of the Bank of Zambia Act in 1994 and the introduction of a new Banking and Financial Services Act (1996).

The liberalization of the financial sector led to the establishment of six new banks between 1992–95, before the banking sector crisis in the latter part of the 1990s led to the collapse of no less than nine banks between 1995 and 2001, at an estimated cost of 7 per cent of GDP to taxpayers and depositors (Maimbo, 2002 and Martinez, 2006). The banking sector crisis in the late 1990s actually reflected gaps in the regulatory framework, corporate governance failures, as well as inadequate capitalization of financial institutions that skewed financial incentives towards risk taking at the expense of depositors and financial stability.

A second wave of reforms commenced in 2002, following the Financial Sector Assessment Programme (FSAP) conducted by the IMF and the World Bank. This second wave of reforms was encapsulated in two Financial Sector

Development Plans (FSDP I and II) that largely focused on enhancing the legislative framework governing the financial sector, improving the market infrastructure of the financial sector through the establishment of a credit reference bureau and the development of the payment system, and promoting financial inclusion (i.e. the participation of a wider number of household and firms in the financial sector through the utilization of financial services). More recently, these reforms have included the introduction of a Bank of Zambia (BoZ) policy rate and the graduation of monetary policy implementation to targeting interest rates rather than monetary aggregates. In the area of financial sector supervision, capital requirements for banks have been increased substantially, while interest rate caps have also been introduced by restricting the maximum lending margins that banks and non-bank financial institutions can charge customers above the BoZ policy rate. Appendix 1 provides a chronology of some of the key financial sector developments in Zambia.

The financial sector reforms have had a positive impact on financial sector development, although the pace and nature of reform has varied across the sector. For example, the reform and development of the banking sector has tended to outpace the development of the pension and insurance industry and the capital market, reflecting the importance of the banking sector in the economy. Two standard measures of financial sector development are the ratio of money supply (e.g. broad or narrow money) and private sector credit to Gross Domestic Product (GDP) – although the ratio of private sector credit to GDP is often seen as being more indicative of financial deepening, (Demirguc-Kunt

Figure 7.1 Measures of financial deepening in Zambia 1996–2012

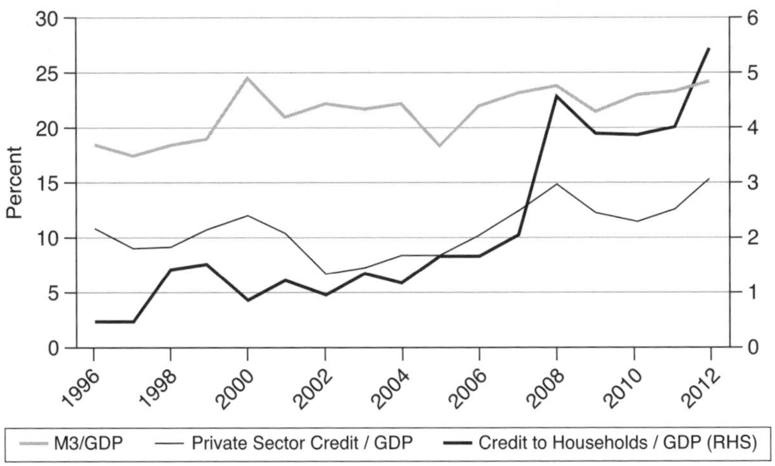

Source: Bank of Zambia

133

Figure 7.2 Private sector credit expansion and real GDP growth, 1996–2012

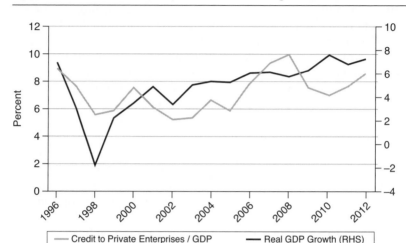

Legend: — Credit to Private Enterprises / GDP   — Real GDP Growth (RHS)

Source: Bank of Zambia and Central Statistical Office

and Levine, 2001). These ratios are captured in Figure 7.1 and show that Zambia's financial sector has deepened. The banking sector crisis of the late 1990s had a negative impact on financial sector development between 1996 and 2001. Thereafter, the financial sector developed and the ratio of private sector credit to GDP rose sharply up until the financial crisis of 2008. In 2012, the various measures of financial deepening indicated in Figure 7.1 had gone back to or surpassed their levels in 2008. The expansion of credit to private households has been a key driver of this expansion.[3]

The increase in financial deepening was further supported by the expansion in banking infrastructure and the provision of financial services to the public, particularly over the 2005–12 period. Over this period, there has been an appreciable increase in technological infrastructure, such as point of sale terminals, automated teller machines (ATMs), and clients using mobile banking services. The number of depositors and borrowers in commercial banks increased by an annual average rate of 82 per cent and 58 per cent respectively between 2004 and 2012. There has also been an increase in the number of employees in the financial sector from 3,466 in 2004 to 6,600 in 2012, an annual average increase of 8.6 per cent. Between 2009 and 2012, the number of mobile banking customers increased by 320 per cent to 530,786, while the number of customers using Internet banking services increased by 191 per cent to 24,468, suggesting that the application of technology is beginning to lower the cost of accessing financial services. However, financial inclusion in Zambia remained relatively low at 37 per cent, and this issue is addressed in Section 7.3.

7.2.4 *Economic growth and resource mobilization*

From a macro-economic perspective, the trends in real GDP growth over the period of reform have largely coincided with the trends in financial sector deepening. During the 1990s, economic growth was volatile with an average annual growth rate of only 0.7 per cent. However, over the next ten years economic growth strengthened, particularly after 2002, rising to an annual average growth rate of 2.7 per cent. Figure 7.2 shows that between 1996 and 2002, the expansion of credit to private enterprises as a percentage of GDP exhibited a downward trend, before accelerating thereafter until the global financial crisis struck in 2008. Annual real GDP growth has averaged 6.2 per cent between 2003 and 2012, with growth rising to 7.6 per cent in 2010 from 5.1 per cent in 2003. This strong growth has been supported by an increase in both savings and investment in the economy.

Figure 7.3 shows that gross national savings as a percentage of GDP declined precipitously between 1996 and 2001 and then recovered strongly thereafter, rising to 24.8 per cent of GDP in 2009. However, investment as a percentage of GDP rose steadily over this period, rising to 25.5 per cent in 2003 and remaining relatively flat thereafter. Between 2009 and 2012, Gross National Savings declined to 15.2 per cent of GDP, but this decline was compensated for by an increase in external borrowing, current and capital transfers from abroad (i.e. external savings). Much of the increase in investment has come from foreign direct investment (FDI) flows into the mining sector – through both debt and equity. The growth in FDI flows and private sector external

Figure 7.3 Gross fixed capital formation, gross national savings, and external borrowing

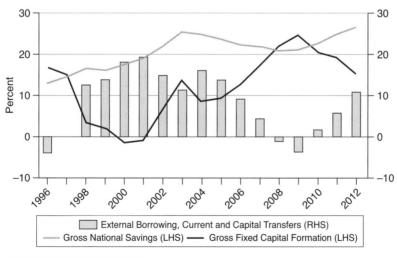

Source: Central Statistical Office (CSO)

Figure 7.4 FDI and private sector external debt 1999–2012

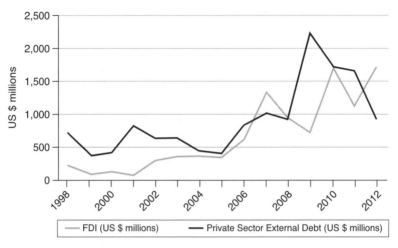

Source: Bank of Zambia (BoZ)

debt is shown in Figure 7.4. Between 2004 and 2012, FDI inflows grew by an annual average rate of approximately 34 per cent.

Zambia's recent financial and economic history thus points to the positive role that financial sector development has on economic growth. There is now, in fact, a large body of theoretical and empirical evidence that supports the proposition that financial sector development is important for economic growth. The World Bank (2007 and 2011), for example, has provided comprehensive research with specific reference to Africa that demonstrates the increasingly important role that financial markets play in resource mobilization and economic growth. This is particularly so in countries that are able to foster competitive environments that promote innovation and expand the range and use of financial services.

However, perhaps the most compelling evidence on the complexity and importance of the relationship between finance and growth is the recent global financial and economic crisis, in which the near collapse of key financial institutions and markets had far reaching implications on commerce and trade across the globe and pushed the world economy into recession.

7.3 The role of financial markets in resource mobilization in Zambia

Over the past 40 years, theoretical and empirical developments in the area of financial economics have deepened our understanding of the nature of financial institutions in market economies and the role that they play in resource mobilization and economic growth. The fundamental insight of financial economics is the notion that in any prospective financial contract, information asymmetries between the contracting parties gives rise to a divergence of incentives that can lead to the breakdown of trade and the exchange of assets. In effect, information asymmetries can frustrate the workings of the price system in allocating resources to their most efficient use. Information asymmetries represent a cost that must be borne to facilitate trade. Relative to a world in which information asymmetries did not exist, this reduces the overall welfare of society.

These theories of information costs are relevant to the challenge of resource mobilization in Zambia because they help us to understand the nature of the financial sector in the country and the constraints that we observe. This includes aspects such as the dual nature of the financial sector with respect to access to financial services, the role of competition in potentially reducing costs and improving (or reducing) the quality, range and availability of services as well as the very structure of the financial sector itself. They also provide important insight into what the appropriate policy response should be if we are to optimize domestic resource mobilization and enhance the role of the financial sector in economic development. This is because they provide a framework for understanding the competing incentives faced by financial institutions and firms in entering into financial contracts, and it is the resolution of these competing incentives that best describes, or gives rise to, the financial relationships and institutions that we observe. Section 7.3.1 outlines the theoretical framework which underpins many of the empirical models which have been used to describe the financial sector that we actually observe in both developed and developing countries. This section can be skipped for those less theoretically inclined. Sections 7.3.2 to 7.3.4 then describe Zambia's financial sector in detail, with specific reference to some relevant theoretical and empirical literature.

7.3.1 *A framework for understanding resource mobilization*

Financial markets facilitate the allocation of resources from savers to investors. In discussing the role of financial markets in resource mobilization, a distinction is made between financial institutions that intermediate or act as a bridge between savers and investors and the capital market (e.g. the LuSE), where savers and investors can be said to interact directly. The financial sector in Zambia can be split into three broad categories: the pensions and insurance companies that are regulated by the PIA; bank and non-bank financial institutions that are regulated by the Bank of Zambia (BoZ); and the LuSE, that is regulated by the Securities and Exchange Commission (SEC). Figure 7.5 outlines the framework within which we discuss the role of the various financial institutions in resource mobilization in Zambia.

Figure 7.5 A framework of resource mobilization in Zambia

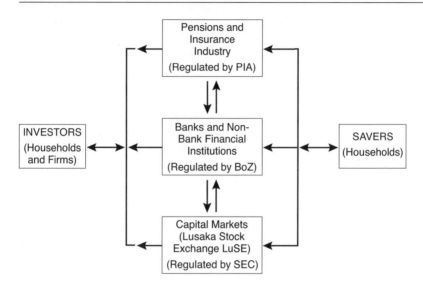

The term 'information costs' is, in fact, a very broad term incorporating the *ex-ante*, current, and *ex-post* costs of financial transactions. Another useful way of presenting information costs is to view them as costs associated with hidden action – agency costs – or hidden information –asymmetric information costs (Harris and Raviv, 1991). However, information costs are probably best explained through some specific examples: In 1970, George Akerlof, now a Nobel Laureate in economics, published a paper entitled *The market for Lemons*, in which he demonstrated theoretically that when buyers have only incomplete information on the quality of second hand cars, sellers will not be able to sell good quality cars since all second hand cars will be marked down and only low quality cars (lemons in US parlance) will be sold. Incomplete information in this case kills the market in good quality second hand cars. The challenge for the used car salesman is to find a way of credibly signalling the quality of the car, for example, by offering some limited guarantee. Akerlof thus demonstrated the challenges of *ex-ante* or asymmetric information costs.

A wider perspective on the implication of information costs was provided by Jensen and Meckling (1976) who argued that a private enterprise could be viewed as a 'nexus of contracting relationships'. A firm's borrowing or debt/equity ratio, sometimes referred to as its capital structure choice, could be explained by the contractual relationships of its key stakeholders. These key stakeholders included the owners of the firm, the managers of the firm, and the workers employed by the firm, who all had a stake in the value of the firm. Jensen and Meckling (1976) demonstrated that information asymmetries between these key stakeholders, with respect to the value of the firm, led to conflicts of interest. For example, where the owners and managers of the firm were different, the managers of the firm typically had more information about the true value of the firm than its owners. The managers therefore had an incentive to extract value from the firm by generating higher non-pecuniary costs. As rational investors would understand that the dilution of ownership in a firm created these costs, they would offer a lower price for acquiring equity in such firms and this lower valuation of the firm was referred to as the agency cost of equity. The conflict of interests between owners and managers thus reflected a challenge of effectively monitoring the operations of managers. Ross (1973) demonstrated that a higher debt equity ratio could reduce such monitoring costs by forcing companies to make regular cash payouts that minimized the misuse of resources. In addition, higher debt levels also increased the risks of bankruptcy, which could act as a disciplinary device on the actions of management who would face some punishment from bankruptcy.

Jensen and Meckling (1976) also demonstrated that there were agency costs that arose from conflicts between shareholders and debt holders (or fixed claim holders) in a firm. These agency costs arose because when debt levels were high, shareholders who had limited liability had an incentive to promote risky investment projects that had high payoffs with a low probability of success. This is because any losses for the shareholders were capped by limited liability while the bondholders would bear the cost of bankruptcy. However, if the projects were successful the shareholders were able to pay off the debt and retain the surplus, effectively shifting the risks to the bondholders. Shareholders therefore had an incentive to promote high yielding, but risky, projects that may have a negative net present value and hence lower the value of the firm – and this lower value of the firm represented an agency cost of debt.

Information costs also arise when it is difficult to verify the output of financial contracts after the contract has been concluded. Townsend (1979) referred to this as costly state verification and highlighted the fact that financial transactions might be inhibited because the providers of funds could not verify the cash-flows that would be used to repay the funds lent due to information asymmetries between the providers and users of funds. Asymmetries in information therefore also gave rise to verification costs such as *ex-post* auditing of borrowers and that such costs also represented agency costs of debt. If these costs were significant they could give rise to credit rationing. This is particularly important in the context of Zambia's financial sector, where the majority of firms are actually small and medium-sized enterprises (SMEs) often with poor or no accounting records.

7.3.2 *Banks and non-bank financial intermediaries*

As indicated in Table 7.1, commercial banks dominate Zambia's financial sector, taking deposits and granting loans and, in this process, carrying out an array of functions that include: delegated monitoring, maturity transformation, payment system services, and the management of credit, interest, and liquidity risk (Freixas and Rochet, 2002). The nature of the functions that banks carry out is partly a solution to the existence of information of agency and asymmetric information costs. Diamond (1984, 1996), for example, demonstrated how the existence of banks can be justified on the basis of delegated monitoring. Due to the existence of information costs, households with savings were unwilling to lend money to those households and firms with investment needs. These information costs could, in fact, reflect several factors, including: difficulty in determining good borrowers from bad borrowers, or in verifying the returns that a business or individual was making once he had been lent money, or because the borrowers had a strong incentive to misappropriate funds because they were better informed about the business and the cash-flows it actually generated.

Banks were able to bridge these information costs by essentially pooling and lowering the risk of default from lending money to investors. By being able to lend funds to a wide variety of clients with diverse risk characteristics, banks were able to lower the risks associated with a unit of funds employed and to monitor the funds employed more effectively than any individual or firm could. With this ability to better monitor and lower risks, banks could offer contracts to depositors or agents with surplus funds, in the form of bank deposits, which provided an assured return. Effectively, these depositors were thus delegating the monitoring function to banks, enabling the flow of finance from agents with surplus funds to those with investment needs in the economy. The depositors were also able to keep banks honest by being able to withdraw their deposits without notice or at short notice.

Diamond's (1984) simple model of delegating monitoring offers important insights into the challenges of domestic resource mobilization. With respect to the mobilization of domestic resources from individuals with surplus funds, the nature of the deposit contract (i.e. the fact that depositors could withdraw their funds without notice) was seen as a disciplinary device on bank management. In the absence of this disciplinary role, savings mobilization could be impaired. The banking sector crisis that Zambia faced in the 1990s, which partly arose from corporate governance failure, is an important example of this. A second aspect of the delegated monitoring model was that banks adopt a technology that lowered risks of default through the diversification of their risks – which was achieved by dealing with a large pool of borrowers. The inference here is that any failure of this technology or the inability of banks to lower risk, would impact on resource mobilization. The existence of agency and asymmetric information costs as described in Section 7.3.1 represents such an impediment.

Over the past few years, Zambia's banking sector has in fact registered strong growth and this is consistent with the improvements in financial sector deepening described in Sections 7.2.2 and 7.2.3. More recent developments in the non-bank financial institutions (NBFIs) are also encouraging. The number of NBFIs has increased from 49 in 2005 to 107 in 2012. This growth is accounted for by the increase in the number of *bureaux de change* from 32 to 57 and microfinance institutions (MFIs) from 4 to 35, over the same period – with much of this growth taking place between 2007 and 2012. The growth in MFIs is particularly welcome as it suggests that the information costs associated with MSMEs are being addressed and supports the modest increase observed in financial sector inclusion in Zambia as a whole. However, the default rates for NBFIs were not significantly higher than those for commercial banks.

This increase in domestic resource mobilization has largely been underwritten by an improved macro-economic environment, which has delivered lower inflation; lower budget deficits – and declining interest rates; improved supervision of the financial sector, with higher capital requirements and improved corporate governance standards; and an improved legislative framework for commercial transactions incorporating changes in company law as well as the introduction of commercial courts and enhancement of the arbitration process. All of these factors have acted to reduce information costs in the financial sector, thereby facilitating (easing) the flow of credit in the economy.

However, despite the increase in domestic resource mobilization, many companies remain credit constrained for both formal and informal firms. This is in a large part reflected in the nature of businesses in Zambia. The World Bank's 2009 *Investment Climate Assessment* for Zambia indicates that large-scale companies accounted for only 14 per cent of businesses surveyed with MSMEs accounting for 86 per cent. A comprehensive Zambia Business Survey (ZBS) conducted by the Zambia Business Forum, the World Bank, FinMark Trust and the Zambian Government through its Private Sector Development (PSD) Programme (Zambia Business Survey, 2008), found that Zambia's private sector was dualistic in nature, with the majority of firms being MSMEs operating in the informal sector (i.e. those employing less than 50 employees). Many of these MSMEs were in fact micro enterprises, were unregistered with any regulatory agency and operated predominantly in the agriculture sector (70 per cent of MSMEs) and operated in the rural areas (81 per cent of MSMEs). Most MSMEs were in fact home based and were either self-employed individuals or family enterprises.

The bulk of MSMEs in Zambia therefore have very severe information costs associated with poor record keeping, low financial literacy, and the fact that they operated in a sector (agriculture) that was prone to significant external shocks. The ZBS (2008) indicated that only 7 per cent of MSMEs were banked for business. Given the importance of information costs in resource mobilization, it is therefore not surprising that many firms are credit constrained. The information asymmetries of MSMEs was further compounded by the fact that they largely traded with individuals unlike their large-scale enterprises which were not only more diverse in terms of the sectors they operated in but over 60 per cent of large enterprises supplied other large enterprises in addition to trading directly with individuals, small businesses, and the government. Increased trading with formal sector enterprises, particularly when these trading partners themselves had access to finance, can be seen as another avenue of reducing information costs and of increasing financial inclusion.

The dualistic nature of Zambian businesses does in fact find itself reflected in the dualistic nature of access to, and the provision of, finance for households and firms. This duality in the financial sector can be understood at two levels. The first level is that many companies are excluded from the financial sector altogether. At the broader level of the population as a whole, work by FinMark Trust (2009) on financial inclusion in Zambia indicates that financial inclusion has increased only modestly from 33 per cent in 2006 to 37 in 2009. This can be seen as a reflection of the nature of businesses in Zambia and their high information costs. However, credit constraints can also be observed within the universe of banked firms themselves, in that MSMEs in this set of firms do not have the same access to credit as their larger counterparts. Credit to banked MSMEs was only 5.3 per cent of outstanding private sector credit at end-December 2010 compared to 48.4 per cent for large firms, while consumer loans accounted for 44.4 per cent.

From a theoretical standpoint, the duality observed in Zambia's financial sector can also be understood as a consequence of existing information costs. Macho-Stadler and Perez-Castrillo (2001) demonstrate, based on the signalling hypothesis of Ross (1977), that in circumstances where risk-neutral investors cannot easily discern the quality of firms (i.e. due to information costs), firms have an incentive to signal their quality through debt. They demonstrate that a separating equilibrium can be defined in which good quality firms are able to acquire debt, while bad quality firms are not. This can be equated to the financial exclusion observed in Zambia, where only 37 per cent of households utilize either formal or informal financial products. However, they go further than this and also demonstrate an equilibrium in which all firms carry some level of debt and the level of debt is positively correlated with relative firm quality and negatively correlated with the probability of default. This can be equated to the dichotomy observed in the banking sector, where large firms are able to access credit much easier and on more favourable terms than small firms.

7.3.3 *The pensions and insurance industries*

The pensions and insurance industries can be seen as the second pillar of Zambia's financial sector and are an important source of long-term capital. The asset and liability structure of pensions and insurance companies differs from that of banks and the concept of delegated monitoring does not adequately explain the information costs and the incentive structures that they face – this is particularly true for insurance companies. Pension funds can be seen as providing size and maturity transformation, mobilizing savings by issuing non-transferable financial claims and buying real and financial assets such as property, stocks and bonds, as well as deposits in the banking system. This type of intermediation reflects the fact that individual surpluses do not necessarily match individual deficits and savers may have a shorter time horizon for their deposits than investors. Although banks also provide size and maturity transformation, they differ from pension funds in that they have assets (loans) which are not necessarily marketable, for example in Zambia.

The standard deposit contract issued by banks differ from standard insurance contracts in that they do not protect against liquidity shocks – which are not verifiable because of information symmetries. Diamond and Dybvig (1983) present a model of intermediation based on the provision of liquidity insurance. Insurance companies issue liabilities in the form of conditional contracts to depositors or savers who wish to protect themselves against specific liquidity shocks. On the asset side of their balance insurance companies invest in real and financial assets to secure a return that meets their expected liabilities at any given time.

Both the pension and insurance industries have grown in Zambia in recent years, as demonstrated in Figure 7.6. Pension fund assets have registered a rapid growth rate over the past decade. Total pension fund assets, for the voluntary private sector schemes, rose from K214 billion in 1999 to K3,668.4 billion in 2012, or 3.5 per cent of GDP. This represented an annual average growth rate of approximately 25.3 per cent in nominal terms. If we take account of inflation, the real average annual growth rate over the same period was approximately 8 per cent. If we include the assets of the National Pensions Scheme Authority (NAPSA), which is a compulsory scheme for all formal sector workers, total assets of the pension industry stood at K10,009 billion at in 2012.

The important role that pension funds play in resource mobilization, particularly for long-term funds, is demonstrated by the composition of pension fund assets (see Figure 7.8). At end 2012, 37 per cent of pension fund assets were invested in fixed interest securities, which included Treasury bills and other short-term securities, GRZ bonds and other longer dated securities; 12 per cent were invested in equities (both listed and unlisted), and 24 per cent was invested in property.

Figure 7.6 Total assets of pension industry (voluntary schemes) and insurance industry

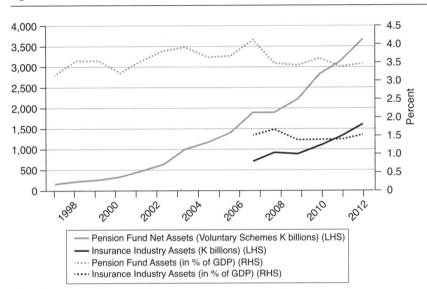

Legend:
— Pension Fund Net Assets (Voluntary Schemes K billions) (LHS)
— Insurance Industry Assets (K billions) (LHS)
···· Pension Fund Assets (in % of GDP) (RHS)
···· Insurance Industry Assets (in % of GDP) (RHS)

Source: Bank of Zambia, Pensions and Insurance Authority

A critical challenge facing the pension fund industry in Zambia, as in other countries, is the challenge of actuarial deficits. This is a much greater challenge for the public sector pension funds than private sector pension funds. Actuarial deficits essentially mean that the present value of assets of a given pension fund are less than the present value of assessed liabilities (i.e. expected future contracted pension payments). The fundamental driver of actuarial deficits, particularly with respect to private pensions is the fact that many of these pensions are defined benefit schemes (e.g. where pension payouts are based on an employee's final salary), rather than defined contribution schemes (where the pension payout is correlated with what the pensioner and his employee has put into the scheme). Pension contributions by existing workers are not sufficient to meet the pension liabilities falling due. Clearly this puts great pressure on the ability of pension funds to ensure they can secure a reasonable return on their investments that helps them to meet their liabilities. Addressing this issue will require a combination of measures, which include increased contributions from both employers and employees and improving the returns on assets under management.

The insurance industry has undergone some significant changes in recent years, following the establishment of the PIA, which include the separation of life insurance from general insurance. Consolidated data for the insurance industry indicates that total assets have grown from K704.4 billion in 2007 to K1,603.4 billion in 2012, or by 128 per cent. However, as a percentage

Figure 7.7 Distribution of insurance industry assets, 2012

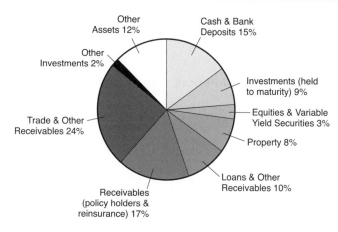

Source: Pensions and Insurance Authority

of GDP, the total assets of the insurance industry were just 1.5 per cent in 2012. In December 2010, approximately 63 per cent of the total assets of the industry were accounted for by investment in: trade and other receivables, receivables from policyholders and re-insurance; cash and bank deposits; and loans (see Figure 7.7). Investment in fixed income securities and equities was negligible, suggesting that there is potential for the insurance industry to play a stronger role in financial intermediation through investment in the debt and equity markets. An additional feature of Zambia's insurance market is that life insurance companies tend to have a more

Figure 7.8 Distribution of total pension fund assets, 2012

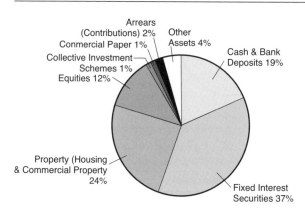

Source: Pensions and Insurance Authority

diversified asset base than the general insurance companies. Life insurance companies have approximately 56 per cent of their assets invested in current assets, while for general insurance companies current assets account for around 80 per cent of assets.

7.4 Debt and equity markets: the Lusaka stock exchange

The Lusaka Stock Exchange (LuSE) represents the market in which savers and investors interact directly, without the use of a financial intermediary, either through the issuance of debt or equity. This is often referred to as an arm's length relationship, but it is important to note that the regulatory framework and rules governing the capital markets are critical for successful resource mobilization. Our discussion of information costs suggests that companies that are able to trade on the LuSE are those that have been able to minimize their information costs. The stringent listing requirements for any company wishing to have its shares or debt traded on the exchange can all be seen in the context of addressing costs associated with hidden action (agency costs) and hidden information (asymmetric information costs). In this regard, the principle of companies complying with strong accounting standards, transparency in the reporting of their financial affairs, and employing best practice corporate governance arrangements – all work to reduce information asymmetries between savers and investors. Given the

Figure 7.9 Stock market developments, 1995–2012

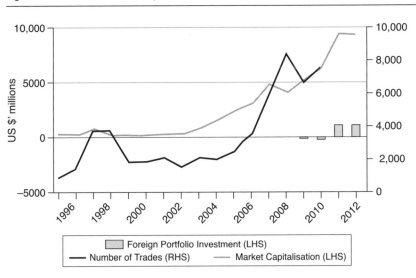

Source: Lusaka Stock Exchange

fact that most companies in Zambia are small and micro enterprises with high information costs, it is no surprise that LuSE is in fact dominated by large-scale companies.

LuSE has registered a phenomenal growth rate since its inception in 1994 (see Figure 7.9). Market capitalization has increase by an annual average rate of 37.2 per cent per annum between 1999 and 2012, in US dollar terms, while market capitalization has risen from $US280 million in 1999 to $US9,327 million in 2012. The return on the index, reflected in the growth

Table 7.2 Bond issuance at LuSE

Year	Type of Company	Type of Issue	Pricing	Tenor	Value US$ Equivalent
1999	Zambian Breweries*	Rights issue			9,022,243
2000	Farmers House	Corporate bond	8.64%	3-4 years	1,000,00
2001	Baobab School	Debenture	–	–	1,500,00
	Farmers House	Rights issue			1,979,904
2002	Arcades	Convertible debenture	10.00%	4.5 years	1,500,000
	Zambian Breweries*	Rights issue			16,510,374
2003	Barclays Bank Plc*	Capital note	91 TB + 1.25%	11 years	10,922,396
	Lunsemfwa Hydro Power	Corporate bond	Libor + 3%	6 years	7,000,000
2004	Copperbelt Forestry Co.	Corporate bond	7.00%	4 years	1,000,000
2006	Farmers House*	Rights issue			10,484,985
2007	Development Bank of Zambia*	Medium term note	182 TB + 2.5% 182 TB + &	5 years 3–5 years	15,847,575
	Investment Bank Plc*	Medium term note	3.5%		10,077,500
	Lafarge Cement*	Medium term note	182 TB + 1.2%	5 years	27,000,000
	Copperbelt Energy	Initial public offering	440		28,669,127
	Cavmont Capital*	Rights issue			4,791,393
2008	Zambeef Products*	Rights issue	5,500		20,665,520
	Celtel*	Initial public offering	640		136,310,483
	Zanaco*	Initial public offering	470		28,715,247
	Standard Chartered Bank*	Medium term note		10 years	10,239,670
	Barclays Bank*	Medium term note	182 TB + 3%	2 years	35,838,844
	Bayport*	Medium term note		2 years	19,455,372
	Zanaco*	Preference shares			4,237,173
2009	Zambia Sugar Plc*	Rights issue	280		54,225,855
	Investrust Bank Plc*	Medium term note	182 TB + 3.5%	3 years	5,355,808
	Investrust Bank Plc*	Medium term note	182 TB + 4%	6 years	9,640,454
2010	Farmers House*	Corporate bond Rights issue	5,202.75	12 years	15,653,751
2011	Investrust Bank Plc*	Rights issue	16		5,319,139
	Zambeef Products*	Rights issue	2,975		20,672,421
	Zambian Breweries*	Rights issue	1,950		69,353,115
	First Quantum Minerals*	Zambian depository receipts	4,700		17,150,483
2012	CCHZ*	Rights issue			17,279,580

Source: LuSE
** US $ equivalent calculated using end-year (December) monthly average exchange rate.

in the index itself, has registered an annual average growth rate of 23 per cent between 1999 and 2012. The LuSE has also seen an increase in the number of bonds and other securities issued by private sector corporations (both financial and non-financial institutions, see Table 7.2).

However, although LuSE market capitalization at 46.8 per cent of GDP is as large as the total assets of the financial intermediaries (banks, pension and insurance companies) the capital market remains very shallow. While there has been increased activity in terms of the number of companies raising capital on LuSE, the secondary trading of bonds (both government and private sector) and other securities also remains very limited. In order for the debt and capital market to play a larger role in resource mobilization, there needs to be both an increase the supply of securities on the exchange (both debt and equity), as well as an improvement in the secondary trading of bonds, particularly government bonds of which there is a plentiful supply, with outstanding bonds at end 2012 representing 7 per cent of GDP. The enhancement of secondary trading of securities on the exchange, particularly bonds and other debt instruments, should improve liquidity. However, both of these challenges are not in the direct control of LuSE. Resolving them will therefore require increased coordination between the regulatory authorities that superintend the financial sector (primarily BoZ, the SEC and the Ministry of Finance).

7.4.1 *Finance and resource mobilization: issues and challenges for Zambia*

Zambia's financial sector has grown over the past ten years and this is reflected in the measures of financial sector depth, the increasing number of financial institutions, both bank and non-bank, offering financial services to the public, and the increased range of financial products. However, the financial sector continues to be dominated by a low level of financial intermediation; lack of financial services in rural areas; high bank charges and account requirements; poor credit culture; lack of long-term funding; weak regulatory framework for non-bank financial institutions; fragmented financial sector laws; and underdeveloped financial markets. The majority of companies and individuals also remain excluded from the financial sector. Further, if Zambia is to sustain the high levels of economic growth necessary to achieve higher middle-income status by 2030, much higher levels of investment must be achieved and sustained over a long period of time. These challenges require further deepening of the financial sector and the enhanced mobilization of domestic resources.

We have argued in Section 7.3 that the nature of Zambia's financial sector, in terms of institutional arrangements and the effectiveness of financial intermediation, is shaped by information costs. These information costs are pervasive and therefore to enhance domestic resource mobilization and financial sector development in general, they must be addressed in a comprehensive manner. We have observed that one of the critical functions that the banking sector plays in domestic resource mobilization is that of delegated monitoring between savers and investors and maturity transformation by taking short-term deposits and creating long-term assets (loans). These functions ameliorate information costs that would otherwise stifle economic activity. The banking sector dominates the financial sector in Zambia and must continue to play a central role in domestic resource mobilization by being able to better perform its delegated monitoring and maturity transformation function.

The pension and insurance industry plays a critical role in the mobilization of long-term financing and in helping to manage liquidity shocks they are also able to bridge rigidities in maturity transformation by the banking sector. The mobilization of long-term financing is a critical challenge that the financial sector must meet, given the required investment in infrastructure development is critical if Zambia is to achieve and sustain levels of economic growth of above 7 per cent over the next two decades. This will require that the pension and insurance industry plays a much stronger role in the financial sector, by helping to reduce information asymmetries in the financial sector and by implementing measures that safeguards the solvency of financial sector institutions, particularly pension funds. Overall financial sector development plays an important role in economic growth and development. As the Zambian economy is dominated by MSMEs, the financial sector must therefore also address the significant credit constraints that MSMEs face. Again, this will require the amelioration of the significant information costs that MSMEs face, as well enhancing the role of competition in driving financial sector inclusion.

We can summarize the key challenges that need to be addressed in enhancing financial sector development in general and domestic resource mobilization in particular, as revolving around efforts to address the various information costs that we have identified in Section 7.3. These challenges can be addressed through interventions at three levels: (1) Enhancing the legal and institutional framework governing the financial sector; (2) encouraging more effective competition that promotes financial intermediation and consumer welfare; and (3) promoting financial inclusion as the lack of access to financial services is a significant impediment to the growth of small businesses and the transferability of savings. In 2010, the government adopted a new programme FSDP II (2010–12), that builds on earlier reforms under FSDP I, with a focus on three areas: improving market infrastructure, increasing competition, and increasing financial inclusion. The successful implementation of the core objectives under identified in the FSDP II is thus central to meeting the challenges of resource mobilization and financial sector development in Zambia.

7.4.2 *Enhancing market infrastructure*

Having an appropriate legal and institutional framework is critical in being able to reduce information asymmetries and transaction costs that inhibit the mobilization of savings and the extension of credit. This entails strengthening governance arrangements in the financial sector, including: the adoption of strong disclosure requirements to the public on the performance of financial institutions; streamlining the regulatory framework governing the financial sector so as to minimize information gaps and strengthen compliance; improving the delivery of commercial justice by strengthening the adjudication of commercial transactions in a cost-effective and timely manner; and enhancing the timely availability of information on credit risk through the promotion of credit reference bureaus and the development of the payment system infrastructure. These measures to enhance market infrastructure can be seen as reducing information costs arising from both agency (hidden action) and asymmetric information (hidden information) costs – leading to more efficient financial sector intermediation and enhanced domestic and external resource mobilization.

In this regard, the legal and regulatory reform measures envisaged under the FSDP II offer the opportunity to significantly reduce information and transaction costs in the financial sector. Important milestones include the completion of the review and harmonization of financial sector legislation. This includes changes to the Bank of Zambia Act, the Banking and Financial Services Act, the Building Societies Act, the Securities Act, the Insurance Act, the Companies Act, the repeal of the Money Lenders Act, and the development of Pension and Insurance Regulations. Other milestones include the establishment of a financial intelligence unit, the development of a 'national switch' under which financial service providers can share retail infrastructure, enhancing the framework for crisis management, updating accounting and auditing standards – and extending the adoption of these international standards in cost effective way to MSMEs (FSDP II Project Proposal, 2009). The enhancement of the crisis resolution framework is particularly important in the wake of the global financial crisis, which demonstrated the potential severity, and reach of the collapse of systemically important financial institutions.

7.4.3 *Increasing competition*

A common proposition in economics is that, all things being equal, competition leads to optimum solutions in terms of wealth creation and consumer welfare. In the financial sector the underlying premise is that increasing competition will provide expanded financial services at a lower cost and therefore enhance domestic resource mobilization. An important assumption that underlies this proposition is the absence of information asymmetries or costs – and yet we have seen in Section 7.3 that in financial markets, information costs can be pervasive with significant adverse consequences on resource mobilization. The second key challenge in enhancing domestic resource mobilization in Zambia is therefore that of ensuring that there is effective competition in the financial sector. This should involve more effective oversight of the financial sector by the Zambia Competition and Consumer Protection Commission (ZCCPC) that protects consumers against predatory lending practices and the abuse of bargaining power by financial institutions.

It is also important that structural factors that contribute to high transaction costs in the financial sector are also addressed. This includes addressing the high legal costs that are associated with entering and exiting financial contracts, in terms of both financial outlays and time taken, and developing the insurance industry so that it is better able to contribute to the management of liquidity risk and provide a more reliable source of long-term funding. In this regard, strengthening the Pension and Insurance Authority is critical by enhancing its regulatory framework and ensuring that it has the necessary complement and calibre of staff will be critical for further deepening of the financial sector. The solvency of long-term pension funds, both public and private, also needs to be addressed by transforming schemes from defined benefit to defined contribution schemes and by increasing contributions to close actuarial deficits.

Again, the programmes adopted under the FSDP II offer an important platform to address some of these issues. Under the goal of increasing competition, activities under FSDP II include: (1) increasing market efficiency through better collateral registration and enforcement as well as the enhancement of consumer protection; (2) increasing transparency by enhancing credit reference services and strengthening the legal and regulatory frameworks for their provision; (3) developing human capital in the financial sector and improving financial literacy to enhance the knowledge and use of financial services; and (4) streamlining the role of state-owned financial institutions. Properly implemented, these measures are all-important in improving the efficiency of the financial intermediation process, again because they will tend to lower both agency and asymmetric information costs.

7.4.4 *Financial inclusion*

Access to financial services in Zambia remains a significant challenge. The overall level of access of adults to both formal and informal financial services remains low at 37.3 per cent in 2009, up from just 33.7 per cent in 2005. Access to formal financial services was much lower at 23.2 per cent in 2009 from 22.4 per cent in 2005, while the percentage of the adult population that was banked was just 13.9 per cent in 2009, down from 14.6 per cent in 2005. This low level of access to financial services in Zambia reflects a combination of factors that include: poor infrastructure, low savings, and high information costs. Increasing access to finance is, therefore, the third important challenge in deepening the financial sector and increasing domestic resource mobilization. This will require a significant investment in financial sector infrastructure and, given the fact that Zambia has one of the lowest population densities in sub-Saharan Africa, this will require a significant investment in technology. Increased savings will need to be encouraged by ensuring that financial savings are not punished, through the prevalence of negative real interest rates, particularly for small (non-corporate) depositors. In this regard, monetary policy has an important role to play in ensuring that inflation is maintained at low, single-digit levels.

There are a number of programmes currently being implemented that should help to expand financial inclusion and these include: (1) promoting the use of technology such as mobile banking and improving financial literacy; (2) strengthening the microfinance industry by enhancing prudential regulations and developing credit reference services for small borrowers; (3) enhancing rural finance through the use of innovative products such as warehouse receipts/certificates as collateral and identifying rural finance gaps in the agriculture supply chain; and (4) utilizing the development finance institutions to expand access to development finance as well as housing finance. Beyond these specific measures, it is important to note that financial inclusion is likely to be impacted by the other measures undertaken to improve market infrastructure as well as expand competition.

7.4.5 *Quis custodiet ipsos custodes – Who watches the watchmen?*

In the first or second century AD, the Roman satirist Juvenal posed the question of who would guard the guardians when reflecting on the impossibility of enforcing moral behaviour on women – his substantive point being that the guards would be equally susceptible to women's charms. In more modern times, this question has been posed in relation to the challenges of democratic governance and the need for the separation of powers. This quote has relevance for the financial sector as well, in that regulators also need to operate within a framework that is open, transparent and accountable to the public, because information asymmetries also impact on the ability of the regulatory authorities to perform their functions effectively.

The supervision of the financial sector, for example, impacts on resource mobilization (both domestic and external) because weak financial institutions ultimately lead to inefficient intermediation, higher costs, a narrower reach, and higher risks of default that can significantly set back financial sector development. This was demonstrated by the banking crisis that Zambia experienced in the mid to late 1990s and the more recent global financial crisis. The existence of information asymmetries means that the management of the incentive structures faced by different financial institutions and actors, including the regulatory authorities, is critical for the common good.

Monetary policy also has an important role to play in enhancing domestic resource mobilization. This is because a monetary policy framework that is characterized by an independent central bank with a credible and transparent decision-making process, can help alleviate information costs, strengthen the transmission of monetary policy and anchor inflation expectations at low levels. Low levels of inflation ultimately support the financial sector development and domestic resource mobilization by helping to maintain the value of money and thereby minimizing the tax associated with financial transactions using fiat money. In this regard, care should be taken to ensure that recent monetary policy measures, such as those taken to limit lending margins, are implemented in a manner that does not lead to financial disintermediation, but support financial inclusion and the core monetary policy goals of price and financial system stability.

7.5 Conclusion

The increased mobilization of financial resources is critical if Zambia is to finance the investment it requires to generate higher economic growth and achieve a significant reduction in poverty. The existence of significant information costs in the financial sector gives rise to conflicting incentives and coordination failures that hamper resource mobilization. The financial sector is also at the centre of the transmission mechanism of monetary policy and links macro-economic policies, namely the control of inflation and promotion of economic growth, to micro-economic policies relating to the allocation of resources and the access of households and firms to financial products and services.

The FSDP is an important framework for addressing the challenges faced by the financial sector in mobilizing internal and external resources. The specific focus on enhancing market infrastructure, competition issues, and financial inclusion, in the FSDP II offers prospect of changes that will help lower information costs in the financial sector and help to enhance the mobilization of both domestic and external resources for economic development more effectively. The development of the secondary market for government securities is also important, particularly for the mobilization of long-term resources. In this regard, efforts to review the tax structure, as well as to consolidate government bonds are important above and beyond their direct benefit to the mobilization of domestic and external resources.

The BoZ must, therefore, continue to play a central role in financial sector development because this has a direct impact on the efficacy of monetary and supervisory policy and the ability of BoZ to achieve its ultimate objective of price and financial system stability.

Appendix

Chronology of Selected Financial Sector Development Measures 1992–2013

Measure	Date
100% export retention scheme introduced for exporters	March 1992
Commercial Bank interest rates liberalized	September 1992
Unified exchange-rate system introduced	December 1992
Open market type operations in primary Treasury bill auctions introduced	January 1993
28-day Treasury bill auctions introduced	March 1993
91-day Treasury bill auctions introduced	August 1993
182-day Treasury bill auctions introduced	August 1993
Bank of Zambia foreign exchange dealing system introduced	December 1993
Foreign exchange Control Act revoked	January 1994
The Banking and Financial Services Act (BFSA) Chapter 387 of the Laws of Zambia enacted	June 1994
Government bond auctions introduced	December 1994
Daily BoZ open market operations in credit and deposit auctions introduced	March 1995
Off-tender (non-auction) window abolished. All Treasury bill auctions to be conducted with commercial banks	December 1996
The Bank of Zambia Act No. 43 of 1996 enacted	December 1996
Introduction of the Book-entry trading system in Government securities, with a view to improving secondary trading	August 1997
Government bonds listed on the Lusaka Stock Exchange (LuSE)	March 1998
18-month Government bonds re-introduced	October 1998
Re-admission of eligible institutional investors to directly participate in Treasury bill and Government tenders	April 1999
Implementation of risk-based supervision framework	1999
Zambia Electronic Clearing House established with the view to improving and modernizing the payment system	September 1999
Introduction of longer-term Government securities (273-day Treasury bill and 24-month Government bond)	October 2000
BoZ re-admits individuals and corporate entities into the primary auction of Government securities	April 2001

Measure	Date
BoZ re-opens the off-tender window for Government securities to the public on non-competitive basis	November 2001
BoZ implements Broad-based Interbank Foreign exchange Market	July 2003
Introduction of Real Time Gross Settlement System	June 2004
Introduction of 3 and 5 year Government bonds	August 2005
Introduction of 7, 10, and 15 year Government bonds	August 2007
Enactment of the National Payment System Act	2007
Reduction of statutory Reserve Ratio from 8% to 5% and core liquid assets ratio from 9% to 6%	2011
Increase in minimum capital requirements for local and foreign owned banks from the equivalent of $US2.4 million to $US20 million (K104 billion) and $US100 million (K520 billion) respectively	2012
Introduction of Bank of Zambia policy rate	April 2012
Debut Sovereign rating by Fitch and Standard and Poors	2012
Introduction of Statutory Instrument No. 33 as amended by Statutory Instrument No. 78 prohibiting the quoting and pricing of goods and services in foreign currency	2012
Introduction of lending margins for banks and non-bank financial institutions tied to the BoZ Policy rate. CB Circular No. 25/2012	December 2012
Increase in statutory reserve ratio from 5% to 8%	January 2013
Amendment of the Bank of Zambia Act 1996 to allow for the monitoring of Balance of Payments	2013
Introduction of Statutory Instrument No. 55 on the monitoring of Balance of Payments	2013
Launch of the International Finance Corporation (IFC) Medium-Term Note Programme with issuance of a debut K150 million bond (in rebased Kwacha)	September 2013

Notes

1. Director, Economics Department, Bank of Zambia.
2. In January 2013 the Kwacha was rebased by dividing all Kwacha values by 1,000. Data in this paper reflects un-rebased Zambian Kwacha.
3. Our definition of private sector credit includes lending to: private enterprises, public enterprises operating on a commercial basis; households; and non-bank financial institutions.

References

Akerlof, G. (1970). The market for lemons: Quality uncertainty and the market mechanism, *Quarterly Journal of Economics*, 84:3 488–500.

Beck, T., Maimbo S.M., Faye, I., and Triki, T. (2011). *Financing Africa: Through the Crisis and Beyond*. Washington, DC: World Bank.

Demirguc-Kunt, A., and Levine R. (eds) (2001). *Financial Structure and Economic Growth: A Cross-Country Comparison of Banks, Markets, and Development*. Cambridge, Massachusetts: MIT Press.

Diamond, D. (1984). Financial intermediation and delegated monitoring. *Review of Economic Studies*, 52: 647–664.

Diamond, D. (1996). Financial intermediation as delegated monitoring: A simple example. *Federal Reserve Bank of Richmond Economic Quarterly*, 82:3 51–66.

Foster, V., and Dominguez, C. (2010). Zambia's infrastructure: A continental perspective. *Africa Infrastructure Country Diagnostic (AICD)*. Washington, DC: World Bank.

Freixas, X., and Rochet, J. (2002). *Microeconomics of Banking*, 5th Edition. Cambridge, Massachusetts: MIT Press.

FSDP II Project Proposal (2009). FSDP Secretariat. Available at: <http://www.boz.zm/FSDP/FSDPProjectProposal.pdf> (last accessed March 2014)

Harris, M., and Raviv, A. (1991). The theory of capital structure, *The Journal of Finance*, 46:1 297–355.

Honohan, P., and Beck, T. (2007). *Making Finance Work for Africa*, Washington, DC: World Bank.

Jensen, M., and Meckling, W.R. (1976). Theory of the firm, managerial behavior, agency costs, and ownership structure. *Journal of Financial Economics* 3: 305–60.

King, R. G., and Levine, R. (1993). Finance and growth: Schumpeter might be right, *Quarterly Journal of Economics*, 32: 513–542.

Maimbo, S. M. (2002). The diagnosis and prediction of bank failures in Zambia, 1990–98, *Development Policy Review*, 20:3 261–278.

Martinez, J. (2006). Access to financial services in Zambia, *World Bank Policy Research Working Paper* 4061. Available at: <http://www.ksri.bbs/files/research02/wps4061.pdf>

Ministry of Energy and Water Development (2010). *The study for power system development master plan in Zambia*.

Rajan, R., and Zingales, L. (1998). Financial dependence and growth. *American Economic Review*, 88: 559–587.

Ross, S. A. (1973). The economic theory of agency: The principle's problem, *The American Economic Review*, 63:2 134–139.

Shleifer, A., and Vishney, R.W. (1997). A survey of corporate governance. *The Journal of Finance*, Vol. LII:2 737–783.

Townsend, R. (1979). Optimal contracts and competitive markets with costly state verification. *Journal of Economic Theory*, 21: 265–93.

World Bank (2009). *Zambia – Second Investment Climate Assessment: Business Environment Issues in Diversifying Growth*. Washington, DC: World Bank.

8

Post-crisis Financial System Regulation: Implications for Zambia

Austin Mwape

8.1 Introduction

This chapter is about lessons learned from the global financial crisis and how they can help structure regulation and supervision of banks in Zambia. The crisis has been an advanced economy phenomenon and, to a large extent, post-crisis reforms are motivated by the need to fix what went wrong in those economies. It is quite clear that the reform agenda has gone global and there is a desire to have the new standards applied uniformly across jurisdictions. In embracing the unavoidable, countries such as Zambia have a responsibility to meaningfully assess the implications of these reforms on their financial sector, bearing in mind the different stages of financial sector development and the unique macro-economic circumstances. This philosophy has guided the views expressed in this chapter.

The chapter is divided into eleven sections. Section 8.1 gives a short introduction, while Section 8.2 gives some basic principles of financial sector regulation, effectively offering some perspective to the remainder of the chapter. Sections 8.3 to 8.8 give an overview of the Zambian financial system focusing on financial depth, development complexity, competition, and how the system weathered the global financial crisis. Sections 8.9 and 8.10 examines the new global thinking on financial system regulation post-global financial crisis and analyses the implications of the new thinking and the emerging challenges for financial system regulation and supervision in Zambia. Section 8.11 offers some concluding thoughts.

8.2 Basic principles of financial regulation

Following the global financial crisis of 2007–09, there is now no ambiguity in that the goal of all development effort is the growth of the real economy, and that the financial sector is only useful to the extent that it helps deliver stronger and more secure long-term growth. Financial intermediation is necessary for economic growth. However, the financial sector needs to be regulated so as to keep it safe and stable. The crisis has exposed the importance of the quantum and quality of regulation as opposed to the pre-crisis view that the reduction of the burden of regulation would inevitably allow the financial sector to deliver more growth. As noted by many observers, it is now evident that financial markets do not always self-correct, that signs of instability are not easy to detect in real time and that the costs of instability can be huge[1].

In effect, a revisit of the basic rules that guide the regulation and supervision of banks has become inevitable if the risk of financial instability is going to be reduced or meaningfully managed going forward. This calls for a multifaceted intervention structured around strong governance institutions and arrangements. Structuring of the ground rules for a good governance environment engages several stakeholders including, among others, lawmakers, politicians, private sector and the public.

The global financial crisis aside, the experience of bank failures in Zambia during the mid-1990s, and the impact that these failures had on small depositors and the disruption in liquidity provisioning to needy sectors, are still fresh in the minds of many.[2] Therefore, enhancements in the governance of banks and other financial institutions are seen as a possible remedy for reducing the probability of a recurrence of such events.

Clearly, financial stability is about resilience and measures to facilitate this should be put into place well in advance. Capital, liquidity, sound infrastructure and strengthened resolution arrangements are just some of the critical elements that need to be solidly in place. An array of policies remains key to ensuring financial stability with the micro- and macroprudential dimensions attracting most of the attention in the post-crisis era. To complement these, good monetary and fiscal policies are important for consumer protection, safeguarding of the financial infrastructure, and improved market discipline through enhanced transparency and strong accounting standards. These are key contributors to financial stability and it is for this reason that key principles, meant to help minimize financial instability, are structured around these areas.

Because financial stability concerns have become a global phenomenon, global basic principles have also been designed to help guide the structure of bank regulation and guide the conduct of supervision. While uniformity in application of these rules is not a norm, consistency and alignment to the rules by jurisdictions is encouraged in order to reduce incentives for regulatory arbitrage across jurisdictions.

The Basel Core Principles for Effective Banking Supervision constitute the most recognized and accepted minimum standards for sound supervisory practices and are considered universally applicable. The September 2012 version of the standards has incorporated lessons from the recent global financial crisis and other important regulatory developments. The revised principles have been reorganized to highlight the difference between what supervisors do and what supervisors expect banks to do. They have embraced emerging trends to accommodate systemically important banks; macropru-dential issues and systemic risk; crisis management, recovery and resolution; and corporate governance, disclosure and transparency.

There are 29 Principles, split into two thematic groups with Principles 1–13 addressing supervisory powers, responsibilities and functions, while Principles 14–29 address supervisory expectations of banks, emphasizing the importance of good corporate governance and risk management as well as compliance[3]. This chapter therefore highlights, in Section 8.8, the issues that arise within the wide variety of institutional settings, historical context and political environment in which banks operate in Zambia within the locale of the new standards and principles as promulgated by the Basel Committee on Banking Supervision (BCBS).

8.3 The Zambian financial system: Overview of how it weathered the financial crisis

8.3.1 *Key policy issues*

Patrick Honohan (2007) notes that the desire of any developing country is to structure policy interventions in the financial sector that will help it transform in a manner that ensures that modern technology, organizational innovation, and internationalization are exploited to the maximum in a manner that ensures that investible funds are well allocated to underpin growth and to protect against any future risk.[4]

He suggests a two-pronged approach for policy in designing a framework that would help strengthen African financial sectors:

- Long-term growth requires focusing on the larger and more formal parts of the financial system.

- As growth-enhancing policies begin to have their effects, improving the access of low-income households and micro-entrepreneurs to finance should become an additional central focus of financial sector policy.[5]

By implication, policy intervention should focus on those measures that would 'speed' up the deepening of the larger formal components of the financial system. In this regard, focusing on measures that would enhance the operations of the banking sector would be an appropriate policy strategy in Zambia considering that the banking sector accounts for more than 90 per cent of total financial sector assets.[6] This approach, however, does recognize the need for this policy focus to be complemented by deliberate measures to extend the reach of basic savings, payments, credit and insurance services for people on lower incomes and for the smallholder farms and micro-enterprises that provide their livelihood.

8.4 Financial system regulation and supervision in Zambia

In Zambia, financial system regulation and supervision targets the conduct of banking and financial services in order to maintain financial system stability[7] and provide safeguards for investors and customers of banks and financial institutions. As noted in Section 8.8, the framework leverages internationally accepted standards, particularly those promoted by the BCBS and sibling committees responsible for other components of the financial system.[8]

Whereas supervisory policies target the maintenance of financial system stability,[9] there is no formal criterion that defines what is meant by 'financial system stability' in any of the statutes concerned with the regulation of the various components of the financial system in Zambia. For this reason, there is inbuilt discretion in the application of this terminology by authorities.

The type of financial service being provided determines the appropriate authority responsible for regulating a financial service provider. Consistent with this, companies conducting banking business and certain defined financial services are regulated under the Banking and Financial Services Act (BFSA) with the Bank of Zambia being the principal supervisory authority. Other authorities regulating and supervising other financial service providers include the Pensions and Insurance Authority (PIA), the Securities and Exchange Commission (SEC), and the Ministry of Finance.

8.5 Structure of the Zambian banking sector

During the past two decades, the banking sector in Zambia has experienced substantial structural changes, partly driven by the changes in the general economic environment. Changes in the performance of the Zambian economy, determined particularly by the mining sector, have been the key drivers of

Figure 8.1 Personal (per cent of net loans & advances), and non-performing loans (per cent of net loans and advances)

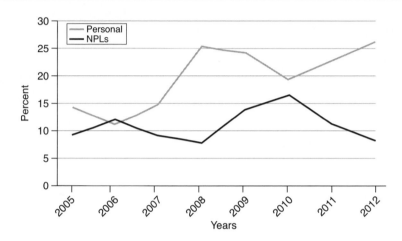

this change. Improvements in the supervisory and regulatory architecture, including the modernization of the Bank of Zambia (BoZ) Act and the Banking and Financial Services Act (BFSA), were also a factor. In particular, the BFSA was substantially revised and updated in 1995 and later refined in 2000 and 2005 following the Zambian banking problems of the mid-1990s.

As returns on Treasury bills (TBs) declined over the years and the household and corporate balance sheets strengthened, there was a significant shift

Figure 8.2 Net loans and advances (per cent of total assets) and Treasury bills (per cent of total assets)

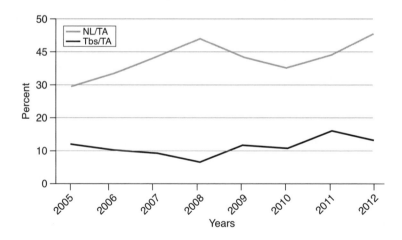

towards credit expansion, particularly with the salary-based (personal) loans, a new innovation, increasing from 11.3 per cent in 2006 to account for about 25.6 per cent of the banking industry's total loans as of the end of December 2008. The proportion slightly declined between 2008 and 2010, possibly on account of lagged spillover effects of the global financial crisis, before reverting to 26.2 per cent as at end December 2012 (Figure 8.1).

As banks appeared to reposition following the spillover effects from the global financial crisis, between 2008 and 2010, net loans as a proportion of total assets decreased to 35 per cent at end December 2010 after registering an increasing trend between 2005 (29.7 per cent) and 2008 (44.3 per cent). Net loans have since recorded some recovery reaching 45.6 per cent by end December 2012. Treasury bills (TBs), as proportion of total assets, eased up to reach 13 per cent at end December 2012 from a low 6.8 per cent in 2008, after steadily declining from 12 per cent registered in 2005 (Figure 8.2).

Increased fiscal discipline on the part of the Zambian Government reduced the attractiveness of TBs as an investment option. Conversely, private sector credit as a percentage of GDP has been steadily increasing over the years, peaking at 14.3 per cent at end December 2008 before declining to 10.7 per cent at end December 2010, following the global financial crisis. Private sector credit has since recovered to 13.5 per cent at end December 2012 and now exceeds the pre-crisis levels of 7.3 per cent and 9.3 per cent of GDP achieved in 2005 and 2006 respectively. The December 2012 figure is still marginally below the 14.3 per cent peak attained in 2008 (Figure 8.3).

Figure 8.3 Bank deposits, bank assets, and banking claims on the private sector as per cent of GDP

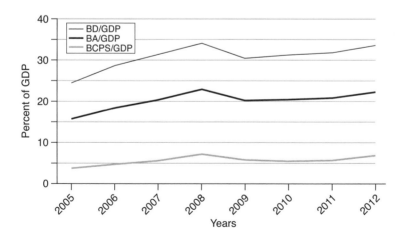

Generally, the sector was growing with both the ratio of bank assets and bank deposits to GDP showing remarkable growth after recording declines in the 1990s. Bank assets as a ratio of GDP grew by 6 percentage points to above 30.9 per cent in 2012, from about 24.3 per cent in 2005. Bank deposits as a ratio of GDP also grew by about 5 percentage points to 22.7 per cent in 2012 from 17.2 per cent in 1998. These positives aside, access to finance remains a challenge in Zambia with 62.7 per cent of the household sector (Zambian adults) still having no access to finance in 2009.[10] This, however, does present an improvement over the 2005 figure of 66.3 per cent of Zambian adults being financially excluded.[11]

8.6 Financial soundness indicators[12]

8.6.1 *Capital adequacy*

Zambia's industry average regulatory capital to risk-weighted assets ratio (CAR) at 24.4 per cent was above the SADC average of 19.9 per cent as at end September 2010 (see Figure 8.4).

Zambia had the highest core (Tier 1) capital to risk-weighted assets ratio in SADC at 20.3 per cent compared with the regional average of 15.9 per cent.[13]

The two ratios also favourably compare with the BCBS set standard of 8 and 4 per cent respectively. The higher ratio levels should be expected given the high proportion of Government Securities (GS), particularly TBs, on banks' balance sheets in Zambia. GSs receive a risk weight of zero in the capital adequacy computation. TBs as a ratio of total assets have been on an increasing trend since 2008 (Figure 8.2). The high ratios do not

Figure 8.4 Capital adequacy ratio at September 2010

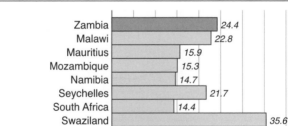

necessarily provide a positive spectacle as they indicate increasingly constrained credit to the private sector with potentially negative consequences on growth.

8.6.2 *Quality of assets*

Net non-performing loans (NPLs) to total loans at 15.8 per cent remained high and way above the SADC average of 5.9 per cent as at end September 2010. Two banks in Zambia, one local- and one foreign-owned, accounted for 68 per cent of the banking sectors total.

8.6.3 *Earnings and profitability*

Zambia's banking sector earnings and profitability improved with return on assets (ROA) recovering to 3.1 per cent in 2010 after experiencing a decline to 1.3 per cent from 4.7 per cent in 2009 and 2008 respectively. Over the same period, the average SADC region ROA ratios declined to 2.4 per cent in 2010 from 5.1 per cent in September 2008. This ratio was a marginal improvement on the 2.3 per cent recorded in September 2009. Zambia's average ROA for 2010 was also marginally above the average recorded by SADC countries.

Zambia's banking industry return on equity (ROE) also significantly recovered in 2010 to 17 per cent after registering a 29.7 percentage point drop to 3.2 per cent in 2009 from 32.9 per cent recorded in 2008. The average ROE for SADC in 2010 at 22.9 per cent was an improvement over the 2008 21.1 per cent ROE recorded in 2009. This, however remained below the 30.5 per cent ROE recorded in September 2008. For 2009 and 2010, Zambia's ROE remained below that of the SADC average.

8.6.4 *Liquidity*

Zambia's banking industry's average liquid assets to total assets ratio of 43.4 per cent was quite high and was above the regional average of 27.9 per cent as at end September 2010. Excess liquidity phenomenon is quite a common feature across the region and in most African financial markets.

8.7 Financial depth, development and complexity

8.7.1 *Financial depth*

The trend in financial depth of the Zambia financial sector has fluctuated with the ratio of M2 to GDP[14] remaining within the 15 per cent to 25 per

Figure 8.5 Financial depth

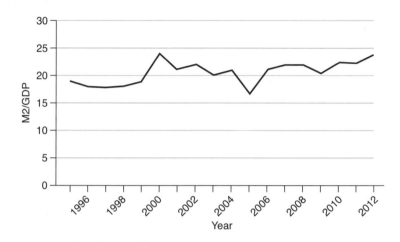

cent band between 1995 and 2008 (see Figure 8.5). There was a notable upward trend from 1996–2000 before the ratio fell. However, since 2005 the ratio has been steadily increasing to reach 23.8 per cent at end December 2012. The average ratio of liquid liabilities to GDP in Zambia has, however, remained consistently below the 32 per cent average in Africa – 49 per cent in East Asia and Pacific and 100 per cent in high-income countries (Honohan (2007), p. 27).

The decline in the ratio in the early and mid 1990s was partly due to the banking sector crisis, which saw the closure of close to ten banks, which collectively accounted for about 8 per cent (7.8 per cent) of GDP[15]. The bank closures impacted adversely on both the stock of deposits and private sector credit in Zambia, considering that the closed banks accounted for about 25 per cent of the banking sector's liquid liabilities.[16].

Recently, however, both deposits and private sector credit have been growing at a relatively accelerated rate (see Figure 8.3) with the entry of new banks, which by the end of 2012 had increased to 19 from 12 in 2000.

8.7.2 Financial development

The ratio of bank claims on the private sector to nominal GDP is used to measure financial development. This ratio gives some indication of the extent to which economic activity in the private sector, and indeed the economy, is financed by the banking system.[17]

Indications are that the financial sector has been developing with a sustained upward trend, notable from 2003. The ratio has increased to 13.5 per cent in 2012 following a decline during the post global financial crisis

Figure 8.6 Financial development

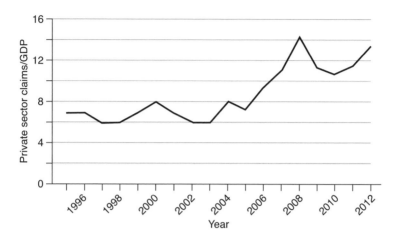

period when ratios of 11.4 per cent and 10.7 per cent were recorded in 2009 and 2010 respectively as against the period peak ratio of 14.3 per cent in 2008 (Figure 8.6).

8.7.3 *Financial complexity*

The Zambian financial sector has become relatively more complex over the years with the ratio of currency to M1[18] registering a steadily declining trend over the years to reach 33.8 per cent in 2012 from a peak of approximately

Figure 8.7 Financial complexity

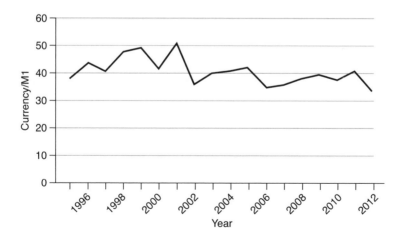

51 per cent in 2001. This ratio had been on an increasing trend from the 1990s until the early 2000s (Figure 8.7).

8.8 Competition

Theory suggests that competition among banks does have implications for risk-taking behaviour, financial regulation as well as financial stability. Competition is good, particularly taking into account the concern that the cost of borrowing and bank charges in Zambia are very high.

Zambia has, in the recent past, experienced a second wave of interest in the banking sector with the number of licensed banks increasing to 19 in 2012 from 12 in 2000. This is an increase of about 58 per cent over a relatively short period (12 years). There are a number of divergent views on the implications of this development on competition in the Zambian financial sector.

There is a school of thought that advocates for the increase in the nominal number of banks as a possible solution to the high cost of doing business within the banking sector. This view posits that numbers will increase competition and thus cause banks to improve efficiency and reduce costs. Competition is effectively viewed in the narrow sense where increased nominal numbers inevitably translates into an increase in effective competition. It is conceivable however that the new entrant(s) could fail to meaningfully contribute to the sector becoming contestable.

In Zambia, segmentation is quite apparent in the banking sector, with discrimination and differentiation in terms of products, services and related costs quite evident across segments (Mwape 2005). For this reason, the impact of new entrants on competition is likely to be different depending on the segment affected by such entrants. Entry into the dominant segment, comprising mainly of subsidiaries of large internationally active banks, will probably yield positive results on the general competition in the industry because such entrant will be contestable should issues of collusion be assumed away.

On the other hand, entry at the tail end of the banking sector may not meaningfully impact on competition for the sector. In effect, the tail-end segment of the banking sector competes for the residual business, which is characterized by higher inherent risks. Expected returns will, by design, be low, implying that new entrants may have a higher probability of contributing negatively to financial sector stability. Such entry into the sector will inevitably increase the general cost of supervision as it will require enhanced oversight.

For this reason, one would support the view that for competition to be meaningful in the financial sector, measures that impact on size and scale of operators in the non-contestable tail end of the banking sector may be required. For example, the recent consolidation of the Nigerian banking system resulting from the increase in minimum capital requirements is seen by some commentators as a possible way of reducing rent-seeking and increasing professionalism by the elimination of numerous inherently inefficient small banks.[19]

Consequently, the argument for or against entrance into the banking sector does not have clear-cut answers. The issue of competition and whether or not the Zambian banking sector is overbanked requires a tailor-made solution taking into account the uniqueness of the Zambian banking sector. The sector does need new players to contest certain segments. In the same vein, entry into some other segments needs to be streamlined given the lack of contestability and the implicit higher supervisory costs associated with such entrants.

8.9 New global thinking on financial sector regulation post-crisis: Implications for Zambia

8.9.1 *Governance failure and the global financial crisis*

The G20 London summit of 2009 identified major failures in the financial sector and in financial regulation and supervision as having been fundamental causes of the global financial crisis. There has therefore been a shift in policy design with a view to address the weaknesses identified as inherent to the current regulatory architecture. A key objective of current reform proposals is to minimize the risk of a repeat of a global crisis of the scale witnessed in 2007.

8.9.2 *Impact of first- and second-round effects of the crisis*

In Zambia, given the relatively weak financial market linkages with the global economy and the recently enhanced capital adequacy levels in the financial system, the financial sector reasonably escaped the first-round effects of the financial crisis, with the financial condition of the banking sector remaining good with average capital adequacy levels for the sector at 16 and 10 per cent for Tier 2 and Tier 1 respectively in the immediate aftermath of the crisis.[20] However, capital adequacy aside, the Zambian banking sector remained vulnerable to second-round effects with the quality of the banking sector's loan book deteriorating. NPLs, as a per cent of net loans, increased to 14.1 per cent at end December 2009 from 7.7 per cent at end December 2008 respectively. NPLs continued to deteriorate, peaking at 16.8 per cent at end December 2010. The quality of the loan book has, however, been improving during the post-crisis period with the ratio of NPLs to net loans and advances declining to 11.4 per cent and a 8.6 per cent as at end December 2011 and 2012 respectively. (Figure 8.1)

8.9.3 *Lender of last resort and crisis management*

The global financial crisis has witnessed notable innovation in central bank relations, not only with the traditional banking sector, but also with the entire corporate world. Various rescue financial packages were devised that covered a whole range of financial and non-financial corporate entities in a bid to salvage the imminent free-fall of the financial system. In effect, the conduct of monetary policy and the lender-of-last-resort (LOLR) function were revolutionized.

Zambia does not have tested and well-structured contingency arrangements to deal with either solvency or liquidity problems of a systemic nature in the financial sector. Lessons learned from the global financial crisis reveal the importance of flexibility and creativity in a central bank faced with a crisis situation. Central banks in advanced economies have been credited with being creative and forceful in extending their mandates to address the recent financial crisis.[21] This ability has implications on future governance arrangements surrounding central bank operations.

Leverage and discretion of the form exercised by advanced-economy central banks would create a serious source of risk of abuse should attempts be made to replicate such initiatives in environments with weak governance institutions. For such discretion to be transposed and embraced in jurisdictions such as Zambia it is necessary to design an attendant robust accountability framework to go with it. Effectively, the entire legal and general governance framework relating to the financial system will have to undergo significant review in order to ensure that, should such a need ever arise, there will be in place adequate firewalls to enhance transparency and *ex-post* accountability.

These concerns aside, the BoZ should be in a position to supply liquidity efficiently when markets, and particularly solvent institutions under its supervision, are under stress.[22] Experience of tensions in the advanced financial markets have confirmed the need for central banks, irrespective of the depth and development of the financial markets they oversee, to review their capacity to provide liquidity broadly and flexibly under stressed conditions. During the immediate post-crisis period, the Zambian financial sector had evidence of emerging problems, particularly in the quality of loans.

At the time, the emerging problems appeared to be localized to a few banks – i.e. both local and foreign. However, it is quite clear that this development posed a serious source of risk to the entire financial system. For this reason, the medium- to long-term require a coordinated initiative and response in the form of robust arrangements to deal with banks that may become weak on account of the adverse spinoffs from future global financial crisis or indeed any other externality.

Such arrangements would require Treasury (Ministry of Finance) involvement as they may concern insolvency issues of a systemic nature, which BoZ may not be in a position to legally address, coupled by balance sheet limitations. Inevitably, there will be a need to strengthen the framework for dealing with failure resolution, deposit insurance, cross-border arrangements for dealing with foreign-owned banks that may be facing stressed states, and so forth. The task for BoZ will therefore be to ensure that these initiatives are embraced, localized, and implemented in a timely manner to give assurance that BoZ and government will be in a position to deal with external systemic sources of stress to the financial system.

A major challenge for BoZ will relate to its ability to deal with distortions arising from the segmentation problem inherent to the availability of liquidity and functioning of the inter-bank market in Zambia. On an aggregate level, there is evidently excess liquidity in the inter-bank market but with distortions in the ability of banks to access it at the micro level due to a variety of factors, including current asymmetries relating to information on the existing financial condition of banks. Such asymmetries are likely to grow in crisis states.

Emergency liquidity assistance arrangements should accommodate 'partial' or segmented funding constraints, as these remain a source of systemic problems. Special arrangements for segments of the banking sector have to be structured carefully and possibly discreetly in order to manage the risk of possible stigma. Stigma sometimes sends the wrong signal that banks accessing assistance from BoZ are weak, even if such assistance is being extended under well-structured standing facilities for meeting fractional funding needs by banks. Such perceptions may impair the effectiveness of these initiatives. There will also be issues of moral hazard arising from such arrangements that will require to be managed.

8.9.4 *Financial Sector Contingency Plan*

In its 2010 budget, the Government of Zambia announced that, in consultation with the BoZ, it would embark on putting in place a Financial Sector Contingency Plan (FSCP) to address the systemic stability risk posed by the global financial crisis. The expectation was that the Treasury (MOF) would assumes a more active role in meeting the funding needs of a rescue package where this is found to be necessary.

It was also intended that the Treasury assume an equally active role in rescuing systemically important institutions that are insolvent but are found to be *too big to fail*. This is because a systemic problem in the financial sector could overwhelm the capacity of BoZ balance sheet to accommodate it. This reasoning is consistent with the principles on which stimulus packages in developed financial markets were framed, where such packages were firmed up with the financial backing of the Treasury.

This proposal comes with its own challenges in countries such as Zambia where the Treasury faces serious budgetary constraints. The ability of the Treasury to source funding in a *timely* manner for a rescue package for the financial sector, should such a need arise under present arrangements, remains questionable. Additionally, the fact that interventions of this nature inevitably entail the commitment of public funds to rescue mismanaged private interests, the conditions under which such bailouts are made will also be important. Logically, the Treasury will be interested in assurance that public funds made available in this manner are recoverable. Inevitably the robustness of the contingent safeguards surrounding such bailout initiatives will be critical.

Developed economies are able to mobilize resources on the international financial markets more easily than economies such as Zambia. Even though Zambia now has a credit rating which has, in principle, made it relatively easier for a country like Zambia to tap into the international financial markets for funds in times of need, a credit rating on its own may not guarantee access to such funds in states where the fundamentals in a country are not favourable. Even if Zambia can borrow, the price for such debt would be affected by the unfolding dynamics in the commodities (copper) markets and the perceived impact on the long-term financial strength of the country. Clearly, therefore, mobilizing resources in a timely and cost-efficient manner, to finance a rescue package for the financial sector by the Treasury, will remain a major challenge.

In practice, complementary funding contingent solutions have to be structured to address this problem. Such solutions may have to deviate in some way from the common arrangements popular in advanced economies in which the Treasury is playing a significant primary role financially. In Zambia, the interim role of the Central Bank in the financing and management of a possible rescue of the financial sector in the case of a systemic threat, should it arise, may have to be enhanced in a material way.

For example, a contingent rescue plan can be backed by the balance sheet of the Central Bank during the intervening period, given the reality that the Treasury would not be in a position to provide the required financial resources on a scale similar to the packages that were rolled out in advanced economies in a *timely* and *cost-effective* way.[23] The Treasury, however, could still assume a residual role in that it will forgo the potential dividend that BoZ is required to declare should the Central Bank make a loss on account of such financial intervention. Further, the Central Bank's rescue-related expenses could be appropriated as a government liability redeemable post-crisis. This will enable the government to have time to structure reimbursement modalities from future budget cycles.

8.10 Post-crisis reforms and implications for bank regulation in Zambia

Generally, the proposed reforms are two-pronged, targeting both the micro and macro components of bank regulation. At the micro or bank level, regulation intends to raise the resilience of individual financial institutions to periods of stress. At the macro level, the objective is to address system-wide risks that can build up across the banking sector as well as the procyclical amplification of these risks overtime. The two approaches are interrelated with enhanced resilience at the micro level contributing to reduction in risks of system-wide shocks. The issues are discussed *seriatim* below, not necessarily in their order of importance.

8.10.1 *Strengthening the capital base of financial institutions*

A key contributor to the global financial crisis was the excess build-up in off- and on- balance sheet leverage at financial institutions with the attendant gradual erosion of the level and quality of the capital base.[24] This culminated in the inability of banks to effectively absorb financial losses.

For this reason, the new rules prescribe capital adequacy requirements for banks and financial institutions that are significantly above those applied in the past, emphasizing the enhancement of the quality and quantity of Tier 1 capital.[25] In addition, a *dynamic* capital mechanism meant to generate an additional buffer within the Tier 1 capital band at the top of the cycle has been introduced.[26] In effect, the new reforms have made common shares and retained earnings the predominant form of Tier 1 capital.[27]

In Zambia, concerns currently exist regarding the quality and transparency of capital at banks and financial institutions. In particular, the quality of retained earnings poses challenges due to difficulties in the provisioning practices and inadequate enforcement of the provisioning regulations. The quality of the accounting infrastructure has also been an issue in certain instances due to absence of arm's length relationships between some financial institutions and their external auditors. Further, historically, there has been a paucity of accounting skills in Zambia, which has also impacted on the effectiveness of the internal audit and accounting function at particularly the small banks and corporations in general.[28]

Because of this, the capital cushion that some banks build up through retained earnings lacks transparency. This has made the role of the reserve account, created under Section 69 of the BFSA, questionable with regard to its ability to effectively complement common equity in banks' capital structure. This concern arises from the fact that the reserve account will have been built up from retained earnings whose quality remains questionable.[29] For this reason, the conclusion by BCBS that 'under the current capital standards banks could display strong Tier 1 ratios whilst having limited tangible common equity' does apply to some banks in Zambia.[30]

Another problem faced by the banking sector relates to high stamp duties on paid-up capital for corporations that is charged by Patents and Companies Registration Agency (PACRA). As recently as December 2010, PACRA was still charging a 2.5 per cent stamp duty on paid-up common equity. There is no doubt that the high stamp duties create incentives for banks and financial institutions to keep their common equity to the minimum prescribed by regulation and use retained earnings and general reserves to build up their Tier 1 capital base.

Further, banks and financial institutions are not required to have their authorized capital fully paid up as long as the minimum capital threshold required by regulation is met by the paid-up component of the authorized capital. Where authorized capital exceeds the required paid-up common equity as stipulated by regulation, banks will opt to hold paid-up common equity to the extent of the amount prescribed by regulation.

This problem is amplified by the fact that, in Zambia at the moment, there is no regulatory guidance on the proportion of minimum common shares that is required to be held by a bank in its Tier 1 capital structure. This is compounded by the way common shareholders' equity is defined by the Capital Adequacy Regulations (CAR), which, in addition to common shares, include contributed surplus, retained earnings, general reserves, and the statutory reserves fund. For this reason, the quality of capital, particularly Tier 1 capital at banks and financial institutions remains difficult to determine with certainty.

A key issue relates to some of the components included in primary (Tier 1) capital. Sections 16(e) and (f) of SI 184 include general reserves and statutory reserves as key components of primary or Tier 1 capital. A general reserve in the Zambian context relates to appropriated retained earnings that reflect additional potential losses based on 'an assessment of the bank's overall situation by its management'.[31] This capital component, going by the way SI 184 defines it, has elements of encumbrance and appears to be less subordinate than paid-up common shares. It is quite clear that this particular 'reserve' is specifically meant to accommodate possible losses that could not be specifically identified but that are estimated based on a bank or the experience of a financial institution's management. Effectively, it is an estimate based on 'expected losses', as inferred by management, and in a way may be likened to a specific loan-loss provision made by banks.

Assuming prudence in management's estimation of such a reserve, there should be minimal deviation of actual additional loss incurred by a bank that is not aligned to specific loan accounts, from the general loan loss provision as provided for in the reserve account. The availability of such a reserve to cushion unexpected losses is thus compromised. For this reason, the quality of this capital component comes into question, thus placing its eligibility to be included in Tier 1 capital in doubt. It is quite clear, therefore, that common equity remains subordinate to this reserve and hence superior from a prudential perspective.

Another concern that inevitably rationalizes the need to review SI 184 of 1995 relates to its failure to provide a definition for reserve account even though it does provide a definition of general reserves. On the other hand, the principle act, the BFSA, has no provision that refers to a general reserve. It rather has provisions that deal with the reserve account with a different definition from that given to general reserves in SI 184, the Capital Adequacy Regulations. Whereas the reserve account has attributes that would reasonably pass for consideration in Tier 1 capital, assuming away the underlying governance concerns of transparency and tangibility highlighted above, the definition of general reserves would not for the reason outlined below.

Basel Capital Accord (Basel 1) requires that, where general provisions or general loan-loss reserves do not reflect a known deterioration in the valuation of a particular asset or assets, such reserves will qualify for inclusion in Tier 2 and not Tier 1 capital.[32] Strictly speaking, the thrust of Basel 1, which is the basis on which the Zambian capital adequacy regulatory framework is designed, would be to exclude such capital from consideration as a Tier 1 component. Following from this, therefore, it is quite apparent that shortcomings do exist in the design of the current regulatory framework for capital adequacy.

Recent efforts to revise upwards the minimum paid-up capital for banks and other financial institutions have also had inherent implementation difficulties. In December 2006, the Bank of Zambia issued a Gazette Notice[33] revising the minimum required paid-up capital for banks and other classes of financial institutions. The required paid-up minimum capital for banks was increased to K12 billion from K2 billion.[34] However, Section 7 of the same Gazette Notice requires banks that do not meet the minimum capital requirements at the coming into force of the Notice to 'enter into negotiations with BoZ to progressively build up its *primary* capital and not *primary paid-up capital*'.

This requirement created problems in causing banks to increase their paid-up capital to K12 billion since primary capital as defined by SI 184 of 1995 is much broader than primary paid-up capital, which is just one among the other many components.[35] What this has meant is that banks have conveniently translated the required K12 billion minimum paid-up capital requirements to mean primary capital, which includes paid-up common equity plus other relatively less subordinate capital items already discussed.

The implications of this confusion can be seen from the obtaining regulatory capital positions for banks in Zambia as at end December 2009. Out of a total of 16 operating banks, nine – or 56 per cent – had paid-up common shares that were below the minimum required primary paid-up capital of K12 billion. This is in spite of the fact that all banks in Zambia were required to have increased their minimum capital requirements to the minimum prescribed by Gazette Notice No. 682 by 30 June 2008. Of the nine banks, four are subsidiaries of large internationally active banks operating in Zambia. On the other hand, should one interpret Section 7 of Gazette Notice No. 686 to be the relevant provision for compliance purposes, only one bank had the broader primary capital marginally below K12 billion as at end December 2009.

Clearly, a fresh review of the capital adequacy requirements in tandem with the proposals being made through the Basel group will be prudent and appropriate in the Zambian situation. Such review should have the objective of enhancing the need for banks to hold more common equity in their primary (Tier 1) capital structure and re-align Gazette Notice No. 682 to ensure that it addresses the intent of the revisions to the Capital Adequacy Regulation amendments of 2006, which was to increase the minimum primary paid-up capital that banks hold. The new capital requirements of 2012 have also not meaningfully addressed the technical challenges inherent in Gazette Notice No. 682.

It will also be necessary that existing disincentives that could be discouraging banks from holding relatively more common equity in their Tier 1 capital structures, such as PACRA stamp duties, are addressed through the financial sector reforms being spearheaded under the Financial Sector Development Plan (FSDP) phases. The reforms should also address matters relating to the auditing and accounting infrastructure. This could go a long way in making compliance relatively more cost-effective and manageable.

8.10.2 *Procyclical effects and capital requirements*

Basel II capital regime is considered to have inherent procyclical effects, and a concerted effort was made in the post-crisis period to adapt it so that procyclicality is avoided. This is in addition to the introduction of separate measures to achieve overt countercyclicality (Turner Review, p. 59). It has now been acknowledged that the way in which capital requirements and the actual level of capital vary through the business cycle is as important as the absolute minimum level of capital. Basel III has been designed to address this, amongst other problems. [36]

The present approach to capital adequacy regulation in Zambia, even though based on the Basel I framework, still has elements of risk sensitivity. The framework has inbuilt inherent procyclicality as it does produce somewhat higher capital requirements for financial institutions when economic conditions deteriorate as risks will have inevitably increased. It also logically follows that prudent financial institutions will be expected to become more cautious in the extension of credit during such downturns. Effectively, the quantum of credit to the private sector is likely to reduce during a downturn.

The immediate post-crisis period witnessed a decline in lending in Zambia. The proportion of net loans and advances to total assets, which had increased to 44.3 per cent in 2008, declined to account for 38.7 per cent in December 2009 – representing a decline of about 12 per cent or 5.6 percentage points. By the end of 2010, this ratio had declined to 35 per cent before recovering to 39 per cent and 45.6 per cent in December 2011 and 2012 respectively. In the same vein, the proportion of the less risky assets, Treasury bills (TBs), which had been on the decline, notably in 2007 (17.3 per cent) and 2008 (13.8 per cent), began to edge upwards to account for 25.5 per cent and 21.1 per cent in 2011 and 2012 respectively. This represents an increase of 52 per cent or 7.3 percentage points between 2008 and 2012 compared to a decline of 10.9 percentage points or 44 per cent between 2005 and 2008 (Figure 8.8).

Clearly, the banks' balance sheet structure was changing, a possible indication that banks were repositioning by partly shifting into a less risky asset, TBs, to accommodate medium-term lagged effects of the global financial crisis on business at the local level. In effect, the Zambian financial system remains vulnerable to cyclicality events arising from both external and internal sources.

The main feature of the proposed countercyclical capital regime is to have required and actual capital held by financial institutions increase in good

Figure 8.8 Net loans, advances, and Treasury bills as per cent of total assets

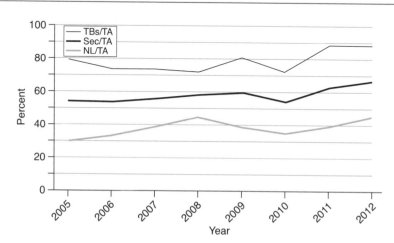

times when loan losses are below long-run averages. This, it is argued, would create capital cushions that could be drawn down during economic downturns as losses increase.[37] The benefits of this approach include the likely decrease in the probability of bank default given the better alignment of capital with expected default risk through the economic cycles. Such innovation will also minimize the need for public authorities to take intervening measures to prevent widespread bank failures of systemic proportions, given that there will be a decrease in the probability of system-wide bank failures.

The proposed methodology requires the use of long-term data horizons to estimate probabilities of default, the introduction of a downturn loss-given-default (LGD) estimates and the appropriate calibration of the risk functions, which convert loss estimates into regulatory capital requirements.[38] Banks should be required to conduct stress tests that consider the migration of their credit portfolios in a recession.

To determine the appropriate levels of capital buffers and how to reasonably present the impact is basically a choice between discretion-based, as against formula-based, capital buffer determination regimes. Under the discretionary framework, authorities would use judgement and discretion to determine the required capital buffers having regard to the macro-economic cycle and other macro-prudential concerns. As regards the formula-driven system, a predetermined metric will determine the appropriate capital buffer for the individual banks as well as the financial system.[39]

The latter, metric-based approach would be the most attractive in the case of Zambia given the weak governance institutions (Mwape 2005). A subjective approach would be vulnerable to possible abuse given the risk of regulatory capture. The metric approach would, however, also face serious challenges, particularly in terms of data requirements and availability, in addition to the paucity of the appropriate modelling skills to accurately prescribe the necessary capital buffer requirements.[40] In light of these difficulties, *a blend* between the two approaches could be most appropriate for jurisdictions such as Zambia.

The dynamic provisioning concept, as applied by the Spanish, is another attractive regime. This regime uses a statistical method to allow for losses inherent in a portfolio that have not yet materialized with provisions building up higher than would normally be required during an economic upswing. The buffer built up during this period would consequently be available to absorb losses incurred during an economic downswing, effectively providing a cushion to the potential impact on capital during the downturn.

Dynamic provisioning, even though attractive, does pose serious challenges in terms of the potential impact it might have on perceptions in small, bank-dominated financial markets such as Zambia. The effective understatement of profits and consequently the capital adequacy obtaining at a bank through dynamic provisions may trigger asymmetric inferences by market stakeholders that may work against a bank. As markets develop and deepen, dynamic provisions may create noise that may destabilize an otherwise 'sound' financial institution and possibly pose risks to financial system stability. This framework would therefore require having a parallel sound framework to manage the inherent risk that come with the largely *ex-post* features given its reliance on past events to predict future likely losses in the banks.[41]

The other worry is that the regime rests on shaky robustness considering that it controls for certain present and future state dynamics in the financial system. Such dynamics may impact loan quality and effectively reduce, or indeed increase, loan-loss probability in a way that significantly deviates from the average exhibited over the relevant inference period. For example, the current Basel III initiatives and the follow-on refinements in the overall financial institutions' regulatory architecture post the global financial crisis are going to materially impact on the way banks are regulated. This will in turn also affect the conduct of business by banks. In effect, the loan-loss experience of the past decade may not accurately mirror the likely loan quality at banks in future states. Robust stress testing that captures a whole array of possible future states might be a more feasible solution.

8.10.3 *Offsetting procyclicality in published accounts*

Considering the attractiveness of including an overt countercyclical element in capital requirements, a problem arises regarding whether or not published accounts and the calculations of required capital by financial institutions should capture this. Basel II, under its *Market Discipline Pillar*, Pillar III, advocates for the periodic publication of financial institutions' accounts as a means for instilling transparency and consequently market discipline in the financial institutions. A forward-looking provisioning regime has become an attractive policy innovation following the global financial crisis. BCBS is thus advocating for a change in accounting standards towards an expected loss (EL) approach in order to 'improve the decision usefulness and relevance of financial reporting of stakeholders, including regulators'.[42]

It follows therefore that with an overt countercyclical element, the published accounts will include an adjustment for events whose occurrence is based on probability and expectations. Where the expected event for which adjustment has been taken infers adverse information, it may create damaging noise for the financial institution concerned and possibly the financial system. Whereas it is at present considered reasonable not to include anticipated or probable future events in published accounts for both the trading and banking books but to reflect the facts of the situation as at the balance sheet date,[43] the above proposals suggest otherwise.

There are arguments that suggest that the inclusion of an offsetting procyclicality element in the published accounts would create incentives for such accounts hiding the effects of bad management decisions. This would arise because a management that is able to make provision in advance for future possible losses could use such provisions to hide losses whose causes are idiosyncratic. The complexity of discerning and making a distinction between such losses and those that are due to externalities would pose serious challenges to both regulators and other stakeholders such as shareholders.

However, the mere existence of the risk of management hiding incompetence does not negate the need to have provisions that embrace possible future events arising from volatility-driven macro-economic dynamics. It might be possible to put in place a mechanism to broadly distinguish between states of systemic downturns and those of idiosyncratic developments that may adversely impact the financial condition of individual institutions. This should be the challenge for regulatory authorities going forward.

Even though this proposition sounds ideal, there are some concerns with regard to the inherent potential it has to fuel procyclicality. In the case of the banking book, it is argued that provisions in good times are likely to be below the expected losses that might arise from existing long-term loan contracts and from customer relations over a complete economic cycle. This may lead to relatively higher declared profits, which could generate a number of concerns.

Firstly, the higher profit levels will enhance financial institutions' lending capacity by enabling them to carry relatively more loans on the books as a result of higher capital levels arising from this profitability. The key concern is that the arising credit expansion may not be commensurate with the longer-term capital adequacy of the bank.[44] Secondly, the higher profits may translate into higher bonuses, thus possibly creating incentives for management to grow the asset base further. It is argued that published accounts will be able to address the management incentive whilst a countercyclical capital regime would be able to offset the first impact.[45]

Without delving too much into the details of the solutions to this problem, it is necessary to examine the relevance of this analogy to the Zambian situation. Loan contracts in Zambia are relatively short-term. Even though there is a notable lengthening of the loan period to terms exceeding one year in recent times, traditionally bank loan contracts have been relatively short-term in Zambia, as in most African financial markets.[46]

Therefore, in the long term, loan contracts are likely to be adjusted to take into account the changing circumstances during the short term and thus declared profits and the arising consequences on capital are likely to adjust in tandem with the dynamics in the economy. Even though a lag remains feasible between firming up of changed contracts and the changes in real economy dynamics, the short-term nature of the loan contracts provides a window for banks to adjust quickly. It is therefore possible for prudent institutions to adequately manage their loan book through the cycle with minimal procyclical effects on the condition of the bank. For this reason, the current practice of provisions reflecting known information on the quality of the loan book remains adequate in the Zambian environment at least for the medium term. As it is, based on this regime, banks have been able to carry reasonable provisions anchored on assessed present quality of the loan book.

In Zambia, banking activity is dominated by on-balance sheet transactions particularly in the banking book. Because of this, the transmission process for the global financial crisis has been relatively slow and hence reasonably predictable. It therefore follows that prudent financial institutions were able to reposition themselves to deal with the risks arising from the global financial crisis in a meaningful way. For this reason, micro aspects of risk management competence at the financial institution level remained relatively more important over the period of uncertainty. Regulatory focus and intervention while acknowledging the long-term importance of macro-prudential supervision will have to prioritize improving risk management at the institutional level in the medium term.

Having regard to the issues highlighted above, proposals to set aside a non-distributable *economic cycle reserve* while sounding plausible should be structured in such a way that it does not unnecessarily cause banks to unduly carry excess and idle capital on its books.[47]

Already banks and financial institutions in Zambia are required, under Section 69 of the BFSA, to maintain a Reserve Account to which a prescribed amount is transferred out of the net profits of each year before any dividend can be declared and after due provision has been made for tax.[48] Clearly the reserve fund does significantly complement the available cushion to a bank in times of stress. To the extent that the required minimum paid-up capital required by regulation is 'adequate', it becomes feasible to build up a reasonable reserve fund cushion during the times that banks are making profits. This arrangement carries some remote elements of procyclicality given the direct link of the reserve fund build-up to the profitable performance of a bank. Banks are normally profitable during the boom periods.

8.10.4 *Gross leverage ratio back stop*

BCB has agreed to introduce a simple, non-risk-based leverage ratio to supplement risk-based capital requirements. The ratio is meant to contain the build-up of excessive on- and off-balance sheet leverage in the banking system to avoid destabilizing the deleveraging process.[49] The case for a gross leverage ratio arose partly from the experience during the global financial crisis when assets considered to be low risk on account of their liquidity features turned out to be illiquid and thus riskier than initially envisioned. Effectively, banks discovered that the capital held against these assets was inadequate.

Further, the inbuilt judgement-driven capital allocation under some advanced modes of Basel II introduced disparities in assessed risk between banks and supervisors. This led to what the FSA describes as 'creeping regulatory concessions' on required capital. The simple leverage ratio is therefore considered as a backstop on this deficiency.[50]

In Zambia, CAR does not specifically require financial institutions to maintain a minimum gross leverage ratio. This appears to be a defect in design of the CAR (1995) rather than the intent of the law. Section 83(4) of the BFSA empowers BoZ to prescribe the minimum required regulatory capital for banks. According to Section 83(4), the minimum required regulatory capital to be prescribed by BoZ should not be less than 6 per cent of a bank's or financial institution's assets, contingent liabilities and other exposures. Effectively therefore, the law does put a *gross leverage ratio cap* on the required regulatory capital for banks.

The CAR regulations do not capture this legal dimension. It has therefore become feasible for a bank in Zambia to comply with present CAR requirements as prescribed by SI 184 while remaining in breach of the cap prescribed by the principle act under section 83(4). An adjustment for this requirement to the capital adequacy levels for banks in Zambia for the end period December 2009 showed that, if the requirements of Section 83(4) of the BFSA were to be enforced, five banks, three of which can be considered as being systemically important, would be found to have deficient capital.

The defect in the Statutory Instrument aside, it can be argued that a gross leverage ratio remains attractive in Zambia, particularly taking into account the data problems the country is likely to face should it prefer the relatively more sophisticated regimes under Basel II. The advantage with a gross leverage ratio is that it will be relatively easy to apply and monitor.

8.10.5 *Containing liquidity risk: in individual banks and at the systemic level*

The crisis demonstrated that strong capital requirements, even though a necessary condition for banking sector stability, are not sufficient on their own. They need to be complemented with a strong liquidity base backed by a robust supervisory oversight framework.

To address this problem, BCBS has been working on two regulatory standards for liquidity risk targeting internationally active banks. Firstly, a Liquidity Coverage Ratio[51] (LCR) has since been introduced in January 2013 aimed at promoting the short-term resilience of the liquidity risk profile of institutions by ensuring that they have sufficient liquidity to survive any acute stress scenario lasting for a month.[52] Secondly, a Net Stable Funding Ratio[53] (NSFR) is being floated, intended to capture structural issues related to funding choices. The idea of the NSFR is to promote resilience over longer-term horizons by creating additional incentives for banks to fund their activities with more stable sources of funding on an on-going structural basis.[54]

For Zambia, there is merit in considering the introduction of such a standard at the institutional level. Such a standard would be appropriate and preferred, given that liquidity concerns are generally structural in nature and not systemic, due to the historical excess liquidity that obtains in the Zambian financial system. It is necessary though that the value of the ratios as a means for identifying possible sources of macro-prudential liquidity risk is retained. This will continue to assist BoZ to devise appropriate measures to guide the management of such risks by individual banks or the system.

Funding source stability for banks and the system will be a key factor going forward and should therefore be a focus of regulatory innovation in Zambia.

8.10.6 *Institutional and geographic coverage: economic substance, not legal form*

The new capital and liquidity requirements discussed in the sections above might increase incentives for regulatory arbitrage with possibility of bank-like activities migrating outside the regulatory boundary to escape the new requirements.[55] Potential destination for such arbitrage activities would be the so-called 'shadow banking system' in which bank-like activities are carried out but are not subject to regulation.[56]

In Zambia, the impact of such migration on financial system stability will remain negligible in the medium term. As the case is with most African countries, the non-bank financial services sector remains a relatively small component of the formal financial system in Zambia. Banks presently dominate formal financial sector activity both in terms of assets and leverage.[57] Because of this, the adequacy of bank regulation remains the most important ingredient in the stability of the Zambian formal financial sector in the medium term. Further, the relatively more significant non-bank financial institutions – such as the Development Bank of Zambia (DBZ), the Zambia National Building Society (ZNBS) and the Zambia National Savings and Credit Bank (ZNSCB) – are now also regulated by the Bank of Zambia.

Additionally, the insignificance of the trading book for banks in Zambia, even though not ideal from a developmental perspective, will continue to shield the banking sector from exposure to this source of risk in the medium term. Moreover, there are now efforts being made to harmonize the different laws governing operations of different financial institutions under the Financial Sector Development Plan (FSDP). The affected laws include the BFSA, the Pensions and Insurance Act, the Securities Act and the Companies Act. It is also worth acknowledging that efforts to coordinate the supervision of financial institutions based on economic substance do exist through the collaborative MOUs that have been signed across regulatory authorities such as the Bank of Zambia, the Pensions and Insurance Authority and the Securities and Exchange Commission. Such interventions are likely to help deal with regulatory arbitrage between different authorities.

To this extent therefore, the regulatory boundary problem as presented in the advanced economies only remains important in the regulatory reform agenda for the longer term rather than within the immediate and medium term in countries such as Zambia. Conduits such as special investment vehicles (SIVs) and other forms of securitized lending that were common avenues for regulatory arbitrage in advanced financial markets are to a large extent not that developed in the Zambian financial markets.

8.10.7 *Deposit insurance and bank failure resolution*

Even though the new measures addressing capital, accounting, and liquidity coverage will reasonably help reduce failure probability, there will still remain a residual risk of bank failure that requires contingent measures. For this reason, deposit insurance will remain relevant to protect small depositors in bank failure states. Additionally, robust bank failure resolution will be necessary for the orderly winding up of failed banks.

Depositor confidence is important to the stability of the financial system. Authorities in advanced economies instituted extraordinary measures during the global financial crisis to ensure confidence by effectively extending deposit insurance to all deposits including those that were technically not covered under existing deposit insurance arrangements.[58]

Conversely, safety-net arrangements do affect incentives of both banks and their creditors particularly depositors. Banks will have the incentive to take on more risk where the risks of a run arising from confidence problems are reduced by deposit insurance. The opposite will happen where safety net arrangements are weak or non-existent. Depositors will also have little incentive to monitor banks where deposit insurance exists or strong safety-net arrangements are present. Barth, James, et al. (2006) notes that safety net arrangements, particularly deposit insurance, may facilitate risk taking to the extent that it encourages depositors to relax their monitoring efforts in addition to reducing or eliminating any risk premium in their cost of funds.

Plans to introduce deposit insurance in Zambia have been on the agenda for some time. There is already a Depositor Protection Bill, which provides for the establishment of a Deposit Protection fund and a Deposit Protection Corporation. The introduction of deposit insurance on its own might not significantly reduce the risk of failure of small banks (*Tinies*) in view of some structural problems, such as the distribution of deposit liabilities held by this category of banks. Banks that fit the 'small' or '*Tiny*' description in the Zambian context have notable funding diversification problems and have an inherently volatile deposit liability structure.[59] In these banks, institutional investors, who may not receive adequate coverage from the proposed deposit insurance scheme, do account for a significant proportion of deposit liabilities. In effect, Tinies will remain vulnerable to the risk of large deposit withdrawals by any one of the significant uninsured depositors responding to adverse information. This implies an inherent significant exposure to funding risk that could easily translate into liquidity distress.

In the context of Tinies, therefore, it is difficult to see how deposit insurance will remedy the volatile nature of the structure of their funding. These banks would have to rely on prudence in funding risk management at the institutional level with a leaning towards restructuring their liabilities so that deposit base is more diversified. Ingenuity in product design will also help to attract household depositors/borrowers, who tend to be more complacent not only because they are likely to be covered by the proposed deposit insurance scheme, but also because they tend to be less aware of the risks inherent at banks.[60]

In Zambia, this situation has meant that the costs of funds for some Tinies are much higher than the published average savings rates for the sector. This is because institutional depositors have the muscle to negotiate or even dictate higher than average rates on their deposits. In recent times, for example, it has become quite common for large depositors to request 'collateral' on their deposits with Tinies or banks that are wrongly or rightly perceived to be having problems. This arrangement further constrains the ability of the affected institutions to source funding from, say, the inter-bank market, where the pledged (encumbered) collateral would be the equivalent, in quality, to that which would be eligible for purposes of sourcing inter-bank liquidity.

Generally, however, it is important that a deposit protection scheme backed by a robust failure resolution regime is put in place as a means to enhance residual confidence problems at banks. This has proved to be a critical tool to deal with confidence problems even though it may not impact on institutions in the same way due to idiosyncratic factors such as the size of a bank.

8.10.8 *Macro-prudential analysis*

A deficiency that has been identified in today's approach to financial system regulation is the failure to acknowledge the importance of the link between macro-economic performance and financial system stability. Macro-prudential analysis should, according to present thinking, form the basis for a whole array of supervisory responses to developments in the economy that may adversely impact on financial system stability. This approach has rationalized the need to, among other things, extend regulatory concern to the role played in the financial system by different institutions, whether or not such institutions are at present subject to prudential requirements. The key issue of concern should be how such institutions are likely to contribute to systemic risk in the financial system.

In Zambia, this deficiency exists as present focus of regulation is on the financial condition and conduct of business by individual financial institutions with little structured focus on systemic issues. Admittedly, though, there is a semblance of *ex-post* inference made to concerns of a systemic nature in the banking and non-bank financial sectors. This is done by way of consolidation of some indicative variables such as the balance sheet, income statements, capital adequacy calculations, etc. What is currently missing, though, is the failure to analyze developments in key macroeconomic variables in a structured way with a deliberate alignment of such developments to the stability of the financial system. However, plans are in place to establish a function within BoZ to address this deficiency.

8.10.9 *Risk management and governance*

Even though there has been an acknowledgement of the need to shift focus from firm specific analysis to systemic developments, the need for improvements in the effectiveness of risk management and firm specific governance has been acknowledged as still vital to overall stability in the financial system. This is particularly important in the Zambian financial market, where firm specific problems are quite pronounced at some financial institutions due to weak governance institutions compounded by both regulatory and political capture factors.

There is evidence to suggest serious shortcomings in internal risk management at some institutions with glaring failings at board level. A catalogue of inspection reports at BoZ does indicate problems in the capacity and ability of some boards at both banks and non-bank financial institutions to identify and constrain excessive risk taking by institutions at the micro level. Such shortcomings and the failure to deal with them do create problems for regulation, as these practices tend to contaminate the financial system as they get transmitted to other institutions through bad precedence setting. To deal with this problem, regulatory innovation has turned to prefer a more active role for financial institution regulators in determining the technical competences of senior risk managers. The adequacy of the governance structures for risk oversight is also receiving attention with a desire to see a more direct relationship between senior risk management and board risk committees.

In Zambia, even though current laws require BoZ to subject all persons concerned in the management of a bank to be subjected to a fit and proper test, this has not been strictly followed.[61] In practice, this probity test has historically been restricted to mainly two positions in financial institutions – i.e. the Chief Executive Officer (CEO) and the Chief Finance Officer (CFO). In effect, banks have traditionally had great leverage in determining the suitability of persons they consider for any of the other managerial portfolios including that of risk management.

Further, the only committee at board level that may oversee the risk management issues, that is required by law to be in place at every bank, is the Audit Committee of the Board.[62] Where risk committees exist, this has basically been an internal governance arrangement of the bank concerned and not a measure prompted by law.

Clearly there will be a need for a closer review of the practice and the law to ensure that BoZ assumes more responsibility in these areas than is at present apparent from practice and law. Further, it will also be necessary for the BFSA to be amended so that the law officially acknowledges the growing importance of risk management in banks both at board and executive levels if high standards of risk management in banks and other financial institutions are to be achieved.[63]

8.10.10 *Regulation of large complex banks*

The story behind the recent global financial crisis is anchored on complexity and high leverage in the securitized model of credit intermediation in advanced economies. Central to the crisis origins was the trading book of banks and investment banks where large losses were incurred on structured credit and credit derivatives. Due to uncertainty of the exact scale of the potential losses, confidence in the financial markets became impaired, creating serious systemic liquidity problems.

Follow-on debate is focused on whether or not there should be institutional separation between narrow banking and investment banking particularly for regulatory purposes.[64] What is becoming a consensus is that there is a case for the review and determination of the appropriate relationship between the different types of banking and securities market activities going forward. It has also been argued that, whereas the risks posed by the securitized credit model should not be ignored, acknowledgement has also been made that banks can equally take excessive risk by making high-risk loans which they hold on their own banking book balance sheet, as much as acquiring securities originated by others. For this reason, due to the interconnectedness of modern financial markets, the solution will not necessarily lie in an exclusive approach, but rather focus should be on the extension of the regulatory boundary to cover all financial activity which might create systemic risk.

In the Zambian situation, this argument remains relevant. Whereas acknowledging the reality that the securitized credit model and the related problems it generated are primarily an advanced economy phenomenon, the reality that the banking book does generate risks that may pose risks of comparable magnitudes[65] makes the solutions being proposed and debated relevant. Going forward, regulation should focus on the risks that financial activity might generate whether or not such activity lies on or off the balance sheet of a regulated financial institution. Financial system systemic risk generation should also be a factor in the determination of which institutions to regulate whether or not such institutions qualify to be called banks or financial institutions in the strictest sense.

8.10.11 *Regulation and supervision of cross-border banks*

The recent global financial crisis has also raised questions with regard to the robustness of the existing regime for the regulation and supervision of cross-border financial institutions. The current regime has relied on the home supervisory authority to ensure soundness of the overall institution. It has been noted, mainly through the failure of Lehman Brothers, that global investment banks are inherently interconnected. This makes it difficult for individual national entities to survive when the group fails, even if such entities operate in subsidiary form, given the huge importance of confidence factors in the market.

This revelation is quite important for certain jurisdictions, Zambia included, where a sense of regulatory comfort has been derived from the legal requirement for internationally active banks and financial institutions to operate as subsidiaries and not as branches of their respective parent companies. By so doing, it has been felt that the extent to which the impact of failure at group level would be transmitted to the local subsidiaries will be limited with the subsidiary host authorities able to shield the local operation from the full impact of such failure. However, as the Lehman Brothers case has demonstrated, confidence factors can be equally important and may actually impact on the subsidiary operation in a manner similar to the effects that such failure would have on an entity operating as a branch.

Compounding this problem has been the questions recently being raised regarding the extent of operational independence of the subsidiaries of regional and international banks that have a presence in the Zambian financial market. A practice has been established whereby some financial institutions, banks in particular, have intra-group relations that BoZ view as not being conducted at arm's length. A case in point relates to existing intra-group management contracts that have been significantly contributing to the operating costs at some bank subsidiaries.

BoZ commissioned an investigation into the extent of the problem. It has been established, for example, that in 2009 management fees accounted for 9.3 per cent of the banking sector's operating expenses compared to 5.5 per cent in 2005.[66] Significantly contributing to the industry total growth rates were two foreign-owned banks that registered annual average growth ratios of 25 per cent and 15.6 per cent respectively. Further, it has also been established that, compared to salaries and employee benefits (SEB), management fees grew much faster in the period 2007–09 recording average annual growth of 44.9 per cent compared to 26 per cent for SEB, effectively reversing the trend prior to 2007, when the average rate of growth for SEB was ahead of that for management fees. Over the four-year period 2005–09, nominal management fees increased by 289 per cent, with the inflation rate trailing behind the growth rate in management fees, implying substantial increase in real terms.[67]

The inference here is that management fees are effectively exerting more pressure on net earnings of banks compared to staff expenses. The report has also observed that a partial explanation for this can be attributed to the fact that growth in staff related expenses at subsidiaries of foreign banks was constrained by several factors, including the non-replacement of staff at these banks resulting in the respective head offices getting more involved in managerial decision-making at their subsidiary operations. It is also quite evident, at least at one subsidiary of a large internationally active bank, that management fee payouts were responsible for some of the significant losses incurred at the bank.

Because these fees are tax allowable in Zambia as against dividends that are not, a possible incentive could be that this avenue will become a preferred channel for transferring shareholder income and possibly liquidity, to prop up group stressed liquidity states, following the widespread liquidity problems that followed the financial crisis in advanced financial markets, where these groups have a major presence.

The BoZ report also notes that the deductibility of management fees gives rise to a tax benefit equivalent to 35 per cent or 45 per cent of the fees paid. The fees further benefit from a 15 per cent withholding tax (WHT), deductible at source, given that they are paid to a recipient, the holding company, who is not based in Zambia. Since management contracts require that fees are paid net of taxes, Zambian subsidiaries of foreign banks are effectively made to absorb the amount of WHT paid. In this regard, as management fees increase, it follows that the amount of WHT that Zambian subsidiaries of foreign banks have to absorb increases. This has apparently been the situation obtaining over the period of interest – i.e. 2005–09. BoZ concluded that the tax deductibility of management fees was an incentive to banks to pay management fees over dividends, for which this relief is not available, thus effectively enhancing distributable profits.

Clearly, the problems outlined above reinforce the case for the need for regulatory authorities to create incentives to ensure that there is clear distinction in the way subsidiaries of foreign banks operate with a view to ensuring that intra-group transactions are done at arm's length. A number of possible solutions to this problem are being considered by the authorities in Zambia. These include:

   i. A need to strengthen the governance structures at subsidiaries, particularly the role of the local management and Board in the subsidiaries' decision making process;

  ii. A need for subsidiaries to seek authority and justify the management fees structure from BoZ;

 iii. Banks should be required to utilize available local expertise in areas where they are assessed to have relative strength; and

  iv. Management fees should not be tax deductible

To address concerns such as the ones outlined above, some regulatory intervention initiatives are focused on structuring frameworks for international coordination, emphasizing issues of mutual national concern. The Financial Stability Forum has thus defined the objective that all major cross-border financial institutions should be covered by a 'college of supervisors'. Zambia, being host to some subsidiaries of key regional and internationally active banks from South Africa, Nigeria and the United Kingdom, has been party to some of these supervisory colleges, particularly the ones arranged by the FSA.

There is some scepticism being expressed as regards the potential success of these colleges in spite of the good intentions behind their proposed establishment. Although it is envisioned that they will contribute to improved flow of useful information between home and host country supervisors, there still exist important inherent limitations, particularly in dealing with cross-border crisis situations. In the Zambian situation, a conflict of supervisory interest can be inferred from the intra-group management contract problem referred to earlier. Whereas the home supervisory authority may be more inclined to have enhanced liquidity transfers into their jurisdictions from subsidiary operations of the groups they oversee, host supervisors, as the case is at present with the BoZ, are more inclined to structuring ways and means of ring-fencing liquidity at the local subsidiary operational level to mitigate concerns arising from the risk of adverse spillover effects from deteriorating liquidity states at group level.

8.11 Conclusion

The recurrence of financial crises globally demonstrates existence of serious knowledge gaps between financial sector dynamics and the overarching financial sector oversight infrastructure. It is quite evident that perfecting the interface between financial sector regulation, supervision, and financial sector stability has proved difficult over the years. Evidently the level of financial sector depth, development, and complexity also appears to be important, particularly with regard to the speed with which financial sector problems permeate different financial systems. These realities have implications on the ultimate impact that a crisis will have on a financial system and the type of solutions that authorities can meaningfully structure to address such a crisis.

The contrast between the impact of the crisis on advanced economies and less developed countries such as Zambia lays credence to this school of thought and brings out the reality that no one solution would fit the financial sector dynamics of all countries. It makes sense, therefore, for countries to structure tailor-made solutions to address possible sources of financial sector instability. Conscious efforts should be made to localize the financial sector interventions in order to ensure that financial sector policy development and the structuring of the regulatory architecture fully embrace the dynamics inherent to the domestic situation. Globally accepted practices should be treated as 'good' guiding principles with a candid evaluation and alignment of the policy wish list with country-specific dynamics, including the state of the human and financial resource strength on the ground. This should also extend to a reality check on the absorption capacity of such 'good' guiding principles by a country, taking into account the strength of governance institutions on the ground.

Notes

1. Duvuri Subbacharao (2011); FSA, Turner Review (2009); IMF (2009).
2. Approximately K110 billion of public funds or 7.8% of GDP were provided to problem banks in the form of liquidity support during this period (Bank of Zambia).
3. BCBS, September 2012.
4. Patrick Honohan et al. (2007) p. 4.
5. Ibid. p. 5.
6. Honohan (2007) observes that 'banks will remain at the heart of African financial system' for some time.
7. See Bank of Zambia Act (1996) (Section 4) for functions of the Bank of Zambia.
8. The committees include the Committee on Payment and Settlement Systems, the Committee on the Global Financial Systems, and the International Association of Deposit Insurers.
9. See Section 4(1) of the Bank of Zambia Act.
10. FinMark Trust et al., June 2010, p. 62.
11. Ibid.
12. The SADC average figures in this section are based on the SADC Secretariat review of Financial Soundness Indicators for the member countries.
13. As explained later, in Section 8.10.1 of this chapter, the core capital ratio of Zambian banks could be overstated considering the problems related to the tangibility of elements that qualify as core capital.
14. Need to note that this ratio had increased to 24 per cent as at end December 2012. (http://www.quandl.com/WORLDBANK/ZMB_FM_LBL_MQMY_GD_ZS).

15. The ratio of money broadly defined (M2) or liquid liabilities (currency plus demand and interest-bearing liabilities) to gross domestic product (GDP) are used as a proxy for financial depth. An upward trend in this ratio infers a financial sector that is growing faster than the real sector and hence proxy's deepening of the financial sector. Conversely, a financial sector with growth that lags behind that of the real sector will indicate a declining financial sector (Shallowness).

16. Bank of Zambia estimates.

17. Limiting these variables to the banking system is unlikely to materially distort our inference given the significance of banks to the Zambian financial system. Ratio is regarded as a good proxy as it assumes that lending to the private sector is relatively more productive than lending to government.

18. The ratio of currency to the narrow definition of money (M1), currency ratio, is used to proxy the complexity of the financial structure. The trend in this ratio throws some light on the state of the financial structure in Zambia and how it has evolved over time. The lower the ratio the better as it is indicative of relative diversification of financial assets and liabilities within an economy. A low ratio effectively signals a wider use of financial assets other than cash in transacting business.

19. Honohan (2007), p. 15.

20. It is important to note that deficiencies exist in the implementation of capital adequacy standards in Zambia. It is therefore possible that the capital adequacy levels may have been overstated.

21. Cooley and Philippon (2009), p. 277.

22. It is worth noting that the BoZ Act does not pose a legal constraint on BoZ to only extend LOLR liquidity assistance to solvent banks. In effect, insolvent banks can also legally receive liquidity assistance from BoZ under Sections 41 and 42. The BoZ Act is silent on the financial condition of the bank or financial institution that should be eligible to access an LOLR facility from it, even though the BoZ LOLR Policy of March 2010 restricts eligibility for emergency liquidity assistance to solvent banks or financial institutions (See Section 6(ii) of BoZ LOLR Policy).

23. The monetary policy implications of such a move will have to be carefully evaluated and taken into account.

24. BCBS, Draft Report on Strengthening the Resilience of the Banking Sector, December 2009, p. 1.

25. The FSA are already applying a set of guidelines that imply a revision of the minimum core Tier 1 capital to 4% from 2% with indications that Tier 1 capital will also be adjusted upwards to 8% from 4%. It should also be noted that in 2013 the FSA was contemplating easing the rules for new banks to start up, with a caveat that such banks would be allowed to fail in an orderly manner. This measure is expected to enhance competition.

26. The additional buffer is equivalent to 2–3% of core Tier 1 capital. Such capital requirements can be increased in a variety of ways including through the required capital adequacy ratio adjustments or by way of increasing the risk weights attached to each asset category (*Turner Review*. p. 57).

27. Basel (2009) notes that, under the previous capital adequacy standard, banks could

hold as little as 2% common equity to risk-based assets before applying regulatory adjustments.

28. A recent case in point is the rejection of audited accounts for publication by the BoZ due to a misrepresentation of the financial condition of the bank in question by its external auditors. Whether or not the misrepresentation was on account of a genuine error, it does justify the concerns expressed regarding problems in the auditing and accounting infrastructure in Zambia.

29. Section 69 of the BFSA requires banks in Zambia to transfer to a Reserve Account part of retained earnings in a manner prescribed by SI 182 of 1995, the Reserve account regulations. Regulation 3 of SI 182 requires a bank or financial institution to maintain a reserve fund and out of retained earnings of the distributable profits from the current financial year, before any dividend is declared, transfer to the Reserve Fund a sum equal to not less than:

    a) Fifty per centum of such profits, whenever the amount of the reserve fund does not exceed half its paid-up equity capital; or

    b) Twenty per centum of such profits or such sum as shall make the amount of the reserve fund equal to the paid-up equity capital, whenever the amount of the reserve funds exceeds half of its paid-up equity capital but is less than the paid-up capital.

30. Basel Committee on Banking Supervision, Consultative Document, *Strengthening the Resilience of the Banking Sector,* issued for comments by April 2010, December 2009, p. 4.

31. SI 184 of 1995.

32. The Basel Capital Accord further notes that, where provisions or reserves have been created against identified losses or in respect of an identified deterioration in value of any asset or group or subsets of assets, they are not freely available to meet unidentified losses which may subsequently arise elsewhere in the portfolio and therefore do not possess an essential characteristic of capital. Such provisions or reserves should therefore not be included in the capital base (Basel Capital Accord 1988, p. 5).

33. Republic of Zambia, *Government Gazette* No. 5546 of 29 December 2006. Gazette Notice No. 682 of 2006.

34. Section 2 of Gazette Notice No. 682 of 2006, The Banking and Financial Services Act (Capital Adequacy) Notice, 2006 states that, 'A bank shall commence operations with a primary paid-up capital of not less than Kwacha Twelve Billion, or such other higher amount as maybe prescribed by the Bank of Zambia from time to time and shall maintain this minimum amount at all times.'

35. Primary or Tier 1 capital as defined by the Capital Adequacy Regulations, SI No. 184 of 1995 includes, in addition to paid-up common shares, the following items: eligible preferred shares; contributed surplus; retained earnings; general reserves; statutory reserves and minority interests (common shareholders' equity).

36. A capital adequacy regime is procyclical if its operations tend to encourage or necessitate business responses that exacerbate the strength of the economic cycle. If capital requirements tend to fall in periods of strong lending growth and low credit losses, this can tend to accentuate the boom with well-capitalized banks able to expand lending aggressively. Conversely, if capital requirements rise in

recessions, banks facing capital constraints may cut back lending, making the recession worse.

37. Op. cit., *Turner Review*, p. 61.
38. BCBS, op. cit., 2009, p. 8.
39. BCBS has settled on two specific proposals. One is based on the use of the highest average probability of default (PD) estimate applied by a bank to each of its exposure classes as a proxy for a downturn PD; while the other is based on the use of an average of historic PD estimates for each exposure class.
40. The Bank of Zambia has in recent times (see 2010 budget) significantly reduced its training budget due to serious financial constraints. This is likely going to adversely impact on the quality of a wide spectrum of services the Central Bank provides to the public in general and the financial sector in particular during the medium to long term.
41. For example, in June 2000 the Banco de España introduced a dynamic provision for Spanish banks and other credit institutions which aims to ensure that aggregate annual provisioning – including the dynamic provision – equals average annual net losses suffered in the banking system in the last decade (*Turner Review*, p. 63).
42. BCBS, 2009, op. cit., p. 8
43. Banking books allow for provisioning only where there are known events of credit quality deterioration or where it is reasonable to infer that such events have already occurred even if evidence in respect of individual loans is not yet available in the banking system.
44. The assumption here is that the regulatory capital adequacy ratio requirements remain unchanged over the period of concern.
45. See *Turner Review*, op. cit., p. 66.
46. Honohan (2007) notes that, the lack of long-term finance in African financial markets is partly a reflection of the long-term risks and partly an endogenous response to the need for monitoring and reconstructing. This problem is further compounded by the lack of long-term resources available for investment (p. 16).
47. The non-distributable economic cycle reserve is required to set aside profits in good years to anticipate losses likely to arise in the future (*Turner Review*, p. 66).
48. SI 182 of 1995 operationalizes Section 69 of the BFSA. Section 3 of SI 182 requires banks and financial institutions to transfer to the Reserve Account a sum equal to not less than:
    a) 50 per cent of such profits, whenever the amount of the reserve fund does not exceed half of its paid-up equity capital; or
    b) 20 per cent of such profits or such sum as shall make the amount of the reserve fund equal to the paid-up equity capital, whenever the amount of the reserve fund exceeds half of its paid-up equity capital, but less than the paid-up equity capital.
49. BCBS, Basel III: December 2010 (rev June 2011), p. 69.
50. *Turner Review*, op. cit., p. 67.
51. This ratio identifies the amount of unencumbered, high-quality liquid assets (HQLA) an institution holds that can be used to offset the net cash flows it would encounter under a short-term stress scenario. The scenario entails both institution-specific

and systemic shocks built upon actual circumstances experienced (BCBS, Framework for Liquidity Risk Measurement, December 2009).

52. BCBS, Basel III: The Liquidity Coverage Ratio and Liquidity Risk Monitoring Tools; January 2013.

53. This ratio measures the amount of long-term stable sources of funding employed by an institution relative to the liquidity profiles of the assets funded and the potential for contingent calls on funding liquidity arising from off-balance sheet commitments and obligations. The standard requires a minimum amount of funding that is expected to be stable over a one-year time horizon (BCBS, IFLRM, December 2009).

54. BCBS, op. cit., December 2009, p. 2.

55. When regulation is effective, it may adversely impact on the operations of the regulated, thus creating incentives to cross the regulatory boundary.

56. The shadow banking sector comprised of institutions that borrowed short-term in rollover debt markets, leveraged significantly, and lent and invested in longer-term and illiquid assets. Unlike banks, these institutions were inherently vulnerable to runs, as they were not covered by any safety nets that are normally designed to prevent runs in banks. In 2007 and 2008, the shadow banking system experienced a serious run that led to the collapse of a significant part of this unregulated financial system (see Viral V. Acharya et al. 2009). *Turner Review* (op. cit., p. 70) also observes that US investment banks, which formed a significant part of the shadow banking system had, over time, developed into very large, highly leveraged institutions, performing significant maturity transformation, but were not subject to the same regulatory regime as banks.

57. Honohan et al. (2007) observe that the non-bank formal financial system controls relatively far smaller resources compared to banks, a phenomenon typical of low-income countries, not only those in Africa.

58. In the UK deposit insurance before the failure of Northern Rock covered the first £2,000 of each person's retail deposit at any one bank and 90 per cent of the balance up to £35,000. This was considered inadequate to prevent a retail deposit run and was consequently revised upwards to coverage of 100 per cent of the first £50,000 of each person's retail deposit with each bank (£100,000 for a joint account). Further, government in the UK ensured that depositors suffered no loss during the crisis period even in situations where deposits were higher than available insurance (*Turner Review.* p. 74).

59. The predominance of institutional investors in a majority of small banks in Zambia remains a source of potential volatility. As Dziobek et al. (2002) notes, institutional investors are relatively sophisticated, have access to banks' financial information, and have a fiduciary responsibility to safeguard their assets. As a result, they are prone to shifting investments and hence such investments are volatile (p. 71).

60. It is worth noting here that such an approach does have its own downside as the asymmetry of information on the quality of projects available for financing increases the smaller and relatively more informal that the target clientele becomes. This effectively implies an adverse effect on the Tinies' balance sheets.

61. Section 31(1) of the BFSA disqualifies a person from being elected a director or to be appointed a CEO, CFO or manager of a bank if that person is not a fit and

proper person to hold the relevant office in relation to integrity and professional expertise.

62. Section 67(1) of the BFSA requires the directors of each bank or financial institution to establish an audit committee of the board.

63. It should be acknowledged, though, that BoZ has issued *Risk Management Guideline* and relies on moral suasion to enforce this.

64. Narrow banks perform classic retail and commercial banking functions, and have access to retail deposit insurance and the lender of last resort facilities. On the other hand, investment banks are significantly involved in risky trading activities and are normally excluded from access to retail deposit insurance and from lender of last resort facilities.

65. The US banking crisis of 1929–33 is cited as having been more severe than today's crisis, even though it did not have a serious global dimension. The crisis was part driven by the excessive localization of credit capacity and credit extension, which is a feature common in the Zambian financial system today.

66. Bank Supervision Department, 2010.

67. Ibid.

References

Acharya, V. V., Richardson, M. (eds), (2009). *Restoring Financial Stability, How to Repair a Failed Financial System.* New York: John Wiley & Sons, Inc.

Alexander, K. (2004). Corporate governance and banking regulation. *Cambridge Endowment for Research in Finance Working paper 17.* Cambridge: University of Cambridge Press.

Bank of Zambia (2010). *Preliminary Report on Management Fees Paid by Zambian Banks to Their Group.* Bank Supervision Department (19 January).

Bank of Zambia (2010). *The Bank of Zambia Lender of Last Resort Policy* (March).

Barth, J., Caprio, Jr., G and Levine, R. (2006). *Rethinking Bank Regulation.* New York: Cambridge University Press.

BCBS, Basel III (2010, 2011). *A Global Regulatory Framework for More Resilient Banks and Banking Systems* (December 2010: rev June 2011).

BCBS, Basel III (2013). *The Liquidity Coverage Ratio and Liquidity Risk Monitoring Tools* (January).

BCBS (2012). *Core Principles for Effective Banking Supervision.* BIS (September).

BCBS (2009). *Draft Report on Strengthening the Resilience of the Banking Sector* (December).

BCBS, IADI (2009). *Core Principles for Effective Deposit Insurance Systems.* BIS (June).

BCBS (1988). *International Convergence of Capital Measurements and Capital Standards.* Basel Capital Accord.

BCBS (2009). *International Framework for Liquidity Risk Measurement, Standards and Monitoring.* Consultative document (December).

Brunnerneier, M., Crocket, A., Goodhart, C., Persaud, A.D., and Shin, H. (2009). *The Fundamental Principles of Financial Regulation.* London: Centre for Economic Policy Research (June).

Cooley, T. and Philippon, T., (2009). The bail out. In: Acharya, Viral V., and Richardson,

M. (eds) *Restoring Financial Stability: How to Repair a Failed Financial System*. New York University, Stern Business School, Wiley Finance.

Dziobeck, C., Hobbs, J.K., Marston, D. (2002). Toward a framework for systemic liquidity policy. In: Enoch, C., Marston, D., Taylor, M. (eds) *Building Strong Banks Through Surveillance and Resolution*. Washington, DC: International Monetary Fund.

Financial Services Authority (2009). *A regulatory response to the global banking crisis. The Turner review*. (March).

Finmark Trust and African Heights (2010). *FinScope Zambia 2009 Survey Top Line Findings, Final Report*. (June).

Goodhart, C., and Illing, G. (eds) (2002). *Financial Crisis, Contagion and Lender of Last Resort. A Reader*. Oxford: Oxford University Press.

Government of Zambia (1995). *The Banking and Financial Services (Capital Adequacy) Regulations*. Statutory Instrument 184.

Government of Zambia (1995). *The Banking and Financial Services (Reserve Account) Regulations*. Statutory Instrument 182.

Government of Zambia (1996). *Bank of Zambia Act No. 43 of 1996*, Lusaka: Government Printers.

Honohan, P., Beck, T. (2007). *Making Finance Work for Africa*. Washington, DC: World Bank.

International Monetary Fund (2009). *The Implications of the Global Financial Crisis for Low-Income Countries*. Washington, DC: International Monetary Fund.

International Monetary Fund and World Bank (2005). *Financial Sector Assessment. A Handbook*. Washington, DC: International Monetary Fund.

Mbaku, J.M. (2006). *Governance and poverty alleviation in sub-Saharan Africa* in *Governance and Pro-Poor Growth in sub-Saharan Africa*. AERC Seminar Papers, Senior Policy Seminar VIII. Dakar: Senegal (March).

Mwape, A. (2005). *An Examination of the Relationship between Ownership Structures and Risk in Banks: Bank Governance and Regulation in the East and Southern African Region*. Ph.D Thesis. University of London.

Republic of Zambia (2000). *Banking and Financial Services Act*.

Republic of Zambia (2006). *Gazette Notice 682*.

Republic of Zambia (2006). *Government Gazette 5546* (29 December).

Standard Chartered Bank (2009). *Standard Chartered Global Focus, Monthly analysis of economic and financial market developments* (April).

Stiglitz, J., and Weiss, J. (1981). Credit rationing in markets with imperfect information. *American Economic Review* 71(3): 393–410.

Subbarao, D. (2011). *Financial sector regulation for growth, equity and stability in the post-crisis world*. Inaugural address at the First CAFRAL-BIS International Conference. Mumbai (15 November).

III

The Supply Side: Production, Trade, and Infrastructure

9

Mining in Zambia: Revitalization and the Challenges of Inclusive Prosperity[1]

Christopher S. Adam, Alexander Lippert, and Anthony Simpasa

9.1. Introduction

The history and economics of Zambia is a story of copper mining. From unpromising beginnings, the first half of the 20th century saw Zambia, a country of less than two million people, become one of the 'big five' global copper producers in the world. This period of prosperity was relatively short-lived, however, and was followed by a long steady decline in prices, production and profitability over the final quarter of the century. However, just as the wave was passing, the control and ownership of the industry was brought decisively under public ownership and control of the behemoth conglomerate, the Zambia Consolidated Copper Mines (ZCCM). Such was the importance of the mining sector in the economic and political life of Zambia that by the early 1980s 'ZCCM was the state and the state was ZCCM'. However, a combination of the failure of the state-run model, deteriorating geology and adverse global conditions in the copper industry meant that by the mid-1990s, ZCCM posed such a severe threat to public finances that its re-privatization became inevitable, despite political opposition from many quarters.

The privatization of the mines – helped in no small measure by the surge in global commodity prices since 2003 – heralded a remarkable revitalization of the sector (Figure 9.1). However, the return to profitability has also recast the challenges of securing the returns to the country's natural resource

Figure 9.1 Zambia: A century of copper prices and production

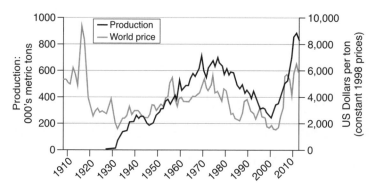

endowment for the citizens of Zambia. With ownership of the rights to exploit copper resources now firmly back in private hands and, more particularly in private foreign hands, the public policy debate is appropriately anchored on the question of how policy should be configured to strike an equitable balance between putting in place the right incentives for the effective development of the mining sector on the one hand and ensuring that an equitable share of the returns to the exploitation of the nation's mineral resources can be secured for the citizens of Zambia.

Any answer to this question must recognize two overriding features that shape the economics of copper in Zambia. Firstly, the changing nature of property rights over mineral resources and the state's options for securing a share of the rents from copper mining must be considered, as well as how different strategies have affected incentives for exploration for and production of copper. Secondly, the strength of linkages from copper to the rest of the economy and how these shape macro-economic policy options must be considered. Copper mining in Zambia is an enclave activity, both technically and spatially, and as mining in Zambia moved deeper underground it became increasingly capital- and import-intensive, so that forward and backward market linkages with the domestic economy beyond the local environs weakened. Fiscal and quasi-fiscal instruments became increasingly more important as tools for capturing and distributing mineral rents. However, as has been documented extensively elsewhere (Adam and Simpasa, 2011), the manner in which these policy instruments were deployed in the 1970s and 1980s had disastrous consequences for the economy and people of Zambia.

In this chapter we argue that the authorities have managed the surge in copper prices since 2003 much more successively than they did 40 years earlier; and while outcomes, especially in the fiscal domain, are still woefully underpowered, our research suggests the local area spillovers may be more substantial than previously thought.

The remainder of this chapter is structured as follows. Section 9.2 provides a brief overview of the history of copper mining in Zambia from the development of the industry in the late 19th century until the nationalization of the mines in the early 1970s. Section 9.3 then describes the attendant macroeconomic consequences of the 1970s and 1980s and the reorientation of economic management in the 1990s under the MMD government. Section 9.4 describes the privatization of ZCCM in the late 1990s. Sections 9.5 and 9.6 discuss the management of the copper price boom that began in 2003 and reports on estimates of the scale of local-level spillover effects from the mining sector. Section 9.7 revisits the debate over the mining tax regime and provides an estimate of forgone revenues arising from fiscal incentives granted to the foreign investors during privatization. Section 9.8 concludes.

9.2 Mining in Zambia: Geology, geography, and politics

9.2.1 *History*

Copper mining in Zambia has its modern origins in British colonial interests in southern Africa at the end of the 19th century. The rich copper deposits stretching from Luanshya in modern-day Zambia to Katanga in the modern-day Democratic Republic of Congo had been known of for centuries but systematic prospecting in the area dates from the height of the 19th century European 'Scramble for Africa', when a wave of small-scale prospectors, licensed by Cecil Rhodes' British South Africa Company (BSAC), converged on the area. Prospecting rights were secured in the system of mutual recognition established by the European powers at the Congress of Berlin in 1884. The Congress defined the limits of the BSAC's concession to the north (thereby ceding rights over the immensely rich surface deposits around Katanga to the Congo Free State, later the Belgian Congo), but in doing so it conferred authority to the BSAC for prospecting over the territory of modern-day Zambia.

Initially, rights were allocated over numerous small concessions establishing an artisanal mining industry, few of which were economic. The decade following the end of the First World War radically altered the prospects for the Zambian copper industry. The continued industrialization of the global economy, and especially the industrialization of war, underpinned a sustained growth in the global demand for copper. But, for Zambia, the real revolution came through a combination of geological happenstance and enlightened public policy. The discovery in the early 1920s of rich sulphide seams beneath the thin oxidized surface layer of ore massively increased the potential commercial value of the ore body and this potential was exploited, thanks both to the granting of new prospecting and mining rights to large commercial operations, most notably Ernest Oppenheimer's Anglo American Corporation, and the decision to extend Rhodes's 'Cape to Cairo' 600 km railway from Victoria Falls to the Copperbelt.

The consolidation of rights and the provision of infrastructure created the conditions where large-scale private capital investment allowed the mining industry to incur the fixed costs necessary to overcome the inefficiencies of artisanal mining and exploit the economies of scale in copper production. Two foreign mining houses, Anglo American Corporation (AAC) of South Africa and the Rhodesian (later Roan) Selection Trust, owned by the American Metal Climax Inc. (Amax), quickly consolidated their grip on the industry and between them established Northern Rhodesia as one of the 'big five' producers (the others being the US, Russia, Chile and Congo/Zaire). Within a decade, Northern Rhodesia had emerged as a major supplier of copper to the world economy, accounting for 10 per cent of world production in the 1930s and 1940s, and reaching its maximum share of almost 15 per cent in 1959 (Figure 9.2).

With this basic ownership structure in place, the industry rode the long post-Second World War boom, with production responding to rising world demand and prices throughout both the Korean and Vietnam wars. At independence in 1964, Zambia could boast of having the highest per capita income in sub-Saharan Africa (albeit one that was very poorly distributed).

9.2.2 Geography, linkages and state ownership

Production peaked at 700,000 tons of copper in 1969. In the same year, delivering on President Kenneth Kaunda's 1968 Mulungushi Declaration (see, for instance, Kaunda, 1968) and reinforced by an intellectual climate that championed the state's capacity to absorb and manage economic risk, the government took its first steps towards state ownership of the mining sector, acquiring a controlling interest in the major mining houses.[2] The feasibility

Figure 9.2 Zambia's market share in global copper market

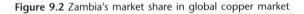

of this model of economic management was further reinforced by the apparent success of the mining industry itself.

Before the emergence of large-scale industry, the Copperbelt region was very sparsely populated – principally by subsistence farmers. To create and sustain an effective supply of skilled labour to the mines, the mining houses had, since the early 1930s, made substantial investment in the training, health and social welfare of its labour force (Robinson,1933; Coleman,1971). By the early 1970s, the Copperbelt was in effect a collection of prosperous company towns populated by a well-educated, well-paid and heavily urbanized labour force that both enjoyed high-quality cradle-to-grave welfare provision, courtesy of the mining houses, and constituted an important source of aggregate demand.

The Mulungushi Declaration was therefore, in part, an attempt to recast this 'company town' model to a national scale. The fundamental problem was simple: the model relied on an unchanged resource base that, unknown to government at the time, was already at its zenith. While state ownership on its own was unable to greatly strengthen backward linkages (although large state-owned, import-substituting industrial conglomerates under the stewardship of INDECO and ZIMCO were created to supply the copper industry), it could and did strengthen forward linkages, principally through the widening remit of the state-owned copper industry and through fiscal means. As it later became clear, however, this strategy was fundamentally unsustainable, and was worsened by the decline in world copper prices.

9.3 The lost decades and the road to privatization

The three decades following the Mulungushi Declaration were a disaster for the mining industry in Zambia and for the economy as a whole. Bad luck played a part: almost as soon as government had acquired majority control of the industry, world copper prices started their long decline, geological conditions began to deteriorate, and the geopolitics of southern Africa severely disadvantaged landlocked Zambia's engagement with the world economy.[3] By the mid-1980s, copper production had fallen sharply and unit costs of mining increased concomitantly, sharply dissipating mineral rents (Figure 9.3).

Poor macro-economic management and the lack of checks and balances required to control the enormous expansion in the unprofitable non-core activities of ZCCM and outright rent-seeking activities compounded the bad luck of falling copper prices. Thus, by the early 1990s, when the one-party state of Kaunda's Second Republic was successfully challenged by the Movement for Multi-party Democracy (MMD), rents in the mining sector in Zambia had been all but eliminated.

Figure 9.3 Copper prices, costs, and rents 1970–2008

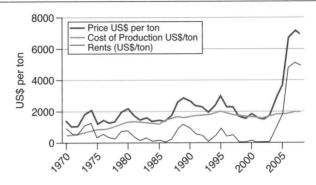

Problems emerged early in the 1970s when world copper prices rose sharply at first and then fell steadily. Treating the temporary positive shock as if it were permanent, and the negative shock as if it were temporary, the authorities failed to save during the boom and sought to sustain absorption (both public and private) during the long slump through extensive external borrowing in anticipation of a rapid recovery in the price of copper (McPherson, 1995). This optimism was obviously miscalculated, as demonstrated by the World Bank's highly overstated copper price projections (Gulhati, 1989).

As the decade continued, it became apparent the Zambian economy had galloped into an abyss, needing urgent adjustment to correct the attendant macro-economic imbalances. However, while the World Bank and other observers began to urge structural and macro-economic adjustment in response to lower world prices, the Zambian Government sought to maintain absorption through a high borrowing strategy. This proved very costly: the ensuing crisis of the 1980s stemmed in large measure from the combination of a failure to save when copper prices were temporarily high and a failure to adjust when they were persistently low. With absorption consistently exceeding GDP through the late 1970s and 1980s, and with output growth declining, the public debt burden grew rapidly, resulting in an accumulation of arrears, both on amortization and interest payments.

As borrowing options dried up in the 1980s, consumption was sustained through a severe squeeze on investment, falling from an average of over 30 per cent of GDP per annum from 1965–74 to 23 per cent per annum in the decade from 1974 and to around 15 per cent per annum by the early 1990s. Mining investment also plummeted, barely covering the depreciation of the capital stock in mining. For example, capital expenditure by ZCCM for its operating units fell from about 30 per cent of total mineral sales in 1983 to less than 10 per cent in 1989. The depletion of non-renewable natural resources during the 1980s (at low world prices) thus financed public and private consumption and was used to service external debt, eroding total national wealth.

The deepening economic crisis from the late 1970s eventually drew the government to seek external assistance. An initial IMF adjustment programme was negotiated in 1978 and again in 1983, but each was met with limited success. Pressures to liberalize the exchange-rate regime and eliminate the severe real exchange rate overvaluation were thwarted by increasingly weakening external and fiscal balances, arguably exacerbated by lower-than-expected donor aid flows. As a result, the price decontrols and removal of subsidies on basic foods in 1986 were accompanied by a rapid nominal exchange rate depreciation that hit the previously protected but politically powerful urban population on the Copperbelt hard. Riots ensued and reform efforts were halted (Bates and Collier, 1993). The denouement of the failed adjustment efforts of the 1980s, and indeed of Kaunda's Second Republic, began in May 1987, when the government broke off relations with the International Monetary Fund (IMF) and adopted a Growth from Own Resources Economic Recovery Programme (ERP). Exchange rate reforms were reversed, price controls reinstated and debt service payments limited. A fundamental macro-economic incompatibility quickly emerged: relative prices, particularly for foreign exchange, became severely distorted, the anti-export bias increased and investment expenditure collapsed further. Unemployment rose dramatically, creating further social pressures. The ERP collapsed in 1989 and a new reform package, very similar in design to the 1983 programme, was agreed with the IMF. This programme was a critical nail in the coffin of the economic and political model of the one-party state of the Second Republic. Within a year, Kaunda had acceded to pressures to hold competitive multi-party elections and in October 1991, Kaunda suffered a landslide defeat at the hands of the Movement for Multi-party Democracy (MMD) candidate, Frederick Chiluba, while UNIP ceded 125 of the 150 parliamentary seats to the MMD, effectively ending UNIP and Kaunda's presence on the Zambian political scene.

9.4 Privatization and recovery

Although the election of 1991 was not fought explicitly on the issue of ZCCM and the copper industry, the change of regime ushered in a shift in thinking about the role of the state in economic management and, as a consequence, in the management of natural resources in Zambia. The realization that the state-driven model had come close to driving the mining sector to extinction saw discussion over the nature of ownership of the mining sector, including the possibility of privatization to foreign investors, emerge into mainstream political debate.

The MMD government immediately embarked on an aggressive programme of macro-economic stabilization and reform, transforming Zambia from one of the most *dirigiste* economic regimes in the 1980s to one of the most liberal. The new government moved rapidly to unify and liberalize the exchange-rate regime (Zambia was one of the first African countries to remove all controls on both the current and capital account transactions), and relax controls on domestic financial markets. Financial sector reforms were accompanied by significant trade liberalization and, at the same time, government embarked on an ambitious programme of privatization. By the mid-1990s, the state had divested itself of the vast majority of the roughly 400 state-owned, non-mining enterprises that had been built up over the preceding 30 years.

Macro-economic stabilization in the early 1990s required steely commitment by government, but this commitment proved difficult to sustain. Weaknesses in governance and mounting political tension within the ruling MMD saw the reformist zeal of their early years in government rapidly dissipate as the political rivalries that had been successfully subordinated to the common objective of overturning Kaunda's and UNIP's hegemony broke the surface, causing the associated goodwill of donors to dissolve. But even without these problems, stabilization would have been hard to sustain as the economy was hit by a sequence of poor harvests and, as copper prices continued to decline, further exposing the parlous state of the mining sector. With official reserves already at the minimum level required to satisfy the IMF and no access to external capital other than through aid flows (including debt rescheduling), adjustment to the deteriorating external conditions was overwhelmingly through continued expenditure reduction, both public and private. The burden of adjustment again fell on aggregate investment and once again growth stagnated. It was against this background that the privatization of ZCCM was launched, with none of the fanfare or evangelism of the non-mining privatization programme but rather an air of inevitability that the end-game had arrived.

Initially, given the totemic position it occupied in Zambian society, the mining sector fell outside the purview of the Zambian Privatisation Agency (ZPA) and indeed was not even considered as a suitable sector for privatization. However, prompted by continued steady decline in world prices, worsening geology, and continued rent-seeking, ZCCM fortunes collapsed precipitously. As indicated earlier, capital expenditure had fallen to less than a quarter of its value in the early 1970s, while production was prematurely halted at a number of mines and no resources were being devoted to prospecting. Between 1997 and 1998, ZCCM's reported pre-tax losses totalled approximately $650 million – almost $US1 million per day. By the time the first components of the ZCCM conglomerate were privatized in 1998, mining output was 42 per cent of its level at independence in 1964 and only one third of its 1969 peak. Crucially, this low output level represented the industry's maximum capacity and not the outcome of an optimal response to below-trend world copper prices (World Bank, 2002).

The steady deterioration of the financial condition of ZCCM dictated both the pace and the options for privatization. No investor was prepared to absorb the whole of ZCCM, so it was decided that the conglomerate would be broken up and sold in a set of separate packages with the state retaining a range of contingent liabilities arising from, among other things, pension and environmental obligations. Moreover, given the heterogeneity and complexity of each unit – and the rapidly changing financial environment – it was deemed impossible to conduct the sale by auction. Component parts were sold through, often opaque, bilateral negotiations with pre-selected preferred bidders, with each sale agreement concluded through a legally-binding and confidential Development Agreement (DA). The process took more than three years, with the final (and, in terms of mining potential, the largest) block of assets – Konkola Copper Mines – finally being sold to the Anglo American Corporation (AAC) in March 2000.[4]

Inevitably the bargaining power lay overwhelmingly in the hands of the eventual purchasers: world prices remained depressed through most of the negotiation period and losses mounted across ZCCM, while a combination of brinkmanship by potential purchasers – frequently based on 'revelations' from the execution of due diligence investigation into the financial accounts of ZCCM – and relentless pressure from the donor community to conclude the process on highly attractive terms (GRZ, 1999), saw both strike prices and the general terms of sale move sharply against the vendor. However, given the pessimistic outlook for the world market prevailing at the time, it was seen as a success to have sold most of the components of ZCCM as going concerns for a positive cash price: the potential problems of negotiating away such generous fiscal terms were heavily discounted.[5] Only when market conditions recovered were the full consequences of the sale conditions became apparent.

9.4.1 *Development agreements and the tax regime*

Though each component of the ZCCM sale was negotiated on a bilateral basis, each mining contract contained broadly similar tax arrangements. By the conclusion of the privatization process, the de facto tax code for mining was as follows:

- Corporate income tax was levied at 25 per cent on taxable profits (compared with 35 per cent for the non-mining sectors);

- The royalty rate was capped at 3 per cent on gross proceeds. In practice, however, all new mining companies paid royalties at a rate of 0.6 per cent;
- Full exemption from import duties on recurrent and capital inputs;
- Interest costs and repatriated dividend income were fully deductible;
- Capital expenditure was fully expensed in the year in which it was incurred;
- Losses could be carried forward for up to 15–20 years.
- Pension liabilities and environmental legacies originally incurred by ZCCM were transferred to the state-owned holding company, ZCCM-IH Ltd;
- Each DA established a 'stability period' of between 15 and 20 years during which the agreed terms and conditions were guaranteed.

A detailed discussion of the mining tax regime in Zambia is discussed in Chapter 5 (Conrad, 2013). Here we review the principal elements. By international standards, the tax structure embedded in the DAs was overly liberal, generous and biased towards the taxation of rents that, at the time of negotiation, were historically low. The effective royalty rate of 0.6 per cent of gross proceeds was particularly low and well below the global average of 2–5 per cent (Pricewaterhousecoopers, 1998) and the IMF estimate of 5–10 per cent for developing countries.

9.4.2 *Summary*

The privatization of ZCCM sought to achieve two financial goals. The first was to stem the operating losses that were borne by the public budget and crowding out already low public expenditure, and the second to reverse the 30-year trend of underinvestment in exploration and production. It was anticipated that with sufficient investment, the mines would return to profitability and remain viable at expected long-run prices, generating public revenue – directly through mineral taxation and indirectly through the local multiplier. Central to the sale strategy, therefore, were the investment commitments made by the new mining companies under the DAs. Although government had limited instruments to enforce investment commitments, capital inflows to the sector have been substantial since privatization and have exceeded the commitments originally anticipated (whether the investment commitments would have been honoured if prices had remained low is a moot point). For instance, between 2003 and 2009, foreign direct investment (FDI) in the mining sector increased to more than 60 per cent ($US4.5 billion) of total FDI in the same period (GRZ, 2010). The bulk of this investment was initially for rehabilitation of existing mining and smelting operations, but was followed by new investment, most notably at KCM in the context of the Konkola Deep Mining Project, and with the opening of the Lumwana mine in Solwezi by the Australian-Canadian consortium Equinox – estimated to be the largest open-pit copper mine in Africa.

9.4.3 Recovery and outlook

In terms of world market conditions, the privatization of ZCCM could not have occurred at a worse time: between the issue of tenders in March 1997 and the decision by Anglo American to relinquish its equity in Konkola Copper Mines in January 2002, world copper prices, in constant US dollars, fell by almost 40 per cent, reaching an all-time low. The average price in 2002 was $US1,514 per ton compared to a previous low of $US1,520 in 1932 and a long-run average for the 20th century of around $US3,560. It was these consistently falling prices that forced repeated re-negotiation downwards of the final sale price of the mining assets.

In retrospect, the Anglo American withdrawal from KCM occurred at the very bottom of the market and the hand-back to government coincided with the turnaround in the copper market, fuelled in the main by the global investment boom led principally by China and other emerging economies and speculative trading by highly leveraged hedge funds. Between 2002 and April 2008, copper prices increased sixfold, from around $US1,500 per ton to over $US9,000 per ton, in current prices. Prices fell back sharply as the global financial crisis unfolded in 2008 – to just under $US3,000 per ton in December 2008 – but recovered quickly and have remained high since. The price boom (and sustained plateau since) has dwarfed anything seen since independence: measured in constant prices, world copper prices at their peak in 2008 were 20 per cent higher than their peak value in 1974 and double the average price since 1920. The only time copper prices were ever higher was when the combatants on the Western Front were hurling millions of copper-tipped shells at each other in 1916 and 1917 (Figure 1).

The combination of above-trend prices and the substantial investment in the sector by new foreign owners has led to a substantial increase in productive capacity and a corresponding fall in unit costs (see Figure 3). Between 1991 and 1999 mining output contracted by 32 per cent and by 2000 annual output was less than 250,000 tons. By 2004 this had increased to 400,000 tons and to well over 500,000 tons in 2007 and 2008. With the start of production in the new open-cast mines of Lumwana and Kansanshi, copper output rose to almost 875,000 tons in 2011, the highest level ever achieved in Zambia.

The privatization of the mines and the increased investment in rehabilitation and new mines has also been accompanied by a substantial expansion of prospecting activity leading to a sharp upward revision in the prospective economic life of the industry. In 1974, for example, it was estimated that copper mines would be exhausted by around 2020: current estimates extend this to at least the final decades of the 21st century. A portion of this increase reflects the application of new mining technology. Recent technological developments in extracting copper from the accumulated waste materials from the past century of mining (the tailings dumps) have, for instance, effectively presented the mining houses with new pre-crushed surface mines which can be 're-mined', but most of the revision reflects an intensification of exploration and prospecting.

For reasons of geology and geography, Zambia remains a relatively high-cost producer, even after the over-burden of ZCCM's extensive non-core activities had been removed. According to World Bank data (2008), the average unit cost of production in Zambia is around $US1,500–$US1,800 per ton, compared with global average of between $US750–$US1,000 per ton, although the Zambian average is likely to fall as the share of output accounted for by the new Lumwana and Kansanshi open-cast mines increases. Given best estimates for copper prices in the long run,[6] the long-run viability of the industry is not in question, although as a marginal producer, the sector remains perennially vulnerable to the volatility in world markets.

9.5 The copper price boom: savings, investment, and the pressures for tax reform

To assess the scale of Zambia's copper price and to explore how the proceeds from the boom were used, Adam and Simpasa (2011) and Lippert (2013) undertake a simple counterfactual analysis.[7] Taking world prices for copper and cobalt in 2002 as the counterfactual, they compute a lower 'bound' estimate of windfall by assuming that in the counterfactual production would have followed a similar path to that which occurred.[8] They compute the 'windfall' as the increase in export earnings at actual world prices relative to their value at the counterfactual price level over the period from 2003 to 2010. Combining the results for copper and cobalt, their calculations suggest that the cumulative net windfall income accruing from copper exports from 2002 to 2010 was approximately $US3.5 billion.[9] In net present value terms this corresponds to around 100 per cent of base year GDP.[10] Clearly, if we assume that some of the rise in output over this period should be attributed to the price boom (as opposed to being the effect of investment in the mines following privatization), then the boom would be even larger. However measured, though, this is a very substantial positive terms of trade shock.

The next step is to consider how the public and private sectors responded to this increase. Adam and Simpasa (2011) use the well-known savings-equals-investment identity to estimate how much of the computed windfall was saved and by whom:[11] they estimate that around half the windfall income generated over the period was saved and of this approximately two thirds was represented by domestic gross fixed capital formation with the remaining third represented by a net increase in foreign assets.

Superficially, this represents a remarkably high overall savings propensity and certainly out of all recognition from the boom of the early 1970s, while the disposition of savings would appear to be consistent with an efficient expenditure response to a temporary resource boom in which savings accumulate initially in the form of foreign assets and then are drawn down to finance domestic capital formation as the limits of the domestic supply capacity dictate.

However, this simple picture is significantly incomplete, since a substantial share of the windfall income accrued to the foreign owners of the mines in Zambia, and a substantial proportion of the measured foreign asset accumulation is, in fact, the repatriation of profits and payment of dividends by Zambia-based mining houses to their foreign shareholders. Adam and Simpasa (2011) suggest that almost 60 per cent of the fixed investment can be directly attributable to (foreign) investment in the mining sector, while almost 90 per cent of all the net capital outflows can be attributed to profit and dividend remittances by the mining houses. Simpasa et al. (2013) estimate revenue forgone during the boom period to be about 5 per cent per annum of current GDP, equivalent to a total of $US2.8 billion or five times the estimated infrastructure investment financing gap of $US500 million (Foster and Dominguez, 2011). This is what is meant locally by the 'cashless copper boom'.

9.6 Measuring the local-level spillover from mining activity.

The preceding analysis suggests that at a macro-economic level, the impact on domestic incomes and consumption of surging copper prices has been relatively weak, principally because the relatively under-powered tax structure combined with the unusual nature of the privatization exercise has left the lion's share of the rent from mining in the hands of the (foreign) private mine owners. However, this is probably not the full story. In this final section we use some innovative econometrics to explore the strength of the local spillovers from the booming mining sector to the Zambian economy – the forward and backward linkages of Hirschman (1958) – drawing on work by one of the authors that uses a 'treatment-effects' framework to estimate spillover effects from mining to the local economy (Lippert, 2013). The analysis shows that these spillovers exist at a local level and are not insubstantial.

The underlying idea is simple: as the mining sector expands production (which is evidenced from Figure 1) its demand for factor inputs (land, labour and capital) increases along with the range of intermediate inputs required in the production process. Some of this demand leaks offshore through imported capital goods, certain skills and so forth, but other components of demand need to be sourced locally, most obviously certain types of labour, but also non-traded intermediate inputs into production such as transport, hospitality and ancillary services. This direct local demand from the mines in turn creates a local-level multiplier. The question is simply, how large are these effects and how are they transmitted?

The transmission of the demand pulse will depend to a substantial degree on prevailing conditions in the local economy. The higher is local demand and the lower is unemployment, the stronger the price effect; on the contrary, when there is widespread local unemployment, we would expect adjustment to be in terms of quantities, on the extensive margin, so to speak. To be more specific, we would expect the immediate effect of the boom to be seen in higher labour demand and increased demand for local services, for transportation, construction, and cleaning services, among other locally supplied inputs. The local multiplier is also likely to be larger when demand is concentrated in goods and services intensive in unskilled labour. Given this, we would expect the local multiplier to weaken as the distance from the mine increases.

Weighing against these is the possibility of substantial local Dutch Disease effects driving up local prices; large inward migration effects and, potentially, adverse environmental effects that together actually reduce relative living standards in mining areas which if strong enough might reduce material living standards. The environmental impact of Zambia's mining sector, for example, is much debated (Fraser and Lungu, 2007) and may adversely affect agricultural productivity and living standards in mining regions (Aragon and Rud, 2013, for a discussion of the environmental effects of mining in Ghana). Hence, whether or not the mineral boom raises welfare measures depends on the extent of the mine's backward linkages and the corresponding local multiplier effect and is, ultimately, an empirical issue.

If the net effect is positive, then we would expect those effects to extend – to some degree – to areas that are either spatially connected or otherwise exposed to the boom. Intuitively, higher purchasing power of the urban population raises the demand for food (locally produced) and results in higher agricultural income and improved living standards for the rural population. Further, there is no reason to expect that backward linkages are confined to the most local environs. The high population density and relatively developed transportation infrastructure of the Copperbelt suggest the presence of strong trade links between mining and non-mining areas that are connected to mining areas by major trunk roads. These non-mining districts may therefore well benefit from increased mine production due to trade links and the local multiplier effect: this effect can be tested.

In order to test the competing hypotheses empirically and identify channels of transmission from mine production to living standard measurements, Lippert (2013) applies an extended 'difference-in-difference' method to local-level data to identify the scale of local spillovers, where here a local area is measured as a parliamentary constituency. He estimates the following regression model:

$$Y_{c,t} = \beta_1 Q_{c,t-1} + \beta_2 T.Q_{t-1} + \gamma X_{c,t} + \alpha_c + \lambda_t + \varepsilon_{c,t}$$

where $Y_{c,t}$ is a measure of living standards in constituency c in year t and $Q_{c,t-1}$ denotes the volume of copper production in constituency c in the previous year. This variable will only be positive if there is a mine in the constituency. $T.Q_{,t-1}$ is the interaction between lagged *aggregate* copper production (for the economy as a whole) and a dummy variable that takes the value one if the respective constituency is located along the copper transportation route, in other words if it is *not* itself a mining constituency but is linked to one by the transport infrastructure. The vector of controls, $X_{c,t}$ includes socio-economic constituency characteristics to control for time-varying observables (age, gender ratio, fraction of rural households, educational attainment, fraction of migrants, etc.) and the direct effect of mine expansion (fraction of mine workers).

The model also includes constituency (α_c) fixed effects, which will control for the host of unobservable constituency-specific fixed factors driving economic well being, and year (λ_t) fixed effects which similarly control for time-varying unobservable factors that are common across all constituencies (for example, the effect of changes in macro-economic policies). $\varepsilon_{c,t}$ is the error term. In this framework, then, β_1 is the main coefficient of interest and measures the average change in living standards in response to a 10,000 metric tons increase in local copper production. The coefficient β_2 measures the impact of higher aggregate mining activity in constituencies that do not host a mine but are connected to the industry by a principal transportation route. In other words, it is a measure of the 'line-of-rail' or 'line-of-road' effect of mining.

This baseline model specification imposes the somewhat unrealistic restriction that spillovers are confined to constituencies in which the respective mines are located (or along the specific transport routes). However, the general transport infrastructure is reasonably developed in the mining areas and since, given high population density means that constituencies in the Copperbelt are relatively small in size, we might reasonably expect backward linkages of the mines to extend into neighbouring constituencies. To test this hypothesis and estimate spillovers to non-mining areas, Lippert (2013) considers an alternative measure of 'local output' to mean the combined output of all mines within a certain radius from the centroid of the respective constituency. Extending the radius allows him to identify the average catchment area of the mines.

Table 9.1 provides a summary of the main findings from Lippert (2013) where for convenience and brevity we report only the coefficient estimates on the parameters of interest. The first row of the table measures the impact per 10,000 tons per annum of increased local production on various measures of well being, and the second row the impact on these measures for constituencies along the transport corridors. The rows reported in column [1a] measure the impact on household per capita expenditure for households progressively distant from the epicentre of the production increase.

Several key findings emerge from this analysis. Firstly, while the vast majority of the additional value from mining accrues to final consumers outside the local area, the copper boom does appear to have improved living standards in the immediate surroundings of the mines; increases in local copper production has positive and significant effects on household expenditure, on housing conditions, consumer durable ownership, and child health in mining constituencies and substantially reduces local unemployment. For example, a 10,000 ton increase in constituency-level copper output is associated with an increase in per capita (adult equivalent) expenditure of some 4.2 per cent higher than for households in constituencies not directly exposed to the boom. Similarly, the measured unemployment rate falls by 3 per cent following an increase in local copper production by 10,000 tons. Additionally, the copper boom appears to significantly boost household ownership of wealth-related consumer durables and an improvement in other housing conditions. Moreover, the results on the illness indicator and poverty measures confirm the same effect: according to this analysis increased output of copper from mines in the local community reduces reported illness episodes and reduces overall poverty in mining areas.[12]

Secondly, the positive effects of the boom spill over to the hinterland, more so to neighbouring constituencies, than to those located on the copper transportation routes. Consistent with increasing transportation costs and imperfect labour mobility, the magnitude of spillovers to surrounding areas decreases steadily with distance and becomes statistically insignificant after around 75 km. On the basis of simple averaging, this implies that around two million people reside in the overall catchment area of all the twelve mines on the Copperbelt.

Two other key results – not reported in detail here – emerge from the analysis. These are, firstly, that consistent with the theoretical literature on the Dutch Disease (Cordon and Neary, 1982), relative prices increase slightly in response to the boom but there is little evidence of higher overall

Table 9.1 Estimates of local spillover effects of increased copper production

	[1] Household Expenditure (per capita)	[1a] Local Unemploy-ment rate	[2] Local Unemploy-ment rate	[3] Ownership of Consumer Durables	[4] Housing Conditions	[5] Child Health (illness episodes)	[6] Poverty
Change in Local Output (Q_C) [10,000 tons]	6764***		-0.007***	0.011***	0.014***	-0.005***	-0.008***
Transport x Output (T.Q)	883.00		-0.003***	0.002***	0.001	0.000	-0.001*
Spillover to Non-Mining Constituencies							
Distance:							
10 km		6780.00 ***					
30 km		6310.00 ***					
50km		5882.00 ***					
75 km		4132.00 **					
100 km		2374.00					
R-Squared	0.56	0.10	0.10	0.84	0.47	0.33	0.38
N	745	745	745	745	745	745	745

Notes:
[1] Ownership denotes household ownership of consumer durables (car, mobile phone, TV, DVD player, radio);
Housing conditions defined as access to electricity and potable water
Measures constructed as first factor of principal components analysis of covariates. Illness episodes are a self-reported measure of the number of illness events amongst a household's children
Poverty is measured as proportion of households living at income below that required to purchase CSO minimum consumption basket
[2] Each specification includes constant, district and year fixed effects and household-level controls (household size, education, age and gender mix etc.)
[3] Significant levels [***=1%, **=5%, *=10%]

inflation in mining regions, arguably due to the locally elastic supply of labour (Moretti, 2010). Secondly, the evidence suggests the key channel through which the urban population benefits from the mine expansions is labour demand, and that in turn higher urban incomes are transmitted to the rural hinterland via increased demand for agricultural products and trade links between urban and rural areas.

These findings are robust to different lag structures of local copper production, alternative clustering choices for standard errors, and the exclusion of any particular set of mines from the sample. Estimating the baseline specification for the non-migrant sample shows that the positive spillover effects from increased mine activity are not driven by selective migration and can indeed be attributed to strong backward linkages of the mines.

9.7 Renegotiating the tax code

Although we can identify a significant local multiplier from the mining sector to the economy of the Copperbelt, its scale is modest at best: the mining sector remains a classic enclave, the rents from which accrue overwhelmingly to the mine owners. A small share is retained as onshore investment in the sector but the majority has been remitted offshore in the form of profits. The combination of high rents and weak linkages means the burden of securing some of these rents for the benefit of the local citizenry therefore must lie with the tax system. However, as noted above, the taxation arrangements negotiated as part of the Development Agreements during privatization eviscerated any buoyancy from the tax regime (Table 9.2). Despite experiencing the largest copper price boom in its history, the tax take as a share of GDP remained more or less constant throughout the boom, at just under 18 per cent, with the only revenue accruing directly from the mining sector coming from the royalty on production.[13] Conventional profit taxes in the mining sector yielded precisely zero revenue to government as the twin effects of large loss carry-forward provisions afforded to the mining houses and the provision for full expensing of investment expenditure reduced the tax liability to zero.

The failure of the tax system to extract any substantial revenue during the early years of the copper boom increased the pressure on government to re-define its relationship with the mining industry. Populist opposition to the mining privatization, or more particularly to foreign ownership and control in the sector, has been on the increase and in early 2007 government sought to re-negotiate the development agreements (DAs) with the mining houses but without halting the burgeoning investment in exploration and exploitation in the sector that followed the ZCCM privatization. Since most DAs included clauses securing the terms for periods of not less than ten years,

Table 9.2 Zambia: Central Government Revenue, 2001–12, per cent of GDP

	2001	2002	2003	2004	2005	2006	2007	2008	2009	2010	2011p	2012p
Total Revenue and Grants	24.8	26.2	25.0	23.8	23.6	21.6	23.0	23.2	18.9	19.6	22.5	20.9
Tax Revenue	19.1	17.9	18.0	18.3	17.2	17.2	17.7	17.6	14.6	16.4	19.3	16.6
Other Revenue	0.5	0.3	1.4	0.8	0.4	0.9	0.7	1.3	1.4	1.4	1.6	2.6
Grants	5.7	8.3	7.0	5.5	6.4	4.4	4.6	4.3	2.9	1.8	1.6	1.7
Total direct tax on mining (% of Revenue)	0.3	0.1	0.2	0.1	0.7	0.7	9.0	10.8	6.8	11.6	16.6	24.1
Total mining taxes inc. royalties (% of GDP)	**0.1**	**0.0**	**0.0**	**0.0**	**0.1**	**0.1**	**1.6**	**1.9**	**1.0**	**1.9**	**3.2**	**4.0**

Source: IMF Article IV, 2012 Table 3

the government initially sought to establish a revised code for new mining investment by re-negotiating the existing agreements one-by-one, but this proved difficult and it reverted to a more direct legislative strategy, announced in the 2008 Budget (GRZ, 2008a), which repealed the Minerals and Mining Act 1995 and cancelled the pre-existing DAs, thereby establishing a new fiscal regime for the sector through the enactment of the Minerals and Mining Act (GRZ, 2008b).

The new tax code introduced in the 2008 Budget had two objectives. The first was to shift the tax code decisively in favour of generating a larger revenue flow to government from the mining sector, and the second was to improve the buoyancy of the system in boom times. To achieve this a number of elements were introduced: (i) an increase in the mineral royalty rate on base metals from 0.6 per cent to 3 per cent of gross revenue; (ii) the reduction of capital allowances from 100 per cent expensing to 25 per cent expensing; (iii) an overhaul of the taxation of corporate income (profits) involving an increase in the base rate from 25 per cent to 30 per cent combined with a variable profit component that would increase to 45 per cent if taxable profits exceeded 8 per cent of revenues; (iv) a graduated windfall tax levied at progressively higher rates as the world price of copper broached price thresholds;[14] (v) a 15 per cent withholding tax on interest, royalties, management fees and payments to affiliates and subcontractors; and (vi) a 15 per cent duty on the export of unprocessed copper.

The result of the reforms was to significantly increase the presumptive effective tax rate on mining, both on average and especially when world prices were elevated. Assessment by the IMF suggested that at prevailing 2008 copper prices and aggregating over all instruments, the average effective tax rate on mining in Zambia rose from around 31 per cent to 47 per cent, taking Zambia from being one of the lowest to one of the highest tax regimes amongst developing countries, although much of this increase was due to high prevailing prices and the accompanying strong progressivity of the graduated windfall tax. Given the accumulated losses still being carried forward against tax liabilities, the actual tax yield was somewhat lower.

Nonetheless, the 2008 measures immediately drew sharp criticism, from the mining houses and their representatives and from the international donor community, including the IMF, and have over the next four years been modified and revised. The graduated windfall tax was withdrawn and 100 per cent expensing of capital expenditure restored, but the variable tax rate was retained on the statutes while government stood its ground on the basic royalty and even increased it further to 6 per cent in the 2012 Budget, a tenfold increase over the rate prevailing in the DAs, sufficient, on IMF projections made at the time of the 2012 Article IV mission, to generate an additional 1.5 per cent of GDP in revenue at prevailing world prices. As Table 2 indicates, the IMF anticipated that the new regime (combined with sustained world prices) would start to generate substantially higher tax revenues for government. As yet, this is still to be realized. The actual total tax yield accruing from royalty payments in 2012 was about $US300 million (1.3 per cent of current GDP), lower than the previous year's take of 1.4 per cent.

The struggle since 2008 to put in place an effective tax regime highlights the serious challenges in implementing mining tax regimes that are capable of generating revenue for government but also limit disincentive effects on mining companies. The pragmatic shift towards royalty-based taxation and the re-introduction of withholding taxes on cross-border payments has served to secure a current revenue stream as well as obviate administrative difficulties and informational asymmetries that arise in administering a pure rent-based tax, including the risk that taxable profits can be easily shifted out of the jurisdiction by mining companies who typically have better information and more sophisticated financial management and audit systems than the government can afford.[15]

However, this has come at the cost of moving further from what economic theory would see as a first-best non-distortionary taxation of pure rent. Furthermore, this shift was far from smooth and government was challenged at each turn – with mining houses threatening legal action against government's negation of the stability clauses in the DAs and, in extremis, disinvestment. The retreat by government to cede the more egregious distortions created by the graduated windfall tax defused much of the tension. The likelihood is that the bulk of revenue over the coming years will come from the royalty but eventually as the high front-loading of investment expenditure tapers off and loss carry-forward and investment offsets against taxable profits decline, the conventional profit tax begins to yield revenue to government.

This episode reveals much about the politics of the economic management of mineral resources and how, even in a relatively unified and peaceful environment present in Zambia, negotiations over both the privatization of ZCCM and the re-negotiation of the tax regime were suffused with suspicion. There has been no call for re-nationalization of the sector. Parliamentary and popular opposition did coalesce around the charge that, at least viewed from the middle of the copper price boom, foreign mine owners had received too favourable terms during privatization and that as a consequence, government's primary objective was to redress the balance.

9.8 Conclusions

It has often been said that it was Zambia's good fortune to be 'born with a copper spoon in its mouth', although for much of the 50 years since independence in 1964 natural resource dependence has been more of a curse than a blessing. The central economic challenge facing Zambia at the time of independence and the central challenge now and in the future is to find the right model for the efficient exploitation of its natural resource endowment and the equitable distribution of the rents, between various current stakeholders and between present and future generations.

Since independence, there has been a radical shift in the way the state has sought to exploit this endowment. Initially, the prevailing view was that state ownership of the industry offered the best means of capturing and distributing the rents to the people of Zambia. The traumatic 25-year failure of the state to efficiently manage the volatility in the copper market and its fundamental inability to avoid the dysfunctional rent-seeking that flourished in the state-dominated economy meant that when the pendulum eventually swung away from state ownership and control, it did so decisively. Thus, while the sale of ZCCM proved successful in re-invigorating the mining industry and staunching the state-owned company's mounting losses, it did so by not only divesting the state of the direct responsibility for managing the industry but did so on terms which more or less eliminated its capacity to share in the future rents from the sector, at least over the medium term.

The sustained boom in the copper sector since 2003, which has been described in the popular press and by opposition politicians in Zambia as a 'cashless boom' – one in which the people of Zambia saw few of the benefits from the boom, either in terms of employment or other transfers, but bore the costs associated with the appreciation of the exchange rate – starkly illustrated how much the previous decades of mismanagement had forced the government's hand during the privatization process. Given that Zambia is a relatively high-cost producer, rents in the mining sector are likely to remain modest so that, barring a major expansion in (low-cost) production from open-cast mines, revenue flows will necessarily be limited, but nonetheless, the capacity of the mining sector to generate between 2 per cent and 4 per cent of GDP per annum in revenue – estimates towards the lower end of the IMF's medium-term projections – would represent a very substantial improvement in fiscal condition compared to the late 1990s, when ZCCM's losses were approaching 10 per cent of GDP per annum. Thus, while the recovery in revenue was (and is) never likely to be transformative for Zambia, it will allow government to pursue a public investment programme commensurate with its level of development potentially without excess debt accumulation.

The boom also allowed for two vitally important and positive developments for the mining industry and the economy as a whole. The first is that the favourable price conditions meant that the investment commitments made by the new mine owners at the time of privatization were not just realized but substantially exceeded. Mining industry investment is powerfully procyclical and for once in its history, conditions in the sector combine with reasonable macro-economic stability and a broadly credible economic policy regime to allow a substantial and efficient mining investment boom to occur.

Existing mines and supporting plant were rehabilitated, new activities, most notably the Lumwana mine, were brought on line, while the intensification of exploration activity identified substantial new economic reserves of copper and other minerals on the fringes of the Copperbelt and North Western Zambia, where First Quantum Minerals is developing a large-scale Kalumbila Trident mining project. This undertaking promises to open up the region and substantially increase Zambia's global copper market share. Thus, barring a catastrophic collapse in the long-run price of copper, the recent copper boom has allowed the mining industry in Zambia to be reset, and although Zambia will remain a relatively high-cost location, the investment boom has served to stabilize and lower unit mining costs and leaves the industry better placed to generate profits in medium term and to confront the imminent short-run decline in world prices.

The second major effect of the boom was the re-negotiation of the tax code. The boom starkly exposed the imbalance in the distribution of gains from positive price developments. The re-negotiation of the mining code was far from straightforward but represents a crucially important milestone in economic policymaking in Zambia, both to the extent that the government was able to put in place a new code which, broadly speaking, shifts the balance somewhat in the direction of the revenue imperative without undermining the requirements of a competitive tax regime, and to the extent it was able to modify and fine-tune the code in response to criticism and reactions from stakeholders.

Huge challenges still remain in Zambia. There are enormous challenges in overcoming the legacy of the past mismanagement of the economy, including deep poverty, substantial inequality and a badly depleted public infrastructure. There is also the challenge of managing expectations about future public spending capacity when needs are so high but the rents from mining are likely to remain modest. However, the period since privatization has seen a number of encouraging developments including the rehabilitation of the mining sector and a clear articulation of a coherent strategy for growth and development of the non-mining sector. Realizing this strategy will be a formidable challenge but there is little doubt that Zambia is likely to exit this boom in a stronger position than it entered it and in a much stronger position than it exited previous copper price booms.

Notes

1. This paper draws heavily on earlier papers by the authors (Adam and Simpasa, 2011) and Lippert (2013).
2. In August 1970, government acquired a 51 per cent controlling stake in the Roan Selection Trust and Anglo American's operations in Zambia, creating Roan Consolidated Mines (RCM) and Nchanga Consolidated Copper Mines (NCCM). In 1982, RCM and NCCM were merged to create ZCCM. At that point, the Government of Zambia held 60 per cent of the equity, AAC 27 per cent and the remainder was held by a range of private investors.
3. During the 1980s Zambia's geographical isolation was exacerbated by regional political crises that cut off natural transport routes through (the then) Southern Rhodesia, Angola and Mozambique and South Africa, while the economic crisis in Tanzania at the time severely reduced the throughput at the port of Dar es Salaam.
4. Less than two years after acquiring KCM, Anglo American announced its decision to withdraw completely from the mining industry in Zambia, after almost 80 years as the dominant player in the sector, with Vedanta Resources PLC, an Indian mining company listed in London, acquiring the controlling stake in KCM in 2004.
5. In each of the sales, government retained an indirect minority equity share in the mining sector through its majority ownership of ZCCM Investment Holdings (ZCCM-IH), an investment company charged with the management of legacies arising from former ZCCM operation including debt consolidation, pension fund obligations and the environmental legacies. These operations were to be funded through dividend income arising from minority equity participation and revenue sharing or 'price-participation' arrangements.
6. The World Bank, for example, sees copper prices remaining at around $US7,000 / ton (constant prices) for the foreseeable future (World Bank Commodity Price Forecast Update, July 2013).
7. Further evidence on estimated revenues foregone from the boom can also be found in Simpasa et al. (2013).
8. As is clear from the production data in Figure 1, this leads to a highly conservative or lower-bound estimate of the scale of the boom. An alternative would be to assume that the additional recovery in output was itself partly due to boom-inspired investment.
9. Around 90 per cent of this accrued from the copper price boom and the remainder from the boom in cobalt.
10. Exactly how much depends on the discount rate. Discounting income back to 2002 at 5 per cent implies a windfall of 110 per cent of initial GDP whereas a discount rate of 10 per cent lowers this to around 86 per cent.
11. They decompose the savings-investment identity (in which savings is represented by gross domestic fixed capital formation including any change in inventories plus net foreign asset accumulation by the public and private sectors. Assuming a counterfactual investment rate equal to the actual rate in 2002, windfall investment and windfall foreign savings, from both public and private sources is then computed.

12. Notwithstanding high-profile evidence suggesting a deterioration in direct health and safety conditions in the sector (Human Rights Watch, 2011).
13. In 2007, for example, royalty payments of approximately $US20 million were raised from proceeds of $US3.4 billion, a yield of precisely 0.6 per cent, as established in the Development Agreements.
14. A royalty was to be levied at a rate of 25 per cent on gross proceeds when the copper price exceeds $US2.50/pound ($US5,600 per ton); at a rate of 50 per cent when the copper price exceeds $US3.00/pound ($US6,720 per ton); and 75 per cent in excess of $3.50/pound ($US7,840 per ton).
15. The government also enacted a new law aimed at curtailing misreporting of export earnings and other international transactions (GRZ, 2013).

References

Adam, C. and Simpasa, A. (2011). Copper mining in Zambia: from collapse to recovery in Collier, P. and Venables, A.J. (eds) *Plundered Nations? Successes and Failures in Natural Resource Extraction.* London: Palgrave Macmillan.

Aragon, F.M. and Rud, J.P. (2013). Modern industries, pollution and agricultural productivity: Evidence from Ghana. *IGC working paper* April 2013.

Bank of Zambia (various years). *Annual Report.* Lusaka: Bank of Zambia.

Bates, R. and Collier, P. (1993). The politics and economics of policy reform in Zambia. *Journal of African Economies* 4(1): 115–143.

Coleman, F. (1971). *The Northern Rhodesia Copperbelt, 1899–1962.* Manchester: Manchester University Press.

Corden, W.M. and. Neary, J.P. (1982). Booming sector and de-industrialisation in a small open economy. *The Economic Journal* 92(368): 825–848.

Davis, J.M. (ed). (1933). *Modern Industry and the African.* London: Macmillan.

Foster, V., and Dominguez, C. (2011). Zambia's infrastructure: A continental perspective. *Policy Research Working Paper* WPS5599. Washington, DC: World Bank.

Fraser, A. and Lungu, J. (2007). *For Whom the Windfalls? Winners and Losers in the Privatisation of Zambia's Copper Mines.* Lusaka: Mine Watch Zambia.

Government of the Republic of Zambia [GRZ] (1999). Zambia Letter of Intent. Memorandum of Economic and Financial Policies. Washington, DC: International Monetary Fund.

GRZ (2008a). *Budget Address.* Lusaka: Government Printers.

GRZ (2008b). *Minerals and Mining Act 2008,* Lusaka: Government Printers.

GRZ (2010). *Foreign Private Investment and Investor Perception in Zambia.* Lusaka: Bank of Zambia, Zambia Development Agency and Central Statistical Office.

GRZ (2013). *The Bank of Zambia (Monitoring of Balance of Payment) Regulations,* 2013. Statutory Instrument (SI) No 55.

Gulhati, R. (1989). Impasse in Zambia: The economics and politics of reform. *World Bank Economic Development Institute Development Policy Case Studies* 2.

Hirschman, A.O. (1958*). The Strategy of Economic Development.* New Haven, CT: Yale University Press.

IMF (2008). Zambia: Request for three-year agreement under PRGF: Staff assessment *IMF Country Report* 08/187.

IMF (2012). Zambia: Article IV Report *IMF Country Report* 12/200.

Kaunda, F. (2002). *Selling the Family Silver: The Zambian Copper Mines Story* Kwa-Zulu Natal: Interpak Books.

Kaunda, K. (1968). Zambia's economic reforms. *African Affairs*, 67 (269): 295–304.

Lippert, A.B. (2013). *Spillovers of a Resource Boom: Evidence from Zambian Copper Mines* M.Phil. Economics Dissertation, University of Oxford (unpublished).

McPherson, M.F. (1995). *The Sequencing of Economic Reforms: Lessons from Zambia*. Paris: Special Program of Assistance for Africa.

Moretti, E. (2010). Local multipliers. *The American Economic Review* 100(2), 373–377.

PricewaterhouseCoopers (1998). *Comparative Mining Tax Regimes: A summary of Objectives, Types and Best Practices*. London: PricewaterhouseCoopers.

Robinson, E.A.G. (1933). The economic problem. In: Davis. J.M. (ed). (1933) *Modern Industry and the African*. London: Macmillan.

Simpasa, A., Hailu, D., Levine, S., and Tibana, R. (2013). Capturing mineral revenues in Zambia: Past trends and future prospects, *UNDP Discussion Paper* August.

World Bank (2002). Zambia: Privatisation Review, Facts, Assessment and Lessons. *Report prepared at the request of the Minister of Finance and National Planning*.

10

Agriculture and Land

Jonathan Pycroft, Mulenga Musepa, Francis Ndilila, and Sherman Robinson

10.1 Introduction

Zambia is well endowed with the resources for agricultural development, possessing a favourable climate, abundant arable land, and labour and water resources. Yet the country has barely begun to unlock the potential of agriculture to contribute to economic growth and poverty reduction. The yield rate for maize is 2.0 tons per hectare, which is above the least developed countries (LDCs) average of 1.4 tons per hectare, but below the southern African average of 3.6 tons per hectare.[1]

The current state of the sector shows that agricultural development is neither straightforward nor inevitable. With a new government having recently been elected, there is an important opportunity to rethink agricultural policies. This chapter seeks to address some specific, current issues in Zambian agriculture, focusing on the policy options available, each of which is briefly introduced here.

The technology used in Zambian agriculture today is, in most cases, very basic. Despite the great wealth of technological developments that are known to raise agricultural productivity, few are available to the majority of poor farmers. Two such issues are addressed: farm equipment and fertilizer use. Both are areas where many smallholder farmers can realistically aspire to make improvements. The upgrading of farm equipment requires investment, which can be hampered by poor functioning of both the credit and the output markets. The role that cooperatives may be able to play is also considered, as is the role of appropriate tools and animals.

The main policy influencing fertilizer use is the fertilizer subsidy, which significantly lowers prices for many farmers. The question of how beneficial the subsidy is on yield is investigated, and suggestions are made as to how the provision of subsidized and non-subsidized fertilizer could be better coordinated.

Maize is the largest crop in Zambia and the staple food throughout the country. One policy that previous governments have adopted intermittently is to ban the export of maize, which is intended to increase the quantity available for domestic use. This is questioned in light of the disincentive effect that it has for farmers choosing to produce maize in the first place.

This chapter is structured as follows. Section 10.2 presents a background to Zambian agriculture, which includes an overview of the sector. In addition, new research is presented that shows that there is some bias against agriculture in the current tax policy. Section 10.3 addresses specific agricultural policy issues in turn: farm equipment, fertilizers, and the maize export ban. The final section concludes, drawing together the key messages from the chapter.

10.2 Background to Zambian agriculture

10.2.1 Overview

Agriculture employs 67 per cent of the labour force, even though it contributes only 21 per cent of GDP (World Bank, 2007; Bertow, 2007).[2] The sector also supplies the agro-manufacturing industries, which account for 84 per cent of manufacturing value-added, and together, agriculture and agro-processing account for 12 per cent of export earnings (ibid.).

The history of the sector still has implications in the present day. During colonial times, development of agriculture was geared towards serving the mining sector (Robinson et al., 2007). The Maize Control Board, which was first established in the 1930s, continued to be widely influential following independence, asserting certain principles for the agricultural market. These included an emphasis on maize production, despite the fact that half the country was poorly suited to growing it, and state control of consumer prices, which served to keep urban food prices low (Kean and Wood, 1992). The government also guaranteed producer prices, based on production costs, which protected the industry from imports (ibid.). In practice, the policy produced a pro-urban bias, with rural farmers being somewhat placated by government subsidy of farm inputs (Robinson et al., 2007).

The Chiluba government of the early 1990s sought to reduce government involvement in the sector. Some price controls and subsidies were removed, and farmers were encouraged to grow crops appropriate to their region

(Chizuni, 1994). However, the initial fervour for free market doctrine cooled and, in later years, government returned to having some active role in the sector. The specific policies adopted included fertilizer subsidies and maize export bans, both of which are addressed in this chapter.

Today, Zambian agriculture is dominated by smallholder farmers, of which there are around 800,000 (Kodamaya, 2011). Steady population growth has led to declining farm sizes, with cultivated land per person falling by nearly half between the 1960s and 1990s (Jayne et al., 2003). These are typically very small-scale with three-quarters of farm households cultivating two hectares or less (Bertow, 2007).

Geographically, there is enormous untapped potential. Of the country's 752,000 square kilometres of landmass, 58 per cent is suitable for arable use but of this only about 14 per cent is currently under cultivation (GRZ, 2006). Furthermore, although the country accounts for an estimated 40 per cent of the water resources in the region, only about 6 per cent of irrigation potential is utilized (Bertow, 2007), making agriculture predominantly rain-fed and highly prone to the vagaries of weather, and thereby wide variations in output.

All regions of Zambia could be described as having low population density; however, the northern parts of Zambia are characterized by high rainfall and generally acidic soils. On the other hand, the eastern parts of Zambia receive good rains, have fertile soils, but are characterized by higher population densities, while central Zambia is lowly populated, has good rains and fertile soils. The dominant crops in the different regions (and areas of irrigation) can be seen from the country map in Figure 10.1 below.

Figure 10.1 Dominant farming systems across Zambia

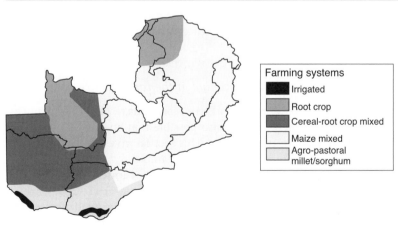

Source: FAO (2010)

Figure 10.2 Food production index

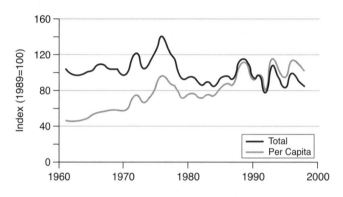

Source: WRI (2006)

The lack of technological development has contributed to modest productivity in the sector. The following graph (Figure 10.2) shows that food production per capita has changed between the late 1970s and late 1990s.

Of course, not all rural households are farming households, but generally rural households receive the majority of their income from agriculture. Jayne et al. (2003) shows that, on average among each of the poorest three income quartiles of households, less than 25 per cent of their income is derived from non-farm sources. At least in the short- to medium-term, growth in agriculture is likely to lead to greater poverty reduction. Diao et al. (2010) compare an agricultural-led development strategy and an industrial-led development strategy using CGE model analysis. The overall conclusion is that agricultural growth is more beneficial to the poor, as they would participate more in the growth process. Therefore, while non-farm activities offer a route out of rural poverty for some, agriculture will remain central to the rural economy for many years to come.

10.2.2 *Is there a bias against agriculture in the tax system?*

The structure of the tax system can favour or damage given sectors. This may be consciously chosen but it is also possible that an industry is advantaged or disadvantaged unintentionally. This section investigates the impact of the overall tax structure on agriculture in Zambia.

There is a history of high agricultural taxation. Farmers were the most heavily taxed group in the 1970s and 1980s (Robinson et al., 2007), which concurred with the general pro-urban policy bias mentioned above. The modelling work in this section investigates whether any such bias exists today.

Predicting which industries would benefit the most from removing certain taxes (or all taxes) can be tackled using a computable general equilibrium (CGE) model. A CGE model is based around a core data set, which represents the flows of resources between agents in an economy (known as a SAM). The CGE model links these different agents, estimating how they respond to one another. The different agents of the economy are linked together as a system. This means that when there is a 'shock' to the system, such as removing a tax, the model can simulate how the economy would respond.

Once the CGE model is set up, the different tax types can be removed. Removing commodity taxes from the economy, the model can show which industries are advantaged or disadvantaged, relative to other sectors. In this study, we are especially concerned with whether the agriculture sector (or parts of it) is advantaged or disadvantaged relative to other sectors by the tax system. In the model, agriculture is split into two categories: traded and non-traded. Traded agriculture is defined as agricultural production that is more than 15 per cent exported or more than 15 per cent imported. All other types of agriculture are classed as non-traded. The modelling methodology and results are explained in more detail in the Technical Appendix (available at www.csae.ox.ac.uk/books).

The results of removing all commodity taxes (i.e. VAT, excise and import duties) in the Zambia CGE model are shown in Table 10.1 below.

Focusing on the results for agriculture, one sees that the tax system does not contain an overall bias against agriculture. However, the model shows that there is a bias against traded agriculture (exports and imports). Conversely, there is a small bias in favour of non-traded agriculture, i.e. agriculture that is produced and sold domestically.

The lesson from this modelling exercise is that there is a bias against traded agriculture due to the overall tax system. Export earnings from agriculture are an important way of expanding the sector, and agricultural exports are an important component of overall exports. Importers and exporters already face obstacles such as high transport costs. Therefore, the bias against traded agriculture is some cause for concern.

The underlying bias against traded agriculture arising from the overall tax

Table 10.1 Percentage change in real value added from removal of all commodity taxes

	BASE VALUE Billions of Kwacha	Removing taxes percentage change from BASE
Traded agriculture	2260	2.82%
Non-traded agriculture	5213	-1.23%
All agriculture	7474	-0.01%
Manufacturing & services	30,513	-0.01%
Total – All production	37,987	-0.01%

system does suggest that it would be reasonable to support this part of the sector, or at least not legislate against it. We will return to this theme when specific policies are addressed. For example, the ban on maize exports operates against farmers wishing to engage in it. The fertilizer subsidy works in favour of those that apply fertilizer or are beginning to introduce it. Understanding that there is some underlying bias against traded agriculture and in favour of non-traded agriculture is worthwhile when addressing policy issues for the sector.

10.3 Policy issues I: Technology

There is an abundance of agricultural technologies that are known to effectively raise productivity. However, for various reasons, much of the technology is not used on the majority of Zambian farms. Indeed, many farmers primarily use only simple farming implements such as the hand hoe. Technologies such as fertilizer, improved seeds, or water management techniques are also underutilized.

In general terms, technological investment is costly, whether this means buying draught animals or fertilizer. In the right circumstances, there is a role for loans to be made available for such investment. Otherwise, the farmer must be in a position to retain some profit from one harvest to the next. Whether one is considering repayment of loans or retention of profits, it is important that the price received by the farmer is sufficiently high to encourage this.

This section focuses on two aspects of technology. Firstly, the farm equipment used, especially whether farms are using hand hoes or draught animals for ploughing. Secondly, the promotion of fertilizer and the fertilizer subsidy programme.

10.3.1 *Farm equipment*

The farm equipment employed on Zambian farms varies, with relatively wealthy farms tending to plough their soil with oxen, whilst many use a simple hand hoe. For the southern and eastern regions of Zambia, home to some 420,000 smallholders, the proportions are as follows: 60 per cent practice hand hoe agriculture, 25 per cent plough with borrowed or rented oxen, and 15 per cent have their own draught animals (Haggblade and Tembo, 2003). In some cases, farms have regressed in the level of technology employed: many have been forced to revert to hand hoes having previously used draught animals. The key reason for this is that Corridor disease, a tick-borne ailment, destroyed much of the cattle population (IFAD/FAO/FARMESA, 1998). The fact that much of the grazing land is communal makes the problem worse as disease spreads more quickly between herds.

Weeding with a hand hoe is considered to be the toughest job on the farm, and is usually carried out by women (ibid.). With draught animals, the weeding time per acre is reduced from two to four weeks to two to four days (ibid.), which is why the adoption of (or reversion to) farming with draught animals is widely believed to be the key to improving yields.

If returns to investment in draught animals (and other farm equipment) are high, the question arises: why it is not happening already? What are the constraints faced by the farmer? Four possible answers are considered: (i) credit market failure, (ii) output market failure, such as low prices received by the farmer, (iii) the lack of cooperatives, and (iv) the appropriateness of the available production technology. Each is addressed in turn.

The credit market requires both willing borrowers and willing lenders. While there is no obvious magic bullet to spur productive lending, Kabaghe (2010) proposes some of the key issues. The uncertainty in the agricultural market could be reduced with less government intervention (including removing the maize export ban) and a strengthening of the legal framework. Many lenders have a poor understanding of agricultural markets, which leads to over-cautious lending (or lack thereof). On the farmers' side, many could make themselves more attractive to lenders were they to enhance their capabilities of carrying out a financial analysis and risk management.

For many, the functioning of the output market (ii) appears to be a serious constraint. The farmers face uncertainty with regard to prices and legislation (outlined in FSRP/MATEP, 2006). Middlemen can therefore exploit the lack of information about the price at major markets to limit the profit of the farmer. However, this particular information problem is largely being solved by the use of mobile phones, which improves rural farmers' information about urban prices, giving them more bargaining power than before.

An innovative solution from Ethiopia that is worth watching is the recently established Ethiopian Commodity Exchange, which provides a marketplace for buyers and sellers, where both are assured of 'quality, delivery and payment' as well as dissemination of market data, clear trading rules and a dispute settlement mechanism (IFPRI, 2008). It would be worthwhile investigating whether a similar institution could be set up for Zambia.

The potential for cooperatives to raise agricultural investment and productivity is clear. For example, a smallholder with a modest field will not afford a tractor, and even if they could, it would not be fully utilized. However, if a sufficient number of such farmers cooperated, they may be able to afford a tractor and make good use of it. With respect to purchasing inputs, such as fertilizer, a cooperative would have some collective bargaining power. The same strength in volumes argument applies when selling output to traders.

Despite these theoretical advantages, historically, attempts to operate cooperatives in Zambia have had little success in bringing major benefit to the members. Following independence in the 1960s, cooperatives were actively promoted, supported by government-sponsored initiatives. Though some of these were genuine grassroots organizations, others were created to take advantage of government funds (Ojermark and Chabala, 1994). The Kaunda government made further attempts at top-down imposition of co-operative structures, which failed to bring the hoped-for benefits (ibid.). Questions remain about the effectiveness of cooperatives today, though success stories have been reported (Farm Radio, 2008). A useful direction for further study would be to compare different cooperatives and investigate whether there are best practice concepts or rules of thumb that could be adopted more widely.

The fourth consideration is the appropriateness of available technology, with some innovations being suggested that could benefit many farms. Some gains could be made if different production tools were produced for men and for women (ibid.). Another example is the introduction of donkeys. Firstly, donkeys are cheaper than oxen, but also, it is sometimes believed (rightly or wrongly) that women are not capable of working with oxen. The same is not true for donkeys (ibid.). Encouraging such developments, and helping to establish the trade links necessary to deliver them, could help promote their use.

Ultimately, a farm that relies on the hand hoe for production will never be highly productive, and will require backbreaking work, largely carried out by women. Changing this production method is a key part of developing the sector. This section has outlined the key constraints that are worth investigating further.

10.3.2 *Fertilizer and fertilizer subsidies*

Efficient fertilizer use has long been understood to have great potential to raise agricultural productivity.[3] Limited nutrients in the soil limit the potential growth of crops. Fertilizer provides additional nutrients, which, if used properly, raises farm productivity.

Recognizing this, the government introduced a Fertilizer Support Programme, which is designed to 'improve access of smallholder farmers . . . to agricultural inputs in adequate and timely amounts', as well as improving the competitiveness of the private sector in their supply and distribution of such inputs (GRZ, 2002). This intervention was introduced against a backdrop of only 20 per cent of farm households using fertilizer (ibid.).[4]

The main Fertilizer Support Programme provides a 50 per cent subsidy for the farmer. The intention is to assist 200,000 smallholder farmers. In a separate programme, a Food Security Pack is distributed free to those households most in need.

A World Bank briefing about the previous government's promotion of fertilizer (World Bank, 2006) noted that these programmes use around half of the agricultural budget, questioning the extent to which this was justified. In addition, the briefing notes that the timeliness of deliveries was not as good as private sector deliveries (ibid.). Xu et al. (2009) calculate that fertilizer that is acquired 'on time' doubles the maize response rate to the fertilizer. The same study also notes that over 30 per cent of households report late delivery of fertilizer. This suggests that there would be large returns to efforts to improve the logistical arrangements of distribution.

The subsidized fertilizer clearly causes problems for private sector suppliers, who cannot compete with a 50 per cent subsidy. Therefore, they may choose to delay transportation to certain rural areas until they are sure that there will be no subsidized fertilizer in that region. This suggests that if government were able (a) to fix the pattern of distribution in advance, and (b) to disseminate the information quickly (such as posting the planned distribution in newspapers and on a web site), then private fertilizer providers would be better placed to respond, thus benefiting the farmers that need such supplies.

There is no doubt the subsidy does help many farmers. The benefits do not reach the whole sector, but are targeted at certain regions and at those who can afford at least 50 per cent of the cost. While the help is good for those who receive it, it inevitably distorts the market, and stifles the distribution of non-subsidized fertilizer.

The previous government considered this policy as a stepping stone towards complete removal of government from the agricultural market (GRZ, 2002). Some kind of gradual shift is sensible (rather than sudden shocks that would be difficult to adapt to), though it is unclear how such a transition would continue. Xu et al. (2009) propose a reduction in the intensity of fertilizer application – firstly, because of their finding that maize yields respond well to fertilizer, but this response is subject to diminishing returns, and secondly, that the subsidy budget could then be distributed to more farmers. In whatever manner the subsidy is allocated, it should be provided in a transparent fashion that causes as little distortion to the market as possible.

Beyond straight subsidies, other factors are important in promoting fertilizer use, such as education and the proximity to paved roads (Jayne et al., 2006). Both of these can be directly promoted by government, with extension agents explaining the benefits of fertilizer and its application to a wider group of farmers and the on-going road-building programme facilitating fertilizer distribution. Some argue that the returns to research and extension are higher than for straight subsidies (e.g. Chapoto, 2010).

10.3.3 *Modelling fertilizer subsidies*

The CGE model used above was adapted to allow analysis of fertilizer use. This allowed farmers to choose to produce with more or less fertilizer, dependent on the price. The full results are in the Technical Appendix (available at www.csae.ox.ac.uk/books). The results suggested that without the subsidy, the overall use of fertilizer for agricultural crops could fall by around 13 per cent, though this would clearly be greater for those farmers directly affected. The estimated fall in overall output was around 1 per cent. One point to note is that the model allows farmers who purchase less fertilizer to re-allocate resources to other inputs, such as hiring more labour. In practice, the extent to which this is possible would depend on the producer in question, and would vary across regions and throughout the year. The overall conclusion is that a substantial fall in fertilizer use would be expected, along with a noticeable fall in output.

10.4 Policy issues II: Maize export ban

In some years, previous governments have introduced a ban on the export of maize. In principle, the ban on maize exports is implemented whenever there is a shortage of domestic production. The rationale is simply that maize should not leave the country when Zambians are facing a shortage. However, this straightforward conclusion is questioned when one delves a little deeper into the issue. The largest problem is that it discourages farmers from growing

Figure 10.3 Domestic demand curve for maize

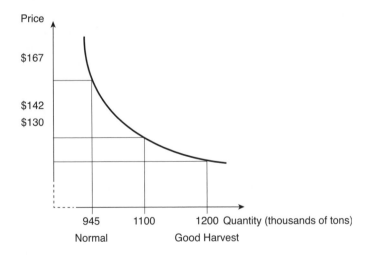

maize in the first place, and so may in fact reduce domestic availability, rather than increase it.

International trade tends to reduce the variability in producer income, where production is subject to external influences. In the case of agriculture, production is heavily dependent on the weather (an external influence). Favourable weather leads to a bumper harvest. If all this extra production is placed on the domestic market, prices can fall dramatically. Rather than benefiting from the extra volume of production, farmers' incomes can fall, because of these low prices. This situation is explained in Figure 10.3 taken from a Food Security Research Project (FSRP, 2006) presentation, which shows approximate values for Zambia maize harvests and prices. Firstly, note that in a normal year there is little incentive to export as the price is high ($167/ ton[5]). Secondly, compare the situation in a normal year to a good harvest. Production rises from 0.945 million tons to 1.200 million tons. If all of this extra production is placed on the domestic market, the price collapses to $130/ton.

If trade is restricted, then domestic producers are forced to sell at the domestic price. However, if farmers are able to export, the price fluctuation can be moderated. This is represented by the middle position on the curve. One hundred thousand tons is exported, leaving 1.1 million on the domestic market (which is above the average of 945,000 tons). The domestic price falls, but only to $142/ton. This operates similarly to a floor price, which smooths the income received by the farmer.

The price fluctuations in Zambia are dramatic. Haggblade (2006:2) categorizes harvests from 1994 to 2005 into four groups dependent on the quantity of production. The average prices per ton of maize during those years were as follows:

- excellent harvest $127
- good harvest $156
- moderate harvest $174
- bad harvest $206

In particular, note that during a bad harvest, domestic maize prices are very high. This suggests that there would be little incentive to export during a bad harvest year. Farmers would tend to find it much more profitable to supply the domestic market.

Trade openness can also help to smooth prices in bad harvest years by encouraging imports. In this case, the high domestic price would attract imports into the country, adding to the availability on the domestic market. This would moderate the price rise, helping to smooth consumer expenditure. Both in times of very high and very low production, openness to international trade helps to smooth both producer income and consumer prices.

10.4.1 *Technological potential*

Not restricting farmers to the domestic market would also encourage higher levels of production. With export restrictions, farmers face the risk of a price collapse. This risk discourages farmers from investing in new technology. Such investment could be purchasing a draught animal to aid ploughing, acquiring fertilizer, or being able to purchase fungicide, if required. Large-scale farms could invest in irrigation equipment. There are many known technologies that could be more widely employed in Zambia, were the conditions right. One such technology is improved seeds, which are used widely throughout most of the developing world. As can be seen from Figure 10.4, sub-Saharan Africa has not yet adopted this technology to the same extent as other regions (though adoption has grown rapidly).

This does suggest that large increases in productivity are possible in Africa with existing technology. Improving incentives for farmers to make use of technologies, such as improved seeds or irrigation systems, could substantially raise productivity. The main point is that technology exists that could boost agricultural production, if it were worthwhile for the farmers to adopt it.

10.4.2 *The nature of the maize export ban*

In principle, the ban is introduced when the harvest is poor, the idea being that, in times of crisis, the priority is to feed the domestic population. However, the ban also restricts farmers' behaviour. In fact, there is only a downside for the farmer, which discourages the production of maize in favour of other crops.[6]

The difficulty for the farmer is exacerbated by the capricious nature of the ban. A look at the history of the ban shows how it increases uncertainty

Figure 10.4 Improved varieties of cereals, usage 1980 and 2000 per cent of cereal area

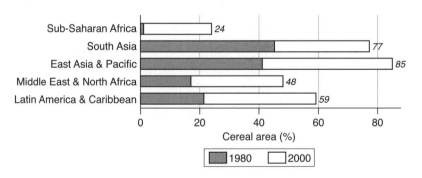

Source: Evenson and Gollin (2003); FAOSTAT (2006) cited in World Bank (2007:52)

for the farmer. Restrictions on imports and exports were removed in 1994 as part of a series of economic reforms. Contrary to this general policy of allowing cross-border trade, the export ban on maize was first introduced in 1996 (Seshamani, 1998). Maize export bans were also in place in the following years: 2003, 2005, 2006 (removed later in year), 2007, and 2008.[7] The ban ought only to come into force in shortage years, but there is no clear rule for when it should be imposed. This leaves farmers waiting on political decisions as to whether they will be allowed to supply foreign clients.

The bureaucratic requirements for exporting include obtaining a certificate of fumigation, which is used to get a phytosanitary clearance certificate, which in turn is used to get an export permit that can be used only once (Whiteside, 2003). There are reports of local officials behaving as if there was a maize ban, even in times when it is not government policy (ibid.).

An important point about the ban is that it is only truly effective against those exporting large quantities through the main border posts. Smaller quantities can be exported through informal channels regardless of official policy, though there are increased risks and costs of doing so (ibid: 38–40; Times of Zambia, 2004). Therefore, while the ban reduces maize exports, it does not eliminate them.

A final note about this policy is that imposing an export ban encourages Zambia's neighbours to do the same, as Malawi did in 2008 (CFSC, 2008). Especially in remote parts of the country, food can sometimes be made available more easily from imports, rather than from domestic sources. Dorosh et al. (2009) argues persuasively that an 'open borders' policy offers an inexpensive method of promoting stability in both food prices and consumption, with significant benefits being felt by low-income consumers. The government may wish to work with Zambia's neighbours to establish the principle that cross-border trade will be permitted within the region as a method of improving food security.

10.4.3 *Modelling the maize export ban*

The investigation of the effects of the maize ban was investigated using the CGE model (outlined in Section 10.2.1 and in the Technical Appendix, available at www.csae.ox.ac.uk/books.). The effects of the ban were entered into the model in the following ways. Firstly, a ban lowers the price obtained from exporting. Recall that the ban does not completely remove the possibility of exporting, because it is only partially effective (informal trade still continues) and because it may not be in place for the entire year. Therefore, in the simulations the price of exports was raised by 10 per cent,[8] which caused an increase in quantities exported.

Secondly, consistently lower prices and greater risks results in less investment in agriculture, and less adoption of new technology. In order to simulate this possible side-effect a 'medium-term' simulation was proposed. In this simulation, as well as the export and domestic price increases, the quality of technology is also improved. A modest increase of 2 per cent in total factor productivity (TFP) across the sector was simulated, which increases the productivity of the sector for given inputs.

A final point to note is that both exports and imports of maize are usually small components of production and consumption. For example, in 2006 (the year used for our base model), out of a total production of maize of K4,256 billion, an estimated K167 billion, (4 per cent) was exported, while a mere K21 billion was imported (IFPRI, 2006). More details of the simulations are given in the Technical Appendix (available at www.csae.ox.ac.uk/books).

Under these conditions, unsurprisingly, the results project an increase in exports, specifically, a rise of K81 billion, or 77 per cent. Less certain is the response of maize provided to the domestic market. The simulation suggests that domestic production would rise sufficiently (by 3.2 per cent) such that the quantity of maize available domestically would also rise (by 1.2 per cent). The rise in exports is more than compensated by the increase in total production.

While the actual magnitudes of these effects would vary from year-to-year, depending on the harvest, changes in the foreign prices and so on, the general point is an important one. The domestic availability of maize is likely to be at least as high without the maize ban. Over the medium term, domestic availability could even be improved by allowing exports.

Although, within a single season, the ban may slightly increase domestic availability, by depressing the price received by farmers, it reduces the incentives to produce in the first place. Additionally, reducing the price received by farmers makes it more difficult for them to maintain and upgrade their methods of farming, suggesting that potential productivity gains are being discouraged.

At first glance, the maize export ban appears to be increasing the availability of maize in Zambia. However, the lower price received by farmers also results in less incentive to produce and less incentive to invest in better technology.

As noted in Section 10.2.2, the tax system is already biased against agricultural exporters. Adding this further risk of an export ban as an additional burden, serves little short-term purpose, and seems to be harmful in the medium-term.

The price mechanism is already effective in reducing exports. During times of poor harvest, domestic prices are very high, making exporting unattractive. A ban that was strictly imposed only at such times would have little impact on domestic supply. Therefore, it would seem a better choice to remove restrictions on farmers, so they know in advance that they can export, should the domestic price fall. At a minimum, any ban would only be imposed with regard to clearly laid out criteria, which would remove much of the uncertainty that farmers now face.

Removing restrictions on maize exports can moderate price changes in an inexpensive (or indeed profitable) way. The analysis in this section suggests that the stability that this would offer to farmers would encourage production and so not only raise exports, a worthwhile goal in itself, but would also raise domestic supply, which is the key concern of government.

A concerned government wanting to act in times of food crisis has many other positive options available. Food shortages are typically regional shortages. If purchasing power in that region also falls, which is likely as agriculture is also the major source of income, then denying exports would do little to encourage supply to the affected region. One solution would be a cash-for-work scheme that would restore some purchasing power to the region. Medium-term solutions would include encouraging domestic trade through improved infrastructure and better pricing and quality information. Though there is insufficient space to explore these options in detail, the point is simply to note that governments have other, more effective, options available to them. Such options are worth pursuing in preference to a maize export ban that does little to help the immediate problem and discourages production in the future.

10.5 Conclusion

This chapter has focused on a few key issues for Zambian agriculture, drawing out how policy could be used to benefit the sector. The chapter has utilized a computable general equilibrium (CGE) model to analyze a number of issues. The first use of the model was to demonstrate that the commodity tax system has an inbuilt bias against traded agriculture in favour of non-traded agriculture.

In terms of policy issues, there are many areas of agricultural development that would benefit from more attention. However, there are limited funds coming from government and donors, which should be spent in such a way that promotes, not harms, other initiatives in the sector. More importantly, the regulations affecting the sector must be designed to incentivize farmers to develop themselves.

With these ideas in mind, the first specific topic addressed was farm equipment. There is a clear need to introduce, or re-introduce, draught animals to those farms that rely solely on simple tools. The section suggested four constraints that prevent farmers from making such investments. These range from the functioning of the credit markets and the output markets to the benefits from cooperatives and the appropriateness of the available technologies.

The second topic was the use of fertilizer and the fertilizer subsidy. Fertilizer is known to boost yield rates if used correctly, and deserves to be encouraged. The model simulations estimate the scale of the reduction in fertilizer usage and output that would result from the removal of fertilizer subsidies. At the moment, the distribution of the subsidized fertilizer competes with and somewhat stifles privately sold fertilizer. Efforts to promote more transparency with regard to subsidized fertilizer would have significant benefits for farmers.

The third topic was the maize export ban. When active, such a policy lowers the price of maize, making farmers less willing to produce it at all. Worse still, historically, the precise basis on which the ban was introduced was unclear. The concern is that allowing exports reduces the supply to the domestic market, which is the primary concern of the government. However, the research presented here suggests that with exports being permitted the domestic availability of maize would be at least as high, if not higher, because of the higher overall production induced.

The more general point regarding maize prices is that low maize prices benefits the urban poor at the expense of the rural poor. One of the consequences of low prices to rural farmers has been the lack of investment in much of the agriculture sector and farmers struggling to re-invest following a shock. Higher prices received by rural farmers would help this situation. In the medium-term, this would also help urban consumers, if the result were a more productive sector that was more resilient to shocks.

The agriculture sector is still the economic base for the majority of Zambians. The sector clearly has a long way to go to reach its full potential. There are no cheap, quick fixes available. However, steadily improving policies, to strengthen agricultural markets and to incentivize farmers to invest, can encourage much-needed growth.

Notes

1. The values are average yields for maize between 2005 and 2009. The southern African average is largely driven by South Africa (FAOSTAT, 2011, available at: http://faostat.fao.org/).
2. This sub-Saharan African average is that agriculture accounts for 15 per cent of value added (World Bank 2007: 341). Comparable estimates of labour force percentages in agriculture in SSA are scarce (ibid: 320–21).
3. For example, in 1973, the Food and Agriculture Organisation established a Commission on Fertilizers (FAO Council Resolution 2/61).
4. Note that previously fertilizer had been common for maize production in Zambia according to figures from 1987 (Heisey and Mwangi, 1996, p 8).
5. These are average prices. In reality, the typical price of maize is seasonal, with prices low from June to September, rising to a peak in February (FSRP, 2006).

6. Diversification into other staple crops might help food security. For example, Dorosh et al. (2009) advocate increased production of cassava. However, diversification away from maize would likely involve non-staples as well.
7. Sources: *Times of Zambia* (2004), *Independent Online* (2005), Reuters (2006), Reuters (2007), *All Africa* (2008).
8. This reflects the magnitude suggested in FRSP (2006).

References

Bertow, K. (2007). Impact of IMF and World Bank policies and EPAs on smallholder farmers in Uganda, Zambia, and Ghana. University of Giessen, December. Available at: <http://germanwatch.org/handel/euaf07pe.pdf>, (last accessed March 2014).

CFSC (2008). Malawi Press Review, May 2008, Centre for Social Concern, Lilongwe, Malawi. Available at: <http://www.africamission-mafr.org/kanengomai08.htm> (last accessed March 2014).

Chapoto, A. (2010). Agricultural Productivity in Zambia: Has there been any Progress? *ACF/FSRP Research Presentation to the Zambia National Farmers Union Congress*, Mulungushi Conference Centre, Lusaka, 6 October.

Chizuni, J. (1994). Food policies and food security in Zambia. *Nordic Journal of African Studies* 3(1): 46–51.

Diao, X., Peter H., and Thurlow, J. (2010). The role of agriculture in African development. *World Development* 38(10): 1375–1383.

Dorosh, P., Dradri, S. and Haggblade, S. (2009). Regional trade, government policy and food security: Recent evidence from Zambia. *Food Policy* 34: 350–366.

East Africa: Trade to Gain Despite Ban on Exports, All Africa (2008) 3 June. Available at: <http://allafrica.com/stories/200806030051.html> (last accessed February, 2010).

Evenson, R.E., and Gollin, D. (2003). Assessing the impact of the green revolution, 1960 to 2000, *Science*, 300(5620): 758–62.

FAO (2010). Country Profiles: Zambia, Food and Agriculture Organisation. Available at: <http://www.fao.org/countryprofiles/index.asp?lang=en&iso3=ZMB&subj=4> (last accessed February 2010).

Farmers' Cooperatives Help Zambian Farmers Survive and Thrive. Farm Radio (2008) Scripts Package 83, Script 8, March. Available at <http://www.farmradio.org/english/radio-scripts/83-8script_en.asp> (last accessed March 2011).

FSRP (2006). Overview of maize production & marketing trends. *Presentation, Food Security Research Project*, Lusaka, Zambia, (February).

FSRP/MATEP (2006). Making maize markets work for Zambian small farmers, traders & consumers, Presentation for Ministry of Agriculture and Cooperatives Outreach Workshop, (28 November, 2006), *Food Security Research Project (FSRP) and Market Access, Trade and Enabling Policies Project* (MATEP).

GRZ (2002). *Fertilizer Support Programme 2002–04*, Government of the Republic of Zambia (February).

GRZ (2006). *Fifth National Development Plan 2006–10*, Government of the Republic of Zambia (December).

Haggblade, S. (2006). Maize price projections for Zambia's 2006/07 marketing season. *Policy Synthesis, Food Security Research Project – Zambia* (June).

Heisey, P. and Mwangi, W. (1996). Fertilizer use and maize production in sub-Saharan Africa. *CIMMYT Economics Working Paper 96–101*. Mexico: CIMMYT.

IFAD/FAO/FARMESA (1998). The potential for improving production tools and implements used by women farmers in Africa. A Joint Study by the International Fund for Agricultural Development, the Food and Agriculture Organisation, and Farm-level Applied Research Methods for Eastern and Southern Africa.

IFPRI (2006). *A Social Accounting Matrix (SAM) for Zambia*. Washington, DC: International Food Policy Research Institute (IFPRI), 2006.

IFPRI (2008). Ethiopia's commodity exchange opens its doors. *International Food Policy Research Institute Press Release*, available at: <http://www.ifpri.org/pressrel/2008/20080414.asp> (last accessed March 2011).

Independent Online (2005). *Drought keeps Zambia from exporting maize*. Available at: <http://www.iol.co.za/news/africa/drought-keeps-zambia-from-exporting-maize-1.235581#.U7a6xqz-bZ9>.

Jayne, T.S., Govereh, J., Xu, Z., Ariga, J. and Mghenyi, E. (2006) Factors affecting small farmers' use of improved maize technologies: Evidence from Kenya and Zambia. Presented at *Symposium on Seed-Fertilizer Technology, Cereal Productivity and Pro-Poor Growth in Africa: Time for New Thinking?* International Association of Agricultural Economics Tri-Annual Meetings, Gold Coast, Australia, August 12–18, 2006.

Jayne, T.S., Takashi Y., Weber, M.T., Tschirley, D., Benfica, R., Chapoto, A. and Zulu, B. (2003) Smallholder income and land distribution in Africa: Implications for poverty reduction strategies. *Food Policy* 28: 253–275.

Kabaghe, C. (2010) Is credit and input distribution the answer to increased crop production and incomes in Zambia? *Presentation to the Economics Association of Zambia Public Forum*, Pamodzi Hotel. (08 April, 2010). Available at: <http://www.aec.msu.edu/fs2/zambia/Ag_Fiance_Input_Markets.pdf> (last accessed March 2011).

Kean, S. and Wood, A.P. (1992) Agricultural policy reform in Zambia: The dynamics of policy formulation in the Second Republic. *Food Policy*, 17(1): 65–74.

Kodamaya, S., (2011) Agricultural policies and food security of smallholder farmers in Zambia. *African Study Monographs*, 42: 19–39.

Lofgren, H., Harris, R.L. and Robinson, S. with Thomas, M. and El-Said, M. (2002) *A Standard Computable General Equilibrium (CGE) Model in GAMS*. Washington, DC: International Food Policy Research Institute (IFPRI).

Minde, I., Jayne, T.S., Ariga, J., Govereh, J. and Crawford, E. (2008) Promoting fertilizer use in Africa: Current issues and empirical evidence from Malawi, Zambia, and Kenya. Presentation at the *Southern Africa Regional Conference on Agriculture Agriculture-led Development for Southern Africa: Strategic Investment Priorities for Halving Hunger and Poverty by 2015*. Grand Palm Hotel, Gaborone. (8–9 December 2008).

Ojermark, P. and Chabala, C. (1994) The development of independent cooperatives in Zambia: a case study. *FAO*, Rome (Italy). Available at: <http://www.fao.org/docrep/003/v4595e/v4595e00.htm> (last accessed March, 2011).

ReliefWeb (2006). *Maize prices remain low*. Available at: <http://reliefweb.int/report/

zambia/fews-zambia-food-security-update-oct-2006-maize-prices-remain-low> (last accessed July 2014).

Reuters (2007). *Zambia says floods leave 1.4 million people hungry*. Available at: <http://uk.reuters.com/article/2007/03/27/idUKL2721868320070327> (last accessed July 2014).

Robinson, P., Govereh, J. and Ndlela, D. (2007). Distortions to agricultural incentives in Zambia. *Agricultural Distortions Working Paper* 40, World Bank: Development Research Group.

Times of Zambia. *Maize Smuggling Continues*, (26 April, 2004).

Venkatesh, S. (1998). The impact of market liberalisation on food security in Zambia. *Food Policy*, 23(6): 539–51

Whiteside, M. with Chuzo, P., Maro, M., Saiti, D., and Schouten, M-J. (2003). Enhancing the role of informal maize imports in Malawi food security. *Consultancy report for the Department for International Development* (DFID) (December, 2003).

World Bank (2006). *Fertilizer Toolkit: Promoting Effective and Sustainable Fertilizer Use in Africa: Zambia Government Programs to Promote Fertilizer*. Washington, DC: World Bank.

World Bank (2007). *World Development Report 2008: Agriculture for Development*. Washington, DC: World Bank.

WRI (2006). EarthTrends: The Environmental Information Portal, World Resources Institute: <http://earthtrends.wri.org/text/agriculture-food/country-profile-204.html> (last accessed February 2010).

Xu, Z., Guan, Z., Jayne, T.S. and Black., R. (2009). Factors Influencing the Profitability of Fertilizer Use on Maize in Zambia. *Policy Synthesis* No.32, Food Policy Research Project – Zambia, February 2009, available at: <http://www.aec.msu.edu/agecon/fs2/zambia/index.htm> (last accessed February 2011).

Disclaimer

The views expressed are purely those of the authors and may not in any circumstances be regarded as stating an official position of the European Commission.

11

Energy Policy

Alan Whitworth

11.1 Introduction

Every economic and social sector needs adequate, reliable and affordable energy input to grow.

(Republic of Zambia, 2006: 131)

The energy sector covers a wide range of subsectors, from charcoal production, biofuels, and solar energy through to fuel and electricity. It is not possible to properly address all the economic issues in the sector here. This chapter focuses on two subsectors – fuel and electricity – which are of particular significance for the formal economy and external competitiveness, where government is the main player, and where reform can make a real difference to sector performance. In both cases it will be shown how political developments in the 1960s and 1970s, such as the Unilateral Declaration of Independence (UDI) in Rhodesia and President Kaunda's 'African socialism', profoundly shaped current institutions, policies, and technology. While much of the economy has been liberalized since the 1990s, the fuel and power subsectors remain essentially unreformed; government remains the dominant owner and operator. Mismanagement and lack of maintenance and investment in the absence of competition have led to frequent supply disruptions in both subsectors and to some of the highest fuel costs in Africa. There is widespread public agreement that policy has failed.

This chapter shows that in both subsectors some obvious (to economists, if not to the public) reforms can be expected to both improve reliability and reduce real costs. Beginning with fuel, this would mean removing the protection of the pipeline and refinery from competition by private oil marketing companies importing finished products by road and rail. The chapter goes on to show the importance of allowing electricity tariffs to increase to levels sufficient to attract private investment in new generation and transmission facilities.

11.2 Fuel[1]

The cost and reliability of fuel supplies are critical to the competitiveness of all economies and to citizens' well being. Fuel, the country's largest import, has been a major constraint to growth in Zambia since the 1960s. Fuel costs have been among the highest in the world, while increasingly frequent shutdowns at the Indeni refinery have caused extensive supply disruptions. Continued operation of Indeni will require substantial investment. Following Total's withdrawal from Indeni, there are increasing doubts over the economic viability and reliability of the pipeline and Indeni.

This section examines the problems in the subsector and considers whether Zambia should switch to importation of finished fuel products. After briefly describing current institutional arrangements, the section examines why fuel costs are so high in Zambia and considers how they can be reduced. It goes on to look at the implications of relying on a single pipeline and refinery for reliability of supplies and questions the role of Government in the subsector, before concluding with the issues of taxation and price control.

11.2.1 *Current fuel sector institutions*

The government (GRZ) has been the main actor in the Zambian fuel sector since the 1960s. With sanctions against the Ian Smith regime in Rhodesia disrupting oil imports, it was decided to construct a 1,710-km pipeline to transport petroleum products from Dar es Salaam and to build a refinery in Ndola. The TAZAMA pipeline, commissioned in 1968, is jointly owned by the Zambian (66.7 per cent) and Tanzanian (33.3 per cent) governments. The Indeni refinery, a simple, hydro-skimming refinery with a design capacity of 1.1 million tonnes per year, was commissioned in 1973. It has been 100 per cent owned by GRZ since it acquired Total's 50 per cent stake in 2009.[2] A blend of whole crude and finished products, known as 'spiked crude', is imported and then refined and separated to meet the Zambia market mix. Procurement is handled by the Ministries of Energy and Water Development and Finance.[3] The CIF (cost, insurance, and freight) cost of fuel procured under the supply contract (with IPG) covering the years 2008 and 2009 amounted to $US741.8 million.[4]

The 50 million litre capacity Ndola Fuel Terminal, adjacent to the refinery, is used for storing and managing the distribution of refined products and is also 100 per cent owned by GRZ (and managed by TAZAMA Pipelines Ltd). Except for during breakdowns and supply disruptions at Indeni (when finished products are imported directly, mainly by road), all Zambia's fuel needs since 1973 have been supplied through the pipeline and Indeni.

Indeni does not purchase crude oil feedstock itself or own and sell the products it produces. Instead, it operates on a tolling arrangement. GRZ is the supplier and proprietor of the feedstock and owner of the products produced and lifted from the refinery. Finished products are sold to 27 private licensed oil-marketing companies (OMCs), which distribute them throughout Zambia, mainly by road tanker. While OMCs are allowed to import finished products, since 2008 they have attracted 25 per cent import duty, whereas Indeni only pays 5 per cent duty on its feedstock. With, in effect, a monopoly in fuel importation and processing, the Energy Regulation Board (ERB) determines maximum retail fuel prices (except for sales to mines and certain other industries).

Zambians have relied on the pipeline for fuel imports for so long that few are aware that there may be lower cost alternatives. The pipeline and refinery are widely regarded as valuable national assets and it is taken for granted that a pipeline is the most economic way of importing fuel; there is little public debate on alternatives. However, they can only be considered genuine assets if they provide real economic value to the country in the form of lower fuel prices and/or more reliable supply than alternative import arrangements. If this is not the case, they should be regarded as sunk costs and written off. The evidence below on costs and reliability casts serious doubt on the value of the pipeline and Indeni.

11.2.2 Fuel prices

Table 11.1 and Figure 11.1 show that in June 2008 Zambia had much the highest retail pump prices in the southern African region. This was largely

Table 11.1 Southern Africa comparative diesel prices, June 2008

Diesel/Gasoil (US$/litre)	Bots	Malawi	Mozam	Nam	RSA	Swaz	Tanz	Zambia
Product Basic Cost	1.19	0.96	1.05	1.04	1.04	0.99	1.05	1.48
Transport, Service Differential	0.08	0.22	0.01	0.01	0.01	0.02	0.01	0.09
Govt. Levies, Duties, Taxes	0.06	0.34	0.16	0.19	0.24	0.26	0.44	0.55
Oil Company Margin	0.05	0.08	0.12	0.05	0.05	0.05	0.09	0.11
Dealer Margin	0.06	0.06	0.09	0.05	0.08	0.06	0.05	0.07
Retail Pump Price	1.44	1.67	1.43	1.34	1.42	1.37	1.63	2.30

Source: BP (2008)

Figure 11.1 Southern Africa comparative diesel prices, June 2008

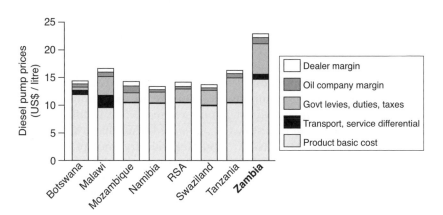

attributable to two factors: higher product basic costs and taxes. As taxes are not a cost to the economy, merely transfer payments, they are of much less concern than Zambia's product basic costs and are discussed below.[5]

It is no surprise that Zambia's product basic costs are higher than those of its coastal neighbours because of the greater distance over which imports have to be transported. Of concern, however, is that, at $US1.48/litre, Zambia's costs were significantly higher than in landlocked Malawi ($0.96), Botswana ($1.19), and Swaziland ($0.99).[6] It is noteworthy that, of these countries, only Zambia imports fuel through a pipeline; the others use a combination of road and rail transport.

To examine why Zambia's costs are higher we can look, in turn, at two of the three main stages in the supply chain: the crude procurement process and refining.[7] Beginning with procurement, a recent study by an oil and gas downstream logistics expert noted that the 'contractual arrangements and supply/procurement details are not altogether transparent' (Matthews, 2010: 11). The study compared how much GRZ actually paid for all Zambian feed-stock cargoes in 2008 and 2009 (CIF Dar es Salaam values) with 'normal' prices, i.e. with reference values for crude [derived from free on board (FOB) spot market prices at source] and for typical transportation and insurance costs for the distances involved. The study concluded that in most cases 'actual CIF costs, Dar were markedly higher than the reference prices. The average differential between actual and reference cost for all 11 cargoes 2008–09 was $96/tonne for Murban crude [$127/tonne for gasoil], amounting to a total of some $43 million [$50 million for gasoil] over the period' (Matthews, 2010: 22).

'The total "overcharge" vs good international practice was . . . $93 million over the two years' (Matthews, 2010: 22), or 12.5 per cent of total CIF costs

($741.8 million). In other words, it appears that poor procurement practices by GRZ result in substantially higher crude import costs (to Dar es Salaam) than necessary.

Turning attention to the refining stage, as compensation for its capital and operating costs Indeni receives a processing fee from GRZ. In late 2009 this fee was $61.10 per tonne of feedstock or $8 per barrel based on average 2008–09 feedstock composition. This fee is incorporated in the cost-plus price formula for retail pump prices. 'This is an extraordinarily high processing fee for a simple hydroskimming refinery . . . it is difficult to see how $8.00 per barrel can be justified . . . in an old plant that is significantly amortized' (Matthews, 2010: 24–25). Assuming industry 'good practice' costs of $4.00 ($2.00 operating and $2.00 capital) per barrel, 'the total saving if good practice were achieved . . . would amount to an annual saving of $13.7 million per year based on the three years, 2007–09 average throughput' (Matthews, 2010: 25).

An additional significant cost included in the price structure is the allowance for 'Refinery loss' at 10 per cent of throughput. 'In a hydroskimming refinery, the total fuel and loss . . . should be no more than 4 to 5 per cent maximum' (Matthews, 2010: 25 (based on Wijetilleke and Ody, 1984)).

A 5 per cent excess loss 'is equivalent to some $17 million per year at 2008–09 prices for crude oil' (Matthews, 2010: 25).

These findings of an industry expert suggest that the arrangement whereby the government is the monopoly importer and refiner of fuel is highly inefficient and that, as a result, pump prices are much higher than they need to be. Table 11.2 summarizes the potential reductions in pump prices if

Table 11.2 Estimated impact of identified supply chain cost savings on final pump prices, ZKw/litre

Product	(1) Crude Procurement Good Practice Saving $112.62/t (2008–09)	(2) Refining Cost/Fee Good Practice Saving $30.55/t	(3) Refinery Fuel & Loss Good Practice 5%	Total Pump Price Saving ZKw
Petrol				
before tax	466	114	145	725
after tax & fees	741	181	230	1,152
Kerosene				
before tax	501	123	156	780
after tax & fees	532	130	166	828
Diesel				
before tax	528	129	165	822
after tax & fees	626	154	195	975

Source: Matthews (2010:26)

internationally accepted industry 'good practice' could be achieved in the three areas identified and quantified above: crude procurement (saving $112.62 per tonne), refining cost ($30.55 per tonne saving), and refinery fuel and loss (5 per cent of throughput). The savings for petrol, kerosene, and diesel are shown both before and after 2009 taxes and fees. Total potential savings are in the range ZKw 725–822 and ZKw 828–1,152 per litre before and after tax respectively. Based on 2009 prices they are equivalent to reductions in (after tax) pump prices of 19 per cent for petrol, 21 per cent for kerosene, and 17 per cent for diesel.

This illustrates the potential savings from 'good practice' operation of the current Zambian system. However, even if Indeni were operated optimally, its costs would still be higher than those achieved in modern large-scale refineries.

> Economies of scale are particularly important for refining . . . As a basic rule of thumb, a refinery needs to have a processing capacity of at least 100,000 barrels a day (or 5 million tonnes a year) to be economic in a liberalized market . . . A sub-economic-scale refinery is unlikely to be able to compete with product imports from large and efficiently run refineries.
>
> (Kojima et al., 2010: 19–20)

With its capacity of just 1.1 million tonnes a year, Indeni is clearly a 'sub-economic-scale refinery'. The only way it can survive is through public subsidies and/or tariff protection. As shown below, Indeni receives substantial protection from imports – at the expense of the consumer.

11.2.3 *Reliability of supplies*

The costs to the economy are not limited to higher pump prices. Because all Zambia's fuel requirements are imported through the pipeline, whenever there is an unplanned shutdown fuel supplies are disrupted throughout the country. The phenomenon of long queues outside petrol stations countrywide has become increasingly common as a result of failure to maintain and invest in the pipeline and refinery.[8] The withdrawal of Total, which provided much of the technical services, from Indeni in 2009 raises the prospect of increased supply disruptions in the future unless substantial investment is undertaken.

Reliable estimates of the amount of investment required just to maintain the current level of operations of the pipeline and Indeni are elusive. However, GRZ has struggled to finance Indeni in the past and the fiscal situation suggests that public funding will continue to be a constraint (Whitworth, 2012). Public investment in the pipeline or refinery is therefore likely to crowd out expenditure on basic social services (for which GRZ is clearly responsible). This calls into question the appropriateness of direct government involvement in commercial fuel operations.

Another concern is that the refinery cannot adapt to the changing requirements of the Zambian market for fuel products. On one hand, new engines (in the mines and imported cars) require 'cleaner' fuels (i.e. low sulphur diesel, higher octane petrol). On the other hand, supply of quality 'black' products such as furnace fuel oil for the mines and other industries is sometimes problematic for Indeni, depending on feedstock composition.

11.2.4 *Role of government*

In most oil importing countries fuel supplies are seen as the responsibility of the private sector; there is rarely a market failure or security reason for government involvement. While it may have been necessary during the UDI period in Rhodesia, GRZ's prominent role in the Zambian fuel sector appears anachronistic today. On one hand, GRZ is responsible for procuring the feedstock, paying TAZAMA and Indeni to transport and refine it respectively, and selling finished products to OMCs. On the other hand, it is responsible for regulating the sector and fixing maximum prices. Not only is there a conflict of interest between the two roles, but the former (commercial) role can undermine regular functions of government. For example, on occasion, release of budgeted funds to ministries has been delayed because feedstock contract payments have taken priority. Also, delays in adjusting pump prices when world feedstock prices are rising have led to fiscal losses on fuel operations, at the expense of regular government functions.

This might be acceptable if it were demonstrated that GRZ was performing well in terms of fuel costs and reliability. However, as noted above, Zambia has higher basic product costs than its neighbours and frequent supply disruptions. International experience suggests that few governments are equipped to conduct commercial operations efficiently. The track record of Zambian parastatals is particularly weak, even by African standards. The evidence above suggests that this applies equally to fuel. Continued GRZ involvement in fuel operations appears hard to justify given that: (i) substantial investment is required in the subsector just to maintain – let alone improve – current operations; (ii) scarce public resources are urgently needed elsewhere for basic public services; and (iii) the private sector will invest (in the right policy environment).

11.2.5 *Monopoly concerns*

The state currently has a monopoly over fuel importation and processing in Zambia. This raises a number of concerns. Firstly, in economic theory, monopoly is associated with higher prices resulting from both the exploitation of market power and lower incentives to cut costs. The figures in Section 11.2.2 appear consistent with the theory. Secondly, relying on the pipeline for *all* Zambia's fuel requirements means that the entire country is affected by breakdowns. Allowing competition in fuel importation would greatly reduce the risk of major supply disruptions. Thirdly, even if procurement, the pipeline and the refinery were all run efficiently, there would still be substantial costs and risks involved in distributing finished products from a *single* point – Indeni – throughout a country as large as Zambia. For many parts of the country direct importation is likely to be more economic. For example, Chipata is 900 km by road from Ndola but only 140 km from Lilongwe, the capital of Malawi. Given that Malawi has historically had significantly lower fuel costs than Zambia, Eastern Province may be able to procure fuel more cheaply through Malawi.[9] Finally, instead of relying on competition to keep prices down, the monopoly structure of the fuel industry has compelled GRZ to establish retail price controls managed by the ERB. As discussed below, these are not working well.

These concerns are the inevitable result of importing fuel via a single pipeline and using import duties to prevent competition. This raises the question of whether importation via pipeline is the most appropriate arrangement for Zambia.

11.2.6 *The alternative: Direct import of finished products*

There are two main alternatives to current arrangements: (i) (re-)conversion of the pipeline to a clean products line to enable it to carry finished products and (ii) direct import of finished products by OMCs via road and/or rail. Importing finished products by pipeline would eliminate the need for refining and the inefficiencies at Indeni identified above.

However, conversion to a clean products line would require further public investment, assuming that TAZAMA remains in public ownership. Also, the disadvantages associated with: (i) monopoly; (ii) government involvement in commercial operations; and (iii) national distribution from a single point would remain.

The potentially more attractive alternative is liberalized direct importation of finished products by OMCs. Instead of just buying products from Indeni for internal distribution, OMCs would be free to procure fuel on the world market and transport it from Indian Ocean ports to Zambia by road, rail, or both.[10] This is how most landlocked African countries import fuel. It is also how GRZ has responded when Indeni has been shut down for extended periods; OMCs were given temporary waivers of import duty.

There are a number of potential advantages relative to current arrangements. The most obvious one is the introduction of competition into a sector where it is sorely needed. There would be competition both between OMCs themselves and between different ports and transport routes. So, suppliers to, say, Eastern Province, using Durban might be competing against suppliers using the ports of Nacala or Beira. Costs should come down as a result of both the need to compete/survive and the transport savings from serving different provinces from the nearest/most convenient ports. The potential for cost savings is illustrated by the fact that on the occasions when Indeni has been closed, the differential import duty on finished products has been suspended and OMCs have been able to import fuel at lower cost than Indeni; once Indeni resumed normal operations punitive duties (currently 25 per cent) are imposed on direct imports in order to protect Indeni revenues.

The other obvious benefit of competition is that it would eliminate the countrywide fuel crises that currently result from unplanned shutdowns at Indeni. Securing fuel from multiple sources is a much safer risk strategy than relying solely on Indeni. If one OMC experiences supply disruptions others can fill the gap.

Another advantage of allowing competition is that it would allow GRZ to withdraw from active operations in the fuel sector to focus on policy and regulation without turning a public monopoly into a private one. Meanwhile, the simple presence of competition would reduce, if not eliminate, the need for price controls on fuel.

A common counter-argument is that importing fuel by road tankers instead of by pipeline would increase road maintenance costs. While true for the region, it would not necessarily apply inside Zambia. As noted above, finished products are currently distributed by road (and, to a much lesser extent, rail) throughout Zambia, starting from Indeni. Direct importation would open up the possibility of, say, Eastern and Southern Provinces receiving supplies through Malawi and Zimbabwe/Botswana respectively, greatly reducing use of Zambia's own roads. While increased road maintenance costs would be a legitimate concern for Zambia's neighbours, these should be covered by appropriate road user charges in those countries and therefore reflected in Zambia's import costs.

In order to close the pipeline and switch to direct imports of finished products there would have to be investment in new storage capacity on the part of both GRZ (to ensure strategic reserves) and OMCs. While the Copperbelt could be covered by converting Indeni storage products to finished products, investment would be required at Ndola Fuel Terminal. New capacity would be needed in Lusaka and at some provincial depots. Switching over would have to be a gradual process. Moreover, OMCs will not be prepared to invest without certain safeguards, for example over taxation and pricing policy.

11.2.7 Taxation

Fuel taxation is an important source of government revenue in most countries.[11] Not only is it relatively easy to collect,[12] but it can support other policy objectives such as cutting imports, energy efficiency, and reducing carbon emissions, etc.

After several years of relative stability, fuel taxation policy in Zambia has been erratic in recent years. Table 11.1 shows that in June 2008 Zambia had much the highest government levies, duties, and taxes in southern Africa, at 55 US cents per litre. While taxes had been among the highest in the region for some time, this was aggravated by the impact of the jump in international oil prices in mid-2008 on Zambia's *ad valorem* fuel taxes. *Ad valorem* taxes are levied as a fixed percentage of import values, whereas most of Zambia's neighbours have *specific* tax rates that do not vary with world prices. GRZ cut excise duty rates on petrol and diesel twice between June and September from 60 per cent and 30 per cent to 36 per cent and 7 per cent respectively. Duties were cut to defuse public concern at increasing pump prices. In effect, GRZ cut duties to offset the impact of rising world prices. However, even though world prices fell sharply within a few months of their mid-2008 peak, duties (and pump prices) were not revised until January 2010. Moreover, the increase was modest: diesel excise duty was only raised from 7 per cent to 10 per cent (cf. 30 per cent pre-June 2008), while petrol duty was unchanged.

The combined impact of: (i) reductions in excise duty and (ii) falling world prices and import volumes following the global financial crisis was that monthly fiscal revenues from oil products (customs, excise and value added tax (VAT)), which had averaged about $US25 million per month between January 2007 and mid-2008 (peaking at $US60 million in mid-2008), declined to an average of about $US15 million in 2009 (Matthews, 2010: 22).[13] The timing of the decrease was unfortunate because it aggravated a general decline in government revenue resulting from the global crisis and other developments (Whitworth, 2012).

As in many countries, recent changes in fuel taxation appear to reflect a political desire to keep fuel prices low. As noted in Chapter 12, fuel prices are a key factor in transport costs so revenue maximization should not be the sole criterion in determining tax rates. However, if fuel taxes are to make a sustainable contribution to government revenue they must be stable and predictable.

One way of moderating price fluctuations while sustaining revenue would be to replace *ad valorem* taxation with *specific* (fixed) rates per litre. Whereas *ad valorem* taxes cause domestic prices to increase (or decrease) by more than increases (or decreases) in world prices, specific taxes are countercyclical. They are also harder to evade because the rates are fixed and known, and there is no scope for under-invoicing. However, rather than adjusting taxes, a more sustainable way of reducing fuel prices (without damaging GRZ revenue) is to reduce basic product *costs* through increased competition and efficiency.

11.2.8 *Price control*

Whenever a market is characterized by monopoly there is a case for statutory price controls to protect consumers. As noted above, the importation and refining of fuel for the Zambian market is a pure monopoly. The ERB, therefore, determines ex-Ndola Fuel Terminal prices periodically using a cost-plus formula.[14] The principle of cost-plus pricing is that the final price should cover all costs in the supply chain plus a 'fair' profit margin.[15] However, this system was effectively suspended between late 2008 and January 2010, seemingly in response to political pressure. Despite significant increases in world prices, pump prices were not adjusted at all during 2009. The cost of the delay in adjusting pump prices was borne by: (i) government[16] which, in addition to cutting excise duty, used scarce fiscal resources to subsidize oil consumers; and (ii) OMCs, whose margins were frozen in nominal terms. Pump prices were frozen again following the 2011 elections. With rising world oil prices unbudgeted fuel subsidies cost $US145 million (0.7% of GDP) in 2012 and $US220 million (1%) in 2013 before fiscal pressures forced their abandonment in May 2013. This calls into question ERB's independence and the usefulness of price control in current circumstances. Of course, if competition from direct imports was allowed, there would be no need for price control.

11.2.9 *Conclusions*

Zambia no longer has the highest pump prices in the region. However, this is not a result of improved efficiency. Instead, it is the result of a sharp reduction in excise duties and the use of price controls to prevent or delay increasing import prices feeding through into pump prices. The costs of suppressing fuel prices have been borne by the Treasury, contributing to the deterioration in Zambia's fiscal performance, and by those people affected by the resulting cuts in public expenditure (as well as by OMCs).[17] Given Zambia's fiscal prospects, this is not a sustainable strategy.

Bringing fuel prices down permanently will require efficiency improvements, which cut basic product costs. The data presented above suggests that there is considerable scope for cutting costs, particularly if Zambia ends its total dependence on TAZAMA and Indeni, and switches to direct import of finished products by OMCs. Not only could such competition cut costs, but it could also increase the reliability of fuel supplies and allow GRZ to withdraw from commercial operations.

Public concern over high fuel prices in Zambia usually takes the (misguided) form of demands for public subsidies. GRZ has often given way to such demands, at substantial fiscal cost. There is little public understanding that the underlying reason for high fuel prices is that for decades GRZ has been protecting a highly inefficient pipeline and refinery monopoly from competition. This inefficiency is implicitly recognized by GRZ (though not the public) in the form of the 25 per cent import duty on finished products, which is solely intended to protect Indeni, not to raise revenue. GRZ ownership and protection of a fuel supply monopoly is anachronistic in what is otherwise one of Africa's most liberal economies. Giving up the monopoly and allowing the direct import of finished products, by eliminating the difference in import duty between crude (5 per cent) and finished products (25 per cent), should result in a significant reduction in fuel costs and prices with little reduction in GRZ revenue.

An understandable reason for GRZ's reluctance to liberalize the fuel sector is that 320 jobs would almost certainly be lost at Indeni and 260 at TAZAMA. Both organizations can be expected to resist liberalization. However, it is important to understand that new jobs would be created, both directly in OMCs and indirectly through the improved competitiveness of the Zambian economy resulting from permanently lower fuel prices. Moreover, almost all Zambians will benefit from lower fuel prices resulting from improved efficiency.

This section suggests there is a strong *prima facie* case for radically altering Zambia's fuel import arrangements. However, while there are complaints whenever increases in world prices are passed on to pump prices, the Zambian public is largely unaware of the scope for sustainably reducing fuel costs (and improving reliability of supply) through domestic policy reform. The pipeline and Indeni are still seen as national assets long after their main rationale – sanctions against Rhodesia – ended; public discussion focuses on how they should be operated, rather than on whether they are still needed. A properly informed public debate is long overdue.[18]

11.3 Electricity

It is widely believed in Zambia that the country has some of the best river resources and hydro-electric potential in Africa, and should, therefore, be a major exporter of power to the region. Instead, it has been experiencing persistent load shedding since 2007. Apart from the Kariba North Bank extension, there has been no significant investment in generation capacity since 1977. What went wrong?

In reality, Zambia's hydro-electric potential is relatively modest. It is only ranked tenth on the African mainland in terms of technically exploitable (eleventh for economically exploitable) hydropower potential, far behind countries such as Democratic Republic of Congo, Ethiopia, and Cameroon (Japan International Cooperation Agency, 2010: Table B.20).[19] Nevertheless, while it may never be a major exporter, Zambia should have little difficulty achieving self-sufficiency in power. Much of the explanation for the poor performance is straightforward, although there is little public understanding of the issues.

This section shows how developments in mining resulted in Zambia having virtually the lowest electricity tariffs in Africa – well below the level necessary to attract private investment. With the government having insufficient resources to provide basic health and education services, let alone to invest in power, this made load shedding unavoidable when mining demand increased following privatization and the copper boom of the 2000s. It goes on to discuss how the power deficit can be addressed through demand management, trade, and investment in new generation capacity. The importance and challenges of increasing tariffs are highlighted, and the roles of the public and private sectors discussed. The section concludes by questioning the realism of GRZ plans for rural electrification.

11.3.1 *Historical background*

To understand the poor performance of the electricity subsector some history is necessary, particularly the role of the mining industry. The key trends are illustrated in Table 11.3. Ninety-five per cent of Zambia's electricity is generated by three hydro-electric power stations:

1. Victoria Falls, commissioned in 1938, installed capacity of 108 MW since 1972;

2. Kariba North Bank, commissioned in 1960, 600 MW;

3. Kafue Gorge Upper, commissioned in 1971, capacity of 900 MW since 1977;

They were built primarily to meet the expanding needs of the copper mining industry.

Table 11.3 shows that, in 1975, mining accounted for 66 per cent of domestic energy consumption (42 per cent of total sales, including exports).

The commissioning of Kafue Gorge Upper more than doubled generation capacity. As a result, substantial 'surplus' capacity became available (illustrated by the widening gap between installed capacity and peak load between 1975 and 1978 in Table 11.3); much of the increased energy was exported to Zimbabwe.

Had copper production grown as anticipated, this surplus would have steadily decreased and further generation capacity would have been required

Table 11.3 ZESCO capacity, sales, and tariff time series

	Installed Capacity (MW)	Peak Load (MW)	Mining Sales (GWh)	Domestic Sales (GWh)	Export (GWh)	Total Sales (GWh)	Copper Prodn* ('000 MT)	Residential Tariff** (Kwacha/KWh)	Residential Tariff*** (US cents/KWh)	Mining Tariff**** (US cents/KWh)
1975	1,200	718	2,300	1,190	2,010	5,500	619	1.40	–	–
1976	1,326	735	2,600	1,222	2,278	6,100	713	1.40	–	–
1977	1,476	734	2,879	1,229	2,392	6,500	660	1.40	–	–
1978	1,656	762	3,841	1,425	2,523	7,789	656	1.40	–	–
1979	1,656	778	3,987	1,481	2,734	8,202	585	1.70	–	–
1980	1,656	764	4,027	1,416	3,156	8,599	612	1.70	–	–
1981	1,656	804	4,190	1,434	3,531	9,155	586	1.70	–	–
1982	1,656	846	4,257	1,657	3,756	9,670	580	1.70	–	–
1983	1,656	852	4,293	1,697	3,168	9,158	575	2.13	–	–
1984	1,656	851	4,249	1,749	2,810	8,808	522	2.13	–	–
1985	1,656	860	4,138	1,714	3,218	9,070	479	3.63	–	–
1986	1,656	890	4,465	1,815	2,575	8,855	459	7.00	–	–
1987	1,656	912	4,459	1,864	966	7,289	483	7.00	–	–
1988	1,656	919	4,434	1,961	1,233	7,628	422	7.00	–	–
1989	1,656	866	4,289	1,860	148	6,297	451	7.00	–	–
1990	1,656	926	4,251	1,970	986	7,207	427	14.46	–	–
1991	1,656	943	4,094	2,070	2,108	8,272	377	17.35	–	–
1992	1,656	993	4,239	2,155	95	6,489	442	1.56	0.91	–
1993	1,656	1,003	4,313	2,108	855	7,276	402	5.38	1.19	–
1994	1,656	1,018	4,142	2,122	1,066	7,330	366	5.70	0.85	–
1995	1,656	1,010	4,123	2,238	1,397	7,758	344	7.00	0.81	–
1996	1,656	1,028	4,149	2,401	816	7,366	327	10.00	0.83	–
1997	1,656	1,090	4,047	2,384	695	7,126	302	33.68	2.57	–
1998	1,656	1,126	3,879	2,603	528	7,010	256	42.10	2.26	3.08
1999	1,656	1,069	3,620	2,262	586	6,468	266	58.94	2.47	3.08
2000	1,656	1,085	3,218	2,985	857	7,060	312	73.68	2.37	2.69
2001	1,656	1,088	3,519	2,578	1,591	7,688	358	85.47	2.37	2.72
2002	1,656	1,118	3,707	2,909	649	7,265	376	85.47	1.98	2.74
2003	1,656	1,255	3,870	3,168	434	7,472	360	90.00	1.90	2.76
2004	1,698	1,294	3,952	3,520	188	7,660	423	90.00	1.88	2.77
2005	1,698	1,330	4,091	3,516	265	7,872	470	100.00	2.24	2.84
2006	1,698	1,393	4,499	3,389	472	8,360	514	100.00	2.78	2.90
2007	1,698	1,605	4,748	3,537	191	8,476	522	100.00	2.50	2.94
2008	1,698	1,478	4,773	3,678	74	8,525	612	127.00	3.39	3.98
2009	1,819	1,483	6,413	3,887	321	10,621	696	178.00	3.53	4.14
2010	1,659	1,580	6,331	3,475	578	10,384	852	250.98	5.21	4.48
2011	1,812	1,571	5,252	5,265	707	11,022	879	250.70	5.16	5.60
2012	1,854	1,681	5,554	4,763	980	11,297	na	250.70	4.88	5.60
2013	2,034	1,695	5,929	4,917	1,083	11,929	na	250.70	4.65	5.60

Source: Energy Regulation Board, except as indicated below
* Source: Bank of Zambia
**Metered Residential Tariff Rate E3 until 1993 (source: Energy Statistics Bulletin), Rate R2, consumption between 100 and 400 KWh, since 1994 (source: ERB)
***US cent equivalent only calculated since market determined exchange rate policy adopted in 1992
****Tariff charged by CEC to privatized mines, including mark-up of about 0.8 US cents on ZESCO charge to CEC. Source: CEC. Tariffs prior to privatization are not available.

by the 1990s. However, following the nationalization of the mines in 1972, investment in mining virtually dried up. Initially, production levels (which peaked at 747,500 tonnes in 1969) were sustained; however, with minimal investment, falling copper prices from 1975, and poor management, production started to decline in the late 1970s. By the time the mines were privatized in the late 1990s, production was just 256,000 tonnes (in 1998). As a result, instead of the anticipated increase, mining electricity consumption dropped to 3,218 GWh in 2000 from 4,027 GWh in 1980.

By contrast, domestic *non-mining* sales increased fairly steadily from 1,416 GWh (35 per cent of mining sales) in 1980 to 2,985 GWh (93 per cent of mining sales) in 2000 – reflecting the growth in the urban economy.[20] Despite this, the decline in mining sales meant that Zambia had a substantial surplus of generation capacity over domestic demand until the 2000s. In other words, for some 30 years domestic demand for power was effectively unconstrained and there was little urgency over new investment.

Surplus capacity meant there was little pressure on ZESCO[21] to maintain real tariff levels. Economic pricing principles require that energy prices cover not only the direct costs of operating and maintaining the system but also a return on the capital investment. However, until the 2000s, the Zambian Government was much less interested in earning a return on its investment in ZESCO and other parastatals than in providing a public service. As the mines were also publicly owned until the late 1990s and tariff increases are always unpopular with the public, as long as ZESCO was able to cover its operating costs and did not ask for public funds, GRZ preferred to minimize tariff increases.[22]

As noted above, ZESCO's generation capacity is nearly all hydro-electric. The distinctive characteristic of hydro schemes relative to thermal generation (coal, oil, gas) is that they have very high capital costs, but low operating costs. This meant that throughout the 1980s and 1990s, with no pressure from its shareholder for an economic return on the capital *already* invested and (with spare capacity) no need for *new* investment, ZESCO was able to comfortably cover its operating and maintenance costs with low tariffs. Because the lack of pressure to increase tariffs persisted for so long – as illustrated in Table 11.3 – residential tariffs fell to the exceptionally low level of below 1 US cent per KWh in the mid-1990s. While tariffs increased significantly following the establishment of the Energy Regulation Board (ERB) in 1997, at about 2.5 US cents per KWh, they were still virtually the lowest in Africa (see Table 11.5).

Following privatization of the mines, the picture changed dramatically. Substantial investment in the mines and the copper price boom led to a rapid recovery in copper production from 256,000 tonnes in 1998 to 879,000 tonnes in 2011. In turn, this meant a rapid increase in the demand for power, wiping out the surplus capacity and exports. Mining sales rose from 3,218

GWh in 2000 to 4,748 GWh in 2007, while system peak load increased from 1,085 MW to 1,605 MW over the same period. With total installed capacity of only 1,698 MW, there was an insufficient cushion to allow for maintenance shutdowns. As a result, with new mining loads coming on stream (taking mining sales to 6,331 GWh in 2010), demand has exceeded supply since 2007 and Zambia has experienced persistent load shedding in peak hours.

Warnings from ZESCO since the 1990s that without new investment in generation capacity Zambia would face load shedding elicited little response from the government until the mid 2000s, by which time it was too late. Until Zambia established macro-economic stability and received debt relief under the Heavily Indebted Poor Country (HIPC) initiative, GRZ was in no position to raise finance itself for power projects. While legislation had been enacted to allow private investment in power generation, with tariffs well below the level needed to provide a positive return on investment, there was little private interest.[23]

11.3.2 Addressing Zambia's power deficit

Table 11.4 presents a summary of the base case load (demand) forecast prepared for ZESCO as part of a recent power system development planning exercise, along with known installed capacity once expansion projects currently underway are completed (see below). The anticipated rapid growth in demand is largely driven by continued expansion of the mining sector. The surplus/deficit column is simply the difference between forecast peak demand and installed capacity. However, this ignores the requirement to periodically close generation units for planned maintenance and allowance for unplanned outages, and therefore significantly underestimates ZESCO's capacity deficit.

Even without allowing for outages, and even after the commissioning of

Table 11.4 ZESCO load forecast, 2010–30

Year	Confirmed Installed Capacity (MW)	Domestic Peak Demand (MW)	Surplus/ Deficit (MW)	Domestic Sales (GWh)
2010-11	1,908	1,801	107	9,932
2011-12	1,908	2,080	-172	11,853
2012-13	1,908	2,214	-306	12,542
2013-14	2,268	2,299	-31	12,947
2014-15	2,268	2,438	-170	13,784
2021-21	2,268	2,893	-625	15,749
2030-31	2,268	4,068	-1,800	20,823

Source: JICA (2010)

Kariba North Bank Extension (360 MW) in 2013, ZESCO faces a substantial and growing capacity deficit. This must be addressed through a combination of demand management, trade, and investment in new capacity.

11.3.3 *Demand management*

There are a number of obvious demand management measures. Firstly, as illustrated in Table 11.5 and discussed below, ZESCO tariffs have been exceptionally low, encouraging wasteful consumption. While mining loads are price-inelastic, the substantial tariff increases required to attract investment should dampen demand by other consumers. Secondly, with more than a third of its customers un-metered in 2006 and an excessive level of outstanding debtors, there is considerable scope for reducing demand through improved utility management practices. Thirdly, there is also substantial scope for improving energy efficiency: 'Compact Fluorescent Lamps can enable energy savings of up to 80 per cent for residential customers' (World Bank, 2008: 8). ZESCO plans to distribute 1 million lamps are projected to cut peak demand by 50 MW (World Bank, 2008: 9).

11.3.4 *Trade in energy*

The energy deficit since 2007 has been partially met through imports, mainly from Democratic Republic of Congo. A second 220-kV transmission line to Democratic Republic of Congo is being constructed by Copperbelt Energy Corporation (see below) to facilitate increased imports. However, as Zambia's power supply crisis has coincided with a crisis throughout southern Africa, there is little prospect of meeting all the shortfall through imports. Moreover, until the August 2010 tariff increases, the wholesale price of imports (5 US cents per KWh in 2010) exceeded most of ZESCO's retail tariffs.

Table 11.3 shows that Zambia exported substantial energy until 1986 – as much as 39 per cent of total sales in some years. However, this was essentially disposal of surplus energy that could not be sold domestically; it was not seen as an important revenue source. As domestic demand increased, exports tailed off. With new investment in generation and growing regional demand, energy could, again, represent an export opportunity for Zambia.

The regional energy market has been transformed in recent years by two major developments: the establishment of the Southern African Power Pool and the advent of democracy in South Africa. While there had been limited bilateral energy trading within the region for decades, the 1995 Inter-governmental Agreement establishing the Southern African Power Pool created the first common power grid between the 12 member countries[24] and a formal common market for electricity under the auspices of the Southern African Development Community (www.sapp.co.zw). The aim was to optimize the use of available energy resources by expanding electricity trade, reducing energy costs, and providing greater supply stability for national utilities. The initial facilitation of bilateral contracts was supplemented in 2001 by a short-term spot market in non-firm electricity contracts, utilizing the Internet to conduct trades, and subsequently by increasingly sophisticated market developments. ZESCO is an active member of the Power Pool but, with little surplus generation capacity available for export, it has yet to fully exploit the potential benefits of increased energy trade.

The impetus for establishing the Power Pool was greatly strengthened by the entry of South Africa – by far the largest energy market in Africa – into the regional market following the end of its apartheid isolation. Domestic supply problems since 2008, combined with the environmental imperative to reduce its dependence on coal-fired generation, have greatly increased South African demand for 'clean' energy, such as hydro-electricity. Tariffs more than doubled between 2008 and 2010 to facilitate investment and the regulator approved further increases in residential tariffs equivalent to 10.5 US cents per KWh from mid-2012 (www.eskom.co.za).[25] The increase in South African demand and tariffs appears to represent a ready market for Zambian energy exports. It raises the intriguing possibility that investment in new capacity could be justified on the basis of South African, rather than Zambian, tariffs.

11.3.5 New capacity

Zambia has an estimated hydropower potential of about 6,000 MW, of which less than 2,000 MW has been harnessed (Republic of Zambia, 2006: 131). A rehabilitation programme enabled ZESCO to upgrade capacity at Kafue Gorge Upper from 900 MW to 990 MW, and at Kariba North Bank from 600 MW to 720 MW from 2010. The extension to Kariba North Bank further increased installed capacity by 360 MW from 2013 at a cost of about $US420 million.

These projects should enable ZESCO to meet most of the anticipated load growth and reduce load shedding over the medium term. However, supply will only be fully secure once the 750 MW Kafue Gorge Lower scheme is completed at a cost of at least $US1.5 billion. This will both eliminate the domestic capacity deficit and enable Zambia to once again become a significant energy exporter.[26]

11.3.6 Public or private finance?

Zambia's current power stations were all publicly financed and the power utility, ZESCO, remains a public enterprise. Not surprisingly, therefore, many Zambians have called for government investment in new power generation. However, purely public investment is no longer a realistic option. When the last major energy investment, Kafue Gorge Upper, was embarked upon in the late 1960s, Zambia was a lower-middle-income country with significant public revenues from the mining industry to invest. The subsequent economic mismanagement and collapse wiped out GRZ's 'fiscal space'. While improved management since the early 2000s and debt relief have increased fiscal space somewhat (Whitworth, 2012), essential public services such as education, health, and water remain severely under-funded. As electricity is a 'less essential' service and given the proliferation of independent (i.e. private) power producers worldwide in recent years, it is more appropriate these days for investment in new capacity to be financed by the private sector.

However, whereas until recently GRZ preferred keeping tariffs low to earning a financial return on public investment in the power sector, private investors demand a commercial return on their capital. Private finance will not be forthcoming unless investors believe that real tariff levels will increase substantially – to at least 7.5 US cents per KWh.[27] The challenge for GRZ is not just to increase tariffs, but to persuade potential investors and financiers that the increase will be permanent. It is important to distinguish here between the two main domestic markets for electricity, mining, and non-mining. We begin with the latter.

11.3.7 Non-mining tariffs

Table 11.5 shows that, until recently, Zambia had the lowest residential, commercial, and industrial tariffs in Africa. At roughly half the regional average, they barely covered operations and maintenance costs, and were well below the minimum level needed to induce private investment.

Increasing non-mining (particularly residential) tariffs is complicated by public resistance, owing to a number of factors. Firstly, tariffs have been at such low levels for so long that the Zambian public considers this normal; they are unaware that tariffs are much higher in the rest of the world. Secondly, there is little understanding of the link between low tariffs, lack of investment, and load shedding. Thirdly, the five-year-plus lag between tariff increases and the resulting increase in generation makes consumers reluctant to pay more now when the benefits are so far into the future. Finally, there is widespread dissatisfaction with ZESCO service levels, reflecting both low revenues and poor management.

As illustrated above, the combination of declining real tariffs, lack of investment in generation capacity, and rapid growth in mining loads since 2000 made load shedding in peak hours virtually inevitable – regardless of ZESCO performance. However, ZESCO's problems have been compounded by poor management. In recent years ZESCO performance has been characterized by many of the problems typically associated with African parastatals: political interference; frequent changes in the board and senior management;

Table 11.5 Comparison of typical effective residential, commercial, and industrial tariffs in sub-Saharan Africa, 2003–08 (US cents/KWh)

Consumption	Residential 100 KWh	Commercial 900 KWh	Industrial 100 KVA
Benin	13.6	15.1	10.7
Botswana	7.5	7.2	4.0
Burkina Faso	20.0	26.7	15.0
Cameroon	10.9	11.4	9.2
Cape Verde	25.8	21.8	17.7
Chad	30.0	44.7	38.8
Congo, Dep. Rep.	4.0	11.0	14.6
Congo, Rep.	16.0	10.7	11.2
Cote d'Ivoire	11.9	16.9	10.7
Ethiopia	4.1	8.3	4.7
Ghana	8.2	13.9	6.4
Kenya	14.8	21.7	15.1
Lesotho	7.2	9.3	3.3
Madagascar	3.0	25.3	10.5
Malawi	4.0	6.9	3.1
Mali	26.6	23.2	
Mozambique	6.8	8.0	5.1
Namibia	11.7	14.0	13.6
Niger	14.1	13.2	9.3
Nigeria	3.4	5.0	5.1
Rwanda	14.6	17.2	17.2
Senegal	23.8	22.8	15.8
South Africa	3.6	7.7	2.7
Tanzania	6.7	8.0	5.4
Uganda	21.4	21.9	17.0
Zambia	**2.9**	**4.4**	**2.5**
Zimbabwe	4.3	5.7	

Source: Briceno-Garmendia and Shkaratan (2011)

the absence of clear commercial objectives and practices; overstaffing; lack of maintenance; poor cost control; inadequate tariffs; and poor customer care, etc.

The cumulative results of the above are reported in the 'Revised ZESCO's Cost of Service' report to the ERB. Following an analysis of ZESCO's costs, revenues, and financial performance, the report highlighted five key issues (IPA Energy Consulting, 2007):

- five straight years (2002–06) of operating losses;
- cash-flow problems indicated by increasing total receivables and total payables;

- more than one third of customers were not metered;
- a 'very rapid run-up of staff costs', with the average cost per employee doubling every two years between 1999 and 2004;[28]
- 'significant under pricing of mining loads' (discussed below).

The tariff comparison with other African utilities in Table 11.5 represents an unanswerable case for a permanent real increase in tariffs.[29] However, the damage to ZESCO's public reputation resulting from persistent load shedding and from press reports of extravagant salaries, the use of ZESCO resources for political purposes, and subsidized electricity for staff, etc. made it difficult for the ERB to approve the order of increase required to attract investment. ZESCO applications for tariff increases invariably attract considerable criticism in the press.

While public opinion lagged behind, the need for economic tariffs to attract investment was increasingly recognized within government. GRZ committed itself to achieving 'cost reflective' tariffs as part of its 2008–11 International Monetary Fund (IMF) programme, though the term was not precisely defined (IMF, 2008). The ERB approved significant tariff increases between 2008 and 2010. Residential tariffs increased to 5 US cents per KWh in August 2010 for monthly consumption up to 400 KWh (the R2 rate shown in Table 11.3) and 8 US cents above 400 KWh (www.erb.org.zm). While tariffs had yet to reach cost reflective levels, Zambia was no longer the outlier shown in Table 11.5. The ERB approved further increases in principle from 2011. However, the ERB board was dismissed following the 2011 elections and there were no further increases between 2010 and early 2014 – representing a significant real decrease in tariffs.

11.3.8 Mining tariffs

Table 11.3 shows that mining sales represented 61 per cent of total electricity sales in 2010 and that the recovery in mining accounts for most of the increase in sales since 2000. Without this, there would be no urgency to expand generation capacity.

There are two main categories of mining load: privatized mines and new mines. For the privatized mines ZESCO supplies power at the *wholesale* level to Copperbelt Energy Corporation (CEC), which acquired Zambia Consolidated Copper Mines' transmission and distribution network in 1997, and which retails power to the individual mines. The (then publicly owned) mines benefited from low tariffs throughout the 1980s and 1990s while ZESCO had surplus capacity. These tariffs were then entrenched during the privatization negotiations. The Cost of Service report[27] found a 'significant under pricing of mining loads'. It estimated that in 2006/7 ZESCO was 'selling to CEC at a loss of about one half a US cent/KWh' and that the average mining tariff would have to increase by 29 per cent to reach 'cost reflective' levels (IPA Energy Consulting, 2007: 9). In 2008 ZESCO negotiated a 35 per cent increase in the CEC tariff.

Two major new copper mines, Kansanshi and Lumwana, commenced operations in 2005 and 2008 respectively. Kansanshi's demand is expected to reach 72 MW and Lumwana's 90 MW (Japan International Cooperation Agency, 2010). At full operation their combined peak load of 162 MW will be equivalent to 10 per cent of the entire 2011 system peak load. ZESCO sells power directly to both mines at individually negotiated tariff rates. Although meeting these significant new loads requires ZESCO to bring forward investment in new generation capacity and/or to import energy, the negotiated (retail) tariffs in 2006 were *below* the (wholesale) rate at which ZESCO sold to CEC (IPA Energy Consulting, 2007: 9).

The initial failure to negotiate commercial tariffs with the privatized and new mines appears to reflect the legacy of subsidized tariffs to the mines during the 1980s and 1990s when they were in public ownership. However, there can be no justification for subsidizing private mines, especially when their growing energy demands are crowding out non-mining loads and imposing an urgent requirement for investment in new capacity. To ensure its long-term financial health and sustainability, and to enable investment to proceed, ZESCO doubled mining tariffs (which do not require ERB approval) from 2.84 US cents per KWh in 2005 to 5.60 cents in 2011 (Table 11.3).

11.3.9 *Public or private ownership?*

Even with increasing tariffs, ZESCO's track record gives few grounds for confidence that the utility will be able to turn around its operational and financial performance while remaining in public ownership. To an outsider, ZESCO appears a prominent candidate for privatization. Given a suitable policy environment and economic tariffs, GRZ could raise substantial sums from sale of its assets, which could then be re-invested in sectors such as health, education, water, and roads, which clearly belong in the public sector. Yet, despite its poor public reputation, there appears to be little public or political support for 'unbundling' (i.e. separating the generation, transmission, and distribution functions), let alone for privatizing, ZESCO. Public ownership remains surprisingly popular in Zambia, reflecting both President Kaunda's 'African socialism' and the controversial record of the privatization programme of the 1990s.[30]

11.3.10 *Increasing access*

'Zambia has an overall national electrification rate of 20 per cent, with about 40 per cent of the population in urban and peri-urban areas and only 2 per cent of the rural population having access to electricity' (World Bank, 2008: 4). The Rural Electrification Authority (REA) was established by GRZ in 2003 to promote and finance rural electrification projects. It is financed by a 3 per cent levy on non-mining electricity consumers, which is currently equivalent to about $US2.5 million a year. Grants are provided to project developers in rural areas based on economic and financial criteria. The REA Rural Electrification Master Plan aims to increase the electrification rate to 51 per cent by 2030 at a cost of some $US50 million annually (REA, 2010).

While the aspiration to increase the electrification rate is understandable, the 51 per cent target appears unrealistic for two reasons. Firstly, Zambia is one of the largest, most sparsely populated countries in Africa. This makes most extension of the grid into rural areas uneconomic; the costs of extending transmission and distribution lines over long distances will hardly ever be recovered from the small number of potential customers.[31] Substantial subsidies – far in excess of the REA levy – will therefore be required. Secondly, 50.7 per cent of the rural and 10.2 per cent of the urban population was 'extremely poor' in 2006 (Central Statistical Office, 2009: 20). Such people struggle just to meet their basic food requirements; for them electricity will always be an unaffordable luxury, no matter how much tariffs are subsidized.

The only grid extensions likely to be economically viable are those that involve relatively short distances and either: (i) high population density or (ii) commercial loads. In practice, they will be largely confined to urban and peri-urban areas. There is little prospect of many Zambians living far from the ZESCO grid getting connected. Instead, they will have to rely, if anything, on generators or on stand alone systems based on diesel, solar, or (occasionally) mini-hydro sources of power. However, unit costs for such schemes are usually much higher than for ZESCO; economic, financial, and management constraints make it unlikely that more than a tiny proportion of the rural population will benefit.

11.3.11 Conclusions

GRZ bears much of the responsibility for the load shedding experienced throughout Zambia since 2007. By allowing tariffs to fall to exceptionally low real levels, it rendered investment in power generation economically and financially non-viable, while consumers took subsidized tariffs for granted. Despite warnings that new generation capacity was urgently needed, GRZ was reluctant to take the necessary, but politically unpopular, measure of substantial tariff increases to encourage investment. The populist emphasis on rural electrification and increasing access distracted attention away from the need for investment in generation.

By the time the need for tariff increases was properly understood within government, it was too late to avert load shedding given that a typical hydro station takes at least five years to construct.[32] Moreover, strong public opposition (reinforced by ZESCO mismanagement) meant that tariffs could only be increased gradually. The onset of load shedding in 2007 appeared to focus minds: tariffs subsequently increased in stages to their highest real level in over 30 years, with residential tariffs reaching 5 US cents per KWh in 2010. While tariffs were yet to reach 'cost reflective' levels, investment prospects improved considerably – reinforced by the prospect of being able to export surplus energy to South Africa (and the region) at the much higher tariffs applied there. The announcement in 2010 that the Kafue Gorge Lower scheme will proceed with Chinese (public and private) finance, and strong private sector interest in other schemes, such as Itezhi-Tezhi, suggested that the corner had finally been turned. However, the election of a more populist government in 2011 and the freezing of tariffs until (at least) 2014 illustrates that recent progress remains fragile.

Appendix

Figure 11.A1 Retail prices of diesel in sub-Saharan Africa in February 2010 ($US per litre)

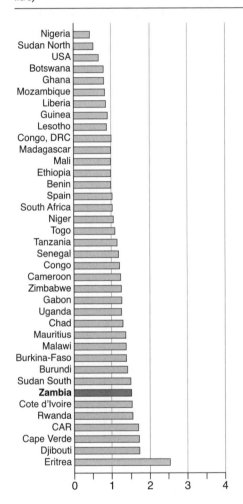

Source: World Bank Africa Transport Unit.

Notes

1. The fuel section draws heavily on Matthews (2010). Helpful comments from Robert Masiye and Bill Matthews are gratefully acknowledged.
2. Total acquired its shares from Agip, the original project developer, in 2001. Between 2002 and 2007 Total was responsible for procurement of the petroleum feedstock for Indeni.
3. In October 2007 the Zambian government appointed TAZAMA Pipelines Ltd as its agent to manage the procurement of feedstock on its behalf.
4. Equivalent to 9.3 per cent of total FOB imports, worth $7,967 million over the two years (IMF, 2010)
5. As noted below, excise duties on fuel were cut sharply later in 2008. Despite this, Appendix 11.1 shows that Zambia still had among the highest pump prices for diesel in sub-Saharan Africa in February 2010. As pump prices include taxes, which differ markedly between countries, they are a poor guide to *cost* differences.
6. While comparable data for June 2008 is not available, British Petroleum data for August 2006 shows Zambian product basic costs were 13 per cent higher than in Lesotho and 4 per cent higher than in Zimbabwe.
7. Data on the efficiency of the pipeline, the middle stage, is not publicly available.
8. The 'refinery was shut down for a total of 113 days in 2007 compared to 119 days in 2006. The shutdowns in 2007 were mainly driven by the shortage of feedstock whereas in 2006 shutdowns were mostly attributable to technical problems' (ERB, 2007: 20).
9. Similarly, Livingstone is 800 km from Ndola, but only 10 km from Zimbabwe and 70 km from Botswana. Much of Northern Province is closer to Tanzania than to Ndola.
10. Even if Indeni achieved the above 'good practice' savings 'through investment and enhanced operational procedures, it would only just compete with road tanker supply' (Matthews, 2010: 41).
11. For example, in Uganda fuel taxes averaged 2.2 per cent of GDP between 1991 and 2006 (Cawley and Zake, 2010: 111).
12. This applies to Zambia in particular because excise duty is collected at a single point: Indeni. A switch to direct import by OMCs would require collection at border posts.
13. Fuel taxes represented 2.4, 2.7, and 1.4 per cent of GDP in 2007, 2008, and 2009 respectively (author's calculation from Zambia Revenue Authority data).
14. Although there is a degree of competition at the distribution, wholesale, and retail levels, the ERB also issues 'indicative' pump prices which the OMCs observe (Matthews, 2010: 16).
15. A common criticism of cost-plus pricing is that by covering all costs it 'rewards' inefficiency and provides little incentive to cut costs.
16. The fiscal loss/unbudgeted subsidy in 2009/early-2010 was $US90 million (IMF, 2010: 37).
17. Most of whom are unaware that their public services have been crowded out by fuel subsidies.
18. Following the 2011 elections a Commission of Inquiry on the ERB was set up to

assess, *inter alia*, how fuel prices could be reduced. While its report was never published, the Commission was understood to oppose liberalization largely for fear of public reaction to the 580 jobs that would be lost at Indeni and TAZAMA.

19. Zambia's technically exploitable hydro potential of 30 TWh/year compares with figures of 774 TWh/year for Democratic Republic of Congo, 260 TWh/year for Ethiopia, and 115 TWh/year for Cameroon (Japan International Cooperation Agency, 2010).

20. Growth in domestic sales over the period would have been more rapid had it not been for the closure of a number of manufacturing parastatals in the 1990s.

21. The Zambia Electricity Supply Corporation (ZESCO Ltd) was established as a parastatal company under the Companies Act in 1970.

22. By forgoing a commercial return (dividend) on public investment in the power system, the government was effectively subsidizing electricity consumers. As most electricity is consumed by the mines and the urban population, the income distribution effect was regressive.

23. Lunsemfwa Hydropower Company, which owns Mulungushi (20 MW) and Lunsemfwa (18 MW) hydropower stations, is the sole independent power producer selling electricity to the national grid. It accounted for 1.6 per cent of total national supply in 2005 and 2006.

24. All countries south of, and including, Democratic Republic of Congo and Tanzania are members, although Malawi is not connected to the grid.

25. At an exchange rate of $US1 = Rand 7.50.

26. The Finance Minister announced in August 2010 that GRZ was negotiating a 'public private partnership' with Sino-Hydro Power Company of China to construct Kafue Gorge Lower. Sino-Hydro would have a 65 per cent equity stake and ZESCO 35 per cent, while the China Africa Development Fund would provide loan financing of $US1 billion (Times of Zambia, 14 August 2010; available at: af.reuters.com/article/topNews/idAFJOE67C0I220100813). The 2012 GRZ Budget provided $US175 million for ZESCO's equity stake. As of early 2014, the scheme was expected to be commissioned in 2019.

27. The Cost of Service study estimated that if residential tariffs were to be 'cost reflective' they needed to increase from 3.05 US cents per KWh (2006/7 rate) to 7.55 cents. World Bank calculations estimate a long run marginal cost for new Zambian hydro generation of 7.5–7.8 cents (Vennemo and Rosnes, 2008).

28. Both the customer/employee and cost/employee ratios compared poorly with other utilities in the region.

29. Poor electricity consumers are partially protected through a subsidized 'lifeline block' of 100 KWh per month.

30. In 2009 78 per cent of Afrobarometer respondents supported the statement 'The government should retain ownership of its factories, businesses and farms', while only 3 per cent agreed 'It is better for government to sell its businesses to private companies and individuals' (Afrobarometer, 2009).

31. Unless there is a large commercial load such as a mine.

32. While thermal capacity, such as gas turbines, could have been installed as a temporary measure, with unit costs well in excess of tariffs this would only have compounded ZESCO's financial losses.

References

Afrobarometer (2009). Afrobarometer Round Four Zambia Survey Results. Available at: <http://www.afrobarometer.org>. Lusaka: Synovate Zambia.

Briceno-Garmendia, C. and Shkaratan, M. (2011). Power Tariffs: Caught between Cost Recovery and Affordability. *Policy Research Working Paper 5904*. Washington, DC: World Bank.

British Petroleum (2008). *Southern Africa Comparative Diesel Prices,* June (internal document).

Cawley, C. and Zake, J. (2010). Tax Reform. In: Kuteesa, F., Tumusiime-Mutebile, E., Whitworth, A. and Williamson, T. (eds) *Uganda's Economic Reforms*, pp. 103–128. Oxford: Oxford University Press.

Central Statistical Office (2009). *Monthly Bulletin,* December. Lusaka: Republic of Zambia.

Energy Regulation Board (2007). *Energy Sector Report 2007*. Lusaka: Energy Regulation Board.

International Monetary Fund (2008). *Request for a Three Year Arrangement under the Poverty Reduction and Growth Facility*. Washington, DC: International Monetary Fund.

International Monetary Fund (2010). *Zambia: Fourth Review under the Three-Year Arrangement under the Extended Credit Facility, Requests for Waiver of Non-observance of Performance Criteria and Modification of Performance Criteria, and Financing Assurances Review*. Washington, DC: International Monetary Fund.

IPA Energy Consulting (2007). *Revised ZESCO's Cost of Service*. Edinburgh: IPA Energy Consulting.

Japan International Cooperation Agency (JICA) (2010). *Study for Power System Development in Zambia*. Tokyo: JICA.

Kojima, M., Matthews, W., and Sexsmith, F. (2010). Petroleum markets in sub-Saharan Africa. *Extractive Industries for Development Series No. 15*. Washington, DC: World Bank.

Matthews, W. (2010). *Analysis of the Fuels Industry in Zambia*. Background paper for the Zambia Public Expenditure Review. World Bank. Unpublished mimeograph.

Republic of Zambia (2006). *Fifth National Development Plan: 2006–2010*. Lusaka: Republic of Zambia.

Rural Electrification Authority (2010). *Rural Electrification Master Plan*. Lusaka: Rural Electrification Authority.

Vennemo, H. and Rosnes, O. (2008). Powering-up: Costing power infrastructure investment needs in Africa. *Background Paper No: 5,* Africa Infrastructure Country Diagnostic. Washington, DC: World Bank.

Whitworth, A. (2012). *Creating and wasting fiscal space: Zambian fiscal performance, 2002 to 2011*. Lusaka: Zambia Institute for Policy Analysis and Research.

Wijetilleke, L. and Ody, A. (1984). World refinery industry, need for restructuring. *Technical Paper No: 32*. Washington, DC: World Bank.

World Bank (2008). Increased access to electricity services project. *Report No: 41308 – ZM*. Washington, DC: World Bank.

12

Transport Policy

Gaël Raballand and Alan Whitworth[1]

12.1 Introduction

While the performance of the transport sector is critical for growth and competitiveness everywhere, it is particularly important for landlocked countries such as Zambia. The central issues in the transport sector revolve around how the country should respond to the sharp deterioration in what was a relatively well-developed transport infrastructure in the 1970s. The proceeds from copper mining financed the construction of both the railway to Durban during the colonial era and an extensive road network during the early years after independence. However, the decline in mineral exports from the late 1970s, and the impact of both macro-economic and sector mismanagement on maintenance funding, meant that transport infrastructure deteriorated sharply during the 1980s and 1990s. Rapid economic growth since 1999, driven by the revival of mining and improved macro-economic management, has enabled a start to be made on restoring the road network. However, much remains to be done, particularly if the railways are to be restored to their former glory.

Recent government plans and budgets have emphasized the priority attached to transport infrastructure investment. The roads subsector has been the largest beneficiary of growing fiscal space in recent years. With large sums likely to be invested in the sector over the medium term it is vital that transport policy and investment decisions are soundly based.

There appears to be a broad public consensus, reflected in the Fifth and Sixth National Development Plans, that all transport infrastructure existing in the 1970s should be restored to its original condition and then extended (with new rail routes and upgrading of unpaved roads). This chapter challenges this consensus and attempts to dispel some myths about transport in

Zambia. It shows how recent developments – particularly the development of a competitive trucking industry between Zambia and South Africa – have undermined the competitiveness of the railways, calling into question the need for two rail systems. It also shows that the government is unable to maintain the existing road network, let alone an upgraded one.

The key issues and choices in Zambia's transport sector can be divided into two (overlapping) categories – external and internal. As a landlocked country heavily dependent upon trade, the efficiency and costs of its international transport corridors are vital. Zambia has little influence over developments in neighbouring countries through which the corridors pass, but still has important decisions to make. The chapter focuses, in particular, on the issue of road versus rail for copper exports.

While decisions on external transport can be based essentially on technical and economic considerations, those on internal transport are more complex: political economy considerations, such as integration of a large country and delivery of social services to rural areas, complicate the picture. As in many countries, the economics and the political economy of transport investment in Zambia often conflict. While road-upgrading projects are invariably popular, in a large, sparsely populated country like Zambia, with low traffic volumes, few projects produce acceptable rates of return using conventional economic appraisal methods. This can lead to pressures to adopt over-optimistic assumptions or to neglect economic appraisal.

Most of the road network was built in the 1960s and 1970s when Zambia was one of the richest countries in Africa in per capita terms. The chapter addresses the thorny issue of whether Zambia can still afford to maintain the whole network to desired standards. It shows how political pressures to pave roads are crowding out maintenance expenditure. Unless public expectations for road standards are moderated it will not be possible to maintain the entire network.

12.2 External transport

12.2.1 Background

Being landlocked, Zambia is dependent upon transport corridors through neighbouring countries for access to sea ports. Looking at a map it appears to have a wide choice, with access to Beira and Nacala ports in Mozambique, and Walvis Bay and Lobito (once the link to the Benguela railway line is restored) on the Atlantic. In practice, virtually all Zambian trade uses the 'North South Corridor': either (and mainly) south through Zimbabwe and Johannesburg to Durban, or northeast to Dar es Salaam. Until the 1990s most freight was transported by rail, using railway lines specifically built to transport Zambian copper exports. Today, for reasons discussed below, road is the predominant transport mode – even for copper. This is illustrated in Figure 12.1.

Zambia's landlocked status is widely regarded as a major impediment to trade and economic growth. However, it is offset somewhat by the fact that international road transport prices to and from Zambia are among the lowest along international corridors in Africa. In June 2006 road transport prices in Zambia fluctuated between $US1.35 and 1.65 per km for a truck with an average payload of 33.9 tonnes, depending on the backhaul rate. This translated into a transport tariff of between 3.7 and 5.6 US cents per tonne kilometre (tkm), which is comparable to South African rates (Raballand et al., 2008).[2] A different source, based on systematic trucking surveys, confirmed that Zambia benefits from some of the lowest transport rates (along the Copperbelt-Durban corridor) among African landlocked countries (Figure 12.2) (Teravaninthorn and Raballand, 2008).

These low rates reflect the highly competitive trucking industry that has developed between South Africa and Zambia since the collapse of apartheid in 1991. The lifting of economic sanctions led to a boom in South African

Figure 12.1 Zambia international and regional trade, 2005–06

Oil – POL* by pipeline – 0.20 mtpa Dar es Salaam	Total trade 4.1 mtpa Excl DRC transit				
	Imports 2.3 mtpa		Exports 1.6 mtpa		
	Rail 0.60	Road 1.70 (74%)	Rail 0.53	Road 1.07 (67%)	
Origin/Destination	Rail	Road	Rail	Road	
South Africa	0.320	1.065	Nom.**	0.455	44.9%
Zimbabwe	0.13	0.060	Nom.**	0.245	7.5%
Tanzania	0.025	0.090	0.010	0.01	3.3%
DRC	0.015	0.120	0.020	0.20	8.6%
Namibia	0	Nom.**	0	Nom.**	0%
Transit DRC (est)	0.11	0.275	0.05	0.075	
International via Gauteng/Durban	0.15	0.151	0.18	0.143	15.2%
International via Dar es Salaam	0.04	0.236	0.17	0.148	19.4%
International via Beira	0	0.028	0	0.019	1.1%

*POL is Petroleum, Oil and Lubricants.
**Nominal (Nom.) means a very insignificant volume (a couple of trucks a day).

Estimated freight transport flows 2005/2006 (million tonnes pa)
Source: Raballand et al. (2008)

exports (and investment) throughout southern Africa, mostly transported by road. In contrast to its neighbours, from which trucks usually return empty, the revival of Zambian copper exports has meant that trucks are able to carry loads in both directions – significantly reducing transport prices.

While current road transport unit rates are relatively low, the long distances from Zambia to the coast mean that further cost reductions are important for competitiveness. Where might these come from? Economists usually look to investment in extending or upgrading conventional transport infrastructure (road, rail, bridges, etc.) to reduce costs. Using simulations with vehicle operating cost data from Zambian operators along the North-South Corridor,

Figure 12.2 Comparison of transport prices in selected countries and routes, 2006–07

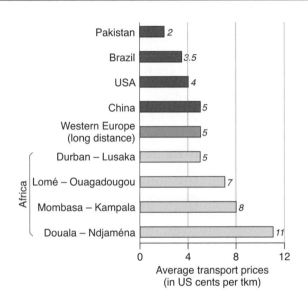

Source: Teravaninthorn and Raballand (2008)

Table 12.1 Expected impact of alternative measures on transport costs and prices in Southern Africa

Measures	Decrease in transport costs	Decrease in transport prices[1]
Rehabilitation of road from fair to good	-3/5%	-2/3%
20% reduction in border-crossing time	-3/4%	-10/15%[2]
20% reduction in fuel price	-10%	-5/7%
20% reduction in informal road payments	-1%	±0%

Source: Teravaninthorn and Raballand (2008), based on interviews with truck operators

it was found that the two most important determinants of transport prices in southern Africa are border-crossing time and fuel costs (Teravaninthorn and Raballand, 2008). Table 12.1 shows that while upgrading the condition of a corridor road from 'fair' to 'good' is expected to decrease transport prices by 2–3%, 20% reductions in border-crossing time and fuel prices can generate much larger reductions.[3]

12.2.2 *Border crossing*

Goods being transported along the North-South Corridor spend up to one third of total transport time at border crossings (Curtis, 2009). In 2008 it took an average of 39 hours for a truck to transit northbound and 14 hours southbound through Chirundu, the main crossing between Zambia and Zimbabwe (and 34 hours and 11 hours respectively, for Beitbridge). Delays mainly affect the clearance of consolidated loads, i.e. loads that have multiple consignors or consignees. On average, it took over 60 hours to clear a north-bound consolidated load (there were virtually no southbound consolidated loads) in Chirundu. Single entry break-bulk loads (which are loaded on to a flat deck trailer and then tarped) took around 40 hours to clear, both north- and southbound. The main source of northbound delays was the Zambia Revenue Authority, which took an average of 17.4 hours to process a truck and its documents (Curtis, 2009).

If Zambian international transport prices are to be significantly reduced, it is essential that clearance procedures are simplified and border-crossing time reduced. This was the motivation for opening a one-stop border post at Chirundu in December 2009. The idea is that customs and immigration procedures are only completed once, instead of being repeated on both sides of the border. However, it is too early to assess the impact on reducing border delays; international experience demonstrates that building facilities is easier than implementing institutional reforms.[6] There are plans to construct similar one-stop posts at the main border crossings with Tanzania, Malawi, and Botswana.[7]

12.2.3 *Fuel costs*

Zambian fuel prices are among the highest in Africa. As discussed in Chapter 11, until 2008 this was owing to both high import costs and high fuel taxes relative to the rest of Africa. However, fuel taxes were cut sharply in 2008. The high diesel prices in February 2010 illustrated in Appendix 11.A1 are largely attributable to Zambia's highly inefficient fuel importation arrange-ments. Instead of importing finished products by road or rail like most landlocked countries, Zambia imports crude oil through a pipeline from Dar es Salaam that is then processed at the Indeni refinery before being distributed throughout the country. Inefficiencies at all stages in the chain (purchasing crude, pipeline, refinery and distribution) mean that Zambia has substantially higher fuel costs than necessary.

As a result, Zambian transport operators pay higher fuel prices than in most other countries in the region, undermining their competitiveness. Zambian companies which operate regionally have lower fuel costs than those which only operate in the domestic market because trucks can fill their tanks outside Zambia.[8] As discussed in Chapter 11, there is considerable scope for reducing domestic transport costs by liberalizing fuel importation.

12.2.4 Railways

Railways have played a crucial role in Zambian history. The first railway line was built during the colonial era to export Northern Rhodesian minerals via South Africa. The capital city owes its location to its original function as a railway junction, while the vast majority of urban Zambians live along the 'line of rail'. When sanctions against the Ian Smith regime in (Southern) Rhodesia closed the line in the 1960s, the Tanzania Zambia Railway (TAZARA) line to Dar es Salaam was built to provide an alternative route for Zambian copper (and other trade) to the Indian Ocean.[9]

Until the copper mines were privatized in the late 1990s nearly all Zambian copper was exported by rail. Both the mines and the railways were government owned and transport competition was discouraged; the road network was in such poor condition that road transport was not an option anyway. Today, most copper is exported by road. The decline in rail traffic began long before privatization. Total traffic carried by Zambia Railways fell from more than 6 million tonnes in 1975 to below 1.5 million tonnes in 1998, and was just 690,000 tonnes in 2009. While TAZARA's design capacity was some five million tonnes per year, freight traffic peaked at 1.2 million tonnes in 1986, averaged about 600,000 tonnes during the 2000s (TAZARA, 2010) and dropped to just 383,000 tonnes in 2008/09 (Table 12.2).

Table 12.2 RSZ and TAZARA freight traffic, 2007–10 ('000 tonnes)

Traffic Category	RSZ				TAZARA			
	2007	2008	2009	2010	2006/07	2007/08	2008/09	2009/10
Exports	144.5	265.8	119.8	127.4	199.5	215.5	140.5	230.2
o/w copper	*161.5*	*238.1*	*187.6*	*114.2*	*151.7*	*148.5*	*107.1*	*201.6*
Imports	218.5	224.1	250.7	338.8	207.7	227.6	214.3	203.8
Local	202.8	73	119.4	94.4	131.3	84.5	28.2	89
Transit (non-mineral)	135.8	91.4	13.2	79.4				
Total	**863.1**	**892.4**	**690.7**	**754.2**	**538.5**	**527.6**	**383.0**	**523.0**

Source: RSZ, CPCS Transcom Limited (2010) and TAZARA (2010)

This is of concern to the Zambian Government (GRZ) for two main reasons. Firstly, the loss of much of the copper trade has reduced the profitability of both rail systems, with implications for public finances, investment, employment and freight rates. Secondly, the switch to road has increased road maintenance costs (which are largely borne by the government) and has implications for traffic congestion, safety, and the environment, etc.

Several factors explain the switch from rail to road. One key development – independent of the railways – that, arguably, triggered the switch was the steady decline in copper production following the nationalization of the mines in 1972 and falling copper prices. The fall in production from 712,000 tonnes in 1976 to 255,000 tonnes in 1998 caused a substantial drop in revenue for the railways that could not easily be replaced, severely undermining their finances. This compounded the lack of investment and maintenance, which was characteristic of most Zambian parastatals. Following privatization of the mines, the railways lost their monopoly over copper traffic. However, they were slow to adjust to the changing market and competition from the trucking industry. Managers, many of whom were political appointees, were reluctant to reduce staffing in response to falling revenues because GRZ regarded the railways as an important source of employment; so labour costs came to consume about 60% of revenues.

The reduction in copper traffic from the 1970s initiated a vicious circle of decline for the railways. Lower revenues meant fewer funds for maintenance and investment. Deferral of maintenance led to the progressive deterioration of the rail infrastructure. As a result, derailments became increasingly frequent and speed, reliability and security all declined, damaging customer confidence in the railways. Meanwhile, the combination of growing trade with South Africa and upgrading and rehabilitation of the trunk road network from the turn of the century (see below) enabled competition from trucks to develop. For the first time there was a viable alternative to rail transport and the switch from rail to road began. Falling traffic volumes meant higher unit prices were required to cover fixed costs. However, tariff increases would only accelerate the switch from rail to road.

Copper production rebounded strongly – reaching 879,000 tonnes in 2011 – following privatization and the worldwide copper boom. However, there was little rebound in rail traffic for a number of reasons. The strong competition from trucks and the deterioration in the railways have already been noted. Also, much of the increased production came from two major new mines, Kansanshi and Lumwana, both of which are located west of the original Copperbelt, more than 170 km from the nearest railway. Finally, following substantial investment in smelting capacity, by 2010 virtually all Zambian copper was exported as cathode. Being a higher value, lower volume product than concentrate, reliability and the time taken to market are particularly important for cathode exports – making road transport more competitive. Together, the above developments have transformed the economics of road versus rail in Zambia.

With GRZ in a state of fiscal crisis throughout the 1980s and 1990s, there was no possibility of an injection of public funds. Not surprisingly, by the turn of the century both railways had accumulated substantial financial losses and maintenance backlogs. To try and address the situation, in February 2003 GRZ signed a 20-year concession agreement with NLPI Ltd of South Africa to operate Zambia Railways, which was renamed Railway Systems of Zambia (RSZ). The concessionaire relieved GRZ of responsibility for financial losses and committed to invest at least $US14.7 million in the first five years. Freight traffic (754,000 tonnes in 2010) was far below expectations in the NLPI Ltd financial proposal and a fraction of traffic volumes in the 1970s. Copper concentrate exports increased from 8,331 tonnes in 2004 to 238,109 tonnes in 2008 before falling back to 114,200 tonnes in 2010 (Table 12.2). RSZ withdrew completely from inter-mine traffic, which had traditionally been important, because it could no longer compete with trucks.

A stakeholders' meeting in January 2010 chaired by the Ministry of Communications and Transport revealed serious concerns on the part of the mines over RSZ's capacity limitations (insufficient locomotives and wagons); reliability (outdated infrastructure and poor maintenance); transit times (average of 30 days to Durban);[10] uncompetitive rates relative to road rates (particularly for Durban); poor security of rail shipments; and weak coordination between RSZ, TAZARA and Spoornet (Engman, 2010). The government also expressed concern over the performance of the concessionaire from time to time, though this may partly reflect unrealistic GRZ expectations about potential traffic volumes when the concession was signed (CPCS Transcom Ltd, 2010). This is representative of the growing disillusionment with rail concessions in sub-Saharan Africa. With a couple of exceptions,[11] concessions have failed to perform as anticipated, sometimes because of unrealistic expectations, sometimes because of incompetent concessionaires selected through an inadequate concessioning process and sometimes a combination of both (World Bank, 2006).

Following its victory in the September 2011 elections, the new Patriotic Front government started reviewing a number of commercial deals undertaken by the previous Movement for Multi-party Democracy government. In September 2012 the Minister of Finance announced a Cabinet decision 'to compulsorily acquire the concession rights that were granted [to RSZ] . . . necessitated by RSZ consistently acting in a manner prejudicial to the interests of the nation through the mismanagement of the Zambia Railways infrastructure and rolling stock' (*Zambian Economist*, 2012). Responsibility for network operations and management was to be transferred to Zambia Railways Ltd, the GRZ holding company.

The implications of suddenly terminating the concession are unclear at the time of going to print, but are likely to be considerable. The concession was originally prompted by management failures when Zambia Railways was operated as a parastatal; it is not obvious that the situation has improved. GRZ will presumably resume responsibility for paying staff and covering financial losses. Since NLPI also operates the service from Victoria Falls through Zimbabwe to South Africa, the prospects for continued operations may be dependent on reaching an amicable agreement with NLPI.

The situation at TAZARA, which is jointly owned by the Zambian and Tanzanian governments and still operated as a parastatal, appears to be worse than at Zambia Railways. Despite a rebound in 2009/10, freight volumes have fallen precipitously (Table 12.2)[12] to a point where the operational viability of the system is in doubt. While financial data is not publicly available, TAZARA is believed to be in financial crisis and largely dependent on (tied) grants from China. 'TAZARA requires an investment of $US 208.999 million to sustain its operations' (TAZARA, 2010: 19). With annual turnover averaging just $US37 million between 2007/08 and 2009/10, there is little prospect of recapitalization on this scale. To avert collapse, the two governments approached the Chinese Government – which financed and built the railway – about the possibility of concessioning TAZARA to a consortium of Chinese enterprises (TAZARA, 2010: 6). The outcome is not known. TAZARA's fundamental problem is that, even if it were well capitalized and managed, the rationale for its existence largely disappeared once sanctions against Rhodesia were lifted and the border re-opened. With Zambia Railways itself having substantial surplus capacity, it is doubtful whether there is sufficient traffic for one railway, let alone two.

The fundamental economic choice that Zambia has to make in the rail subsector is whether or not to invest further public resources. There is a widespread presumption that rail is the most economic (and environmentally friendly) means of transporting Zambian mineral exports. Because rail was traditionally used for exporting copper and because the infrastructure already exists (a sunk cost) it is assumed that, with the right investment and management, rail must be competitive with road. The recent shift to road transport is seen as a temporary aberration, especially now copper production has returned to the levels of the 1970s and is expected to continue growing.

Recent experience casts doubt on this thinking, which ignores the implications of the emergence of a competitive trucking industry that did not exist 20 years ago. At current low volumes, the minimum rail freight rates required to achieve financially viable operations are higher (despite sunk costs) than equivalent road rates (despite high border-crossing and fuel costs).[13] Given its longer transit times and reliability problems, rail is simply not competitive with Zambia's comparatively low trucking rates. To achieve a satisfactory return, new investment in rail needs to improve services sufficiently to attract substantially increased traffic volumes, but without significantly increasing prices.[14]

It is often suggested that one reason truck rates are competitive is that trucks do not pay for the full cost of the damage they inflict on Zambia's roads (or environmental, congestion, and safety costs). If the extra costs to government of maintaining trunk roads exceed the taxes and user charges collected from trucks this would represent a government subsidy to the industry. This is sometimes used as an argument for government intervention – either to invest in the railways or to force the mines to use them.

While there is a strong suspicion that trucks loaded with mining products are failing to cover their costs, there is no hard evidence available. Because they can often refuel outside Zambia (where prices are lower), the value of fuel taxation paid by trucks is not known. Nor is it known how much of the revenue collected from trucks is actually used to repair the damage they cause (and how much is spent on other roads). The Road Development Agency claims that damage to the roads owing to overloading has been greatly reduced as a result of recent investment in weighbridges. However, there are no estimates of the damage caused to the roads (let alone the environment) by mining loads, which can be significant even without overloading. Even if it were demonstrated that trucks are being subsidized, estimating and valuing the impact of mining loads and then reforming road user charges may well be a more economic solution than investment in railways.

Ensuring trucks fully cover the cost of the damage they cause to the roads is critical. If road user charges go up substantially – and are enforced – this may be sufficient to attract the mines back to rail without further public expenditure. However, investing in railways should not be an *alternative* to proper road management and user charges.

In the long term, the case for rail may depend less on Zambian mines than on developments across the Democratic Republic of Congo (DRC) border in Katanga Province. Almost all DRC production of copper and cobalt is currently exported through Zambia, mainly by road. Whereas virtually all Zambian concentrate is smelted/refined into cathode prior to export (for which road transport is more competitive), much DRC copper is exported as concentrate. Being some three times the volume of cathode and one third of the value, concentrate is better suited to rail than to road transport. Moreover, copper production requires imports of dangerous goods and chemicals, for which rail transport is more appropriate. Copper production is growing even faster in DRC than in Zambia. Having exported 405,000 tonnes of copper and cobalt in 2011, copper exports exceeded 900,000 tonnes in 2013 (IMF, 2014). Given that transporting DRC copper exports through Zambia in 2011 required some 375 trucks daily (*Mining Weekly*, 2011), growing DRC copper production appears to represent both a serious threat to Zambia's roads and an opportunity for its railways to recover lost traffic.

However, this cannot be taken for granted. Even for concentrate, significant investment to improve the reliability of rail services will be required to successfully compete with trucks. Such investment will be risky for two reasons. Firstly, increased DRC investment in smelting may reduce both the volumes transported and the competitive advantage of rail. Secondly, Angola had almost completed the rehabilitation of the 1,344-km Benguela Line from Lobito to the DRC border by early 2014 and the Angolan and DRC railway companies were discussing restoring the link to Lubumbashi (Business Week 2013). Once restored, the Lobito corridor would be a shorter route to the coast with the potential to divert much DRC copper production away from Zambian railways (and roads).[15]

There are significant risks in investing in Zambian railways largely on the basis of growth in DRC copper production. Thorough economic and financial appraisal – and probably long-term contracts with mines in DRC and inter-governmental agreements – will be required before significant new investment can be justified.

GRZ has emphasized the need to revive Zambia Railways and TAZARA, and reverse the switch from rail to road transport for some time. However, the only significant investment so far is the 37-km link from Chipata to the Malawi rail network, which connects to the Mozambican port of Nacala, which was commissioned in 2010 at a cost of some $US10 million. The Sixth National Development Plan includes plans not only to recapitalize TAZARA, but also to build a number of completely new rail lines. These include connecting TAZARA to both the Nacala system and to Lake Tanganyika, and extending the Zambia Railways system from Chingola to Solwezi (to serve the new Kansanshi and Lumwana mines), from Livingstone to Kazungula, and from Kafue to Lion's Den in Zimbabwe (Republic of Zambia, 2011a).

While there is private sector interest in constructing lines from Solwezi to both the Namibian border[16] and to Chingola,[17] the economics and the case for public investment in some of the proposed lines appear weak.[18] In the case of both Zambia Railways and TAZARA, established rail systems were virtually bankrupted under public ownership and, in the former case, have proved difficult to revive under private management. Spending scarce public resources on constructing completely new lines from scratch, when GRZ has been unable to revive Zambia Railways and TAZARA, is extremely risky.

Railways typically only consume 30 per cent as much fuel as trucks per tonne kilometre. If, as many predict, real fuel prices increase significantly over the long term this will clearly improve the economics of rail relative to road transport. If the proposal in Chapter 11 to liberalize the procurement of Zambian fuel imports is adopted, this is likely to increase demand for rail services. The combination of increased copper production in DRC, the extension of the Copperbelt into northwest Zambia and rising fuel prices could make investment on certain rail routes an attractive business proposition at some stage. However, the track record of government involvement in railways strongly suggests that such decisions are best left to the private sector, with GRZ playing a purely facilitating role.

Rather than attempting to *reverse* the switch from rail to road, perhaps GRZ should *embrace* it. Unless it can be demonstrated that trucks impose significant hidden costs on the economy,[19] the emergence of a competitive trucking industry appears to have cut Zambian international transport costs substantially – surely a welcome development? Instead of trying to persuade the mines to switch to rail, GRZ should focus on ensuring that the key trunk roads are upgraded and maintained to the standard needed to carry growing mineral exports, while also ensuring that costs are fully recovered through appropriate road user charges and fuel taxation.

12.3. Internal transport

12.3.1 *Background*

The central issues in internal transport are shaped by the country's geography and history. Zambia is one of the largest, most sparsely populated countries in the world. Not surprisingly, therefore, it has one of the highest lengths of road network in Africa: (i) per capita and (ii) per Dollar of gross domestic product (GDP).[20] One obvious implication of this is that financing maintenance of the network is more difficult than elsewhere.

A large part of the road network was constructed during the first decade after Independence in 1964. At the time, Zambia had one of Africa's most prosperous economies and was classified as a middle-income country.[21] With healthy tax revenues from the mining sector and negligible debt, the new government could afford to embark on a major programme of public investment.[22] Decisions on which roads to build were driven primarily by President Kaunda's 'one Zambia, one nation' policy, with its emphasis on integrating the whole country. The resulting network owed little to economic considerations, comprising both economically viable roads (connecting the main towns and to neighbouring countries) and low traffic volume roads designed to promote national unity. Nevertheless, with the finances of a middle-income country, it was probably affordable at the time.

As of 2011, Zambia had a total road network of 67,523 km. A 'core road network' (CRN) of 40,454 km of trunk, main, district, urban and primary feeder roads has been identified as the minimum network required to be maintained continuously. A breakdown of the network by road type is presented in Table 12.3. Of the core network, 9,403 km have an asphalt (paved) surface, while 31,051 km have a gravel or earth surface.

Table 12.3 Zambian road network

Road type	Responsible agency	Estimated Network (km)	CRN Paved (km)	CRN Unpaved (km)	CRN Total (km)
Trunk	RDA	3,116	3,024	92	3,116
Main	RDA	3,701	2,205	1,496	3,701
District	RDA	13,707	1,362	12,345	13,707
Urban	RDA	5,597	2,812	2,785	5,597
Primary feeder	RDA	15,311		14,333	14,333
Secondary feeder	MLGH*	10,060			
Tertiary feeder	MLGH*	4,424			
Park roads	ZAWA**	6,607			
Community roads	MLGH*	5,000			
Total		**67,523**	**9,403**	**31,051**	**40,454**

* MLGH is the Ministry of Local Government and Housing
** ZAWA is the Zambian Wildlife Authority

Source: Road Development Agency, Zambia Highway Management System

With its high ratio of road length to population and GDP, maintaining the road network was always going to be relatively difficult in Zambia. However, it became much more difficult as a result of the country's sharp economic decline following the nationalization of the copper mines in 1972 and the general economic mismanagement up to the turn of the century (Hill and McPherson, 2004: Ch. 2). Collapsing revenue combined with the extension of government activity led to large fiscal deficits and accumulation of debt. As a result, discretionary fiscal resources dried up; there was virtually nothing left over after paying wages and debt service. Inevitably, road maintenance was a casualty of the economic collapse. Maintenance funding was negligible between the 1970s and mid-1990s.[23] A survey of 8,800 km of trunk, main and district roads in 1995 found that only 20 per cent were in 'good' condition, 29 per cent were in 'fair' condition, and 51 per cent were in 'poor' condition. Ninety per cent of feeder roads were in poor condition (World Bank, 1997: 12).

As discussed below, both the GRZ fiscal position and road maintenance funding have improved significantly in recent years. Nevertheless, Zambia today has to maintain an 'over-engineered' (see below) road network which has suffered over 20 years of neglect. This raises the question: 'Can Zambia still afford the road network of the 1970s?'

Serious attempts to restore Zambia's roads began in the 1990s. They covered both reform of the institutional framework and a rehabilitation programme. While Zambia was an extreme case, the problem of inadequate maintenance funding was common throughout Africa; few governments were able to provide adequate funding through the budget. To tackle this, donors, through the World Bank led Road Maintenance Initiative (RMI), pushed for a new model across Africa. Instead of relying on the budget for maintenance, governments were encouraged to introduce 'fuel levies', the proceeds of which were credited to a 'road fund' earmarked for road maintenance. Earmarking the proceeds was presumed to make fuel levies more acceptable to road users than conventional taxes.

The RMI institutional model essentially comprised two new institutions outside the public service: (i) a 'road fund agency' to manage and allocate the fund; and (ii) a 'road development agency' to plan and manage maintenance and other work. Zambia signed up to the RMI, introduced a fuel levy and passed legislation to establish a Road Fund in 1994. Today, the key road sector institutions are the National Road Fund Agency (NRFA) and the Road Development Agency (RDA), which were established by legislation in 2002 and became operational in 2005. NRFA reports to the Ministry of Finance. Until 2012, RDA reported to the Ministry of Transport, Works, Supply, and Communications, which had overall responsibility for roads policy.[24] However, in September 2012, President Sata announced that RDA would henceforth report instead to State House 'in order to address corruption allegations at the agency' (*Lusaka Times*, 2012).

12.3.2 *Road sector investment programme*

In parallel with these institutional reforms, donors and GRZ drew up a Road Sector Investment Programme (RoadSIP I), initially covering the period 1997 to 2007. It included both rehabilitation and upgrading of parts of the network and periodic and routine maintenance, with an emphasis on gradually reducing the proportion of the network in poor condition. RoadSIP I was the basis for the substantial GRZ and donor funding that was required to rehabilitate the road network. It was succeeded by RoadSIP II, covering the period 2004 to 2013. The start of RoadSIP II was accompanied by a revised Road Sector Policy to guide expenditure. Road Fund resources were to be allocated in the following order of priority:

1. Routine and periodic maintenance of all core roads classified as being in good and fair condition;
2. Counterpart funding of donor-funded and rehabilitation programmes;
3. Administrative costs for the Road Transport and Safety Agency (RTSA), NRFA and RDA (Republic of Zambia, 2003:10).

Given the large backlog of deferred maintenance, the civil works programme to be financed under RoadSIP II was to focus on rehabilitation of roads classified as being in poor condition. The government would develop and adopt consistent selection criteria and specifications for road programmes and for maintenance standards to ensure that scarce financial resources were applied to highest priority programmes. Priorities would be established on the basis of:

1. Net present value (NPV) divided by cost or economic rate of return (ERR) for main and trunk roads; the threshold value of the NPV/cost or ERR would be subject to agreement with stakeholders;
2. Multi-criteria ranking for feeder, community and national parks access roads developed during RoadSIP II;
3. All roads rehabilitated under RoadSIP would be placed under annual routine and periodic maintenance (Republic of Zambia, 2003:11).

12.3.3 Funding trends

Table 12.4 shows that, since 1996, substantial resources have been spent on rehabilitating the road network. Initially, the main source of funds was the GRZ budget, through both direct funding of rehabilitation projects and the fuel levy (Box 12.1). Levy proceeds were in the range of $US7–15 million annually through 2003, but have increased substantially since 2004 – reaching $US78.8 million in 2011. Significant progress on restoring the network only got going from 2000 when donor funding scaled up substantially, reaching

Table 12.4 Road funding, 1996–2011 ($US million)

	GRZ Projects	Fuel Levy	ORUCs	Domestic Sub-total	External	Total
1996	13.4	8.8		22.1	7.9	30.0
1997	14.3	10.3		24.6	11.5	36.1
1998	27.0	12.4		39.4	4.3	43.7
1999	21.6	8.5		30.0	6.7	36.7
2000	19.9	7.3		27.2	37.0	64.1
2001	12.4	9.3		21.8	53.3	75.0
2002	9.9	10.6		20.5	67.6	88.1
2003	11.6	8.3		19.9	62.4	82.3
2004	4.9	24.1		29.0	47.1	76.1
2005	5.6	39.2		44.9	52.6	97.4
2006	19.8	55.7	4.9	80.3	79.4	159.8
2007	33.8	56.2	5.2	95.2	59.6	154.8
2008	26.0	51.2	45.1	122.2	91.4	213.6
2009	59.3	61.9	45.1	166.3	40.0	206.3
2010	100.8	68.7	45.5	215.0	28.3	243.5
2011	310.4	78.8	64.2	453.4	194.9	648.2

The 2009 Fuel Levy figure includes $US18.3 million of prior year arrears
NRFA income from interest and exchange rate gains is included with ORUCs

Source: NRFA and Ministry of Finance (domestic), own estimates (external).

$US91.4 million in 2008. The programme was mainly donor-funded between 2000 and 2005. However, following a striking jump in GRZ project funding, the programme has again been mainly domestically funded since 2006. Other road user charges (ORUCs),[25] which have been credited to the Road Fund since RTSA took over responsibility for their collection in 2007, have also become a significant source of funding – $US64.2 million in 2011.

The domestic share of road funding accelerated sharply from 2009, reaching 88% in 2010. This was a result of two main developments. Firstly, GRZ funding through the budget for specific road projects increased from $US26.0 million in 2008 to $US59.3 million and $US100.8 million in 2009 and 2010 respectively. Secondly, much donor funding for RoadSIP II was suspended in 2009 following the discovery that RDA had signed contracts committing itself to expenditure of more than double the $US180 million approved in the 2008 GRZ budget. As discussed below, this led to a major audit of RDA being undertaken by the Auditor General.

Table 12.4 shows a substantial increase in total road funding from $US30.0 million to $US243.3 million between 1996 and 2010. However, this is dwarfed by the dramatic increase in expenditure to $US648.2 million in 2011. While road expenditure started accelerating from 2005, the September 2011 presidential and parliamentary elections added further impetus. Both domestic and external funding increased sharply for numerous new upgrading and rehabilitation projects signed during 2010 and 2011. GRZ project funding tripled from $US100.8 million in 2010 to $US310.4 million in 2011. Much of this was for an unbudgeted $US170 million programme to rehabilitate urban roads, which was announced a few months before the elections and financed through short-term foreign commercial borrowing. External funding increased from $US28.3 million to $US194.9 million. This was largely attributable to a new financier to the road sector, the Development Bank of Southern Africa, which disbursed $US151.1 million to five upgrading projects in 2011.

Increasing expenditure on roads was seen as a key element in the ruling Movement for Multi-party Democracy (MMD) party's strategy for winning the 2011 elections. Greatly improved macro-economic performance and increasing fiscal space (see below) meant the increase was financeable. In the event, the MMD lost the elections. However, the multi-year contracts signed before the election effectively committed the incoming Patriotic Front government to further increases in road expenditure. Despite containing few new commitments, the 2012 GRZ budget for roads exceeded $US850 million (Republic of Zambia, 2011c).

12.3.4 *Rehabilitating the core road network*

One of the main objectives of RoadSIP II was to bring the CRN into a 'maintainable condition' by 2013, i.e. once rehabilitation was carried out, only

Box 12.1 Fuel levy

Given GRZ's poor record of funding for road maintenance, adoption of a fuel levy was made a condition for donor support of RoadSIP. Initially, in 1994, the levy was set at about 1 US cent per litre for petrol and diesel, increasing to about 4.5 cents in 1996. Since then, part of the excise duty on petrol and diesel (up to a maximum rate of 15 per cent of the wholesale price) collected by the Zambia Revenue Authority (ZRA) has been designated as fuel levy. It is paid into the GRZ consolidated fund ('Control 99') along with all other ZRA revenue, but is earmarked for *routine road maintenance*. The Budget Office then transfers funds to the NRFA, although the amounts transferred do not necessarily match revenues.

While they have increased substantially in recent years, reaching $US68.7 million in 2010 (Table 12.4), Levy proceeds are not based on – and have never been nearly sufficient to meet – Zambia's road maintenance requirements. Being *ad valorem*, they fluctuate with world fuel prices. They are also subject to political decisions, such as the reduction in diesel excise duty from 30 per cent (15 per cent for fuel levy) to 7 per cent in 2008 in order to reduce pump prices (see Chapter 11). As of April 2010 fuel levy was equivalent to 8.8 and 11.3 US cents per litre for diesel and petrol respectively – among the highest rates in the region (Gwilliam, et al. 2008: 17). Total fuel taxes (customs duty, excise duty, and value added tax) were equivalent to 23.0 and 39.1 US cents per litre respectively.

While data is not available, it is widely acknowledged that international trucks largely avoid Zambian fuel taxes by filling their fuel tanks before entering and after leaving Zambia.[26] As illustrated in Appendix 11.A1, diesel prices are significantly higher in Zambia than in neighbouring countries, mainly because of inefficiencies in the pipeline and refinery (see Chapter 11). Reducing diesel prices through liberalizing fuel imports would reduce the incentive to purchase diesel outside Zambia and should lead to increased fuel levy collections.

routine and periodic maintenance would be required to maintain the network in 'good' or 'fair' condition. Initially, priority was given to roads carrying the most traffic, i.e. trunk and main roads. As a result, the proportion of the *paved* network in 'poor' condition was reduced from 21 per cent in 2004 to 6 per cent in 2009 (RDA, 2009: 9–11). Using the revised criteria adopted in 2008 (see below), the poor proportion was just 1 per cent.

By contrast, the proportion of the unpaved network in poor condition increased from 74 per cent in 2004 to 79 per cent in 2009 (using the original criteria). The proportion of urban roads (excluded from the above figures) in poor condition was 69 per cent for paved and 50 per cent for unpaved in 2009 (RDA, 2009: revised criteria). So, whereas good progress had been made on the paved network, unpaved and urban roads had continued to deteriorate. The substantial increase in road funding in recent years was only sufficient to restore the paved network.

With the RoadSIP II targets for unpaved and urban roads well off track and with much donor funding still suspended, GRZ commissioned consultants in 2011 to assess the situation and revise the programme. The report

Table 12.5 Cost of rehabilitating CRN in poor condition

	Km	Cost/km $US	Cost $US million
TMD* paved	66	1,000,000	65.9
Urban paved	1,949	750,000	1,461.9
TMD* unpaved	8,917	75,000	668.8
Urban unpaved	1,393	30,000	41.8
Primary feeder unpaved	12,613	30,000	378.4[28]
Total	**24,938**		**2,616.8**

* TMD stands for Trunk, Main and District roads

Source: Republic of Zambia 2011b:7.

noted that to bring the entire CRN to a maintainable condition, over 2,000 km of (mainly urban) paved and nearly 23,000 km of unpaved roads would require rehabilitation (Republic of Zambia, 2011b: 7). Table 12.5 shows that, on the basis of recent contract prices, this would cost in the order of $US2.6 billion, of which a substantial amount is for the rehabilitation of urban paved roads.[27] In revising RoadSIP II it is necessary to consider both the financial prospects and the economics of rehabilitating the CRN.

12.3.5 Maintenance needs and prospects for road sector funding

Recognizing that the economic return to maintaining existing 'maintainable' roads is invariably higher than for rehabilitation and upgrading, the 2003 Road Sector Policy gave priority to routine and periodic maintenance of roads in good and fair condition. Therefore, in assessing the likely availability of funding for rehabilitation it is necessary first to estimate maintenance requirements.

Using recent actual contract prices and costs, the RoadSIP II revision exercise estimated the average annual cost of maintaining the CRN – assuming that the entire network was brought to a maintainable condition. For the unpaved and urban networks this was, of course, largely hypothetical. The annual cost of maintaining the paved and unpaved networks is estimated at $US106.5 million and $US133.3 million respectively, in 2011 prices (Table 12.6). In principle, maintenance expenditure should be fully financed from the fuel levy and ORUCs. However, despite recent increases, their combined value was still only equivalent to $US143 million in 2011 (Table 12.4).

What are the prospects of achieving the substantial increases in domestic financing required to maintain the unpaved network? Tax revenues from fuel have fluctuated wildly in recent years,[29] making it difficult to project future fuel levy proceeds. However, with relatively high fuel levy rates by regional standards, with Zambia's retail fuel prices already being among the highest in Africa (Appendix 11.A1), and given the political sensitivity of fuel prices,

Table 12.6 Estimated average maintenance cost for the core road network

Road Type	Paved	Unpaved	Total
Trunk	36.9	1.2	28.1
Main	18.8	13.5	32.3
District	8.5	66.3	74.8
Urban	42.3	25.1	67.4
Primary feeder		27.2	27.2
Total	**106.5**	**133.3**	**239.8**

Routine and periodic maintenance, $US million per year
Source: Republic of Zambia 2011b: Table A1-6

there appears to be little prospect of significant increases in fuel levy. Collection of ORUCs is considered good by regional standards, so, again, there appears little scope for further large increases. For both fuel levy and ORUCs the likeliest scenario is that they will grow in line with traffic volumes.

If maintenance expenditure is confined to the proceeds of fuel levy and ORUCs this will cover little more than the maintenance of the 9,400 km paved network and the rest of the CRN will steadily disintegrate. What other potential funding sources are there? In theory, GRZ could borrow (domestically or overseas) in order to plug the maintenance funding shortfall; current debt levels are unusually healthy following the Heavily Indebted Poor Country (HIPC) initiative and the Multilateral Debt Relief Initiative (MDRI), so GRZ can afford to increase its borrowing. However, few lenders will be prepared to finance a purely recurrent activity such as road maintenance, particularly given Zambia's poor track record in debt-management. It is a well-established budgeting principle that recurrent expenditure should be financed from recurrent revenue (such as taxes and ORUCs), while borrowing should be used for investment (including road rehabilitation) and dealing with economic shocks.

The obvious alternative is for GRZ to supplement fuel levy and ORUCs proceeds by providing funding earmarked for maintenance through the recurrent budget. As noted above, GRZ direct project funding of the road sector has increased rapidly in recent years, reaching $US310.4 million in 2011 (Table 12.4). This suggests that, with good medium-term prospects for growth and tax proceeds, Zambia should be able to fully finance the $US240 million required to maintain the entire CRN (Table 12.6) from recurrent, domestic sources without too much difficulty – provided, crucially, that GRZ is prepared to genuinely prioritize maintenance over new road investment.

However, GRZ direct funding in Table 12.4 is for specific upgrading projects and switching it to maintenance looks problematic. While GRZ stated policy as set out in the Road Sector Policy prioritizes maintenance expenditure, there has been a growing divergence between policy and practice in recent years. For as long as donors were providing most of the finance for RoadSIP II, they were able to ensure that funds were allocated in line with the Road Sector Policy/economic priorities. This meant prioritizing roads carrying the most traffic (i.e. trunk and main roads) for rehabilitation and resulted, as noted above, in most of the paved network being restored to good or fair condition.

GRZ fiscal space started to increase significantly from 2007[30] and the road sector has been one of the prime beneficiaries; domestic funding in Table 12.4 increased from 0.8 per cent to 2.4 per cent of GDP[31] between 2003 and 2011. With the paved network largely fixed by 2006, under RoadSIP II these additional resources should have been used to start rehabilitating those parts of the unpaved and urban networks with relatively heavy traffic – and then to maintain them. However, contrary to the Road Sector Policy, most of the additional GRZ road funding since 2007 has been used to extend the paved network.

Even if the policy were strictly implemented from now on, there would be little short-term impact on maintenance funding. The Auditor General found that over-commitments by RDA in 2008 were approximately $US200 million, leading to serious cash flow problems (Republic of Zambia, 2010). By the end of 2010, the total level of commitments for locally funded road-work activities had reached about $US254 million (Republic of Zambia, 2011b: 7). Until these contractual commitments are cleared there appears to be little prospect of switching GRZ direct funding from projects to rehabilitation and maintenance.

RDA's 2011 Work Plan foresaw the start of upgrading or rehabilitation of 900 km of existing roads to fully engineered paved roads, in addition to 700 km of such projects which were signed earlier and continued into 2011 and beyond. This represented an increase in the length of the paved network (6,600 km excluding urban roads) by nearly a quarter (Republic of Zambia, 2011b: 13).

The Mongu–Kalabo road alone is estimated to cost $US260 million – more than total expenditure on the entire road sector in 2010. While this road is partly financed by a loan from China, GRZ has to provide a significant proportion of the cost as 'counterpart funding' through the budget. In addition, some projects are fully funded by GRZ.

The extent of RDA contractual commitments and the step increase in GRZ project funding in 2011 together raise doubts as to whether GRZ will meet the $US100 million annual shortfall in maintenance funding for the unpaved CRN, let alone the $US2.6 billion needed to bring the CRN to a maintainable condition. Contrary to stated policy, new upgrading projects appear to be crowding out maintenance expenditure and contributing to the continued disintegration of the unpaved network.

12.3.6 *The economics and political economy of road investment*

These new road-upgrading projects are of concern not only because of their financial impact in crowding out maintenance expenditure, but also because of doubts over their economics. Although the Road Sector Policy states that expenditure priorities will be established on the basis of economic criteria (Republic of Zambia, 2003: 11), the reality is different. There is no tradition of basing investment decisions on economic appraisal in Zambia. As noted above, economic considerations had little influence over the expansion of the road network in the 1960s and 1970s. In any case, with negligible discretionary resources (after paying salaries and debt service) available for public investment throughout the 1980s and 1990s, any capacity GRZ might once have had to conduct economic appraisal has long since disappeared.

No government has the resources to undertake all road project proposals simultaneously. Computer software such as Highway, Development and Management (HDM)-IV[32] has been developed to enable governments, road agencies and donors to prioritize projects and maintenance expenditure on the basis of objective data and economic criteria, i.e. as required by the Road Sector Policy. However, the resulting priorities often conflict with political priorities, such as the Zambian pressure to pave. Not surprisingly, therefore, there are many cases across Africa of parameters/assumptions being manipulated in order to provide an economic justification for proposed investments.[33] Highly optimistic assumptions explain why few impact evaluations have been conducted of African road investments and why those that have been carried out rarely record the level of benefits assumed at appraisal. Although RDA operates HDM-IV, it has little impact on decision-making.[34]

In October 2010 President Banda launched the construction of the Mongu–Kalabo road. Although the contract distance is only 34 km, because the route is across the Zambezi flood plain it is expected to cost $US260 million, making it one of the most expensive rural roads per kilometre in the world.[35] Clearly, political considerations continued to outweigh economics in the allocation of road funding.[36] The pressure to upgrade roads increased still further following the 2011 elections. In 2012, President Sata launched the Accelerated National Roads Construction Programme to upgrade 37 roads (8,200 km) to bitumen standard at an estimated cost of $US5.3 billion over five years (The Post, 2012).

The economic viability of any road-upgrading project is largely a function of traffic volumes. While, say, paving a gravel road reduces vehicle operating costs (such as fuel and maintenance) and travel time, some minimum level of traffic is required if the value of these savings over time (project benefits) is to exceed the costs of upgrading. A World Bank study refers to 'the widely accepted minimum traffic threshold of 300 vehicles per day to make paving of roads economically viable' (Gwilliam et al., 2008: 36). A study using country data extracted from trucking surveys in HDM-IV demonstrated that high service levels[37] are not economically viable for roads with less than 150 loaded trucks per day (Teravaninthorn and Raballand, 2008). In Zambia this threshold is probably only achieved on the trunk/main network, mainly between Chirundu and Solwezi and possibly Kazungula/Livingstone and Lusaka.

Interestingly, the First Highway Programme in Zambia recommended the following thresholds/surface standards for different traffic levels back in the 1960s:

- *earth* surface, with occasional gravelling if required, for roads with traffic volumes of *less than 20 vehicles per day*;
- full *gravel* standard for roads with *20–150 vehicles per day*;
- *bituminous* surface for roads with *more than 150 vehicles per day* (World Bank, 1997).

Because Zambia is one of the largest and most sparsely populated countries in Africa, only a small proportion of its roads carry 150 vehicles per day, let alone 300, and these are already paved. The implication is that few upgrading projects are justified on economic grounds. The above thresholds have been largely ignored by Zambian governments since independence; many roads have been paved despite having traffic levels well below 150 vehicles per day.[38] As a result, Zambia had the highest proportion of 'over-engineered' roads (paved roads with less than 300 vehicles per day) in a survey of 21 African countries (Gwilliam et al., 2008: 37). In other words, much funding of the road sector has been wasted because the vehicle operating cost savings from paving cannot outweigh the extra construction costs, even in the long term. The proportion of over-engineered roads will increase further as a result of the new upgrading projects contracted since 2010.

By contrast, regular maintenance nearly always has good economic returns, as illustrated by the following generic example based on representative regional data (Gwilliam et al., 2008: 34):

Poor road maintenance . . . increases the long-term costs of maintaining the road network. Keeping up . . . a maintenance regime for a low-volume sealed road for 15 years costs about USD 60,000 per km. If the road is not maintained and allowed to deteriorate over the 15 year period, it will then cost about USD 200,000 per km to rehabilitate it so rehabilitating paved roads every ten to twenty years is more than three times as expensive in cash terms, as maintaining them on a regular basis, and 35 per cent more expensive in terms of net present value discounted at 12 per cent per year.

Why is GRZ continuing to pave roads at the expense of maintenance despite their poor economics? This issue is not unique to Zambia. While economists would like to see road investment and expenditure allocation decisions made largely on the basis of transparent economic criteria (e.g.

using HDM-IV), few governments operate this way – especially in Africa. Political considerations usually dominate resource allocation decisions. Road investments are invariably popular throughout Africa. They are one of the most visible ways for governments to demonstrate they are 'doing something' about development. Cutting ribbons on upgraded roads attracts much better publicity for politicians than just maintaining roads in their current state. Nobody ever objects to a road project, partly because they are unaware of what expenditure it is displacing – its opportunity cost.

It is widely assumed by the public, politicians and donors alike that road investments reduce poverty by cutting vehicle operating costs, which, in turn, lead to lower transport prices, higher farm incomes, and increased investment and employment, as well as improved service delivery. In reality, only the first link in the chain – between road investment and reduction of vehicle operating costs – can be taken for granted and is relatively automatic. Whether operating cost savings get translated into lower transport prices depends on the degree of competition in the trucking industry, which depends, in turn, mainly on formal/informal rules in the industry and on traded volumes. In an uncompetitive environment with low traded volumes reducing vehicle operating costs is unlikely to lead to corresponding reductions in transport prices. The volumes of agricultural produce traded in rural areas of Africa are generally low by international standards – particularly in sparsely-populated Zambia – making it unlikely that cost savings will be passed on.

Moreover, even where a competitive market and high volumes (say, 1,000 tonnes a day) result in lower prices, a potential investor may require more than a 10–20 per cent reduction in transport prices before deciding to invest. Even if transport costs account for (a comparatively high) 20 per cent of total production costs, cutting transport prices is unlikely to reduce total production costs by more than 4–5 per cent, which may not be sufficient to elicit increased investment, employment and poverty reduction. Transport is just one factor in the production function of the service provider.

In much of the developing world the benefits from road investments as perceived by the public and politicians are much higher than those measured by economists. As it is usually perceptions that count, this creates considerable pressure on governments to undertake new road projects – regardless of the economics – and to favour new/upgraded roads over maintenance of existing ones. The public is largely unaware of the poor economics of paving projects and of the trade-off between upgrading and maintenance. The demand, therefore, is for paved roads.

Given the political attraction of paving roads in Zambia, it is not surprising that their dubious economics is largely ignored. Instead, projects are justified on such grounds as: (i) traffic will increase substantially after the road is opened; (ii) upgrading is needed for national integration; (iii) there will be important social and developmental benefits which are not captured by conventional economic analysis; and (iv) the road will open up new trade (e.g. with Angola). While there can be some validity to such arguments, they are rarely backed up with evidence – they are simply asserted. There is no process whereby the economics is explicitly adjusted to incorporate such considerations.

As noted above, where traffic volumes are below 150 vehicles per day the cost (in present value terms) of paving a gravel road exceeds that of maintaining it in good or fair condition. However, given Zambia's track record in road maintenance, the public understandably has little confidence that gravel roads will be properly maintained. As newly paved roads do not require significant maintenance for 5–10 years (depending on workmanship and traffic) there is less risk that they will deteriorate. This adds to the pressure to pave. However, the more GRZ succumbs to such pressure the less resources will be available for maintenance – further undermining confidence.

Zambia's geography compounds such pressures. Because of its size the people of, say, Western Province see little benefit from road improvements in Eastern Province (and vice versa). This creates political pressure for regional 'equity' in the allocation of resources. This can be a particular problem for road maintenance funding. While technical and economic considerations would focus funds on those roads and regions with the heaviest traffic, because this is seen as inequitable, NRFA has been pressurized into distributing maintenance funding evenly across the country. When maintenance funding is inadequate to begin with, this can result in resources being spread too thinly to have much impact.

12.3.7 What can be done?

While significant progress in rehabilitating the paved network has been made in recent years, the Zambian road sector is still in crisis. The increases in fuel levy and ORUCs are sufficient to maintain little more than the paved network. Meanwhile, the unpaved and urban networks have continued to deteriorate. It has been estimated that some $US2.6 billion is needed to achieve the RoadSIP II target of restoring the entire CRN to a maintainable condition, while an additional $US100 million a year would be needed to maintain it. The rapid increase in GRZ funding of road projects since 2006, combined with encouraging prospects for economic growth, suggest that sufficient resources could be found to maintain the entire network and to start rehabilitating the unpaved and urban networks. However, instead of maintenance and rehabilitation (and contrary to stated policy), most of the additional GRZ funding – and substantial foreign borrowing – is being used to pave a small proportion of the unpaved network.

The political pressure to pave is effectively crowding out maintenance and rehabilitation expenditure. A small proportion of Zambians are benefiting from a few upgraded roads at the expense of the majority of the rural population, who are dependent upon unpaved roads, which continue to disintegrate. Their poor economics means that upgrading projects are slowing growth by crowding out investments with higher returns. As well as crowding out GRZ maintenance funding, the emphasis on paving has indirectly crowded out donor funding to the sector. Attempting to reconcile the Road Sector Policy, on the one hand, with the political pressure to pave on the other almost certainly contributed to the substantial over-commitment of resources by RDA in 2008, to the subsequent crisis (see below), and to the withholding of donor funding (Table 12.4).

What can be done to reverse the deterioration in the unpaved and urban networks? Addressing the above funding gap must involve a combination of increasing the resources available (both domestic and foreign) for rehabilitation and maintenance, and scaling back demands. The most obvious and urgent step is for GRZ to adhere to the 2003 Road Sector Policy – in particular to stop embarking on uneconomic upgrading projects and ensure that additional domestic funding is genuinely prioritized for maintenance and rehabilitation. By clearly demonstrating its commitment to maintenance and to the allocation of resources on economic criteria, GRZ would also unlock the donor resources that have been frozen since 2009.

Resisting the urge to upgrade roads will not be easy, requiring a mindset change on the part of many Zambians. The public has totally unrealistic expectations for the road sector. Having got used to roads being 'over-engineered' since independence, there is a widespread expectation that all trunk, main and district roads should, ultimately, be paved. There is little understanding that most new upgrading projects are uneconomic, that rehabilitating the entire CRN is unaffordable, or that paving crowds out rehabilitation and maintenance. Adhering to the Road Sector Policy will require strong political leadership, therefore.

While strict adherence to the policy should release increasing GRZ and donor funding over time, this will not be sufficient to close the funding gap. Optimizing the condition of the network with the resources available must, therefore, involve a combination of lowering service standards and measures to improve efficiency/reduce unit costs. If these prove insufficient, the only option may be to reduce the length of the network.

12.3.8 Service standards

One obvious way of stretching limited financial resources across the network is to reduce costs by adopting lower standards. It is useful to distinguish here between *construction* standards and *maintenance* standards. Beginning with construction, it is widely believed that high standards are necessary to achieve high economic impact. As noted above, paving roads is only economic when traffic levels exceed certain thresholds. In the case of gravel and earth roads, it has been demonstrated that construction/rehabilitation of rural roads to standards suitable for trucks is rarely economic because such roads are: (i) expensive to build relative to the income generation they make possible; (ii) expensive to maintain and, in the absence of a sustainable framework for maintenance, soon disappear; and (iii) usually 'underused'. A study covering 50 villages in Burkina Faso found that of 47 rural access roads to villages, 19 had no motorized vehicle traffic at all – despite 'intermediate means of transport' of up to 100 motorcycles, 250 bicycles, and 100 pedestrians a day (BDPA and Sahel Consult, 2003). Similar issues arise in Zambia.

It is widely assumed that, by reducing vehicle operating costs for trucks, road investments make transport more affordable for farmers and road users. However, farmers may still not be able to afford to use a truck if they only have a small agricultural surplus to market. Moreover, as noted above, vehicle operating cost savings may not be passed on to users through lower tariffs if trucks face no competition.[39]

Road infrastructure has an impact on service delivery through two main channels. The first – which is less significant than usually thought[40] – is the impact on vehicle operating costs: roads in bad condition increase the fuel consumption and maintenance costs of trucks. The second impact – more critical, but often neglected – is on timeliness and supply chain reliability: poor road quality can (occasionally) cause breakdowns and service interruptions.

Turning to maintenance standards, in 2008 RDA reviewed the criteria for classifying the condition (good/fair/poor) of the paved network using HDM-IV. It found that 'the present RoadSIP II roughness criteria was too high compared with the maintenance options limits, thereby increasing the expenditure to maintain the network unnecessarily' (RDA, 2009: 3). As a result, RDA increased the roughness thresholds for good/fair/poor from International Roughness Index (IRI) <3/3 <IRI <6/IRI >6 to IRI <4.5/4.5 <IRI <9/IRI> 9 respectively. Applying the revised thresholds to the condition of the paved network in 2009 resulted in the proportions of good/fair/poor condition changing dramatically from 18 per cent/76 per cent/6 per cent to 75 per cent/24 per cent/1 per cent respectively (RDA, 2009: 8).[41] While data is not available, the maintenance and rehabilitation cost savings implied by the re-classification are substantial and indicate the importance of appropriate standards for the efficiency of road expenditure.

Under RoadSIP I and II, RDA's objective has been to increase the share of roads in good and fair condition. However, the economic benefits (in the form of vehicle operating cost savings) from improving road conditions from fair to good are much lower than for improvement from poor to fair; costs associated with poor road conditions are much higher than for roads in fair condition. This suggests that RDA should focus on minimizing the proportion of roads in poor condition rather than increasing that of good roads. With only 1 per cent of the paved network classified as poor under the revised criteria, the priority now should be on maintaining the paved network in its current condition.

What about feeder roads? Primary feeder roads constitute 46 per cent of the CRN unpaved network, of which 88 per cent (over 12,000 km) were in poor condition in 2009. The cost of rehabilitating this network is estimated at $US378 million in 2011 prices (Table 12.5). Even if funds were available, it would be hard to justify such a large investment as motorized traffic levels on these roads are very low – typically less than 20 vehicles per day (Republic of Zambia, 2011b: 15).

It is commonly assumed that most rural households in Africa are not connected to markets and therefore need a road passable by a truck. Much investment in feeder roads seems to be based on the belief that this is a necessary condition both for income generation and for providing social services. However, there is little empirical evidence to support this belief.[42] Despite the poor condition of the feeder roads, analysis of the 2010 and 2011 Zambian Crop Forecast Surveys shows that most smallholder farmers with surplus maize to market 'either sell their maize directly on their farms or travel very short distances to sell their maize to private buyers', even in remote areas (Chapoto and Jayne, 2011: 10). Maize sellers estimated that there were from 7.4 to 9.0 traders buying maize directly in their villages, pointing to 'a reasonable degree of competition in village-level maize buying and that the transport and market failure problems commonly attributed to smallholder conditions in Zambia are much less of an issue than previously thought' (Chapoto and Jayne, 2011: 17).

There is a continuum of integration into markets for most households in Africa. Although a road may be impassable for cars, a motorcyclist can dismount and walk around the trouble spot in the road and then continue his trip. Most rural populations are connected to markets *somehow*; connectivity is not either zero or one. Transport connectivity is only one component of rural development – and not necessarily the most important. This may explain why investments in rural roads have rarely had the anticipated impact on poverty reduction, as found in a study of Burkina Faso, Cameroon, and Uganda (Raballand et al. 2010a). While no such evaluation has been conducted in Zambia, the results would probably be worse as Zambia is less densely populated than Cameroon and Uganda (implying less traffic).

Road upgrading is not the only answer to connectivity problems in rural areas. From a transport service provider perspective, purchases from small farmers cannot increase significantly without load consolidation and agglomeration at the local level. Load consolidation decreases the need for a road accessible by truck to every farm and increases value-added for farmers. Roads for trucks should only be extended to where local agglomeration occurs (small towns or large collection points). With larger volumes to transport and more rotations (because of more rapid turnover and better road conditions), increased competition between transport operators may emerge – helping to reduce transport prices (Raballand et al., 2010a).

The following proposal in the RoadSIP II report makes a lot of sense (Republic of Zambia 2011b: 15):

> Because the primary concern of users of the feeder road network is to be able to pass safely and easily at most, if not all, times of the year, the current system of measuring condition based on road surface roughness is inappropriate. A system based on 'passability' along the network for normal motorised traffic, e.g. a small pick-up, would be more useful. Planning of road improvements at local level would then be focused on a network approach whereby general maintenance plus spots that were difficult to pass would be targeted for attention with the aim of increasing the overall network passability score. The system would also pay attention to linkages so that improvements were not undertaken on roads with no linkage to higher levels of the network. This would put priority on addressing bottlenecks such as stream crossing or swampy areas that can render a whole road length unusable.

This should not only cut unit costs by perhaps two thirds, but also lead to faster removal of bottlenecks causing long road closures and high transport costs in rural areas.

Because the Zambian public has such high and unrealistic expectations for the road network, there is a danger that moves by RDA to lower standards will be misinterpreted as poor performance and resisted. It will be important to undertake an information campaign, therefore, to carefully explain the reasons for the change.

12.3.9 *Unit costs*

For many years Zambian unit costs for road construction and maintenance were among the highest in Africa, reflecting, *inter alia*, that Zambia is a high cost economy generally and the lack of competition among contractors following the low level of expenditure on roads between the 1970s and 1990s. However, a comparison with Tanzania and Malawi suggests that unit costs have recently increased throughout the region and that Zambia may no longer be out of line (Republic of Zambia, 2011b).

Nevertheless, an investigation of RDA by the Auditor General (following RDA's over-commitment of its 2008 budget) in 2009 showed that unit costs are substantially higher than they need be. Detailed procurement, financial and technical audits revealed widespread inefficiency in RDA management of road contracts and produced other disturbing findings.

On procurement, these included:

- lack of drawings and condition surveys;
- poor-quality contract documents;
- lack of transparency in the selection of RDA bid evaluation committees;
- a tendency of RDA tender boards to ignore bid evaluation committees' recommendations, contrary to procurement rules;
- engineer's estimates were not used when conducting evaluations, making it difficult to ascertain the reasonableness of bids;
- lack of contract negotiation meetings.

On *financial* and *technical* aspects, the audits highlighted:

- contracts were sometimes running without supervision;
- poor contract administration leading to delays and additional costs;
- 'Poor quality works were observed on most of the contracts reviewed';
- non-submission of performance bonds meant contractors were not penalized for non-performance;
- delays in payments to contractors and consultants resulting in interest charges and standing time;
- irregular instructions were given to contractors, such as payment to RDA staff and servicing of RDA vehicles;
- inadequate progress reports;
- decisions on contract price variations were not always justified by the contractor;
- where RDA supervised contracts, supervision funds were paid through the contractor, raising issues of objectivity (Republic of Zambia, 2010).

Following submission of the Auditor General's report to Parliament in 2010, new RDA and NRFA boards and chief executives were appointed. The new RDA board and chief executive were themselves dismissed, along with many senior managers, following the change of government in 2011. The report suggests that, once the management and staffing issues are resolved, it should be possible to reduce unit costs significantly.

12.3.10 *Reducing the core road network*

Even if service standards are lowered and unit costs cut, without a substantial increase in GRZ maintenance funding it is unlikely that resources will be sufficient to rehabilitate and maintain the entire unpaved and urban parts of the CRN. The logical response would be to scale back the length of the network to a level that is financeable. However, this would be extremely difficult politically; ministers will be most reluctant to announce that particular roads are being abandoned.

12.4 Conclusions

This chapter has highlighted two dilemmas facing the Zambian government – whether to intervene in the railways and what kind of road network can be afforded. The economics of Zambian railways has been fundamentally transformed since the 1990s. Political developments in South Africa, economic liberalization in Zambia and rehabilitation of the trunk road network have enabled a highly competitive trucking industry to develop along the North–South Corridor. As a result, Zambian importers and exporters enjoy some of the lowest trucking costs per tonne-kilometre in Africa – comparable to South African rates. Meanwhile, the steady decline in the railways (originally triggered by the collapse in copper exports) and the export of copper in cathode form has made it extremely difficult for the railways to compete with trucks on either price or reliability, despite the recovery in mining. TAZARA is heavily in debt and appears to be on the brink of bankruptcy.

These developments raise serious doubts as to the fundamental long-term viability of the railways. Without substantial investment and improved management it is hard to envisage the railways ever again being competitive with trucks. Yet further public investment (in order to compete with private truckers) is hard to justify when there are so many other demands on public finances. The only market failure arguments for public intervention arise from concerns that the costs imposed on the economy by trucks (increased road maintenance and traffic congestion) are not fully recovered through taxes and other charges. Unfortunately, data is not available to quantify these costs. However, reforms to road user charges and road investment may well be more cost-effective ways of tackling such concerns than investment in railways.

A major uncertainty is the impact of increased copper exports from DRC on Zambia's transport infrastructure. If these continue to be transported in concentrate form by truck this will greatly increase the number of trucks on Zambian roads. The volumes may be sufficient to justify investment in the railways. However, if Congolese copper is processed (in DRC or Zambia) and exported as cathode the impact would be much less. Moreover, once the link between Lubumbashi and the Benguela Line is rehabilitated, Congolese exports may not need to transit through Zambia at all. Until things become clearer, it will be very hard to justify significant new public investment in Zambia's railways. Unless the private sector shows interest in investing, Zambians may have to reconcile themselves to the collapse of one of the rail systems.

Things are no simpler in the roads subsector. There is a large gulf between government ambitions to rehabilitate and upgrade the road network, on the one hand, and the resources available on the other. The fundamental problem is that Zambia is too poor and sparsely populated to maintain the entire 40,000 km CRN to desired standards, let alone the other 26,000 km of feeder, park and community roads. Apart from some urban roads and the trunk roads connecting Lusaka and the Copperbelt to Chirundu/Livingstone/Kazungulu/Nakonde, few roads carry (or have the prospect of carrying) sufficient traffic to economically justify being paved or maintained in a 'good' condition.

Despite the substantial increase in both road user charges and external financing in recent years, this has only been sufficient to restore and maintain the paved network. The unpaved and urban networks have continued to deteriorate. While the improving fiscal situation means that the government should be able to finance the additional $US100 million per annum needed to maintain the rest of the network through the budget, most GRZ funding has been – contrary to the Road Sector Policy – earmarked for extending the paved network. Not only is this crowding out rehabilitation and maintenance expenditure, but also most paving projects are simply uneconomic. 'In a situation where part of the road network is effectively disappearing because of lack of maintenance, to add big capital–intensive projects which are economically unsound is a waste of scarce resources' (Republic of Zambia, 2011b: 12).

There appears little prospect of raising sufficient funds to rehabilitate the unpaved and urban roads and then maintain the entire CRN to the standards assumed in RoadSIP II. Failure to face the facts has led to attempts to stretch limited funds 'equitably' across the whole country instead of prioritizing them. As a result, resources have been spread too thinly and wasted. Improving the unpaved and urban networks will require the recognition that they cannot be restored to the standards of the 1970s. To use the limited funds effectively, standards must be lowered and unit costs reduced. In the case of feeder roads, even if finance was available, traffic levels are too low in most cases to justify the costs of rehabilitation. Instead of trying to achieve conventional road roughness targets, it will be necessary to move to a system based on 'passability'.

Notes

1. Helpful comments from Gary Taylor on the internal transport section are gratefully acknowledged.

2. This was reconfirmed in 2010. Engman (2010) found that most trucking companies charge around 4 cents per tkm for southbound and 6.5 cents per tkm for northbound traffic.

3. Simulations were carried out based on trucking surveys conducted in 2007/08, which enabled the computation of total operating costs and the breakdown of vehicle operating costs. Road rehabilitation gains were estimated in HDM-IV (see below) using trucking survey data and were then compared with total vehicle operating costs. Border-crossing costs were estimated using the value of time for trucks sitting idle at borders.

4. Decreases in transport costs and prices differ since some cost savings are retained by truck operators.

5. The reduction in border-crossing time enables increased vehicle turnarounds (and revenues) which, with strong competition along this corridor, leads to significant reductions in transport prices.

6. Interviews with importers and freight forwarders cross-checked with customs data indicate that border-crossing time had yet to improve as of mid-2011.

7. Their economic viability will depend on traffic levels. An investment of more than $US5 million is difficult to justify where border crossings handle less than 50 second-hand trucks a day, remaining less than an average of two days at the border. One-stop border posts are only economic where traffic is high (more than 100 trucks daily) and delays are long. This suggests that Chirundu and Beitbridge may be the only viable candidates along the North–South Corridor.

8. The costs of Zambian regional operators were $US1.35 per km or 4.0 US cents per tonne km in 2007, below those of South African-based operators (Raballand et al. 2008).

9. The oil pipeline was built for the same reason.

10. Average transit times in 2005/06 to Durban were estimated at 21 days by rail and 7–9 days by road. Times to Dar es Salaam were 18 days and 8.5 days respectively (Raballand et al. 2008: 9).

11. Such as CAMRAIL in Cameroon and SITARAIL in Ivory Coast.

12. Konkola Copper Mines is the only major mine still exporting via TAZARA.

13. This assumes that the main trunk road network is properly maintained.

14. A pre-feasibility study on the proposed North West railway extension from Chingola to Solwezi used a railway tariff of US 15 cents per tkm as a competitive tariff with road, which is clearly unrealistic. Railway prices in the Southern Africa region, for general freight on lines carrying 0.5–1 million tonnes, are typically of the order of US 3.3 cents per tkm (Raballand et al. 2008).

15. A possible new spur connecting the Benguela Line directly to Zambia could also divert Zambian copper exports, particularly from the new northwest Copperbelt.

16. In February 2011 a South African consortium commenced a $US4 million feasibility study of the 1,000-km line (*The Post*, 2011a).

17. North West Rail, a Zambian company, has plans to build a 405-km line at a cost of about $US500 million (*The Post*, 2011b).
18. Connecting TAZARA to Nacala would involve substantial costs to cross the Luangwa valley. It would also be dependent on the Malawi railway system, which is likely to remain in a poor condition for the foreseeable future.
19. Estimating the true costs of trucking operations should be a priority for research.
20. At 6.4 km per 1,000 inhabitants and 21.4 km per $US1 million of GDP, Zambia is ranked sixth out of 44 sub-Saharan African countries for both classifications (Raballand, 2010b, based on World Development Indicators).
21. In 1964 Zambia had the fourth highest GDP per capita in sub-Saharan Africa after South Africa, Gabon and (South) Rhodesia (www.NationMaster.com).
22. Much of Zambia's public infrastructure, not just roads, dates from this period (Sardanis, 2003).
23. GRZ 'maintenance expenditure was only 12 per cent of the total network requirements in 1991, estimated then at $US 33 million equivalent' (World Bank, 1997).
24. The Road Transport and Safety Agency (RTSA) was established at the same time as NRFA and RDA.
25. This refers to road and driving licences, weighbridge fees and fines, and international transit fees.
26. The only fee that foreign trucks cannot avoid is the international transit fee (and road user charges). At $US10 per 100 km, trucks going from DRC to Durban or Dar es Salaam and back would pay fees of $US117 and $US214 respectively. At 2009 rates, fuel levy and total fuel taxes – if paid – for the same journeys would have been about $US24 and $US95 respectively for Durban and $US44 and $US174 for Dar es Salaam.
27. The cost estimate for urban roads in Table 12.5 is subject to a particularly wide margin of error, being based on a limited sample of contracts.
28. In practice, feeder roads would be improved incrementally through spot improvements over a number of years using a network approach rather than fully rehabilitated link by link, as assumed here.
29. Combined revenues from customs, excise and VAT on fuel were $US308 million in 2007, $US410 million in 2008, $US208 million in 2009 and $US350 million in 2010 (authors' calculations from ZRA data).
30. This was owing to the combined effect of improved fiscal management, HIPC/MDRI debt relief, increasing mining tax and GDP growth (Whitworth, 2012).
31. Rapid economic growth meant that real GDP was 67 per cent larger at end 2011 than at the start of 2003.
32. HDM-IV is the software most widely used for road investment and maintenance appraisal by road agencies and donors.
33. For example, traffic growth is inflated, costs are reduced, routine maintenance is assumed to take place (despite poor track records), road life is extended and the value of time for cargo is inflated.
34. 'Economic analyses are usually carried out for large projects but this is often in a perfunctory way and if the results show that the investment is not justified, this is often ignored' (Republic of Zambia, 2011b: 12).
35. 'On average the cost of building a tarred road in the rest of the country is ZKw 5

billion per kilometre, here because of the complicated terrain it will cost ZKw 60 billion per kilometre'. President Rupiah Banda quoted at the ground-breaking ceremony (*Lusaka Times*, 2010).

36. Whereas most of Zambia's traditional donors require a sound economic case for project financing, following debt relief, GRZ is increasingly able to access loans from agencies which are less concerned with economic viability.
37. A paved road with two standard lanes.
38. 'There is evidence of overinvestment in Zambia's main road network . . . analysis suggests that 65 per cent of the main road network does not have the traffic levels that warrant paving' (AICD, 2010).
39. At low traffic volumes there is no possibility of competition between truck operators.
40. See Teravaninthorn and Raballand (2008).
41. A similar downward revision of standards for the unpaved network resulted in the proportions of good/fair/poor for 2009 changing from 10 per cent/11 per cent/79 per cent to 7 per cent/29 per cent/64 per cent respectively (RDA, 2009a: 11).
42. Raballand et al. (2011), using a randomized experiment in Malawi, demonstrate that, as villagers can afford very limited amounts for bus rides, a road in good condition does not necessarily lead to increased bus services or use.

References

AICD (Africa Infrastructure Country Diagnostic) (2010). *Zambia's Infrastructure: A Continental Perspective*. Washington, DC: World Bank.

BDPA and Sahel Consult (2003). *Stratégie Nationale du Transport Rural au Burkina Faso*. Burkina Faso: Ministère des Infrastructures des Transports et de l'Habitat du Burkina Faso, Ouagadougou.

Business Week (2013). *Congo Rail Seeks to Link Copper Mines to Angola's Lobito Port*. Available at: <http://www.businessweek.com/news/2013-10-16/congo-rail-seeks-to-link-copper-mines-to-angola-s-lobito-port/>.

Chapoto, A. and Jayne T. (2011). Zambia farmers' access to maize markets. *Food Security Research Project Working Paper* 55. Lusaka: Food Security Research Project.

CPCS Transcom Limited (2010). *Zambia Railway Concession Review Study*. Unpublished report.

Curtis, B. (2009). The Chirundu Border-Post. *Sub-Saharan Africa Transport Policy Discussion Paper 10*. Washington, DC: Sub-Saharan Africa Transport Policy Program.

Engman, M. (2010). *The Role of Trade and Transport Issues in the Competitiveness of Zambia's Copper Industry*. Washington, DC: World Bank.

Gwilliam, K., Foster, V., Archondo-Callao, R., Briceno-Garmendia, C., Nogales, A., and Sethi, K. (2008). The Burden of Maintenance: Roads in Sub-Saharan Africa. *Africa Infrastructure Country Diagnostic Background Paper 14*. Washington, DC: The World Bank.

Hill, C. and McPherson, M. (2004). *Promoting and Sustaining Economic Reform in Zambia*. Boston, MA: Harvard University Press.

International Monetary Fund (2014). *IMF Country Report No. 13/94*. Available at: <http://www.imf.org/external/pubs/ft/scr/2013/cr1394.pdf>.

Lusaka Times (2010). *RB flags off K1.2trn Mongu -Kalabo Road works*. Available at: <http://www.lusakatimes.com/2010/10/18/rb-flags-k12trn-mongu-kalabo-road-works/>.

Lusaka Times (2012). *President Sata launches Link Zambia and declares that he has taken over RDA contracts*. Available at: <http://www.lusakatimes.com/2012/09/20/president-sata-launches-link-zambia-declares-rda-contracts/>.

Mining Weekly (2011). *DRC transport infrastructure needs more investment focus*. Available at: <http://www.miningweekly.com/article/drc-transport-infrastructure-needs-more-investment-focus-2011-06-21>.

Raballand, G., Kunaka, C., and Giersing, B. (2008). The impact of regional liberalization and harmonization in road transport services: A focus on Zambia and lessons for landlocked countries. *World Bank Policy Research Working Paper 4482*. Washington, DC: World Bank.

Raballand, G., Macchi, P., and Petracco, C. (2010a). *Increasing Efficiency in Rural Road Investment. Lessons from Burkina Faso, Cameroon and Uganda*. Washington, DC: The World Bank.

Raballand, G. (2010b). Welfare of Roads Investments Impact – The Case of Zambia. *Background paper for the Zambia Public Expenditure Review*. Mimeo.

Raballand, G., Thornton, R., Yang, D., Goldberg, J., Keleher, N., and Müller, A. (2011). Are rural roads investments sufficient to generate transport flows? Lessons from a randomized experiment in rural Malawi and policy implications. *World Bank Policy Research Working Paper Series 5535*, Washington: The World Bank.

Republic of Zambia (2003). *Road Sector Policy*. Lusaka: Ministry of Finance and National Planning.

Republic of Zambia (2010). *Report of the Auditor General on the Road Development Agency for the period January 2006 to September 2009*. Lusaka: Office of the Auditor General.

Republic of Zambia (2011a). *Sixth National Development Plan, 2011–2015*. Lusaka: Ministry of Finance and National Planning.

Republic of Zambia (2011b). *Road Sector Investment Programme II, 2004–2013, Bankable Document – Addendum 2*. Lusaka: Ministry of Communications and Transport.

Republic of Zambia (2011c). *Estimates of Revenue and Expenditure, 2012*. Lusaka: Ministry of Finance and National Planning.

RDA (Road Development Agency) (2009). *2009 Road Condition Report*.

TAZARA (Tanzania Zambia Railway Authority) (2010). *Rail Sub-Sector Review Paper for the Fourth Joint Infrastructure Sector Review*. Mimeograph.

Teravaninthorn, S. and Raballand, G. (2008). *Transport Prices and Costs in Africa*, Washington, DC: World Bank.

The Post (2011a). *Epinsan, govt sign pact over railway in N/Western*. Available at: <http://www.postzambia.com/post-read_article.php?articleId=17873>.

The Post (2011b). *Govt restores Kavindele's North West Rail licence*. Available at: <http://www.postzambia.com/post-read_article.php?articleId=18459>.

The Post (2012). *Sata launches phase one of the Link Zambia 8000 Project*. Available at: <http://www.postzambia.com/post-read_article.php?articleId=28959>

Whitworth, A. (2012). *Creating and Wasting Fiscal Space: Zambian Fiscal Performance, 2002 to 2011*. Lusaka: Zambia Institute for Policy Analysis and Research.

World Bank (1997). Staff Appraisal Report: Republic of Zambia – Project to Support a Road Sector Investment Program. *Report No. 16539-ZA*. Washington, DC: World Bank.

World Bank (2006). *Review of Selected Railway Concessions in sub-Saharan Africa*. Washington, DC: World Bank.

Zambian Economist (2012). *Compulsory Acquisition of Railway Concession Rights*. Available at: <http://www.zambian-economist.com/2012/09/compulsory-acquisition-of-railway.html>.

13

Trade Policy and Trade Facilitation in Zambia

Massimiliano Calì, Chungu Kapembwa,
and Emmanuel Mulenga Pamu

13.1 Introduction

Zambia is an open economy with a lowly diversified export base, dominated by one export: copper. As shown once again by the recent global downturn, this export structure bears the typical problems of commodity dependence in terms of exposure to volatile international prices and 'Dutch Disease' type effects (Corden and Neary, 1982; Sachs and Warner, 1999). Zambia has been trying to diversify from mining, promoting the expansion of non-traditional exports (NTEs). While the country has been relatively successful in favouring the growth of NTEs, it still remains a copper-dependent economy with a thin export basis outside copper. Moreover, new challenges have emerged (and are still emerging), which may not allow trade policy to follow a business-as-usual strategy in the next few years; in addition, services exports have been relatively sidelined by government policies (except, to some extent, in the case of tourism), which may be an important shortcoming to be addressed for a small, landlocked economy such as Zambia.

This chapter addresses these issues (re-)considering the direct and indirect challenges faced by trade (and trade-related) policy towards effective and sustainable export diversification. The chapter has been divided into seven sections: it starts with an overview of the trade sector in Zambia, including the description of the historical trajectory of trade and trade policy in the country; it then moves on to identify the sectors which have the major export potential (in the short, as well as in the longer, term). On the basis of this identification the following sections examine the challenges facing such sectors which can be addressed through trade policy and through complementary trade-related policies; Section 13.6 focuses on those trade barriers that may not be biting currently but are likely to emerge in the medium term. The chapter ends with some conclusions.

13.2 Overview of the trade sector

13.2.1 *Trade policy*

In the course of the 1990s, Zambia embarked on a process of extensive economic reforms aimed at liberalizing a much-regulated economy. The trade regime had been relatively liberal already since the 1990s and in 1996 the average most favoured nation (MFN) tariff was further slightly reduced from 13.6 per cent to 13.4 per cent.[1] Customs duty rates ranged from 0 per cent to 100 per cent prior to 1991 and by 1998 tariff categories had been reduced to four, with rates of 0, 5, 15, and 25 per cent (see Tables 13.1 and 13.2). During the World Trade Organization (WTO) Uruguay Round, Zambia bound all its tariff lines on agricultural products, 97 per cent of which are bound at a ceiling rate of 125 per cent. More than 180 non-agricultural products have been bound at rates ranging from 30 to 60 per cent.

Table 13.1 Main trade-related reform measures, 1991–2009

Year	Policies
1991	Normal tariff levels reduced to a range of 0–50%
1993	Normal tariff levels reduced to a range of 0–40%
1994	All controls on curent and capital accounts abolished
1995	Import sales tax changed to import VAT
1996	Nominal tariff levels reduced to a range of 0–25%/ SADC Trade Protocol signed
2000	COMESA FTA signed, with zero duty for trade among participating members

Note: No sigificant policy change has occurred after 2000

Table 13.2 Main indicators of tariffs, per cent at 2005

	Tariff bands	Share of tariff lines	Share of imports	Share of customs revenue
Raw materials	0–5	21	30	0
Capital goods	0–5	14	24	15
Intermediate goods	15	33	26	36
Finished goods	25	32	21	48

Source: CSO, quoted in World Bank (2005)

311

In 2004, there were an estimated 6,234 tariff lines at the harmonized system eight-digit level. These tariffs are offered on a most-favoured-nation basis to other WTO member states. Over 50 per cent of imports are subject to very low tariffs (between 0 and 5 per cent). The highest tariffs are applied to consumer goods, in particular light manufacturers, beverages and tobacco, textiles, apparel, leather and food products. Within the framework of the WTO, Zambia has bound tariffs on all agricultural products at 125 per cent; about 4 per cent of industrial products are also bound at rates ranging between 35 and 60 per cent.[2]

Zambia's trade policy has remained substantially unchanged since the liberalization process began in 1992 after the Movement for Multi-party Democracy (MMD) assumed office. The country's aim was to pursue an outward-orientated, export-led trade strategy based on open markets and international competition. Government efforts to become an export-led, private sector-based economy were re-affirmed in the Fifth National Development Plan (FNDP) (Government of Zambia, 2006). One of the main objectives of the FNDP was to mainstream trade into Zambia's national development plan with the goal of improving the quality of locally produced goods and services, and to increasing the country's share in world exports.[3] Core FNDP programmes include funding for improvements in standards, quality assurance, accreditation and metrology, export promotion, domestic trade, and competition.

This view is reflected in the stated objectives of Zambia's trade chapter in the FNDP, i.e.

- to transform the Zambian economy into a diversified and competitive one that is well integrated into the international trading environment;
- to stimulate and encourage value addition activities on primary exports as a means of increasing national earnings and income flows;
- to stimulate investment flows into export oriented production areas in which Zambia has comparative and competitive advantages;
- to assist domestic firms to increase their levels of efficiency and, therefore, withstand increasing competition in the domestic market.

According to the FNDP, the aim of government is to create a link between primary extraction and industrialization through value addition, especially production meant for the export sector. In addition to the liberalization process, Zambia has sought to expand the access to markets by signing trade agreements at bilateral and regional levels, as well as by engaging more fully in the multilateral negotiations within the Doha Development Agenda. Zambia has been a member of the Common Market for Eastern and Southern Africa (COMESA) since 1982 and the Southern African Development Community (SADC) since 1980, when it was known as the Southern African

Development Coordination Conference. Zambia also enjoys preferential market access in high-income countries through its status as a Least Developed Country (LDC) and African country. For instance, Zambia has duty-free quota free (DFQF) market access into the USA through the Africa Growth Opportunity Act (AGOA), into the European Union (EU) through the Everything But Arms (EBA) initiative and into Canada through the Canadian Initiative.

Currently, Zambia is also in the process of negotiating an Interim Economic Partnership Agreement with the EU under the framework of the Eastern and Southern Africa (ESA) configuration. Zambia's market access offers 'backloads liberalization'[4] on products that attract 15 per cent and 25 per cent customs duties. The effects of trade diversion should be partly offset by the launch of the SADC Free Trade Agreement (FTA) in August 2008, which should level the playing field between the EU and Zambia's major source of imports, South Africa (Fessehaie, 2008).

13.2.2 *Non-traditional exports*

In the last decade, merchandise NTEs as a whole have grown exponentially, from $US260 million in 2000 to over $US1,200 million in 2008 (Table 13.3). However, NTEs as a percentage of total merchandise exports have also exhibited significant fluctuations, especially as a result of fluctuations in the value of traditional exports. The proportion of merchandise NTEs to total exports increased from 9 per cent in 1992 to 38 per cent in 2002 and has fallen to 23 per cent in 2008 (Table 13.3). This recent fall in the share of NTEs has essentially been a consequence of the steep growth in the prices of metals – copper in particular.

The growth of NTEs is in line with the country's desire to lessen its dependence on the export of copper and cobalt. In fact, export diversification is one of the main objectives of Zambian trade policy. By removing export controls and gaining improved access to markets, the trade policy reforms of the past two decades appear to have helped encourage such diversification. However, the performances of the NTEs are subject to both internal and external constraints, which have continued to hamper their growth. According to the analysis of the Zambia Development Agency (2008), internal sources of vulnerability include supply capacity and diversification constraints, narrow product range and low investment levels, poor infrastructure and financial constraints, as well as the high cost of production. Inadequate availability and difficult access to trade and development finance, as well as high interest rates, have also had a negative impact on NTEs. In addition, relatively under-developed infrastructure, lack of accredited testing laboratories and quality assurance for NTEs, and the high cost of freight contribute to high costs making it difficult for exporting firms to take advantage of global opportunities. External factors have to do mainly with competitiveness as a result of

Table 13.3 Zambian traditional and non-traditional merchandise exports, 2003–08

	2003	2004	2005	2006	2007	2008
Total NTEs (US$ min)	415	485	565	757	826	1,208
NTE Growth %	12.72	16.8	16.66	33.85	9.16	46.24
Total Metal Exports (US$ min)	669	1,358	1,644	3,084	3,400	4,000
Metal Export Growth %	19.46	103.11	21	87.57	10.25	17.66
Total Exports Growth %	16.79	70.06	19.86	73.82	10.04	23.25
NTEs as % of Total Exports	38.29	26.3	25.6	19.71	19.56	23.2
Total Exports (US% min)	**1,084**	**1,844**	**2,210**	**3,841**	**4,227**	**5,210**

Source: Zambia Development Agency and Bank of Zambia

exchange rate volatility, the global market environment, tariff and non-tariff barriers, such as product standards tariff escalations, and tariff peaks (Zambia Development Agency, 2008).

The NTEs are concentrated in agricultural commodities, agro-processing and mineral-based manufacturing sectors. Their export growth has been sustained over the past 15 years with the main increases achieved in primary agricultural commodities and engineering products (Table 13.4). The good performance of NTEs is mainly owing to a combination of good harvests and improved international prices for selected commodities. For example, growth in exports in the animal sector was largely attributed to an increase in production, increased openness of regional and international markets and improved markets access, and aggressive marketing (dairy). With regard to engineering products, growth was mainly owing to increased market access. The major export markets include South Africa, the largest principal market for cables, copper rod, and aluminium, followed by Kenya, Tanzania, Zimbabwe, Malawi, Botswana, Namibia, and Democratic Republic of Congo. Other markets were Uganda, the Philippines, Switzerland, Hong Kong, India, Mauritius, and Mozambique, and new markets, particularly in West Africa and the Middle East.

Despite the generally upward trend the performance of the merchandise NTE sector over the last three decades has been varied. Textiles and clothing started off very promisingly but have progressively become less competitive internationally with the emergence of less expensive textile and garments industries in China and the Far East, which are often in direct competition with Zambian textiles (Zambia Development Agency, 2008). The decline of the textiles sector has been precipitated by the dismantling of the global apparel quotas under the Agreement on Textiles and Clothing in 2005, and by the increased imports of second hand clothes into the country.[5]

However, exports of agricultural, agro-processed and non-copper mineral products, notably precious and semi-precious stones, have continued to expand. Zambia has also embarked on an ambitious promotion of tourism

Table 13.4 Export earnings by non-traditional exports (NTEs), 1998–2008

	1998	2000	2003	2005	2006	2007	2008
Animal products	4.15	3.37	3.59	2.13	2.3	5.18	7.86
Building materials	8.58	8.67	11.14	8.45	14.53	7.91	35.68
Chemical & pharmaceutical	6.90	7.05	9.67	20.57	20.22	38.32	93.33
Engineering products	31.67	20.61	29.09	96.42	288.59	210.50	225.70
Floriculture	32.86	33.86	22.40	32.09	17.84	38.25	26.91
Garments	0.42	0.39	0.16	0.45	0.32	7.18	8.08
Gemstones	11.59	15.44	23.68	31.61	18.70	30.33	35.16
Handicrafts	0.16	0.25	0.15	0.18	0.55	0.59	1.25
Horticulture	20.56	27.36	45.97	20.51	23.02	37.25	36.35
Leather & leather products	3.13	4.33	3.35	3.96	4.85	5.83	10.14
Non-metallic minerals	0.53	1.14	2.60	1.13	2.43	3.46	6.87
Other manufactures	3.09	4.36	15.40	22.22	24.51	38.93	29.24
Petroleum oils	6.81	0.44	18.41	14.36	13.06	20.49	26.34
Primary agriculture	62.25	37.10	97.91	196.98	176.91	182.70	247.64
Processed & refined foods	49.41	35.55	43.88	66.93	103.57	115.00	108.42
Textiles	42.37	36.03	25.98	26.94	19.58	15.22	18.52
Wood products	3.19	3.89	2.96	3.47	4.50	5.02	14.76
Sub-total	**287.66**	**239.85**	**356.34**	**548.39**	**735.33**	**786.42**	**932.28**
Re-exports	3.66	3.96	3.58	3.67	4.84	25.49	215.36
Scrap matal	4.21	5.10	3.70	6.76	5.45	4.94	9.60
Mining	12.23	7.33	44.60	3.11	2.36	2.40	48.28
Total visible NTEs	**307.76**	**256.24**	**408.22**	**561.93**	**747.97**	**819.26**	**1205.51**
Electricity	5.63	7.39	6.96	3.76	9.23	7.33	3.30
Total NTEs	**313.39**	**263.63**	**415.18**	**565.69**	**757.20**	**826.59**	**1208.81**
Copper and cobalt	**629.74**	**521.10**	**669.23**	**1644.20**	**3084.10**	**3400.30**	**4000.80**
Total merchandise exports	**943.13**	**784.73**	**1084.40**	**2209.89**	**3841.30**	**4226.89**	**5209.61**

Source: Zambia Development Agency

and other service sectors as part of its diversification and general economic development effort. The sectors that seem to have benefited the most in recent years include the primary agriculture, building materials, engineering products, and processed and refined foods, as well as chemical and pharmaceutical products, and wood products. The agro-based NTEs increased from $US30 million in the early 1990s to $US276 million in 2004 to $US420 million in 2008.

The increase in the floriculture sector is mainly attributed to increased investments in the sector, thus resulting in increased export quantities and earnings. Part of the growth is attributable to the increase in the production hectarage of the existing farmers who are trying to take advantage of expanding opportunities in the EU, as well as the South African market. However, the floriculture sector continues to face key challenges, including occasional council and local authority crop levies; downward fluctuation of prices per stem on the Aalsmeer Auction Floor in the Netherlands; high interest rates; exchange rate fluctuations; low-quality fresh flowers owing to prolonged use of the same rose bushes resulting in flowers being sold at less-than-market-average prices; widespread use of outdated growing techniques and inappropriate technology; and lack of medium- (three to five years) and long- (over five years) term finance to develop infrastructure and improve production facilities. The decline in 2008 was mainly owing to reduced production in response to a drop in global demand (Zambia Development Agency, 2008). The general decrease in horticulture exports over the past few years has largely been attributed to decline in production volumes following the liquidation of one of the main players in the industry. This had also seen reduced out-grower activity in the sector. The high freight costs have also adversely affected the competitiveness of the Zambian flower and vegetable industry. This has been compounded by the high cost of aviation fuel, and high landing and handling charges in the destination markets (Zambia Development Agency 2007, 2008).

With this in mind, the Export Development Act of 1985 (amended in 1993) was intended to pave the way for the development and promotion of non-traditional products. The Act established the Export Board of Zambia (EBZ) to implement the provisions therein. The stated objective, based on the country's natural resources endowment, is to diversify away from traditional exports into agriculture and tourism, although the country's geography and the type of labour available raise questions about the ease of moving into agriculture. The urban (and mining) nature of Zambia's population, the lack of access to the sea and the related high costs of accessing foreign markets, along with the uncertain prospects for world agricultural reform, suggest some caution about relying on agriculture. As we argue below, there are a number of reasons that make the diversification objective worthwhile; the rest of the chapter is mainly concerned with the way in which trade policy and complementary policies may encourage the development of such diversification into NTEs.

In terms of the geographical composition of the merchandise NTEs, regional markets have become increasingly important for Zambia's NTEs, displacing the traditional EU market with the Democratic Republic of Congo and South Africa becoming the biggest markets for Zambia NTEs over the last few years. Table 13.5 shows the major export destinations for merchandise NTEs. The largest absolute increase in exports occurred for those countries that are members of both COMESA and SADC (i.e. mainly South Africa and Democratic Republic of Congo).

The services sector is an important part of Zambia's trade diversification strategy. That is confirmed by the growth of services exports, which have almost trebled since 2002 (Figure 13.1). This growth has occurred after a decade of stagnation and has been larger than that of merchandise NTEs over the same period, suggesting that services hold an important potential

Table 13.5 Non-traditional exports by selected regional grouping, 1999–2009 ($US million)

	1999	2000	2001	2002	2003	2004	2005	2006	2007	2008	2009
AFRICA	210.7	146.6	160.6	199.2	188.7	500.0	453.0	548.2	759.8	762.6	818.6
COMESA	764.6	78.9	74.4	84.3	96.6	259.3	270.7	288.6	397.0	470.2	528.2
SADC	197.2	136.1	141.4	189.1	178.3	486.9	433.6	497.6	723.6	728.4	777.3
EU	77.6	65.5	82.0	63.7	63.6	88.2	121.4	106.8	123.0	78.7	59.5

Source: Central Statistical Office

for contributing to the growth of the NTEs in Zambia. However, Zambia remains a net services importer with imports (mainly transport, freight and insurance linked to imports of goods into the country) three times larger than exports.

Exports are dominated by transportation and travel services, in particular tourism, whose receipts have more than doubled between 2000 and 2008 – also benefiting from the diversion of Victoria Falls tourism from neighbouring Zimbabwe into Zambia following the economic collapse of the former (Table 13.6). While transport and travel represent over three quarters of total service exports, other sectors, such as communication and insurance, display promising growth rates.

13.3. The export potential: current and future scenarios

Broadening the export base away from traditional mineral exports has become key under Zambia's development strategy and consequently emphasis has

Figure 13.1 Total imports and exports of services ($US million)

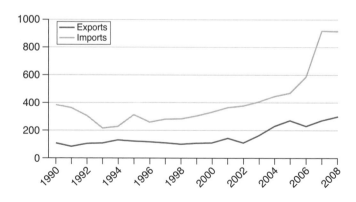

Source: UNCTAD (2011)

Table 13.6 Imports and exports of services by sector ($US million)

	1990	2000	2003	2005	2006	2007	2008
Total exports	**106.8**	**115.0**	**165.0**	**273.3**	**228.1**	**273.4**	**297.0**
Transport	65.1	42.6	42.6	85.9	86.3	90.9	104.8
Travel	12.8	66.5	87.7	98.4	110.0	137.8	146.0
Other services	28.9	5.9	34.7	89.0	31.8	44.6	46.2
Communic.	NA	0.1	4.5	12.0	13.2	14.7	14.5
Insurance	3.9	5.1	6.8	8.0	8.5	9.5	10.1
Total imports	**386.1**	**334.6**	**403.4**	**470.8**	**588.4**	**914.8**	**911.1**
Transport	284.2	202.3	234.9	272.9	315.2	412.0	507.1
Travel	54.1	43.6	48.6	58.0	68.0	55.7	64.0
Other services	47.8	88.7	119.9	139.9	205.2	447.1	339.9
Construction	NA	34.7	39.9	35.4	82.2	282.4	150.4
Insurance	19.5	19.8	28.1	43.7	53.2	72.9	92.0

Source: UNCTAD (2011)

been placed on product, as well as market diversification. This focus on diversification can be justified in light of the economic curse of natural resource booms owing to a re-allocation of resources away from the most dynamic sectors of the economy and towards the natural resource sector (Corden and Neary, 1982; Sachs and Warner, 1999). Although the recent copper price boom has also been accompanied by a growth of Zambian NTEs, Calì and te Velde (2007) provide some evidence of adverse effects of the boom on NTEs growth mainly via the appreciation of the real exchange rate. Moreover, diversification appears to be generally associated with export growth. For example, Hummels and Klenow (2005) find that around 60 per cent of exports growth in larger economies is explained by the (product) extensive margin, i.e. the number of new products exported.

The importance of export diversification has been underscored once again by the recent global downturn. Calì and Kennan (2009) show that trade was most adversely affected in those LDCs whose exports are concentrated in oil and minerals. These include Zambia whose exports were severely affected by the crisis mainly through the negative impact on copper (but other export products were not spared either). This weakened the performance of the export sector and created a serious trade deficit during the year (Ndulo et al., 2010).

The key message is that trade diversification is important. Given Zambia's endowments, there are a number of options to diversify away from the traditional sectors: non-traditional exports based on value addition in the copper sector, and agro-based and non-agro-based exports and services exports. These sectors have been identified as holding potential for diversification by previous studies (International Trade Centre, 2005; World Bank, 2005), which also highlight their own challenges and risks.

NTEs based on value addition in the copper sector consist mainly of copper wire and copper rods, which are part of the engineering products. These exports are dominated by one company, ZAMEFA, whose main export markets are regional, including South Africa, Democratic Republic of Congo, Kenya and Senegal, and, to a lesser extent, Europe (Sweden).

Non-agro-based exports with potential, as identified by the Government of Zambia (GRZ) (2006) and the World Bank (2005) include manufactured products, such as cement, lime, other building materials, sugar, gemstones, and processed foods, such as maize flour, as well as textiles. However, if this potential is to be realized there is a need to address the risks and challenges that these sectors face. These include inadequate access to affordable credit for investment; high costs of transport to final markets; cumbersome customs procedures; inefficient tax rates and administration; institutional weakness; difficulties in conforming to international product standards and volatility of the exchange rate (Government of Zambia, 2006; World Bank 2005).

The other group of products with an export potential is the agro-based NTEs, which represent a large chunk of merchandise NTEs. These include, in particular, animal products and primary agricultural products, such as cotton lint, cotton yarn, flowers, vegetables, tobacco, and other horticultural products. These sectors have the most potential among merchandise exports to reduce poverty as they are relatively labour intensive. However, according to GRZ (Government of Zambia, 2006) they still suffer from restrictive customs procedures, drought (owing to dependence on rain-fed agriculture and limited utilization of irrigation), sanitary and phyto-sanitary standards requirements, competition from other countries, poor infrastructure, disease persistence, high cost of production, and exchange rate volatility.

Although the traditional diversification sectors are very important, relying only on the current NTEs may not be enough in the long run for an effective and sustainable diversification process. Zambia needs to actively develop new competitive export sectors, including in services. These sectors are particularly appealing to a landlocked country with high transport costs and a small internal market like Zambia. These characteristics tend to impose high penalties on several goods' exports, but much less on services (Qureshi and te Velde, 2008). This need towards expanding the importance of services in Zambian trade has also been recognized by Mattoo and Payton (2007a). The main current services exports of Zambia are concentrated in tourism (exports of services via consumption abroad, 'mode 2' of services exports in WTO terminology) and to some extent in the export of services via the temporary movement of natural persons abroad, particularly health and education professionals (so-called 'mode 4').[6]

However, exports via cross-border supply (mode 1) may also hold some potential, for example through call centres and business process outsourcing (BPO) given the relatively low labour costs and the English proficiency of a sizeable part of the workforce. The rising importance of this type of services exports is confirmed by the rapid growth in communications exports in the last decade (Table 13.6).

Despite this potential, the services sector has, so far, been fairly sidelined in the diversification process with the possible exception of the tourism subsector, which has been receiving active attention from the government over recent years. Successful development of the services sector requires the development of requisite infrastructure and reforms accompanying legislations taking into account national interests and commitments undertaken in the various trade agreements the country is party to (Ministry of Commerce, Trade and Industry, 2009). Zambia is also actively engaged in negotiations on trade in services at the WTO.

Investment opportunities also exist in the energy sector and this is particularly important in view of the projected power deficits in southern Africa in the future. Zambia's potential for more hydropower generation plants can lead to future export revenue generation through increased power exports in the region. Currently, the Itezhi-Tezhi Hydro Electric Project, the Kafue Gorge Lower Hydro-Electric Project, the Zambia-Tanzania Interconnector, and the Zambia-Namibia Interconnector projects are underway. However, there is still potential for more power generation capacity for the private sector to invest in and government should put in measures to encourage private sector investment.

While geographical diversification is also important for export growth (Amurgo-Pacheco and Pierola, 2008), access to the main markets is already guaranteed by the web of international agreements of which Zambia is part. However, in the diversification process it is of primary importance that the identification of the priority sectors and products intersects with that of markets. In particular specific distinction of distant high income and regional markets need to be made in order to define the types of firms and products able to export in each sector category and market. This will also help the country specifying the type of technical assistance, technology, and other strategies required to develop any potential sector with great export potential.

13.4 Challenges for trade policy

On the basis of the export potential identified, this section looks at the challenges facing such sectors that can be addressed through trade policy. This is divided into standard trade policy dealing mainly with tariff measures and non-tariff-related trade policy.

13.4.1 *Standard trade policy measures*

To the extent that standard trade policy aims to achieve low tariff barriers in the country's main potential markets, Zambia has fared pretty well in this area. Since 1994, Zambia has been granted preferential access to various industrial country markets such as the USA (under AGOA); the EU (under the Everything-but-Arms Initiative), as well as the Chinese, Japanese, Canadian, and other market access initiatives as a result of being a Least Developed African country. Given that tariff liberalization and access to market are already fairly advanced in Zambia, market access has not been a limiting constraint on export growth, as most of Zambia's exports face zero or low tariffs and qualify for preferential access to the major developed countries and regional markets.

This list of preferences provides Zambia with duty-free access for most of its existing exports. However, for the bulk of Zambia's exports (copper and raw materials) the MFN tariffs are either zero or extremely low, so tariff preferences are not relevant. This is not the case with most NTEs, for which preferential access is relevant and Zambia benefits from the existing pattern of preferences. This degree of preferences may partly explain the good performance of NTEs in the past decade but it is likely to decrease as the trading partners reduce their MFN tariffs as part of the Doha Development Agenda and continue signing new bilateral and regional trade agreements.

As the country moves forward and seeks to achieve the goals set out in Part 13 of the *National Development Plan 2006–2010* and the *Vision 2030*, which seeks to transform the country into a *'prosperous middle-income Nation by 2030'*, Zambia will need to implement trade strategies that maximize the exploitation of opportunities and benefits presented by all market access arrangements, including the Economic Partnership Agreement (EPA), which is currently under negotiation.

Moreover, utilization of available preference schemes has been very weak. The low uptake of preferences is owing mainly to low domestic supply capacities, and also partly the result of difficulty in meeting external quality and standards requirements (discussed in the next section). The low domestic supply capacities are partly owing, in broad terms, to (i) lack of access to water, fertilizer, high yielding variety seeds, extension services, financial services, and marketing; (ii) a customary land tenure system that does not allow secure land rights and long-term investment in land development; and (iii) inadequate infrastructure (rural roads, storage facilities, marketing infrastructure, power, and telecommunications services) (World Bank, 2005).

Just as with access to markets, improving the already liberal import regime represents a second order challenge for Zambian trade policy. Capital goods and other inputs to Zambian producers tend to face low tariffs, mainly concentrated in the 0–5 per cent range. However, the World Bank (2005) argues that some features of the actual tariff structure, such as the high average tariffs (19 to 23 per cent) on light manufactures, tend to create an anti-export bias on the export of these products, both statically (incentives for domestic producers to serve the higher price domestic market rather than the world market) and dynamically (by shielding the producer from world competition, high tariffs reduce incentives to innovate).

13.4.2 Non tariff-related policy

While standard trade policy measures are likely to be of second order importance, non-tariff-related policy appears to be more important for Zambian exports. This is owing to the fact that non-tariff trade barriers (NTBs) often represent binding constraints to the country's exports. The application of NTBs has greatly reduced the effectiveness that preferential market access provides for developing and least developed countries such as Zambia. Most developed countries have resorted to using NTBs such as standards, phyto-sanitary and environmental standards in place of tariffs to protect their domestic markets from exports from developing countries. For example, sanitary and phyto-sanitary (SPS) measures were used to restrict fish exports into developed countries from Kenya, Mozambique, Tanzania and Uganda for several years in the late 1990s. In addition, African meat exports to the Americas, dairy products to the EU and animal exports to Japan face SPS restrictions, which are considered discriminatory because the restrictions were dependent on inspections at a particular time and not specific. Other examples are limitations on residue left on product for export to the EU, where even advanced countries such as the USA complain about the standards for aflatoxins (Mutume, 2006). Other studies such as Mold (2005) have also shown the impact of NTBs on African exports, where they found that NTBs are being applied in a systematic pattern and that this has had a negative impact on the exports of African countries.

Manufactured exports from developing countries are often also affected by stringent rules of origin and this potentially reduces the impact of trade preferences and diversification on mono-economies such as Zambia because they are very prohibitive.[7] This is particularly so because in many cases the rules of origin prevent developing countries from sourcing their inputs from the most competitive sources. An example is the EU's offer of duty-free access to clothing exports from the Maldives only if the fabric and cloth are made there. This is an impossible requirement for a tiny country where clothes made from Chinese cloth would face high tariffs in the EU (ICTSD, 2005a).

The International Centre for Trade and Sustainable Development (ICTSD) (ICTSD, 2005b) also indicated that rules of origin governing preferential access of fish caught within the exclusive economic zone (EEZ) of African, Caribbean, and Pacific (ACP) countries meant that for fish to be considered as originating in ACP, they would have to be caught within 12 nautical miles of the shore or, if outside this boundary, they must be caught on an ACP- or EU-registered vessel, sail under an ACP or EU flag, the crew must include at least 50 per cent EU and/or ACP nationals, and the vessel must be at least 50 per cent owned by EU/ACP nationals.

Once LDCs add value they export their products at MFN and face tariff escalations. This suggests that Zambia needs to supports negotiating efforts towards more liberal rules of origin within the main trade agreements, especially with the EU, which has fairly restrictive rules of origin mechanisms.

At the regional level, Imani Development (Austral, 2007) indicates that the NTBs that have been identified range from a wide variety of non-tariff charges to restrictive trading practices and policies, and cumbersome customs and administration procedures and practices. Other common NTBs associated with COMESA and SADC countries are Technical Barriers to Trade and the SPS measures.[8] NTBs at the regional level result from countries having different standards, which in some cases entail that there are no equivalence and mutual recognition. Other countries in the region, such as the Democratic Republic of Congo, have sought a derogative on obligations under the regional trade agreements and are able to impose NTBs on exports from Zambia.

Some of the NTBs that affect Zambian exports in the region are summarized in Table 13.7. A recent study by Keane et al. (2010) found that NTBs in the SADC region have a more negative impact on intra-SADC than on extra-SADC trade. This suggests that SADC countries, including Zambia, tend to be less able to adjust to NTBs than other exporters to the southern African region.

For these reasons, Zambia needs to continue supporting the regional mechanisms put in place under both SADC and COMESA to progressively remove and eliminate regional NTBs, as well as those at multilateral level. In countries in the region which are not part of the SADC and COMESA FTA, such as Democratic Republic of Congo, bilateral agreements should be negotiated to improve and increase market access. For example, Democratic Republic of Congo – which is an increasingly relevant export market for Zambia – has not yet started implementing the regional protocol on trade and still imposes its own customs and other trade-related duties.

As mentioned above, modes 2 and 4 are the modes where Zambian services exports are currently concentrated and which may hold the most potential given the country's factor endowment. Zambia has a fairly large supply of relatively unskilled idle labour (with good English language skills), which is likely to be an advantage for 'mode 2' type of exports and also, to some

Table 13.7 Non-tariff barriers (NTBs) affecting Zambian exports to SADC and COMESA

Non-Tariff Barrier	Export Products Affected by NTBs
Quantitative Restriction	Sugar; Rice and Textiles
Technical Barriers to Trade	a) Coffee exports to South Africa are restricted based on the level of Ocratosin in the coffee b) Export of detergent pastes to Zimbabwe was sometimes prevented due to lack of instructions for users in the two main Zimbabwean local languages
Custom Procedures	South Africa requires SADC certificates of origin prior to shipment of exports
Sanitary and Phyto sanitary Regulations	Beef and leather products cannot be exported to South Africa because of poor standards of abattoirs and the fact that foot and mouth disease is believed to be endemic in Zambia
Costly Quality Assurances	Flowers and horticultural products
Unfavourable Business Climate	High cost of finance; high interest rates discourage production of export goods; poor transport infrastructure and lack of storage facilities
Public sector involvement in exports	Exports of maize to countries in the region that experienced deficits, predominantly exported by the Food Reserve Agency, a public sector agency reponsible for food reserves
Export Restrictions	Maize and maize products

Source: NTB Survey IMANI (2007)

extent, for 'mode 1'. The country is already a fairly important exporter of health and educational services via mode 2 in Africa but a lot of its potential in this type of exports seems still untapped if compared with other developing countries, such as the Philippines and India. In addition, the natural amenities the country is endowed with, such as the Victoria waterfalls, the game parks and the mild climate, along with the relative security of the country, represent an important potential for the growth prospects of the tourism industry.[9] While there are no evident trade policy constraints with respect to mode 2, exports via mode 4 are, by far, the most restricted of services exports. That effectively constrains the ability of Zambia to develop one export sector where it has some comparative advantage, especially in semi- and low-skilled labour, which are also the most restricted areas within mode 4 trade. One way to facilitate the development of those exports while minimizing their potential negative effects (mainly in terms of brain drain) could be to promote revolving guest worker schemes as proposed, for instance, by Amin and Mattoo (2007). The exact design of the scheme may need to be worked out in more detail in the case of Zambia, but what appears clear is that Zambia has an interest in developing more guest worker schemes, mainly at bilateral and/or regional level.

Aside from the constraints imposed by NTBs in destination countries, Zambia also faces trade-related domestic constraints to exports. In particular, services themselves – far from being only important potential exports – also represent key inputs for production and exports in the Zambian economy (Arnold and Mattoo, 2007). Indirect costs for Zambian firms, which are mostly a result of services inputs into production, account for 22 per cent of gross value added – twice as much as the share of labour costs and the second highest share among a large sample of developing countries analyzed by Eifert et al. (2005). Often, access to relatively inefficient services inputs limits the productivity of Zambian firms. For example, Arnold et al. (2008) estimate that if Zambian firms had the same access to telecommunication services as their South African counterparts, their productivity would be 13 per cent higher. Similarly, Zambian firms would be 6 per cent more productive if they enjoyed the same access to financial services as the average South African firm. Mattoo and Payton (2007b) argue that these types of constraints can be addressed partly through international services trade negotiations in two ways. Firstly, Zambia could enhance the commitment to reform at the multi-lateral level (i.e. within the General Agreement of Trade in Services in the WTO). This would allow the country to bind the reforms in key sectors, as well as to reassure potential services investors of the stability of the invest-ments in Zambia. Secondly, and perhaps more importantly, the government could deepen the integration in services at the regional level, in both SADC and COMESA. Such enhanced integration would allow service providers to exploit those economies of scale typical of the provision of services such as telecommunications and transport, and could create a common market for professional services.

13.5 Trade-related complementary policies

Trade policy is relevant for export diversification but at least as important are those trade-related complementary policies, which are necessary to tackle the binding constraints to exports and doing business in Zambia in general. In spite of the gains made in economic growth and macro-economic stability, such constraints appear to keep private sector investments down, thus stifling modernization and the increase in competitiveness of the firms.

The main constraints have been identified by both the World Bank (2005) and GRZ (Government of Zambia, 2006). A lot of them relate to inefficient services inputs, which, as mentioned above, constrain the productivity of Zambian firms, including exporters. While trade-related policies can help improve the quality and the access to these services, complementary domestic policies have possibly an even more important role to play in this respect. Firstly, infrastructure services, especially transport and telecommunications, are not adequate to overcome the country's difficult geography; there are long distances to profitable markets and a lack of access to the sea. This finding is confirmed by the World Bank Enterprise Surveys, according to which transportation is a more important constraint for firms in Zambia than for firms in the average low-income or sub-Saharan country (World Bank, 2011a). Moreover, as shown in Table 13.8, Zambia has a much lower level of Internet bandwidth than the average for low-income and sub-Saharan African countries, with higher-than-average Internet prices. Prices of fixed line telecommunications are also higher than average. With only three lines per 100 people, Zambia's fixed-line teledensity remains at half the average in sub-Saharan Africa (WTO, 2009). However, prices of mobile services, where the market is liberalized are below average (with higher penetration).

The strengthening of transport services is inherently linked to the development of physical infrastructure, part of which is currently being addressed by the North–South Corridor project which is connecting Zambia to the north and to the south of the SADC region. However, the lack of appropriate regulation appears also to be a constraint to the efficiency of the air-transport sector (Schlumberger, 2007), which is important for perishable exports, such as horticulture and floriculture. Differently from road transport, the major reasons behind the poor performance of the telecom sector seem to lie in the persistent de facto monopoly over the fixed-line network and in a relatively ineffective regulatory system with the regulator (Communications Authority of Zambia) having little control over the monopolist Zamtel (Arnold et al.,

Table 13.8 Information and communication technology (ICT) indicators, 2000 and 2007

	Zambia		LICs	sub-Saharan Africa
	2000	2007	2007	2007
International internet bandwidth (bits/second/person)	0	3	26	36
Price basket for mobile service (US$/month)	4.6	8.9	5.7	12.6
Price basket for residential fixed line (US$/month)		14.6	11.2	11.6
Price basket for internet service (US$/month)		78.6	29.2	43.1
Price of call to United States (US$ for 3 minutes)	2.57	1.41	2	2.43

Source: World Bank – ICT at a glance

2007). In tackling these constraints it is important to bear in mind that sequencing of reforms usually matter. For instance, it usually makes sense to open up sectors like telecommunications and banking to competition once an effective regulator is in place. Arnold et al. (2007) suggest that on the basis of international experience stimulating some competition before privatizing the telecom monopoly is usually better to increase the number of main-lines.

Secondly, the access to and the cost of, financial services – especially credit – remain important constraints to the operations of firms in Zambia. Access to finance is indicated by 14 per cent of Zambian firms surveyed by the World Bank in 2007 as the main constraint to their growth. Credit is costly in Zambia, with interest rates on loans often much higher than the inflation rate. Only large firms are able to borrow at lower-than-average rates, while small firms appear to be generally credit constrained (de Luna Martinez, 2007). According to a survey of the Bank of Zambia [quoted in de Luna Martinez (2007)], only 2.5 per cent of small firms would rely on bank lending if they faced a crisis in their business. This restricted access to credit is partly the reason for low investments in modern technology by Zambian firms and by exporters in particular. The FNDP (Government of Zambia, 2006) recognizes this problem and aims to establish an accessible and affordable export financing facility. According to the World Bank (2011b) 'Doing Business Indicators' the regulatory environment for getting credit is now relatively efficient, with Zambia ranking sixth among the countries surveyed in 2010 (up from fourteenth in 2009).

Thirdly, the relatively low levels of productivity of Zambian firms are also owing to a generalized scarcity of skilled labour. Although only 4 per cent of firms indicate inadequate educated workforce as the main constraint to growth, this share is higher than for the average low-income or sub-Saharan country (World Bank, 2011a). Moreover, the lack of skilled labour is particularly constraining for exporting firms, which are directly exposed to international competition. A carefully designed investment in technical and vocational training driven by the actual needs of the export sector would be an important step in providing Zambian firms with access to an internationally competitive labour force in the relevant sectors.

Fourthly, as we have seen above, NTBs tend to stifle Zambian exports, essentially because of the inability of exporters to meet standard requirements of foreign markets. This constraint applies to most Zambian NTEs and to both regional and international markets. A key reason behind such inability is the lack of appropriate standards and certification facilities in the country. The proposal of the FNDP to strengthening and de-centralizing the administration of testing and certification of SPS standards goes some way towards addressing this issue, although much remains to be done.

Fifthly, Zambia has historically had a fairly unconducive business environment for firms, ranking consistently at the bottom of the Doing Business

Figure 13.2 World Bank 'Ease of Doing Business' rankings 2010 and 2011

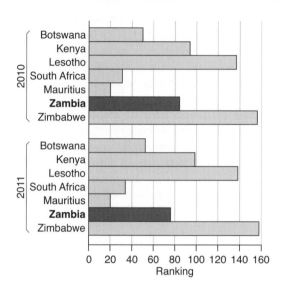

Source: World Bank (2011b)

Indicators (DBI) ranking. However the government has, in recent years, taken several steps to soften this constraint in many areas, including through the establishment of the Zambia Development Agency (ZDA), which is a one-stop facility for investment and export promotion; the approval of the Information and Communications Technology (ICT) policy, the enactment of the Tourism and Hospitality Act and the Zambia Tourist Board Act; the reduction in the number of days required for business registration and days taken to obtain a visa or employment permit; and a reduction in the number of days to export or import goods.[10] Such measures have contributed to a significant improvement in the DBI ranking. As Figure 13.2 indicates, the country's ranking improved to position 76 in 2011 from position 84 in 2010.[11]

This dynamicity compares favourably with most countries in the SADC region and although Zambia continues to lag well behind the regional leaders (Mauritius, South Africa, and Botswana), the improvements in the past few years confirm that the country is moving in the right direction in most of the areas. However, the cost of trading across borders remains an area where Zambia continues to perform poorly, with the time and costs to clear imports and exports well above the regional averages and an overall ranking in the lowest quintile. This is despite the recent streamlining of customs-clearing procedures and the reforms including the establishment of a one-stop border post at Zambia's busiest border post, Chirundu, a pre-clearance facility, accreditation of compliant clients and the automation of custom systems. Further reducing the high costs of trading across borders should be a trade-related priority for a country that already suffers a high penalty owing to its relative isolation from large markets.

13.6 Future perspectives on trade policy

Dealing with probable future challenges is as important as dealing with current challenges for Zambian trade policy. A number of trade barriers that may not be currently biting yet are likely to emerge in the medium term as new trade-related issues relevant to Zambia. Turning such potential barriers into an opportunity would require both good planning and enough (technical and financial) resources. The contours of these future barriers will clearly depend on the types of sectors where Zambian exports will be concentrated in. The specific exports where Zambia will compete internationally are obviously impossible to predict as they are likely to emerge as an endogenous process of 'self-discovery' (Hausmann and Rodrik, 2003). However, we can identify potential barriers to exports in a couple of broad sectors – agriculture/ agro-industry and energy – which are likely to represent important export opportunities for Zambia in the near future.

Firstly, given the priority of export diversification into (mainly) agricultural based products, the emergence of private standards is likely to be one such barrier. Private standards are an established set of rules that must be met usually in order to achieve better access to markets, the ability to sell to certain buyers and/or qualification to use a particular label or logo. Among these standards, ethical and environmental standards are becoming increasingly important, especially in the primary agriculture and agro-processing sectors. These labels convey information on the products to which consumers attach a particular value (e.g. the production techniques used to produce a certain product have minimized the carbon dioxide emissions). This provides a further element of differentiation for goods, with an associated price premium over other similar products. Examples of labels that use such standards include Fair Trade, Rainforest Alliance, GlobalGap and Soil Association Organic. The size of the market for ethical and environmental standards is already noticeable. Ellis and Keane (2007) report evidence from a number of sources for the UK market, which is one of the most important destinations for several Zambian NTEs. A survey by the Co-operative Bank (2007) found that 6 per cent of the UK adult population are committed consumers of ethical products and services – up from 5 per cent in 2003. These consumers shop for ethical products on a weekly basis and spend an estimated annual £1,600 per household on ethical food and drink. A market research study conducted by Nielsen (2007) in the UK found that 33 per cent of survey respondents actively tried to buy Fair Trade products as of July 2007, whereas 21 per cent actively tried to buy ethically-produced or ethically-grown products, 57 per cent tried to buy local products, and 17 per cent tried to buy organic products.

The share of these labels in total consumption is still relatively low, but it is steadily growing. The National Consumer Council (2006) found that household spending on ethical goods and services in the UK almost doubled between 2001 and 2006. This growth is expected to continue in the future as these goods tend to be considered 'luxury' goods, whose consumption increases more than proportionately with income. Standards are an increasingly important way to differentiate agro-based produce and are also becoming a requirement to access supermarket chains in certain products. Moreover, for a number of agricultural products ethical and environmental consumption already represents an important share of the market. That is also the case for some NTEs, which are important for Zambia, for example the cut flowers sector, where, in 2007, 9 per cent of UK imports were under the 'Fair Trade' label.

Zambian exporters are currently not particularly involved in these export markets, except for the horticulture sector, where the lack of easy port access has forced the Zambian export industry to compete internationally by supplying high-value exotic and out-of-season fresh and minimally-processed vegetables to EU retail markets. These markets demand compliance with the European retailers' private standard for Good Agricultural Practices (EurepGAP, now GlobalGap) as a pre-condition for entry. The high costs of compliance with such a standard have made it hard for Zambian smallholder producers of fresh vegetables to participate in the export chain (Graffham and MacGregor, 2007).

These high costs are one of the obstacles that would need to be tackled by Zambia to develop standard compliant production. While lack of compliance to ethical and environmental standards is not currently a binding constraint for most Zambian exports, this may restrict access to increasingly important and lucrative export markets in the future as the consumption of such products increases. The development of a standard compliant production requires commitment and vision on the side of both the producers and the government. Providing adequate technical information and financial resources to help cover the fixed costs of compliance for producers are likely to be important public policy interventions that may help this type of production take off (Eyhorn, 2007). In general, raising awareness about the types of benefits that the development of such production may bring about is likely to be necessary if these types of exports are to become important NTEs in Zambia.

Emission controls are another area that may involve trade-related challenges for Zambia. The eventual further development of emission trading and/or of pollution cap systems may partly change the structure of international trade, providing incentives to reduce the emission intensity of production, as well as to increase the production of alternative energy. These are actually broader than solely trade objectives but they have clear implications for future ability to trade. Reducing the emission intensity of production may involve technological changes that take a long time to implement and the government has a role to play in facilitating the process.

Given its factor endowments a more promising route for Zambia to take advantage of the development of carbon trading schemes could be to invest in the production of renewable energy. As mentioned above, hydro-electric power is currently a potential major source of energy for Zambia but other sources could also become important in the future, such as solar power and ethanol. The former could rely on the low population density of the country, as well as to great solar exposure. The latter would rely to the transformation of sugar, which Zambia is able to produce relatively competitively. The development of this production would require the establishment of proper incentives by the government, as well as the provision of adequate infrastructure for the transportation of such energy. This production would have clear exports implications. Not only could such production increase the ability of Zambia to export emission rights should an emission-trading scheme be implemented, but it would also allow Zambia to increase its exports to the region in view of the projected power deficits in southern Africa.

13.7 Conclusions

The biggest trade challenge for Zambia in the next few years is for it to reduce its dependence on copper by fostering the development of NTEs. As copper production and prices increase, the role of copper in exports has become more important despite the steady increase in NTEs. There are a number of options to facilitate the growth of NTEs. As far as standard trade policy is concerned Zambia should strengthen its negotiation efforts with regional organizations such as SADC, COMESA and other non-regional institutions, such as the EU, etc. Attention should be focused on those groups of merchandise exports with the highest potential, i.e. NTEs related to the copper sector (mainly copper-based engineering products) and agro-based NTEs, including primary agriculture, horticulture, and floriculture. However, Zambia should also have a keen interest in the development of its services export sector, which, given its factor endowment, is likely to be a potentially advantageous sector to develop, especially via mode 2 and mode 4 services trade. In fact, the sector has been relatively sidelined in the diversification process save the case of tourism. Investment opportunities also exist in the energy sector and this is particularly important in view of the projected power deficits in southern Africa in the future.

Zambia enjoys fairly good market access in goods, as traditional tariff barriers faced by its exports are low in the main markets. However, NTBs often represent a constraint for Zambian exporters; in particular, such as SPS and environmental standards, which most developed countries have been increasingly using to protect their own markets. There is also need to address the issue of stringent rules of origin, which has tended to reduce the impact of trade preferences. Zambia also needs to strengthen trade-related complementary policies such as the achievement of macro-economic stability through prudent monetary and fiscal policies. A number of challenges also need to be addressed, particularly relating to poor infrastructure, low levels of productivity, the high cost of telecommunication and the high cost of finance, to name but a few.

Finally, a number of trade barriers that may not be currently biting are likely to emerge in the medium term as new trade-related issues relevant to Zambia. Given the priority of export diversification into (mainly) agricultural-based products, the emergence of private standards and emission controls are likely to be two such important barriers. Turning these into opportunities would require both good planning and enough (technical and financial) resources.

Notes

1. Most favoured nation (MFN) treatment refers to the principle of not discriminating between one's trading partners. The MFN tariff is a normal, non-discriminatory tariff charged on imports (which excludes preferential tariffs under free-trade agreements and other schemes or tariffs charged inside quotas).
2. Binding is a commitment not to increase a rate of duty beyond the agreed 'bound' level. Once a rate of duty is bound, it may not be raised without compensating the affected parties. Effectively applied rates are obviously equal or smaller than the bound rates.
3. The FNDP includes a chapter on Commerce and Trade were the government outlines its plans during the plan period.
4. Under the tariff phase down schedules, Zambia offered to remove tariffs on at least 85 per cent of their trade towards the end of the agreed liberalization period.
5. Other sub-Saharan countries with more competitive textile sectors than Zambia's, such as Lesotho, Madagascar and Mauritius, have still been able to benefit from preferential access to the US market through AGOA, partly displacing exports from Zambia to those markets. Zambia has eventually started to provide raw materials for the textile exports of other African countries.
6. Although there is no reliable, updated data on the number of Zambians providing services via mode 4, te Velde (2006) suggests that this type of export has some

importance, especially in health and education (mainly through nurses and teachers). One proxy, albeit imprecise, for the level of exports via mode 4 is the value of remittance receipts, which, in 2007, stood at $US59 million (Manenga et al., 2010). That is 0.5 per cent of GDP, thus still representing a relatively small inflow, but its share in GDP has been growing steadily over the past few years.

7. Laws, regulations, and administrative procedures determine a product's country of origin. A decision by a customs authority on origin can determine whether a shipment that falls within a quota limitation qualifies for a tariff preference or is affected by an anti-dumping duty. These rules vary from country to country.

8. SPS measures or regulations are implemented by governments to protect human, animal, and plant life and health, and to help ensure that food is safe for consumption.

9. For example, anecdotal evidence suggests that the relative stability of Zambia has been partly responsible for the rapid increase in tourism in the area of Livingstone, which has increasingly become the basis for exploring the Victoria waterfalls for tourists concerned with the economic and political unrest in Zimbabwe.

10. For example, in 2006, the Patents and Companies Registration Office (PACRO) introduced a web-based, licence-free software application. PACRO also automated the business registration process and opened a Customer Service Centre to serve as a one-stop shop for business customers. An interactive website was established which allows customers to download application forms and complete them before visiting the office. During the period under review the government instituted further measures to de-centralize company registration to Ndola and Livingstone. Between 2005 and 2008 the time it took to register a business was reduced from over 30 days to one day (WTO, 2009).

11. In fact, the surveys for DBI are conducted the year before. So, for instance, the data for the 2010 indicators really refer to the end of 2009.

References

Amin, M. and Mattoo, A. (2007). Migration from Zambia: Ensuring temporariness through cooperation. *World Bank Policy Research Working Paper* 4145. Washington, DC: World Bank.

Amurgo-Pacheco, A. and Pierola, M.D. (2008). Patterns of export diversification in developing countries: Intensive and extensive margins. *World Bank Policy Research Working Paper* 4473. Washington, DC: World Bank.

Arnold, J., Guernazi, B., and Mattoo A. (2007). Telecommunications: The persistence of monopoly. In: Mattoo, A. and Payton, L. (eds) *Services Trade and Development: The Experience of Zambia*. Washington, DC and Basingstoke: World Bank and Palgrave Macmillan.

Arnold, J. and Mattoo, A. (2007). Services in the Zambian economy. In: Mattoo A. and Payton, L. (eds) *Services Trade and Development: The Experience of Zambia*. Washington, DC and Basingstoke: World Bank and Palgrave Macmillan.

Arnold, J., Mattoo, A., and Narciso, G. (2008). Services inputs and firm productivity in sub-Saharan Africa: Evidence from firm-level data. *Journal of African Economies*; 17: 578–599.

Calì, M. and Kennan, J. (2009). The Effects of the Global Financial Crisis on exports in Least Developed Countries. *Paper presented at the AERC conference on Rethinking African Economic Policy in Light of the Global Economic and Financial Crisis.* Nairobi.

Calì, M. and te Velde, D. W. (2007). Is Zambia contracting 'Dutch Disease'? *ODI Working Paper 279.* London: Overseas Development Institute.

Co-operative Bank (2007). *The Ethical Consumerism Report.* Available at: <http://www.co-operativebank.co.uk/images/pdf/ethical_consumer_report_2007.pdf> (last accessed 10 April, 2011).

Corden, W. M. and Neary, J. P. (1982). Booming sector and de-industrialization in a small open economy. *Economic Journal*; 92: 825–848.

de Luna Martinez, J. (2007). Financial services: Dealing with limited and unequal access. In: Mattoo, A. and Payton, L. (eds) *Services Trade and Development: The Experience of Zambia.* Washington, DC and Basingstoke: World Bank and Palgrave Macmillan.

Eifert, B., Gelb, A. and Ramachandran V. (2005). Business environment and comparative advantage in Africa: Evidence from the investment climate data. *Working Paper 56.* Washington, DC: Center for Global Development.

Ellis, K., Keane J. (2008). A review of ethical standards and labels: Is there a gap in the market for a new 'Good for Development' label? *ODI Working Paper 297,* London: Overseas Development Institute.

Eyhorn, F. (2007). *Organic Farming for Sustainable Livelihoods in Developing Countries? The Case of Cotton in India.* Zurich: vdf Verlag.

Fessehaie, J. (2008). Zambia and the EPA. *Trade Negotiations Insights* 7: 8–10.

Government of Zambia (2006). *Fifth National Development Plan.* Lusaka: Government of Zambia.

Graffham, A. and MacGregor, J. (2007). Impact of EurepGAP on small-scale vegetable growers in Zambia. *Fresh Perspectives, Agrifood Standards and Pro-Poor Growth in Africa*; 3.

Hausmann, R. and Rodrik, D. (2003). Economic development as self-discovery. *Journal of Development Economics*; 72: 603–633.

Hummels, D. and Klenow, P.J. (2005). The variety and quality of a nation's exports. *The American Economic Review*; 95: 704–723.

Imani Development (2007). *Inventory of Regional Non Tariff Barriers: Synthesis Report.* Pretoria: Imani Development.

International Trade Centre (2005). *Identification of Priority Sectors for Export Promotion in Zambia.* Geneva: International Trade Centre.

International Centre for Trade and Sustainable Development (2005a). EU to modify rules of origin for trade preference schemes. *Bridges Weekly Trade News Digest*; 9: 8.

International Centre for Trade and Sustainable Development (2005b). European proposal on preferential access rules targets fisheries. *Bridges Trade BioRes* 5: 4–5.

Keane, J., Calì, M., and Kennan, J. (2010). *Study on Impediments to Intra-Regional Trade in sub-Saharan Africa.* London: Overseas Development Institute.

Mattoo, A. and Payton, L. (2007a). *Services Trade and Development: The Experience of Zambia.* Washington, DC and Basingstoke: World Bank and Palgrave Macmillan.

Mattoo, A. and Payton, L. (2007b). Services trade for Zambia's development: An overview. In Mattoo, A. and Payton, L. (eds) *Services Trade and Development: The Experience of Zambia*. Washington, DC and Basingstoke: World Bank and Palgrave Macmillan.

MCTI (Ministry of Commerce Trade and Industry) (2009). *Commercial Trade and Industrial Policy*. Lusaka: Government of the Republic of Zambia.

Mold, A. (2005). *Non Tariff Barriers – Their Prevalence and Relevance for African Countries*. Addis Ababa: UNECA, Africa Trade Policy Centre.

Mutume, G. (2006). New barriers hinder African trade. *African Renewal*; 19: 19.

National Consumer Council (2006). *A Consumer Perspective on Sustainable Consumption*. Available at: <http://www.ncc.org.uk/nccpdf/speeches/NCC079_a_consumer_perspective_on_sustainable_consumption.pdf> (last accessed 10 May 2011).

Ndulo, M., Mudenda, D., Ingombe, L., and Muchimba, L. (2010). *The Effects of the Global Financial Crisis on Zambia*. London: Overseas Development Institute.

Qureshi, M. and te Velde, D. W. (2008). *Working Smart and Small*. London: Commonwealth Secretariat.

Sachs, J.D. and Warner, A.M. (1999). The big push, natural resource booms, and growth. *Journal of Development Economics*; 59: 43–76.

Schlumberger, C. (2007). Air transport: Revitalising Yamoussoukro. In: Mattoo A. and Payton, L. (eds) *Services Trade and Development: The Experience of Zambia*. Basingstoke: Palgrave Macmillan.

Stevens, C., Meyn M., and Kennan, J. (2007). Duty-Free, Quota-Free Access: What is it Worth? *ODI Project Briefing* 10.

te Velde, D.W. (2005). *Temporary Movement of Natural Persons in EU Trade Agreements: Issues, Existing Provisions and Options for EPA Negotiations*. Paper prepared for Second Meeting of the COMESA Technical Working Group of Services Specialists for the Regional Services Assessment, Mauritius.

UNCTAD (2011). International trade in services statistics, online database. Available at: <http://unctadstat.unctad.org/ReportFolders/reportFolders.aspx?sCS_referer=&sCS_ChosenLang=en> (last accessed 4 May 2011).

World Bank (2005). *Zambia Diagnostic Trade Integration Study*. Washington, DC: World Bank.

World Bank (2011a). *Enterprise Surveys*. Available at: <http://www.enterprisesurveys.org/Custom/Default.aspx> (last accessed 30 April 2011).

World Bank (2011b). *Doing Business Indicators*. Washington, DC: World Bank.

World Bank (2011c). *ICT at a* glance. Washington, DC: World Bank.

WTO (World Trade Organization) (2009). *Trade Policy Review Report by the Secretariat*. Geneva: WTO Secretariat.

Zambia Development Agency (2007). *Exporter Audit 2007*. Lusaka: Zambia Development Agency.

Zambia Development Agency (2008). Exporter *Audit 2008*. Lusaka: Zambia Development Agency.

IV

Public Service Delivery and the Political Economy of Reforms

14

Is There a 'Populist Threat' in Zambia?[1]

Nic Cheeseman, Robert Ford, and Neo Simutanyi

14.1 Introduction

Michael Sata's remarkable victory in the 2011 presidential elections answered some questions about Zambian politics and raised many more. The victory of the Patriotic Front (PF) over the incumbent Movement for Multi-party Democracy (MMD) demonstrated that it was possible for an opposition party to harness mass support in order to defeat an established incumbent. At the same time, Sata's effective use of populist appeals showed that a leader willing to speak to the issues that voters care most about could mobilize a vast support base, even when competing in a political landscape that was far from free and fair.[2] But it was less clear what Sata's ascent to the presidency meant for the future direction of Zambia's economic and political policy. His supporters hoped for more jobs, more money in their pockets, and an economy under greater Zambian control. Foreign investors feared that the new president would castigate them as foreign 'infestors' and make it more costly, and more difficult, to do business in Zambia. For their part, donors worried that by introducing populist policies President Sata would undermine the prudent economic policies that had helped the country to secure debt relief and economic growth under his predecessors. They also fretted that if the great popular expectations inspired by Sata's victory were not met, political instability would ensue.

It is easy to see how each of these distinctive dispositions towards Sata's presidency emerged. Populist leaders, such as Bolivia's Eva Morales and Venezuela's Hugo Chavez, typically build their support by reaching out to people directly, bypassing party and state structures in order to construct very personalized forms of linkage to the electorate (Weyland, 1999; 2001). They do this by connecting emotionally to voters, highlighting the most pressing issues that they face, and promising simple solutions. When explaining the economic hardship of the poor, and the failures of previous regimes to improve the lot of 'normal' people, they often blame foreign enemies, who become catch-all scapegoats for the country's ills (Knight 1998). In the case of the aforementioned Latin American leaders, it has often been the USA that has borne the brunt of populist scorn.

Populist movements typically share three features that are particularly important from the point of view of development and democracy. Firstly, because populists have a tendency to promise the earth, they generate great excitement amongst their supporters and often struggle to deliver on their promises in the long run – although, admittedly, this hardly distinguishes them from any other set of political leaders. Secondly, populist governments' critical attitude towards foreign engagement in the economy often make them more reluctant to accept advice from organizations such as the International Monetary Fund (IMF) and the World Bank (although this is not always the case, see Roberts 1995; Weyland, 1999). Taken together, these two features mean that populist presidents are particularly likely to respond to pressure for rapid improvements by adopting unsustainable economic policies that have negative long-term consequences. Thirdly, because populist leaders often develop fanatic support they are often able to use their personal appeal to undermine institutional checks and balances, thus increasing the risk of both poor economic management and democratic backsliding.

Michael Sata followed some, but not all, of these classic populist tropes. His campaigns reached an impressive number of people as the PF leader used a helicopter to traverse the country, connecting through his personal charismatic appeal. And careful research conducted before each meeting allowed him to speak to the particular issues facing each constituency. He drew on his reputation as a 'man of action' to argue that he would be able to quickly solve people's most pressing problems, thus encouraging the PF's rank and file support base to dream that his election would transform their standard of living. Like Chavez and Morales, his rhetoric also gave international investors cause for thought. Particularly in previous election campaigns, Sata was fiercely critical of the role played by the Chinese government, calling for a 'Zambianization' of key natural resources, such as copper, water, and land. More specifically, the PF had pledged to increase taxes on the mining sector, while improving the working conditions for Zambians employed by foreign firms. It was therefore natural that donors feared a rejection of Western economic orthodoxy, while foreign investors became increasingly conscious of their exposure to political change.

But much of the debate on Zambia under Sata has not paid much attention to the composition of Sata's support base and what they actually want. The PF has risen to prominence by articulating the needs and desires of ordinary Zambians, and has often modified its position in line with the change public mood. The political attitudes of the wider population and of PF supporters, in particular, can therefore help us to understand the policies that Sata is likely to pursue while in office. This chapter reviews the available evidence from national representative surveys and finds that, in general, Zambians are particularly supportive of populist policies. PF supporters, in particular, favour high levels of government intervention in the economy and are keen to see greater state control of key industries.[3] We find that some of the fears of donors and foreign investors are not without foundation. The great pressure on President Sata to deliver public services and 'money in people's pockets' will make it extremely difficult for the PF to contain spending within manageable levels, while the strong public support for state intervention means that the government is likely to come under intense pressure to implement subsidies and handouts, especially in urban areas. Although such policies would alleviate the short-term suffering of Zambians, they may also increase the country's debt burden and introduce distortions into economy, two trends that undermined the country's economic performance in the 1980s. But we also find that in many ways the PF does not fit the classic populist model. Most notably, the president's supporters do not blame China for Zambia's ills and actually see foreign investment as a positive development. Moreover, there is no evidence that ordinary PF voters are more authoritarian, or more willing to support the personalization of power, than the average Zambian. This suggests that the new government has no need to alienate foreign investors, and that President Sata will have some significant incentives to retain and respect the principle of plural politics.

Indeed, the composition of the PF's support base suggests that there may also be many positives to come out of President Sata's government. By mobilizing support on the basis of a populist strategy, he has managed to build a party that does not rely on ethnic appeals and has a genuinely diverse support base. The PF's rule is therefore less likely to descend into the sort of divide-and-rule politics that has undermined national unity and political stability in nearby Kenya and Malawi. That Sata's urban popularity has been based on his ability to recognize the needs of poor urban dwellers, such as unemployed youth, retirees, retrenched workers, industrial workers, and those in the slums, also suggests that the PF's economic policy may be comparatively pro-poor, which is a particular concern of international donors, such as the Department for International Development (DfID) of the UK. Of course, leaders are not always guided by the wishes of rank and file members, as the declining popularity of the former MMD government and President Frederick Chiluba demonstrates. Moreover, the centralization of power under the Zambian constitution and the weakness of key democratic institutions mean that the country is particularly vulnerable to the idiosyncratic decisions of the president. But to the extent that the PF follows the wishes of its supporters, fears of a 'populist threat' in Zambia may be exaggerated.

14.2 The rise of the Patriotic Front (PF)

Michael Sata arrived at a populist stance through a process of trial and error. When he first split from the MMD government after hearing that he would not be outgoing President Frederick Chiluba's choice of successor, his support base was largely limited to his Bemba 'homelands', leading Scarritt (2006) to suggest that the PF was at the very least a 'potentially ethnic' party, while Erdman (2007) concluded that it was best understood as an essentially Bemba party. However, having only polled three per cent in the 2001 elections Sata was forced to rethink his strategy, and it was at this point that his approach began to change. Sensing widespread frustration among slum-dwellers and the urban workers who felt let down by what they saw as the 'broken promises' of the government, Sata recognized that there was an opportunity to take support away from the ruling party in urban areas (Larmer and Fraser, 2007). Drawing on his reputation as a political 'street-fighter' during his days in the United National Independence Party (UNIP) and as District Governor of Lusaka, he set himself up as a man with his finger on the pulse of the street and the slum.[4]

Significantly, during the period that Sata was casting around for a new political image, the role of the Chinese government and investors in Zambia was becoming a salient political issue. The Zambian government offered generous terms to private investors in order to attract desperately needed international capital amidst the economic gloom of the 1990s, when copper prices were low (Rakner 2003). However, when copper prices increased as a result of rising global demand many Zambians came to see these deals as exploitative. Most notably, the considerable proportion of copper revenues leaving the country meant that high copper prices did little for the Zambian exchequer.[5] However, contrary to popular perceptions, this was not the work of the Chinese. Of the 11 'packages' originally sold by Zambia Consolidated Copper Mines (ZCCM), only Chambishi was bought by Chinese investors and the nature of the deals owed more to pressure from British, Canadian, Indian, and South African players (Adam and Simpasa, 2011). Despite this, China quickly emerged as the main target of Zambian discontent – perhaps because stereotypes regarding the poor conditions for Chinese workers in China, coupled with the lack of integration of Chinese bosses and workers into Zambian society, made Chinese firms a more salient and vulnerable target (Lee, 2010). Even before Sata began to lash out against 'foreign infestors', Zambian mine workers had accused Chinese mine-owners of showing a disregard for health and safety, and Chinese companies had been criticized for bringing in Chinese labour, so contributing to the problem of unemployment in Zambia (see Larmer and Fraser, 2007; Muneku, 2009; Mutesa, 2010).

China quickly became the foreign target against which Sata sought to develop his image as the defender of Zambia's national interests. As with most populist leaders, the PF leader was more eloquent and specific when talking about who was to blame for Zambia's economic plight than he was on the question of who deserved to benefit from the country's resource wealth and exactly what should be done to put the situation right. Ahead of the 2006 elections, Sata engaged in a number of activities deliberately intended to bait the Chinese government, making trips to Taiwan to source party funding and ultimately announcing that if elected he would recognize Taiwan. Such statements drew an angry response from the Chinese government, which threatened to sever diplomatic ties to Zambia if Sata's pledge was carried out. The PF also promised that they would force Chinese companies to employ Zambian workers, to pay them a living wage, and would impose a 'windfall tax' on all mining companies to enable the country to benefit from the boom in copper prices as a result of increased Chinese demand. According to Larmer and Fraser (2007), Sata's dynamic and charismatic delivery, and his clearly articulated set of streamlined policies, enabled Zambians to imagine him as a decisive, effective, and transformative leader.

Despite not joining the United Democratic Alliance (UDA), a coalition that brought together a number of the most significant opposition parties, Sata came second in the presidential poll, although he still fell 373,098 votes short of the MMD's Levy Mwanawasa, who comfortably secured his re-election. But the upward momentum of the PF was confirmed when the party swept the board in local elections in a number of urban centres (Larmer and Fraser, 2007). Although little research was conducted on the actual attitudes to the Zambian electorate, it became commonplace to credit Sata's strong performance to his attacks on foreign investors. However, in the 2008 presidential by-election, which followed the untimely death of President Levy Mwanawasa, Sata was careful to respond to the national mood of mourning by edging closer to the centre-ground, and was rewarded with 38.1 per cent of the vote, just 1.96 per cent behind the successful MMD candidate, Rupiah Banda.[6] From the available electoral data, it is impossible to tell whether the improvement in Sata's performance owed more to the further spread of the PF's message or to Banda's failure to capture the public mood and a low turn-out. But what could not be called into question was that from an embarrassing seventh place in 2001, Sata had established the PF as the second party of Zambian politics.

As with the 2006 election, much of the scholarly analysis of the campaign stressed the 'populist' nature of Sata's support. In one of the only analyses of the 2008 general elections to be published, Cheeseman and Hinfelaar (2010) found considerable evidence to back up Larmer and Fraser's (2007) earlier thesis that Sata's ability to mobilize support was underpinned by his ability to identify a message that resonated with poor and disenfranchised Zambians across ethnic lines. Significantly, in 2008 Sata won a majority of the presidential vote in a number of high-density urban constituencies (the units in which the presidential ballot is broken down) outside of Bemba-speaking areas, most notably in Lusaka Province, but also in the Central and Eastern Provinces.

This is not to say that Sata's support was all 'populist'. Cheeseman and Hinfelaar also found that between 2006 and 2008 Sata's share of the vote increased by as much in Bemba-speaking rural areas as it did in urban areas. They therefore concluded that the key to Sata's success was his ability to simultaneously mobilize separate ethnic and populist constituencies. Cheeseman and Larmer have subsequently referred to this distinctive combination of ethnic and populist support as ethno-populism (2013). Running an ethno-populist strategy is particularly complicated because while the two constituencies may overlap, as is likely to be the case in the Copperbelt, where Sata receives support from some Bemba-speaking trade unionists, the core interests of the two groups are not wholly compatible. For example, cheaper food for urban workers usually means lower prices for rural producers. In this sense, what is interesting about the PF is that it developed not one support base, but a number of different support bases – all held together by different forms of loyalty to Michael Sata.

But this caveat notwithstanding, the PF did develop a form of Zambian populism that rested on two key pillars. First, and most important, was the assumed capacity of the government to intervene in the economy in order to improve the lives of ordinary citizens. Sata's approach focused on economic conditions and the responsibility of government to improve conditions on the ground. As with all populists, his worldview was an explicitly interventionist one: the government can make things better for ordinary Zambians, and it can do so quickly. As presented by the PF during its campaigns, the market was not something to be left to its own devices in order to rationalize the economy and direct resources into the country's most productive sectors. Instead, the market was viewed as something that could be controlled by the government of the day in order to enrich the nation. Put simply, although Sata was willing to advocate lower taxes, his general approach was not to emphasize the value of removing political distortions within the economy – a classic preoccupation of the IMF and the World Bank – but to argue that political intervention was necessary to resolve market failure. For the PF it was not enough to wait patiently for steady economic growth to raise living standards; quality of life could be improved in the short term through food subsidies, increases in wages for workers, and greater expenditure on public services.

The second key pillar of the PF's populism was Sata's high-profile criticism of international partners. Populists require a common enemy around which to rally supporters, and the growing influence of China in Africa provided Sata with an easy target. Moreover, by depicting the MMD as being in collusion with foreign governments, and hence complicit in the country's economic hardship, Sata was able to build a psychological wall between 'them' and 'us'. This strategy was particularly effective because it framed the choice that voters had to make on his terms: Zambians could either vote for the MMD and another five years of foreign dependency, or they could take control of their own destinies by voting for the PF. Although Sata later modified this line by promising to maintain Zambia's ties with China if he was elected, it was by painting a picture of Chinese exploitation and western dependency that Sata positioned himself as the defender of the national interest. In the process, he promoted a form of Zambian nationalism, stressing common interests rather than narrow sectional appeals; even if this message varied for effect according to local context.

14.3 Zambian political attitudes

It is easy to see why Sata's brand of populism was able to excite voters and worry donors in equal measure. The upturn in economic fortunes of the Zambian Government has been built on two main foundations. Firstly, greater Chinese demand resulted in rising copper prices and a revival of the mining sector and related industries. Secondly, the massive debt relief secured by the Mwanawasa government meant that money could be diverted from debt repayment towards infrastructure projects and public services. Significantly, under Mwanawasa, the government earned international respect as a reforming administration with a reputation for cutting back on corruption, controlling inflation, and balancing the budget. As a result, Zambia became a much more attractive destination for foreign investors, while donors re-engaged with the country following the later years of the Chiluba administration, when many foreign partners scaled back their activities as a result of rampant corruption and democratic backsliding. There are elements of Sata's nationalistic populism that clearly threatened to undermine both of these foundations and to undo Mwanawasa's hard work.

But politicians only ever implement their pre-election promises selectively. So in thinking through what a populist president means for policy in Zambia we need to move beyond campaign slogans to understand the PF's priorities. Sata clearly has a pragmatic side, as demonstrated by the moderation of his anti-Chinese rhetoric in recent years and his earlier decision to position himself as the right person to complete the work of the much more conservative Mwanawasa following the former president's untimely death in 2008. In power, then, Sata is likely to seek out a compromise between what is desirable and what is achievable. The policies he settles on are likely to be strongly shaped by political realities – such as the importance of Chinese investment to Zambia's economic well being, whatever he may have said in the heat of the campaign – and the priorities of Zambian voters.

It is therefore important to ask exactly what Zambian voters want and what sorts of policies these demands might give rise to? Is there general sympathy for a populist position or is this limited to PF supporters? Does Sata's support base agree with all of his ideas or only some of them? To answer these questions we analyse data from the Afrobarometer, a large-scale attitude survey that is designed to be nationally representative and is conducted on a face-to-face basis in respondent's language of choice. The fourth round of the Afrobarometer covered 19 countries between March 2008 and June 2009; the data we use here was collected in Zambia between 2 and 24 June 2009, and is based on a survey of 1,200 individuals aged 18 and over.[7] We examine this data in two stages. Firstly, we consider the general responses of Zambians in order to assess the level and nature of populist attitudes in the population. Secondly, we adopt a narrower focus to assess the specific support base of the PF.[8]

The Afrobarometer asks a wide range of questions, so we are able to test simultaneously the effect of several different factors. We begin by assessing popular attitudes towards the economy under MMD rule, to see whether voters disagree with the IMF- and World Bank-approved reforms implemented under the Mwanawasa and Banda administrations, and are generally sympathetic to their reversal. Firstly, we look at what people thought about national and personal economic conditions in 2009 through a battery of six questions that ask respondents about personal and national economic conditions in 2009, a year prior, and their impression of what was likely to happen in 2010. Secondly, we assess voter poverty levels, using a set of five questions that measure how often respondents go without basic essentials, such as food, water, and fuel. We tested how these items are related to each other using factor analysis, a technique which examines whether the responses to different items suggest they are driven by a single common underlying variable, or several have several distinct drivers. In this case, factor analysis confirmed that a single underlying poverty factor drives responses to all the separate items, suggesting that different forms of poverty in Zambia tend to have a common underlying pattern. We therefore combine these items into a single standardized poverty scale.[9] We also employ a range of questions that ask Zambians for their specific views on the economic performance of the MMD. Zambians were asked whether they think economic reforms have helped or harmed most Zambians, and whether they think that reforms should be abandoned or that the hardships they generate should be accepted. Zambians were also asked about government performance in several economic areas, including job creation, poverty reduction, inflation, inequality, and privatization. We also look at views of foreign influence in Zambia using a number of questions that ask whether particular countries or institutions have too much influence, and how much foreign non-governmental organizations (NGOs), foreign businessmen, investors, and donors – including China – are helping Zambia.

Just as important as the rejection of foreign assistance is support for higher levels of government intervention, particularly in the economy. We investigate this by employing eight measures to look at whether Zambians favour private provision of services, government provision, or a mix of the two. These areas are: agricultural markets; (currently) state-owned businesses, schools, and clinics; job creation; crime control; purchase and sale of copper; and agricultural credit. But donor fears about the policy implications of Sata's populism are not constrained to the economic realm; another source of concern is the potential rejection of democratic methods. We employ a set of nine items that tap Zambian support for various aspects of democratic practice, such as the election of leaders, respect for political rights and civil liberties, recognition of the value of opposition parties and dissenting views, and the protection of institutional checks and balances. We also assess the extent of dissatisfaction with existing institutions and the ruling class. The Afrobarometer provides us with two key ways of capturing such dissatisfaction. Firstly, we look at the levels of trust in a range of Zambian institutions, including the presidency, parliament, the police, the courts, the electoral commission, and the ruling and opposition parties. Secondly, we look at perceptions of the prevalence of corruption in five Zambian institutions: the presidency, parliament, the police, the courts, and the tax office.

Finally, we look at the distribution of support for populist attitudes in Zambia. Are these simply held by urbanites or by certain ethnic groups affiliated to Sata, or are they held more generally? And is there any evidence that those with populist attitudes think more 'nationally' and so are less swayed by ethnic political appeals? To assess whether President Sata's government may have a positive impact on national unity we deploy two measures – firstly, a question that asks whether respondents identify primarily with their ethnic group, with the Zambian nation, or equally with both and secondly, a question that asks whether political leaders should look to help all Zambians or focus on the interests of their own group.

14.4 Assessing the extent of support for populist policies in Zambia

We can broadly divide the set of populist beliefs outlined above into two main groups: economic elements, concerning the current state of the Zambian economy and the desire to radically reform it with activist state intervention, and socio-political elements concerning disaffection with Zambia's political and social institutions, dissatisfaction with democracy, and support for undemocratic alternative governments. Table 14.1 presents the overall levels of support for various economic populist ideas among Zambians.

Table 14.1 reveals widespread support for many economic populist ideas. Zambians were strongly negative about national economic conditions under the MMD, although this was tempered somewhat by a perception that things have started to improve and optimism about further progress. Such overtly negative evaluations are likely to have been shaped by the timing of the survey, which was conducted in 2008–09 – a period in which copper prices

Table 14.1 Economic populism in Zambia, 2009

Measure	Support for populist position (%)
National economic conditions	
Negative about present condition	72
Conditions worse than a year ago	37
Conditions will be worse in a year's time	32
Personal economic conditions	
Negative about present conditions	58
Conditions worse than a year ago	31
Conditions will be worse in a year's time	31
Experience of poverty – gone without several times or more food	46
Water	33
Medicine	54
Cooking fuel	30
Cash income	82
Views of current economic policies	
Economic reforms should be abandoned	46
Economic reforms hurt most Zambians	82
Government handling managing the economy badly	74
Government handling job creating badly	86
Government handling improving living standards for the poor badly	84
Government handling keeping prices down badly	90
Government handling narrowing income gaps badly	89
Not very or not at all satisfied with government privatization policy	77
Demand for an activist state*	
Agricultural markets	62
State-owned businesses	80
Schools and clinics	81
Job creation	71
House building	49
Crime control	71
Purchase and sale of copper	75

* per cent agreeing that the government should have the main responsibility for provision in each area.

had fallen from around $9,000 to around $3,500 per metric ton with negative consequences for Zambia's economic outlook. However, our survey findings are in line both with the responses given to a survey conducted in 2006, and qualitative reports of the attitudes of ordinary Zambians both before and after this period (Larmer and Fraser, 2007), and therefore seems to reflect a deeply rooted and consistent trend. It is important to note that this does not necessarily mean that the reform agenda of the MMD was not working. Rather, it may be that the slow pace of 'trickle-down' meant that those at the grass roots felt no direct benefit from the country's improved macroeconomic situation, and so were naturally doubtful about the MMD's claims to have put Zambia back on track. Zambia's strong economic performance over the last two years, with economic growth averaging between 5 and 6 per cent, may have helped lift the mood of many voters, although they remained deeply unhappy with the status quo. This is no doubt related to the fact that the constituency of impoverished voters in Zambia, the chief target of populist appeals, is very large. More than a third of Afrobarometer respondents reported regularly going without water or cooking fuel; half regularly going without food or medicine; and four-fifths reporting regularly going without any cash income. Proposals to subsidize food or fuel prices are likely to play particularly well with such voters.

Zambian voter dissatisfaction with the MMD's economic record was also profound. Between 74 and 90 per cent of respondents rated the government's performance on each economic issue negatively, suggesting something close to a national consensus that the MMD government was a failure in economic terms, despite the relative improvement in the economy since the re-introduction of multi-party politics. Similarly, high proportions of Zambians agree that economic reforms have hurt most Zambians, but the Zambian people are more cautious with regard to whether the current reform effort should be abandoned entirely: almost as many people accept the need to continue the reform process and accept the hardships it generates as believe it should be abandoned. However, it is clear that even voters who wish to see the reforms continue do not think the Zambian Government is implementing economic policy well. Put another way, it would seem that Zambia's steady economic growth has not actually made a difference to the lives of ordinary Zambians. There appears to have been no sense at the grass roots that growth was being translated into more jobs or higher wages. Official statistics support this story. According to the Central Statistical Office, despite recording economic growth of around 6 per cent between 2002 and 2010, poverty levels remained high, averaging 65 per cent during the same period.

The Afrobarometer also reveals a very deep pool of support for an activist state in Zambia: a large majority of Zambians continue to favour a strong role for the state in nearly every aspect of the economy. This is no doubt reflective of a history of intensive state intervention in the economy during

349

the tenure of UNIP, which ruled Zambia for 27 years after independence. During the period of UNIP one-party rule (1972–91) President Kenneth Kaunda established a soft version of African socialism, in which private enterprise was curtailed and large businesses and industries were brought under the control of the state. The basic modus operandi of the UNIP regime thus encouraged ordinary Zambians to look to the state to resolve their economic difficulties. Attitudes to the state in Zambia today reflect this legacy. Between 60 and 80 per cent of Zambians believe the government should have sole responsibility for the provision of most resources, including control over the economically critical copper industry (75 per cent) and of agricultural credit (77 per cent). Large majorities also believe that job creation is the province of the state, not the private sector (81 per cent). There is a smaller minority who believe in a mixed economy, with both the government and private business playing a role, but only a vanishingly small proportion of Zambians believe that private enterprise should drive economic provision. Only in house building do we see evidence of a more mixed view. This is somewhat surprising given that Zambians suffered consistent economic hardship during the one-party state era, when the government was heavily involved in the economy and presided over a series of economic disasters, failing to deliver either jobs or services. However, it does reflect a wider trend in Africa in which people first and foremost want their states to be the engines of development. Significantly, we see little variation in attitudes to the state across different age groups, suggesting that these findings are not simply a legacy of the way in which older Zambians were 'socialized' during the UNIP years, nor can they be explained easily as the expression of the younger Zambians' impatience for jobs and services. Rather, it appears that frequent periods of populist mobilization by leaders or movements promising state-led development have encouraged people to believe that the government is the best vehicle for advancing their interests – even if it has failed to do so thus far. At the same time, international financial institutions have wholly failed to build a domestic constituency in favour of a more market-based economy in Zambia, perhaps in large part because many Zambians have yet to experience the benefits of economic growth directly. Tellingly, much of the blame for previous economic difficulties appears to have been placed on individuals or political parties, rather than on the notion of state intervention itself (Larmer, 2007). As a result, many Zambians are still waiting for a government to fulfil the promises first made by UNIP way back in the 1960s.

Table 14.2 summarizes the picture in relation to the socio-political attitudes including concerns about foreign influence; low trust in Zambian institutions, perceptions of corruption, and negative views of democracy and the practices associated with it. Surprisingly, despite the attention Sata and the PF have given to the allegedly malign influence of foreigners in Zambia, there is little evidence of strong antiforeigner sentiment in the

Table 14.2 Socio-political populism in Zambia, 2009

Measure	Support for populist position (%)
Negative perceptions of foreign influence	
Foreign non-governmental organizations (NGOs)/ donors have too much influence	28
Foreign businesses and investors have too much influence	26
Foreign NGOs help Zambia little or not at all	14
Foreign businesses and investors help Zambia little or not at all	25
China helps Zambia little or not at all	17
USA helps Zambia little or not at all	16
Institutional trust	
Low trust in president	56
Low trust in parliament	51
Low trust in Electoral Commission	57
Low trust in ruling party	62
Low trust in opposition parties	53
Low trust in police	49
Low trust in courts	37
Perceptions of corruption*	
Office of the President	38
Parliament	32
Government officials	44
Police	55
Tax officials	46
Support for antidemocratic principles and practices	
Don't use elections to choose leaders, find alternative method	22
Political parties are divisive, better if there are fewer	26
President should not be accountable to parliament	34
Opposition parties should cooperate with government, not criticize it	64
Media should not criticize government	17
President alone should make laws, not parliament	22
President should not be subject to rule of law	26
President should not be subject to term limits	14
Opposition to the rule of law	
People do not have to respect court decisions	27
Police do not have the right to enforce the law	24
Tax office does not have the right to make people pay taxes	23
Dissatisfaction with democracy and support for alternatives	
Zambia not a democracy/not at all satisfied with democracy	23
Approve of one-party rule	17
Approve of military rule	7
Approve of one-man rule	5
National versus ethnic loyalties	
More Zambian than ethnic group	25
Politicians should serve all Zambians, not just own group	60

* Proportion of respondents who answered that 'most' or 'all' of those working in the institution are corrupt

broader electorate. This is not to say that there is no constituency here for Sata to mobilize: between 15 and 30 per cent of Zambians express hostility towards foreigners and international organizations, with the greatest hostility towards business investors. However, Sata's targeting of China would seem to have been of limited utility, as the majority of his compatriots (51 per cent) regard China as 'somewhat' or 'very' helpful to Zambia. So although the PF may continue to use China to demonstrate its 'Zambianist' credentials, there is limited appetite for this within the wider electorate. Indeed, it may well have been the realization that many Zambians were positive about the role of foreign actors – not least those that rely on Chinese investment for their jobs – that persuaded Sata to soften his language in the last few years. However, it is important to note that the overall level of knowledge in this area is very low – more than a third of Zambians answered 'don't know' to each of these questions, suggesting the average Zambian voter feels that they know too little about the role foreigners play in Zambian society to make an informed judgement.

Low Zambian hostility to foreigners and international institutions does show up in another question, however. Zambians were asked who they blamed for the current economic condition of their country in an open-ended question where they were free to offer any answer. Nearly three quarters blamed the current MMD administration under Rupiah Banda (31 per cent), or the previous MMD administrations of Levy Mwanawasa (7 per cent) or Frederick Chiluba (36 per cent). Only around 7 per cent named foreigners or international organizations as the main cause of economic distress. Zambians lay the blame for their economic woes at the door of the presidential palace, not at the door of the IMF branch office or the Chinese embassy. There is, therefore, only very limited support for the existence of an aggressively Zambian nationalist populism, in contrast to the typical story that commentators have told to explain the increase in the PF's popularity between 2001 and 2008.

Given the relatively high evaluations of foreign governments, it is striking that Zambians expressed very low trust in their domestic political institutions, with clear majorities saying they had little or no trust in the president, parliament, the electoral commission, and both ruling and opposition parties (Table 14.2). This suggests that there was considerable popular disaffection for 'antisystem' parties, such as the PF, to exploit. Significantly, trust levels were lowest for the president and the ruling party, and somewhat higher for the opposition, which is the reverse of the general pattern: of the other countries surveyed by the Afrobarometer, only in Zimbabwe are opposition parties more trusted than the ruling party, a clear sign of the depths to which the MMD had fallen in the eyes of Zambian voters. However, Zambians do show somewhat higher trust in their legal institutions – the police and the courts. A slim majority at least somewhat trust the police and nearly two-thirds express some confidence in the judiciary, suggesting that while there is considerable 'antisystem' sentiment, Zambians do not believe that all of their key institutions are equally suspect.

A similar picture emerges with regard to corruption. Zambians are relatively subtle in their understanding of graft and associated practices, in that while they perceive widespread corruption, they typically do not regard their institutions as being entirely corrupt. The most common answer in each case is that there are 'some' rotten apples in each body. However, a significant minority of Zambians were considerably more cynical: between a third and a half of respondents regard each institution as mostly or entirely corrupt, with the police, the tax office, and the government bureaucracy cited as being the worst offenders.

Given the negative evaluations of government performance and the widespread perception that the administration was blighted by corrupt officials, one might naturally expect Zambians to have lost faith in democracy. Yet only 23 per cent of Zambians say they are 'not at all satisfied' with democracy, or believe that Zambia isn't a democracy at all. On the various substantive items dealing with democratic practice, the proportion choosing the authoritarian option is consistently at or below one quarter of survey respondents. Large majorities of Zambians support multi-party competition, a free press, and agree with the principle that presidents should be accountable to parliament and constrained by the rule of law. An overwhelming majority favour term limits for presidents, perhaps reflecting former President Frederick Chiluba's unpopular (and ultimately unsuccessful) attempt to secure an unconstitutional third term in 2001. Large majorities also agree that their own behaviour should be constrained by the rule of law. Zambians overwhelmingly believe that court decisions should be binding, that the police have the right to enforce laws, and that the tax department has the right to collect taxes, despite the low levels of trust they have in these institutions. Thus, while the Zambian population may be positively predisposed to populist messages, they are likely to reject authoritarian demagogues. There is no evidence in the survey data that Zambians are willing to sacrifice democracy for development.

In summary, if and when the PF government intervenes in the economy it is likely to enjoy considerable public support. There may be powerful business lobbies in the capital, but they lack a national constituency. But Zambians do not reject market solutions because they are seen to be 'foreign' or because they are hostile towards the IMF or World Bank. Rather, they reject market solutions because they believe that they have not improved the lot of the common man. They want a more interventionist government to put this right, but not at any cost: democracy and the rule of law remain concerns close to the heart of the average citizen.

14.5 The social distribution of populism

Clear support for populist ideas is therefore evident in a number of policy areas, but we have yet to assess just how important populism is to the PF's ability to mobilize support, or to consider how populist attitudes are distributed throughout society. To take the latter question first, although Zambia has never experienced a serious incident of ethnic conflict, multi-party elections have demonstrated significant patterns of ethnic voting. Zambia's many ethnic groups come together to form four main language groups, Bemba, Tonga, Lozi, and Nyanja, and these communities tend to support different political parties.[10] For example, recently the third party of Zambian politics, the United Party of National Development (UPND), has been criticized for being a 'tribalist' Tonga party, with little support outside of Southern Province. Meanwhile, the failure of the MMD to retain the support of Bemba speakers, especially during the Mwanawasa presidency, undermined the legitimacy of the government in the sizeable 'Bembaphone' parts of the country. In turn, when the PF first emerged many interpreted it as an ethnic vehicle through which Sata intended to build support by tapping into the sense of disenfranchisement of his kinsmen. So is Sata's presidency likely to exacerbate existing regional–linguistic divisions because of its strong Bemba support? Or can the catch-all nature of populist appeals act as a unifying force on Zambia's diverse and fragmented political landscape? We answer this question in two stages, first by analyzing the social distribution of populist attitudes and then by evaluating the composition of the support base of the PF itself.

To do this we employ regression analysis on a selection of the items we have employed above. Table 14.3 shows the results of regression analysis of three attitudes that are related to a populist disposition. It is not straightforward to model the populist belief system, as in reality it has a number of

Table 14.3 Social distribution of economic populist attitudes, 2009

	National economic performance	Abandon economic reforms	State intervention scale
Urban	**-0.30 *****	0.09	**0.24 +**
Bemba	**-0.31 *****	**0.29 ***	0.18
Completed secondary school	0.07	-0.05	**-0.58 *****
Post-secondary school	0.13	0.15	**-0.89 *****
High political discussion	**-0.26 ****	**0.21 +**	**-0.26 ***
R^2	0.04	0.01	0.05
N	1,193	1,132	1,200

Ordinary least squares regression. Significant predictors in bold: $+ < 0.01$; $^*P < 0.05$; $^{**}P < 0.01$; $^{***}P < 0.001$

different components – support for a charismatic leader, discontent with the current economic reforms, a lack of patience, and faith in the transformative power of the state – not all of which have been captured by survey data. Here we focus on state intervention, which is perhaps the most fundamental component of the populist voter in Zambia. But we also consider two other attitudes, hostility to the MMD's programme of economic liberalization and negative views of the Zambian economy because they are likely to render individuals more receptive to populist appeals. The latter two are measured using individual items, but we evaluate support for state intervention using an additive scale that sums up all of the areas where Zambians think government should play the main role.

We tested a wide range of demographic factors, but few turned out to have any relationship with populist attitudes or wider economic discontent. Populist views seem quite widely diffused through the Zambian population, rather than concentrated in particular segments of society. Only a few variables emerge as significant predictors, and even these do not show consistent effects on all our measures. In line with previous studies that have traced the historic evolution of urban radicalism among the Bemba community and mine workers of various ethnicities (Larmer 2007), we find that Bemba respondents and Zambians living in urban areas tend to be more critical of the country's economic performance, and that Bemba speakers are more willing to advocate abandoning the MMD's economic reforms. However, there is considerable agreement on the need for new economic policies among all ethnic communities. Moreover, we find that on the critical question of state intervention, Bembas are no more likely to take up a populist position than respondents from other groups.

There is some evidence that the politically engaged are more likely to hold populist views – those who say they discuss politics regularly express more populist views on all three items. However, those Zambians who have at least completed secondary education are markedly less keen on state economic intervention. Whether this is a result of a greater awareness of the benefits markets bring, a lesser reliance on state services, or a greater awareness of the failings of the present Zambian state – or something else entirely – is not clear, but the strength of the relationship suggests that increasing education levels in Zambia may gradually erode Zambians' currently strong attachment to a state-dominated economy. Note that this is very unlikely to be an age or cohort effect – we tested for age effects throughout and found no evidence for significant differences between age groups.

Table 14.4 shows a similar analysis conducted on selected socio-political populist attitudes. We use factor analysis to condense the multiple questions on the issues of trust, foreigners' role in Zambia, and views of authoritarian government into a single scale.[11] This factor analysis confirms that responses to the multiple questions on these issues move together, suggesting they are

Table 14.4 Social distribution of socio-political populist attitudes, 2009

	Trust in state institutions	Foreigners help Zambia	Satisfaction with democracy	Support for authoritarian alternatives
Urban	**-0.46*****	0.01	**-0.27 ****	-0.01
Bemba	**-0.29*****	0.001	**-0.39 *****	-0.07
Tonga	-0.15	-0.01	0.13	**-0.16 ***
Lozi	**-0.15***	**-0.50 *****	0.04	0.15
Urban Bemba	**0.27****	-0.12	0.24	0.01
Urban Tonga	**0.32***	-0.20	0.03	**0.26 ***
Age 30–44 years	-0.05	0.14	-0.04	-0.05
Age 45–59 years	**0.16***	0.05	-0.10	-0.05
Age 60+ years	**0.20***	0.03	0.03	-0.15
Completed secondary school	**-0.19****	0.02	0.09	**-0.21 *****
Post-secondary school	**-0.19****	0.08	0.05	**-0.32 *****
High political discussion	**-0.20****	0.001	-0.06	-0.03
R^2	0.14	0.05	0.05	0.04
N	1,198	913	1,118	1,192

Significant predictors in bold: $*P < 0.05$; $**P < 0.01$; $***P < 0.001$

being driven by a single underlying factor, which forms the basis of our analysis. Satisfaction with democracy is measured using a single item, with four categories: not a democracy/not at all satisfied, not very satisfied, fairly satisfied, and very satisfied. Again, three out of the four issues we examine here show little social differentiation. This is also true for attitudes towards the rule of law and corruption, which are not presented here for reasons of space. Only one attitude shows a strong pattern of social differentiation: trust in the institutions of the state. Urban Zambians, Bemba, younger Zambians, those with higher education levels and those who discuss politics typically express lower trust in Zambia's institutions. Perhaps unsurprisingly, it is some of the same groups, namely the Bemba and those living in urban areas, which are particularly dissatisfied with Zambian democracy. However, neither group is supportive of authoritarian alternatives: where the only significant predictor is education, educated Zambians reject authoritarianism even more strongly. The same pattern is not found on the other items. There is virtually no social differentiation at all on the issue of how much help foreigners are providing to Zambia. Similarly, there seem to be few sections of Zambian society that are consistently more supportive of authoritarian views.

There is thus no clear ethnic divide in terms of support for populist policies. When it comes to perceptions of the role played by foreigners and the need for state intervention, Zambians are united. The effective implementation of populist policies could therefore have a unifying impact. It could be argued that the close association between the Bemba group, certain aspects of populism, and the PF, could taint Sata's populism with an ethnic brush in the eyes of other Zambians. But while voters in winner-takes-all political systems are always less likely to trust a president who is not 'one of their own', there are good reasons for thinking that this may not undermine the wider acceptance of populist policies. For one thing, the Bemba community's responsiveness to populist messages cannot be reduced to their support for Sata; rather, it is rooted in a set of complex historical processes. Owing to patterns of migration to the mines, Bemba became the *lingua franca* on the Copperbelt, with high numbers of Bembas rotating between rural and urban areas with the season and the availability of paid labour (MacMillan, 1993; Ferguson, 1999). As a result, members of the Bemba community had greater exposure to urban political currents, and have consistently played a leading role in Zambian urban and political life. From the 1940s onwards, Bembas took up senior positions within the trade union and nationalist movements, and have been at the forefront of urban politics ever since (Bates, 1971; for more on Zambian civil society see Bartlett, 2000). In turn, the sacrifices made by the community to secure independence and to mine copper, the country's only significant natural resource, led to complaints that the community had not been rewarded appropriately for its efforts. It is this sense of entitlement, coupled with greater exposure to the radicalizing influence of trade union politics, which has rendered Bemba voters more susceptible to populist appeals that promise to improve the lot of urban workers (Larmer, 2007). Although the way that Bemba leaders have presented this underlying sense of entitlement has often led to criticism of tribalism, the fact that contemporary Bemba support for populism is typically not expressed in ethnic terms means that it is less likely to trigger discomfort in other communities, although this could easily be reversed if President Sata is seen to discriminate against other communities by appointing a Bemba-dominated cabinet.

It is also important to note that the Afrobarometer survey suggests that Bemba speakers are also more likely to view politics in national, rather than ethnic, terms. In the post-colonial period the strong urban presence of the community, and the use of the Bemba language by many non-Bembas in urban areas, facilitated the assimilation of individuals from a range of different groups, leaving the Bemba the most cosmopolitan ethnic group in Zambia. That these processes have shaped the perceptions of rural Bemba, as well as their urban counterparts, can also be explained by the group's distinctive past; generations of cyclical migration have established particularly strong ties between Bembas in urban and rural areas, facilitating the exchange of people and ideas. Thus, although Bemba speakers may be hoping to do particularly well out of having a co-ethnic in State House, there is no evidence that they wish to be rewarded at the expense of national unity. Rather, the fact that the Bemba community tends to express its political demands in terms of populist policies rather than patrimonial pleas means that it employs a political language that other communities can buy into. This point also has significant implications for the pressures that the PF is likely to face when in office: if it is true that Bembas tend to support Sata because he is a populist, rather than supporting populism because it happens to be the policy of Sata, then Bembas may join other ethnic groups in criticizing the government if it fails to deliver – unless, of course, the president can find ways to channel sufficient public appointments and resources back to keep his home areas satisfied no matter how the government performs on national issues.

This leads us neatly on to the first question highlighted above – just how important is populism to Michael Sata's support base? Will the PF lose popularity if it back-tracks on its policy pledges or is the party really just a collection of ethnic networks that will support President Sata whether he intervenes in the market or not? To answer these questions we test all the different populist attitudes in a logistic regression model of support for the PF among all Zambians who reported voting in the 2008 presidential election (Table 14.5). A logistic regression is used because the outcome we are looking at

Table 14.5 Logistic regression models of support for the Patriotic Front (PF), 2009

Variable	PF support (baseline model)	PF support (attitudes model)
Intercept		
Urban/rural (reference; rural)		
Urban	**1.96** ***	**1.56** ***
Ethnicity (reference: other)		
Bemba	**3.09** ***	**2.93** ***
Tonga	**-2.58** ***	**-1.75** ***
Lozi	0.18	0.06
Urban* Bemba	**-2.10** ***	**-2.42** ***
Urban* Lozi	**-1.65** *	**-1.67** **
Age (reference < 30years)	–	–
Age 30–44 years	**-1.04** ***	**-1.24** ***
Age 45–59 years	**-1.04** ***	**-1.17** **
Age 60+ years	**-1.17** ***	-0.73
Discuss politics	**0.56** *	0.47
Government economic policies have hurt most Zambians		**0.22** *
Support for rule of law		**0.38** **
Trust in Zambian instititions		**-0.77** ***
Government performance on economic issues		**-0.57** ***
Perceptions of corruption in Zambian institutions		**0.39** *
N	851	777
Pseudo R²	0.34	0.43

Significant predictors in bold: *$P < 0.05$; **$P < 0.01$; ***$P < 0.001$

has two values: supporting the PF or supporting someone else. The coefficients we show give an indication of how different variables influence the probability that an individual Zambian voter will support the PF rather than voting for one of the other parties. Two models are reported: a baseline model, including all the significant demographic predictors of PF support, and an attitudinal model, which adds in all the significant attitudinal predictors of PF voting. The baseline demographic model reveals strong urban–rural, age, and ethnicity effects that explain quite a lot of the variance in PF support. As geographical voting patterns would suggest, Sata received his greatest support from voters that were younger, were Bemba speakers, and lived in urban areas. In contrast, Tonga voters were particularly reluctant to give him their votes. Despite the general appeal of populist parties, then, ethnic identities still constrained political behaviour. Yet, support for the PF was not all about ethnicity. Lozis and Nyanjas did not discriminate against the PF as Tongas did, and if we rely on demographic factors alone our model is not a bad fit, but fails to provide a comprehensive account of the factors that drive PF support (pseudo R^2 of 0.34).

To see this more clearly, consider our second model, which assesses how significant populist attitudes were to Sata's electoral success. We find five attitudes that were associated with a greater tendency to vote for Sata and the PF. These include both economic and socio-political aspects of populism. Including all five populist attitudes in the final model significantly improves our model fit, which means that this set of populist beliefs was an important driver of support for the PF. This is important because it means that President Sata cannot simply rely on ethnic loyalties and patron–client networks to retain power. The populist platform that he campaigned on was absolutely critical to his victory and failure to make good on his promises could seriously impair the PF's chances of re-election. However, it is also worth noting that the coefficients for the demographic factors in our model hardly change when populist beliefs are added in. This individual level evidence fits with previous interpretations of the PF as an ethno-populist party (Cheeseman and Hinfelaar, 2010; Cheeseman and Larmer, 2013). Sata draws more support both from two main constituencies: certain ethnic and demographic groups – young people, urbanites, Bemba – whatever their beliefs, and those who hold certain populist beliefs – in particular disaffection with Zambia's ruling institutions and discontent over economic performance – whatever their background.

The specific populist attitudes that predict support for the PF tell us much about the hopes and values of the government's support base. Those who rated the performance of the incumbent MMD government on economic issues poorly, and those who believed economic reforms have harmed most Zambians, were significantly more likely to support the PF. Similarly, those who had little trust in Zambia's institutions and those who regarded the people who work in such institutions as being corrupt are also attracted to the main opposition party. However, the PF did not only mobilize the cynical: support for the rule of law was also significantly correlated with PF support. As previewed above, PF supporters may have believed that the Zambian state was performing poorly, but they did not desire an attack on the state; rather, they sought the reinvention of the state as a better functioning, law-governed democracy. Further evidence for this interpretation comes from the absence of any correlation between dissatisfaction with democracy or support for authoritarian alternatives and voting for the PF. Zambians wanted a man of action, but not a demagogue.

14.6 Populism, democracy, and the market

If President Sata is to fulfil the demands of his support base he will need to increase the level of state intervention in the economy and also to improve economic performance, especially as it affects urban workers. As we have seen, PF supporters' suspicion of the market is not driven by a desire to exert greater control over foreign investors. Instead, it has its roots in the widespread belief that recent economic gains have not aided ordinary people or been fairly distributed. In part, this is a legacy of Chiluba's second term in office, when corruption escalated and the MMD's populist and democratic credentials were undermined. Against this backdrop, it is perhaps unsurprising that many Zambians believe that economic liberalization served as a pretext for corruption and that the far-reaching privatization programme was rolled out principally to reward the president's allies and supporters. It is also important that most Zambians have yet to feel the direct benefits of economic growth. The reforms implemented by the MMD may have laid the foundation for Zambia's current economic recovery by opening up the economy to competition and foreign investment, but in the 1990s they also inflicted a miserable combination of job cuts, wage freezes, and tax increases on the Zambian people (Simutanyi, 1996; Craig, 2001). Memories of the hardships of that time run deep. Thus, ordinary Zambians remain unconvinced of the IMF- and World Bank-approved policies implemented (if at times only partially) by previous presidents. But Zambians do not blame international actors for their plight. Rather, they locate the blame for what they see as the country's economic mismanagement closer to home. President Sata's followers do not want to cut the country off from the rest of the world; they are simply searching for an alternative vision of economic development that will insulate them from uncertainty and economic insecurity. It is this, not antiforeigner sentiment, that underpins grass-roots support for nationalization. Given this, President Sata will not be driven to reject international finance and advice by his own supporters — if this occurs, it will come from the President himself.

Our survey findings suggest two different economic risks in the years ahead. The first is that the PF may spend beyond Zambia's means if it attempts to live up to its campaign promises to cut taxes, put more money in people's pockets, and improve public services. As we have seen, Zambians expect direct intervention in the economy, and they expect it to improve their material conditions. This desire, coupled with the intensity of excitement and expectation that greeted President Sata's victory, will make it extremely difficult for the PF to adopt a cautious approach to economic reform and government spending. Yet, given that government revenue is unlikely to increase significantly in the short-to-medium term, it will be difficult for the PF to deliver much more than the MMD without increasing government borrowing. This is significant because although the debt relief secured under President Mwanawasa means that Zambia is far better placed to borrow than it used to be, there is a danger that taking on a greater debt burden will make it harder for the government to maintain its spending commitments, especially if the value of copper falls in the medium term.

The second main risk is that the strength of public support for government intervention in the economy will lead to the adoption of short-termist policies that will distort the market and so undermine the prospects for long-term economic growth. Under the one-party state, Zambia became a classic case of 'urban bias', in which the UNIP government deliberately depressed food prices in order to subsidize the cost of living to urban residents and so stave off the prospect of unrest (Bates, 1981). Although this policy enabled UNIP to retain power in the short term, it also undermined the incentives for rural farmers to produce, which, in turn, led to a fall in agricultural exports and a rise in the cost of food in the medium term. As a result, the subsidy ended up hurting both rural communities and the very urban dwellers it was intended to assist. President Sata will come under similar pressure to intervene in the economy in order to alleviate the difficulties of those in the slums. Rural Bembas are also likely to press their claims, and are unlikely to be satisfied unless the government maintains the agricultural subsidies imposed by the MMD and also provides visible and large-scale projects to combat their relative marginalization. PF leaders are therefore likely to find it very difficult to resist the introduction of a range of distortionary policies, from fertilizer subsidies in rural areas to cheap food in urban locales. Such interventions are not always a source of economic disaster: fertilizer subsidies introduced by the Malawian government helped to increase agricultural production and thus to break a cycle of underproduction and famine. But if the mutual compatibility of such interventions and their long-term economic effects are not well thought through they are likely to produce negative unintended consequences, become a burden on the budget, and stifle innovation.

Happily, there is no evidence that in their desire for rapid change PF supporters would sanction undemocratic behaviour. If anything, they were more ardent democrats than MMD supporters: 71 per cent agreed that everyone should obey the law. This suggests that they are less likely to tolerate democratic backsliding and the theft of public resources. On the face of it, then, President Sata's government has strong incentives to deepen Zambia's democratic gains. But this could be a misleading finding. The enthusiasm of PF voters for democracy and the rule of law was, in part, a reflection of the fact that in 2009 the party was not in government. To argue in favour of greater constraints on the president and bureaucrats was thus to argue in favour of limiting the power of the MMD and to strengthen the hand of opposition leaders, such as Sata. We do not have data on the attitudes of PF supporters since the party won power and are therefore in no position to comment on whether or not power corrupts, but it is heartening that PF supporters also had no truck with authoritarian alternatives: 91 per cent reject one-man rule and 86 per cent reject one-party rule.

Of course, it is impossible to know to what extent the desires of PF supporters would shape the policies pursued by a PF government. African political parties are notorious for their lack of internal democracy and the degree to which they are controlled by their leaders (Carothers, 2006). It is conceivable that President Sata will interpret his electoral victory as an endorsement for all of his party's policies and will be emboldened to pursue an even more radical agenda in power. It is also possible that the PF will misread the hopes and values of its supporters, compromising democracy in the struggle to promote development in a way that may well disappoint the party faithful.

However, it is also conceivable that President Sata will be a more pragmatic president than his image as a radical 'man of action' suggests.[12] In his last round of international trips before the 2011 election, he went to great pains to reach out to foreign donors. For example, during a visit to Oxford University, Sata positioned the PF as a responsible party with which the UK could do business. In a speech peppered with terms such as 'good governance', 'human rights', and 'gender equality' he argued that Zambia required the support of foreign partners if it is to meet its economic aims. Now that the PF is in power, the same logic would suggest that the President will need to find an accommodation with China, the IMF, and the World Bank. Despite the PF's eye-catching positioning, then, the election of a 'populist' government in Zambia may result in as much continuity as it does change.

Notes

1. This chapter was written prior to Michael Sata's victory in the 2011 elections and has been subsequently modified to take his election into account, but the original analysis has not been rewritten.
2. Zambia was rated as 'Partly Free' in 2010 by Freedom House (see www.freedom house.org).
3. For a discussion of how similar processes have played out in the South African context see Halisi, 1998; Sitas, 2008.
4. Gould, J. (2007) Zambia's 2006 elections: the ethnicization of politics? *Nordic Africa Institute*; 26: 5–9. Available at: http://www.nai.uu.se/ (last accessed February 2012).
5. Alastair Fraser, 'Mining income to state just $71 million over 5 years', *Mine Watch Zambia*, 26 February 2007. For information on Zambia's mines during this period see http://minewatchzambia.com (last accessed 23 October 2012).
6. BBC News (2006) Zambia's mourning turns political. Available at: http://news.bbc.co.uk/1/hi/world/africa/7582398.stm (last accessed 24 October 2012).
7. For more information see www.afrobarometer.org.
8. We also tested the influence of these factors in a logistic regression of PF versus MMD support in a model limited to those who supported one of the two main parties. The pattern of findings is broadly the same as that reported here. The scale is constructed from the predicted factor scores for each individual. The scores are standardized with a mean of 0 and a standard deviation of 1. This means that about 68 per cent of respondents will score between –1 and 1, while 95 per cent will score between –2 and 2.
9. A fifth language group, the Lunda-Kaonde, is also significant, but there are insufficient numbers of this group in the survey to examine their attitudes and behaviour separately. For a detailed discussion of Zambia's language groups see Posner (2005).
10. The trust in state institutions factor is built from items asking about trust in the president, parliament, Electoral Commission, local government councils, the governing party, the police, and the courts. All of these items load together on a single factor, which explains 60 per cent of the variations in responses, and which we call 'trust in state institutions'. The 'foreigners help Zambia' factor is built from items asking about how much four international actors – China, USA, international investors, and international NGOs – have helped Zambia. One factor again explains 60 per cent of the variance here, suggesting Zambians tend to have a generally positive or negative view about outside interventions, but do not distinguish very much between different actors. Analysis of the individual items reveals little social differentiation. The 'support for authoritarian alternatives' factor is built from support for three authoritarian alternatives to democracy: military rule, one-party rule, and one-man rule. Once again, a single factor explains 60 per cent of the variance, suggesting Zambians who support one form of authoritarian government tend to also support others.
11. See Chirambo, 1999 for an interesting discussion of democracy as a limiting factor on populism in Malawi. Halisi, 1998, discusses the relationship between citizenship and populism in South Africa.

References

Adam, C. and Simpasa, A. (2011). Copper mining in Zambia: From collapse to recovery. In: Collier, P. and Venables, A. (eds) *Plundered Nations? Successes and Failures in Natural Resource Extraction*. Basingstoke: Palgrave, pp. 304–350.

Bartlett, D.M.C. (2000). Civil society and democracy: A Zambian case study. *Journal of Southern African Studies*; 26: 429–446.

Bates, R. (1971). *Unions, Parties, and Political Development: A Study of Mineworkers in Zambia*. New Haven: Yale University Press.

Bates, R. (1981). *Markets and States in Tropical Africa: The Political Basis of Agricultural Policy*. Berkeley, CA: University of California Press.

Carothers, T. (2006). *Confronting the Weakest Link: Aiding Political Parties in New Democracies*. Washington, DC: Carnegie Endowment for International Peace.

Cheeseman, N. and Hinfelaar, M. (2010). Parties, platforms, and political mobilization: The Zambian presidential election of 2008. *African Affairs*; 109: 51–76.

Cheeseman, N. and Larmer, M. (2011). Ethnopopulism in Africa: Mobilizing support in diverse and unequal societies. *Democratization* ahead-of-print: 1–29, <http://dx.doi.org/10.1080/13510347.2013.809065>.

Chirambo, R. M. (2009). Democracy as a limiting factor for politicized cultural populism in Malawi. *Africa Spectrum;* 442: 77–94.

Craig, J. (2001). Putting privatization into practice: The case of the Zambia Consolidated Copper Mines Ltd. *Journal of Modern African Studies*; 30: 389–410.

Ferguson, J. (1999). *Expectations of Modernity: Myths and Meanings of Urban Life on the Zambian Copperbelt, Perspectives on Southern Africa*. London: University of California Press.

Halisi, C.R.D. (1998). Citizenship and populism in the new South Africa. *Africa Today*; 45: 423–438.

Knight, A. (1998). Populism and neo-populism in Latin America, especially Mexico. *Journal of Latin American Studies*; 30: 223–248.

Larmer, M. (2007). *Mineworkers in Zambia: Labour and Political Change in Post-Colonial Africa, 1964–1991*. London: I.B. Tauris.

Larmer, M. and Fraser, A. (2007). Of Cabbages and King Cobra: Populist Politics and Zambia's 2006 Election. *African Affairs*; 106: 611–637.

Lee, C.K. (2010). Raw encounters: Chinese managers, African workers, and the politics of casualization in Africa. In: Fraser, A. and Larmer, M. (eds) *Zambia, Mining and Neoliberalism: Boom and Bust on the Globalized Copperbelt*. Basingstoke: Palgrave Macmillan, pp. 127–152.

Macmillan, H. (1993). Historiography of transition on the Zambian Copperbelt – another view. *Journal of Southern African Studies*; 19: 681–712.

Muneku, A.C. (2009). Chinese investments in Zambia. In: Baah, A.Y. and Jeunel, H. (eds) *Chinese Investments in Africa: A Labour Perspective*. Accra: Africa Labour Resource Network, pp. 160–202.

Mutesa, F. (2010). China and Zambia: Between development and politics. In: Cheru, F. and Obi, C. (eds) *The Rise of China & India in Africa*. London and New York: Nordiskaafrikainstitutet and Zed Books, pp. 167–180.

Posner, D.N. (2005). *Institutions and Ethnic Politics in Africa*. Cambridge: Cambridge University Press.

Rakner, L. (2003). *Political and Economic Liberalisation in Zambia*. Stockholm: The Nordic Africa Institute.

Roberts, K. (1995). Neoliberalism and the transformation of populism in Latin America: The Peruvian case. *World Politics*; 48: 82–116.

Scaritt, J. (2006). The strategic choices of multi-ethnic parties in Zambia's dominant and personalist party system. *Journal of Commonwealth and Comparative Politics*; 44: 234–256.

Simutanyi, N. (1996). The politics of structural adjustment in Zambia. *Third World Quarterly*; 17: 831–837.

Sitas, A. (2008). The road to Polokwane? Politics and populism in KwaZulu-Natal. *Transformation: Critical Perspectives on Southern Africa*; 68: 87–98.

Weyland, K. (1999). Neoliberal populism in Latin America and Eastern Europe, *Comparative Politics*; 31: 379–401.

Weyland, K. (2001). Clarifying a contested concept: populism in the study of Latin American politics. *Comparative Politics*; 34: 1–22.

15

Rationality, Cosmopolitanism, and Adjustment Fatigue: Public Attitudes to Economic Reform in Zambia

Michael Bratton and Peter Lolojih

15.1. Introduction

Technocrats usually take the lead in formulating and managing policies for economic development. In aid-dependent African countries, the relevant inner circle of policy actors includes senior officials in national central banks and ministries of finance, as well as advisors from international financial institutions and development assistance agencies. In this elite-centred process, few opportunities arise for the citizens of African countries to express their views in economic policy debates. Indeed, when it comes to economic reforms, the opinions of the man in the street and woman in the fields are rarely sought and seldom considered.

This chapter seeks to cast light on the neglected realm of public attitudes to economic reform. With a focus on Zambia, it asks four basic research questions: What do ordinary citizens think about the package of market-oriented reforms that shaped the economic policy agenda after the country's transition to multi-party democracy in 1991? How has public opinion evolved over time on key policy questions regarding limits to state intervention and the introduction of market mechanisms? Who among Zambians supports or opposes the reforms associated with economic stabilization and structural adjustment? What factors – not only demographic, but also economic or political – explain popular demand for economic reform, if any, and mass perceptions of whether benefits are being supplied?

To anticipate the results, we find that public opinion towards economic reform in Zambia is a mixed bag. As a whole, Zambians neither embrace nor refuse the orthodox package of reforms introduced by the Chiluba government (1991–2001) and sustained under the Mwanawasa presidency (2001–08). Instead, they distinguish among specific policy measures, accepting some and rejecting others. And, with only minor modifications, popular policy preferences are largely consistent over time. Among social groups, rural dwellers are more likely to be satisfied with economic reform policies than urbanites for reasons that we explore below. Perhaps the most original finding concerns the influence of 'cosmopolitanism' – an individual's openness to globalization, for example, through information and communication technology – as an explanatory factor driving support for market-oriented policies. Otherwise, such support is barely formed in Zambia and is difficult to explain.

Our inquiry is animated by an interest in different types of rationality. Do Zambians mainly use economic or political reasoning to arrive at attitudes to reform? We demonstrate that individual citizens use both sorts of criteria in making up their minds about whether a structural adjustment programme is appropriate and effective in Zambia. But which criterion matters more? On the demand side (do citizens want economic reform?), political factors, such as satisfaction with democracy and approval of the president's job performance, are relatively more important. And, although economic considerations are pre-eminent on the supply side (do citizens think the government is delivering the benefits of reform?), a complete explanation also requires reference to political factors, including an individual's partisan identification with political incumbents. The chapter ends with a discussion of the implications of our results for the political management of economic reform programmes.

15.2. Economic versus political rationality

In order to frame an investigation about policy choice and performance, it is useful to draw a basic distinction between two forms of rationality. On one hand, economic rationality is the approach of technocrats who apply standard cost-benefit tests to determine which one of several policy options provides maximum output for the least expense. On the other hand, political rationality derives from the worldview of politicians who assess policy alternatives in terms of expected impacts on political support and longevity in office (Medard, 2002; Geddes, 2003; van den Berg and Meadwell, 2004). Although both forms of rationality are based on instrumental reasoning, the former is driven by detached fiscal calculation and the latter by a passionate urge to retain political power.

With reference to the policy choices of African governing elites, political calculations have repeatedly trumped economic rationality. Reflecting on the first several decades of independence, researchers from the African Economic Research Consortium (AERC) identify a 'syndrome' of anti-growth policies – including a closed economy, price distortions, and market regulation – which they describe as 'control regimes' (Ndulu and Collier, 2007). Robert Bates (2008: 74) argues that:

> Control regimes effectively . . . lowered the continent's rate of economic growth. That these policies nonetheless remained in place reflects the political advantages they conferred: resources that authoritarian elites could employ to ameliorate political tensions, to recruit political clients, and to build political machines, and thereby remain in power.

In this light, policies aimed at structurally adjusting African economies in the 1980s and 1990s represented a heroic effort to impose principles of economic rationality on a thoroughly politicized policy environment. That these programmes met their goals with only scattered and sporadic success is testament to the strength of patronage – a key element in the logic of political rationality. Because, on its own, a strategy of 'getting the prices right' rarely worked in isolation, international development agencies turned attention to democratic reforms and good governance, an approach to economic development that can be thought of as 'getting the politics right'. In conjunction with domestic protest against corruption, repression and mismanagement, international pressures over the past two decades helped to open up politics in Africa and, in a good number of countries (including Zambia), to prompt a transition to multi-party electoral democracy. A puzzle remains, however: if there is an 'elective affinity' between authoritarian political institutions and control policies (Bates, 2008: 73), then does democratization create conditions for the adoption of economically rational, market-oriented policies?

Recent analyses of elite orientations to policy reform in Africa warn about the persistence of politically motivated 'neo-patrimonial' practices (van de Walle, 2001; Cammack, 2007). The implication is that political considerations remain paramount among policy actors, even in liberalized political environments [but see von Soest (2006) and van Donge (2009)]. Medard (2002: 386) characterizes the result as 'a politically rational particularistic mode of redistribution through patronage, allowing for a middle-term reproduction of the regime'. With specific reference to Zambia, Szeftel (1982: 5) speaks of politics as taking a 'clientelist form in which patronage constitutes an important mechanism through which political supporters often obtain access to state resources in return for helping patrons obtain access to public office itself'.

This chapter approaches competing forms of rationality from the bottom up rather than the top down. It asks how citizens in Zambia's electoral democratic regime regard the policy agenda of economic reform. We assume that ordinary people are pragmatic in arriving at preferences, favouring policies that actually work to their benefit. From this perspective, it is economically rational for citizens to lend support to policies that lead to macro-economic growth and improved living standards, while rejecting policies that fail to achieve these goals. As for political motivations, it is also rational for clients to cultivate close ties to individuals and organizations that wield power, notably the incumbent president and the ruling party. By demonstrating political loyalty, thus helping patrons retain office, clients signal that they are worthy beneficiaries of the official patronage machine.

But how can these different forms of reasoning be captured and measured for purposes of research?

On one hand, citizens refer to existential economic experiences in judging the suitability and impact of government policies. For example, they may consider their own satisfaction (or not) with living conditions – present, past, or future – in deciding whether they prefer a market or state-based approach to economic management. Or, instead of adopting an egocentric perspective, they may base emerging policy preferences on their own judgements about the current, retrospective, and prospective performance of the national economy writ large. If the literature on economic voting in non-African countries is any guide, popular policy preferences will be shaped – 'sociotropically' and 'retrospectively' – by the condition of the national economy in the immediate past (Kinder and Kiewiet, 1981; Lewis-Beck and Stegmaier, 2000). The logic of any such economic referendum is that, based on recent experience, citizens will support the candidate or policy that delivers the most tangible material benefits.

On the other hand, citizens also use daily political life as a source of cues for appraising economic reform. They know whether the government that introduces a reform policy has been legitimately elected, extending cooperation to the authorities or withholding it accordingly. In this regard, approval of economic policy reform may depend on an individual's diffuse feeling about an ideal political regime, expressed as 'support for democracy' (Klingemann, 1999; Schedler and Sarsfield, 2007). Or, citizens may use a more specific assessment of how well the democratic procedures of a particular elected regime in their country are actually working – an attitude commonly referred to in the literature as 'satisfaction with democracy' (Anderson and Guillory, 1997; Diamond, 1999). Even more specifically, acceptance of an economic policy package may hinge on whether the individual citizen has voted for intends to vote for, or otherwise identifies with the incumbent party in power. Partisans are likely to give their preferred party the benefit of the doubt on policy matters, whereas opponents are prone to be unduly critical. Finally, given that political 'big men' continue to loom large, even in elected governments in Africa, citizens may base their acceptance of a prevailing policy regime on whether they feel close to patronage. In particular, if voters share an ethnic or party identity with the president, it is rational for them to support his or her policies because they stand to benefit from his/her largesse.

15.3 Data

To test these propositions, data is drawn from the Afrobarometer, a comparative series of national public opinion surveys on democracy, markets, and civil society conducted by a network of independent researchers.[1] Over the previous ten years, the Afrobarometer has conducted four surveys in Zambia, dated 1999, 2003, 2005, and 2008. Fieldwork for the most recent survey occurred from 13 to 28 October 2008, i.e. the period immediately before the special presidential election occasioned by the death of Zambia's third president, Levy Mwanawasa.[2] In addition, observations on selected items are available from surveys under a democracy promotion project conducted by a donor agency in 1993 and 1996.[3] With these sources, it becomes feasible to describe Zambian attitudes to economic reform, track the evolution of these opinions, distinguish reform supporters from reform opponents, and test competing explanations about the formation of economic attitudes.

15.4 Economic policy and performance

After 1991, the Zambian Government undertook far-reaching economic policy reforms aimed at liberalizing the national economy. Key policy measures included the deregulation of foreign exchange controls, removal of consumer and producer subsidies, reductions in import tariffs, and, most importantly, the privatization of state-owned enterprises, notably in the strategic copper sector. Under pressure from donors to rein in government spending, successive governments adopted a cash budget (Chiluba) or an activity-based accounting system (Mwanawasa), and developed an explicit poverty reduction strategy (IMF, 2002, 2006; Seshamani, 2002). By prosecuting his predecessor for theft of public resources, Mwanawasa sought to publicize his government's expressed commitment to rooting out corruption. In a vote of confidence in Mwanawasa's calls for good governance and poverty reduction, international financial agencies relieved over 90 per cent of Zambia's previously crippling external debt.

These policy developments, along with a quadrupling of the international price of copper between 2003 and 2006, helped to stabilize and build the country's economy. As Table 15.1 indicates, Zambia has maintained an average annual GDP growth rate above 5 per cent in the current decade, peaking at 6.2 per cent in 2006 and 2007 (Central Statistical Office, 2009). The mining sector's share of economic output also grew, albeit marginally, from 6.2 per

Table 15.1 Gross domestic product (GDP), Zambia, 2000–08 (at constant 1994 prices)

Year	Total GDP (K billion)	GDP per capita (K)	GDP growth rate (annual percent)
2000	2,499	255,213	3.6
2001	2,621	259,806	4.9
2002	2,708	260,138	3.3
2003	2,847	264,930	5.1
2004	3,000	270,528	5.4
2005	3,160	276,215	5.3
2006	3,357	284,507	6.2
2007	3,564	293,054	6.2
2008	3,770	300,966	5.8

Source: Lusaka: Central Statistical Office, *The Monthly*, 70: January 2009

Table 15.2 Inflation trends, Zambia, 2000–08

Year	Year on Year Inflation Rate (percent)
2000	30.1
2001	18.7
2002	26.7
2003	17.2
2004	17.5
2005	15.9
2006	8.2
2007	8.9
2008	16.6

Source: Lusaka: Central Statistical Office, *The Monthly*, 70: January 2009

cent in 2000 to 8.3 per cent in 2008. During this expansion, Zambia also enjoyed a falling rate of inflation from 30.1 per cent in 2000 to 8.2 per cent in 2006 (see Table 15.2). A recent spike in inflation (to over 16 per cent by December 2008) can be attributed mainly to rising import costs exacerbated by the depreciation of the local currency and an upward spike in crude oil prices.

While the period from 2000 to 2008 was a positive time for the Zambian economy, fundamental challenges remain. Even though the incidence of absolute poverty is said to have dropped nationally in the urban Copperbelt, it rose or held steady in Central, Northwestern, and Western Provinces (Central Statistical Office, 2006a). Moreover, the estimated proportion of unemployed persons increased steadily, with jobless rates highest among young people in urban areas. As only 17 per cent of employed adults report holding a job in the formal sector, most Zambians continue to rely on self-employment or unpaid family labour (Central Statistical Office, 2006b). Of greatest concern is the fact that cuts in social expenditure led to declining living standards. Compared with other countries around the world, Zambia slid on the Human Development Index from the 81st percentile in 1990 to the 91st percentile in 2008 (United Nations Development Program, 2009). The International Monetary Fund (IMF) recently issued the grim reminder that 'poverty is still widespread in Zambia with 68 per cent of the population falling below the poverty line' (2006: 3).

15.5 The preferences of Zambian citizens

How well do popular policy priorities match the Zambian government's economic policy? A suitable starting point to this inquiry is an open-ended question that asked Afrobarometer survey respondents to spontaneously identify 'the *most important problems* facing this country that the government should address'. Up to three responses were recorded in the respondents' own words. Summary trends are presented in Figure 15.1.

Three priorities consistently top the popular policy agenda: unemployment, healthcare, and education. Healthcare was uppermost in Zambians' minds in 1999: it accounted for 17 per cent of all responses and was mentioned by 38 per cent of all respondents. In both 1999 and 2008 education ranked in third place. Over time, however, unemployment surpassed both healthcare

Figure 15.1 Most important national problems: Trends in public opinion, Zambia, 1999–2008

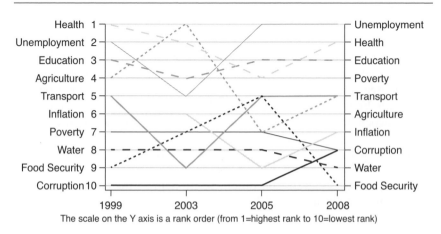

The scale on the Y axis is a rank order (from 1=highest rank to 10=lowest rank)

and education; by 2008 it accounted for 16 per cent of all responses and was mentioned by 48 per cent of all respondents.

Other notable trends include the elevation of concerns about poverty alleviation (from rank seven to rank four), even after the Zambian Government published its first Poverty Reduction Strategy Paper in 2002. Anxiety about inflation tended to fall by mid-decade, only to rise again by 2008 – a trend that mirrors the actual path of inflation, as officially reported by the Central Statistical Office (see Table 15.2). And, in a somewhat surprising result given the escalation of maize meal prices in 2008 (Jayne et al., 2008), popular unease about food security first rose steadily between 1999 and 2005, but then dropped off sharply in the most recent survey. Notwithstanding this last result, the overall tendency is for Zambians to grant increasing priority over time to economic worries about poverty and unemployment.

The rise of unemployment as the nation's leading policy problem can be traced to the closure of copper mines, the retrenchment of workers in industries exposed to foreign competition, and the weakening of the Zambian currency. These trends, including a recent reversal in copper prices, have intensified as the world economy entered a drastic slowdown during 2008. High petroleum prices in early 2008 also contributed to inflated costs of production, prompting some companies to reduce staffing levels as a measure to control costs. When Zambians indicate the rising salience of unemployment, they appear to be referring to formal employment and to be discounting gains in full- and part-time job availability in the expanding informal sector.

As for education, Zambians are concerned about limited access to public schools, colleges, and universities, as well as with high costs. The recent government policy to allow all Grade 9 pupils who obtain a full certificate to proceed to Grade 10, has been received with mixed feelings. Although the policy provides opportunity for more pupils to complete secondary school, the capacity of the education system in terms of teaching staff, infrastructure, and learning materials cannot guarantee high standards in education. The Fifth National Development Plan (FNDP) 2006–2010 is therefore targeting three educational priorities: recruitment of teachers; procurement of materials; and the construction of classrooms and teachers' houses. The government is estimated to need to recruit 5,000 additional teachers per year to reduce the present unfavourable pupil-teacher ratio (Republic of Zambia, 2006).

Although achievements have been recorded in malaria control,[4] Zambian citizen anxiety in respect to health services is well founded. Total expenditure on health fell from $US24 million in 1997 to an average of $US18 million for 2001–05, a situation that has had a negative impact on the provision of good-quality healthcare. Because of low wages and benefits in the civil service, and a poor working environment in the health sector, there has been a massive exodus of medical workers, especially nurses, to other countries. A recent assessment reported that current health workforce levels are only 50 per cent of the required levels (Republic of Zambia, 2006).

Within this socio-economic context, how do Zambians evaluate the various economic policies introduced by successive governments since the country's return to multi-party elections in 1991? We trace public opinion with respect to key components in the stabilization and structural adjustment package. With regard to price reforms, the Afrobarometer surveys ask whether Zambians are willing to pay market prices for consumer goods and fees for education. With regard to institutional reforms, our questions concern the restructuring of the civil service and the privatization of public corporations. All these topics have arisen in policy debates in Zambia in the period 1991 to 2008. And each appears on the popular agenda of the country's 'most important problems' in the guise of widespread and persistent concerns about the quality of education, the costs of inflation, and the shortage of employment.

15.6 Support for price reforms

The establishment of market prices for consumer goods – notably maize meal (Zambia's staple food) – was a top priority item for the Chiluba government as soon as it took office. During the late 1980s, former President Kaunda had made several attempts to remove subsidies on maize meal, which were then the single largest item in the government's growing budget deficit. But the president always backed down in the face of urban protests. Confronted after 1990 with an organized political challenge from the Movement for Multi-party Democracy (MMD), the government of the United National Independence Party (UNIP) abandoned any pretence of adherence to donor-sponsored economic reforms. As the election of 1991 approached, Kaunda fixed maize meal prices, effectively allowing subsidies to balloon to $US1.5 million per day. As soon as MMD won the elections convincingly with more than three quarters of the vote, Chiluba was forced to address this unsupportable drain on the public budget. On 27 December 1991 he announced that subsidies on maize meal would be cut in half – a measure soon followed with the complete removal of all such subventions.

How did the Zambian population react? In this instance, subsidy cuts were not followed by food riots, perhaps because citizens acknowledged that a freely elected government had won a mandate for reform. However, the acquiescence of the citizenry to a key reform measure also reflected a growing acceptance that 'getting the prices right' had the beneficial side effect of ending the shortages of consumer goods that had plagued the country under Kaunda. No longer would Zambians have to line up to buy bread or go without sugar and cooking oil because these commodities were unavailable. When first asked in 1993, a majority of Zambians – some 54 per cent – agreed

Figure 15.2 Popular attitudes to consumer prices: Trends in public opinion, Zambia, 1999–2008

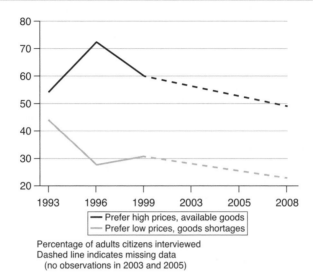

Percentage of adults citizens interviewed
Dashed line indicates missing data
(no observations in 2003 and 2005)

that 'it is better to have goods in the market even if the prices are high'. At the time, significantly fewer respondents – just 44 per cent – agreed that 'it is better to have low prices even if there are shortages of goods' (Figure 15.2).[5]

While popular sentiment about consumer prices fluctuates in Zambia, a pro-reform preference has prevailed consistently. As Figure 15.2 shows, almost three quarters of Zambians chose the 'high prices/available goods' option in 1996, as did three fifths in 1999. The question about market prices was not asked in 2003 and 2005 surveys, but by October 2008 some 49 per cent of Zambian adults continued to favour market pricing. While this proportion was no longer a majority, the gap between supporters and opponents of this policy more than doubled from 10 percentage points in 1993 to 26 percentage points in 2008.

One interpretation of the observed trend is that Zambian citizens accept free market pricing, but with increasing reluctance over time. By 2008, one quarter of the survey respondents (28 per cent) said that they 'didn't know' what kind of policy regime they preferred, agreeing with neither market nor controlled prices for consumer goods. Because there is no correlation between age and support for market prices, we can discount the possibility that only older people, i.e. those who remember the shortages of the 1980s, are the main (but dwindling) supporters of market pricing. Another possibility is that, with the appearance of high-end supermarkets in Zambia's urban areas, many people are becoming disillusioned with an economic policy regime that makes available plentiful luxury goods but at prices that working people cannot afford.

We turn now to another example of price reform, in this case for educational services. In return for standby agreements with the IMF and programme loans from the World Bank, the Kaunda government slashed spending on social programmes. Schools found themselves without textbooks and health clinics ran out of essential drugs. As maintenance was deferred, buildings and equipment began to show signs of wear and tear. In short, there was 'a wholesale deterioration in the productivity of the government machine' (Gulhati, 1989: 31). At the same time, the government introduced cost-recovery measures, such as service fees at hospitals and clinics, and expanded school fees at all levels of the education system. Yet, even as households faced increased costs for social services, a majority of Zambians expressed a willingness to shoulder some of the burden. In response to the 1993 survey, almost three quarters (73 per cent) of respondents agreed that 'it is better to raise educational standards, even if we have to pay school fees'. Barely a quarter (27 per cent) associated themselves with the view that 'it is better to have free schooling for our children, even if the quality of education is low' (Figure 15.3).

By the late 1990s, however, international agencies revised donor strategy for educational development, placing emphasis on mass access to basic schooling (World Bank, 2001, 2008). As neighboring countries like Malawi (1994) and Uganda (1996) introduced universal primary education (UPE), the prospect of rescinding entry-level school fees began to enter policy debates in Zambia. Fulfilling a pledge made in the 2001 election campaign, the Mwanawasa administration adopted UPE as government policy for grades one to seven of primary school in 2002.

Figure 15.3 Popular attitudes to school fees: Trends in public opinion, Zambia, 1999–2008

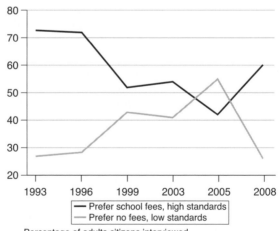

Percentage of adults citizens interviewed

As a probable consequence of this policy shift, the pattern of public opinion on school fees abruptly changed: the majority of Zambians who had favoured market pricing for high-quality education through 2003 (54 per cent) disappeared in favour of a new majority (55 per cent) who favoured free education in 2005.[6] In a striking result from the most recent survey, however, this new preference did not last: by October 2008, Zambians again reversed themselves, with 60 per cent once more supporting the pro-market position on school financing. Note, however that more urban dwellers, compared with their rural counterparts, prefer paying school fees in order to raise educational standards.[7]

One likely reason for tolerance of school fees is that Zambians perceive declining educational quality under the UPE policy: preferences for free education are negatively correlated with perceptions that the public education system suffers problems with poor teaching and overcrowded classrooms.[8] Instead, Zambians are apparently willing to countenance the payment of school fees in return for better education. In practice, nominally 'free' education is still associated with indirect costs, for example for school uniforms, books and supplies, private tuition, and Parent Teacher Association fees (Petrauskis and Nkunika, 2006).[9] In short, the efficacy of the UPE policy in relieving parents of the financial burden of educating their children remains to be demonstrated.

15.7 Opposition to institutional reforms

If Zambians evince pro-market attitudes toward price reforms, do they also support pro-market institutional reforms? In this case, they clearly do not. Take civil service reform, for example. In its first budget, the Chiluba government made a commitment to drastically reduce the size of a public sector bloated by the profligate distribution of patronage jobs. This policy was prompted by the realization that government ministries were ineffective, undisciplined, and hardly responsive to the needs of the public; personnel cutbacks were also consistent with conditions imposed by international lenders in return for promises of future debt relief. The idea was to rehabilitate run-down state bureaucracies by reducing the size of the establishment and improving professionalism and efficiency. Even as some public employees would unavoidably lose their jobs, others would become better trained, paid, and motivated.

The government announced a Public Service Reform Program (PSRP) in 1993. By 2006 it had resulted in a number of achievements: a reduction in the size of the public service from 139,000 in 1997 to 104,000 in 2000 (before increasing again to 115,000 in 2004); the appointment to key technical and professional positions of competent and qualified staff; a rationalization of the salary structure; the promulgation of new terms and conditions of service;

a new disciplinary code; and new procedures for hiring and firing personnel (Republic of Zambia, 2006).

However, the effort to retrench employment in the public service immediately ran into a headwind of public opposition. In 1993, two thirds of Zambians interviewed agreed that 'all civil servants should keep their jobs even if paying their salaries is costly to the country'; only one third agreed that 'the government cannot afford so many public employees and should lay some of them off' (see Figure 15.4). The reasons are not hard to find: with the government being the largest employer in the economy, and with unemployment perceived as the leading national problem, many ordinary people viewed with alarm the prospect of livelihood losses. Moreover, resistance was widespread, not only in Zambia, but in other southern African countries.[10] The desire to protect civil service employment in Zambia was equally shared among urbanites and rural dwellers over the period 1999–2008. Moreover, in 1996, individuals without a government employee in their household were no less likely to oppose the policy than individuals who were directly dependent on a regular government paycheque.

Over time, public opposition has dissolved only slightly. From a peak in 2003, when three quarters opposed civil service cutbacks, some three out of five Zambians still withheld support in 2008. The gap on this issue between reform supporters and reform opponents widened slightly between 1993 (34 points) and 2008 (39 points).

In sum therefore, Zambians have long preferred the state to intervene actively in the economy in order to create jobs. A growing pro-state

Figure 15.4 Popular attitudes to civil service reform: Trends in public opinion, Zambia, 1999–2008

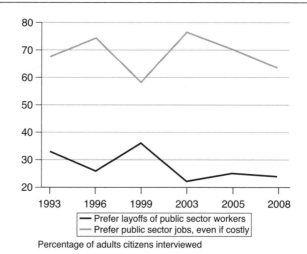

Percentage of adults citizens interviewed

orientation comes through clearly when survey respondents are asked, 'Who should take the main responsibility for providing jobs? Is it government, private business, individuals, or some combination of these providers?' In 1993, a clear majority of Zambians (57 per cent) considered that the government had sole responsibility for creating jobs in their country, with a further 33 per cent thinking that the government shared responsibility for job creation with private businesses and individuals. The overall proportion preferring some role for the state in job creation actually rose between 1993 and 2008 (from 90 per cent to 95 per cent). But, the proportion favouring the state alone began to fall (from 57 per cent to 47 per cent), with a growing proportion (from 33 per cent to 48 per cent) now recognizing job creation as a responsibility shared between the public and private sectors and with citizens themselves.

In the light of popular concerns about civil service reform, it comes as no surprise that Zambians also resist the privatization of state-owned enterprises (SOEs) – a policy that stirred up vigorous policy debate and intermittent labour unrest. The thrust of Zambia's privatization programme, perhaps the most ambitious in sub-Saharan Africa, occurred between 1993 and 2003. More than 250 SOEs were sold to private (mostly foreign) investors, mainly in the agro-processing, manufacturing, and financial sectors (Zambia Privatization Agency, 1993, 1997, 2001). Because copper exports are the strategic mainstay of the economy – accounting for 54 per cent of export earnings in 2008 – the government was slow to cede control of the mining sector. After lengthy stop-start negotiations, the Anglo-American Corporation (AAC) eventually purchased the largest copper mining divisions including Nkana, Nchanga, and Konkola in March 2000 (Craig, 2001). But the AAC pulled out of these investments in 2003 over concerns about profitability and was succeeded in 2004 by an Indian-based multinational conglomerate,

Table 15.3 Ownership in the mining sector, Zambia, 2008

Mining Company	Private Shareholder (share)	ZCCM-IH share
Mopani Copper Mines	Carlisa Investments Corporation (90%)	10%
Chambishi Metals	Enya Holdings (90%)	10%
Konkola Copper Mines	Vedanta Resources (79.4%)	20.6%
Luanshya Copper MInes	Enya Holdings (85%)	15%
NFC Africa Mining	China Non-Ferrous Metal Mining (85%)	15%
Lumwana Copper Project	Equinox Copper Ventures (95.5%)	4.5%
Kansanshi Mining	First Quantum Minerals (79.4%)	20.6%
Copper Energy Corporation	Zam-Energy (85%)	15%
Chibuluma Mines	Metorex Limited (85%)	15%
Ndola Lime Company	Carlisa Investments Corporation (90%)	100%

Source: ZCCM-IH Investments Profile, http://www.zccm-ih.com.zm

Vedanta Resources. As shown in Table 15.3, the Government of Zambia now holds only small minority stakes in most of Zambia's mining companies. It exercises remaining nominal control through an 86.7 per cent share in the Zambia Consolidated Copper Mines-Investments Holdings, a holding company (Fraser and Lungu, 2008).

From the outset, and before the privatization programme was fully launched, Zambians were already wary. In 1993, some six out ten concurred that 'the government should retain ownership of its factories, businesses, and farms', with only four in ten agreeing that 'it is better for the government to sell (these assets) to private companies and individuals' (Figure 15.5). As the consequences of privatization became apparent, including an influx of foreign corporations and the closure of previously protected enterprises, popular dissatisfaction grew. Anti-privatization sentiment rose to a peak by 1996 (68 per cent), as did the spread between pro- and anti-privatization views by 1999 (to a 37-point gap). While opinion has moderated slightly in the current decade, Zambians now oppose privatization almost as much as they shun civil service reform. Indeed, citizens who presently reject one category of institutional reform are also likely to reject the other.[11]

Perhaps the politically charged issue of foreign ownership of the country's copper mines drives Zambian opinion towards privatization. The 2008 survey posed an additional question: 'As you may know, the government has reduced its role in the economy, for example by privatizing the mining companies. Overall, how satisfied are you with the way this policy works?' As the distribution of responses – 35 per cent satisfied ('very' or 'fairly'), 62 per cent

Figure 15.5 Popular attitudes to privatization: Trends in public opinion, Zambia, 1999–2008

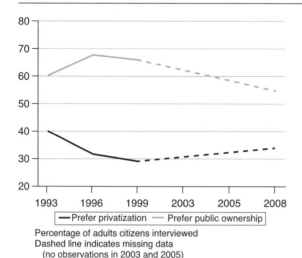

Percentage of adults citizens interviewed
Dashed line indicates missing data
(no observations in 2003 and 2005)

reported not ('not very' or 'not at all') – mirrors broader anti-privatization sentiment, we infer that the Zambians generalize from their attitudes regarding the strategic minerals sector. Note also that dissatisfaction with privatization correlates highly with an individual's expression of opposition to the sale of government assets.[12] And the 2008 result reflects the crystallization and deepening of anti-privatization sentiment compared with 2002 (when 39 per cent were satisfied, 51 per cent were not, and 10 per cent didn't yet know).

As with the provision of public employment, however, there is trace evidence that Zambians are also recognizing that the state cannot shoulder all economic tasks. Asked who should bear the main responsibility for buying and selling copper, the same overwhelming majority of Zambians in 2008 (90 per cent) as in 2002 (91 per cent) cited *some* role for the state. But the proportion favouring the state alone fell dramatically over this time period from a high of 76 per cent to just 48 per cent. In this respect, public opinion is begrudgingly granting a role in managing strategic commodities to the private sector, if not in place of the state, then at least in partnership with it.

15.8 Adjustment fatigue

On balance, therefore, Zambians neither holistically accept nor completely reject an orthodox package of structural adjustment reforms. Instead, they prefer to pick and choose among component policies, supporting some but opposing others. In general, we have found evidence that Zambians are willing to accept price reforms that require the payment of prevailing market rates for consumer goods and education services. However, we have also noted a strong streak of resistance to reforms that require the restructuring of economic institutions. By saying 'no' to job cuts in the civil service and to the sale of public corporations, people express persistent attachments to the state as the principal provider of employment.

Given this mixed record, we wonder what overall conclusions Zambians draw about outcomes from a continuous period of economic reform. What balance of costs and benefits do they attribute to the implementation of a market-oriented policy package? In particular, do Zambians display signs of 'adjustment fatigue'? In Latin America, according to Nelson (1989: 7):

> . . . the combination of prolonged austerity and economic liberalization . . . generated . . . sustained internal political conflict . . . (At minimum) continued economic stagnation or decay . . . destroyed popular confidence in the government's ability to manage the economy, as well as confirmed initial skepticism of the effects of the policies urged by external agencies.

As Zambia has recently experienced growth rather than stagnation, and has encountered only mild civil unrest around economic policy issues since the 1980s,[13] we do not expect to find citizens turning diametrically against a market economy in the mould of Argentinians and Venezuelans (Quispe-Agnoli, 2004). However, the success of populist politicians such as Michael Sata, who dispense a message of international protectionism and wealth redistribution suggests that there is an audience in Zambia that is primed to try an alternative development strategy (Larmer and Fraser, 2007; Cheeseman and Hinfelaar, 2009).

Figure 15.6 tracks public opinion on reform outcomes, revealing a remarkably clear and recurrent pattern. Over the course of the past decade, less than a quarter of Zambians have ever thought that 'the government's reform policies have helped most people; only a few have suffered'. By contrast, about three quarters have consistently reported that 'the government's economic policies have hurt most people and benefited only a few'. Writ large, this almost invariant trend can be read as a sustained overall vote of no confidence in the structural adjustment agenda.

Implied in this result is an assumption that economic reforms have negatively affected the distribution of wealth. Figure 15.7 shows that people are happier with the provision of social services than with the management of the economy. Nevertheless, Zambians are particularly concerned about social inequality, as represented by a growing income gap between rich and poor. Asked in 2008 to evaluate government performance on a range of development tasks, Zambians draw sharp distinctions. A majority judges the government to be performing well at addressing educational needs, reducing crime, fighting corruption, and improving health services.[14] But under a half say

Figure 15.6 Popular attitudes to reform outcomes: Trends in public opinion, Zambia, 1999–2008

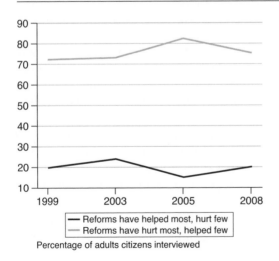

Reforms have helped most, hurt few
Reforms have hurt most, helped few

Percentage of adults citizens interviewed

Figure 15.7 Popular assessments of government performance, Zambia 2008

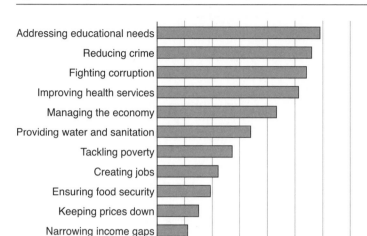

"How well or badly would you say the current goverment is
handling the following matters?"
Percentage of survey respondents saying "very well" or "fairly well"

the same about its performance at managing the economy, providing water
and sanitation services, and tackling poverty.[15] Less than a quarter approve
government performance at creating jobs, ensuring food security, and controlling inflation. In important respects – especially creating jobs – these assessments reflect unsatisfied public demand for the solution of important national
problems.

Notably, the government is given the lowest grade for 'narrowing income
gaps between the rich and the poor'; just 11 per cent of Zambians think the
elected authorities are performing well at this development task. In all three
surveys where the question was asked (2003–08), 'narrowing income gaps'
always ranked low; but, by 2005 and 2008, concerns about social inequality
first joined and then displaced 'creating jobs' at the very bottom of popular
performance rankings. In this light, we can understand why, over time,
Zambians have attached growing importance to poverty as an important
national problem (see Figure 15.1). Even if gross domestic product (GDP) per
capita is on the rise and destitution has eased in some provinces, people
apparently perceive poverty in relative, as well as absolute, terms and are
disturbed by the unequal distribution of gains from recent economic growth.

Under these circumstances, it is difficult to find a mass constituency in
Zambia for a rigorous economic reform agenda. At the same time, however,
Zambians have shown a good deal of forbearance towards government's
economic policies. As Figure 15.8 indicates, even though most survey

Figure 15.8 Popular attitudes to economic reform: Trends in public opinion, Zambia, 1999–2008

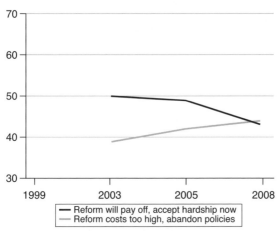

Percentage of adults citizens interviewed

respondents did not support the reform programme, a slim majority (50 per cent) were, nonetheless, willing to endure it, agreeing that 'in order for the economy to get better in the future, it is necessary for us to accept some hardships now'. In 2003, only a minority (39 per cent) had had enough; they felt instead that 'the costs of reforming the economy are too high; the government should therefore abandon its current economic policies'. While the difference between patient and impatient citizens tightened slightly in 2005 (49 per cent versus 42 per cent), reform proponents could still claim that a plurality preferred to stick with the programme. However, in a substantively and statistically significant shift in 2008, slightly more Zambians (44 per cent) now want the government to abandon its prevailing package of economic policies than are willing to grant more time for the government to deliver results (43 per cent).[16] It would appear that, after almost 18 years of economic reform, and despite objective improvements in the performance of the economy, most Zambians now feel the pangs of adjustment fatigue.

15.9 Towards explanation

This chapter turns from a description of Zambian public opinion to an explanation of its origins. On the demand side, we want to know what explains the degree of popular support for economic reform policies. On the supply side, we are interested in accounting for the extent of popular satisfaction with government's management of the economy. As discussed earlier, we hypothesize that, in making their minds up about the desirability and efficacy of economic reform, citizens will make both economic and political calculations. The remaining puzzle is which of these competing rationalities offers the better explanation.

To make popular demands operational for research purposes, we create an additive index of support for economic reform. It comprises the number of reform policies – consumer prices, school fees, civil service cutbacks, and privatization – that individuals support.[17] The supply-side indicator of satisfaction with economic reform is an average construct of the respondent's opinion of how well or badly the current government is managing the economy and tackling poverty.[18] As indicated in Figure 15.7, Zambians are split on the matter of overall economic management (43 per cent positive) and dubious about the effectiveness of the government's anti-poverty strategy (only 27 per cent positive).[19]

To measure the extent to which citizens use a calculus of economic rationality, we select public opinions on four key economic factors: the country's present economic condition, the individual's present living conditions, the country's past economic condition (compared with 12 months ago), and the individual's expected future living conditions (estimated in 12 months time).[20] The argument here is that citizens will reason from their own economic circumstances in calculating their stances towards reform. We expect that socio-tropic (i.e. country-level) conditions, both present and retrospective, will have more formative effects on reform attitudes than egotistic (i.e. personal) considerations. However, we guess that future expectations about personal well being may also have some effect.

We also select four political factors as indicators of political rationality. Support for democracy is a standard item used in barometer surveys worldwide to tap an individual's ideal regime.[21] Similarly, satisfaction with democracy is a familiar comparative item that asks, 'overall, how satisfied are you with the way democracy works in (your country)?'[22] We expect that supportive and satisfied democrats are more likely to favour the policies implemented by a freely elected government. The third political factor is the performance of the president, which is a measure of popular perceptions of the chief political executive's job performance over the previous year.[23] Given the timing of the October 2008 survey in Zambia, respondents were asked to comment on the job performance of late President Levy Mwanawasa, who died in August 2008. As a final indicator of political rationality, we examine whether an individual stated an intention to vote for the candidate of the incumbent MMD party in the presidential election of 30 October 2008. The logic of the last two indicators is that citizens are expected to use considerations of personal and party loyalty, especially to the national patron-in-chief, in calculating whether economic policies are likely to serve their interests.

Table 15.4 Components of cosmopolitanism, Zambia, 2008 (Pearson's R correlation matrix)

	Index of Cosmopolitanism‡	Computer	Internet	Mobile Phone	Remittances
Computer	.822***				
Internet	.807***	.892***			
Mobile phone	.693***	.403***	.361***		
Remittances	.442***	.169***	.190***	.101**	
Languages	.439***	.105***	.100**	.252***	.085**

‡ A one-factor principal components solution produces a reliable 5-item index
 (Cronbach's alpha = .662)
*** 0 = < .001, ** p = < .01

As with any multivariate analysis of survey data, controls are necessary for demographic factors. Relevant to economic reform in Zambia – substantively, as well as statistically – are residential locale (urban or rural), gender, age, and education. All these standard markers are included in the multivariate models that follow.

In addition, we have developed a novel indicator of the extent to which an individual has a global – as opposed to local – orientation towards the world. We call this orientation 'cosmopolitanism'. It is measured by an index of five items: the first measures the number of languages an individual speaks; the remainder measure the frequency of an individual's computer, Internet, and mobile phone use, as well as the frequency with which he or she receives money remittances from outside the country.[24] Table 15.4 indicates that these five items together comprise an average index of cosmopolitanism: while computer use is most central to the index and multilingualism most peripheral, all, nonetheless, cohere into a reliable scale.[25] We predict that cosmopolitan Zambians will be more open than their parochial compatriots to a market reform agenda.[26] And, while education and cosmopolitanism are highly correlated,[27] they should not be conflated. Instead, we expect that even Zambians with low levels of education may be able to learn about economic reform through new interactions with a global environment.

15.10 Explaining support for reform

What, then, explains support for economic reform – limited as it is – among Zambians? Table 15.5 displays results of an ordinary least squares regression analysis. Explanatory factors that attain statistical significance, of which there are only three, are highlighted in bold font.

Table 15.5 Support for economic reform, explanatory factors, Zambia, 2008 (Ordinary least squares regression)

	B	S.E.	Beta	Sig.
Constant	1.1000	.388		.005
Economic factors				
Country's present economic condition	**-.080**	**.040**	**-.077**	**.046**
Your present living condition	.043	.042	.040	.314
Country's economic condition 12 months ago	.029	.044	.022	.510
Your living conditions in 12 months time	.084	.043	.067	.051
Political factors				
Support for democracy	.037	.065	.019	.564
Satisfaction with democracy	**.117**	**.042**	**.093**	**.005**
Performance of the president	-.047	.050	-.031	.343
Intend to vote for incumbent party	-.043	.092	.015	.640
Demographic controls				
Gender (female)	-.034	.074	-.015	.647
Locale (rural)	.046	.083	.020	.581
Age	-.004	.004	-.034	.297
Education	-.058	.031	-0.77	.061
Cosmopolitanism	**.266**	**.062**	**.183**	**.000**

Adjusted R square = .033   Standard error of the estimate = 1.112

The first notable result is that, on the demand side, economic factors apparently matter little. In deciding whether they want policy reforms, Zambians seemingly make scant reference to economic conditions. The perceived condition of the national economy actually has a negative effect on support for economic reform, which is the opposite of what we expected. It seems that the better the economy is seen to be doing, the less Zambians demand reform. This perverse result is barely statistically significant. Moreover, as inferred earlier, future expectations about personal living conditions have a more positive effect on demand for reform than any other economic factor. But this predictor falls short of statistical significance.

By contrast, a political factor is in play. If Zambians are satisfied with democracy, they are significantly more likely to want economic reforms. We interpret this result to mean that policies arrived at through democratic methods are able to attract support by virtue of their procedural legitimacy. In other words, a democratically elected government is able to sell reform measures more effectively to its constituents than a government that is not so elected. This result generalizes the observation made earlier about the relative ease with which the Chiluba government withdrew maize meal subsidies without provoking the violent unrest that had always accompanied Kaunda's efforts to implement this reform. Nor did the later removal of subsidies on fertilizer and fuel provoke political unrest, though perhaps for other reasons. The constituency of fertilizer-using peasant farmers is scattered countrywide and is not well organized; the owners of taxis, minibuses, and factories can easily pass on the burden of higher fuel prices to customers. However, our analysis suggests political reasoning based on satisfaction felt with democracy also plays a role.

Strikingly, a demographic factor provides the best explanation of who among Zambians demands reform. It seems that support for market-oriented policies is mainly an attribute of cosmopolitans. By far the most influential factor in the equation, cosmopolitanism has a stronger and more significant influence than either economic or political rationality. And it is distinct from education – a statistically insignificant predictor in this model. How might this influence work? We speculate that Zambians who use information and communications technology, for example the 56 per cent who say they use a mobile phone every day (see Table 15. 6), have access to economic knowledge that helps build support for reforms. In other African countries, farmers who use mobile phones are able to gather and compare crop prices across a range of markets before deciding when and where to sell (Aker, 2007; Hahn and Kibora, 2008; Molony, 2008). Similarly, people who maintain contacts outside their home village or neighbourhood, for example through travel, remittances, or exchanges with people who speak other languages, are more likely to be exposed to debates about the 'magic' of the market.

All of these results must be tempered, however, by a recognition that support for economic liberalization in Zambia is barely formed and difficult to explain. Even an exhaustive model with four economic, four political, and five demographic predictors accounts for a mere 3 per cent of the variation in popular support for economic reform. We can only conclude that public opinion on this matter remains inchoate: political rationality and cosmopolitanism aside, there are few patterns that point to the formation of strong demands either for or against reform. Instead, Zambians of all walks of life remain undecided about the suitability of market reforms to their country's development needs.

Table 15.6 Use of information technology, Zambia, 2008

| | How often do you use the following? | | |
	Computer	Internet	Mobile Phone
Never	61	67	13
Less than once a month	10	9	3
A few times a month	12	12	8
A few times a week	9	8	20
Every day	7	4	56

Percentage of adult Zambians

15.11 Explaining satisfaction with reform

Whether or not they explicitly called for it, Zambians received a strong dose of market reform between 1991 and 2008. This is not to say that the Chiluba and Mwanawasa administrations fulfilled all the policy conditions required by aid donors or fully moved the country from a planned to an open economy. Because the Zambian government encountered obstacles and engineered reversals during the implementation of the economic adjustment programme, caution is warranted in discussing popular evaluations of the supply of reform. For example, a Fertilizer Support Programme (FSP) launched during the 2002–03 agricultural season re-introduced subsidies and required smallholder farmers to form marketing cooperatives. In the run-up to the 2006 election, the MMD government broke the public budget to disburse funds through the Food Reserve Agency to buy up a bumper maize crop. Subsidies for fuel were re-introduced in 2008 to offset the escalating international price of crude oil. Thus, in commenting on their government's performance in liberalizing the economy, Zambians are undoubtedly judging the product of a partial and incomplete reform process.

With this caveat in mind, we now seek to explain satisfaction with economic reform using the same method, format and structure of explanatory factors as before. Regression results are shown in Table 15.7.

The supply-side model is more powerful as it explains one quarter of the variance in popular satisfaction with the government's management of the reform programme. Moreover, as predicted, both economic and political rationality play formative roles in shaping this aspect of public opinion. And, whereas cosmopolitanism heightens satisfaction, rural residential location is even more influential. We discuss each explanatory strand in turn.

Firstly, we consider economic factors. As predicted, an individual's sociotropic assessments of the macro-economy strongly and significantly shape his or her satisfaction with reform. The better the country's perceived economic condition, the more likely is a Zambian to say that the government is doing a good job at managing the national economy and alleviating poverty. This rational calculus rests primarily on the country's current economic status, though evaluations of past economic conditions and expectations of future personal living standards play modest reinforcing roles. But the strongest (and only significant) effect is a direct line of economic reasoning from country-level economic conditions to satisfaction with reform. In this light, the dramatic contraction of the world economy in 2009, which occurred after fieldwork for the Afrobarometer Round 4 survey was complete, is likely to spill over into Zambia in the form of future dissatisfaction with economic reform.

Secondly, Table 15.7 indicates that political rationality also matters. Three

Table 15.7 Satisfaction with economic reform, explanatory factors, Zambia, 2008 (Ordinary least squares regression)

	B	S.E.	Beta	Sig.
Constant	.084	.231		.715
Economic factors				
Country's present economic condition	**.206**	**.024**	**.294**	**.000**
Your present living condition	.013	.026	.017	.624
Country's economic condition 12 months ago	.041	.026	.047	.118
Your living conditions in 12 months time	.030	.026	.035	.247
Political factors				
Support for democracy	.022	.039	.017	.567
Satisfaction with democracy	**.096**	**.025**	**.111**	**.000**
Performance of the president	**.119**	**.030**	**.116**	**.000**
Intend to vote for incumbent party	**.355**	**.055**	**.190**	**.000**
Demographic controls				
Gender (female)	-.002	.044	-.001	.962
Locale (rural)	**.182**	**.050**	**.115**	**.000**
Age	.001	.002	.009	.770
Education	.028	.019	.053	.140
Cosmopolitanism	**.093**	**.037**	**.095**	**.012**

Adjusted R square = .252   Standard error of the estimate = ??

of four political factors have strong, positive, and statistically significant connections to popular approval of reform outcomes. Zambians who are satisfied with democracy, or who approve of the president's performance, or who vote for MMD are all likely to approve of the government's track record at economic management. It is insufficient for citizens to simply prefer democracy in the abstract as an ideal regime; in Zambia, there are too many professed democrats who say they support democracy but who disapprove of the consequences of the reform programme, such as deepening inequality. Instead, to endorse reform outcomes, citizens must also express approval of the actual performance of the democratic regime, the incumbent party, and the top political leader. Indeed, they use approval of these actors and institutions as heuristic shortcuts in arriving at favourable evaluations of economic reform.

But which matters more: economic or political rationality? Not shown in Table 15.7 is the amount of variance explained by each bloc of factors. When regressed alone on satisfaction with economic reform, the four economic variables explain over 16 per cent of variance; the four political variables exactly 12 per cent; and the five demographic controls less than 4 per cent. This sub-analysis suggests that economic rationality is probably more important than political rationality in a citizen's calculation about the costs and benefits of reform. However, it also confirms that a supply-side explanation is deficient without reference to both economic and political reasoning, and it also hammers home the necessity for studying reform processes within an interdisciplinary political economy framework that makes room for, and grants credence to, both types of rationality.

Thirdly, and finally, we consider demographic controls. As indicated, we again find that cosmopolitans are champions of reform, being more than willing parochials to approve reform outcomes. One possible mechanism is that the liberalization of exchange control regulations has eased the flow of foreign currency remittances from Zambians working abroad, thus inducing a gratified response from recipients. Another possible connection concerns the liberalization of the mobile phone market, which has not only enabled Zambians to communicate more easily, but also helped to build a constituency for market reforms. In Zambia, where there are 73 languages (seven of which are considered to be the main ones), the ability to speak more than one language provides an opportunity for accessing perceptions on reform initiatives across language barriers. Once again, we confirm that cosmopolitanism substitutes for education, as education is not shown to be significant (Table 15.7). The spread of mobile phones is apparently having a democratizing effect in which individuals with less education are able to use new technologies to learn about economic reform and formulate their own opinions about its outcomes. However, the use of computers and the Internet probably presupposes a certain level of formal education that has yet to become widespread in Zambia.

We cannot close without noting the strong effect of residential locale on economic satisfaction. Other things being equal, rural dwellers are 18 per cent more likely than urban dwellers to express satisfaction with the reform programme. We can speculate about this highly significant result. Perhaps rural dwellers have benefited from market reforms, for example as farmers encounter better rural-urban terms of trade or improvements in the delivery of agricultural services. During the 2005–06 farming season, a 65 per cent increase was recorded in output of maize, with the benefits of increased sales accruing to farmers, including smallholders. Moreover, there have been greater increases in informal employment in the agricultural sector compared with the non-agricultural sector.

Alternatively, perhaps rural dwellers know little about the national economic reform programme and simply go along with whatever policies the government proposes. Certainly, there is evidence that, like other long-standing ruling parties in Africa, MMD has fallen back on a rural base of support. By targeting subsidies under the FSP at small farmers in rural cooperatives, much as UNIP did before, the ruling party resorted to tried and true patronage techniques. Moreover, in the run-up to the 2008 presidential election, Rupiah Banda, then Acting President and MMD candidate for the presidency, announced a reduction of 75 per cent on the price of fertilizers. The Afrobarometer's 2008 pre-election survey indicated that MMD would do well in rural Northwestern, Western, and Eastern provinces, and fare badly in the urban Copperbelt and Lusaka provinces, predictions later borne out in the official election results (Electoral Commission of Zambia, 2008).

15.12 Conclusions

We have reviewed popular attitudes to economic policy reform in Zambia from 1993 to 2008, a period marked by political and economic liberalization, and by hints of economic recovery and improved public management. Yet, despite such positive objective changes, adult Zambians have yet to subjectively embrace an orthodox agenda of economic policy reform.

Most clearly, we observe fixed public opposition to institutional reforms that aim at reducing the role of the state in the economy. In 2008 (as in 1993), three out of five Zambians opposed the privatization of state-owned enterprises and civil service reform. These opinions were accompanied by a rise in mass concern about unemployment as the nation's 'most important problem'. At the same time, however, we detect a growing public recognition that the state cannot create jobs on its own and that private individuals and firms make important contributions, too.

This study also reveals that initial public tolerance of price reforms is wearing thin. To be sure, a majority of Zambians, after briefly flirting with support for universal free schooling, once again express willingness to pay for higher educational standards. But, whereas a majority also once accepted market pricing for consumer goods, only a minority takes this stance today. Indeed, we characterize the major trend in economic opinion in Zambia as one of growing adjustment fatigue. Most Zambians are convinced that the government's economic policies have hurt more people than they have helped and have contributed to widening income inequalities. For the first time, a slim plurality of Zambians is now ready to abandon the reform programme.

In explaining the sources of these economic opinions, we isolate three distinctive factors in ascending order of importance. Firstly, rural dwellers, who may have benefited from recent reversals of market policies in agriculture, say they are more satisfied with policy performance than their counterparts who live in urban areas. Secondly, offsetting this demographic tilt, we find that Zambians who have shrugged off local ties in favour of a cosmopolitan worldview, typified by their use of mobile phones and the Internet, are also inclined to support a market-led economy.

Thirdly, and most importantly, we find that the development of popular economic opinion depends on political, as well as economic, calculations. Obviously, the public's views on the performance of the economy shape popular evaluations of the official policy regime. But, if Zambians also feel politically close to the president and ruling party – which we interpret in terms of anticipated access to patronage – then they are more likely to accept policy reform and think that reforms are working well.

What are the policy implications of this cluster of attitudes? How can reformers within Zambia build a political constituency that will sustain a market economy in the long run? Given that popular attitudes to economic reform are highly instrumental, there is no substitute for economic performance. From a public opinion perspective, the acid test for any policy measure is whether it generates well-paid formal sector jobs in urban areas – a requirement that is unlikely to be met without infusions of private investment capital. To the extent that new jobs require the use of information technology, their creation will, in turn, encourage the emergence of cosmopolitan reform coalitions that will build a base of support for a market economy.

At the same time, greater policy attention is required to poverty alleviation and income distribution. Governments, however, can lift up the poor and effectively regulate the excesses of private markets only if the state apparatus is first reformed. Thus, despite popular resistance, the Zambian government should persist with efforts to streamline and professionalize the civil service. Developmental outcomes will only be obtained when Zambians can put more faith in the universal application of a rule of law than in the particularistic rewards of a patronage system. If state institutions were competent and trustworthy, a blanket policy of privatization would be unnecessary and could be replaced with various kinds of public-private partnership. The global financial crisis of 2009 has already put an end to the 'Washington consensus' in favour of this sort of emergency experimentation. Under these circumstances, there is now opportunity for international donors and lenders to recommend policies that converge with the expressed preferences of Zambian citizens.

Notes

1. Afrobarometer surveys are conducted in up to 20 African countries on a regular cycle. Because the instrument asks a standard set of questions, countries can be systematically compared and trends in public attitudes can be tracked over time. Coordination for Afrobarometer activities is provided by the Centre for Democratic Development (CDD-Ghana), the Institute for Empirical Research in Political Economy (IREEP-Benin), and IDASA (South Africa). Advisory and support services are provided by Michigan State University and the University of Cape Town. Data is collected by national partners in each African country. In Zambia, fieldwork was led by the Department of Political and Administrative Studies, University of Zambia, in conjunction with Steadman Inc., a market research firm based in Nairobi, Kenya.
2. The Afrobarometer Round 4 survey in Zambia was based on a national probability sample of adult Zambians (18 years or older) distributed proportionally across all

nine of the country's provinces. Based on Central Statistical Office population projections for 2008, a multi-stage, stratified area cluster sampling approach was used. Interviews were conducted with 1,200 respondents but 99 cases were discarded owing to the low quality of interviews, yielding a final sample of 1,101 persons (and a margin of sampling error of plus or minus 3 percentage points at a 95 per cent confidence level). The respondents were balanced in terms of gender and had a median age of 29 years. Most of the respondents (63 per cent) were rural residents while the remainder (37 per cent) were urban-based. According to respondents' preferences, the interviews were conducted in English (the official language) or in a local language (Chinyanja, Chibemba, Chitonga, Silozi, or Kikaonde). The reader should be aware, however, that owing to violations of Afrobarometer sampling protocols by the service provider (Steadman Inc.), the 2008 data is based on a sample that is somewhat younger, more educated, employed, and wealthy than the national population.

3. The study was conducted on behalf of the Zambia Democratic Governance Project of the US Agency for International Development. The methodology included both focus groups and exploratory surveys. Some questionnaire items now included in Afrobarometer surveys were first tested in surveys in Zambia in 1993 and 1996. Results from this research are reported in Bratton and Liatto-Katundu (1994) and Bratton (1999). See also the *Political Reform Series* at http://www.afrobarometer.org/archives.html.

4. The malaria incidence rate per 1,000 fell from 400 in 2000 to just above 200 in 2004. Deaths caused by malaria dropped from 9,367 in 2001 to 4,765 in 2004. This progress is mainly attributed to the shift in treatment policy from chloroquine to arteminisin-based therapy (Coartem) and improvements in the laboratory services (UNDP, 2007).

5. As with all policy preferences discussed in this section, the questions were posed in a balanced, 'forced choice' format using mutually contradictory statements, which we find a more reliable metric than a univalent Likert scale. The interviewer read both statements to the respondent and asked '*which* statement is closest to your view'. Responses were recorded on a five-point scale, allowing for 'agree' or 'agree very strongly' with either statement and a middle category for 'agree with neither' and 'don't know'. We calculate descriptive statistics by aggregating the 'agree' and 'agree strongly' responses to the pro-reform, market-oriented option.

6. This switch in public opinion also occurred in Botswana, where the majority who favoured market pricing for high-quality education in 2003 (52 per cent) was replaced by a new majority who favoured free education in 2005 (57 per cent).

7. For example, 65 per cent urban versus 48 per cent rural in 2003; and 67 per cent urban versus 52 per cent rural in 2008.

8. Pearson's $r = -142***$ and $-0.087***$ respectively. As the 2008 survey did not ask about particular aspects of service delivery, we used 2005 data for these estimates.

9. Pearson's $r = -0.153***$.

10. In 2005, for example, 86 per cent in Lesotho, 77 per cent in Botswana, and 64 per cent in South Africa preferred to maintain public sector jobs regardless of cost.

11. Pearson's $r = 0.115***$.

12. Pearson's $r = 0.330***$.

13. The main exception is sporadic work stoppages on selected mining compounds and in educational and health institutions, including the country's biggest referral hospital (the University Teaching Hospital). These disputes have usually been resolved through negotiation.

14. As noted earlier, public appreciation of government performance in the education sector may be associated with improvements in student enrolment rates (9 and 10 per cent per annum since 2000 at basic and secondary levels respectively) and infrastructure development (2–3 per cent annual increases in the number of schools). As for crime and corruption, the creation of new agencies and policies, such as community policing, victim support units, integrity committees, and whistleblower protections, may have boosted public approval.

15. For the most part, assessments of government performance in 2008 differ little across urban and rural areas. This regularity holds, even for job creation, which might be expected to be a predominantly urban issue, and food security, which might be expected to be mainly a rural issue. However, urban dwellers are relatively more satisfied with water delivery and rural dwellers with corruption control.

16. Owing to the margin of sampling error inherent in probability surveys, patient and impatient respondents are statistically indistinguishable in 2008. Note, however, that patience with economic reform is lower in Zambia in 2008 (43 per cent) than in neighbouring countries like South Africa (46 per cent), Tanzania (51 per cent), and Malawi (66 per cent).

17. The index of *support for economic reform* ranges across a five-point scale from 0 to 4 policies.

18. Managing the economy and tackling poverty are correlated at Pearson's $r = 0.627$***.

19. The construct of *satisfaction with economic reform* also employs a five-point scale from 'very badly' through 'fairly badly', 'don't know', and 'fairly well' to 'very well'.

20. All economic factors are also measured on five-point scales: the first two factors from 'very bad' to 'very good'; the second two factors from 'much worse' to 'much better'.

21. The question asks, 'Which of these statements is closest to your own opinion? 1. Democracy is preferable to any other kind of government. 2. In some circumstances a non-democratic government can be preferable. 3. For someone like me, it doesn't matter what kind of government we have.' Those choosing statement 1 are held to support democracy.

22. On a five-point scale ranging from 'not at all satisfied' through to 'not very satisfied', 'don't know', and 'fairly satisfied' to 'very satisfied'.

23. On a five-point scale from 'strongly disapprove' to 'strongly approve'.

24. The dualistic distinction between parochialism and cosmopolitanism has a long history in sociological analysis. Far from signifying an evolutionary process of modernization, however, these contrasting modes of personhood can co-exist in modern settings (Merton, 1957). Our conception of cosmopolitanism centres on information and material linkages rather than on the personal 'styles' of self-presentation emphasized in a recent analysis of Copperbelt society in Zambia (Ferguson, 1999).

25. Cronbach's Alpha = 0.662.

26. Using an index constructed at the country level, Norris and Inglehart (2009) demonstrate that exposure to global communications boosts attachments to democratic reforms.
27. Pearson's r =0.610***.

References

Aker, J. (2007). *Does Digital Divide or Provide? The Impact of Cell Phones on Grain Markets in Niger*. Berkeley: University of California, Department of Economics.

Anderson, C. and Guillory, C. (1997). Political institutions and satisfaction with democracy: A cross-national analysis of consensus and majoritarian systems. *American Political Science Review* 91: 66–81.

Bates, R. (2008). *When Things Fell Apart: State Failure in Late-Century Africa*. New York: Cambridge University Press.

Bratton, M. and Liatto-Katundu, B. (1994). A focus group assessment of political attitudes in Zambia. *African Affairs*; 93: 535–563.

Bratton, M. (1999). Political participation in a new democracy: Institutional considerations form Zambia. *Comparative Political Studies*; 32: 549-588.

Cammack, D. (2007). The logic of African neopatrimonialism: What role for donors? *Development Policy Review*; 25: 599–614.

Central Statistical Office (2006a). *Living Conditions*. Available at: <http://www.zamstats.gov.zm> (last accessed December 2009).

Central Statistical Office (2006b). *Labor Force Survey, 2005*. Available at: <http://www.zamstats.gov.zm> (last accessed December 2009).

Cheeseman, N. and Hinfelaar, M. (2009). *Parties, Platforms and Political Mobilization: The Zambian Presidential Election of 2008*. Oxford: Oxford University Press.

Craig, J. (2001). Putting privatization into practice: The case of Zambia Consolidated Copper Mines Limited. *Journal of Modern African Studies*; 39: 389–410.

Diamond, L. (1999). *Developing Democracy: Toward Consolidation*. Baltimore: Johns Hopkins University Press.

Electoral Commission of Zambia (2008). *2008 Elections: Final Presidential Results*. Available at: <http://www.elections.org.zm> (last accessed December 2009).

Ferguson, J. (1999). *Expectations of Modernity: Myths and Meanings of Urban Life on the Zambian Copperbelt*. Berkeley: University of California Press.

Fraser, A. and Lungu J. (2008). *For Whom the Windfalls? Winners and Losers in the Privatization of Zambia's Copper Mines*. Lusaka: Civil Society Trade Network of Zambia/ Catholic Centre for Justice, Development and Peace (CSTNZ/CCJDP). Available at: <http://www.minewtachzambia.com> (last accessed December 2009).

Geddes, B. (2003). *Paradigms and Sandcastles: Theory Building and Research Design in Comparative Politics*. Ann Arbor: University of Michigan Press.

Gulhati, R. (1989). *Impasse in Zambia: The Economic and Politics of Reform*. Washington, DC: World Bank.

Hahn, H.P and Kibora, L. (2008). The domestication of the mobile phone: Oral society and the new ICT in Burkina Faso. *Journal of Modern African Studies*; 46: 87-109.

International Monetary Fund (2002). *Zambia: Poverty Reduction Strategy Paper*. Available at: <http://www.imf.org/external/NP/prsp/2002/zmb> (last accessed December 2009).

International Monetary Fund (2006). *Memorandum of Economic and Financial Policies: Review of Recent developments and Performance under the PRGF-Supported Program*. Washington, DC: International Monetary Fund.

Jayne, T., Chapoto, A., Minde, I., and Donovan, C. (2008). The 2008/09 food price and food security situation in Eastern and Southern Africa. *International Development Working Paper*, November. East Lansing: Michigan State University.

Kinder, D. and Kiewiet, D. (1981). Sociotropic politics: The American case. *British Journal of Political Science*; 11: 129–141.

Klingemann, H. D. (1999). Mapping political support in the 1990s: A global analysis. In Norris, P. (ed) *Critical Citizens: Global Support for Democratic Governance*. New York: Cambridge University Press.

Larmer, M. and Fraser, A. (2007). Of cabbages and king cobra: Populist politics and Zambia's 2006 election. *African Affairs*; 106: 611–637.

Lewis-Beck, M. and Stegmaier, M. (2000). Economic determinants of electoral outcomes. *Annual Review of Political Science*; 3: 183–219.

Medard, J.F. (2002). Corruption in the neo-patrimonial states of sub-Saharan Africa. In: Heidenheimer, A. and Johnston, M. (eds) *Political Corruption: Concepts and Context*. New Brunswick, NJ: Transaction Publishers.

Merton, R. (1957). *Social Theory and Social Structure*. Glencoe, Illinois: Free Press.

Molony, T. (2008). Running out of credit: The limitations of mobile telephony in a Tanzanian agricultural marketing system. *Journal of Modern African Studies*; 46: 637–658.

Ndulu, B. and Collier, P. (2007). *The Political Economy of Economic Growth in Africa, 1960–2000, 2 vols*. New York: Cambridge University Press.

Nelson, J. (1989). *Fragile Coalitions: The Politics of Economic Adjustment*. Washington, DC: Overseas Development Council.

Norris, P. and Inglehart, R. (2009). *Cosmopolitan Communications*. New York: Cambridge University Press.

Petrauskis, C. and Nkunika, S. (2006). *How Free is Free Education? The Cost of Education in Lusaka*. Lusaka: Jesuit Centre for Theological Reflection.

Quispe-Agnoli, M. (2004). Reform fatigue: Symptoms, reasons, and implications. *Economic Review*. Atlanta: Federal Reserve.

Republic of Zambia (2002). *National Decentralisation Policy 'Towards Empowering the People'*. Lusaka: Office of the President – Cabinet Office.

Republic of Zambia (2005). PSRP – *Public Service Management Component*. Lusaka: Cabinet Office.

Republic of Zambia (2006). *Fifth National Development Plan (FNDP), 2006–2010*. Lusaka: Ministry of Finance and National Planning.

Republic of Zambia (2008). *CSO Monthly*; 68

Republic of Zambia (2009). *CSO Monthly*; 70

Schedler, A. and Sarsfield, R. (2007). Democrats with adjectives: Linking direct and indirect measures of democratic support. *European Journal of Political Research*; 46: 637-659.

Seshamani, V. (2002). *The PRSP Process in Zambia*. Brussels: Economic Commission for Africa.

Szeftel, M. (1982). Political graft and the spoils system in Zambia: The state as a resource. *Review of African Political Economy*; 9: 4–21.

UNDP (United Nations Development Program) (2007). *Zambia Human Development Report*. Ndola: Mission Press

UNDP (United Nations Development Program) (2009). *Human Development Indices: A Statistical Update, 2008*. Available at: <http://hdr.undp.org/en/statistics> (last accessed December 2009).

van de Walle, N. (2001). *African Economies and the Politics of Permanent Crisis, 1979–1999*. New York: Cambridge University Press.

van den Berg, A. and Meadwell, H. (2004). *The Social Sciences and Rationality: Promise, Limits and Problems*. Rutgers, NJ: Transaction Publishers.

van Donge, J.K. (2009). The Plundering of Zambian resources by Frederick Chiluba and his friends: A case study of the interaction between national politics and the international drive towards good governance. *African Affairs*; 108: 69–90.

von Soest, C. (2006). How does neopatrimonialism affect the African state? The case of tax collection in Zambia. *GIGA working paper* 32. Hamburg: German Institute of Global and Area Studies.

World Bank (2001*). Chance to Learn. Knowledge and Finance for Education in sub-Saharan Africa*. Washington, DC: World Bank.

World Bank (2008). *Abolishing School Fees in Africa: Lessons Learned in Ethiopia, Ghana, Kenya and Mozambique*. Washington, DC: World Bank.

Zambia Privatization Agency (1993). *Progress Report* # 2 (January 1 to June 30).

Zambia Privatization Agency (1997). *Progress Report* # 10 (January 1 to June 30).

Zambia Privatization Agency (2001). *Progress Report* # 18 (January 1 to June 30).

16

Achieving Better Health Outcomes Through Innovative Strategies and Results-focused Interventions

Collins Chansa, Mirja Sjoblom, and Monique Vledder

16.1 Introduction

The Government of the Republic of Zambia envisions a country where all Zambians have 'equity of access to cost-effective, quality healthcare as close to the family as possible' (Ministry of Health, 1992). Zambia's journey to improving health service delivery dates back to 1991/1992 after the re-introduction of multi-party politics. The health sector reforms have seen many faces, but the prime motivation has been to improve efficiency and effectiveness in the provision of health services. The various reforms have been implemented in several areas of service delivery (including disease-specific areas) and focused on de-centralization of health service provision and reorganization of institutional arrangements; healthcare financing (aid harmonization and alignment alongside vertical projects); and pharmaceutical supply chain management. In the last few years, the health reform process has focused on strengthening governance structures and public-private partnerships.

16.1.1 *Achievements and challenges*

In recent years, the coverage of key health interventions has increased in most of the major public health priorities, including immunization, malaria,

HIV/AIDS, and tuberculosis (TB). For example, the national coverage for fully immunized children has been above 90 per cent between 2008 and 2010 (Ministry of Health, 2011a). Malaria parasitaemia in children aged 0–59 months dropped from 22 per cent in 2006 to 16 per cent in 2010, while the percentage of households owning at least one insecticide-treated net increased from 38 per cent in 2006 to 64 per cent in 2010 (Ministry of Health, 2010b). The percentage of pregnant women who received a complete course of intermittent preventive treatment (IPT) for malaria increased from 59 per cent in 2006 to 70 per cent in 2010, while the percentage of households covered by indoor residual spraying (IRS) increased from 10 per cent in 2006 to 23 per cent in 2010 (Ministry of Health, 2010b). Furthermore, by June 2012 over 400,000 HIV/AIDS-positive people were now on antiretroviral drugs (ARVs) while 44,000 new smear-positive TB cases were detected and treated during the period 2004–2012.

The increase in disease-specific funding in the last decade, through initiatives such as the US President's Emergency Plan for AIDS Relief (PEPFAR), the Global Fund to Fight AIDS, Tuberculosis and Malaria (GFATM), and the Global Alliance for Vaccines and Immunization (GAVI) Alliance, has contributed to these achievements. The motivation behind these programmes, which gained prominence in the early 2000s, is to control major public health diseases, such as malaria, HIV/AIDS, and TB, which contribute most to high disease burdens in developing countries.

As the disease deficit has been addressed and intervention service coverage has increased, there has been a positive development in maternal and child

Figure 16.1 Progress and gaps in attaining MDGs 4 and 5 in Zambia

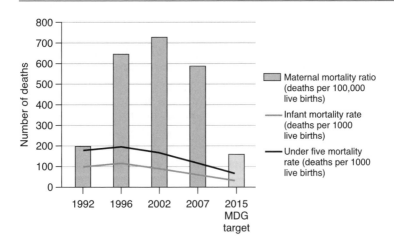

Source: Zambia Demographic and Health Surveys 1992, 1996, 2002, 2007

health outcomes. As shown in Figure 16.1, between 2002 and 2007, the infant mortality rate (IMR) per every 1,000 live births decreased from 95 to 70 deaths, while the under-five mortality rate (U5MR) decreased from 168 to 119 deaths per 1,000 live births (CSO, 2009). The neonatal mortality rate decreased from 37 to 34 deaths per 1,000 live births, while the maternal mortality ratio (MMR) reduced from 729 to 591 deaths per 100,000 live births during the same period (CSO, 2009). The national HIV prevalence among the 15–49 years age group declined from 16 per cent in 2002 to 14.3 per cent in 2007 (CSO, 2009).

Despite these gains, Zambia is unlikely to achieve the health-related Millennium Development Goals (MDGs) by 2015. If the progress in reducing child and maternal mortality is maintained at the same pace (1990–2011 pace), Zambia will only attain MDGs 4 and 5[1] after the year 2040 (Lozano et al., 2011). This is because the annual rates of reduction (2.1 per cent for U5MR and 2.5 per cent for MMR) for the period 1990–2011 are significantly lower than the annual rates of reduction required to achieve the MDGs targets (4.4 per cent for U5MR and 5.5 per cent for MMR) (Hogan et al., 2010; Rajaratnam et al., 2010; Lozano et al., 2011).[2]

It should also be noted that there is a need to improve the equity in access to healthcare in Zambia. Beyond the national aggregate trends, major inequalities in coverage, utilization, and health status exist (CSO, 2009; IHME, 2011). As shown in Figure 16.2, utilization of maternal and child health services is higher among the rich despite ill health being concentrated among the poor.[3]

In summary, the data we have presented so far tell us that there has been substantial, but insufficient, progress in disease-specific outcomes to guarantee the attainment of the health-related MDGs. Inequalities in intervention coverage, utilization, and health status persist and have stalled progress. Against this backdrop, accelerated efforts will be required to achieve the health-related MDGs by 2015 and address the bottlenecks for providing the population with equity of access to cost-effective, quality healthcare.

16.2 Looking forward: key policy issues in the immediate-to-long-term future

While the disease-specific programmes have made a large contribution to improvements in health outcomes in recent years[4] by focusing on the low-hanging fruits, most programmes have not had the objective to create an efficient and sustainable health system.

To some extent disease-specific funding has contributed to the weakening of the overall health system as a result of strict earmarking (ring-fencing) with various conditionalities, skewing of funding to a few diseases (malaria,

Figure 16.2 Inequities in utilization of maternal and child health services and child health outcomes

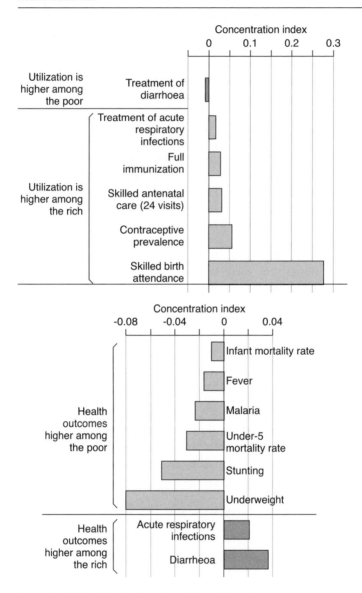

Source: World Bank, 2012. Health Equity and Financial Protection Report

HIV/AIDS, TB), and creation of different planning and implementation structures that are linked inadequately to those existing in the country (Cheelo et al., 2008).

Resources have often been provided off-budget, meaning that it is not channelled through the government, but rather through non-governmental organizations (NGOs) and international agencies. The share of donor resources that were transferred through the Ministry of Health (MOH) in Zambia decreased from 63 per cent in 2003 to 29 per cent in 2006 primarily as a result of the inflow of vertical funds (Maher, 2010). One of the reasons why donors prefer to channel their resources outside the health sector is because of the governance issues in the sector, which will be discussed in detail in Section 16.2.2, and the consequent inefficiencies in the health sector.

In comparison to other developing countries and those in sub-Saharan Africa (SSA), Zambia generally has poor health outcome indicators, even though the level of investment is relatively high. This is shown in Table 16.1. For example, Zambia has the 21st highest U5MR amongst the 195 United Nations Children's Fund (UNICEF) countries and territories worldwide (UNICEF, 2012). This is despite the fact that it has per capita total health expenditure and per capita government health expenditure that are higher than the average for developing countries.[6]

Table 16.1 Key demographic and socio-economic indicators

	Zambia	Developing countries	Sub-Saharan Africa
Under-five mortality rate per 1,000 live births	119*	63	121
Infant mortality rate per 1,000 live births	70*	44	76
Maternal mortality ratio per 100,000 live births	591*	290	500
Percentage HIV/AIDS prevalence (15–49 years age group)	14.3*	0.9	4.8
Life expectancy at birth (years), 2010	49	68	54
Percentage of one-year-old children immunized against measles, 2010	91	84	75
Percentage of under fives with fever receiving malaria drugs (2006–2010)	34	19	39
Percentage of skilled attendant at birth, (2006–2010)	47	66	5
Per capita general goverment health expenditure	26**	16**	24**
Per capita total health expenditure	44**	43**	56**

UNICEF Statistics and Monitoring 2012 except for
* 2007 Zambia Demographic and Health Survey and
** World Health Organization Global Health Observatory

Source: UNICEF Statistics and Monitoring 2012 (www.unicef.org/statistics) except for *2007 Zambia Demographic and Health Survey; **World Health Organization Global Health Observatory

The shift of scarce clinical health workers from comprehensive health-care to disease care is also a major issue (Cheelo et al., 2008). In fact, the human resources crisis in Zambia appears to have worsened at a time when the flow of external/donor resources to support Zambia's health sector (primarily through vertical programs) have increased dramatically (World Bank, 2009b). The overall trend has been that as total per capita health expenditures increase with the addition of more funding into the health system, the proportion of personnel expenditure (PE) to total health expenditures declines (even as the proportion of PE to MOH expenditures increases). In short, it is the inability of the vertical financing to formally finance PE that causes 'so much money chasing so few workers' (World Bank, 2009b).

There is also initial evidence that there may be issues in sustaining the results of disease-specific programmes in the long run. In Zambia, malaria cases increased by 34 per cent between 2009 and 2010, after the previously reported reductions (Ministry of Health, 2011a; United Nations, 2012). While the reasons behind this resurgence are many, the fragility of the malaria control programme has been brought to the fore (United Nations, 2012).

Given the issues with disease-specific funding, a fundamental rethink of the current strategic approach to health service delivery is necessary. The GFATM, which is one of the main donors of disease-specific funding in Zambia and elsewhere, has itself recognized its inadequacies and has initiated extensive reforms aimed at transforming the way it operates, and how it can increase the effectiveness of its grants on people's lives.[5] This is also recognized in the Africa Investment Case, a document that implores African leaders and their regional and global partners to focus their attention and resources on health investment that works and on strengthening health systems for better health outcomes in SSA. It calls for increases in investments to be matched with greater effectiveness and efficiency, and the need for country-led investment decisions (HHA, 2011).

Taking a leaf from the Africa Investment Case, this chapter discusses four strategic areas for health system strengthening, namely health financing; governance and accountability; results and value for money; and technology and health. These areas are part of the Zambia National Health Strategic Plan for the period 2011–2015 (Ministry of Health, 2011c) and accentuate the key areas of policy focus in the immediate-to-long-term future. Based also on the evidence that we have gathered, these areas present us with a clear conviction on where we think the health reforms could have the largest effect on health outcomes in Zambia. If implemented correctly, interventions in these four areas can help to address both the supply and demand sides of health service delivery, leading to improvements in universal coverage and health status.

16.2.1 *Health financing: Improving resource mobilization, allocation, and use*

Level of health expenditure

Over the period 2000–10, Zambia has been spending an average of 6.3 per cent of its gross domestic product (GDP) on health (Figure 16.3). This is higher than low-income countries (LICs) and low–middle-income countries (LMICs) around the world, which have been spending an average of 4.7 per cent and 4.3 per cent of their GDP on health respectively. However, in comparison with other countries in SSA, Zambia's total expenditure on health as a percentage of the GDP is slightly lower than the SSA average of 6.4 per cent over the same period. In other terms, the per capita total health expenditure (THE) has been $US44, which is lower than the SSA average of $US56,

Figure 16.3 Level of health expenditure

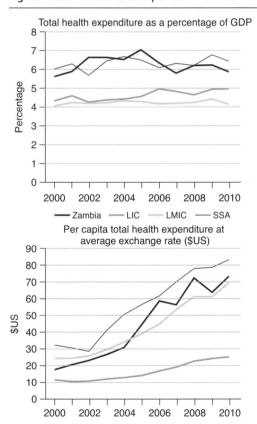

Source: World Health Organization, Health Expenditure Series

but higher than other LMICs ($US43) and LICs ($US16) around the world during the period 2000–10.

Composition of health expenditure

During the period 1995–2006 the major sources of health financing in Zambia were government tax and non-tax revenues (on average, 29.2 per cent), donor financing (26.3 per cent), private health insurance, and employer-funded schemes (12.4 per cent), and households (32.1 per cent) (Ministry of Health, 2009). This is illustrated in Figure 16.4, which demonstrates three important characteristics of the financing environment: the high share of expenditure that is financed by donors; the substitution between government and donor expenditures; and the high and almost constant households' out-of-pocket expenditures on health over the last 15 years, despite increased inflow of donor financing.

General government health expenditure

The share of health in total government expenditure in Zambia between 2010 and 2012 was, on average, 8.7 per cent, far below the Abuja target of 15 per cent (Government of Zambia, 2010, 2011, 2012). In per capita terms, general government expenditure on health (GGHE) was, on average, $US26 per capita between 2000 and 2010 compared with LICs, which spent $US6; LMICs, which spent $US16; and SSA countries, which spent $US24 (Figure 16.5). This implies that government or public health spending in Zambia is higher than other LICs and LMICs around the world, as well as SSA countries.

Figure 16.4 Percentage shares of total health expenditures by funding source, 1995–2006

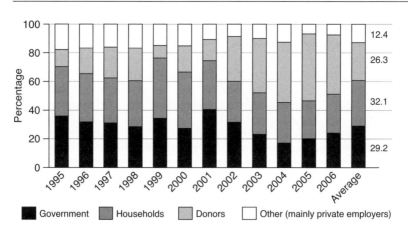

Source: Ministry of Health 2009

Figure 16.5 Per capita general government expenditure on health at average exchange rate ($US), 2000–10

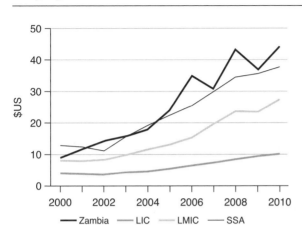

Source: World Health Organization, Health Expenditure Series

Comparison of health expenditure to health outcomes

As mentioned previously, Zambia compares poorly with other LICs and LMICs around the world in selected key child health outcomes (U5MR and IMR) and life expectancy at birth, despite its relatively high health expenditure. This is outlined in Figure 16.6 and also in Table 16.1. It implies that higher health expenditures do not necessarily lead to better health outcomes and, imperatively, the Zambian Government should improve efficiency in resource allocation and use. However, it is important to conduct further analysis on other factors that can influence the cost of providing healthcare, such as the size of the country, topography, and geographic characteristics, population distribution, disease burden, and epidemiological profile, etc. Whatever the case, the regional comparison has revealed that there is scope for Zambia to put its high health expenditure to more efficient use.

Out-of-pocket health expenditure and household capacity to pay for healthcare

In the Zambian context, where households make sizeable contributions to healthcare financing, it is also important to understand who gets sick and, out of those getting sick, who pays the highest levels of out-of-pocket expenditure on health. An analysis of the last six nationally representative Living Conditions Monitoring Surveys shows that the poorest population quintile bears the brunt of the disease burden (reported illness), accounting for 21.5 per cent of the reported illnesses compared with 16.0 per cent reported by the rich over the period 1991–2006 (Cheelo et al., 2010). The disease burden

Figure 16.6 Child health outcome indicators and life expectancy at birth

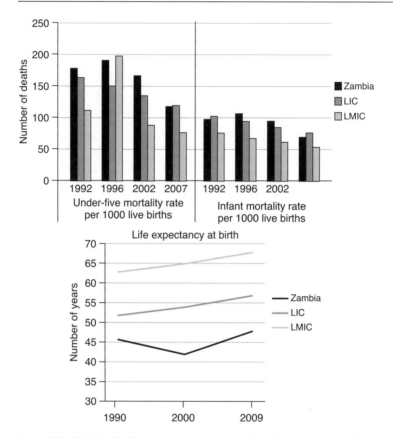

Source: WHO Global Health Observatory Data Repository and Zambia Demographic and Health Surveys 1992, 1996, 2002, 2007

borne by the poorest quintile increased by 4.7 per cent, while it decreased by 5.3 per cent for the richest quintile of the population, illustrating a growing disease burden on the poor during the review period (Cheelo et al., 2010). Out-of-pocket expenditure on health as a share of household's capacity to pay[6] was also highest for the poor (quintiles 1 and 2) and lowest for the rich (quintiles 4 and 5), even though there was a declining trend over the survey years. The largest component of out-of-pocket spending in 2006[7] was payments on medicines (58.1 per cent), and payments to formal health facilities (16.4 per cent).

Thus, Zambia's health financing system is characterized by high out-of-pocket spending on health, which is incurred at the point of service delivery when a person is already sick, making it highly inequitable as such payments are incurred predominantly by the poor and sickly, rather than the rich and healthy. With multiple years of economic growth rates of more than six per cent, the Zambian Government should promote both contributory and non-contributory programmes to protect the large population of poor people. A comprehensive healthcare financing strategy highlighting supplementary ways of generating new funding, equity, and access to care is inevitable.

Alternative healthcare financing mechanisms

Social health insurance

There are various ways to increase the protection of the poorest from catastrophic health expenditure (Picazo, 2009). One contributory health insurance programme that the Zambian Government is currently considering is social health insurance (SHI). SHI is a system of healthcare financing where the policyholder is obliged or encouraged to make contributions to an insurance fund that operates within a government-regulated insurance framework (http://stats.oecd.org/glossary/detail.asp?ID=2487). In order to sustain the operations of the insurance fund, policyholders are usually required to make mandatory contributions in proportion to their income. SHI encourages solidarity among its members through income and risk-pooling. SHI differs significantly from private health insurance (PHI) in that PHI is often characterized by voluntary contributions and for-profit commercial coverage, and does not uphold the solidarity and risk-pooling principles advanced by SHI (Jost, 2001; Colombo and Tapay, 2004).

SHI schemes normally provide some benefits to members and accredited providers in government, as well as the private sector by encouraging active purchasing of health services, which stimulates supply-side improvements across accredited facilities (Wagstaff, 2007). At present, the Zambian government is acting like a 'passive' purchaser of health services, with little knowledge of what it is 'buying' in terms of outputs, and who is receiving the health service outputs. In sharp contrast, SHI pays, or reimburses, health facilities only upon rendering services to members, at an agreed-upon price (the fee schedule). The active purchasing mechanism compels the creation of an institutional separation of 'purchasing of healthcare' from 'healthcare delivery' and this, in turn, influences positively, the way health services are provided in accredited health facilities (Wagstaff, 2007). SHI also encourages the growth of the health sector as private providers will be attracted by the prospect of profits to establish health service delivery outlets in remote areas to cater for the needs of SHI members.

However, SHI also raises a number of challenges and concerns. The availability of fiscal space to meet government SHI obligations is a major concern.

A key risk in the implementation of SHI is whether the government has the wherewithal to pay its contribution as an employer of civil servants in the SHI fund. Another major concern is whether it is feasible to reach the poor, who, overwhelmingly, are employed in the informal sector, with a programme that relies on collecting revenue through payroll taxes. Informality in employment is widespread in Zambia, with about 90 per cent[8] of the entire labour force in the informal sector, the majority of whom are self-employed or working as unpaid household workers (International Labour Organization, 2008). Many countries that have operated under the assumption that SHI would lead eventually to expanded coverage to poorer segments of the population have been disappointed when this has not been the case. This is because it is challenging to have the population that works in the informal sector pay contributions and enrol (Wagstaff, 2007).

The extent to which increased payroll taxes due to mandatory contributions affect the competitiveness of the economy is also an open question. It has been observed that mandatory contributions, such as the ones being envisioned under SHI, tend to 'casualize' employment because it adds to the costs of doing business. Furthermore, there are a number of design and implementation challenges related to institutional capacity, administration costs, and so forth, which are essential to the success of SHI. Despite these concerns, however, some low-income countries in Africa and Asia have shown that SHI can be implemented and it is therefore worth exploring as one option to increasing social protection in Zambia (Lagomarsino, et al., 2012).

Community-based health insurance

A variation of SHI that may be an option for consideration in Zambia is community-based health insurance (CBHI). CBHI schemes have been increasing in Africa in the past 20 years and they involve community members pooling financial or in-kind contributions (mostly agricultural produce) to cater for health payments through specified government or private health providers. CBHI schemes have a number of benefits, including increasing access to services (especially those that are highly valued to the community) and providing financial protection to groups that are normally excluded from traditional SHI schemes. For Zambia, CBHI schemes can be used to provide health insurance cover for the informal sector. This would complement the SHI scheme by providing cover to roughly 90 per cent of the people in the informal sector compared with the 10 per cent of the people in the formal sector that would be covered through the SHI scheme.

CBHI has been implemented in Rwanda and it is one of the few countries that have almost achieved universal coverage (Sekabaraga et al., 2011). The Rwandan government reports that 91 per cent of the country's population belongs to one of three principal health insurance schemes of which CBHI schemes (mutuelles) cover about 80 per cent of the population (WHO, 2010a). Other examples are Ghana, India, Indonesia, Kenya, Mali, Nigeria, the Philippines, and Vietnam where the main SHI schemes have been complemented by CBHI schemes leading to increased government health expenditures, coverage of more people, expanded service coverage, and decreased out-of-pocket expenditures (Lagomarsino, et al., 2012). On the contrary, the main challenge with CBHI schemes is how to expand coverage to attain universal coverage. Within the communities, the contributions might not be affordable to all the community members' resulting into a small financial pool to provide for the required health insurance cover and greater inequities. It is also worth noting that in most of the countries operating CBHI schemes, there have been substantial subsidies provided to the CBHI schemes by the government's and external development partners, which might not be sustainable in the long run.

In conclusion, there is scope for Zambia to improve efficiency in resource allocation and use, while SHI and/or CBHI schemes can be potentially be implemented as alternative means of health financing. A combination of approaches tailored to the needs of the country should be articulated and implemented through a comprehensive health financing strategy. The key issue is to treat health insurance as a heterogeneous and context-specific product with a clear understanding of the demand (*ex ante*), including both individual and household-level characteristics, which play an important role in the demand for health insurance. Broadening the perspective outside the health sector is another route to protecting the poor from catastrophic health expenses. The existing social protection programmes should be re-designed to make them more efficient and effective.

16.2.2 *Improving governance and accountability*

While improved service delivery is often associated with increased funding to the health sector, of particular importance is how much public health spending contributes to better health outcomes (World Bank, 2009a). As pointed out previously, Zambia has higher per capita total health expenditure than other LICs and LMICs, but the health system still remains weak and its health indicators are no better. It is apparent, therefore, that money alone is not enough to achieve better results. In recent years, it has been increasingly recognized that good governance is equally important in ensuring effective healthcare delivery and that returns to investments in health are low where governance issues are not addressed (Lewis, 2006). This implies that emphasis on funding should be accompanied by concerns for governance issues.

Service delivery is both a technical and governance issue, and the extent to which governments assume this fundamental responsibility in a satisfactory manner is of critical importance (UNDP, 2011). Consequentially, and as examined below, poor governance appears to be holding back the provision of quality healthcare in Zambia. This is not to suggest that Zambia has not done anything to improve governance in the health sector, but weaknesses in most governance institutions have been observed for some time. Ironically, Zambia was one of the pioneers of health reforms in Africa, which started as far back as the early 1990s when health service delivery was de-centralized, and the health sector wide approach (SWAp) was implemented (Lake and Musumali, 1999). To date, the SWAp still provides the context and policy framework for the overall health system, and a number of systems and structures have been established to coordinate and manage relations and resources in a consultative manner. However, despite the early promise of the SWAp in promoting transparency and accountability, the health reform objectives have not been fully met (Lake and Musumali, 1999). The problems can be attributed to poor governance in the health sector instigated by weak partnerships, poor alignment, and harmonization (Ministry of Health, 2008a), poor transparency and accountability, a weak health system, and inadequate policies and regulation (UNDP, 2011).

A deeper understanding of governance issues and mechanisms to address them is, therefore, imperative. The World Health Organization (WHO) is clear on its definition of governance which is 'ensuring strategic policy frameworks exist and are combined with effective oversight, coalition building, the provision of appropriate regulations and incentives, attention to system-design, and accountability (WHO, 2007). This suggests that health sector reforms in Zambia and around the world should focus on organizational reforms, systems development, and accountability. In addition, health system stewards should go a mile further by understanding how health systems operate in their own specific country contexts in order to govern them appropriately (Mikkelsen-Lopez et al., 2011).

A review of the literature provides us with the key elements of governance. These are accountability, effectiveness/efficiency, equity, ethics, existence of standards, incentives, information/intelligence, participation/collaboration, policy/system design, regulation, responsiveness, rule of law, transparency, and vision (Mikkelsen-Lopez et al., 2011). These elements of governance are not new and the Zambian Government and all stakeholders are aware of them. As observed in the 2011 *Human Development Report for Zambia*, there has been a systematic erosion of governance institutions in Zambia, which, in comparison with most countries, is below average (UNDP, 2011). The private health sector is also small in Zambia and most of the governance structures are concentrated in the public sector with minimal involvement of the private sector. This is unlike other developing countries in the region, where the private health sector is bigger. Health services in Zambia are provided mostly through 1,882 health facilities, of which 79 per cent are public, 14 per cent for-profit, and 7 per cent faith-based (Ministry of Health, 2010a). Governance of health service delivery is further challenged by the repeal of the 1995 National Health Services Act in 2005 without a replacement Act (UNDP, 2011). This implies that there is no legislative framework for the organization of health services in Zambia.

Within the health sector some empirical studies[9] have assessed the magnitude and effect of certain elements of governance on health sector performance in Zambia. These studies have looked at (i) budget and resource management; (ii) individual providers; (iii) health facilities; (iv) informal payments; and (v) corruption. In general, the 2009 *Zambia Health Sector Public Expenditure Review* (PER) suggests that the health system in Zambia was not functioning effectively, mainly as a result of some apparent inefficiencies in the way healthcare services were being delivered. Budget leakages[10] were identified between the district medical office and the health facilities. More than 33 per cent of the district medical offices admitted delaying the release of district grants to health facilities even though they received these resources from the Ministry of Health headquarters on time. About 20 per cent of the health facilities received resources less than their intended allocations, despite 25 per cent of them being indebted. This phenomenon, described as 'local capture' or control of resources by influential members from the district medical office, has also been observed in Uganda (World Bank, 2009b).

The PER also raised concern on the limited availability of essential medical equipment at most of the hospitals and health centres, and high rates of non-functional medical and non-medical equipment, utilities, and transport (World Bank, 2009b). This signifies poor governance and an erosion of the quality of health service delivery. While clinical staff shortages at 41.4 per cent were crippling operations, this problem is further compounded by high rates of absenteeism (21 per cent self-reported) and tardiness (43 per cent self-reported) (World Bank, 2009b). The high rates of absenteeism and tardiness entail a total loss of 4,108 working days per month among the health facilities in Zambia. Patient perceptions on the 'technical' aspects of service delivery (explaining what the procedure or examination was for, and others) was also low (40-42 per cent).

Another assessment was undertaken to specifically measure the extent of vulnerability to corruption in Zambia's pharmaceutical sector using a standardized assessment instrument from the WHO as part of the Good Governance for Medicines (GGM) programme. The assessment was conducted in 2007 and focused on six essential regulatory and supply functions of the pharmaceutical sector: registration of medicines, promotion, inspection, selection, procurement, and distribution. The overall conclusion was that there is a marginal degree of vulnerability to corruption (score 6.9)[11] in the governance of the pharmaceutical sector in Zambia (WHO, 2012). The report further described the situation as volatile as it could become worse if certain issues were not addressed (WHO, 2012). However, Zambia performed better than other SSA countries (Benin, Cameroon, Ethiopia, Kenya, Malawi, and Mozambique) who conducted the GGM assessment. The overall scores for these countries ranged from 3.1 to 5.1, suggesting moderate-to-high vulnerability to corruption. In most of the 26 countries who have used the GGM assessment, control of medicines promotion, selection of essential medicines, and inspection of pharmaceutical manufacturers and distributors emerged as areas with greater vulnerability to corruption (WHO, 2011). For Zambia, promotion and selection were the major issues while the underlying areas of concern were conflict of interest, unethical practices, bribery, favouritism, counterfeit/sub-standard, and theft (WHO, 2012).

The forms of corruption in the pharmaceutical sector in Zambia are similar to the known forms of corruption in the pharmaceutical sector around the world, which are bribery, falsification of safety data, and theft in the distribution chain (WHO, 2010b). Corruption in the pharmaceutical sector negatively affects access and quality of healthcare leading to a health loss which reduces governments' capacity to provide good quality essential medicines and more unsafe medical products find themselves on the market (WHO, 2010b). With pharmaceutical expenditures accumulating about 15 per cent of the total public healthcare costs in Zambia, losses due to corruption can translate in real economic losses.

The performance measures on governance discussed above are often complemented by perceptions on corruption. Traditionally, health sectors in many countries are perceived as corrupt – a reflection of the overall inability of the institutions in most governments to provide essential services (Lewis and Pettersson, 2009). For Zambia, the allegations of corruption in the health sector in 2009 led to the withdrawal of significant amounts of donor funding. This is shown in Figure 16.7, which highlights a massive reduction in donor releases to the basket at the Ministry of Health from 83 per cent in 2008, a year before the scandal, to 39 per cent in 2009 and 0 per cent in 2010. Revelations of financial misappropriation in the health sector has also contributed to the erosion of public and donor confidence in public institutions, and the ability of these institutions to deliver quality health services (UNDP, 2011).

However, the declining trend in basket funding since 2006 suggests other reasons besides the alleged corruption of 2009. Some of the reasons are: (i) increased donor preference for project or vertical programmes; (ii) movement from basket funding to general budget support at the Ministry of Finance; (iii) a change in the priorities of donors from health to other sectors; and (iv) the global financial and economic crisis of 2008–09. However, in whichever way one looks at this issue, it is important to take advantage of the lessons

Figure 16.7 Donor commitments and releases to the basket, 2006–10

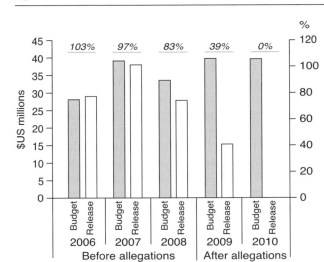

Source: Ministry of Health Basket Reports, 2006 to 2010

learned from the alleged corruption. To date, overall funding to the health sector has reduced, there is very low public and donor confidence in governance institutions in the health sector, loss of Zambia's reputation in implementing SWAPs, and a proliferation of project funding. It also demonstrates the fragile nature of donor–recipient countries' relationships, which only seem to flourish when things are going well, with no ownership of the problem by donors when one arises. All these issues have implications on policy design, regulation, and service delivery in the health sector.

Having identified the weaknesses in governance, it is extremely important for the Zambian Government and its partners to systematically address these issues in a prioritized and timely manner. The starting point would be to restore confidence in the governance institutions in Zambia by putting in place suitable legislation and regulatory frameworks, viable systems, and competent personnel with attractive remunerations to manage the governance structures. The focus should be on improving health service delivery by resolving both supply- and demand-side governance issues. A routine monitoring and evaluation system with performance indictors on governance should also be institutionalized to continuously assess the magnitude and effect of all the elements of governance on health sector performance. The donors should also resolve issues of poor alignment and harmonization to allow for development aid to be more effective.

16.2.3 *Achieving results and value for money*

The section on governance above outlines the importance of good governance in ensuring effective healthcare delivery and obtaining maximum returns from investments in health. Inefficiency is a serious concern in the Zambian health sector and widespread evidence exists to show this. It has been demonstrated, for example, that there is significant inefficiency in resource use in hospitals in Zambia (Masiye, 2007). Zambian hospitals are generally operating at 67 per cent level of efficiency, implying that significant resources are being wasted (Masiye, 2007). As reported in the previous section, shortages in staffing levels continue to be a challenge and this problem is compounded by high levels of absenteeism and tardiness, which further reduce the actual availability of staff in post. Eliminating absenteeism and tardiness would translate to a gain of 187 full-time equivalent staff, enough to staff 21 rural health centres in Zambia (World Bank, 2009b). Revelations of financial misappropriation in the health sector in 2009 further justifies the current calls for more results and value for money in the health sector.

The new government in Zambia, which was elected on a transparency agenda, is also under pressure from the general public and donors to deliver on its electoral promises of reduced corruption and improved health service delivery. Additionally, the global financial and economic crisis of 2008–2009 has contributed to a more general international trend to stronger scrutinize the use of donor resources. Thus, it is no surprise, therefore, that the overriding argument among the policymakers and development partners in Zambia today is that 'productivity enhancement' needs to be systematically built in the health initiatives in Zambia (World Bank, 2009b). As Lewis (2006) observes, where incentives for strong performance either do not exist or are undermined by ineffective management, productivity, and performance suffers.

To increase the productivity of health workers, the National Health Strategic Plan 2011–2015 aims to strengthen the overall health system with a focus on results. One of the key initiatives is the introduction of performance-based financing (PBF). PBF assumes a range of mechanisms designed to enhance the performance of the health system. PBF differs from other approaches to organizing health services as it is the purchaser rather than the service provider that defines the range, quantities, and quality of the services to be provided, location, and the evaluation process (Loevinsohn, 2008). In order for PBF to work, clear lines of responsibility and division of tasks between (a) service providers, (b) financier or purchasing agency, and (c) the regulator have to be established (Canavan et al., 2008). Business plans and contracts also have to be drawn up with an agreement between the three parties on the outputs and expected quality on which performance is rewarded (Canavan et al., 2008).

Figure 16.8: Theoretical considerations behind PBF

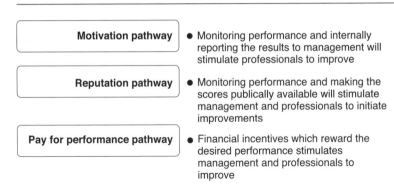

Nowadays, PBF initiatives are being implemented by several developing countries and are grounded on the hypothesis that linking financing to performance contributes to improvements in access, quality, and equity of access (Canavan et al., 2008). PBF mechanisms are now on the increase primarily because of continued dissatisfaction with the gap between investment and outcomes, and the desire to pilot alternative funding modalities that promote autonomy, independent management, and improved services (Blanchett 2003, cited in Canavan et al., 2008, p. 1). On the contrary, input-based health financing systems are increasingly being considered to be too centralized and that they produce variable results contingent on willingness, capacity, and motivation of the recipients and providers of the services (Loevinsohn 2006, cited in Canavan et al., 2008, p. 1). The theoretical underpinning behind PBF initiatives is based on three distinguished pathways to performance improvement, which are outlined in Figure 16.8 (Klundert, 2010).

The literature further suggests some key success factors for implementing PBF schemes in developing countries. These include (i) strong political and management support; (ii) room for change and innovation to maximize efficiencies; and (iii) a strong health information and reporting system that provide valid and reliable figures (Eldridge and Palmer, 2009). To date, there is an increasing body of evidence showing that PBF mechanisms are working in Africa leading to stronger health systems, stabilized and/or decreased costs of providing services, increased service coverage, and improved quality (Canavan et al., 2008). In addition, the shift in organizational culture to a more results oriented way of working has contributed to increased levels of staff motivation and innovations in service delivery (Canavan et al., 2008; Soeters et al., 2006).

Zambia has, in the past, experimented with PBF through performance-based contracting in the health sector. The landmark was achieved in 1996 when the Central Board of Health (CBoH) was established to improve health service delivery in line with management reform and accountability to the consumer. However, while the systems and structures to monitor performance were put in place, performance monitoring was poor and rewards were not contingent on performance (Chansa, 2009). This contributed to the dissolution of the CBoH in 2006. However, within the period of its existence, the CBoH did explore ways of fostering performance improvements in remote districts (Furth, 2006). For example, the performance-based incentives pilot study that was conducted in 2004 examined the effect of incentives on health workers' performance in the Luangwa and Chongwe districts (Furth, 2006). The study found that staff responded positively to performance-based awards (financial and non-financial), leading to improvements in staff motivation (Furth, 2006). The study recommended the introduction of performance-based incentive programmes in Zambia.

To date, various forms of PBF programmes have been implemented in Zambia, though at small scale. This includes the Cordaid and European Union-funded PBF programmes in Catholic health facilities and US Agency for International Development (USAID) programmes through Care International, Plan International, and the Centre for Infectious Disease Research in Zambia (Ministry of Health, 2011b). The MOH is also piloting a World Bank-financed results-based financing (RBF) project in 10 districts with controls in 20 other districts. This project seeks to catalyse the country's efforts to reduce under-five and maternal mortality, and adopts all the three pathways to performance improvement (motivation, reputation, and pay-for-performance) as outlined earlier (Ministry of Health, 2011b). The other component of the project is operational research through a fully-fledged impact evaluation (quantitative and qualitative) aimed at informing policy on the performance of the PBF approach in the Zambian context.

Besides its promise and emerging evidence some studies have questioned the underlying rational and actual effect of PBF initiatives (Eldridge and Palmer, 2009; Ireland et al., 2011). These studies call for a clearer discussion on the PBF concept and question the appropriateness of implementing PBF schemes in less developed countries where health systems are weak (Eldridge and Palmer, 2009). They also question the achievability of performance targets by contending that performance targets may adversely affect the performance of providers in a way that is detrimental to longer-term health system development (Eldridge and Palmer, 2009). In addition, PBF is viewed by some authors (Ireland et al., 2011) as merely a financing mechanism and refute claims that it is a strategic tool that can be used to reform the entire health sector. The basis of their argument is that results-based and economically-driven interventions do not, on their own, respond adequately to patient and community needs, upon which health system reforms are based (Ireland et al., 2011).

However, other authors (Meesen et al., 2011) are sceptical about the critics of PBF and contend that PBF mechanisms can catalyse comprehensive reforms and help address structural problems in public health systems, such as low responsiveness, inefficiency, and inequity. We also observe that the challenges that have been identified by critics of PBF are manageable as demonstrated by countries like Rwanda and Burundi (Meesen et al., 2011).

Through the impact evaluation of the Zambia World Bank-financed RBF pilot project, it will be possible to evaluate the impact of PBF. This will help to provide answers to some critics of PBF (Eldridge and Palmer, 2009), who appeal for more case studies detailing field experiences, success factors, and the potential advantages and disadvantages of PBF. The impact evaluation of the Zambia World Bank RBF project has been planned at baseline, process, and end-line (intervention and two control groups), and this should be able to take care of confounding and variations during the implementation period. So far, some initial results from a pre-pilot in Katete district, which has been in implementation since 2009, shows improvements in incentivized and non-incentivized indicators ranging from 6 per cent to 54 per cent (Dusseljee et al., 2011). An external data verification exercise also shows improvements in data collection and accuracy, while an independent qualitative review showed a wide range of innovations and increased motivation at health facility level (Dusseljee et al., 2011).

It is the country's expectation, therefore, that the World Bank RBF pilot project would provide an empirical analysis of the impact of RBF initiatives. If successful, the Zambian government intends to scale up RBF initiatives countrywide. Whatever the case, this pilot project provides an opportunity for learning and determining the best way of financing health services in Zambia and Africa at large.

16.2.4 New technologies and health

There has been an explosive growth rate in mobile cellular phone subscriptions in SSA over the past decade (from almost 2 to 45/100 people during the period 2000–2010 (World Bank, 2010). This means that many people who were previously excluded by the 'digital divide' now have access to new technologies (World Bank, 2010). It is expected that this growth rate will be sustained as the financial barriers to ownership of a cellular phone decreases with increased market liberalization, large telecom investments in the region, more efficient network equipment, and affordable handsets (United Nations, 2009). What is noteworthy in Africa is the relatively high number of mobile cellular subscriptions, while other means of communication, such as the Internet and fixed phones, are still relatively uncommon. In many countries the mobile phone is the most important information, communication, and technology (ICT) tool before the computer. The region is already pioneering new applications of mobile technology in areas such as mobile banking and micro-insurance, prompting some experts to predict that Africa may be the new centre for innovation when it comes to mobile phones (Hermsan, et al., 2012).

This African meta trend is also present in Zambia and is likely to affect how health services will be provided in the future. In Zambia the number of mobile cell subscriptions has increased dramatically in the last decade, even though the country still has a slightly lower mobile cellular penetration rate of 38 subscribers per 100 people compared with the SSA regional average of 45 subscribers per 100 people as of 2010 (see Appendix, Figures 16.A1 and 16.A2) (World Bank, 2010). The Internet, which as of June 2011, was being used by six per cent of the Zambian population, remains much lower than mobile phone access (Miniwatts Marketing Group, 2012). However, overall access to telephones (fixed line and mobile), radio, and Internet is more challenging in rural areas (Ministry of Communications and Transport, 2007). This is attributed to inadequate telecommunication infrastructure and high access costs (Ministry of Health, 2008b). Availability of electricity in rural areas of Zambia is also poor, which further reduces expansion programmes and use of ICT (Ministry of Health, 2008a; 2008b).

Linking ICT to health – the mobile health revolution

The potential benefit of the mobile phone for improving access to healthcare and enhancing healthcare delivery in Africa is clear, but the opportunity may be particularly promising in a country such as Zambia, which faces severe health access challenges because of its large surface area (the landmass equals that of France and the UK combined), a history of concentration of economic activity, as well as public service along the railway line and relatively poor infrastructure in rural areas. The large gap in health outcomes between rural and urban areas, both when considering the health status of the population, as well as health system outcome indicators, could be overcome as mobile phones reach remote populations and make real-time communication and two-way information exchanges possible. Thus, mobile technology in Zambia does not only have the potential to add efficiency and efficacy to existing systems, but also to reach remote and marginal populations with healthcare services and public health information.

An increasing number of developing countries are using mobile health (mHealth)[12] solutions to address their health needs. Pilot programmes are popping up in many countries, even though very few applications have been taken to scale. Rigorous evaluations of these efforts are also in their infancy. The main areas of application include: (i) education and awareness; (ii) remote data collection; (iii) remote monitoring; (iv) communication and training of health workers; (v) diagnostics and treatment support; and (vi) disease and epidemic outbreak tracking (Vital Wave Consulting, 2009). Within the East, Central, and Southern Africa (ECSA) region health ministers at the forty-sixth ECSA Health Ministers' Conference resolved that all members states should develop national e-policies and strategic plans that address the health sector by 2010 (ECSA Health Community, 2008). For Zambia, a national ICT policy was launched in 2007 with the objective of driving the development and use of ICT in the entire economy, including the health sector (Ministry of Communications and Transport, 2007). Since then, a number of mHealth initiatives have been launched, mostly in the areas of remote data collection, diagnostic and treatment support, and monitoring.

Several initiatives utilizing mobile devices to collect actionable health data have shown promising results in Zambia. One initiative, the EpiSurveyor,[13] was piloted successfully in 2006 by the WHO and DataDyne.org (the technology partner), resulting in more timely and accessible healthcare data, and making it easier to strengthen district level healthcare programmes, such as immunizations and responses to disease outbreaks. Since 2009, USAID/DELIVER has been using the EpiSurveyor to collect health information on malaria supply-chain management, diagnosis, and case management (Frost and Thidiane, 2010). This is being implemented as part of the USAID/Deliver 'End-User Verification' malaria programme monitoring activity. While there has been no rigorous evaluation of the programme in Zambia so far, results from a similar project in Ghana show reduced time and costs for data entry, analysis, and implementation of end-user activities (Frost and Thidiane, 2010). As of April 2012, the EpiSurveyor was being used in more than 170 countries worldwide, making it the most widely-used mHealth software.[14]

Another initiative that is currently being piloted in Zambia is the use of smartphones at the health facility level to replace the paper-based pharmaceutical supply chain information system. The aim is to digitalize the supply chain information system and thereby improve the flow of information on drug availability and stock-outs, and patient needs for drugs. The expected outcomes are: (i) increased access to quality essential drugs; (ii) increased accountability and performance monitoring throughout the system; (iii) increased transparency and reduced leakages of medicines; (iv) increased capacity to respond to upsurges in the demand for certain drugs (e.g. during unexpected outbreaks and/or high transmission seasons); and (v) improved forecasting and timely procurements (USAID Deliver Project, 2011; World Bank, 2011).

The other successful mHealth pilot programmes in Zambia is Project Mwana, which has contributed to improved early infant HIV diagnostic services, post-natal follow-up, and care by enhancing communication between the different actors involved. Delays averaging 6.2 weeks for infant HIV test results pose a significant barrier to early infant initiation of anti-retroviral therapy, especially in rural settings in Zambia. Among the infants who contract the virus from their mothers, about 30 per cent die before the age of one year and 50 per cent before the age of two years if no intervention is provided. Project Mwana aims to reduce the delay in receiving HIV test results by establishing a mobile communication system among formal and community health workers that support health services in rural communities (UNICEF, 2010). The project uses RapidSMS, a free and open-source framework for building mobile applications for dynamic data collection, logistics coordination and communication, and leveraging basic short message service mobile phone technology. The pilot, launched in June 2010, operates in 31 clinics and has, to date, relayed more than 3,000 infant HIV test results with reduced turnaround times of around 50 per cent. The aim is to achieve national scale by 2013, with all health facilities offering early infant diagnosis services (UNICEF, 2010).

The results demonstrate the opportunities that mHealth offers and why mHealth should be part of the broader health reform agenda. While Zambia is at an early stage in implementing the mHealth agenda, the examples given exemplify how the application of ICT solutions, and particularly mobile technology, can be transformative for the sector. Looking to the future there are a number of issues that need to be addressed to drive the agenda forward:

- *Strengthen the policy and regulatory environment* – the lack of a sector specific policy and regulatory guidelines for the use of ICT in the health sector in Zambia has contributed to the ad hoc implementation of existing initiatives. It also leaves important questions on data security, and legal and ethical issues related to ICT use open for interpretation. This gap has, and will, continue to contribute to lack of standardization and specifications on ICT infrastructure in the health sector and needs to be addressed urgently.

- *Work towards making pilot programmes sustainable and bring them to scale* – many of the existing initiatives in mHealth are donor-driven, lack standardization, and have not been tested at scale. As a result, the contribution of these systems to better health outcomes is limited to the project objectives and not holistic to the entire health system. A key priority is to ensure that future pilot programmes are sustainable. Scaling-up existing efforts will require closer collaboration with the private sector and other key players in the telecom business.

- *Evaluate and learn* – Many mHealth initiatives in Zambia have not been accompanied by a rigorous evaluation to measure their impact and cost-effectiveness. It is crucial that future pilot programme include strong evaluation components aimed at tracking progress, and implementation challenges. This will help to identify the appropriateness of mHealth solutions at different levels of the health system in the Zambian context.

16.3 Conclusion

In this chapter we have identified health financing, governance and accountability, results and value for money, and technology and health as the key areas for policy interventions in the Zambian health sector in the next few years. In the area of health financing, the evidence shows high out-of-pocket expenditures, which are incurred at the point of service delivery. This makes it highly inequitable as the financing burden is often on the poor and sickly. The chapter discussed some of the pros and cons of two potential options for improving financial inclusiveness in the health sector; these are social health insurance and community-based health insurance. As the government moves this agenda forward it will be important to carefully consider the various options for improving financial protection for the poor, learn from other countries, and evaluate which approach, or combination of approaches, would work well for Zambia. Based on this analysis, a comprehensive health financing strategy highlighting ways of generating additional funding, and promoting equity and access to healthcare should be developed. This strategy and implementation plan should be tailored to the county's context and priorities. Beyond the health sector implementation of a broad social protection scheme could also make a difference.

The other area we examined was governance and accountability. Here, we firstly made the point that money alone is not enough to achieve better health outcomes and that good governance is equally important to ensure efficient and effective healthcare delivery. We also showed that service delivery mechanisms, processes, and institutions are not working effectively as a result of poor governance. Some of the key symptoms of the lack of adequate systems and controls include the high absenteeism of clinical health workers; a marginal degree of vulnerability to corruption in the governance of the pharmaceutical sector; erratic supply of medicines; low availability and high non-functional essential medical equipment; and local capture of financial resources at district level. Vital pieces of regulatory instruments are also missing. Revelations of financial misappropriation in the health sector has also contributed to the erosion of public and donor confidence in public institutions, and the ability of these institutions to deliver quality health services.

As such, achieving gains in health service delivery depends on how much governance and accountability issues in the health sector are addressed. The starting point would be to develop a legislative framework (a new National Health Services Act) for the organization of health services in Zambia, which, at the moment, is absent. However, the various governance institutions should be strengthened by putting in place conducive regulatory frameworks, viable systems, and competent personnel. The focus should be on improving health service delivery by strengthening both supply- and demand-side governance. A routine monitoring and evaluation system with performance indictors on governance should also be institutionalized to continuously assess the magnitude and effect of all the elements of governance on health sector performance. The donors should also resolve issues of poor alignment and harmonization to allow for development aid to be more effective.

Improvements in health service delivery could also be attained by introducing RBF or PBF initiatives. Experiences from other countries show that such initiatives can improve health outcomes through improved accountability, strengthened health systems, and productivity of health workers. Initial results from the RBF pre-pilot project in Katete, Zambia, also show considerable progress in health output indicators, staff motivation, and service delivery. However, the extent to which these results will be sustained in the other pilot districts remains to be seen. Fortunately, it is expected that the impact evaluation component of the RBF pilot project will provide this answer. Whatever the case, the initial promise of the RBF initiative in achieving results and value for money is worth exploring in Zambia.

Another key area, which has been discussed in this chapter, is the opportunity of using mobile technologies (mobile phones and handheld computers) to improve health service delivery in Zambia. The use of mobile technologies in health is universally referred to as mobile health (mHealth). Zambia faces severe health access challenges mainly as a result of its large surface area, poor infrastructure in the rural areas, and a critical shortage of clinical health workers. These challenges could be answered by mHealth, leading to increased timeliness and accessibility to health information, supply chain management, disease diagnosis and case management, and improved epidemiological surveillance. A few pilot projects in the country have already shown how mHealth initiates can be transformative in the health sector. To drive this agenda forward, it will be important to strengthen the policy and regulatory environment on ICTs, learn from the on-going implementation of mHealth projects, scale-up successful mHealth projects, and sustain them over time.

Our final conclusion, therefore, is that the government and other stakeholders should consider fully exploiting the four areas we have outlined in their quest to improve health service delivery and health outcomes in Zambia. These areas complement each other and not only do they have the potential to add efficiency and efficacy to the existing health system, but they also have the potential to reach remote and marginal populations with healthcare services.

Appendix

Figure 16.A1 Growth of internet users, fixed broadband internet subscribers, mobile cellular subscribers, and telephone lines in sub-Saharan Africa (only developing countries)

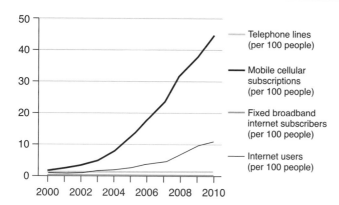

Source: World Development Indicators 2010

Figure 16.A2 Mobile cellular phone subscribers per 100 people

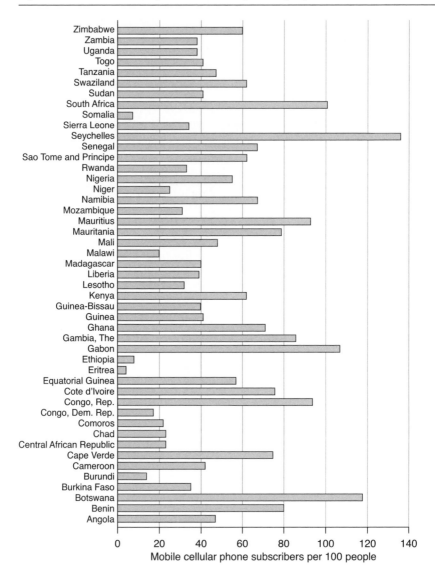

Source: World Development Indicators 2010

Notes

1. MDG 4 is to reduce by two thirds, between 1990 and 2015, the U5MR and MDG 5 is to reduce by three quarters, between 1990 and 2015, the Maternal Mortality Ratio (MMR).

2. Incidentally, progress to reducing MMR in Eastern and Southern Africa would have been greater without the HIV epidemic. This is because of the negative effect of HIV on pregnancy, which creates a higher risk of maternal deaths (Hogan et al, 2010).

3. Even if only half of the selected indicators are statistically significant, these indications of inequalities in utilization and health outcomes between the poor and the rich are undesirable.

4. The concentration indices were estimated using ADePT and data from the 2007 Zambia Demographic and Health Survey, and the 2003 Zambia World Health Survey. The concentration indices capture the direction and degree of inequality. A negative value indicates that the indicator takes higher values among the poor, while a positive index indicates that the indicator takes higher values among the better-off. The larger the index in absolute size, the more inequality there is.

5. A study observed that increased funding for effective malaria prevention interventions has prevented 842,800 child deaths across 43 malaria-endemic countries in Africa (including Zambia) between 2001 and 2010 (Eisele et al. 2012).

6. Expenditure data for developing countries was not available. Data for low–middle-income countries is indicated instead.

7. http://www.theglobalfund.org/en/transformation/

8. http://apps.who.int/nha/database/DataExplorerRegime.aspx

9. http://apps.who.int/nha/database/DataExplorerRegime.aspx

10. Given generally much lower expenditures among poor households, expressing out-of-pocket expenditure on health as a proportion of total household expenditure would not show the burden of health payments by households of different economic status. Thus, out-of-pocket health expenditure has been expressed as a proportion of household's 'capacity to pay'. A household's 'capacity-to-pay' is defined as a household's non-subsistence spending or the effective income that remains after basic subsistence needs have been made.

11. User fees were still in place when this statistics were collected but have since been abolished in Zambia.

12. 2008 Zambia Labour force survey

13. This is through the National Health Accounts survey; the Public Expenditure Tracking and Quality of Service Delivery Survey (PETS/QSDS); the Country Policy and Institutional Assessment (CPIA); and the Good Governance for Medicines (GGM) assessment.

14. A budget leakage is the discrepancy between the authorized health budget and the amount of funds received by intended recipients.

15. The GGM assessment instrument was used to measure the level of transparency and vulnerability to corruption. Qualitative and quantitative information on structural and procedural indicators, and perceptions on the six core functions of the pharmaceutical sector outlined was collected. In each area performance scores were

generated using a scale of 0–10, interpreted as: extreme (0.0–2.0); very (2.1–4.0); moderate (4.1–6.0); marginal (6.1–8.0); and minimal (8.1–10). A consolidated score was finally computed.

16. mHealth is part of the broader eHealth agenda and specifically refers to the use of mobile devices (such as mobile phones and handheld computers) in the health sector. The WHO broadly defined eHealth as 'the combined use of electronic communication and information technology in the health sector'.

17. EpiSurveyor is a mobile phone- and web-based data collection system that is now being used in more than 170 countries to collect information regarding clinic supervision, vaccination coverage, and disease outbreaks, etc. It helps to identify and manage important public health issues, including HIV/AIDS, malaria, and measles.

18. http://www.mhealthinfo.org/project/episurveyor-mobile-health-data-collection

References

Canavan, A., Toonen, J., Elovainio, R. (2008). *Performance Based Financing: An International Review of the Literature*. Amsterdam: Development Policy & Practice, KIT.

Chansa, C. (2009). *Zambia's Health Sector Wide Approach (SWAp) Revisted*. Köln: Lambert Academic Publishing.

Cheelo, C., Chama, C., Kansembe, H., Jonsson, D. and Xu, K. (2010). *Measuring the Distribution of Health Payments and Catastrophic Effects of Health Spending in Zambia: An Analysis of Household-Level Survey Data*. Lusaka: University of Zambia.

Cheelo, C., Chitah, B., Mwamba, S. and Lutangu, I. (2008). *Donor effects on the National AIDS Response and the National Health System: Theme 5 Final Report*. Lusaka: Department of Economics, UNZA.

Colombo, F. and Tapay, N. (2004). *Proposals for Taxonomy of Health Insurance*. Paris: Organization for Economic Cooperation and Development, pp. 1–21.

CSO (Central Statistical Office), MOH (Ministry of Health), TDRC (Tropical Diseases Research Centre), University of Zambia, and Macro International Inc. (2009). *Zambia Demographic and Health Survey 2007*. Calverton, MD: CSO and Macro International Inc.

Dusseljee, J., Chansa, C. and Phiri, C. (2011). *Technical Review of the Katete District Results Based Financing Programme*. A report produced by ETC Crystal on behalf of the World Bank. Washington DC: World Bank.

ECSA (East, Central and Southern African) Health Community (2008). *Resolutions of the 46th ECSA Health Ministers Meeting*. Arusha: ECSA Health Secretariat.

Eisele, T.P., Larsen, D.A., Walker, N., et al. (2012). Estimates of child deaths prevented from malaria prevention scale-up in Africa 2001–2010. *Malaria Journal*; 11: 93

Eldridge, C. and Palmer, N. (2009). Performance-based payment: Some reflections on the discourse, evidence and unanswered questions. *Health Policy and Planning*; 24: 160–166.

Frost, M. and Thidiane, N. (2010). *Zambia: Implementing the End Use Verification survey using mobile phone technology*. Arlington, VA: USAID Deliver project, Task Order 3. Available at: <http://www.mobileactive.org/files/file_uploads/Zambia_EpiSurveyor09_Technical%20Report.pdf> (last accessed 9 November 2012).

Furth, R. (2006). *Zambia Pilot Study of Performance-based Incentives: Operations Research*

Results. Published for the U.S. Agency for International Development Agency (USAID) by the Quality Assurance Project. Available at: <http://www.who.int/management/zambiapilotperformance.pdf> (last accessed 25 October 2012).

Government of Zambia (2010). *Estimates of Revenue and Expenditure*. Lusaka: Government Printers.

Government of Zambia (2011). *Estimates of Revenue and Expenditure*. Lusaka: Government Printers.

Government of Zambia (2012). *Estimates of Revenue and Expenditure*. Lusaka: Government Printers.

Hermsan, E., Banks, K. and De-Waele, R. (2011). *Mobile Trends 2020 Africa*. Available at: <http://www.slideshare.net/rudydw/mobile-trends-2020-africa> (last accessed 30 January 2012).

HHA (Harmonization for Health in Africa) (2011). *Investing in Health for Africa: The Case for Strengthening Systems for Better Health Outcomes*. Available at: <http://www.hha-online.org/hso/system/files/AIC_en_Full.pdf> (last accessed 9 November 2012).

Hogan, M.C., Foreman, K.J., Naghavi, M., et al. (2010). Maternal mortality for 181 countries, 1980–2008: A systematic analysis of progress towards Millennium Development Goal 5. *Lancet*; 375: 1609–1623.

IHME (Institute for Health Metrics and Evaluation), University of Zambia (2011). *Maternal and Child Health Intervention Coverage in Zambia*. Seattle, WA: IHME.

International Labour Organization (2008). *Zambia Social Protection Expenditure and Performance Review and Social Budget*. Geneva: International Labour Organization, Social Security Department.

Ireland, M., Paul, E. and Dujardin, B. (2011). Can performance-based financing be used to reform health systems in developing countries. *Bulletin of the World Health Organization*; 89: 695–698.

Jost, T.S. (2001). Private or public approaches to insuring the uninsured: lessons from international experience with private insurance. *New York University Law Review*; 76: 419–492.

Klundert, J. (2010). *First impressions of the Performance Based Financing Project in Katete*. Rotterdam: Institute of Health Policy & Management, Erasmus University.

Lagomarsino, G., Garabrant, A., Adyas, A., et al. (2012). Moving towards universal health coverage: Health insurance reforms in nine developing countries in Africa and Asia. *Lancet*; 380: 933–943

Lake, S. and Musumali, C. (1999). Zambia: The role of aid management in sustaining visionary reform. *Health Policy and Planning*; 14: 254–263.

Lewis M. (2006). Governance and corruption in public health care systems. *CGD Working Paper* Number 78. Washington, DC: Center for Global Development. Available at: <http://www.cgdev.org> (last accessed 25 October 2012).

Lewis, M. and Pettersson, G. (2009). Governance in health care delivery: Raising performance. *World Bank Policy Research Working Paper* No. 5074. Washington, DC: World Bank.

Loevinsohn, B. (2008). *Performance-Based Contracting for Health Services in Developing Countries: A Toolkit*. Washington, DC: World Bank.

Lozano, R., Wang, H., Foreman, K.J., et al. (2011). Progress towards Millennium

Development Goals 4 and 5 on maternal and child mortality: An updated systematic analysis. *Lancet*; 378: 1139–1165.

Maher, D. (2010). Re-thinking global health sector efforts for HIV and tuberculosis epidemic control: Promoting integration of programme activities within a strengthened health system. *BMC Public Health*; 10: 394.

Masiye, F. (2007). Investigating health system performance: An application of data envelopment analysis to Zambian hospitals. *BMC Health Services Research*; 7:58.

Meesen, B., Soucat, A. and Sekabaraga, C. (2011). Performance-based financing: Just a donor fad or a catalyst towards comprehensive healthcare reform. *Bulletin of the World Health Organization*; 89: 153–156.

Mikkelsen-Lopez, I., Wyss, K. and Savigny, D. (2011). An approach to addressing governance from a health system framework perspective. *BMC International Health and Human Rights*; 11: 13.

Ministry of Communications and Transport (2007). *National Information and Communication Technology Policy*. Lusaka: Ministry of Communications and Transport.

Ministry of Health (1992). *National Health Policies and Strategies*. Lusaka: Ministry of Health.

Ministry of Health (2008a). *Mid-Term Review of the National Health Strategic Plan 2006–2010*. Lusaka: Ministry of Health.

Ministry of Health (2008b). *Joint Annual Review for 2007*. Lusaka: Ministry of Health.

Ministry of Health (2009). *Zambia National Health Accounts 2003 to 2006: General Accounts with HIV/AIDS, TB and Malaria Sub-accounts*. Lusaka: Ministry of Health.

Ministry of Health (2010a). *List of Health Facilities in Zambia 2010*. Lusaka: Ministry of Health.

Ministry of Health (2010b). *Zambia National Malaria Indicator Survey 2010*. Lusaka: National Malaria Control Centre.

Ministry of Health (2011a). *Annual Health Statistical Bulletin 2010*. Lusaka: Ministry of Health.

Ministry of Health (2011b). *Operational Implementation Manual for Results Based Financing (RBF) in Pilot Districts in Zambia*. Lusaka: Ministry of Health.

Ministry of Health (2011c). *National Health Strategic Plan 2011–2015*. Lusaka: Ministry of Health.

Miniwatts Marketing Group. *Internet usage statistics for Africa*. Available at: <http://www.internetworldstats.com/stats1.htm> (last accessed 30 January 2012).

Picazo, O.F. (2009). *Unpublished Report to the World Bank that served as background material to the Draft 2010 Country Health Status Report for Zambia*. Washington, DC: World Bank.

Rajaratnam, J.K., Marcus, J.R., Flaxman, A.D., et al. (2010). Neonatal, postneonatal, childhood, and under-5 mortality for 187 countries, 1970–2010: A systematic analysis of progress towards Millennium Development Goal 4. *Lancet*; 375: 1988–2008.

Sekabaraga, C., Diop, F. and Soucat, A. (2011). Can innovative health financing policies increase access to MDG-related services? Evidence from Rwanda. *Health Policy and Planning*; 26: 52–62.

Soeters, R., Habineza, C., Peerenboom, B. (2006). Performance-based financing and changing the district health system: experience from Rwanda. *Bulletin of the World Health Organization*; 84: 884–889

UNDP (United Nations Development Programme) (2011). *Zambia Human Development Report 2011: Service Delivery for Sustainable Human Development*. New York: UNDP.

UNICEF (United Nations Children's Fund) (2010). *Case Study on Narrowing the Gaps for Equity. Zambia Project Mwana: Using Mobile Phones to Improve Early Infant HIV Diagnostic Services, Post-natal Follow-up and Care*. Nairobi: UNICEF – East and Southern Africa Regional Office.

UNICEF (United Nations Children's Fund) (2012). *The State of the World's Children 2012: Children in an Urban World*. New York: UNICEF.

United Nations (2009). Information economy report 2009: trends and outlook in turbulent times. *A report produced at the United Nations Conference on Trade and Development*. Geneva: United Nations. Available at: <http://www.unctad.org/en/docs/ier2009_en.pdf> (last accessed 25 October 2012).

United Nations (2012). *The Millennium Development Goals Report 2011*. New York: United Nations.

USAID Deliver Project (2011). *The USAID | DELIVER PROJECT Improves Patient Access to Essential Medicines in Zambia*. Available at: <http://deliver.jsi.com/dlvr_content/resources/allpubs/logisticsbriefs/ZM_USAIDelProjImpr.pdf> (last accessed 9 November 2012).

Vital Wave Consulting (2009). *mHealth for Development: The Opportunity of Mobile Technology for Healthcare in the Developing World*. Washington, DC, and Berkshire, UK: UN Foundation-Vodafone Foundation Partnership.

Wagstaff, W. (2007). Social health insurance re-examined. *World Bank Policy Research Working Paper* 4111. Washington, DC: World Bank.

WHO (World Health Organization) (2007). *Everybody's Business: Strengthening Health Systems to Improve Health Outcomes: WHO's Framework for Action*. Geneva: WHO.

WHO (World Health Organization) (2010a). *World Health Report 2010: Health Systems Financing – The Pathway to Universal Coverage*. Geneva: WHO.

WHO (World Health Organization) (2010b). *Good Governance for Medicines Progress Report 2010*. Geneva: WHO.

WHO (World Health Organization) (2011). *The World Medicines Situation 2011 – Good Governance for the Pharmaceutical Sector: 3rd Edition*. Geneva: WHO.

WHO (World Health Organization) (2012). *Measuring Transparency to Improve Good Governance in the Public Pharmaceutical Sector: Zambia*. Geneva: WHO.

World Bank (2009a). *Health and Growth*. A report by the Commission on Growth and Development. Washington, DC: World Bank.

World Bank (2009b). *Zambia Health Sector Public Expenditure Review: Accounting for Resources to Improve Effective Service Coverage*. Washington, DC: World Bank.

World Bank (2010). *World Development Indicators*. Washington, DC: World Bank. Available at: <http://data.worldbank.org/sites/default/files/frontmatter.pdf> (last accessed 25 October 2012).

World Bank (2011). *Electronic Zambia Inventory Control System (eZICS) Project Concept Note*. Unpublished report by the World Bank. Washington, DC: World Bank.

World Bank (2012). *Health Equity and Financial Protection Report*. Washington, DC: World Bank.

17

Housing and Urbanization in Zambia: Unleashing a Formal Market Process

Sylvester Mashamba and Paul Collier

17.1 Introduction

The United Nations (UN) has described decent housing as a human right. Housing also plays a very important part in raising the standard of living of its inhabitants and also contributes greatly to socio-economic development of any nation. In 1996, the Zambian Government went further to state that 'housing is a basic social need and only ranked after food and clothing'. It went further to declare that adequate housing is a prerequisite to national socio-economic development. Good decent housing contributes enormously to better health and enables its inhabitants to carry out other tasks that they would not perform if they were in poor housing. For example, students who live in good and decent housing are better able to carry out their homework than those who live in slums or poor housing.

Housing is the single most expensive investment item that the average family gets to make in their lifetime. Housing also plays a very important role in national economic development, although this recognition is more evident in more developed economies than in Third World economies in general and Zambia in particular. For instance, in Britain, of the recorded £7 trillion of tangible assets, £4 trillion, which is more than 57 per cent, is said to be in the form of housing. In Zambia, however, although accurate figures are not available, the quality and quantity of the total national housing stock is visibly inadequate. The number of Zambians living below the poverty-datum-line (reported to be about 68 per cent) means that most Zambians are not able to afford decent housing by themselves and thus resort to the informal housing market for housing, especially in the urban areas. The huge number of Zambians living below the poverty datum line also means that most Zambians are heavily dependent on rented housing, their employers, public or social housing for decent housing.

The other important role that housing plays in national economic development is in the labour market. Construction of housing units is typically a labour-intensive activity that helps create employment opportunities for the many semi- and unskilled workers in the labour market. Housing construction contributes to national economic development by way of multiplier effects, forward and backward linkages. Multiplier effects refer to the ration of change in the national income (GDP) to initial change in the house construction market investment. For example, an initial investment of $US1,000 may cause an increase in the national income of $US2,500 – in which case the multiplier would be 2.5. In Zambia the multiplier effect was last reported to be approximately 1.16 according to research conducted by the Economics Department at the University of Zambia (UNZA) (UNZA, 1997, p. xii).

On the other hand, backward linkages are measures of the demands created by one economic sector for the products of other sectors. For housing construction, backward linkages usually represent a value, which exceeds the value added by the sector itself – e.g. fuel, wood/timber, and so on. Forward linkages refer to patterns of consumption encouraged by the production of intermediate goods – e.g. office and household furniture, electric goods-fridges, TVs, and so on.

In 2010 the total number of households in Zambia was recorded at 2,640,000 of which 1,300,000 were in urban areas (UNHABITAT 2012). The rapid urbanization taking place in Zambia implies that the country needed to build an average of 1.3 millions houses between 2011 and 2030 to satisfy housing needs. The deteriorating supply and demand imbalances for decent housing, especially in the urban areas, has meant that most urban dwellers (about 70 per cent) now live in slums areas or unplanned settlements, with no basic amenities such as electricity, street lights, water, roads, and sanitation.

In Zambia, it is very clear that the process of formal investment in housing has not taken root. The typical urban house for an average Zambian is a house built in the informal sector on illegal land, thus without title deeds and built without following building regulations and standards. This means that, more often than not, the typical urban house is built in an area that the local authorities will not find favourable to build on, such as the rocky areas of Kanyama or the George compounds of Lusaka. The fact that these slums houses are built on unplanned and illegal land means that the house owners cannot get loans from formal financial institutions to finance house construction and thus have to resort to self, or informal, housing financing.

The failure of the public housing sector agencies to adequately provide housing has only exacerbated the influx of most urban dwellers to to these slum areas (Mashamba, 1990).

What has also come out very clearly in the last decades is that previous public-sector housing delivery systems have completely failed to satisfy the demand for low-income housing. Whereas, the demand for urban housing has been growing in tens of thousands, the supply of housing has been in the mere thousands. The current urban Zambian crisis has been created by two factors. Firstly, there is the question of numbers, that is to say, there are very few houses compared to the demand. Secondly, it stems from the poor quality of most of the available urban housing stock.

Housing provision in 21st century Zambia is evidently in very sharp contrast with historic urbanization in the developed world, for instance in London, England. Whereas, the underlining conditions of migration and income inequalities can be said to be very similar, the rate at which the formal and informal housing markets responded is very different. For instance, whereas, the rates of migration in both London in the early 19th century and in Zambia in the 20th and 21st century can be said to have been similar, the housing supply responses are very different. Whereas, in Europe the response of the housing market to the rising rate of urbanization was to supply formal housing, in Africa, and Zambia in particular, the response has largely been the supply of informal housing.

In London most houses were built for the increasing number of urban ex-peasants who had migrated from the rural areas, by small independent development firms, on freehold land. The fact that the great estates owned almost all the land in London meant that these estates were able to effective control development and thus were able to plan housing development in these estates. The estates not only planned within their own locations, but were able to provide basic infrastructure, such as roads, and then subleased the serviced land or plots to building companies. The companies would then build appropriate housing units, usually using standardized architectural house plans. The most common construction method used to build the 19th century London houses involved labour intensive construction methods. The net result was that many of the massive influx of peasants into London during the 19th century were able to find work in the resultant booming house-construction industry. Indeed, the same phenomenon was repeated and recorded in the miracle cities of Manchester, Chicago and Melbourne (Belich 2009). Further, many of the landlords in the 19th century European housing boom were not large corporations, but were simple retirees who had invested their saving in these housing units, and were usually found living in one and renting out the others.

In Zambia, the situation has been completely different. Firstly, in Zambia, the resultant housing that seems responsive to the increasing urban migrant has been that of the informal housing market with its informal housing product. For example, statistics based on the 2010 census indicate that Zambia has roughly about 1.4 million housing stock, against a rapidly growing population of roughly 13 million people. Whereas its formal housing stock has remained basically static in the last few decades, the population has been growing at an average rate of about 3.0 per cent since independence in 1964, with cities like Lusaka probably growing at about twice the national average. Today, Lusaka is estimated to have a population of over 3 million people, mostly living in the so-called shanty compounds. The situation is not any better in the other cities and urban areas of Zambia. Projections are that Zambia's population will reach 18.8 million by 2015. Unless urgent and immediate steps are taken, Zambia is headed for a housing crisis never witnessed in before, with rentals and house prices expected to reach unprecedented levels.

This chapter, therefore, sets out to try to explain these differences between the housing development in 19th century London at the peak of rural-urban migration and that of 21st Zambia when the same phenomenon is taking place. Here we will adopt the hypothesis that the distinctiveness of housing as a household asset produced by the non-tradable sector exposes it to multiple points of vulnerability not found together either in private consumer goods or in other capital goods. Our hypothesis is that this vulnerability can be addressed by appropriate government policies, which need to be addressed in their totality rather than in isolation, if they are to see the desired results. We suggest the following five vulnerabilities:

1. Affordability of formal housing
2. Clarity in legal rights
3. Financial innovation
4. Supporting infrastructure
5. Opportunities for income

17.1.2 *Affordability of construction costs*

If housing is to be affordable to most people, it is essential that building costs be kept at a bare minimum. The ability of households to afford housing either by way of renting or outright purchase is relative to their income. For example, in Lusaka, the former council-owned low-cost houses in Chilenje South, Libala and Chelstone are going at monthly rents of between K1,500 to K2,500 and selling at between K200,000 to about K350,000 per unit. By the same token, rentals in the informal housing sector are going at about K150 per room to K1,000 per house, with electricity but without piped water. It is difficult, however, to average the selling prices of these informal housing units given the diversity of the state and conditions. However, the price tends to start at about K30,000 to anything up to K500,000, depending upon the size and location of the house. The prevailing rental and selling prices in both the formal and informal housing sectors would suggest that renting and outright purchase of houses is out of the reach of most urban dwellers.

17.2 Building standards

Building standards refer to a set of tests and practices that are used to ensure that the resultant buildings/houses are safe, efficient and sustainable for all. Building standards were first developed in Europe in the early Middle Ages for the protection of residents themselves and their immediate neighbours. For example, the use of thatched roofs was consequently banned as they posed a fire hazard and the fires could spread from one house to the other with ease. Whereas, buildings standards are desirable for the safety and protections of residents, they can be very retrogressive, especially if set very high.

Although the application of appropriate building standards commensurate with the people's incomes helps in protecting the occupants' welfare and their immediate neighbours, inappropriate and very high building standards have a negative effect. It is because of these too high standards in Africa that most households build in the informal housing market devoid of any standards. In Lusaka about 65 per cent of all households live in the informal housing market, where high building standards set by the local authority do not apply. Zambia, like most other Anglophone African countries, merely adopted the then prevailing colonial building standards that the British colonists had applied prior to independence. Although the British colonialists had applied these primarily to a few white colonialists in the colonies in general and Zamia in particular, after independence the newly independent Zambia adopted these standards and applied them almost everywhere regardless of people's income.

It should be noted that when the United Kingdom raised and adopted the high building standards through the Town and Country Planning Act (Parker-Morris Standards) in 1947, which were also applied to all the colonies, average incomes in the UK were substantially higher than those in the colonies. So whereas in the UK the net effect of raising these building standards was an improved set of houses; in the colonies, especially after independence, these standards had the opposite effect. In Zambia, immediately after independence when the pass laws were removed, there was a massive increase in the rural-urban migration rate for which the urban areas in Zambia, especially Lusaka and the Copperbelt towns, completely failed to provide decent and adequate housing set at the British Parker–Morris standards (Mashamba 1990).

The failure by the local authorities in Zambia to build decent houses at the British standards and the ever increasing rate of rural-urban migration meant that more and more migrants were finding their way to Zambia's fast growing informal housing market. Here the house are built using far inferior, but economically more realistic, housing standards that those enforced by the local authorities. Although building standards were never lowered in Zambia, in 1974 the Zambian Government did admit that the prevailing set of building standards in the country were set very high and that the majority of its citizens were now livings in the informal housing sector – commonly referred to as shanty compounds. In 1974, the Zambian Government, with funding and technical support from the World Bank, went further to recognize and upgrade these 'shanty' compounds, but did not lower building standards (Martin 1975).

17.2.1 *Unit costs of inputs*

Building a house requires various inputs, among them finance, labour – both unskilled and skilled – building materials such as cement, roofing sheets, stones and most importantly land on which to build on. Whereas, in comparison with other countries, Zambia can be said to be sparsely populated, getting a plot to build a house in any of Zambia's urban areas can be a nightmare. Consequently, the few plots available are so overpriced that only a few Zambians can afford them.

The high land costs are coupled with high building costs such as cement, roofing sheets and steel. High fuel costs and the fact that Zambia is landlocked mean that all imported building materials are expensive. Although labour can be said to be cheap in comparison with the western and developed world, skilled labour is scarce and often imported, thus making it expensive. For example, it is very common to find Chinese workers doing manual labour on Zambian construction sites. It is common practice to engage foreign, mostly Chinese and South African, workers at most Zambian construction sites, a situation encouraged by the government that says that foreign construction firms perform far better than their local and indigenous counterparts. There is also some evidence that they are cheaper than Zambian firms.

Housing finance is very expensive in Zambia so very few Zambians look to mortgage finance as a viable option. Until recently when the government capped bank-lending rates at 9 per cent, banks and housing finance institutions were lending at over 22 per cent for quite a long time. Admittedly, even at a base of 9 per cent, mortgages in Zambia are still the preserve of an elite few. The majority of Zambians are, therefore, left to fend for themselves in the informal housing market, where houses are built without any financing or building formalities.

17.3 Industrial organization

The construction industry in Zambia is dysfunctional. It is still heavily dependent on foreign construction labour, materials and firms, thereby producing very expensive buildings. The reliance on western labour, technology and materials, therefore, means that the Zambian construction industry is essentially still producing housing for the elite few that can afford it. For instance, whereas the population of Zambia has been increasing in the millions, thus more than doubling from about 3.4m in 1964 to about 9.4m in 1990 and 13.8m in 2010, the annual increase in formal housing stock has been minimal and in the hundreds at best (see Table 17.1). For example, in the 2000, the then Zambian Republican President launched the ambitious Presidential Housing Initiative (PHI), which was charged with spearheading the country's house building programme, and yet the PHI only managed to build 141 housing units of which 102 were said to be low cost and the other 39 were high cost. To further contextualize the country's housing crisis, the 1996 housing policy document estimated that all things remaining equal (they never do), the country needed to build 110,000 housing units every year for the next ten years just to clear the country's backlog for housing. If one then compares the need for housing (estimated at 840,000 units in 1996) against the current levels (of about 400 units) of housing output per year, it becomes very clear that Zambia as a country are nowhere near to solving its housing crisis.

As if the current problems were not enough, it is estimated that about 40 per cent of the population is made up of people aged 15–20 years, meaning that in the next 5–10 years housing demand will increase by at least 20 per cent.

17.4 An interim assessment

It is clear that all the factors mentioned in this chapter, have only helped to make formal housing more unaffordable to most Zambians and thus make informal housing the norm in most Zambian urban areas. At best, what the

Table 17.1 Housing type by percentage

Housing type	1980	1990	2010
Squatter	11%	15%	22%
Upgraded (squatter) units	38%	42%	40%
Site and service	9%	13%	23%
Totals	58%	70%	85%

government has done in the past is to allow for residents to settle in the informal sector, only to formalize the same through upgrading. To date, the predominant policy advice (e.g. Tipple (2000) and Turner (1976)) has been to resolve the housing problem through accepting and encouraging the informal housing process. This chapter will suggest that, on the contrary, there is a need to re-establish formality in the housing market. Only formality can provide the benefits of scale, continuity and legality.

The starting point in re-formalizing the housing market is to focus on affordability. To estimate affordability it is essential to use realistic and reliable urban survey data. Similarly, a minimum unit cost study would also have to be undertaken to compare the cost of building housing that conforms to building standards with that which does not: a discrepancy between these numbers would help to induce policy makers to rethink building standards.

17.5 Legal rights

It is recognized that legal rights affect the housing market in three respects: the ownership, security and marketability of land rights; the extent to which housing can function as collateral; and the rights of tenants relative to landlords.

17.6 Land rights

Urbanization creates value and rising density increases productivity. Because the effect is location-specific, much of the increase in value accrues to the owners of urban land. In Zambia, all the land now called urban was once rural land controlled by chiefs or other traditional leaders. As urban areas grew, more and more surrounding rural areas were absorbed into the urban areas. The surrounding farms, with absent landlords, were always the first to be absorbed into the growing urban areas, but as the residents were occupying the land illegally they did not have legal rights or title deeds. The absence of title deeds or land rights means that tenants have no legal right to the piece of land they occupy. More often than not, the piece of land they occupy is given or, more correctly, sold to them by the ruling party cadres. In some cases, the same piece of land can be sold to two or more unsuspecting residents. Worse still, there are no records to show who land has been sold to. Consequently, there are a number of claims of a single plot in the informal areas.

It would appear that the problem of getting a residential plot lies more with the servicing of land, rather than with the availability of land, suffice it to say that there is still the need to extend the existing boundaries of some of our cities, such as Lusaka. The incapacity of our local authorities to identify, demarcate and service land for house building has consequently led to a number of people moving onto vacant land as squatters. Only after people have moved onto the vacant land and built their houses as squatters do city officials appear eager to provide some form of services to these people.

17.7 Property as collateral

For property to function as collateral, there has to be clarity in the rights to the plot or land. The creditor also has to have the power to foreclose on the property or land in defined circumstances of arrears. This in turn depends upon the law, and the reliability and speed with which courts implement it. The tendency and common experience, however, has been for delays in court proceedings and judicial corruption to make foreclosure unreliable.

17.8 Tenancy

Given the high poverty and unemployment levels in Zambia, more especially in these informal housing areas, it is not surprising that there are more tenants than landlords in these areas. Rentals are by no means cheap, so most residents, especially the working youth and single families, opt to rent rooms rather than houses and flats.

It is important to note that what ultimately determines the price (rental) is the relations between demand and supply of rented accommodation, and in the case of Lusaka, what we notice is that demand far outstrips supply. Whereas there has been a substantial increase in the population (assuming increased population results in effective demand), there has been no corresponding increase in the available housing stock. Another factor that landlords consider when determining rentals is the cost of building, maintenance costs, and other related costs such as ground rents and all other government taxes – because of the informality of this sector most landlords don't pay any form of tax.

Although very high rentals are in themselves very bad, especially for the majority of citizens, they can also act as an incentive to would-be investors. It should be further noted that high rentals do not necessarily mean high profit margins for the landlords, for it could be that the landlords are having to service their (house) building loan, taxes and so on. No doubt, both the government and the ordinary citizens would want to have residential rentals reduced, but to set them below market rates would be to return to the conditions of the Second Republic when Municipal Councils (landlords) collected rentals, but failed to maintain their housing stock. It is also a fallacy to talk of reducing rentals amidst high interest rates, high taxes and a very weak

Kwacha, in an economy where over 75 per cent of the population are living in poverty and struggle to survive day-to-day, let alone be able to save to build a house.

17.9 Support infrastructure

Complementary physical infrastructure and services such as roads, drainage, street lighting, electricity, water, sewerage, coupled with policing, schools, waste disposal and healthcare are a prerequisite to decent housing. Unfortunately, in Zambia local authorities have failed lamentably to provide these. Most of the municipal water and sewage infrastructure was built in the late 1960s and early 1970s, and there has been no notable investment since. In Lusaka, for example, the existing water and sewage plants were built in the late 1960s, when the population of Lusaka was only about 400,000 and yet the same plants are servicing a population that has since grown to over 3 million. It is no wonder that current statistics put the rate of housing informality in Lusaka alone at about 65 per cent.

The failure by the government, through the local authorities, to invest in municipal services meant that even the few available housing plots that the city authorities in Lusaka city have made available have been without municipal services. Take, Chalala, a newly created residential area south of Lusaka catering for medium and high cost houses, for example, where plots were demarcated and sold to residents without services such as piped water and sewerage by the Lusaka City Council. The main roads and bus routes have since been tarred by the Road Development Agency. Residents have had to sink their own individual boreholes for water and septic tanks to discharge their sewerage. The close proximity of the plots and their sheer numbers means that the underground water is heavily polluted and waterborne diseases are very common.

The nature of municipal services such as water and sewerage are that these are best served by a public institution that installs them before the actual building takes place, rather than by individual residents after they have built their houses. For example, in the 1974 Lusaka upgrading scheme a number of houses had to be pulled down to make way for road construction, water and sewerage reticulation, thus adding to the cost of providing for these services.

17.10 Opportunities for income

Apart from being an essential social good, housing also plays an important economic part in our lives. Workers need housing to live in. Housing also generates incomes for landlords who invest in housing, and for the workforce that builds it.

Whereas the intention in the recent sale of public sector houses was to empower most ordinary Zambians to own a house and be home owner-occupiers, the reality on the ground, however, was different. Most of the people who bought the former council and public sector houses have either rented or sold them and opted to live in the shanty compounds. Understandably, some of those that have rented their newly acquired houses have done so for short-term economic reasons, i.e. to raise money to pay off their previous landlords, especially those that bought former company houses, which were sold at much higher prices than the former council houses; or to start some form of business venture.

17.11 Conclusion: From failures of market coordination to failures of policy coordination

Given the scale of the need for housing, it is evident that the government would not be able to afford the investment. This therefore leaves the government with only one option: making the housing market work better. In part this can be done by encouraging the upgrading of existing squatter housing. There is some evidence that in the past this has worked. The Lusaka Upgrading Scheme of the 1970s made a greater impact on the country's housing situation than any other housing programme initiated by any post-independence government.

However, restoration of the formal housing market is essential. This would require a coordinated change in a range of policies. Legal rights would need to be clarified and conferred on land that could be zoned for housing plots. Courts would need to be reformed and streamlined so that land and the buildings on it could readily function as collateral. Building standards would have to be radically lowered to ensure that housing which met official standards was affordable to ordinary urban households. Local authorities would need to have revenue streams, for example generated by the sale of zoned land as in China, from which they could finance the provision of infrastructure for zoned land in advance of house-building. Financial institutions, notably building societies, would need to innovate with mortgages that were indexed to prices and so permitted much lower interest rates and longer repayment periods. Such a package of reforms could unleash house building that would begin to catch up with the enormous backlog that resulted from past policy failures.

There is an urgent need for a national housing policy document that sets out such an agenda. Such a document would set out government priorities and identify the roles of government, the private sector and other major stakeholders in the housing market. The failure by government to effectively implement past official housing policies (such as that officially launched in January 1996) is, however, a source of great concern. Ironically, the government started to discard its own National Housing Policy document immediately after the policy had been announced, when without prior discussion it announced that it was going to sell all council, government and parastatal houses to sitting tenants, a policy measure which had not been mentioned in its housing policy document. It is no wonder that opposition parties at the time accused the government of using the sale of council houses as a political ploy to win votes. Although the idea of selling public housing units is in itself a very positive step, the mere fact that it was not planned for, meant that the long-term effects on the Zambian housing market and the economy had not been carefully thought through. Worse still, rather than sell the council houses at economic prices, so as provide funds to the cash-strapped councils with which to build more houses, council houses were literally given away. As if that was not enough, the government has also taken away most of the other viable income-generating activities from the councils, such as road licenses.

The creation of the PHI was another policy issue that was not mentioned in the 1996 Housing Policy document, again raising questions as to how effective it was and its overall place in the housing market. For example, there has been no explanation of the relation between PHI and the NHA, which most Zambians thought was created to play the role PHI is now playing. Fundamentally, what the government has failed to do is to clearly spell out to the nation the different and complementary roles to be played by both NHA and the PHI in the provision of houses. In the absence of the above, PHI has totally eclipsed the NHA and the emerging private housing sector, which the 1996 housing document claimed was going to take a leading role in the provision of housing.

Although it will also be appreciated that the government has vigorously pursued the policy of empowering Zambians with houses (owner accommodation) it should also be borne in mind that there will always be a category of people who will need rented accommodation. There is therefore a need for polices that enable the provision of such accommodation. The absence of an adequate market for rented accommodation has thus seen a sharp rise in rental rates, especially in the urban areas and Lusaka in particular. With house building cost for a so-called low-cost house now reaching K35m, it is absurd to expect ordinary people to own a house. About 80 per cent of citizens live in poverty, while, on average, the rest earn only around K200,000 per month.

It must also be recognized that there is also the problem of limited capacity to implement housing (and other major) policies at both central and local government. Apart from the obvious factors of financial constraints, there is a need for human capacity, which is always lacking in government. This stems from the fact that both central and local governments offer very poor conditions of services and pay. Although a lot has been said, and in some cases done, about capacity building in the public service, it would seem that as soon as personnel are better trained and equipped, they either leave for the private sector or other countries.

Finally, it would be wrong if we gave the impression that government is unaware of most of the problems highlighted in this chapter as most, if not all, have been well documented in the 1996 national policy document. However, like most things in Zambia, implementation is simply lacking. Unfortunately, policy reacts only to a crisis (crisis management) rather than working to long-term plans. The decision to abandon the National Development Plans has only compounded the lack of planning and capacity to tackle future problems.

Although most Zambians do not have the financial capacity to build their own houses, there are a few investors (either foreign or local) who are interested in building houses for commercial purposes, but are discouraged by the bureaucratic building process and archaic planning laws, such as zoning. Rather than concentrate on building finished houses, government (both local and central) should also make resources available to ordinary citizens to get plots of land for which the government has provided essential public services such as roads and water. Governments should not get into the business of providing houses for its citizens, but should act as a facilitator, and allow the private sector, which has the business acumen and experience, to provide houses. The selling of a one bedroom, low-cost house by the NHA at K33m is itself a manifestation that the days of public sector housing provision are long gone.

Although there have been attempts by the government, through the PHI and the NHA to build more housing stock, the impact of these two institutions has been minimal. Whereas the government's National Housing Policy document talks of a need for 100,000 houses to be built over a 10 year period if we are to satisfy our housing needs, they are currently hoping to supply less than two thousands units per year. At this rate of house construction, we will never satisfy our housing needs.

References

Belich J. (2009). *Replenishing the Earth: The Settler Revolution and the Rise of the Anglo-World, 1783-1939*. Oxford: Oxford University Press.

Martin, R, (1975). Urbanization, squatter settlements and upgrading. *Human settlements in Zambia*. Report of a workshop at the University of Zambia: Lusaka. pp. 67–68.

Mashamba, M.S. (1990). *Informal housing sector and its development in Zambia*. Unpublished Master of Philosopher Degree in Architecture thesis: University of Newcastle upon Tyne.

Mashamba, M.S. (1997). *The construction industry in Zambia: Opportunities and constraints under the structural adjustment programme and the enabling shelter strategy*. Unpublished PhD thesis: University of Newcastle upon Tyne.

Shlomo, A. (2012). *Planet of Cities*. Cambridge, MA: Lincoln Institute of Land Policy.

Tipple, G. (2000). *Extending Themselves. User-initiated Transformation of Government-Built Housing in Developing Countries*. Liverpool: Liverpool University Press.

Turner, J.F.C. (1976). *Housing by People: Towards Autonomy in Building Environments*. London: Marion Boyars.

University of Zambia, Department of Economics (1997). *Housing in Zambia*. Lusaka: University of Zambia.

Index